Edgar A. Poe

Mournful
and
Never-ending
Remembrance

EDGAR A. POE

MOURNFUL

AND

NEVER-ENDING

REMEMBRANCE

Kenneth Silverman

HarperCollins*Publishers*

Designed by Ruth Kolbert

Library of Congress Cataloging-in-Publication Data
Silverman, Kenneth.
   Edgar A. Poe : mournful and never-ending remembrance / Kenneth
Silverman.—1st ed.
     p.   cm.
   Includes bibliographical references and index.
   ISBN 0-06-016715-7
   1. Poe, Edgar Allan, 1809–1849—Biography.   2. Authors,
American—19th century—Biography.   I. Title.
PS2631.S525   1991
818'.309—dc20
[B]   90-56397

92 93 94 95 VB/HC 10 9 8 7 6 5 4

FOR

Jane Compton Mallison

... quod petis hic est,
est Ulubris. ...
—HORACE, *Epistles,* I, xi

CONTENTS

viii · *Contents*

Illustrations insert follows page 244.

Nec morti esse locum, sed viva volare
Sideris in numerum atque alto succedere cœlo.
—VIRGIL, Georgica IV.

(For there is no place of annihilation—but alive
they mount up each into his own order of star,
and take their appointed seat in the heavens.)
—Quoted as the epigraph of "To Arcturus,"
by SARAH HELEN WHITMAN

For *that* which *was not*—for that which had no form—for that
which had no thought—for that which had no sentience—for that
which was soulless, yet of which matter formed no portion—for all
this nothingness, yet for all this immortality, the grave was still a
home, and the corrosive hours, co-mates.
—POE, *The Colloquy of Monos and Una*

Eliza

TO THE HUMANE HEART,
On this night, *Mrs. Poe,* lingering on the bed of
disease and surrounded by her children, asks
your *assistance*; and *asks it perhaps for the last time.*
Richmond Enquirer, November 29, 1811

So theatergoers in Richmond, Virginia, learned about the grave illness and helpless dependents of one of their favorite actresses, Eliza Poe. Assistance was needed, for she was without money or support. Her father had died when she was two, her mother, an actress, nine years later. Her first husband, an actor, was dead; her second husband, the actor David Poe, Jr., had left her. He had also left fatherless the children who waited near her: William Henry Leonard, nearly five years old; Edgar, nearly three; and Rosalie, about a year. Appeals to the humane heart were justified also by Eliza Poe's age. She was twenty-four: young to have been orphaned, widowed, remarried, and deserted; young to now be surrounded by her three children on her deathbed.

Help might be expected, for despite her youth Eliza Poe had played nearly three hundred different roles on the American stage and had become one of the most popular actresses in the country. She had begun performing as a child in England, where she was born, appearing in Birmingham and other theater towns outside of London with her mother, Elizabeth Arnold. As minor British actors had been doing since the colonial period, they emigrated to America, arriving in Boston aboard the ship *Outram* on January 3, 1796. Three months later, Eliza made her American stage debut in Boston, at the age of nine. She sang a new song called "The Market Lass" on a bill that featured her mother in *Mysteries of the Castle.*

Her precocious abilities quickly brought her a reputation. When she began playing small parts later that year, a newspaper critic in Portland, Maine, wrote that she "exceeded all praise. Although a Miss of only nine years old, her powers as an actress would do credit to any of her sex of maturer age."

But from the start Eliza Poe's theatrical success was offset by hard luck. Later in the year, her widowed mother, herself only about twenty-four years old, married a musician named Charles Tubbs, who had sailed with them from England. The couple joined with an actor-manager named Mr. Edgar in forming a troupe of perhaps fifteen players known as the Charleston Comedians. While the company was traveling through North Carolina, Eliza's mother died, possibly of yellow fever, leaving her without parents at the age of about eleven.

For two years or so, Eliza seems to have been under Tubbs's care. She lived the itinerant existence of a provincial actress, traveling from city to city and town to town to play a few days, weeks, or months with companies of varying skill, before audiences of more or less sophistication, in theaters ranging in magnificence from the fifteen-by-seven-foot platform of the Portland Assembly Room, to the marble staircases and gilt boxes of Philadelphia's Chestnut Street Theater, near Independence Hall, seating some two thousand spectators. Touring also meant deepening personal experience, the knowledge gained by selling tickets or working with "Mr. Salenka's learned dog," by squabbles in the company, rowdy galleries, thin houses, a fellow actor's suicide.

Billed as "Miss Arnold," Eliza grew steadily in attractiveness, versatility, and skill. Reviewers often remarked on her prettiness: slight but shapely figure, dark hair, large eyes (Illus. 1). The limited number of playgoers in American towns and cities meant that managers who hoped to fill their houses night after night had to change plays frequently, in turn forcing actors to build large repertoires. By the time Eliza was fifteen she knew about seventy different parts. Most often she was cast in featured brat and ingenue roles, two of which she made especially her own and played repeatedly: the prankish Little Pickle in the farcical afterpiece *The Spoiled Child*; and Biddy Belair in David Garrick's *Miss in her Teens,* a sixteen-year-old promised to an old man in marriage and meanwhile also pursued by an effete fop and a rakish soldier. Fortunately for Eliza, as American theaters of the time offered many plays with songs and music, she was a gifted dancer and singer. She often appeared in a minuet, gavotte, hornpipe, or Spanish fandango. Audiences particularly praised the clarity and innocent sweetness of her voice. A letter writer to a Philadelphia newspaper predicted that in "a short time, she will be unequalled in her profession, with regard to her vocal powers."

At the age of fifteen Eliza moved to repair some of the broken connections in her life, but again with ill luck. While performing in Alexandria, Virginia, she married a teenaged character actor named Charles Hopkins. Billed as "Mrs. Hopkins," she played the Virginia circuit with him for three years, appearing in Fredericksburg, Petersburg, Norfolk, and Richmond. But Hopkins fell ill, perhaps also of yellow fever. Only about twenty years old, he died in Washington in October 1805, the same time of year Eliza had lost her mother.

Eliza resumed her career in Richmond, now eighteen years old and wholly on her own. She often took the role of a lover or wife opposite David Poe, Jr., a twenty-one-year-old actor and dancer. Their training and talents were unequal. The son of a locally celebrated Revolutionary war hero in Baltimore, David Poe had only recently turned to the stage from the study of law, against his family's wishes. His good looks and deep voice promised some success, but his early appearances in Charleston, Savannah, and other southern cities also disclosed a paralyzing stage fright. Newspaper critics routinely reported his floundering in an "abyss of embarrassment" that "plunged him so deep as to deprive him of all power of exertion." Just the same he was paired with Eliza, sometimes partnering her in a slow Scottish dance called a strathspey. In the spring of 1806 they married and she began appearing as "Mrs. Poe."

Likely seeking some permanence, the couple moved east at the end of the Richmond season. After playing briefly in Philadelphia and at the outdoor summer theater in New York, they settled in Boston, where they performed for three successive seasons, of thirty weeks each. Audiences here expected to be entertained in a professional manner. Accordingly, Eliza and David found themselves performing in a handsome theater with cantilevered boxes, holding about a thousand spectators. The mostly English company, nearly twice as large as that in Virginia, offered a rich repertoire. David appeared in such demanding parts as those of Edmund in *King Lear*, Malcolm in *Macbeth*, and Charles Surface in *The School for Scandal*.

The Poes' frequent appearances in Boston over three years made their differing abilities bleakly evident and well known. David was hissed on stage and repeatedly mocked in the press for mumbling, rushing, or forgetting his lines. "Mr. Poe was erroneous in the very first speech in his part: which was the opening of the play," one reviewer remarked, "he was not sufficiently heard, or generally understood." "Mr. Poe [in *Henry IV, Part I*] . . . mutilated some of his speeches in a most shameful manner," another wrote. "Mr. Poe [in *The Finger Post*] was incorrect," said still another, "and did not commit faithfully to memory the part allotted to him—a fault unpardonable." Chiefly, David was derided for lifelessness, perhaps only the outward expression of his dazing nervousness. As one newspaper put it, "Mr. Poe [in *The Provoked Husband*] . . . acted, as usual, quite tamely." Critics occasionally offered him tepid encouragement as "improving." But his reputation for dullness and inadequacy became so firmly established as to make applause itself seem a rebuke. When he showed a spark of life as Sir George Touchwood in *The Belle's Stratagem,* the reviewer commented: "We hardly expected it, and the audience appreciated and rewarded it as a novelty." However bashful his acting seemed, David Poe was proud and somewhat quick-tempered. At one performance he confronted the disapproving audience in what a newspaper called an "obnoxious and insulting way." Another time he turned up in person at the home of a local theater critic in order, the critic said, to "chastise my impertinence."

By contrast, Eliza Poe during her three years in Boston established herself as a featured dancer and one of the most promising young actresses on the American stage. An admired singer as well, she often appeared in sentimental or comic solo songs between the main play and the afterpiece, or concertized at the Boston Coffee House in private programs of vocal and instrumental music. She became particularly associated with a song entitled "Nobody Coming to Marry Me," beginning:

> *Come blind, come lame, come cripple,*
> *Come some one and take me away!*
> > *For 'tis O! what will become of me,*
> > *O! what shall I do?*
> > *Nobody coming to marry me,*
> > *Nobody coming to woo!*

She continued to please by playing ingenues or comic juveniles like Little Pickle, and was praised for romping in tomboy and hoyden parts without gross exaggeration. But she also now had leading roles in major plays—Ophelia in *Hamlet*, Cordelia in *Lear*, Juliet in *Romeo and Juliet.* Moreover, she was cast against the male stars of the American stage, including the "American Roscius" John Howard Payne, the first native professional actor to play Hamlet. Although her performances with Payne were sold out, her critical success was mixed, some critics observing that her proper domain was comedy.

Otherwise reviewers invariably praised not only Eliza's personal beauty and natural talent, but also her understanding of her parts and the tastefulness of her acting. More than anything else they appreciated the generous quality of her career, manifested by her hard work and her wish to entertain her audience and seek its approval. She appeared in every sort of play, from the farce *Mogul Tale: Or, The Descent of a Balloon* to such recent London hits as *Time Tells a Tale* and the very popular melodrama *Tekeli: Or, the Siege of Montgatz.* "She has supported and maintained a course of characters more numerous and arduous than can be paralleled on our boards during any one season," one newspaper editor remarked. "Often she has been obliged to perform three characters on the same evening, and she has always been perfect in the text." "In their performances generally," another writer observed, "few take precedence of this pleasing actress; and for their assiduity, accuracy, and unassuming deportment, with an uniform and studious desire to please, none."

Especially for Eliza, the stay of three years in Boston, as taxpaying residents, meant a unique lull of stability in a lifetime of packing and unpacking. She developed a special fondness for the city, which had favored her since her American debut there as a nine-year-old child singing "The Market Lass." She found time to paint a watercolor sketch that she entitled "Boston Harbour morning 1808." She and David became close friends with another married couple in the company, named Usher—hospitable and generous people with whom they frequently acted (Illus. 2). The Ushers apparently made an odd-looking pair: reviewers tweaked Noble Usher for his "puny dimensions," and his seemingly buxom wife Harriet for depending "so much upon exterior for success." During the summer off-seasons, David and Eliza sometimes traveled south, offering entertainments at the Haymarket Garden in Richmond, sometimes visiting the Poe family in Baltimore. Apparently they brought with them their young son, William Henry Leonard, born on January 30, 1807, just four months after they began performing in Boston.

During their third year in the city the couple had a second son, whom they named Edgar, perhaps after Mr. Edgar, the actor-manager of the Charleston Comedians. As Eliza's pregnancy became pronounced, in the winter of 1808–9, she stopped taking on new roles. Toward the end she appeared only as a supernumerary, for instance among the peasants in *Brazen Masks*. But she acted until about ten days before the birth of Edgar Poe on January 19, 1809, during a winter of violent storms, winds, and ice drifts. Only three weeks later she resumed her busy stage schedule, being specially advertised to feature in her second appearance her acclaimed song *"Nobody Coming to Marry Me."*

The birth of a second child strained the Poes' financial resources, and perhaps their emotional also. David's personal property was assessed in 1808 at only three hundred dollars, and an announcement the same year for a performance to benefit the couple mentions their "severe losses." No sooner did Eliza return to the company than David left it, for some nine weeks. Unhappy about his career and worried about supporting his enlarged family, he headed for Baltimore to seek aid from his parents, perhaps taking the children to be looked after by them for several months. On the way he stopped at the small town of Stockerton, Pennsylvania, between Philadelphia and Baltimore, to visit George Poe, Jr., a first cousin who had married well and was prospering. By George Poe's account, David declared that he had arrived at "the most awful moment of his life." Assuring his wealthy cousin that he had not come to beg, he implored George to meet him the next morning and walked off, George sneered, "with a tragedy stride." But the meeting never happened; each man blamed the other for failing to show up. Instead, David wrote to George from a tavern. Well aware that the Poes scoffed at his pretensions to become an actor, he explained that he considered the profession honorable but had joined it "when a *wild boy*." And he would now abandon it to please George and his family, "provided I could do *any thing* else that would give bread to mine." Accusing George and the other Poes of insensitivity and neglect, he nevertheless presented himself as forced by "extreem distress" to ask a loan of "30, 20, 15, or even 10$." George returned a note saying he did not wish to hear from him again.

Eliza's marriage to David lasted only about another eight months. After finishing their third Boston season, in the summer of 1809, the couple moved to New York, whose Park Street Theater, seating about two thousand, was the largest in the country. Audiences here admired Eliza as a singer, dancer, and comedienne in the snappy adolescent roles she had cultivated, but critics commented often on her unsuitability for weightier parts, judging her "too light for *Ophelia*," "very unequal to *Desdemona*," "not calculated for the serious line." David Poe fared much worse: "a footman is the extent of what he ought to attempt." David found himself caricatured in the press as having a "muffin face," and renamed "Dan Dilly" for thus misspeaking on stage the name *Dandoli*. He responded, as he had in Boston, by threatening the critic, who retorted in print that he respected David but did not fear him: "This we beg to be explicitly understood." David Poe also quickly acquired in New York a reputation for drinking. Under the heading *"Sur un POE de Chambre,"* a newspaper printed scurrilous verses that played on the identity in sound between the name *Poe* and the French word *pot*, meaning either chamber pot or ale mug. The doggerel ended, *Son pere etait pot / Sa mere etait broc, / Sa grand mere etait pinte."*: His [David Poe's] father was an ale mug (or chamber pot); his mother was a pitcher; his grandmother was a pint. The company announced a cast change for a performance on October 20 owing to what it called David's "sudden indisposition," usually a euphemism for drunkenness.

But David Poe was more than indisposed or drunk. Having played in New York just over six weeks, he disappeared from the company, and apparently from the lives of Eliza and of his two children. Why he left them all is unknown, but by the age of twenty-five he had accumulated money problems, parental disapproval, drinking habits, bad reviews, a more successful wife, and children to support. Perhaps simply, as a contemporary wrote, he and Eliza "quarreled and parted." Nothing is known of where David went, or of what became of him.

On her own again at the age of twenty-two, Eliza played in New York about another nine months, until the close of the season in July. By then New York audiences and reviewers had warmed toward her, even in serious roles, and become aware that she was deserted and alone. Benefit performances for her were announced, calling attention to her *"private misfortunes"* and asking mothers especially to give aid, "for the purpose of extricating herself from embarrassments occasioned by having two small children to support out of the scanty pittance of her weekly wages." Aid was more than ever needed, for she was also pregnant again. In December 1810, while in the midst of a new and very busy southern tour, she gave birth to a daughter. She named the child Rosalie, probably after the many characters she had played called Rose, Rosamonda, Rosalie, or especially Rosina, the title role in *Rosina,* one of the parts she most often repeated.

By the following summer Eliza's health was failing. Her tour had started well: as Miss Arnold, Mrs. Hopkins, and Mrs. Poe, she had over the years won an enthusiastic following in the South. Audiences remembered her versatility, beauty, and craft, and greeted her return with delight. "Mrs. Poe's name is a brilliant gem in the theatric crown," one reviewer wrote; "No one has received more than she of the public applause." She acted and concertized in Richmond, Norfolk, Charleston, learning new plays, singing solos, appearing in everything from *Tekeli* to *The Merchant of Venice* to the role of Little Pickle. That she could continue to take this juvenile part suggests that she still seemed very young. But something was amiss. A reviewer in Norfolk, Virginia, recalled Eliza's earlier performances in the place, when she was said to be one of the handsomest women in America: "She never came on stage, but a general murmur ran through the house, 'What an enchanting Creature!'" But now her appearance had changed. Grief had "stolen the roses from her cheeks," the reviewer observed. "Misfortunes have pressed heavy on her. . . . She no longer commands that admiration and attention she formerly did."

Eliza's gaunt look represented more than grief. She was ill, perhaps with some infectious fever. She appeared infrequently when the company opened the Richmond theater in mid-August 1811, and had to be replaced as Rosina during the first week. By the second week of October she stopped appearing at all. Apparently by early November she was bedridden and a charity case. Fellow actors played two benefits for her relief. The manager of the troupe wrote on behalf of her and her children to David Poe's relatives in Baltimore but received no satisfactory reply. Citizens of Richmond, however, responded to appeals to *"THE HUMANE HEART,"* visiting her during her final illness and providing nurses and cooks. She died on Sunday morning, December 8, 1811, and was buried atop the steep slope of Richmond's Church Hill, in the graveyard of St. John's Church.

Eliza's children remained with her during part or all of her illness. They were likely also present at her death, for William Henry Leonard, then nearly five years old, later recalled that she spoke a "long . . . last farewell" to them. He retained a lock of her hair, but Eliza had not much else to give her orphans. What if anything went to the infant Rosalie is unknown. The lapse of a year between

David Poe's disappearance and Rosalie's birth stirred rumors in Richmond that she was Eliza's child not by David but by a lover. To Edgar, then nearly three, there apparently came a miniature portrait of Eliza, some of her letters, and her watercolor sketch of Boston harbor, on the back of which she had written, "For my little son Edgar, who should ever love Boston, the place of his birth, and where his mother found her *best,* and *most sympathetic* friends." Eliza of course left a subtler inheritance as well: the fragmentary knowledge of Tekeli, the Ushers, Dan Dilly, January 3, 1796; the sense of someone who had stirred in a world of singers and dancers, scenery and demon traps; the dim remembrance of herself.

Richmond; John and Fanny Allan.

DECEMBER 1811–JUNE 1815

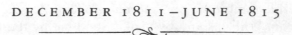

Built on several hills, Richmond in 1811 was a town developing into a city. Its population had doubled in the previous decade to some ten thousand people, of whom nearly four thousand were slaves. As the government seat of rural Virginia, it fittingly centered around the porticoed capitol building, designed by Thomas Jefferson in the form of a Roman temple, whose commanding situation gave a panoramic view of the James River, broken by rocks, small bright islands, and clumps of trees, with here and there the white sails of ships. The river and its falls powered flour mills, and made Richmond commercially promising and important. The first coal mined in America had been dug from deposits on both sides of the James; by now coal was being transported to the center of town by canal boats of eight tons. And from its beginnings Richmond had been a hub of the tobacco trade; by 1819 it supported eleven tobacco manufacturers. Inevitably growth bred nostalgia. Richmond's inhabitants had once been mostly planters with country estates who lived in town for the sake of social pleasures—men, as they were described, of "liberal habits of thinking and acting," and leisure to cultivate them. To the regret of some, a different breed was moving in, men of business and industry, often foreigners.

Among them was the thirty-two-year-old merchant John Allan, also called Jack, Jock, or, as a transplanted Scot, "Scotch" John Allan. A lean man—157 pounds, as he described himself, of "good hard flesh"—he seemed exacting. With his long hooked nose and small keen eyes under shaggy eyebrows, he reminded one contemporary of a hawk (Illus. 3). When just twenty-one, he had formed with his partner Charles Ellis a firm they called the House of Ellis and Allan. From an office, warehouse, and other buildings in the heart of Richmond's business district, they brokered tobacco and sold services and goods in prodigious variety. They undertook to make chains, bridle bits, and keys for ox yokes, to sharpen ploughs, mend scythes. Both piecemeal for local use and in wholesale lots of dozens, sacks, or bales to retailers, they dispensed plaster of paris, white lead, and bladders of putty; shawls, lace, and gilt buttons; herring, apples, and cornmeal; frying pans, coffeepots, and pickle jars; verdigris, wax, and leather; pencil cases, books, locks, wine, toiletries, pewter, and psyches (cheval mirrors), as well as the occasional marble tombstone or "celestial globes." A quite typical order came from Williamsburg by mail: "Send me by the first opportunity Payley's moral philosophy, Cavallo on electricity and a hat. . . . the enclosed string is the size that I wish the hat to be of." Such broad merchandising called for several employees and a separate counting room to handle daily consignments to shippers, warehousing of tobacco and other goods, and a stream of creditors and debtors for transactions often involving thousands of dollars.

The commerce of the House of Ellis and Allan was not only local or regional, but also national and international. The partners took their customers' tobacco as payment for goods dispensed during the year, then shipped the tobacco (and often flour) for sale abroad, where they bought foreign goods for sale in Richmond. Shipments in both directions were large: out went 500 barrels of flour for Cadiz or 86 hogsheads of James River tobacco for Liverpool; back from Cadiz came 438 boxes of cigars or from London £2,000 in flannel, velvet, and blankets. The firm's constant traffic with Bremen, the Azores, Belfast, Halifax, or Gibraltar brought news of international affairs and of schooners, sloops, sea captains, and meant a huge correspondence that ultimately filled 634 fat volumes. Because of the very large market for tobacco in Holland, the partners frequently wrote to Rotterdam, Amsterdam, and Antwerp, and even more often to Dieppe, Bordeaux, Paris, and other cities in France, sometimes called, in their private letters, Frog-land. The far-flung trading demanded political awareness, a cosmopolitan outlook, and occasional trips abroad. Charles Ellis had seen Napoleon in the flesh during a business trip to Paris. John Allan not only spoke of Napoleon's "wonder working genius," but also knew French and sometimes corresponded in it.

John Allan had a reputation for social benevolence—it was later said that he never turned a beggar from his door—and he and his wife, Frances, were theatergoers. A few months after he returned to Richmond from a trip to Lisbon, Frances reportedly joined the several charitable women of Richmond who brought aid to Eliza Poe's sickroom. The day after the actress's death, her infant daughter, Rosalie, was taken in by a Richmond family named Mackenzie. Frances Allan interested herself in the middle child, Edgar. John Allan (and his partner Charles Ellis) at first opposed her, but then yielded to her wishes and wrote concerning Edgar to David Poe's parents in Baltimore. They had taken in their grandson William Henry Leonard, eldest of the three orphans, but either could not afford to care for Edgar also, or else were won over by John Allan's promises to give him a liberal education. However the Allans managed it, they brought Edgar Poe into their home, although they did not formally adopt him.

The three-year-old child entered a vastly different setting from the one he had known of touring and theatrical props, brother and sister, abandonment and poverty. Materially, he was fortunate, for the House of Ellis and Allan provided well. Although profits hung unpredictably on global political events, the effect of weather on crops, and disasters at sea, since coming into existence a decade earlier the firm had generally prospered, enabling the partners to buy and improve Richmond real estate, purchase land (including a thousand acres in Ohio), and form the Marine Insurance Company, with a score of stockholders. These and John Allan's private stockholdings and investments in various banks made for domestic comfort: gilt chairs, globes and engravings (and a print of George Washington), two desks, a four wheel carriage called a coachee, three slaves, a sideboard and set of dining tables richly supplied with barrels of herring, ham, and venison, pounds of chocolate.

The furniture and sweets of course cannot measure how amply the Allans might provide for Edgar's feelings and spirit. In being John Allan's ward, he became dependent on the care and generosity of someone who despised dependence and felt that he had been cheated of care and generosity himself. Born to a pious seafaring family in the seaport of Irvine, Scotland, Allan had emigrated to America at about the age of sixteen. He became a clerk in the Richmond tobacco firm of his uncle, William Galt, the most successful merchant of his day in Virginia, a colorful man who had reportedly fled Scotland for America to escape prosecution for smuggling. Allan felt grateful to Galt for raising him in adolescence and training him in commercial affairs. Yet he also nursed resentment toward his uncle as a hard taskmaster who had denied him an academic education. Galt had kept him "tight to . . . business," he said, and withheld from him many kinds of liberal learning, "on the Ground that it was only a Loss of time &. the possession of them would be of no advantage to me." His resentment was the greater because Galt—a beneficent bachelor who adopted four orphans and supported four more—had not just refused him advantages but also granted them to others. One of Galt's young protégés, Allan felt, received "a better & more expensive Education than ever I had," although "I had stronger claims." For all Galt's help, Allan considered himself self-made, risen in the world, he said, "by my own exertions."

Allan's sense of deprivation gave his code of independence a begrudging, envious quality. His 'Stand on your own two feet' ever registered 'Why should you get what I did not?' In life and in business he required of others what he had given himself: obedience, industry, self-control. Among his favorite words and phrases were "fortitude," "correctness," "undeviating firmness," "perseverance," "good habits," "prudence." His advice to other young men in his position, often repeated in various forms, was "never fail to your Duty to your Creator first, to your Employer next." The success he had reaped made John Allan free to declare his principles, as he also did often: "I am not one of those much addicted to suffer by unavailing regrets"; "I always choose to be on the safe side"; "I as cheerfully forgive as I wish to be forgiven." Avuncular, didactic, and proud of his knowledge of the world, he both felt obliged and found it gratifying to dispense wisdom. He frequently quoted moral saws, cited the sayings of Poor Richard, or invented maxims of his own: "The mind is like a Garden judiciously laid out . . . neglect afterwards . . . permits thorns & weeds to arise, which greatly hurts the fruits."

John Allan had promised the family of David Poe to afford Edgar the liberal education he had not had himself. And in fact the life to which he introduced the child valued intellectual achievement, at least as an outgrowth of practical affairs or as a social ornament. He emphasized that success in business required skill in arithmetic, to make quick and accurate accounts, and in reading and writing, especially the use of correct spelling and grammar and the ability to write a clear, round hand (as he did). Like many Scots of the time, he was also conscious of speaking 'correct' English and tried to rid himself of his broad Scots pronunciation. (Curiously, he retained a burr orthographically, invariably spelling *very* as *verry*.) A knowledge of French, too, had business value owing to the importance of French markets, and even failing that, John Allan said, would "never be less than an elegant accomplishment." Indeed he prized such accomplishments as personal refinements. Despite his uncle's failure to provide him other than a business education, he had on his own, he said, "repaired many Gaps both in general Literature and the Sciences." He bought for the house a flute and a piano forte, and subscribed to Rees's *Encyclopedia.* He often quoted scraps of Cervantes and Swift, or of Shakespeare, whose literary ability he envied: "God! what would I not give, if I had his talent for writing! and what use would I not make of the raw material at my command!" His sense that life had given him stores of worldly knowledge is typical, as is the wish for cultural polish. Yet for all his cleverness in business John Allan's intellectual reach far exceeded his grasp. He at one time began a journal, induced to do so, he said, by "long observation and experience," and hoping to perhaps "serve the cause of Truth & Justice." But he managed to serve truth and justice no better than by such observations as "warm weather for the Season" and "done nothing in Horticulture yet."

John Allan's exacting manner covered not only frustrated longings for self-expression but also a sociability touched with self-indulgence, even dissipation. A legally naturalized American citizen, he relished the civilization and natural beauties of Virginia, "the Estates, the Blacks, Corn & Tobacco," and seems to have hunted, for he owned a bay horse named Saladin and a favorite pointer named Carlo. He also became a member of the local lodge of Masons, a long-lived fraternal organization in Richmond that had officiated in laying the cornerstone of the capitol. He had been born to a pious Presbyterian family, and his uncle William Galt chided him for doing business on Sundays instead of attending church, and for his enjoyment of whist and other card games. In the Allan house, too, liquor flowed freely, the family's bills for 1809–10 including payments for fifteen and a half gallons of brandy, twenty-two and a half gallons of rum, four and a half gallons of whisky, and a quart of gin. Having grown up with four sisters, "Scotch" John Allan felt on easy terms with women, and could be rakish. He spoke now and then of some "verry interesting Belles" in Richmond or of "my old Female Friends." In fact, a few years before taking in Edgar Poe he had likely fathered an illegitimate child, Edwin Collier, whose school expenses he continued to pay.

The care of Edgar Poe depended not only on John Allan but also on his wife, Frances, known as "Fanny" (Illus. 4). Her own history encouraged sympathy for the boy's plight. From the age of ten she too had been an orphan, raised by a guardian. Now twenty-six, she was barely older than Eliza Poe, whom she also resembled in being slight (104 pounds) and girlish. She busied herself sewing, purchasing rugs and mirrors, ordering fruit cake or quarts of strawberry ice cream and custard, not only dedicated to homemaking but in her management also, her husband proudly said, "verry economical." The many spelling errors in her surviving letters suggest a limited education: "I shall endeavor to take your advice" appears as "I shall endevour to take you advices." She brought with her into the marriage her older sister Anne Valentine, a fat and hearty woman who lived with the Allans as "Aunt Nancy." The marriage had remained childless—likely a motive for the couple's acceptance of Edgar— but also playfully affectionate. Fanny's letters to John Allan address him as "My Dear hubby" and "my dear old man," and she enjoyed needling his jealousy. Writing to him during one of his trips, she made a point of reporting that "we had a smart Beau with us"; she wanted him to see, she said, that "I could be as happy and contented without you as you appear to be in my absence." Although often flirtatious and high-spirited, Fanny was also chronically subject to accidents (at one time she fractured her face) and to illnesses that her family and friends believed were often imaginary.

Edgar Poe's new home, then, was amiable and well provided. He would be the responsibility of an unschooled but affectionate young woman of uncertain health, and of a sharp, hard-working merchant whose sententious moralism bespoke his rigorous and resentful demands on personal conduct, but who for all that could be charitable and relaxed. Only later would it appear whether these circumstances and qualities helped a three-year-old boy absorb the loss of his father, the witnessing of the last days and likely the death of his mother, and the separation from his brother and sister. But concerning Edgar's first three years or so with the Allans, only scraps of information survive, and virtually nothing to indicate his feelings:

his name was entered into the family Bible; in the early summer of 1813, amid fears of a British invasion of Richmond, he had an attack of whooping cough and then of measles; sometimes he was called Ned. He liked pets and had playmates, including a young daughter of the Poitiaux family, friends of the Allans, whom he reportedly called his "sweetheart." The Allans clothed him—several tailors' bills survive "to Cuting [*sic*] a suit for Edgar" (for seventy-five cents)—and took him along to White Sulphur Springs, a fashionable spa in the Virginia mountains where they sometimes spent the summer. Beginning to fulfill his promise to educate the boy, John Allan sent him, by the time he was five, to a teacher named Clotilda Fisher, apparently connected to the Allans' church, and after this to the Richmond schoolmaster William Ewing, who reported that Edgar was "charming" and liked the school.

During this time Edgar probably saw his sister, Rosalie, for the Allans lived near the Mackenzie family, who had taken her in. At first she had languished under their care, apparently suffering a serious illness during her second year; John Allan was informed that "poor little Rosalie is not expected to live." Edgar learned of his brother, William Henry Leonard, from David Poe's family in Baltimore. They wrote to thank John and Fanny Allan for their kindness to Edgar and to ask after his welfare. In this way word came to him that his brother spoke of him frequently, much wished to see him, "and is greatly pleased to hear that he is so good as also so pretty A Boy."

London;
The Fall of the House
of Allan and Ellis.

JUNE 1815–JULY 1820

At the age of six and a half, Edgar accompanied the Allans to England. Despite an interruption of trade during the War of 1812, the firm of Ellis and Allan had so much prospered that in 1815 Allan considered buying a steamboat 110 feet long at a cost of twenty-five thousand dollars, that could accommodate fifty passengers. The partners decided on a major expansion by opening a branch house in London, under John Allan's direction, to be called Allan and Ellis.

Fanny Allan balked at making the trip, fearful of the sea and unwilling to break the continuity of their life in Richmond. Allan promised her they would remain abroad at least three years, although he soon saw it would take at least five to be worth the expense of setting up a new establishment and to create trust for the firm in London. Expecting a long stay, he auctioned off a large number of the family's household goods, including mirrors, rugs, beeswax, a spy glass, a chicken coop, and 347 pounds of bacon, bringing more than three thousand dollars. He had a new suit made for Edgar (for two dollars) and bought several books for the boy's use, an "Olive Branch," a "Murray's Reader," and two "Murray's Spelling Books." Edgar, however, seemed to him indifferent to their departure: "Ned cared but little about it, poor fellow," he wrote.

Niggardly accommodations made the thirty-four-day passage to Liverpool uncomfortable. John Allan had to sleep each night, during the entire voyage, on the cabin floor. He had provided some or all of his own stores for the trip, but the captain denied Fanny and Aunt Nancy the privilege of a fire to broil a slice of bacon, severely restricted allowances of water, and, John Allan claimed, stole some of his hams and sold them. During the passage Fanny and her sister became "verry sick," Edgar "a little sick." But Edgar soon recovered. Arrived abroad, Allan sent to Charles Ellis in Richmond two messages that the boy wished to convey through him. For one, he wanted his love given to Mrs. Mackenzie and to his sister, "Rosa." The other message suggests that he had been listening to John Allan's pronouncements on manly fortitude. As Allan reported his words, "Edgar says Pa say something for me say I was not afraid coming across the Sea."

Edgar began his five-year stay with a trip to Scotland. For about six weeks the Allans visited Edinburgh, Glasgow, and Irvine, John Allan's birthplace, where Edgar met his guardian's sisters and uncles. By mid-October the family was installed in London. Allan rented furnished lodgings for six guineas a week at 47 Southampton Row in Russell Square, two streets from the British Museum. Although he determined to find a more convenient and cheaper place, the family remained here for about the next two years. And as they had done in Richmond, they lived well. Allan employed a housekeeper, bought cutlery and silverware, and for a spell hired a chariot, outfitting the coachman's seat with a new lace cushion. He kept his liquor supply well stocked by large purchases—three dozen bottles of choice West Indian Madeira, a dozen bottles of champagne, firkins and casks of beer. Fanny bought herself a parrot, he treated himself to London tailoring—among other items, four capes, two white marseilles waistcoats, a black silk florentine, a "Superfine box Coat." He described for Ellis a contented scene at 47 Southampton Row, himself sitting by a "snug fire in a nice little sitting parlour," Fanny and Nancy sewing, and "Edgar reading a little Story Book."

The London House of Allan and Ellis faltered in getting started, but soon prospered. Allan established the new firm at 18 Basinghall Street and took into his counting house a young assistant named George Dubourg. At first he discovered that, contrary to reports at home, the London tobacco market was depressed and getting worse. The city's commercial life, too, was more complex than Richmond's, with altogether different business methods. As an unfamiliar face, he also found it difficult to get credit and had trouble paying his bills. But in addition to being clever and ambitious, Allan was also persistent and patient. "We must not *dash*," he wrote to Ellis. He soon learned that to get bargains in London one had to buy in large quantities, as he began doing. Soon he was arranging interest rates with banks and making large sales, one tobacco transaction bringing a profit of over seventeen thousand dollars. By 1817 the partners' real estate, stocks, credits, and goods in hand had become worth more than three hundred thousand dollars. Pleased to note that the firm's credit had "attained an eminence which gives me great advantage," he decided to extend his stay. Buying a solid mahogany wardrobe and two chests of drawers (and a copy of Scott's *Rob Roy*), he rented a house nearby, at 39 Southampton Row, for another five years.

While in London, young Edgar Allan—as he was known there—had his first rigorous schooling. He probably attended classes briefly in John Allan's hometown of Irvine, but during most of Edgar's seventh and eighth years, Allan sent him to board with the Misses Dubourg, the family of the firm's eighteen-year-old clerk George. Their school stood on Sloane Street, in Chelsea, about three miles through Piccadilly from the Allans' rented flat in Russell Square. Here Edgar was given a "Separate Bed," a spelling book, geography, and history of England, as well as a seat in church (perhaps Episcopal), with a prayer book and catechism. John Allan naturally paid for them all, and for such other expenses as washing, pens, linen, and shoe strings, receiving reports from the Dubourgs on his state: "Your Son I am glad to say is well & happy."

For part of his eighth and during his ninth years, Edgar boarded at the school of the Reverend John Bransby, at Stoke Newington, four miles from London. As recalled by one of his pupils, Bransby was a portly man, apt at quoting Shakespeare and Horace. Edgar studied Latin, among other subjects, and took dancing lessons. Allan seems to have been pleased with his academic progress. He recorded with satisfaction at various times that Edgar was "a good Scholar" or that he read Latin "pretty sharply." He seems also to have given his ward abundant pocket money; in fact Bransby reportedly thought he allowed the boy an extravagant amount, and by that "spoilt him!" Allan observed Edgar's physical development too, noting that at nine and a half he was "thin as a rasor."

However sharp in his studies or full in pocket, Edgar evidently found his school days in London less rewarding than Allan did, and later remembered them as lonely and unhappy. While boarding at Bransby's, he probably spent the weekends with the Allans, and occasionally came into the city for a day. But living away from his caretakers, under new and unfamiliar custodians, in a strange country, angered and frightened him. How stranded he felt appears in a later account by James Galt, a member of William Galt's family who was fifteen years old and living in Scotland when the Allans visited there in 1815. Galt recalled that John Allan planned to have Edgar educated in Irvine. But Edgar opposed being left in Scotland far from the Allans in London. Later that year, Allan sent Edgar back to Scotland despite his and Fanny's objections, in the company of young James. Throughout the journey, James said, Edgar kept up "an unceasing fuss." At the school in Irvine he sulked, refused to take up his studies, and threatened to return to England. Galt was appointed to keep watch over him and sleep in his room. Had Edgar not been so restrained, Galt believed, he would have tried to make the trip back to the Allans in London alone, although then only seven years old.

Nor can the occasions when Edgar returned to the Allans from Bransby's or the Dubourgs' have been very consoling. His hands full of business, and called away on trips to Bristol, Liverpool, Manchester, and other cities, John Allan found himself without time for his family, "a prisoner in London," he complained, "& almost a stranger in my own house." When his sister Mary came from Scotland for a visit she felt neglected by him and snipped, "my Brother is so much engaged with business that he has no time to gallant ladies." John Allan was not only preoccupied but, so far as concerned Edgar, also insulated by the formality of his goodwill. Several times he told correspondents that Edgar was "a fine Boy" or "a verry fine Boy," and frequently in closing mentioned that he was "quite well." The brief remarks seem at once caring and ritualistic, a combination amounting to the satisfaction taken in performing a charitable Duty. Edgar remained unadopted, and perhaps owing to his anomalous position he did not count outside of Allan's family circle. Relatives of John Allan sometimes sent the boy regards, especially William Galt, "Uncle Galt," as Edgar called him. But scores of friends and associates wrote to Allan in London asking to be remembered to Fanny or Aunt Nancy, without mentioning Edgar, who did not exist for them: "Please present my best respects to Mrs. Allan & Miss [Nancy] Valentine"; "sincere regards to Mrs. Allan her Sister & your own good Self"; "present my best wishes to Mrs. Allan & Miss V." Even one of John Allan's brothers-in-law ended a letter to him from Scotland saying the family there "desires to be Remembered to you Mrs. Allan & Miss Valentine."

Fanny Allan cannot often have been available to Edgar in London either, as she was frequently ill. She had made the trip reluctantly, and once arrived in London felt homesick, "cursedly dissatisfied," John Allan said. She dreamt of her Richmond friends, sent back for hominy, and after a year abroad wished to return. She suffered one misery after another: bad cold and sore throat, swollen face, headaches, croup, attacks of "Catarrh," a fall. She was sometimes confined to her room and nursed by her sister Nancy, sometimes in great pain. John Allan had remained healthy—his body, he said, "hard as a lightwood knot"—and often grew impatient with his wife's many upsets. He noted several times that she was "complaining as usual." In the fall of 1817 her health became so precarious that a physician urged him to take her for the waters and country air at Cheltenham, as he did, spending some time there himself before leaving her in Nancy's care and returning to London. The waters helped but she remained "not Hearty," he wrote, and "complaining." He also took her for a few days to the Isle of Wight to test the salubrious effects of the sea air. Still other times she sought to regain her health by traveling to Devonshire with some of Allan's English business colleagues, or to Dawlish for air and exercise. Occasionally she managed to play a game of whist with her husband or attend a dinner party with him. But her recoveries seem to have been few and momentary. Once when they dined aboard a ship, Fanny was in such good spirits that she raced a group of ladies up and down the decks. For John Allan it was an event, the "first frolic," he said, "I have had for a long time."

A settled home life had come, for Fanny as for Edgar, after the shock of orphanage, and her chronic indisposition perhaps sprang from renewed distress in selling off her household goods and leaving Richmond. That her many complaints had some emotional source seemed clear to George Elwall, the head of a large London firm with whom Allan conducted much business. Elwall and his wife accompanied Fanny during her attempted cure in Devonshire. He flatly told Allan that Fanny had been "spooked by a stupid fellow of a Doctor" into thinking herself ill. He considered her ailments the result of "lassitude consequent on inactivity," and believed that moderate exercise would restore her strength. He was certain, he told Allan, *that she is well.*" As evidence he observed that once when they rode out on the sand beach, her horse refused to go, compelling her to walk a long distance. As a result, "strange to tell," that evening she appeared "in better spirits than I have yet seen her." The next day she complained of feeling sick again, but Elwall attributed her relapse to imagination, "a fancy that she must be ill because she walked so much yesterday." On her part, Fanny bristled at interpretations of her condition as illusory. "I find you are determined," she told John Allan, "to think my health better contrary to all I say."

Often ill and sometime absent, Fanny Allan cannot have offered Edgar much reassurance against the possibility of losing a parent again, or taken much care of him. At times she was thrice-removed, existing only in a report of a report. When she went to Cheltenham with John Allan for several weeks to try a water cure, Edgar's closest contact with her came in a letter from Allan to young George Dubourg. It was through this teenaged clerk that Edgar learned, that John Allan had in closing sent news, that "Mrs. Allan desires her Love to Edgar."

With little warning, after about three and a half years abroad, John Allan found the London tobacco market collapsing. At the beginning of 1819, prices fell sharply, breaking the important firm of Campbell and Bowden: "The effect of such an unsuspected House as this giving way is tremendous," he wrote; "it destroys all Confidence between man & man." He determined to sell whenever he could get an offer, but in the general slowing of trade and rising panic no money was to be had. "The Tobacco Merchants are all marked," he believed, "& I should think . . . they are the destined victims of inevitable ruin." He began appealing to Ellis for funds to get him through the month, urging him to push their debtors for payment. But the remittances he anxiously awaited from Richmond failed to arrive, for business at home had suffered also. State banks in Virginia had begun failing, taking with them many merchants and farmers. The firm of Ellis and Allan stood "as well as a House can do," Allan said, but it had been hurt. In the early spring pressure for money became intense. One London merchant, he noted grimly, fearing his family must go to the workhouse, had hanged himself from the bedpost by a towel.

John Allan's own crisis loomed toward the end of April. *"Hitherto I have held my own,"* he warned Ellis, *"but next week is a trying one, all my resources is exhausted."* He begged his partner for immediate aid: "throw every cent you can rake & scrape into my hands." Allan's realization that the firm had been caught in a network of far larger financial problems at first relieved him of guilt and self-doubt: "In canvassing my intentions & actions as a Merchant," he said, "I have nothing to reproach myself with & this has given me a courage to face & a perseverance to oppose and I hope eventually to overcome all obstacles." Rousing himself, he treated the threat of ruin as a test of his lifelong principles and proclaimed his determination not to falter or despond, and to show nothing of uncertainty. Four years in London had given him "an excellent command of my features," he boasted, *"but then I have had much experience in that way."* To do otherwise than bear up and maintain his composure would unfit him for action, destroy his health, and bring despair. "I . . . always say If we are doomed to Fall let us Fall like men."

The chain of business collapses reached the House of Allan and Ellis on July 17, when Allan stopped payment, unable to meet the firm's debts. Having hardly a shilling left, he asked Ellis to send Fanny some, any, money, "a little Bill . . . to keep us from starving." By October, with the landlord of his Russell Square house dunning him for the rent, he owed some thirty-five thousand pounds. In terms of American currency, the firm's indebtedness was eventually revealed to be nearly $223,000. Despite John Allan's vow to outbrave the situation with energy, conviction, and firmness, this outcome to his London adventure of white marseilles waistcoats and lace-cushioned chariots left him doubting and disillusioned. Privately he now viewed his attempt to set up an overseas house as overreaching, and confided to Ellis that the partners had "erred through pride and ambition," marking themselves for extinction. After settling his affairs, he announced, he would not return to business but would become a farmer or planter.

Luckily, John Allan found many of his creditors disposed to be friendly, willing to give him a year to settle his debts. With their consent, and on the advice of William Galt, he decided to go back to Richmond, where he could see to putting the House in order and paying what he owed. But his trials evidently had taken a physical toll as well. He planned to sail from London in March 1820 but succumbed to a case of "Billious Pleurisy" whose "alarming severity" confined him for a month, then left him weak and forced him to postpone the trip until the summer. To his surprise, Fanny had helped him keep up an appearance of confidence during his crisis by managing to seem unperturbed too, bearing herself, he wrote, "with more fortitude than could have been expected." But having "the greatest aversion to the sea," as he described it, she feared the return crossing. As the time for their departure from England neared, she again became ill.

On July 21, 1820, after a voyage of thirty-six days, John Allan and his family arrived in New York. As if planning to return sometime to England, they left behind with a friend some household goods, including a piano and, it seems, a portrait of Edgar. In concluding the dozens of letters he wrote during his financial disaster, Allan omitted mentioning that "Edgar is quite well," a tag he often routinely added at the end. He omitted Edgar's name once again when informing a correspondent in London that during the very rough voyage Fanny had been extremely seasick and had complained of the extreme heat on their arrival in New York, where she felt so unwell he had to send for a doctor.

Early Ambition;
Jane Stanard; Moldavia.

SUMMER 1820 – SUMMER 1825

Unsettled and financially troubled, the Allans made several moves in Richmond as Edgar grew into his teens. For at least a few months they lived with the Ellises, in a dormered cottage on Second and Franklin streets, before taking a house at Fifth and Clay streets, in the Shockoe Hill district, reportedly a long frame building of two and a half stories, with an acre and a half of garden. From here they moved once more, in 1822 or 1823, to a house given or loaned them by William Galt, at Fourteenth Street and Tobacco Alley, a neighborhood of tobacco warehouses.

During these moves Edgar continued his schooling, this time living at home. Most elementary education in Virginia at the time depended on private academies, of twenty or so male students each, that offered Greek and Latin, French, English composition, math, some science, and occasionally commercial subjects like accounting and shorthand. Until about midway through his fourteenth year Edgar attended the academy of Joseph H. Clarke, a graduate of Trinity College, Dublin. For about two years after that he studied with Clarke's successor, William Burke, an accomplished Latinist who advertised that his academy would serve "to prepare young gentlemen for obtaining an honourable entrance in any University in the United States."

Edgar's schooling in Richmond disclosed and encouraged a gift for language. By the age of thirteen and a half he was reading Horace, and Cicero's *De officiis* (On duty). One classmate recalled that he was always the first in scanning Latin poetry, another that he excelled in "capping verses," an exercise in which the first student quoted a line of Latin verse, and the second had to quote another line beginning with the same initial letter, or the same first and last letters. Edgar also progressed well in French, and began writing satirical and other verses in English, some of which he showed to the other boys. Only one of his early poems survives (in a later transcript), an eighteenth-century-style satire, written when Edgar was perhaps sixteen. Entitled "Oh, Tempora! Oh, Mores!" after Cicero, it caustically portrays a young clerk in a dry goods store. Named Pitts, he is a lower-class pretender to fashion—his "dove-tailed coat, obtained at cost"—and to the arts of seduction: "who so cold, so callous to refuse/The youth who cut the ribbon for her shoes!" Apart from its priority, the poem is notable for its skill in imitation, its scorn toward the clerk as a plebeian vulgarian, and its contempt for the world of merchandising. According to schoolmaster Clarke, Edgar wrote enough fugitive verse to make a whole volume, and wanted John Allan to have it published. But Clarke claimed that he advised Allan to refuse, believing it would harm Edgar at a tender age to be "flattered and talked about as the author of a printed book."

Edgar's accomplishments meant for him not just success but victory. Those who knew him at school later remembered him as blatantly competitive, "eager for distinction," "ambitious to excel," "inclined to be imperious." One classmate said that he "hated a rival." In striving to distinguish himself, he turned to athletics as well. He had returned from England, it was said, with a ruddy face that made him look "like an English boy" (Charles Ellis found the whole family "a little Englishised"), and lithe in body, sinewy and graceful although slight. Another classmate recalled him as "a swift runner, a wonderful leaper, and what was more rare, a boxer, with some slight training," who would invite other boys to hit him forcefully on the chest. He particularly showed off his superior athletic ability in swimming. To a companion at Burke's school he seemed a champion, "the best, the most daring, and the most enduring swimmer that I ever saw in the water." Probably around the age of fifteen or sixteen, he became locally famous for swimming six miles in the James River under a hot June sun and, at least part of the distance, against a strong tide. Beginning from the wharf of a tobacco dealer named Ludlam, and accompanied by a boat containing several boys, he swam downriver to a place called Warwick Bar, emerging from the water with his neck, face, and back blistered.

Not only ambitious for himself, Edgar also desired to lead others. His prowess and daring made him an exemplar to some other boys, such as Thomas Ellis, the son of John Allan's partner, whom Edgar conducted in various escapades and taught to shoot, swim, and skate. "No boy ever had a greater influence over me than he had," Ellis said later. "My admiration for him scarcely knew bounds." At the age of fifteen Edgar became a lieutenant—apparently the second-in-command—of a volunteer company of Richmond boys, the Junior Morgan Riflemen. When the much-loved Marquis de Lafayette, then in his sixties, visited Richmond in October 1824, the young riflemen were appointed to ride in the procession that followed Lafayette's carriage past handkerchief-waving spectators to the Eagle Hotel. In the uniform of his company, Edgar was later reviewed by Lafayette himself. The recognition was doubly appropriate because during the American Revolution, as he knew, his grandfather, General David Poe—father of the actor David Poe, Jr.—had won notice for his self-sacrificing efforts in the hard-pressed Quartermaster Department, sometime paying for supplies out of his own pocket. Lafayette had praised Edgar's grandfather when visiting Baltimore two weeks earlier, singling him out as a friend and ally who had somehow scraped together five hundred dollars to help clothe his troops. After Lafayette's visit, Edgar cosigned, with the Riflemen's captain, two letters to the governor and Council of Virginia, asking on behalf of their company to retain the weapons they had been allowed to draw from the armory.

In wanting to excel and to command, Edgar resembled many other orphans, in whom a feeling of nonexistence and the need to master changeable surroundings often produce a will for power. But even as he tried to transcend what he lacked or had lost, there remained much to remind him of it. In England he had been called Edgar Allan; returned to Richmond, where his status was apparently well known, he was called Edgar Poe. The examples of two nearby orphans emphasized that the Allans had not adopted him. His sister, Rosalie, had been christened by the Mackenzie family, who formally gave her their name. And "Uncle" William Galt brought to America and formally adopted his orphaned relative James, the sixteen-year-old who had allegedly stood guard over Edgar in Scotland. Galt emphatically and publicly referred to the boy as the child "of my adoption and nurture."

At the same time, the celebrity of his grandfather, and much else, served to remind Edgar that he was "Edgar Poe." His brother, William Henry Leonard, by now called Henry, visited him in Richmond twice and wrote at least once (then complained that Edgar failed to reply). Edgar himself visited Rosalie, now called Rose, who was being educated in the fashionable girls' school run by a member of the Mackenzie family. Barely one year old at the time of Eliza Poe's death, Rose believed until the age of ten that her adoptive mother, Mrs. Jane Mackenzie, was her natural mother. She was developing into a hapless, vague-seeming child whose very birthdate was uncertain, listed in the Mackenzie family Bible as "(is said) was born 20 Decr. 1810." Seriously ill in infancy, she continued to be pale and drawn-looking, and according to one of the Mackenzies proved difficult to raise, "she was such a delicate stunted frail little creature." Family members spoke of her as "poor Rose." Edgar's mother also retained some being, for her theatrical reputation survived her. Although Edgar may not have been aware of them, collections of songs published in Richmond in 1817 and in Petersburg in 1824 both included the text and music to her popular specialty number, "Nobody Coming to Marry Me," with the explanation: "As sung by Mrs. Poe, with unbounded applause."

In fact, Edgar continued to seek motherly succor, even as he tried to command his own destiny and to lead others. He felt affectionate toward Fanny Allan, called her Ma, savored the whiff of orrisroot that arose from her bureau drawers. But however loving Fanny's intentions, her continuing illness, worrisome in itself, made her a less than ideal mother: as John Allan said, she was "never clear of complaint." Edgar sought replacements for her. By one account he called Rose's foster mother, Jane Mackenzie, Ma. When about fourteen years old, he became lastingly infatuated with Mrs. Jane Stanard, the warmhearted thirty-year-old mother of one of his schoolmates. Several reliable later accounts report that he went to her for sympathy when unhappy at home, felt consoled and comforted by her, and indeed loved her with "all the affectionate devotion of a son." In one dramatic way she resembled both Eliza Poe and Fanny Allan: she was ill, seemingly a victim for several years of depression. Its source is unknown, but she dwelt unhappily on her own mother's remarriage, and the installation in her father's place of someone she could not respect. Jane's husband chided her for yielding readily to melancholy, and recommended to her "a resigned & *chearful temper*." But she felt incapable of exertion. She suffered, she told him, from a "death-like sickness." Edgar knew her in Richmond for about a year before she died insane at around the age of thirty-one.

Edgar frequently visited Jane Stanard's grave in Shockoe Hill Cemetery. Upset by the loss of this young motherly woman, with its shadow of earlier loss, he grew cross and dejected. His behavior exasperated John Allan and led to clashes at home. Now nearly sixteen, the boy seemed to him transformed, miserable, behaved "sulky & ill-tempered to all the Family." He interpreted Edgar's mood as a sign of thanklessness. He had continued to provide for him, faithfully paying his school bills, laying out eleven and a half dollars for "coats, pantaloons & trimmings," buying him a knife or some calf boots. But he received no appreciation in return: "The boy possesses not a Spark of affection for us not a particle of gratitude for all my care and kindness towards him." When Allan considered the high principles that had governed his own actions, Edgar's coldness and crankiness galled him the more: death itself, he said, would hold no terrors for him, "Had I done my duty as faithfully to my God as I have to Edgar." He did not help the situation by writing to Henry Poe, complaining about Edgar and unfavorably comparing him to his brother: "I feel proudly the difference between your principles & his," he said. In passing he also referred to the rumored illegitimacy of Rose, remarking that "At least She is half your Sister." The remarks seem spiteful and mischievous, bound to create discord. But Edgar's unresponsiveness did more than affront John Allan's pride in his high-minded behavior. Inevitably it reminded Allan that at about the same age he had been kept tight to business and denied the world outside it, reviving old resentments against William Galt: "I have given [Edgar] a much superior Education," he did not fail to point out, "than ever I received myself."

Edgar's failure to feel indebted contrasted, too, with John Allan's three-year struggle to honor the debts of his House. Pressed by creditors, snarled in lawyers and lawsuits, he and his partner had managed by the middle of 1822 to pay off only about one hundred and fifty-five thousand dollars of what they owed, even after sacrificing in a depressed real estate market the most valuable part of their property. They had continued to sell from their store on at least a retail basis, but although they traveled throughout the state pursuing people who owed them money, they had been forced to arrange a final settlement for bankruptcy. Allan apparently managed to survive because William Galt bought the firm's assets and took him in as a secret partner.

On the morning of March 26, 1825, John Allan was at home with William Galt, who owned the house, and Galt's adopted son James. Galt breakfasted on a cup of tea and two small pancakes, then asked the others to help him into an easy chair. They secured him by his hands and under the shoulders when, in John Allan's words, he "suddenly threw back his head & eyes and seemed oppressed." Uncle Galt straightened himself and died.

Said to be the wealthiest man in Virginia, able to ride fifteen

square miles of his own rich land, Galt owned the firm of Galt and
Galt Jr., real estate in Richmond and Lynchburg, plantations in several counties, grist and sawmills, stock in the Bank of Virginia, and
several hundred slaves. To John Allan he bequeathed a one-third
portion of his pew in the Presbyterian Church, the house that Allan
was occupying, and three landed estates: Lower Byrd, containing
about 870 acres, Little Byrd, about 673 acres, and Big Byrd,
amounting to about 4,040 acres. Allan's inheritance was estimated
at three quarters of a million dollars.

The endless dunning and lawsuits abruptly ended, John Allan set
out to buy a new home. By the summer he located a two-story
brick house, which he bought at public auction for fifteen thousand
dollars. Named Moldavia, it had once been owned by the very
wealthy Joseph Gallego, founder of the Richmond milling industry,
whose flour was world-famous. Its eight outbuildings, cultivated
vegetable and flower gardens, grapevines and fig trees, made it more
nearly an estate than a house (Illus. 5). Set on the slope of a hill
and advertised as "more eligible in point of situation perhaps, than
any in the *city*," it offered views of the James River and wooded
hills beyond, as well as the capitol building. The interior shone no
less: a spacious hall and wide mahogany stairway, generously pro-
portioned rooms, a mirrored ballroom with hand-carved mantel, a
tearoom, a notable octagonal dining room, to which the Allans added
rich hangings for the windows and doors, expensive furniture, busts
and paintings.

Aunt Nancy was given a room on the second floor, as was Edgar,
now sixteen and a half and preparing to go off to the university. It
is said that on the front portico of the house, supported by lofty
pillars, hawklike John Allan set a fine telescope he had brought
from London to indulge his interest in astronomy. Around Christmastime he ordered bushels of oysters and casks of whisky. If not
exactly by Industry and Duty, he had recovered from his fall hand-
somely and stood again on his own, only now, as a contemporary
described him, as "Elector of Moldavia."

Difficulties at the University of Virginia and Flight from Richmond.

FEBRUARY 1826 – MARCH 1827

Edgar's enrollment at the University of Virginia, in February 1826, brought his quarreling with John Allan to a breaking point. Located near the village of Charlottesville, sixty miles from Richmond, the school lay in a verdant basin between the Southwest Mountains and the Blue Ridge, the Ragged Mountains rising in the distance. It had opened only the year before, the fulfillment of forty years' thought and planning by its eighty-three-year-old rector, Thomas Jefferson. Architecturally he had designed what he called an "academical village." At one end of a long broad quadrangle he had erected a rotunda-shaped library, modeled on the Pantheon in Rome. Along the sides, like houses fronting a village green, he had built two-story pavilions, each illustrating some famous classical structure. They contained lodgings for the professors above and classrooms beneath, and were linked by one-story dormitories that housed many of the 177 students.

Edgar's conflicts with John Allan did not include his guardian's enthusiasm for academic learning. To have a collegiate education, Edgar said, was something "I most ardently desired." And although the uncompleted construction of the university meant crowded classrooms and plumbing problems, he felt proud to be attending. He observed enthusiastically the progress of the rotunda library as its pillars were completed ("greatly improves the appearance") and books came in ("we have a very fine collection"). The curriculum, too, offered scope for his ambition, especially in languages. By Jefferson's plan, the faculty consisted of eight professors, each heading a school. Edgar enrolled in the schools of ancient languages, taught by Cambridge Master of Arts George Long, and of modern languages, taught by the German George Blaettermann, a handsome curly haired man, careless in dress and appearance. Some students complained of Blaettermann's way of teaching, but Edgar thrived under it; his translations were remembered at the university for having been "precisely correct." Something of his competence in French may be judged by his having withdrawn from the library three volumes of Charles Rollin's *Histoire Ancienne* and two volumes of his *Histoire Romaine,* as well as two volumes of Voltaire. He also studied Italian (and probably some Spanish), and with distinction. According to a later account, Blaettermann once urged his students to render into English verse a portion of Tasso, not requiring the exercise but recommending it as beneficial. At his next lecture he announced that of the entire class only Edgar had done the translation, and complimented his performance. As exams approached, Edgar worked hard, studying he said "a great deal in order to be prepared." At the end of the year, he was listed as having excelled in the examination of both the senior Latin class and the senior French class. Since the new school did not yet grant degrees, these apparently represented the highest student honors.

Edgar sought to be first in other ways as well. Joining the Jefferson Society, a debating club, he acted for a while as secretary and, it was said, "grew noted as a debater." Classmates recalled that he remained an outstanding athlete too, "adept in all gymnastic exercises." One claimed that two or three students, running down a slight slope, jumped nineteen feet, but that Edgar surpassed them with a running broad jump of twenty feet. Whether Edgar pursued his artistic interests in the same competitive spirit is unknown, but he continued to cultivate them. He wrote verse and recited it to friends, and also sketched in charcoal. He reportedly bought a copy of Byron embellished with engravings, one of which he copied onto the ceiling of his room, life-sized, ultimately making a large fresco.

For all Edgar's desiring a university education and success in his studies, a classmate found him moody, frolicsome in his better humor but at times morose. The gloom may in part have arisen from disappointment in his first known romantic attachment. Before leaving Richmond, he had come to care about a girl in the Allans' neighborhood named Elmira Royster. Few details survive, mostly from her later recollections: he was not very talkative, although pleasant when he did talk; introduced her to his brother, Henry, on a trip to Richmond; in a few minutes drew her likeness in pencil; was fond of music. (James Galt also recalled that Edgar sang frequently, "having both a musical and cultivated voice"—resembling in this his mother.) Whatever more Elmira found pleasing about Edgar, she liked him well enough, as she put it later, to have "engaged myself to him." While at the university Edgar wrote to her frequently. But her father opposed the match because of their ages: Edgar was then perhaps sixteen and a half, she only fifteen years old. He intercepted Edgar's letters from Charlottesville, which as a result received no answer from Elmira.

Having to live on his own perhaps also contributed to Edgar's gloom. He was young to be at the university. The average age for beginning students (at least in 1830), was nearly nineteen years; Edgar at the time he entered was only a month past his seventeenth birthday. And student life was chaotic, even dangerous. Jefferson had felt that high-spirited Virginia youth would not be amenable to the tight discipline of Harvard and other northern schools. He established a system of minimal rules and maximum self-governance, hoping students would monitor one another's behavior for the good of all. But his system failed. During a riot in the school's first year, masked undergraduates threw bricks and bottles at professors; a drunken student was charged with hurling through Professor Long's window a bottle filled with urine. The faculty threatened to resign unless the university established "an efficient Police." During Edgar's year, seven students were suspended or expelled for high-stakes gambling, assaults, or drunkenness, and his examination in French had to be rescheduled after "some or all" of the class managed to steal the questions beforehand. And as he reported, "a common fight is so trifling an occurrence that no notice is taken of it." One of his schoolmates, drunk on mint-sling and down about two hundred dollars at cards, accused another player of cheating and whipped him with a cowhide strap. Several scholars besieged the house of a townsman and stripped the clothes off his servant-woman, believing she had "infected the Students with disease." On one occasion Edgar himself was called before the faculty to give information on reports that certain school officials who boarded students also drank and gambled with them in the dormitories. (He testified he had heard nothing about it.)

The violent and dissolute atmosphere unnerved Edgar. Comments about disturbances at the university take up nearly all of the two surviving letters he wrote from the school, betraying his unease in talk of "great consternation" at the school, students' "fear of the Faculty," hopes of doing well "if I don't get frightened." Several incidents he described for John Allan graphically. A student struck by another on the head with a large stone, drew a pistol—"which are all the fashion here," he wrote—that misfired but would otherwise have killed his attacker. One of the most violent of the "great many fights" he witnessed directly: "I saw the whole affair—it took place before my door." A Kentucky student named Wickliffe, once suspended already, dominated another student in a fight, but not content with that "began to bite," Edgar told John Allan. "I saw the arm afterwards—and it was really a serious matter—It was bitten from the shoulder to the elbow—and it is likely that pieces of flesh as large as my hand will be obliged to be cut out."

Reporting this savage biting and other disturbing incidents to John Allan served Edgar for both relief and protest. Passing his own fright on to someone else in some degree reduced it. Even when younger, and perhaps for the same reason, he liked to shock. A son of Charles Ellis recalled an evening at the Allans' house, while a few guests sat quietly at card tables: Edgar covered himself with a sheet and carrying a long cane entered the room as a ghost, intending, Ellis said, "to frighten the whole body of whist players, who were in truth stirred to a commotion." At the same time, Edgar's reports of the harrowing scenes he had witnessed—"I saw the arm afterwards . . . bitten from shoulder to elbow"—sound like indirect appeals for John Allan's reassurance and help. Allan visited the university once during Edgar's stay, likely on business in Charlottesville. Edgar wanted him to return but apparently felt able to tell him so only obliquely. "Perhaps you will have some business up here," he wrote after describing some of the confusion at the school, "and then you can judge for yourself."

What mostly fed Edgar's quarrel with John Allan were his financial problems at the university. During the year he accumulated very large gambling and other debts, a burden he blamed on Allan entirely. According to his later account, Allan sent him to Charlottesville with a hundred and ten dollars, which went immediately to pay for board and attendance at the two schools. Still owing $15 for room rent, $12 for a bed, and $12 more for furniture, payable in advance, he took on debts from the start. In fact, with its grand buildings and substantial faculty salaries, Jefferson's university was the most expensive collegiate school in America, and a costly style of living prevailed. Most students were sons of well-to-do planters, professional men, and merchants. They dressed expensively, waited on by locally owned slaves who shined their shoes and cleaned their rooms, enabling them to maintain while away from home a gentlemanly round of partying, drinking, riding, occasionally even cockfighting. Sent there without enough money for even the academic costs, Edgar said, he was "immediately regarded in the light of a beggar."

A week after arriving in Charlottesville Edgar wrote to Allan asking for more money and for books. Allan replied, he said, with "the utmost abuse," blaming him not only for failing to pay his expenses out of the money he had been given, but even for attending two schools instead of three. Allan did send forty dollars to cover the thirty-nine that Edgar owed, leaving him a dollar for himself. Since he needed books to continue at the university, he said, he got them on credit. Obliged also to hire a servant and pay for wood, washing, and other necessaries, he borrowed money "of Jews in Charlottesville at extravagant interest." Near the close of the school year Allan sent a hundred dollars, but too late and not enough to help. Needing still more, Edgar wrote to Richmond asking a loan from young James Galt, who refused. It was then, becoming "desperate," he explained, that he was driven to start gambling, and so "i[n]volved myself irretrievably."

The truthfulness of Edgar's account, given some five years later, cannot be known, and speculation on its likelihood points for and against. To his charge that John Allan failed to provide adequately for his expenses, it might be said that Allan had always supported him liberally; schoolmaster Bransby, and others, thought Allan overindulged him. Three months after Edgar enrolled at the university, Allan sent him a "uniform coat," six yards of striped cloth for making trousers, and four pairs of socks; pleased, Edgar wrote back that the coat was "a beautiful one & fits me exactly." Yet for all his wealth Allan could also be stingy. When living in London, he put off a visit from two of his sisters in Scotland for the reason, they insinuated, that he "begrudged the trifle they would have consumed during their stay." Feelings of envy and resentment may also have subtly prompted him to repeat with Edgar his own upbringing under William Galt, keeping his ward on a tight rein and withholding advantages he could well afford. On the other hand, against Edgar's claim that he desperately gambled and borrowed to cover essential school costs, it might be said that he needed no special reason to gamble, given the social habits of his classmates and the atmosphere at the school, not to mention John and Fanny Allan's own fondness for whist and other card games. And it is known that near the end of the term he bought on credit for $68, almost the cost of his tuition, not academic necessities but the equivalents of John Allan's marseilles waistcoats, such finery as three yards of "Super Blue Cloth," a set of the "Best Gilt Buttons," and a velvet vest.

No matter whose fault, Edgar returned to Richmond in debt, reputedly for some $2,000 to $2,500. Fanny is said to have greeted him fondly, but others gossiped; he remarked later that he felt ostracized by the notoriety, "taunts & abuse . . . even from those who had been my warmest friends." And after one year his college education was over. He wished to continue, but John Allan apparently refused to support him for another term. (The fact meant no added disgrace; most students attended for only one session, very few ever earned the title of graduates.) Allan permitted (or maybe forced) him to clerk for a while in his countinghouse, although with his huge inheritance he was now withdrawing from the firm. On returning, Edgar faced the added disappointment that Elmira Royster was no longer available. By one later account her parents had sent her away from Richmond; by another, Edgar on his first evening home attended a party at her house, only to find that it marked her engagement.

Most seriously, however, Edgar was pursued for his debts. A schoolmate came to Richmond asking payment on a note of thirty dollars. One Richmond merchant got the constable to begin a court case against Edgar. The constable finding that Edgar lacked property to seize in repayment, the merchant was asked to consider whether to compel Edgar to plead nonage (i.e., legal minority), or have him sent to jail. Edgar found himself, he said, "Every day threatened with a warrant." John Allan refused to pay these or any of Edgar's other debts—the velvet suit, six dollars for a servant in Charlottesville—or even to acknowledge the many demands for payment sent him by Edgar's creditors.

Barely two months after Edgar's return from Charlottesville, the strain between him and John Allan erupted in a two-day confrontation, probably on the eighteenth and the morning of the nineteenth of March 1827. It climaxed more than two years of friction, going back to Edgar's sulky behavior following the death of Jane Stanard. Together with the humiliation he suffered from others in Richmond, and perhaps coming atop his recent loss of Elmira Royster, the set-to was bruising enough to convince Edgar to move out of John Allan's house. Where he stayed is uncertain, but he was able to receive mail and messages at the Courthouse Tavern. After long consideration, he told Allan, he had decided to find a more sympathetic environment, "some place in this wide world, where I will be treated—not as *you* have treated me."

Edgar's departure from Moldavia may have been less headstrong than he made it sound, since he also observed that Allan had thrown him out, "ordered me to quit your house." But his adult personality as it now began defining itself included a reflex for treating his defeats as accomplishments. He declared the reasons for his decision (or compliance) in a letter to Allan, beginning with a curt "Sir," keyed in a tone of lofty resolve, and in fact modeled on the Declaration of Independence. The Revolutionaries of his grandfather's generation, speaking of the British king, had listed how "He has refused," and "He has forbidden," and "He has endeavoured." Edgar, speaking of John Allan, now enumerated how "You take delight in," and "You suffer me to," and "You have moreover ordered."

Edgar's "grievances," as he laid them out for John Allan, were essentially three: that Allan had misled him, restricted him, and rejected him. Allan, he said, had undermined his advancement in the very paths Allan set out for him. Allan taught him to aspire to eminence in public life, led him to expect a collegiate education through which distinction might be attained, but then "blasted my hope" of it. Allan upbraided him for "eating the bread of Idleness" yet subverted his chances of gaining employment, taking delight "in exposing me before those whom you think likely to advance my interest in this world." Allan also restricted him under close supervision at home: "You suffer me to be subjected to the whims & caprice, not only of your white family," he wrote, without giving the details, "but the complete authority of the blacks." The phrase "your white family"—as if he did not feel a part of it—hints at the more encompassing, more oppressive grievance which he set forth, as he did several others, in a paragraph to itself:

> . . . I have heard you say (when you little thought I was listening and therefore must have said it in earnest) that you had no affection for me—

Edgar said nothing further about what he had painfully overheard. Yet his closing comments implied how much he still hoped for Allan's affection. He said he planned to find a job in some northern city, where he might both support himself and save enough to re-enroll at the university. He asked Allan to send to the tavern his trunk, containing his clothes and books, as well as money enough to take him north and see him through for a month, "if you still have the least affection for me." Leaving room for Allan to call him back, he crowded into a postscript at the bottom of the page: "It depends upon yourself if hereafter you see or hear from m[e]."

Allan wrote back to Edgar with angry mockery. "I am not at all surprized," he said, "at any step you may take, at any thing you can say, or any thing you may do." Mimicking Edgar's letter, he began his also with the curt "Sir," and then, correctly observing that the boy had "declared for your own Independance," answered his "list of grievances." Where Edgar blamed him for undermining the very ambitions he had fostered, Allan replied that he had not imagined the preparation for them to require such literary indulgences as the reading of novels and joke books: "it is true I taught you to aspire, even to eminence in Public Life, but I never expected that Don Quixotte [sic], Gil Blas, Jo: Miller & such works were calculated to promote the end." It evidently displeased Allan that Edgar had begun considering literature an enterprise to be valued for itself, rather than as a social grace or help in business. Edgar had misconstrued his comment about "eating the Bread of idleness," he said, which applied not to employment but to taking his education seriously, being intended "to urge you to perseverance & industry in receiving the classics, in perfecting yourself in the mathematics, mastering the French &c. &c."

With his code of obedience and duty to employers, however, what infuriated John Allan was Edgar's complaint of being too closely supervised. He raged over what he perceived as an attack on his authority, the more so as his vision of being resisted, taking in Edgar's complaint of lacking parental love, opened into a spectacle of ingratitude. He replied with a fuming huff of imploded syntax:

> You are a much better judge of the propriety of your own conduct and general treatment of those who have had the charge of your infancy & have watched with parental solicitude & affection over your tender years affording you such means of instruction as was in their power & which was performed with pleasure until you became a much better judge of your own conduct, rights & priveledges than they. . . .

Edgar had warned in his letter, coercively and threateningly, that as he was in "the greatest necessity," his very life depended on John

Allan's compliance: if Allan did not immediately send money, he said, "I tremble for the consequence." Ridiculing this effort to manipulate him, Allan ended by observing the contrast between Edgar's declarations of independence and his groveling entreaties: "after such a list of Black charges," he noted dryly, "you Tremble for the consequence unless I send you a supply of money." Ever quick to inculcate a moral, he had his own warning about black charges: "the world will reply to them." Contemptuously, he left the letter unsigned.

"The world" replied speedily. After a day or two on his own without hearing from John Allan, Edgar felt hopeless. He allowed himself to think (or at least say) that since he had had no reply to his letter, probably his foster father "did not receive it." He wrote again to Allan, but in a different key, this time addressing him not sharply as "Sir," but as "Dear Sir," and beginning humbly enough: "Be so good as to send me my trunk with my clothes." His brief flight outside the Allan household, without food or lodging, similarly brought the accusatory "You" of his first letter down to a forlorn "I": "I am in the greatest necessity, not having tasted food since Yesterday morning. I have no where to sleep at night, but roam about the Streets—I am nearly exhausted—I beseech you. . . . . . I have not one cent in the world to provide any food." John Allan turned over what Edgar sent and wrote on the backside, "Pretty Letter."

Edgar's tale of starvation and homelessness seems clearly enough a bid for reconciliation, but none occurred. Instead, he disappeared. He may have tried to get overseas and persuaded a friend named Ebenezer Burling to join him. According to several later conflicting and embellished accounts, after drinking heavily they managed to get aboard a vessel bound for England, but when Burling sobered up he deserted and returned to Richmond. If the escapade really happened, Edgar may have been inspired to it by the activities of his brother, Henry. Now twenty years old, Henry was seeing the world, serving in South America and elsewhere aboard the U.S.S. *Macedonian,* and writing and publishing some sketches and poems. Edgar did take over his brother's identity and adventures in trying to disentangle himself from his troubles in Richmond. Likely to mystify John Allan and to mislead his creditors, even perhaps his jailer, he sometimes used the alias Henri Le Rennet, a Frenchifying of his brother's middle names, Henry Leonard. To make his whereabouts uncertain, he also created a false trail of maritime roving.

John Allan told his sister that he thought Edgar had "gone to Sea to seek his own fortunes"; a pursuing creditor learned that he had "gone off entirely, it is said, to join the Greeks" in their fight for independence; a relative of Allan later mentioned letters by Edgar sent from St. Petersburg, Russia.

The reality was less exotic, although so natural as to be surprising just the same. Making good on his promise, Edgar had gone north. As the act of an eighteen-year-old struggling to mark himself off from his family, his flight from Richmond does not seem remarkable. But in distancing himself from the Allans he made his way back to Eliza Poe, who on the back of her watercolor painting had instructed him to "ever love Boston, the place of his birth, and where his mother found her *best,* and *most sympathetic* friends."

Boston; Tamerlane; *The Army; Death of Fanny Allan.*

CA. MARCH 1827 – MARCH 1829

For a month or two Edgar seems to have supported himself in Boston by working in a merchandise house, and after that in the office of a small newspaper. He may have been writing, too, and apparently took with him the manuscript of some earlier works when he left Richmond at the end of March. Despite the displeasure of John Allan and the appearance of adolescent confusion, he had been reading Byron and other poets, exploring his imagination, and carefully trying to write poems. Sometime in the spring he turned over what he had written to an eighteen-year-old printer named Calvin F. S. Thomas, whose family may have known David and Eliza Poe. Around June 1827, there appeared in Boston a booklet of forty pages, in paper wrappers, entitled *Tamerlane and Other Poems.* Too inconspicuous to attract any reviews, the work was also published anonymously, its author being identified on the title page only as *"a Bostonian."*

The "little volume," as Edgar called it in his brief preface, consists of "Tamerlane"—406 lines of deathbed confession by the oriental conqueror—and nine much shorter poems. Although the mood throughout is somber, the most insistent theme is that of youth. Edgar began his preface to the reader with the startling claim that most of the poems were written in 1821–22, "when the author had not completed his fourteenth year." Several poems strike the juvenile note in their opening line—"Oh! that my young life were a lasting dream!" ("Dreams")—while in "Tamerlane" the words *young* or *youth* appear ten times, not to mention recurrences of *child, infant,* and *boyhood.*

With their concern also for imagination and reality, self and society, and the meaning of fame, the poems compose a Portrait of the Artist as a Young Man. Especially in Tamerlane, the Tartar warrior, Edgar projected much of his own situation. An orphanlike figure of uncertain parentage, with a "feigned name," Tamerlane hungers for power and command:

> *I was ambitious—have ye known*
> *Its fiery passion? . . .*
> *A cottager, I mark'd a throne*
> *Of half the world, as all my own. . . .*

The ground of Tamerlane's ambition is his conviction of his own genius. Dying, he explains unabashedly that the superior soul knows deeply "the silent tone / Of its own self supremacy." Edgar shared the assurance of personal election he gave to Tamerlane; James Galt later remarked that he was "fully imbued in his early youth with an idea that he would one day become a great writer." The question of greatness so much interested him that he devoted a lengthy footnote to explaining the psychology of esteem. The actions of great men are seen at a distance, he wrote, from which appear only the extraordinary facets of their character. The mundane traits they share with humanity in general go unremarked, therefore seem unconnected with greatness. For this reason, "It is a matter of the greatest difficulty to make the generality of mankind believe that one, with whom they are upon terms of intimacy, should be called, in the world, 'a great man.'" Considering Edgar's circumstances, "the generality of mankind" here sounds much like John Allan under another name.

Although impelled by a rage for transcendence, however, the conqueror retains the longings of the "cottager." Tamerlane recalls, that is, not only the lieutenant of the junior riflemen and the General David Poe-like rebel defying John Allan, but also the suppliant

for Jane Stanard's motherly comforting and for Allan's fatherly care.
Athirst to subjugate empires, Tamerlane at the same time pines for
a simple "matted bow'r" and repose on the "seraph's breast" of a
peasant girl, his adored Ada. His "iron heart," he confides, "In
woman's weakness had a part." The poem does not resolve this
Faustian conflict between aspiration and content, any more than Edgar had. By choosing the throne over the bower, Tamerlane exchanges "A kingdom for a broken—heart" and dies in despair,
homeless. Edgar stated the moral in his preface: "the folly of even
risking the best feelings of the heart at the shrine of Ambition."
But a further remark in the preface suggests that he, like Tamerlane, felt long-sworn to paying the expense of greatness. Should the
volume not succeed critically, he assured the reader, "failure will
not at all influence him in a resolution already adopted." At whatever cost, he would be a poet.

To the conflict over ambition in "Tamerlane," the shorter poems
add a view of the poet as solitary, "alone— / Alone of all on earth"
("Visit of the Dead").* They trace his apartness to several sources,
among them pride, a reiterated and emphatically placed word. The
poet identifies himself not with the "cold" moon overhead but with
the "distant fire" of the "Proud Evening Star, / In thy glory afar"
("Evening Star"). A "wilder'd being," he is also unfitted for the world
by something uncontrolled in his nature, a "chaos of deep passion"
("Dreams"). Always poised for some personal revelation, moreover,
the poems often obscurely refer to some transforming childhood
event that has estranged the poet from ordinary reality. In "Dreams"
it is a unique but transfixing revelation or vision:

> 'Twas once and only *once and the wild hour*
> *From my remembrance shall not pass—some power*
> *Or spell had bound me.* . . .

In "Imitation" the epiphany is less revelatory than traumatic—"Let
none of earth inherit / That vision of my spirit"—perhaps a visita-
tion from the dead, a "waking thought / Of beings that have been."
Elsewhere the cause of alienation is some all-important person or
baneful experience in later life whose legacy of woe forever seals
the poet from the hopeful world of childhood:

> *The happiest day—the happiest hour*
> *My sear'd and blighted heart hath known,*

*For an analysis of the subtle personal content of these poems, see pp. 72–78.

> *The highest hope of pride, and power,*
> *I feel hath flown.* (untitled)

Whether insight, scare, or disappointment, the charged experience has left the young poet preferring the realms of memory, fantasy, imagination, and dream to the mundane world: "Oh! that my young life were a lasting dream. . . . tho' that long dream were of hopeless sorrow / 'Twere better than the dull reality / Of waking life" ("Dreams").

Edgar created this portrait of the artist largely from conventions of romantic pessimism, especially in the works of Byron. Widely printed and reprinted in America, Byron's poems inspired many young American poets to portray themselves as similarly moody, lonely victims of early blight and later world-weariness. How deeply the Byron image impressed Edgar is apparent in his six-mile swim on the James River, emulating Byron's celebrated swim of the Hellespont, and the stories in Richmond that he had joined the Greeks, as Byron had, in their quest for independence. He derived much of the atmosphere and many particulars of "Tamerlane" and his other poems from Byron as well: the blend of ambition and the 'feminine'; the enveloping gloom, pride, and guilt; the picture of a soul damaged from birth and lost beyond redeeming. He named the heroine of "Tamerlane" Ada, after Byron's daughter, and replicated in Tamerlane's desolate return to his bower ("I reach'd my home—my home no more") the language of Byron's *Don Juan*: "He entered in the house—his home no more" (III, liii, 1). Although such direct echoes of Byron pervade the volume, Edgar did not imitate or crib from him merely. In his Byronic depiction of disappointed childhood hopes and of a passionate nature at war with the ordinary may be dimly discerned much of his own experience—his thrown-about beginnings, his unhappy courtship of Elmira Royster, his antagonism to the standards of Ellis and Allan, and his recent break with them ("abroad on the wide earth, / Where wand'rest thou my soul?"). Byron offered Edgar a perspective from which to evaluate his own life and legitimized his experiences as authentic ones for a young poet to have.

By the time *Tamerlane* appeared, in June or July, Edgar was a recent recruit in the United States Army. He had signed enlistment papers on May 26, 1827, giving his age as twenty-two, his height as five feet eight inches, his hair as brown, his occupation as clerk. His name, recently Henri Le Rennet, he gave as Edgar A. Perry. Difficulty in earning a living likely drove him to join; his commanding officer later commented that "he became reduced to the necessity of enlisting into the Service." But his decision seems understandable on other grounds too: his grandfather's association with the Revolutionary army; his own earlier service in the Morgan Junior Riflemen; admiration for the martial ambitions of Byron and of Tamerlane; the prospect of familylike camaraderie.

With whatever complex motives, Edgar enlisted as a private, for a five-year term, in the First Regiment of Artillery. His company (H) consisted of about fifty men, of whom twenty-nine were also privates, commanded by a captain and four lieutenants. Through the summer and fall of 1827 he was stationed at regimental headquarters in Boston Harbor, appropriately called Fort Independence. But in November the company moved to Fort Moultrie, South Carolina, on an island in the main entrance to Charleston Harbor. After some thirteen months the troops shipped again, this time through severe gales, to a large and recently built defense work in Virginia called Fortress Monroe. Mounted with three hundred cannon and doubly protected by a moat, it stood in the entrance to Chesapeake Bay, at Old Point Comfort, a popular vacation spot for residents of Richmond.

Details of Edgar Perry's life and duties during the two years are few. But as the army in this period was not geared to war—the time from 1815 to 1846 has been called the "Thirty Years' Peace"—military life generally concentrated on drills and housekeeping. Just the same, Edgar prospered under army discipline, and again distinguished himself. By early 1828 he had become an "Assistant to the A.C.S." (Assistant Commissary of Subsistence), an officer responsible for arranging the army's food supplies and closely connected to the quartermaster—work similar to that performed by General David Poe as A.D.Q.M., assistant deputy quartermaster of the Continental army. Probably later in the year, Edgar also took on the duties of company clerk, seemingly charged with writing lengthy monthly reports showing the disposition and personnel of each company in the regiment. By the new year he had become an artificer—an office usually occupied by a carpenter, blacksmith, or similar mechanic—and was drawing pay of ten dollars a month. He pleased his superiors. A lieutenant at Fortress Monroe attested that he performed his duties "promptly and faithfully" and that his habits were "good, and intirely free from drinking"; an adjutant there appraised him as "exemplary in his deportment" and "highly worthy of confidence." On New Year's Day, 1829, he was promoted to sergeant major for artillery, the highest possible rank for noncommissioned officers, above sergeant and just below second lieutenant.

For all that, Edgar felt after two years that he had had enough of the army, having served, he said, "as long as suits my ends or my inclination." But he had signed on for five years, the normal period of enlistment. The cost of breaking his agreement was revealed to him by the commanding officer of his company, a Lieutenant Howard. He had found this superior compassionate, a fatherly man who acted from the "goodness of his heart," he said, and "has always been kind to me." Trustingly, he disclosed to Howard his real name and age and his "circumstances," evidently including his orphanhood, his problems at the university, and the quarreling that led him to leave home. Howard promised to discharge him on one condition: a reconciliation with John Allan. Edgar tried to convince the lieutenant that Allan would forgive "even the worst offences," but Howard insisted that Edgar write to him. Edgar surely wanted to end the battle, and wished to leave the army. But he may have balked at making the first move, for it was Howard who wrote to Allan, through a Richmond insurance agent, proposing the double boon of an army discharge and a family reunion. To John Allan, the letter probably represented his first certain news of the boy in two years, since Edgar had accused him of saying privately "that you had no affection for me."

Allan gave his reply in a note he addressed to the intermediary, who sent it to Howard, who handed it to Edgar: "he had better remain as he is until the termination of his enlistment." What little information survives that might explain Allan's hardness shows him in no mood to forgive or to bestir himself. For one thing, for a full year after Edgar left Richmond, he had had to turn away the boy's creditors. For another, he was freed of the duties of business and seems to have grown impatient with other obligations also. His sister Mary in Scotland found him uncaring even about blood relatives and failing to send a letter of condolence upon news of a family friend's death. She wrote protesting his "cavalier manner" of treating her and wondering if he deemed her "worthy of any further intercourse." Later she complained about his casual handling of money left to her and her sister by William Galt, which they apparently asked Allan to look after and invest for them. But he failed to keep his sisters abreast of the state of their inheritance and answered inquiries about it evasively. At ease in Moldavia, John Allan apparently found little pleasure in the thought of Edgar's return.

Edgar now wrote to Allan himself. He put the best face on Allan's willingness to let him wait out the full term of enlistment, attributing it to his mistaken belief that "a *military* life was one after my own heart." But the thought also forced itself on him, he confessed, that Allan simply wanted nothing more to do with him, "that you beleived [*sic*] me degraded & disgraced, and that any thing were preferable to my returning home & entailing on yourself a portion of my infamy." The two years Edgar had spent on his own perhaps prepared him to approach more craftily than before a parent who encouraged independence but resented individuality. Writing in his best hand, and signing himself "respectfully & affectionately," he carefully tempered displays of self-sufficiency with assurances of uncritical obedience. Allan's hopes for him "had always been those of a father," he said, and he desired only to "fulfil your highest wishes." He also called attention to the maturity he had attained: "I am altered from what you knew me, & am no longer a boy tossing about on the world without aim or consistency." He explained that he now felt proud of himself, and believed that much that had seemed doubtful in his behavior would soon be clarified, enabling him to resume his life in Richmond without shame. He only asked Allan to await a sign: "suspend your judgement until you hear *of* me again." By what sign Allan might hear "*of*" him he did not say, beyond proclaiming that it would represent the outcome of heroic ambitions:

> I have thrown myself on the world, like the Norman conqueror
> on the shores of Britain &, by my avowed assurance of victory,
> have destroyed the fleet which could alone cover my retreat—I
> must either conquer or die—succeed or be disgraced.

In his war cry Edgar sounded like no one more than his own Tamerlane. And in fact what he left unsaid in his letter and did not submit to John Allan's judgment was that his certainty of vindicating himself rested on the poems he had been composing, even while in the army. He asked Allan to write Lieutenant Howard "assuring him of your reconciliation" and requesting the discharge.

Edgar received no reply. After three weeks of waiting, he wrote again, methodically summarizing what he had said before. To avoid irking Allan by any hint of complaint, he several times referred to the earlier, unanswered letter as "the letter which you have not received." The nice display of magnanimity was wasted, however, for his second letter also brought no reply. In fact neither letter was as reassuring as he intended. Hard as he tried to seem mature and self-possessed, older habits insinuated themselves. Grown used to manipulating Allan for money, he took the occasion to wheedle: "Pecuniary assistance I do not desire—unless of your own free & unbiassed choice." Accustomed also to playing on Allan's guilt, he threatened: "If you determine to abandon me . . . Neglected—I will be doubly [ambi]tious, & the world shall hear of the son whom you have thought unworthy of your notice." Such attempts to cajole or alarm were not likely to win Allan over. Nor could Edgar control his disappointment and resentment over "the letter which you have not received." He protested that while strangers took a deep interest in his welfare, "you who called me your son . . . refuse me even the common civility of answering a letter." Fearful that he might now be permanently cut off from Allan's support and from the love it still seemed possible to have, he fell back in the end on pleading: "My father do not throw me aside as *degraded*[.] I will be an honor to your name. . . . . . write me my father, quickly."

After six weeks, having passed his twentieth birthday, Edgar wrote to Allan again. Assurances, threats, and pleas having gone unanswered, he tried a new approach, better designed than his soaring prophecies of future greatness to convince the pragmatic Allan of his gratitude and sobriety. His new request, he said, would help Allan to "at once see to what direction my 'future views & expectations' were inclined." He now desired Allan's help in entering the United States Military Academy at West Point. Contrary to his earlier statement that he had been in the army as long as suited him, his plan implied that he wished to continue and advance his career as a soldier. Army regulations required study at the academy for becoming a commissioned officer. He pointed out that, already advanced far in artillery training, and having reached the rank of sergeant major, he could run through his cadetship in six months. Although he was older than other candidates for the academy, he said, Allan's friendships with influential persons, and his own favor among officers at the fort, would easily secure him the appointment.

Edgar sweetened this practical idea with a peace offering to John Allan. In his previous letters he had only alluded to the initial cause of their rupture, avoiding the explosive question between them of whether his debts and disgrace at the university had been brought on by Allan's failure to provide for him adequately, or his own self-indulgence. Humbly he now retracted his earlier insistence that Allan's penury had forced him to borrow and gamble. "I never meant to offer a shadow of excuse," he now said, "for the infamous conduct of myself & others at that place." So far as the fault had indeed been his, he also offered what was in fact the most reasonable accounting of it: "I had never been from home before for any length of time. . . . I have no excuse to offer for my [con]duct except the common one of youth." But for all this level-headed talking and thinking, well calculated to win John Allan's approval, his more ingrained habits had their way once again, certain to provoke Allan's scorn. He made his usual roundabout request for money and typically ended with a challenge. He would await an answer impatiently, he said, for on it depended much of his future life, "the assurance of an honourable & highly successful course in my own country—or the prospect—no *certainty* of an exile forever to another."

Whether John Allan replied to this letter is unknown, but a reconciliation was in the offing. In each of his letters Edgar had repeatedly asked after the health, never anything but uncertain, of Fanny Allan, and repeatedly asked Allan to send "My dearest love to Ma." Although he felt that she tried to provide an affectionate home for him, he may not have written to her during his two years away from Richmond. But he continued to think about her and to desire her concern: "it is only when absent that we can tell the value of such a friend," he wrote to John Allan, "I hope she will not let my wayward disposition wear away the love she used to have for me." In fact Fanny was seriously ill. John Allan had hoped that the family's move to Moldavia might benefit her, as the place was airier and less damp than their previous home. But he saw that the change made "no improvement." After an illness described by a local newspaper as "lingering and painful," Fanny Allan died on February 28, 1829, at the age of forty-four.

Fanny had never lost interest in Edgar's welfare, and in her final illness greatly desired to see him. He apparently secured a military leave, but was not able to arrive until the night after her burial—in Shockoe Hill Cemetery, the graveyard also of the young disturbed Jane Stanard. How keenly he felt Fanny's death would only slowly appear over the next two years. But after the week he spent in Richmond his grief already seems to have been complicated by guilt for having left her: "I have had a fearful warning," he wrote, "&

have hardly ever known before what distres[s] was."

Fanny's death softened John Allan. For the mournful homecoming he bought Edgar a suit of black clothes, as well as some hosiery, a knife, hat, and pair of gloves. After three letters that he "did not receive," he also agreed to support Edgar's plans to be discharged from the army and enter West Point. More important, Edgar wrote, Allan offered what mattered to him most: he "promised me to forgive all." The morning of Edgar's departure brought a small disappointment, however. He went to John Allan's room but found him asleep; unwilling to disturb him, he could not say good-bye. The reconciliation was just the same a relief, and when he returned to Old Point Comfort he wrote to Allan as his "dear Pa," saying that except for Fanny's death he would feel cheered, "much happier than I have for a long time."

Application to West Point; Renewed Quarrel with John Allan.

MAY–NOVEMBER 1829

Entering West Point proved more difficult than Edgar expected, as did his reconciliation with John Allan. Once Allan gave permission for the army discharge, Edgar was obliged to procure a substitute for himself, so that the regiment would not be weakened; as it happened, an experienced sergeant agreed to take his place. The entire process involved official requests and other documents that called on Edgar for information about his birth and parentage. Revealingly, he presented himself as an orphan whose parents had died in the Richmond theater fire of 1809. John Allan then adopted him as his "son & heir."

None of this was true, of course. The savage fire that destroyed the Richmond theater, discussed for years after the event, killed seventy-two people including the governor, but occurred about two weeks after the death of Eliza Poe. Edgar probably fabulated the circumstances of his parents' deaths and his 'adoption' in the hope that a reputable background would strengthen his case for quitting the army and gaining admission to West Point. But his inventions also suggest some shame over his father's desertion and his anomalous position in John Allan's family. On April 15, 1829, he was discharged from the army, and a few days later secured letters of recommendation for the academy from Lieutenant Howard and two other officers. They promised that his education was of "a very high order" and firmly praised his deportment as "deserving of confidence," in fact "unexceptionable."

Back in Richmond by early May, Edgar set to work on the elaborate procedure for becoming a cadet. Applications, including letters of recommendation, were usually made directly to the secretary of war, John H. Eaton. Here John Allan offered help, after his style. Prominent in several of Richmond's social circles, he knew many of the state's leading citizens, several of whom he enlisted to write to the secretary on Edgar's behalf. They included a former governor of Virginia, James Preston, who may have seen some of Edgar's poems, for in addition to promising for the boy a military career of "honorable feelings, and elevated spirit," he recommended Edgar as "a young gentleman of genius and talents—I believe he is destined to be distinguished." Allan induced two other prominent citizens, including the Speaker of the House of Representatives, to write letters for Edgar to take with him when personally presenting his application; both earnestly predicted that Edgar would be "an acquisition to the service."

John Allan himself supplied a testimonial to Secretary Eaton. He took pleasure in observing that at his university examinations Edgar did "great credit to himself." But otherwise, conscious he said of addressing a military man, he assessed Edgar with terse candor. "His History is short. He is the Grandson of Quarter Master Genl Poe of Maryland." Having also cleansed Edgar's past of actors, he set straight his own part in it: "Frankly Sir, do I declare that He is no relation to me whatever." He had interested himself in the boy, he explained, as he had done in many others, because "every Man is my care, if he be in distress." Having made clear the principle that guided him, he asked the secretary's kindness in promoting Edgar's future prospects.

In May, Edgar brought his application to Washington. He learned from the secretary of war that there was a waiting list for appointments to the academy, with some forty-seven candidates ahead of him. Rejections, resignations, and dismissions might be expected, however, and he went away hopeful of being admitted in September. (Officially he was ranked as a "Good" prospect, although some others were listed as "very good" or "highly qualified.") He did not return to Richmond, but instead went to visit his father's family in Baltimore. In July, seemingly at John Allan's prompting, he spoke with the secretary again, walking the thirty or so miles from Baltimore to Washington. Eaton addressed him by name, a promising sign, and told him that resignations and rejections had indeed occurred. But they left him eleventh on the waiting list. The possibility of a September appointment remained, Eaton assured him: vacancies continued to turn up during the opening encampment of the academy, and if they exceeded ten he would immediately be admitted. But if not—he added—Edgar would be among the first on the roll for the following June, when his appointment was certain. Now facing the possibility of a full year's delay in entering West Point, Edgar returned again to Baltimore.

The postponements raised doubts in John Allan's mind about Edgar's efforts and intentions in seeking an appointment. Suspecting Edgar's claim of distinguished military ancestry, he urged him while in Baltimore to "ascertain & get a Certificate" proving that his grandfather had actually served in the American Revolution, and showing where and at what rank. Edgar replied that the facts were "clearly established," and so well known in Washington as to make a certificate unnecessary. Allan's distrust cannot have been allayed by the surprising information Edgar sent from Baltimore, which he feared would have "no very favourable effect if known to the *War* Dept." He had learned, he said, that he was "the grandson of General Benedict Arnold"—a story that perhaps appealed to his view of himself as a Byronic outcast and his inclination to jolt John Allan, but only another fabulation.

As the admission procedure dragged on without result, Allan accused Edgar of misleading him and working on his good nature. Several times Edgar felt compelled to write him, saying he had no way to prove that he had pursued his cadetship energetically. He invited Allan to investigate for himself: "If you doubt what I say & think that I have neglected to use any exertions in the procuring my warrant—write yourself to Mr Eaton & he will tell you that more exertions could not have been." In the glow of reconciliation he had restrained his underlying feeling that John Allan did not appreciate and in fact undermined his efforts. But now his resentment of Allan's distrust broke through. He charged Allan himself with procrastinating. He might have had a June appointment, he

said, but for Allan's inaction: "you will remember that I was under
the impression that you were making exertions to obtain the situation for me, while I was at Old Point & so situated as to be unable
to use any exertions of my own—On returning home nothing had
been done—it is therefore unjust to blame me for a failure, after
using every endeavour, when success was impossible rendered so
by your own delay—."

New clashes over money expanded the reviving quarrel. In May,
when Edgar went to Baltimore from Washington, Allan sent him a
hundred dollars for expenses, with a reminder: "be prudent and
careful." But just a month later Edgar wrote for more money. He
explained that while he was rooming at Beltzhoover's Hotel with
his cousin Edward Mosher, Mosher robbed him of about forty-six
dollars, while he was asleep, of which he recovered ten dollars by
searching his cousin's pockets. Another fifty dollars, he said, had
gone toward paying the seventy-five dollars needed for obtaining
his substitute in the army. Allan doubted the first story, although
Edgar sent him a letter from Mosher acknowledging the theft. The
second story angered him, since Edgar had told him previously that
the cost of obtaining a substitute was twelve dollars, not seventy-
five. Edgar tried to account for the discrepancy in detail. He had
not mentioned the larger amount, he said, because he had not expected it: ordinarily a substitute receives a bounty of twelve dollars
from the commanding officer of a company. But Lieutenant Howard was away at the time of his dismission, when a substitute offered himself for seventy-five dollars; he gave the substitute twenty-
five dollars plus a note for the balance, which he paid when John
Allan sent him the hundred dollars. So, he explained, his need for
more money.

New and still deeper antagonism arose over Edgar's writing. While
in Baltimore he presented himself—his "first attempt at self introduction," he realized—to the prestigious William Wirt, a man of
letters, former attorney general of the United States, and one-time
resident of Richmond. Always eager for the favor of older men,
Edgar was pleased that Wirt treated him politely and asked him to
call frequently, as he did. He asked Wirt's opinion of a new long
poem he had written, probably while in the army. It was a lengthy
astronomical fantasy entitled "Al Aaraaf," parts of which he had
managed to get published in a Baltimore newspaper under the name
Marlow, an apt pseudonym for the author of "Tamerlane." Wirt was
the author of a celebrated biography of Patrick Henry but had never

written poetry nor read much for many years, and he rather flaunted what he called his "ignorance of modern poetry and modern taste." He told Edgar he believed the poem would please modern readers, but doubted that old-fashioned ones like himself would "take." Feeling unqualified to judge, he advised him to get an introduction to some literary critic in Philadelphia, such as Robert Walsh, editor of the *American Quarterly Review.*

Disregarding John Allan's reminder to use his expense money prudently, Edgar ventured to Philadelphia, put up at the Indian Queen Hotel, and went to see Walsh. The editor told him of the difficulty of getting a poem published in America, but promised to notice "Al Aaraaf," if it appeared, in his *Review.* Undaunted, Edgar sent the manuscript to Isaac Lea, a partner in the Philadelphia publishing firm of Carey, Lea, and Carey. Writing about literary matters drew out a capacity for wit and buffoonery that he suppressed in his somberly cautious letters to John Allan. He told Lea that whether the poem got into print or not he was "irrecoverably a poet," and testified to his commitment in some doggerel:

> *It was my choice by chance or curse*
> *To adopt the cause for better or worse*
> *And with my worldly goods & wit*
> *And soul & body worship it—*

Truthfully enough, he stressed to Lea that he had written "Al Aaraaf" under "extraordinary disadvantages," and proposed that his firm publish the long poem together with some shorter works to make a volume.

Returned to Baltimore, Edgar wrote to John Allan, addressing him once again as "Dear Pa," and beginning with a surprise: "I am now going to make a request different from any I have ever yet made." Well aware that Allan believed him to be preoccupied with entering West Point, he tried to blunt the unexpectedness of his request by working up to it. He said he had sent *"a poem"* to William Wirt—whom Allan had known in Richmond—and was enclosing a letter from him giving it a "flattering character." As Wirt advised him to do, he had become acquainted with Mr. Walsh in Philadelphia, who promised to notice the poem. About to make his meaning clear, he explained that he considered John Allan "free from prejudice," willing to help him for good cause, and in agreement with him that at his time of life much could be said for standing *"before the eye of the world."* Nor would increased reputation even

momentarily interfere—he added without mentioning West Point—
"with other objects which I have in view."

Then Edgar sprang his request. If Carey, Lea, and Carey refused
to publish his manuscript at their own risk—as they had invariably
declined "all our American poets"—he desired John Allan to persuade them to publish it, by guaranteeing to repay any loss they
might incur. Such an arrangement would not have been extraordinary, for the profession of authorship was only now coming into
existence in America. Among the few Americans who wrote for a
living, even Washington Irving and James Fenimore Cooper fi-
nanced the production of their own books, hiring the publisher simply
as a printer and distributor, and keeping all the profits. Edgar estimated that publication of his poems would cost one hundred dollars, representing the limit to be lost should not a single copy be
sold. But he assured Allan that more than likely the volume would
earn money, and promised he would always be grateful for his kindness.

What remains of John Allan's reply is the summary he wrote of
it at the bottom of Edgar's letter to him. He wrote back, he said,
"strongly censuring his conduct—& refusing any aid." He did not
disapprove in itself of Edgar's publishing poetry, and later asked to
see his manuscript. But the circumstances and the appeal for patronage made John Allan's reply predictable, especially as Edgar's
request was also mistimed. Allan's wife having died only a few months
before, by the summer he himself was uncharacteristically beset by
ill health, feeling weak and nervous. A widower, he soon became
involved with a woman named Elizabeth Wills and, although the
fact was yet unknown to him, was fathering illegitimate twins, who
would be born to her the following summer. Suspicious of Edgar's
detours and subterfuges and galled by new evidence of his disobedience, he wrote him in July saying, "I am not particularly anxious
to see you."

As Edgar interpreted Allan's words, they amounted to "a prohibition" against returning to Richmond. He wrote home repeatedly,
exhibiting his maturity and willingness to please, making it clear
that he kept on the road to West Point and, more than anything
else now, asking whether Allan wanted him to return. "You would
relieve me from a great deal of anxiety by writing me soon," he
said on one occasion. "I think I have already had my share of trouble for one so young." "By your last letter," he wrote on another,
"I understood that it was not your wish that I should return home—
I am anxious to do so—but if you think that I should not—I only

wish to know what course I shall pursue." As Allan had done before, he sometimes refused to answer Edgar's letters, letting him dangle. Edgar feared that his recent behavior had reawakened old complaints about his debts at the university, indeed that despite the promises to him after Fanny's death Allan remained indignant: "I am conscious of having offended you formerly—greatly—," he wrote several times, "but I thought *that had been forgiven*. At least you told me so—."

As his brief trip to Washington in May turned into an exile from Richmond that lasted through the summer and fall, Edgar found himself stranded in Baltimore, a city of some eighty thousand inhabitants, about five times as many as Richmond. He stayed now at a hotel, now at a boarding house, now with his father's family, "in a most uncomfortable situation," he said, "without one cent of money—in a strange place." He asked and received some money from Allan in July, although it came with the "taunt," as Edgar quoted him, that "men of genius ought not to apply to [his] aid." He continued to apply, however. In August, as he came to acknowledge that his presence in Moldavia was unwanted, he asked Allan to send a trunk he had left in Richmond, adding, "perhaps you will put in it for me some few clothes as I am nearly without." He proposed too that if his entrance to West Point were held up until the following June, Allan would give him enough money to pass the time in Baltimore at a cheap boarding house—"say even 10 even 8 $ pr month." Allan may have agreed, for in November he sent eighty dollars. Edgar wrote back, "truly thankful," he said, and requesting in addition a piece or even half a piece of linen, for his aunt to make up into clothes for him. If he bought the material himself, he let John Allan know, he would be left with nothing for pocket money.

Al Aaraaf

NOVEMBER–DECEMBER 1829

Edgar did more in Baltimore than bide his time. He worked at his poetry, trying to get it published in magazines although uncertain how to do so. He submitted part of a new poem to the *American Monthly,* whose editor printed one stanza as a laughable example of its "sickly rhymes." But excerpts from the poem (eventually called "Fairy-Land") appeared in September in *The Yankee and Boston Literary Gazette,* edited by John Neal, a lapsed Maine Quaker who could claim among many other accomplishments to have debated John Stuart Mill and boarded at the home of Jeremy Bentham, opened a gymnasium where he gave boxing lessons, published sensationalistic novels, and designed his own clothing. Robust and brash—literary friends nicknamed him "Jehu O'Cataract"—Neal called Edgar's efforts "though nonsense, rather exquisite nonsense" and remarked that the author "might make a beautiful and perhaps a magnificent poem. There is a good deal here to justify such a hope."

Coming amid his frustrations in proving himself to John Allan, Neal's comments exhilarated Edgar. They were, he said, "the very first words of encouragement I ever remember to have heard." Privately he had expressed a harsh opinion of the rambunctious Neal, whose literary judgments he considered founded on "sheer impudence." But his reservations evaporated in his elation over Neal's praise. He wrote effusively to the older man as a kindred spirit, telling Neal his literary hopes: "I am young—not yet twenty—*am* a poet. . . . I would give the world to embody one half the ideas afloat in my imagination." Edgar could not have defined himself in such terms to John Allan, nor boasted to him that "I am and have been from my childhood, an idler," and still less told him that "I have no father—nor mother." But amid his trying experiences over the previous two years Edgar had been nurturing a new understanding of his purposes and was coming to see himself as guided, like John Allan, by principles, only by one principle above others. He set it forth to Neal as both the ground of his poetry and a credo: "deep worship of all beauty."

In mid-November, probably only a few weeks after writing to Neal, Edgar found a publisher for his new volume of poems, the Baltimore firm of Hatch and Dunning. Its two young owners offered to print the book and to give him 250 copies. Whether they received financial support from John Allan is unknown, although Edgar had kept trying to win his approval of the publication and promised to send on a copy to Richmond. The work appeared in December, as *Al Aaraaf, Tamerlane, and Minor Poems. By Edgar A. Poe.* Seventy-one pages of thin paper, it made a slim volume, although better printed and more attractively designed than his first collection. Moreover, it did not present him as some anonymous

"Bostonian." He chose rather to identify himself to the public under the name he used in signing his correspondence: Edgar A. Poe. The middle initial, acknowledging but disowning John Allan's name, eloquently resolved his mingled longing and scorn for the man. So he would sign his works ever after.

Edgar retained in revised form five of the nine poems in his first volume. He overhauled "Tamerlane," here dedicated to John Neal, simplifying the involuted syntax, scrapping the footnotes, condensing the hero's long soliloquies on pride and ambition, withal reducing the poem more than 150 lines. He again explored in the new volume the previous motifs of early blight, pride mingled with shame, and the superiority of dreams to reality, but the Byronic idiom is less pervasive than before. Although he told Neal (truthfully?) that most of the poems were written "before I was fifteen," he eliminated the preface too, and with it the earlier insistence on the poet's youth. The volume no longer builds a portrait of the artist, but its occasional playfulness, its notes of new poetic influence (especially John Milton's), and its treatment of several new and more impersonal subjects make his range seem broader and more various than before.

Edgar opened the volume with three epigraphs that hint at the enigmatic quality of several poems to follow. The first, in awkward Spanish from an unidentified play, reads in English:

"Fabio, do you understand what I tell you?"
"Yes, Thomas, I understand it"—"You lie, Fabio"

This teasing of reason is elaborated in the introductory poem of the volume, a carefully orchestrated sonnet on the withering effects of rationalism. From its haughtily damnifying opening, the poem protests (and underscores by reiterated *d*'s) that like Time, the antimystical clarifications of science make nature "dull":

> SCIENCE! *meet daughter of old Time thou art*
> *Who alterest all things with thy peering eyes!*

By robbing matter of spirit, science leaves nature depleted and demythologized:

> *Hast thou not dragg'd Diana from her car,*
> *And driv'n the Hamadryad from the wood. . . .*

In such a devitalized universe, the imagination has no place and must give up its search for "treasure in the jewell'd skies."

Grandly defying the spiritless Cartesian world of science, Edgar created in the next (and major) poem of the volume a universe where "Nature speaks," where flowers whisper, stars tremble, reanimated corpses converse and love. Still more defiantly, he set his scene at the site of a consequential scientific discovery, a bright nova discovered by Tycho Brahe in 1572 that stayed visible for sixteen months, then faded away. Asserting the freedom of the imagination, Edgar merged this star with Al Aaraaf, a wall between paradise and hell depicted in the Koran, where those whose lives have been neither markedly good nor markedly evil must stay until forgiven by God and admitted into paradise. Although the poem is obscure and elliptical in places, its basic action is simple. In Part One God commands the angel Nesace, "ruler" of Al Aaraaf, to convey a message to "other worlds." In Part Two, Nesace rouses the angel Ligeia, and bids her awaken the other thousand seraphs to perform God's embassy. Two souls, however, fail to respond: the "maiden-angel" Ianthe and her "seraph-lover" Angelo, who describes his death on earth and the flight of his spirit to Al Aaraaf.

With Tamerlanian ambition, Edgar here tried to conquer too many worlds at the same time. He not only combined Tycho Brahe's nova with a repository for souls in the Koran, but willfully blended literary traditions and historical facts throughout the poem. Attempted Miltonic grandeur mixes with the orientalism of Thomas Moore's *Lalla Rookh,* fairylike angels kiss and caress, Angelo (Michelangelo) dies in the Parthenon. He compounded the cluttered effect by adding a catalogue of exotic flowers, learned footnotes, songs, bits of angelology and astronomy, raising on the thin narrative base a top-heavy structure of excursions—perhaps what he had in mind when telling Neal that the poem contained "much extravagance which I have not had time to throw away." Labyrinthine syntax, ambiguous pronoun references, and murky transitions also clog the poem's movement and sometimes leave the scene and the speakers uncertain. Not surprisingly considering how much he undertook, Edgar left the poem unfinished, having intended also to bring to Al Aaraaf other Renaissance figures who like Michelangelo had died at around the time of the star's appearance.

Through its many shifts in subject, the poem's constant concerns are the afterlife* and the superior relation of Ideal Love and Ideal Beauty to passion. With its drowsy seraphs, golden air, and banks of exotic flowers, Al Aaraaf is, as Edgar wrote, "a delicate place." Indeed it is a heaven of art and artists. To the Messenger Star have come not only the shade of Michelangelo but also the spirits of lost or buried ancient sculpture, vestiges of architectural ruins engulfed by the Dead Sea, "Friezes from Tadmor and Persepolis." In fact Al Aaraaf is the very home of the aesthetic, the "birth-place of young Beauty." Edgar implied that by means of the messenger star, through beauty, God conveys to the world a glimpse of the divine essence, a sense of the Ideal.

But Edgar also carefully distinguished this beauty from the Ideal. The distinctive oddity of the star is that certain spirits there expire for a second time: re-born on Al Aaraaf, Michelangelo also re-dies there. What subjects even his spirit to imperfection and decay is what first brought death itself into the world—passion. Nesace's embassy to the other stars, although never spelled out, is apparently to warn of the dangers of passion "and so be / To ev'ry heart a barrier and a ban / Lest the stars totter in the guilt of man." But Angelo and the seraph Ianthe fail to heed her summons and repeat the fall of the first couple, "for Heaven no grace imparts / To those who hear not for their beating hearts." And passion is no more compatible with Ideal Beauty than with Ideal Love. Even the noble decorative sculptures of antiquity, although flown to Al Aaraaf as spirits, are poignantly tainted with corruption, "that greyish green / That Nature loves the best for Beauty's grave." Pervaded by genteelly erotic images of flushed cheeks, parted lips, and "glowing Beauty's bust," the poem suggests as much the impossibility as the transcendant value of love beyond sensual passion and corporeality. Human beings and works of art can only aspire after and imperfectly reflect the undying Ideal, never enact or embody it.

Other poems in the volume take ideas about beauty in different directions. "To the River—" sees works of art as at once shiningly transparent and complex, a "bright, clear flow / Of labyrinth-like water." Several of the poems do achieve such an effect, their short stanzas, spacious white page margins, and general compactness conspiring in an effect of lyric simplicity that is belied by their often

* For an analysis of this, and of the more personal content of the volume, see pp. 72–78.

intricate sound patterns. More personally, the untitled poem later called "Romance" transforms Edgar's earlier theme of youthful blight into a contrast between the poet's dreamy youth and careworn later life. In childhood he idly imbibed a sense of romance from nature, depicted as a tutelary "painted [colorful] paroquet" (perhaps a recall of the parrot Fanny Allan bought while in London). But the turbulence of "eternal Condor years" has made music and poetry seem "forbidden things," unless composed in high seriousness and deeply felt. "Fairy-Land" dramatizes the contrast between imagination and common sense, in terms of moonlit and sunlit views of nature. By moonlight, things appear at once known and unknowable, commonplace and portentous:

> Dim vales—and shadowy floods—
> And cloudy-looking woods,
> Whose forms we can't discover
> For the tears that drip all over.
> Huge moons there wax and wane—
> Again—again—again—

But utilitarian daylight makes the visions of night seem comic, as the doggerel rhymes emphasize:

> They [inhabitants of Fairy-Land]
> use that moon no more
> For the same end as before—
> Videlicet a tent—
> Which I think extravagant:

The poem is important for indicating Edgar's ability to treat the same material at one time seriously and at another satirically, and more so for disclosing his growing intention, apparent also in "Al Aaraaf," to create worlds of his own imagining, places between the earthly and unearthly.

Unlike *Tamerlane* two years earlier, *Al Aaraaf* brought Edgar some small public attention. The volume was advertised in a Richmond newspaper by a local bookseller named Sanxay, with whom he arranged for free copies to be made available to any of his old college classmates who might want them. It was also reviewed or noticed in at least four publications in Baltimore and Boston, receiving a gamut of responses. A Baltimore reviewer praised the originality of some of the short poems, but damned the versification as "a pile of brick-bats" and ridiculed the obscurity of "Al Aaraaf": "all our brain-

cudgelling could not *compel* us to understand it." The more unde-
cided reviewer of the Boston *Ladies Magazine* found Edgar sometimes wanting in judgment and perhaps skill, but sometimes also
greatly gifted: "A part are exceedingly boyish, feeble, and altogether deficient in the common characteristics of poetry; but then
we have parts and parts too of considerable length, which remind
us of no less a poet than Shelley." The most favorable judgment
came in a Baltimore newspaper that evaluated the volume in terms
of the widely discussed question of why America had not yet produced a great poet. It observed that the question had in view "some
great being" who would stun the world with a twenty-four-book
epic, and thereby overlooked the daily appearance in America of
strongly imagined poetry in natural language, such as this: "We view
the production as highly creditable to the Country. Throughout,
there runs a rich vein of deep and powerful thought, clothed in
language of almost inimitable beauty and harmony. His fancy is rich
and of an elevated cast; his imagination powerfully creative." The
reviewer urged Edgar on and asked the public to repay his efforts.

West Point

MARCH 1830 – MARCH 1831

In the spring Edgar at last gained admission to West Point. He may
have been helped by John Allan, who elicited a further, influential
letter of recommendation to the War Department. It came from his
partner's brother Powhatan Ellis, a U.S. senator from Mississippi
who wrote to the secretary in March affirming that Edgar's "capacity
& learning eminently qualify him to make in a few years a distinguished officer." Apparently within a week or two Edgar was appointed to a cadetship, beginning in June. With the consent of John
Allan, who presented himself as Edgar's "Guardian," he was asked
to sign articles pledging to serve the United States for five years,
unless sooner discharged.

While awaiting his entrance to the academy, Edgar spent at least
part of the time at Moldavia. The certainty of his appointment per-

haps induced John Allan to permit his stay, but little had changed. Living at close range again, they fought. In Edgar's version of the episode, Allan made demeaning remarks about him at a time when he felt particularly vulnerable. When "my heart was almost breaking," as he retold what had happened, Allan abused "my *family* and myself, under your own roof." Presumably Allan worked over delicate issues like the acting careers of David and Eliza Poe, or Rose's paternity. The irritant was likely a new disclosure about the hundred dollars he had sent Edgar the previous year, fifty of which Edgar claimed to have used in paying for his army substitute. It seems probable that he actually spent the money on other things, for the substitute, Sergeant "Bully" Graves, was now dunning him for a debt. Edgar wrote the sergeant from Richmond explaining that he had tried to get the money a dozen times from John Allan, who "always shuffles me off." He added, imprudently, that "Mr A is not very often sober."

Some sort of truce may have been reached before Edgar left Richmond, as John Allan bought him four blankets and saw him to the steamboat, for a brief return to Baltimore. But the strain continued. Edgar no sooner arrived at the academy, in mid-June, than he received a letter from Allan that charged him with having removed from Moldavia some books and other things that did not belong to him. Edgar denied it, replying he had taken "nothing except what I considered my own property."

The academy's barracks and parade grounds perched on highlands looking down onto the Hudson River, some fifty miles from New York City. Mrs. Frances Trollope, visiting in the year of Edgar's admission, thought the scenery "magnificent," and the buildings, although constructed with governmental uniformity, "so nobly placed, and so embosomed in woods, that they look beautiful"; notes of a French horn accompanying military maneuvers lent the scene, she added, a "deep and solemn sweetness." For all the vernal setting, the academy took earnestly its aim of turning out professional military men. As the secretary of war put it, West Point fostered "those only, who shall evince a disposition and capacity to be of future usefulness to the country."

For the summer encampment Edgar was assigned a tent with three other cadets, one of them the secretary's nephew. The exercises consisted of drills and entrance examinations. New cadets spent the day learning the use of musket, rifle, cannon, and other arms and the preparation of field works and munitions, usually ending with some guard duty. The exams seem to have been elementary, although Edgar reported that several cadets had been found deficient and were released. Because regulations governing conduct and studies were also "rigid in the extreme," he said, of the 130 cadets appointed annually only 30 or 35 graduated. Perhaps as a result of the exams, his own dwindling class contained 104 cadets. He looked ahead confidently just the same. Being older than the other cadets and having previous army and university experience, he wrote to John Allan, "I will possess many advantages."

At the end of August, Edgar and the corps broke summer camp and moved into coarsely furnished barracks to begin the academic part of their education. Drill and parade continued, but most of the day was now devoted to classes and homework. Rising at five in the morning, cadets studied from reveille until seven-o'clock breakfast; from eight until lunch; from two until four in the afternoon (followed by drill, parade, and supper); and from seven until tattoo, at nine-thirty bedtime. The academy's superintendent, Colonel Sylvanus Thayer, wanted the cadets to attain not a smattering of many subjects, but the mastery of a few. Edgar took only French and mathematics (subjects whose usefulness John Allan had stressed), but devoted the entire day to them. Math consisted of descriptive geometry and fundamental algebra (equations of the first and second degree, square and cube roots of equations); French, largely of grammar and translation, with little emphasis on speaking. The French texts included the first volume of *Gil Blas,* which John Allan had criticized Edgar for reading.

Edgar found the study "incessant." Yet as always he wanted to excel, and did so as both linguist and mathematician. In October he was ranked among the "Best" cadets in French, and again in November, when he also received a "Best" in mathematics. Pleased at having, as he said, "a very excellent standing in my class," he distinguished himself again at the general examination in January, when the rigors of the training had apparently reduced his class to eighty-seven cadets (of whom only twenty-four would ultimately graduate). He placed seventeenth in mathematics, and third in French. It pleased him also to find his achievement recognized by his elders. He reported that the military hero General Winfield Scott, a friend of John Allan, had been "attentive" to him, and that he had been "very politely received" by a captain at the academy.

Like his boyhood companions, many of his fellow cadets seem to have found Edgar interesting, and at times amusing. He had culti-

vated an image of himself as a precocious genius, cursed from birth
and recklessly adventurous, and painted the same oversized picture
to his classmates. At the time or in later recollections they described him as being the grandson of Benedict Arnold, as having
run away from his "adopted father," graduated from a college in
England, visited South America, led a "wild, adventurous life, trav-
elling in Europe and the East, and was a seaman, I think, on board
a whaler." A cadet named Thomas W. Gibson later recalled that
Edgar fretted over any joke at his own expense, especially a tale
founded on his being slightly older than his classmates. The story
went that he had really obtained a cadet's appointment for his son
but, the boy having died, had substituted himself. Edgar was not
above horseplay himself. Gibson also recalled that he invented a
scarifying hoax by which they rattled their roommates. Gibson came
into the barracks ranting about having killed "Old K——." Edgar,
with "well-acted horror," accused him of talking nonsense, after which
Gibson returned with a bloodied knife, swinging a bloody gander.
In its desire to shock, the skit recalls Edgar's ghostly masquerade at
John Allan's whist party and his description of the viciously bitten
arm in Charlottesville. Edgar also amused the cadets by lampooning
some of their instructors. He squibbed Lieutenant Joseph Locke, a
teacher of military tactics whose duty it was to report cadets' viola-
tions of regulations.

> *John Locke was a notable name;*
> *Joe Locke is a greater; in short,*
> *The former was well known to fame,*
> *But the latter's well known "to report."*

Edgar continued to write new poems at West Point, and his literary
endeavors and achievements became well known. One cadet, a son
of the editor Sarah Josepha Hale, wrote home quoting to his mother
Edgar's poem on science, and noting that he "is thought a fellow of
talent here."

In all, Edgar acted effectively under the strict regime of West
Point, as he had under the discipline of army life. With its super-
visors and comrades, set meals and routines, punishments and rewards, the academy also made a society of fatherlike and brother-
like persons, indeed a family that was perhaps as intimate and
attentive as any he had ever known. It was in part the orphan who
spoke when Edgar confessed himself contented at West Point, "very

much pleased with Colonel Thayer, and indeed with every thing at the institution."

But the fall brought from Richmond the dramatic and upsetting news that John Allan had remarried. His second wife was Louisa Gabriella Patterson, the daughter of an accomplished New York lawyer, and related to the wife of General Scott. Then fifty-one years old, Allan was her senior by twenty years. He revealed to her before the marriage the birth, in July, of his illegitimate twin sons. Childless during his twenty-six years with Fanny, and now very wealthy, he remained vigorous and evidently desired heirs.

Among its many implications for Edgar, John Allan's marriage meant that others would now receive the attention and comforts he had looked to have himself. However stung, he now more than ever expressed his longing only indirectly. He wrote to Allan sending bland "respects to Mrs A" and, as if to get at least something, asked for a book and some mathematical instruments, hinting that he needed money as well: "my more necessary expenditures have run me into debt." As Allan's marriage had taken place at the Pattersons' house in New York, not far from West Point, he said a visit to him might have been possible. "I was . . . very much disappointed when I heard you had gone on home without letting me hear from you." Two of Allan's Richmond friends had been to the Point during his cadetship, he observed, without adding that Allan had not. "I was indeed very much in hopes that the beauty of the river would have tempted yourself . . . to have paid us a visit."

Edgar's unexpressed worry that he was becoming shut out of John Allan's life was confirmed at the end of the year. Allan sent what he called his final letter, declaring, as Edgar paraphrased it, that he desired "no further communication with yourself on my part." Edgar's unpardonable offense seems to have been his comments to Sergeant "Bully" Graves, his army substitute, that Allan always "shuffled" him off when it came to money and was "not very often sober." Somehow his letter or the remarks became known to Allan. He admitted writing the letter, but in heat, he explained, less than half an hour after their quarrel in Richmond, when, "under your own roof," Allan had abused him and his family and "embittered every feeling of my heart against you." John Allan was proud and touchy, certainly, but it seems unlikely that the slurs alone could have provoked him into estranging himself from Edgar permanently. Edgar and his needs and demands also came from a different life that weighed on the new life and new family he was beginning with Louisa Patterson.

Thrown out and away, Edgar no longer tried to appease John Allan. On January 3 he sent from West Point the longest letter he had ever written, four pages of sarcastic accusatory questions, hot self-defense, and violent countercharges that disgorged months of recent disappointment and years of tactfully-suppressed outrage. He began at the beginning:

> Did I, when an infant, sollicit your charity and protection, or was it of your own free will, that you volunteered your services in my behalf? It is well known to respectable individuals in Baltimore, and elsewhere, that my Grandfather (my natural protector at the time you interposed) was wealthy, and that I was his favorite grandchild—But the promises of adoption, and liberal education which you held forth to him in a letter which is now in possession of my family, induced him to resign all care of me into your hands. Under such circumstances, can it be said that I have no *right* to expect any thing at your hands? You may probably urge that you have given me a liberal education. I will leave the decision of that question to those who know how far liberal educations can be obtained in 8 months at the University of Va. . . .

The truth of it was that Allan had promised and then denied him an education, an assertion he supported by furiously picking anew at the tangle of who did what at the university, detailing for two pages his every financial transaction there, and now rejecting any blame for his debts: "I will boldly say that it was wholly and entirely your own mistaken parsimony that caused all the difficulties in which I was involved at Charlotte[s]ville." It was that Allan gave him one hundred and ten dollars when expenses, at the lowest estimate, were three hundred and fifty dollars, then berated him for not taking more courses. It was that Allan replied insultingly to his request for more books—"if I had been the vilest wretch on earth you could not have been more abusive"—and sent him those he didn't need. It was that in giving him money at the end of the school year, when it was too late, Allan forced him to borrow, gamble, and fall in with a dissolute bunch. He ended up in debt not because he liked to drink and squander, as they did, but because, he said, "it was my crime to have no one on Earth who cared for me, or loved me."

Edgar also traced his life since leaving the university, a course also made needlessly wearing and disappointing by John Allan's indifference and broken promises. Allan gave him no help in getting employment or entering West Point: "I *earned,* myself, by the most humiliating privations—a Cadets' warrant which you could have obtained at any time for asking." After Fanny's death, Allan promised to "forgive all" but sent him off to West Point a beggar, so that he now again found himself in debt. John Allan would remember Fanny's death, of course, and his arrival in Richmond the night after her burial: "If she had not have died while I was away there would have been nothing for me to regret—*Your* love I never valued—but she I believed loved me as her own child."

Edgar wanted revenge too. In concluding his letter he informed John Allan that he was ill, conveying clearly enough that Allan had made him so: "my future life (which thank God will not endure long) must be passed in indigence and sickness. I have no energy left, nor health." He may in fact have been ill, but he found another means also to use his own harm to punish John Allan. After struggling nearly eighteen months to get into the academy, and excelling in his studies, he decided to quit it. He was too exhausted and too strapped for money, he said, "to put up with the fatigues of this place." Since Allan had signed his consent to Edgar's serving in the military for five years, Edgar's withdrawal after six months required his agreement also. Edgar put it cuttingly: John Allan must send his written permission "as my nominal guardian." Allan's refusal would be useless, he added, since he could walk off when he pleased, although without the thirty dollars' traveling expenses he would be given after a formal resignation. In no mood to send polite follow-up inquiries about "the letter which you did not receive," he ended with a warning: "From the time of writing this I shall neglect my studies and duties at the institution—if I do not receive your answer in 10 days—I will leave the point without—for otherwise I should subject myself to dismission."

No letter arrived from John Allan, who considered a reply unnecessary. Instead he wrote a memorandum on the back of Edgar's letter to him, rejecting Edgar's account of their past conflicts as wholly unfair, "the most barefaced one sided statement." He would have helped the boy, he noted, but not on Edgar's own terms and conditions. Apparently he also distrusted Edgar's account of his illness and indigence, for he added that "I cannot believe a word he writes." Edgar's angry inventory of injustices and recriminations left on him a single disgusted impression: "I do not think the Boy has one good quality."

Edgar did as he promised. Under the stern regulations of the academy, cadets were often excused on conduct charges, and he had gotten into disciplinary trouble even before warning John Allan that he would deliberately seek it out. In September he had appeared on a list of cadets who committed the greatest number of offenses for the month. Conceivably he already had received and was reacting to news of John Allan's remarriage the next month. (It is possible that his threat—"From the time of writing this I shall neglect my studies and duties"—was a ploy to account for offenses already committed.) The academy's Conduct Book at the end of the year, several days before he wrote to Allan, lists a total of 106 conduct points against him, a relatively high number that placed him near the bottom of his class, seventy-fourth among eighty-six cadets. In January, following his warning to Allan, he threw himself into the work, piling up sixty-six offenses; the cadet with the next highest number for the month had twenty-one. He was listed as awaiting sentence for "Neglect of his Academic duties."

On January 28, a general court-martial convened at the academy, consisting of six military members, a judge advocate, and president, in Edgar's case a lieutenant from the engineer corps. Edgar was asked whether he objected to being tried by these men. When he replied no, he was arraigned on two charges, each with several specifications. According to the first charge, gross neglect of duty, he was alleged in the first specification to have been absent on named dates some twenty-three times from evening parade, class parade, church parade, reveille roll call, and guard mounting. In the second specification, he was alleged to have been absent from all his academic duties between January 15 and 27. According to the second charge, disobedience of orders, he was accused of failing to obey an order to attend church and another order given him by the officer of the day.

Edgar pleaded guilty to all but the first specification of the first charge. Although it hardly mattered, he apparently did not want to be convicted for what he had not done. Witnesses were sworn in, first to confirm the charges and specifications on which he had pleaded guilty. Some "squad marchers" testified that he had not been at mathematics classes for two weeks, nor at French recitations more than three times in the month. Other military witnesses testified concerning the specifications to which he pleaded not guilty, and verified his failure to appear on various parades or fulfill various orders, as did a cadet named Miller: "the prisoner was reported to me absent from church parade. I asked him if he intended to go to church and he said 'no.' This was equivalent to an order." One of Edgar's roommates was called on his behalf. But there was little to defend, and Edgar declined to offer any defense himself. The military court deliberated and on January 28 found him guilty on all charges. It determined "that the cadet EA Poe be dismissed from the service of the United States."

Before he could leave West Point, however, Edgar had debts to make good. Superintendent Thayer, although known as a strict disciplinarian, had come to like him and recommended that the dismission take effect on March 6, so that his pay would be enough to reimburse his creditors. It amounted to $61, which with other money owed him brought his funds to $85.09. His debts for board, washing, tailor, shoemaker, books, and the like amounted to $84.85, leaving him twenty-four cents.

Edgar remained in the pastoral Hudson River setting until the middle of February. It may have been during the interval that, with Thayer's permission and even contribution, he persuaded 131 of the 232 cadets to put up a dollar and a quarter each to cover the cost of printing a new edition of his poems. The large subscription may have been due to Edgar's reputation as a "fellow of talent," although, as one cadet remarked of it later, "no cadet was ever known to neglect any opportunity of spending his pay."

Edgar left West Point on February 19 and made his way to New York City. Where he stayed and how he survived over the next two months or so are unknown, but traveling thinly clad, "without a cloak," he said, "or an[y] other clothing of importance," he fell ill and became bedridden. Inevitably he turned again, despite "all my resolution to the contrary," he said, to John Allan. Somewhat incoherently, "I hardly know what I am writing," he explained in a wandering, blotted hand that he appealed now not for Allan's affection, "because I have lost that," but to his sense of justice. Viewed fairly, his situation must be seen as entirely Allan's fault. With Allan's permission, he might have resigned, bringing him thirty dollars travel pay—"a single dollar is of more importance to me than 10,000 are to you"; but Allan deliberately refused to answer his letter. "You one day or other will *felll* [*sic*] how you have treated me," he warned. "I have no money—no friends . . . besides a most violent cold on my lungs my *ear* discharges blood and matter continuall[y]." Turning from imperious conqueror to bereft cottager, he feverishly implored John Allan's help: "Please send me a little money—quickly—

and forget what I said about you—God bless you."

From Moldavia the answer seems again to have been silence. Edgar somehow survived in New York for about the next month, perhaps living near Madison Square, seeing to publication of the new volume of his poems, deciding what to do next. Two inconclusive turns in the United States Army had not dimmed for him the allure of Byronic roving and military glory. In March he wrote to Colonel Thayer, asking his help in a further martial venture. "I intend by the first opportunity to proceed to Paris," he said, "with the view of obtaining, thro' the interest of the Marquis de La Fayette, an appointment (if possible) in the Polish Army." He asked Thayer to send an official certificate of his standing in his class and perhaps, as a special kindness, a personal letter to a Paris friend or even to Lafayette himself.

Edgar's plan had more the air of "Tamerlane" than of reality, and he settled for less. He decided to return to Baltimore, not for a visit, but to settle there among his father's family. He explained his thinking with some accuracy. What persuaded him to alter his life, he said, was that he had been, quite inconceivably, replaced: "Mr. Allan has married again and I no longer look upon Richmond as my place of residence."

Poems by Edgar A. Poe

CA. APRIL 1831

Remarks on Childhood Mourning.

───────── ∾ ─────────

Edgar's new volume was published in New York around April, near the time he left the city for Baltimore. It appeared in 124 pages as *Poems by Edgar A. Poe . . . Second Edition,* printed on cheap paper and dedicated "To the U.S. Corps of Cadets." The climax of his early literary career, the work records an inner life of unusual paradox and contradiction.

In calling the book a second edition Edgar presumably meant to exclude from his works the 1827 booklet *"By a Bostonian."* But it might also be called so in the sense that he reprinted several poems from the 1829 volume, including revised versions of "Tamerlane" and "Al Aaraaf." Evidently he had been thinking about the dramatic effects to be rendered by punctuation, for he cut from "Tamerlane" dozens of commas and dashes he had used to indicate the rhythm of the conqueror's speech, reserving them now to mark some special emphasis. At the same time he dropped six short poems and added six new poems, including early versions of important works he would perfect later, such as "To Helen," and early treatments of the eerie landscapes he would make distinctively his, such as "The Doomed City." He also included a meandering prefatory essay, "Letter to Mr.— —," which makes an important statement of aesthetic principles, attacking the idea that poetry concerns ideas or instruction, and defining its aim instead as the production of pleasure. The changes and additions result in a work that, although called a second edition, marks a new self-consciousness and heightened power of imagination and language.

Still, the volume attracted little more attention than one notice and two brief reviews that pronounced it promising but bizarre and obscure. The cadets who had subscribed for the volume seem to have thought even worse of it. Many apparently expected to receive for their money the sort of satirical squibs Edgar had written at West Point. One cadet recalled that his comrades at the academy made merry over passages from the poems as "ridiculous doggerel" and considered the author "cracked." Others disapproved the cheap quality of the book production. Presumably because of the wide margins, another cadet complained that the 124 pages could have been printed in thirty or so. He wrote in his copy, "This book is a damn cheat."

Some of the new poems project already familiar facets of Edgar's poetic personality, reasserting his preference for past to present, dream to reality, myth to science, as in "The Valley Nis": "All things lovely—are not they / Far away—far away?" The conflict between the desire for power and the need for nurture, already dramatized in "Tamerlane," recurs in "To Helen," where the poet is again an adventurer with the instincts of a cottager, a "weary, way-worn wanderer," famously, who longs to be home:

> *On desperate seas long wont to roam,*
> *Thy hyacinth hair, thy classic face,*

> *Thy Naiad airs have brought me home*
> *To the beauty of fair Greece,*
> *And the grandeur of old Rome.*

The lines savor of Edgar's fabrications of his voyages abroad, but more so of his real orphanhood and exile from Richmond. The entire poem turns on the word *home*. Placed for maximum emphasis, suggesting its importance to himself, it stands at the end of the middle line of the middle stanza in the exact middle of the poem.

The clash between independence and dependence takes a strikingly different form in the prefatory "Letter to Mr.— —." Edgar begins by scoffing at received opinion. What usually passes for literary judgment, he says, is no product of individual thought but something stolen by the many from a gifted few: "it may be called theirs as a man would call a book his, having bought it: he did not write the book, but it is his; they did not originate the opinion, but it is theirs. A fool, for example, thinks Shakspeare a great poet—yet the fool has never read Shakspeare." Developed at length, this condemnation of secondhand thought prepares the reader to expect some distinctively independent literary judgments from the author. But what Edgar provides is, unaccountably, a stale attack on the prosiness of Wordsworth, which had been commonplace in English literary criticism for thirty years. Even more surprisingly derivative is his climactic formulation of the aim of poetry:

> A poem, in my opinion, is opposed to a work of science by having, for its *immediate* object, pleasure, not truth. . . .

At the same time that he scorned those who claim the opinions of others as their own, Edgar filched this definition verbatim from Coleridge's *Biographia Literaria*. There Coleridge defines poetry as a kind of composition

> which is opposed to works of science, by proposing for its *immediate* object pleasure, not truth.

More astonishing than the flagrant plagiarism in Edgar's definition is his extra emphasis on its originality: "A poem, in my opinion. . . ."

Many lines in Edgar's three volumes, it deserves being added, are also cribbed or lightly reworked from poems by others. The song in his 1827 volume begins:

> *I saw thee on the bridal day—*
> *When a burning blush came o'er thee,*

The lines come from a poem by a John Lofland, first published in a Philadelphia newspaper in July 1826, beginning:

> *I saw her on the bridal day*
> *In blushing beauty blest.*

In "To Science" (1831 version) Edgar writes:

> *Hast thou not dragged Diana from her car?*
> *And driven the Hamadryad from the wood*
> *To seek a shelter in some happier star?*
> *Hast thou not torn the Naiad from her flood: . . .*

These lines come from an English translation of Jacques-Henri Bernardin de Saint-Pierre's *Études de la Nature:*

> It is Science which has dragged down the chaste *Diana* from her nocturnal car: she has banished the Hamadryads from the antique forests, and the gentle Naiads from the fountains.

Much in "A Paean" echoes a poem called "The Wedding Wake," by George Darley:

> *Be this the funeral song:*
> *Farewell, the loveliest and the best*
> *That ever died so young!*

The opening of Edgar's poem is but a variant of this:

> *How shall the burial rite be read?*
> *The solemn song be sung?*
> *The requiem for the loveliest dead,*
> *That ever died so young?*

Many other examples might be given,* but even these make an unsettling comment on Edgar's claims for independence of thought. To point out the contrast is not to overlook his youth, nor his steeping himself in and absorbing the poetry of his time, nor especially the fact that his poems, taken whole and as a group, read as distinctly his. Yet like his early imitation of Byron, his various pseudonyms, and his appropriating his brother's adventures, Edgar's ease in taking over and passing off as his own the ideas, opinions, and expressions of other people does imply a feeling of not being someone definite. As perhaps the outcome of many early shifts from caretaker to caretaker, it suggests a sense of deficiency in himself and of envy toward others he thought more adequate.

In a still more important respect, Edgar's poems disclose an unfamiliar inner life, difficult to grasp, to which neither his letters nor the known details of his behavior provide access. Outwardly his existence was taken up in a running battle with John Allan over school, money, affection, the army, West Point. But his poems reveal an intense inward preoccupation with death and the afterlife. Death permeates "Al Aaraaf" and other early poems, invading even their language and imagery: "There pass'd, as a shroud, / A fleecy cloud" ("Evening Star"). And death dominates the 1831 volume, whose subjects include a psyche or spirit ("To Helen"), an angel-poet dwelling in heaven ("Israfel"), a corpselike place ("The Valley Nis"), the deaths of women ("Irenë" and "A Paean"), and Death's very kingdom ("The Doomed City").

American culture of the time fostered such a preoccupation, preaching from every quarter the duty of remembering the dead. This so-called cult of memory helped to allay anxieties about the continued vitality of Christian ideas of immortality, and concern that commercial and industrial values had begun to prevail in personal and domestic life. "Society lives to trifles," Emerson com-

---

*"Irenë" draws on a poem called "Edderline's Dream" published in 1829 by the famous English critic John Wilson. Among many similarities in setting, circumstance, and language, where Wilson writes "O, Lady, this is ghastly rest! / Awake! awake, for Jesus' sake!," Edgar, two years later, writes, "Lady, awake! lady awake! / For the holy Jesus' sake!" Some famous lines in "To Helen" apparently derive from a minor writer named John Augustus Shea, whose very popular poem "The Ocean," published in 1830, has the lines: "The glory of Athens, / The splendor of Rome." Shea knew Edgar and seems to have written the poem at West Point, although he had no connection with the academy. Still other examples might be cited.

plained, "and when men die we do not mention them." Even as the growing value of urban land and the health problems of crowded cities dictated the removal of cemeteries to remote locations, keeping the dead out of sight, the bereft more than ever before stored up and treasured mementoes of them—baby shoes, miniature portraits, torn gloves, especially locks of hair, actual body remnants to be preserved as braided rings, or glued to some picture of a weeping willow. A German traveler to America in the 1830s, Francis Lieber, was surprised to see so many people dressed in black, and decided that Americans so much exaggerated bereavement as to cheapen its meaning. He reported a conversation he had near New York with a woman in mourning costume, who told him a distant relation had died. " 'But,' said I, 'I saw you in mourning half a year ago; for whom was that?' 'We were then in mourning for—Mary, my dear,' turning to her sister, 'for whom were we in mourning, then?' "

For sentimentalists of the time, mourning was as much pleasure as duty: "there is a voice from the tomb sweeter than song," Washington Irving wrote. "There is a remembrance of the dead, to which we turn even from the charms of the living." The joys of grief gave rise to a huge popular literature of consolation that included not only works on correct mourning, methods of burial, and the like, but also scores of small volumes of poetry and innumerable lachrymose magazine verses devoted to dead or dying spouses and children, reunions with departed loved ones in heaven, orphans longing to follow their parents into eternity ("Mother,—I love thy grave!," one went; "when shall it wave / Above thy child?").

While this cult of memory helps account for the large number of Edgar's poems on death and the afterlife, it does not explain their special character. He neglected principal elements of the consolation literature of the time, especially its doting on the deaths of children, its delineation of Christian ideas of heaven, and its pervasive moralism. Moreover, death throughout his poems is an ambiguous presence, invariably intermingled with life. The speaker of "Irenë" seems uncertain whether the woman, with her "dreaming eye," is dead or asleep; he tries to rouse her: " 'Lady, awake! lady awake! / For the holy Jesus' sake!' " The dead young bride of "A Pæan" also retains vital signs, reposing "With the death upon her eyes, / And the life upon her hair." Such denial of death of course is ancient and extensive in Western culture, where cosmetics lend

the dead a semblance of life and care is taken to pick a comfortable
coffin. But in Edgar's poems the denial works the other way also.
In "To Helen" and elsewhere, the living are bloodless:

> Lo! in that little window-niche
> How statue-like I see thee stand,
> The folded scroll within thy hand!
> A Psyche from the regions which
> Are Holy-Land!

The person addressed here is at the same time a living woman and
a lifeless statue or spirit of the dead, a psyche.

The landscapes in Edgar's poems have a comparable quality of
death-in-life and life-in-death. Buried beneath luridly lit water, the
doomed city seems a corpse, hideously serene:

> Not the gaily-jewell'd dead
> Tempt the waters from their bed:
> For no ripples curl, alas!
> Along that wilderness of glass—

Yet for all its motionlessness, the deathly place harbors a possibility
of life: "But lo! a stir is in the air! / The wave! there is a ripple
there!" Like the soul of Michelangelo on Al Aaraaf, the city dies
twice, first in its burial beneath the sea, then again in an apocalyptic
descent: "Down, down that town shall settle hence, / Hell rising
from a thousand thrones / Shall do it reverence. . . ." In "Al Aaraaf" itself, brute things and evanescent ideas only seem mute but
are inwardly animate and vocal:

> Ours is a world of words: Quiet we call
> "Silence"—which is the merest word of all.
> All Nature speaks, and ev'n ideal things
> Flap shadowy sounds from visionary wings—

Like this silence of "shadowy sounds," the filmy, slow-motion world
of "The Valley Nis" seems at once eternally still and forever moving. Dramatizing states of unliving-undying and cycles of loss, recovery, and new loss, the poems seem trying to decide whether or
not death is real or permanent.

Other poems announce the poet's wish to rejoin the dead, or his
belief in the possibility of their returning to him. "Israfel" states his
desire to be in heaven, "The Lake" depicts his "infant spirit" self-
destructively drawn to a spot where "Death was in that poison'd

wave / And in its gulf a fitting grave." Contrarily, "Visit of the Dead" remarks the strong will of the dead to revisit earth:

> *Be silent in that solitude,*
> *Which is not loneliness—for then*
> *The spirits of the dead, who stood*
> *In life before thee, are again*
> *In death around thee, and their will*
> *Shall then o'ershadow thee. . . .*

The poet regards such reunions with a fearfully reverential ambivalence compounded of longing and dread. In "Irenë," the dead keep a distrustful watch on the loyalty of the living, remaining dead only as long as they are remembered; if forgotten, they come back in anger:

> *The lady sleeps: the* dead *all sleep—*
> *At least as long as Love doth weep:*
> *Entranc'd, the spirit loves to lie*
> *As long as—tears on Memory's eye:*
> *But when a week or two go by,*
> *And the light laughter chokes the sigh,*
> *Indignant from the tomb doth take*
> *Its way to some remember'd lake,*
> *Where oft—in life—with friends—it went*
> *To bathe in the pure element.*

Given Irenë's resentment, the poet fears as much as wishes her reawakening. Implicitly the function of poetry here is not only to honor the dead, but by commemorating them also to prevent their terrifying return. The poem ends with a morbid plea for Irenë's permanent death and perpetual burial in the devouring tomb:

> *I pray to God that she may lie*
> *Forever with unopened eye . . .*
> *Far in the forest, dim and old,*
> *For her may some tall vault unfold. . . .*
> *Some tomb, which oft hath flung its black*
> *And vampyre-winged pannels back,*
> *Flutt'ring triumphant o'er the palls,*
> *Of her old family funerals.*

The dead are not simply alive but too alive; the problem is to keep them buried.

This peculiar cluster of dead-alive persons, still-moving land-scapes, and deathly dread-longing dominates not only Edgar's three slim volumes of poems but also, to anticipate, his entire literary career. Much of his later writing, despite its variety of forms and styles, places and characters, is driven by the question of whether the dead remain dead. Little of his known behavior during his earlier years, except perhaps his visits to Jane Stanard's grave, indicates much less explains his preoccupation with this question. But its supreme place in his imagination, and its eventual emergence in his behavior as well, invite at least the attempt to understand its personal meaning to him.

The most persuasive and coherent explanation, because it accounts for other prominent features of Edgar's personality also, comes from the modern understanding of childhood bereavement. To summarize this view briefly: adults learn to live with the death of someone they have loved by gradually and painfully withdrawing their deep investment of feeling in the person. But children who lose a parent at an early age, as Edgar lost Eliza Poe, instead invest more feeling in and magnify the parent's image. At the same time they acknowledge the parent's death only superficially. The young child denies the permanence of its loss because, among other things, it cannot comprehend the finality of death, is unable to tolerate the protracted painful remembering and giving up of the loved person that occurs in adult mourning, and feels that the parent's supplies of love and self-esteem are essential to its being; some children believe they cannot survive without the parent. In the luckiest instances, a loving substitute may be available, to whom the young child can immediately transfer its feelings about the dead or dying parent. But neither John Allan nor his wife provided Edgar such a replacement. Lacking a substitute, the child delays or never undertakes the ordeal of attenuating the parent's image, expecting more or less consciously that the parent will return. Freud mentions the remark of a boy of ten after the sudden loss of his father: "I know father's dead, but what I can't understand is why he doesn't come home to supper." This self-contradictory way of thinking is perfectly represented in a later remark of Edgar himself, as reported by a Philadelphia publisher: " 'I believe that demons take advantage of the night to mislead the unwary'—'although, you know,' he added, 'I don't believe in them.' " The statement registers how he understood that Eliza Poe had died but retained far off the belief that she survived.

The modern understanding of established mourning, as it is sometimes called, draws attention to other literary-biographical features of Edgar's poems which likely derive from it. Their simultaneous fear-and-longing to rejoin the lost person is typical of this fixed childhood grief. So is Edgar's fascination in "Irenë" and many later works with monumental burial places, "some tall vault" with "vampyre-winged pannels," caskets and tombs massive enough to prevent the dreaded return of the dead. And much as his person-statue-spirit Helen incorporates in herself the beauty and grandeur of Greek and Roman civilizations, the dead parent of established mourners is not merely preserved in memory but enshrined, intensely idealized as having been gifted, wealthy, aristocratic, famous, and the like. The very existence in the 1831 volume of a new group of poems on dead-alive women and another on animate-inanimate landscapes may have been owing to the death two years earlier of Fanny Allan, with its reverberations of the still earlier deaths of Jane Stanard and Eliza Poe. For the orphaned, the death of someone to whom they have later become deeply attached strains their tolerance of separation and revives feelings about the original loss.

Edgar's underlying denial of death perhaps also helps to explain his easy remolding and evasion of lesser truths, and it gives particular poignancy to his often stated preference for the far off realms of dream and imagination over reality. His simultaneous belief and unbelief, finally, produces not only beings and landscapes at once living and dead, but such other derivatives as images of things at once conscious and unconscious, near and far, present and absent, lost and inalienable, evoking opposed feelings of grief and joy, despair and hope, loss and return, separation and union—expressions of what he himself called his "innate love of contradiction." In the 1831 volume, "The Lake" rests in "conscious slumber," the dead young woman of "A Pæan" receives not a requiem but a song of rejoicing, and several poems take place at points between opposite poles, "Irenë" occurring at "Midnight in the sweet month of June," "Evening Star" at "noontide of summer / And mid-time of night," the young woman of "A Pæan" expiring at midyear, "In June she died—in June." Indeed, to look ahead again, Edgar's split attitude imbues his entire literary career with a spirit of contradiction.

The inability of young children to mourn the death of a parent perhaps seems but one of many ways, if any are needed at all, to account for Edgar's odd, intent imaginings about death. As this biography is not an argument but a narrative, no attempt will be made to 'prove' that the psychoanalytic prototype of the bereaved child applies to him, still less to examine by its light his every word and action. The narrative does often recur to his ideas about death. Yet it does so not in order to demonstrate the truth of a particular view of their origins, but because he continued to pore over them. His absorption becomes increasingly evident, however interpreted. So far as the broad interpretation outlined above is called on at all, it draws strength if not certitude from the many other writers who have testified to the undiminished power in later life of a parent's early death. Somerset Maugham's mother, for instance, died when he was eight years old. A nephew of his recorded the following incident: "A few years ago I was alone with him . . . and his mind sometimes wandered. Suddenly he muttered: 'I shall never get over her death. I shall never get over it.' For an instant I supposed he was referring to my much beloved sister Kate who had died recently, but as he went on talking, I realized that he was thinking of his mother who had been dead for over eighty years." More recently, the American writer Harold Brodkey, whose mother died when he was turning two years old, remarked that the event engrosses him still and that much of his work is an effort to remember her.

Much of Edgar's career, too, may be understood as a sort of prolonged mourning, an artistic brooding-on and assemblage of the fantasies activated by an ever-living past. As no product of his imagination would put to right what had gone wrong or restore what he once possessed, he would begin over and over, repeating in new forms, different imagery, and fresh characters and scenes the dilemma which he presented in his new volume as the peculiar condition of his existence:

> *I could not love except where Death*
> *Was mingling his with Beauty's breath—*

Baltimore;
Maria Clemm;
William Henry Leonard Poe.

APRIL 1831–AUGUST 1831

Citizens of Baltimore boasted that no other city in America or Europe, modern or ancient, had sprung up so quickly to such importance as theirs. From its ample harbor, above which the city and hills beyond spread like an amphitheater, Baltimore clippers sailed for Canton, Buenos Aires, and Marseilles. Only a year before, twenty-four passengers had traveled thirteen miles in an hour and fifteen minutes along the new Baltimore and Ohio Railroad, pushed in a car by the boiler-sized locomotive *Tom Thumb*—the first members of the American public to move over rails by steam power.

The more intimate look and feel of the place also spoke for an improving and expanding urban spirit. As the English statesman Richard Cobden characterized it when he visited in 1835: "Baltimore is the handsomest place I have yet seen—here are the finest monuments—the prettiest girls and the cleanest City in the Union." Universally commented on and visible from a great distance was the noble Doric column erected to the memory of George Washington, a blue-veined shaft of white marble some twenty feet in diameter and a hundred and sixty feet tall, surmounted by a thirteen-foot-high statue of the first president. Conspicuous too was the great Catholic church that housed a six-thousand-pipe organ, the largest in America, its towers crowned with oddly Saracenic cupolas that made it seem as much a Turkish mosque as a cathedral. These and the bustling merchants' exchange, the many hotels, the celebrated markets with their succulent local terrapins and oysters attested to substantial wealth and general prosperity, without ostentation. Most of the comfortable two- or three-story houses were of brick, with steps of fine granite and marble, the widespread red and white making a cheerful effect. Pretty marble fountains and cisterns set here and there supplied ever-flowing streams of pure water and, with the broad streets and white clothing in favor, gave the whole city an appearance of well-built freshness.

Edgar was the fourth generation of the Poe family in Baltimore. His paternal great-grandfather, John Poe, had made his way there after emigrating from northern Ireland before the American Revolution. Three of John Poe's sons fathered branches of the Poe family, one in Georgia and two in Baltimore, including the family of General David Poe. The general had had a varied career in the city. He began as a maker of spinning wheels, served with distinction in the army, sat a year on the Baltimore council, went into bankruptcy after partnership in a rope walk, and in 1814, at the age of seventy-one, took part in a battle in which the Maryland Militia repulsed British invaders. He died two years later, a "Zealous Republican," as a local newspaper put it, "regretted by an extensive circle of relatives, and friends." By then his son David Poe, the actor, had also died or disappeared, but among those the general left behind were his wife and his daughter Maria.

It was to these remnants of the general's family that Edgar now turned. He of course knew them, but had seen little of them. As an infant he had very likely stayed several months with his grandparents in Baltimore, while David Jr. and Eliza toured other cities. But he may well have had no contact with them again until 1829, two years before. Having quit the army, he became stranded by John Allan's silence and, as he said, "succeeded in finding Grandmother & my relations." He had found the general's widow in no position to help him, however, an elderly pensioner, partly paralyzed. He had also found the old woman's daughter, his Aunt Maria, "if possible still worse." Presumably he meant that she had no money, for he seems to have acted as her agent in the transfer of ownership, for nine years, of a twenty-one-year-old slave she had inherited, the very low price of forty dollars suggesting that she could not maintain the young man. Nevertheless it was to Maria that he now turned for help, at her house in Mechanics Row on Wilks Street. By one account it was a small dwelling, of which she occupied only the upper story. Poor, she supported herself and those in her care by taking in sewing, dressmaking, and similar work. But she kept her household, it was said, "wax neat." The tidiness reflected the feel of Baltimore life, but owed still more to Maria's self-sacrificing devotion to Home and Family.

Forty-one when Edgar came to stay with her, Maria was only about three years younger than his mother would have been, had Eliza Poe lived. From all accounts she looked unattractively solid (Illus. 6). "She had the size and figure of a man," an acquaintance commented, "with a countenance that, at first sight, seemed scarce feminine." Her ungainly appearance matched her history, for unlike the Allans, with their coachees, whist parties, and dash of sophistication, she had settled into a graceless existence, barely able to get food and clothing. The sixth child of General David Poe, she had remained single until the age of twenty-seven, probably delaying marriage until his death, which occurred about eight months before. Her husband was a local hardware merchant named William Clemm, Jr. In her choice of him she continued the inbred tradition of the Baltimore Poes, for Clemm had previously been married to her first cousin, Harriet Poe, the daughter of the general's brother. William Clemm brought to his new marriage five children from the first, stepchildren to Maria but also cousins-german. With William Clemm she had three children of her own, who quarreled frequently with their half brothers and half sisters. About eight and a half years after the marriage, William Clemm died, apparently leaving her and the children without property except a parcel of land she received by law, which however he had offered as security on a loan. His relatives offered her no aid, most of them having opposed the marriage to begin with.

An overburdened woman alone in the world, Maria might eke out a bare support taking in piecework, but lacked the social position, training, and connections that might help her do more. Her efforts were also enfeebled by a habit she shared with her deceased brother David and nephew Edgar, a casual even automatic resort to the pity of others. As David, shortly after his son's birth, had fled to a cousin in Pennsylvania pleading for "30, 20, 15, or even 10$," she outright begged and borrowed where she could. Often she presumed on vague or fancied ties, beseeching people related to her no further than in knowing someone she knew. "I am not myself personally known to you," she began one letter to a Baltimore judge, "but you were well acquainted with my late husband, Mr. Wm. Clemm, and also I believe, with many of my connexions." She explained that for a long time ill health had kept her from exerting herself to provide for her family, who were now "enduring every privation." Sounding startlingly like her nephew, she concluded by fishing for a handout: "I do not ask for any material assistance, but the merest trifle to relieve my most immediate distress."

The wax-neat rooms on Wilks Street reversed the values of Moldavia, enclosing a world not of forbearance, honor, and affluence but of complaint, mendicancy, and perennial poor relations. Maria had much reason to complain, for at the time she supported not only herself but also several others who lived with her. For years she had cared for her mother, now about seventy-five years old, paralyzed, and confined to bed, ministering to her, Edgar wrote, with "a Christian and martyr-like fortitude, and with a constancy of attention, and unremitting affection." Maria seems also to have been sheltering at the time her thirteen-year-old son Henry and nine-year-old daughter Virginia, Edgar's first cousins. Named after an infant sister who had died at age two, Virginia was later described as having violet eyes, dark brown hair, and a "bad complexion that spoiled her looks."

Whatever its trials, the situation meant for Edgar the chance for life in a family, after years of lost connections, expulsion, and roaming. Maria was the sister of his father, had known his mother, almost certainly had seen him in his infancy. She represented his best-informed link to a past that had no relation to John Allan, a time when he had toured with his parents from Boston to New York to Philadelphia to Charleston. She was in touch too with the Georgia Poes, who sent affectionate regards through her to Edgar. Other blood relatives lived in and around Baltimore, whom he got to know. They included his sixteen-year-old first cousin Elizabeth Herring, daughter of a local lumber dealer who was married to his father's other sister, also called Eliza. There was also his second cousin Neilson (pronounced Nelson) Poe, some six months his junior, who had studied law and currently owned and edited a newspaper in Frederick, Maryland. He was married to a stepdaughter of Maria Clemm, a child of her husband by his first wife. Together with their penchant for inbreeding, family members also shared, Edgar perhaps especially, a sensitivity about the Poe name. William Poe of Georgia was deeply offended to read in a newspaper about some rascality committed by a young man named Poe. The account, he told Maria, made "the first instance of the name's being disgraced, that has ever met the notice of my eye—I was really mortified when I saw it." The contrary news that "Poe" counted for something in the world did not go unremarked either. The publication of Edgar's 1829 volume inspired Neilson Poe to predict that "*Our* name will be a great one *yet*."

Edgar's settlement in Baltimore also made possible a longer than usual reunion with his brother William Henry Leonard. Descriptions of Henry's appearance differ sharply, one acquaintance recalling his "singular personal beauty," another remembering him as a "slim, feeble, young man with dark inexpressive eyes." In either case he and Edgar were united by their early experiences. Like Edgar, Henry had been born in Boston, although two years earlier, and as an infant had also been left with General Poe's family while his parents toured; he may have spent most of his childhood with them. He often deplored the early death of his mother and, like Edgar, almost certainly was present at her passing in Richmond. The event remained distinct in his memory. He briefly recorded Eliza Poe's last moments in some verses, including her dying kiss and her goodbye:

> *. . . I have had thy last caress,*
> *And heard thy long, thy last farewell.*

He also retained a lock of his mother's hair, which he described in the same poem as "This gift of her I loved so well."

Raised among the Baltimore Poes, Henry joined the navy, or merchant marine, in his late teens, apparently visiting the Mediterranean, the West Indies, South America, and possibly Russia, before returning to the city at around the age of twenty. By then he had developed, like his brother, an interest in writing. He circulated in a young literary and social set, entering Byronic poetry in the albums of young women and giving recitations, proud of his speaking ability. Over the next three years he sailed to Montevideo, worked in a Baltimore law office, and meanwhile published about twenty stories, poems, and sketches under the initials "W.H.P." An acquaintance recalled that his manners were fastidious. But the distresses of the past had obviously been damaging. He began drinking heavily.

Although fostered in different families and cities, and sometimes separated by oceans, Edgar and Henry had tried to stay in touch. Even as a six-year-old child in Baltimore, to recall, Henry spoke of his brother frequently and expressed a great desire to see him, sending through his aunt to John Allan his "best love" to Edgar. Over the years he had written to Edgar himself, and visited him and their sister, Rose, in Richmond, once as Edgar was preparing to go off to the university, another time, in nautical uniform, when he accompanied Edgar and Edgar's friend Ebenezer Burling to see Elmira Royster. On his side, Edgar had turned to his brother several times in his troubles. During his earlier stay in Baltimore, nervously awaiting word from John Allan, he sought out Henry but found him floundering badly, "entirely given up to drink & unable to help himself, much less me." When he fell ill in New York after his court-martial, his ear running, he wrote to Henry for help, but again discovered that "he cannot help me." He clearly admired Henry as an adventurous older brother and understood that their powerful sympathy for each other was the seal of the loss they had endured together. As he explained the bond himself at about this time, "there can be no tie more strong than that of brother for brother—it is not so much that they love one another as that they both love the same parent—their affections are always running in the same direction—the same channel and cannot help mingling."

In fact, like other orphaned brothers and sisters, Henry and Edgar clung so closely together psychologically as to be nearly one person. How intimately their affections 'mingled' appears not only by Henri Le Rennet's borrowing of Henry Leonard's name and exploits, but in Henry's tales and poems as well. Henry named the hero of one of his tales Edgar Leonard, symbiotically combining his own name and his brother's. Not surprisingly, the life story that Edgar Leonard relates is Edgar's but could be Henry's also. "I lost my parents at an early age," he begins, "and was left to the care of a relation. I received a good education, and knew sorrow but by name until I had attained my eighteenth year." The "sorrow" is Edgar Leonard's romance with "Rosalie." Here Henry used the name of their sister to tell the story of Edgar's aborted love affair with Elmira Royster. When Edgar Leonard arrives at Rosalie's house, as may have happened to Edgar at Elmira's, he learns that she is to be married in half an hour. Astonishingly, one of Henry's poems, published as "Original," is virtually identical through three stanzas with a Byronic poem that Edgar published in the *Tamerlane* volume as his own:

> *The happiest day—the happiest hour,*
> *My sear'd and blighted heart has known,*
> *The brightest glance of pride and power*
> > *I feel has flown*—(Henry)

> *The happiest day—the happiest hour*
> > *My sear'd and blighted heart hath known,*
> *The highest hope of pride, and power,*
> *I feel hath flown.* (Edgar)

Henry published another poem under his initials as "*Extract—*'Dreams'." Except in minor features, it too is identical through thirty-four lines with a poem in Edgar's 1827 volume, beginning:

Oh! that my young life were a lasting dream!
My spirit not awak'ning till the beam
Of an Eternity should bring the morrow—(Henry)

Oh! that my young life were a lasting dream!
My spirit not awak'ning till the beam
Of an Eternity should bring the morrow: (Edgar)

It is by no means certain whether the poems are by Edgar or by Henry or represent a collaborative attempt to give their kindred feelings a single voice.

Edgar's cherished reunion with his brother lasted barely six months, for Henry died on the evening of August 1, 1831, and his funeral was held next day at the Wilks Street house. An acquaintance remarked later that he died of "intemperance." Apparently he had not been able to make his way out of the alcoholism that had been plain to Edgar when he found Henry "entirely given up to drink." Henry was twenty-four years old, the same as Eliza Poe when she died. Considering his suicidal slide, the timing may not have been coincidental. Throughout his work runs a vein of melancholy, sometimes despair, and several of his poems concern women who through death abandon their loved ones, who long to join them, "who would like thee be gone, / Who languish here—and for thy brightness pine."

Marriage Hopes;
Early Tales; The Saturday Visiter *Contest.*

AUGUST 1831 – JANUARY 1834

The picture of Edgar's personal life in Baltimore over the next three and a half years must be faint. Until the beginning of 1835, no more material survives for reconstructing how he lived than seven letters by him and shreds of information from others. It is clear that he continued his battle with John Allan (see the next section), and found it nearly impossible to support himself. At various times he unsuccessfully sought work as a schoolteacher and an editorial assistant, and for a spell may even have rejoined the army. The need to earn a living was more acute than ever, for evidently he was considering marriage. He published a few short poems apparently inspired by and addressed to young women in the city, and wrote several verses in the albums of other young women, including that of his cousin Elizabeth Herring. He had addressed two playful acrostics to her during his earlier stay in Baltimore, when she was only about fourteen years old ("Elizabeth, it is in vain you say / 'Love not'—thou sayest it in so sweet a way"). But his more recent visits to her brought objections on three counts from her father, Henry Herring: Edgar was poor, and her cousin, and, like his brother, he drank.

Edgar also had his first serious attachment since his disappointment over Elmira Royster, involving a seventeen-year-old girl named Mary Starr. Knowledge of it is limited to her account, given some fifty years later. Mary said that he visited her every evening for a year, sent notes through his cousin Virginia, and proposed marriage. Her brother, however, disapproved because of Edgar's inability to support himself, let alone a wife, and on her part she found him jealous and explosive, so that they frequently quarreled. One night he failed to appear at her house until after ten o'clock, when despite the late hour they sat on the stoop together. He had been drinking, she recalled, the only time in the year of their close acquaintance when she knew him to take any liquor. A quarrel arose, leading her to run back into her house through an alleyway, frightened, Edgar following. When her mother told her to go upstairs, as she did, he demanded that the woman call her down again, threatening otherwise to go up after her. But Mary's mother blocked the stair doors and persuaded him to leave, and afterward she forbade any further visits from him.

While Edgar's personal life at the time remains mostly lost to view, his increased literary activity appears in the works he published. Baltimore enjoyed some cultural stir, having a large theater and a good concert hall, being the home of such noted architects, artists, and writers as Benjamin Henry Latrobe, Rembrandt Peale, and John Pendleton Kennedy, and supporting in the 1830s twelve or more journals. Edgar had had some contact with the city's literary men earlier and obviously made known to them his precocious claims to large fame. A poem called *The Musiad or Ninead* (Baltimore, 1830) named him alongside other Baltimore poets, and praised his youthful daring:

> . . . *Poe who smil'd at reason, laugh'd at law,*
> *And played a tune who should have play'd at taw,*
> *Now strain'd a license, and now crack'd a string,*
> *And sang as older children dare not sing.*

Likely through Henry Poe, Edgar's broken-off engagement to Elmira Royster also became known to a Maryland journalist named
Lambert Wilmer, who published a three-act play based upon it,
naming his heroine Elmira and remaking Edgar into the lovelorn
and despondent Alphonso, whose tune is "welcome friendly death."

Out of work, Edgar wrote more busily than ever before. Wilmer
recalled that he seemed "constantly occupied by his literary labors."
He turned now to writing fiction, probably in the hope of earning
more money than he might for his poetry. His first published tale
may have been "A Dream," published over the initial *P* in the Philadelphia *Saturday Evening Post* on August 13, 1831. The place and
date of publication matter: Henry had published two poems in the
same newspaper, and Edgar's tale—if he indeed wrote it—appeared
there two weeks after Henry's death, perhaps in response. The narrator tells of having fallen asleep after reading about the "dying
agonies" of the Crucifixion. In his dream he appears to himself as a
Pharisee who has assisted in nailing the Nazarene's palms, hearing
him groan "as the rough iron grated on the bones when I drove it
through." Wandering from the scene of death he hears sluggish waves
of the "Dead Sea" and passes into a vacant street where a wild dog
feasts on a "half-burnt corpse," and a widow prepares a last morsel
for her "dying babe." The whole universe seems extinct: "Nature
mourned, for its parent had died." But through a distant opening
in the heavens he distinctly sees the person he has helped to slay.
He finds himself in a burial ground where a mortuary monument
trembles, topples, and its occupant, as he watches in terror, steps
forth and approaches him. "I saw the grave-worm twining itself
amongst the matted locks which in part covered the rotten scull.
The bones creaked on each other as they moved on the hinges, for
its flesh was gone. . . . He came up to me; and, as he passed, he
breathed the cold damps of the lonely, narrow house directly in my
face." The chasm in the heavens closes, and the narrator awakes
with a shudder.

Although only three pages long, the tale embodies much of Edgar's past, present, and future. So far as it may have been inspired
by Henry's death, its statement that the dead world was mourning

"its parent" suggests a connection in Edgar's feelings between his brother's death and their mother's. It gives narrative form to the differently-shaped fantasies of resurrection earlier prominent in his poetry, and sets the pattern for the main action in much of his later fiction. The wormy corpse breathing into the narrator's face is a figure of the fiction writer as well. Like the cadet devising a scarifying skit with a bloody gander, the writer aims at shocking the reader with pictures of dogs feeding on corpses, visions of decay, in the process relieving by sharing the horror he has confronted or imagined himself. The narrator's inadvertent wandering to the graveyard, as if making his way unconsciously to what he most fears, will be recurrent in Edgar's fiction, as will the device of repeating key words over and over. In the brief compass of the tale, the words *dead* or *dying* appear ten times.

If Edgar did write "A Dream," he almost certainly received nothing for it. But a chance to earn money by his pen came to him from Philadelphia also. In the spring of 1831, the *Saturday Courier* announced a contest to promote American literary development, offering a hundred dollars for "the best AMERICAN TALE." Edgar did not win, but the judges liked what he submitted. On January 14, 1832, five days before his twenty-third birthday, the magazine published, anonymously, the first of his acknowledged tales, "Metzengerstein," a dreamlike narrative of supernatural revenge with strong autobiographical overtones. Like Edgar, the fifteen-year-old Baron Frederick Metzengerstein has been orphaned early in life: "His father, the Minister G——, died young. His mother, the Lady Mary, followed him quickly." More than that, he "stood, without a living relative, by the coffin of his dead mother. He laid his hand upon her placid forehead." Set in the interior of Hungary, the palace Metzengerstein also recalls Moldavia, and in fact the tale concerns the young baron's "hereditary jealousy" of the elderly Count Berlifitzing, which leads him to burn down his stables, where Berlifitzing is consumed.

During the year Edgar also published anonymously in the Philadelphia *Courier* four comic tales, notable for their variety of subject and technique. The flip, staccato "Duke de L'Omelette" relates the death of that nobleman following his horror at being served an ortolan immodestly presented nude, and his defeat of the devil at cards. "A Tale of Jerusalem" is a pseudoscriptural joke in a mock-biblical style. Contrastingly, the unnamed protagonist of "A Decided Loss" finds the morning after his marriage that he has literally lost his breath, and in attempting to hide the fact from his wife runs a gauntlet of comic mutilations and catastrophes. Laid in Venice, "The Bargain Lost" concerns a four-foot-five but rotund metaphysician named Pedro Garcia, who contests the devil's views about the materiality of the soul, instancing a scorn for philosophy and philosophizing repeatedly expressed in the tales. Aside from their bizarre plots, the comedy in these works is zestfully verbal, a cascade of exotic words and absurd names, exclamations and italics, macaronics and funny euphemisms.

Somberly or humorously, all of the tales fantasize ways of surviving death. The premise of "Metzengerstein" is the doctrine of metempsychosis, the transmigration of the soul into a new human or animal body. The murdered old count is weirdly reborn into the figure of a gigantic horse on one of Baron Metzengerstein's tapestries. "Stupified with terror," the baron watches as the cloth image extends its neck and its eyes seem to glow. The Duke de L'Omelette escapes death differently when his corpse is sent by the satanic Inspector of Cemeteries to Baal-Zebub, who resurrects him from an inlaid coffin to play cards. "A Decided Loss" gleefully catalogues all the ways one can die without dying. Having lost his breath but survived, the narrator considers himself "alive with the qualifications of the dead—dead with the propensities of the living." When he tries to run away on a stagecoach, the passengers, thinking him a corpse, throw him out, thereby fracturing his skull and breaking his thighs under the back wheels. An undertaker is sent for, but the narrator slips his burial bands and runs off. Still not dead, he is mistaken for a criminal awaiting execution, and hanged in his stead, then brought to a coroner, who takes off his ears. As he still displays signs of animation, an apothecary is brought in who slits his stomach and eviscerates him. The tale breaks off here, leaving the narrator still "kicking and plunging with all my might," although he has been killed and killed and killed again.

This concern with survival after death helps explain the very many images in the tales related to devouring. To cite but a few examples, the vivified horse on the tapestry of the young baron shows its "gigantic and disgusting teeth," while the baron himself has the "fangs of a petty Caligula" and rides to his death with "lacerated lips, which were bitten through and through." Again, the Duke de L'Omelette is both man and food, and dies while eating. And as the resilient narrator of "A Decided Loss" lies trussed up for burial, two cats chew off his nose. Edgar's fascination with such oral violence, suggesting some primitive rage in him, of course appears as early as his letter on the mutilated arm, "bitten from the shoulder to the elbow," and later in the vultures, condors, and "Time-eaten towers" of his youthful poems. In current psychoanalytic thinking about persons suffering prolonged and unresolved grief, the wish to devour also represents primitive attempts at preserving loved ones, incorporating them so as not to lose them, filling oneself to make up for (and to that extent deny) the loss. The lip-smacking devil in "The Bargain Lost" is just such a gourmand of the dead. He lustily describes the souls he has devoured pickled, fricaseed, or toasted on a fork, including those of Plato, Aristophanes, Catullus, Hippocrates, Quintilian, and especially Terence, "firm as an Esquimaux, and juicy as a German—the very recollection of the dog makes my mouth water."

Edgar was writing other fiction as well. By the spring of 1833 he conceived the idea of gathering his work into a volume called "Eleven Tales of the Arabesque." To unify the collection he decided to present the tales as if read aloud by members of a literary club, and to link them by the members' remarks, designed to burlesque current modes of literary criticism. He tried unsuccessfully to place the collection with the *New England Magazine* and entered six of the tales in a contest sponsored by a Baltimore newspaper, the *Saturday Visiter*. It had announced a prize of fifty dollars for the best tale and twenty-five dollars for the best poem submitted before October 1. To emphasize the unifying frame device, he called the manuscript he sent "The Tales of the Folio Club." He prepared it meticulously, transcribing the tales in print letters with calligraphic clarity. To one of the contest judges it seemed not handwriting at all, but "*printing with a pen.*" For the poetry contest he also submitted a new poem entitled "The Coliseum."

The judges received about a hundred entries. In explaining their decision they observed that the great merit of several of the poems made them hesitate in the award they finally made, to a short poem by a Henry Wilton entitled "Song of the Winds." Many of the tales, they said, were excellent too, but here there was no doubt. They considered Edgar's entire collection of surpassing interest, "distinguished by a wild, vigorous and poetical imagination, a rich style, a fertile invention, and varied and curious learning." He owed it to his own reputation and that of Baltimore, they added, to publish the entire volume. While they thought all his tales equally well done, on the basis of the originality of its conception they chose his "MS. Found in a Bottle."

Edgar's prize-winning tale appeared in the *Visiter* on October 19, followed the week after by the poem he had submitted. "MS. Found in a Bottle" creates a sustained crescendo of ever-building dread in the face of ever-stranger and ever-more-imminent catastrophe. On a voyage from Java aboard a beautiful teak ship freighted with ghee, jaggeree, and some cases of opium, the storyteller learns that the certainties of rationalism provide a feeble account of reality. A furious storm shatters the ship and drowns the crew, although he and an "old Swede" survive on the hulk, lifted sky-high and dropped to an abyss by "the swelling of the black stupendous seas," until hurled by the hurricane onto a dingy black vessel made of some unknown porous material. No one aboard the phantom ship seems able to see the storyteller; he passes unobserved and unable to communicate. The crew seem preternaturally ancient, their knees trembling with infirmity. The gray-haired captain sits alone in a cabin strewn with "mouldering instruments of science, and obsolete long-forgotten charts," emblems of the uselessness of reason. Meanwhile the colossal storm in the surrounding blackness has grown still more fierce. A "chaos of foamless water" rockets the ship toward "stupendous ramparts of ice . . . looking like the walls of the universe." As the ice opens the vessel whirls in immense circles along the "borders of a gigantic amphitheatre," and as it plunges wildly into the whirlpool the narration breaks off.

Edgar made the storyteller a "dealer in antiquities," meaningfully, for the tale he relates illustrates the undying power of archaic consciousness. Despite his positivistic outlook, his "strong relish for physical philosophy," he suffers from "a kind of nervous restlessness" which proves to be the pressure of submerged feeling. Its surfacing in him is marked by several unaccountable events. While aboard the strange ship he experiences "a sensation of familiar things" and the return of "an unaccountable memory." Absentmindedly dabbing at some folded sail with a tar brush, he finds that he has produced the word *DISCOVERY*. His voyage does turn out to be an ordeal of discovery, a movement toward "some exciting knowledge—some never-to-be-imparted secret." The new knowledge of course lies beyond and beneath 'philosophy.' It is knowledge of a world whose existence is proclaimed, in defiance of reason, by ancient beliefs and fears that endure within the self. The colossal porous ship is a living corpse, a thing both material and animate that despite its "worm-eaten condition" is able to "grow in bulk like the living body of the seaman." To the storyteller the captain appears to be both young and ancient: "His forehead, although little wrinkled, seems to bear upon it the stamp of a myriad of years." His speech seems strange and unstrange, near and far: "although . . . close at my elbow, yet his voice seemed to reach my ears from the distance of a mile." The crew are themselves dead in life, gliding about their tasks "to and fro like the ghosts of buried centuries." As his own reason becomes eclipsed, the storyteller himself is drawn into this now-revealed, contradictory realm of the alive in death, threatened with being devoured by "the very teeth of that supernatural sea."

Many of the tale's key words and images reappear in Edgar's near-prize-winning poem, "The Coliseum," which hails the great Roman ruin as a source of poetic inspiration. Where the crew in the tale breathe the "Spirit of Eld," for instance, the building in the poem glorifies the "Memories of Eld." Such resemblances reflect more than composition at about the same time. As Edgar celebrates the Coliseum, it is a ghostly architectural version of the phantom ship, stacked with "phantom-peopled aisles" and resurrected from "buried centuries of pomp." The inner theme of the poem is rebirth, for the seemingly "impotent" relic is in reality a thing of living force and meaning. To the question whether the crumbling fragments are "All," an echo replies:

> *. . . not all!*
> *Prophetic sounds and loud, arise forever*
> *From us, and from all Ruin. . . .*

In continuing to emit wonder, memories, and "more than glory" from its mouldering plinths, the Coliseum is a survivor of death.

On the same day that it published "The Coliseum," the *Visiter* ran a notice, surely with Edgar's compliance and advice, calling for subscribers at one dollar a copy for a volume to be called "The Folio Club." The prize-winning tale was not the best of his productions, the newspaper observed, and all his tales displayed unusual talent, "a raciness, originality of thought and brilliancy of conception which are rarely to be met with in the writings of our most favoured American authors." But only a week after the *Visiter* called for subscribers, it announced that Edgar had "declined" publication by the advertised plan, and intended instead to bring out the volume in Philadelphia. The newspaper did not say so, but what changed his mind was very likely its editor, John Hill Hewitt. As it happened, the "Henry Wilton" to whom the newspaper awarded the prize for the best poem was Hewitt himself. A writer and composer, he entered the contest under a pseudonym, reasoning that as editor of the *Visiter* it "would not look well" to appear a competitor. Edgar already believed that nothing had prevented him from receiving the prize for the best poem but his having won the prize for the best story. When he learned of Hewitt's ruse he was doubly indignant. Maybe trebly, for two years earlier Hewitt had reviewed his *Al Aaraaf* volume scoffingly, remarking that Nature had denied the author "that portion of inspiration essential to the formation of a poet of common order." According to Hewitt, Edgar confronted him in the *Visiter*'s office after the contest, accusing him of having used "underhanded means" to get the prize and of having tampered with the committee. Hewitt said the committee was composed of gentlemen, above being tampered with. Edgar agreed but added, "I cannot place *you* in that category." Hewitt hit him. Edgar staggered, but here, Hewitt said, some friends stopped the fight.

Probably because of his anger at Hewitt, Edgar gave over his Folio Club manuscript to the Baltimore novelist John Pendleton Kennedy. The head of a Baltimore literary club, Kennedy as he neared forty was emerging as the leading depicter in fiction of southern plantation life. The older man admired Edgar's writing and undertook to show his collection to Henry Carey in Philadelphia, the other partner in the firm of Carey and Lea. Meanwhile Edgar managed to publish another part of it, "The Visionary," a tale heavy in Venetian atmosphere involving the double suicide by poison of a mysterious Englishman of exquisite taste, modeled on Byron, and his aristocratic, married mistress. Although anonymous, its appearance in the January 1834 issue of a popular Philadelphia journal, Louis Godey's *Lady's Book,* meant his debut in a monthly magazine of national circulation.

John Allan

In August 1831, about three months after Edgar settled in Baltimore, John Allan's new wife gave birth to the couple's first child, whom they named John Allan, Jr. The birth of his own son and legitimate heir no doubt helped keep Edgar out of mind and at a distance, but not much help was needed. For years Allan had been eager to end his ward's dependence on him, and Edgar's new existence in Baltimore made his claims to affection and aid seem less binding than ever.

Edgar likely had not heard about the birth when he wrote to Richmond that October. But by then he had not seen John Allan since leaving for West Point nearly a year and a half earlier, and already feared that he could no longer consider himself Allan's son. "I am sorry that it is so seldom that I hear from you or even *of* you," he began, "for all communication seems to be at an end; and when I think of the long twenty one years that I have called you father, and you have called me son, I could cry like a child to think that it should all end in this." Throughout their relationship, Edgar's appeals for affection had never been easy to distinguish from requests for the money he had come to accept as a token of it. But now he stressed that his confession of misery over their rupture was no disguised plea for cash, and that he asked nothing for himself: "it is only at such a time as the present when I can write to you with the consciousness of making no application for assistance," he said, "that I dare to open my heart, or speak one word of old affection." Denouncing himself as "the greatest fool in existence," he acknowledged how much John Allan had tried to do for him, how he had repaid Allan's forbearance and generosity with ingratitude, and especially how he understood that the time when he might have appealed further to his goodness was past. "I have nothing more to say—and *this time,* no favour to ask," he concluded. "Altho I am wretchedly poor, I have managed to get clear of the difficulty I spoke of in my last, and am *out of debt,* at any rate. May God bless you."

Edgar's "May God bless you," following on his "I am wretchedly poor," hardly confirms his insistence that he was beyond working on John Allan's pity and guilt. His ill-concealed final plea apparently prompted Allan to send him some money. But although the feelings of disregard and regret Edgar expressed in his letter seem sincere enough, he likely intended them also to set up John Allan for the emergency call he dispatched one month later. "I am in the greatest distress," he began, "and have no other friend on earth to apply to except yourself if you refuse to help me I know not what I shall do." The story he told was brief but dramatic. About two years before he took on a debt that he never expected to have to pay, as it was incurred as much on the account of his deceased brother, Henry, as himself. Nevertheless, eleven days ago he had been "arrested" for the debt. He gave no details, but to emphasize his plight he added that he was in bad health, unable to exert himself on his own behalf. "If you will only send me this one time $80, by Wednesday next, I will never forget your kindness & generosity." And he ended with his familiar warning: "if you refuse God only knows what I shall do, & all my hopes & prospects are ruined forever—."

No evidence of Edgar's arrest has ever been found, and John Allan wavered over responding to his news of it. Three weeks after Edgar wrote, Allan prepared a letter arranging to "procure his liberation" and to have twenty dollars given him, "to keep him out of farther difficulties." But he "neglected," as he put it, to mail the letter for another five weeks. Meantime Edgar rushed off two more petitions, no longer pretending to do more than beg. "If you wish me to humble myself before you I am humble—Sickness and misfortune have left me not a shadow of pride. I own that I am miserable and unworthy of your notice, but do not leave me to perish without leaving me still one resource." By this time he may have learned of John Allan's new son, for he noted that while he was suffering "every extremity of want and misery," Allan was basking in a fullness of existence, "enjoying yourself in all the blessings that wealth & happiness can bestow." His distress over Allan's seeming refusal to help was also conveyed to Richmond by his Aunt Maria, who wrote to Allan at least twice, likely setting down what Edgar suggested or even dictated to her. "I feel deeply interested in him," she explained, "for he has been extremely kind to me as far as his opportunities would permit." She told Allan that her own poverty made it impossible for her to "extricate" him, even though with great difficulty she had procured him twenty dollars. She also assured Allan, from her own knowledge, that except this one case Edgar owed nothing. His present difficulty would be "a warning for him as long as he lives," and if released he would go on to "do well."

With Allan's aid, when it arrived, Edgar apparently paid off the debt. But he had no further contact with his foster father for more than a year afterward. He remained badly pressed for money, and again went to live with Maria, his cousin Virginia, and his grandmother when they moved in the spring of 1833 to Three Amity Street, where Maria seems to have supported herself by dressmaking. To one observer later in the year he seemed careworn, as if "the world was then going hard with him." Again or still broke, he wrote to Allan in April. "It has now been more than two years [actually fifteen months] since you have assisted me," he started, "and more than three since you have spoken to me." Given their long separation he said he felt little hope that his letter would be noticed. Nevertheless he implored Allan to take in the hopelessness of his situation, "without friends, without any means, consequently of obtaining employment, I am perishing—absolutely perishing for want of aid. . . . For God's sake pity me, and save me from destruction."

John Allan's reaction to Edgar's new, and final, appeal was to look over some earlier correspondence with him. He took one letter and wrote a short memorandum on the back of it. It was the letter Edgar had sent from New York after leaving West Point, in which he complained of a bloody discharge from his ear and threatened that "You one day or other will *felll* [*sic*] how you have treated me." Allan began his memorandum by mocking the opening line of Edgar's letter to him—"It has now been more than two years since you have assisted me"—and then his rage erupted in an apoplectic curse: "it is now upwards of 2 years since I received the above precious relict of the Blackest Heart & deepest ingratitude alike destitute of honour & principle every day of his life has only served to confirm his debased nature." He may have become aware of Edgar's budding literary reputation, for he added, with what seems equally admiration and condemnation, "his Talents are of an order that can never prove a comfort to their possessor."

The man with whom Edgar had not spoken for three years was now only fifty-four years old, and fathering a new family. But he had also grown completely gray, his step tottering, the "good hard flesh" deteriorated. Ninety-five-degree heat in Richmond in the summer of 1833 made him feel weak, and in the hope of restoring himself he drove off with his family to Sulphur Springs, the spa in the Virginia mountains to which Edgar had long ago accompanied him and Fanny Allan on summer vacations. Only now John Allan's family included Louisa Allan and two small children, the couple having produced a second son, whom they named after William Galt. The munificence of "Uncle" Galt, as Edgar used to call him, remained in evidence. With the corpulent Miss Nancy, two nurses, two drivers, and five horses the group made, Allan said, "an expensive cavalcade."

Just when Edgar learned of John Allan's illness is unknown, but he may have tried to visit Moldavia early in 1834, not long after the couple had a third child. By then Allan was unable to lie down because of dropsy and confined to an arm chair. For exercise he walked across the room helped by his wife and a servant, leaning on his cane. According to later, second-hand testimony, Mrs. Allan, a strong-willed woman who was said to "never forgive the least slight or disrespect to herself," tried to prevent Edgar from going upstairs to Allan's sickroom, but he rushed past her. When he entered the chamber, according to this account, Allan raised his cane as if to strike him and ordered him to leave. Only a month or so after this episode (if it occurred), a physician had to be called. He applied on Allan's side a large blister plaster. At about eleven o'clock in the morning a week later, on March 27, Louisa Allan heard from his room the cries of one of the children, who had become hurt. When she went in she found her husband dead, sitting alone in his arm chair. She had immediately noticed a difference in his appearance. Her screams brought others to her assistance.

As "Jack," "Jock," or "Scotch" John Allan, he had been a long-time and prominent resident of Richmond, and his death was publicized. The local *Enquirer* observed that among the citizens of the place, "none was better known, none more highly respected." Sometime after his burial, in Shockoe Hill Cemetery, a tombstone went up with an elaborate inscription that in part testified to his humane heart and manly code: "Blessed with every social and benevolent feeling, he fulfilled the duties of Husband, Father, Brother, and Friend, with surpassing Kindness, supported the ills of life with Fortitude, and his Prosperity with Meekness." That like other people he could also be envious, grudging, or tightfisted was of course not commented on publicly, nor were his illegitimate children. James Ellis, a member of his former partner's family, offered a less idealized appraisal when he noted privately that Allan had "not—although the newspapers say so, spent his time in a proper way." Yet Ellis too joined in the general praise for Allan as someone who had been, he said, "ever kind and affectionate to all." His sins, such as they were, "were against himself."

John Allan had drawn up a problematic will, flawed by internal disagreements and nonlegal phraseology. The act seems inconsistent with his careful business habits, and likely resulted from his puzzlement over how to deal with his past. For he added an also inconsistent and colloquial codicil acknowledging the existence of his illegitimate twins, with a shorter addition after one of them died. Louisa Allan renounced any claims under this will, which provided for her husband's surviving illegitimate child. She chose instead to have the courts regard John Allan as having died intestate, and appoint a commission to evaluate his wealth and determine its disposition. The commission assigned the bulk of his estate to his children (presumably only those he had by Louisa), to be held by an executor until they came of age. The executor chosen was James Galt, who as a teenager had stood guard to prevent the still younger Edgar from running back to London from Irvine. Allan also provided an annuity of $300 for Miss Nancy Valentine (plus free board and lodging for life) and bequests to his sisters in Scotland.

What Louisa Allan received for herself was nevertheless formidable, well worthy the Elector of Moldavia, who had not squandered the huge estate bequeathed him by Uncle William Galt. In addition to some bank and railroad stock, she came into a third of her husband's property in Richmond, which consisted of eight houses (including Moldavia), a lumber house, some undeveloped land, and nine slaves (one an infant), with a total value of $59,500. She also received the Lower Byrd plantation, with its livestock and implements as well as some seventy slaves, plus 292 acres of woodland, including the free sawing of fifteen thousand feet of wood annually for the use of the plantation. In addition she got a third part of the Little Byrd and Big Byrd plantations. Like the Lower Byrd, these were working plantations producing saleable crops of cotton, tobacco, and wheat, containing horses, wagons, barrels of beef, carriage houses, and much other property, run by overseers and worked by 150 or more slaves. Within the Big Byrd also lay, it was believed, a gold mine, a third part of whose net proceeds she was also assigned "whenever it shall be worked or leased."

Edgar estimated, probably correctly, that his foster father had been worth three quarters of a million dollars. But neither in his will nor in the codicils did John Allan mention Edgar A. Poe. Nor did the commission appointed by the court recognize his existence. By one account, he went to Richmond after Allan's death and tried to see Louisa Allan, but she would not receive him. He later said that she refused him even his books. Of the stocks and cords of wood, the rights to theoretic gold mines, the eight Richmond houses, there came to him exactly nothing. He might now continue to cry out that he was perishing for want of aid, but no John Allan would appear to upbraid him for evasion, irresponsibility, and disrespect, or to supply school books or mourning clothes or eight or ten dollars for a boardinghouse. Nor could he ever again be only temporarily exiled from John Allan's principled, hawklike love, be only estranged.

The Southern Literary Messenger; *Marriage to Virginia Clemm.*

NOVEMBER 1834–JANUARY 1836

"This is the golden age of periodicals!" The proclamation, by an Illinois magazine in 1831, was premature, a reaction to only the early stage of what would become a six hundred percent multiplication of American periodicals between 1825 and 1850. New printing technologies would feed this huge growth, as well as the diffusion of public education, improvements in eyeglasses, and wider and easier distribution of printed works by a growing network of railroads, whose passengers also welcomed easy-to-read fare that could be dropped in a valise or carpetbag. Many of the mushrooming new magazines would die after a few issues; few would last more than a year or two. But within a quarter century the country would produce altogether some four or five thousand of them.

The swelling enthusiasm for magazine publishing was shared by the energetic Richmond printer Thomas Willis White (Illus. 7). He had begun as an apprentice in the trade at the age of eleven, three years after the death of his father. In August 1834 he launched a new magazine, the *Southern Literary Messenger*. His aim was frankly regional, an effort, he wrote, "to stimulate the pride and genius of the south, and awaken from its long slumber the literary exertion of this portion of our country." He hoped to attract a Southern readership that had often lamented the region's absorption in political discussion to the detriment of belles lettres, and its dependence on Northern writers and publications for reading matter. The last sentence of his inaugural issue was a bugle call: "The South is awakening!"

But so far as White's call was self-congratulatory it was also blustery. A conventionally moralistic man who spoke of "that chaste empress, TEMPERANCE," he sought to offend no one. He designed his magazine to become, as he said, "a source of innocent amusement, and at the same time a vehicle of valuable information." Stressing "pure moral sentiment," his robust-looking, sixty-four double-columned pages therefore offered rather tame reading: verses on "The Power of Faith," short fiction exposing the dangers of parental harshness, essays by anonymous Southerners on jurisprudence or the decay of manners in Virginia illustrated by the current taste for the waltz ("No modest woman ever beheld it for the first time, without the burning blush of shame and confusion"). Whatever its limitations, the *Messenger* was well received. In his first issue White printed letters of encouragement from Washington Irving, James Fenimore Cooper, and other established literary figures, approving his hope of creating a renaissance of Southern letters. Although a Richmond writer speculated that one might more likely sell 5,000 copies of a magazine in New York or Philadelphia than 250 in Richmond, after ten months or so White claimed a subscription list of nearly 1,000.

Despite his success, White had difficulty keeping the *Messenger* afloat. He found himself "Hard-run" for money. Self-educated and a printer by trade, he also felt inadequate to making editorial decisions that involved literary judgments. From the beginning he relied on the advice of more discriminating and better-educated friends, mostly lawyers or professors with literary tastes. He was urged to get the assistance of a trained editor, as he tried to do. But his search was hampered by his ability to pay, and by a pride of possession that made him jealous of titles. After hiring one editor for a while, he identified the man to readers of the magazine not as 'Editor' but as "manager of the editorial department." However concerned about his own inexperience, he wished to stay in firm control of the magazine, and to leave no contrary impression.

A suitable editorial prospect was not far off. Early in 1835, White began hearing from Edgar A. Poe in Baltimore, who wrote to him on the advice of John Pendleton Kennedy. Poe knew of or sensed White's proprietary instinct, for he approached him tactfully, saying "I have no intention of giving you *advice.*" Just the same, as their correspondence drew on into the spring and early summer he plied White with his opinions. Where White feared offending his readers' reverence for what he called "Virginian simplicity"—plain morals in plain language—Poe dismissed this respect as a sham. "Nobody is more aware than I am that simplicity is the cant of the day," he counseled, "but take my word for it no one cares any thing about simplicity in their hearts." Successful English magazines had demonstrated, he explained, that readers really liked sensational subjects treated in a heightened style, even to the point of what is ordinarily called bad taste. "To be appreciated you must be *read,* and these things are invariably sought after with avidity." He advised White to ignore adverse criticism of such works, for their true value "will be estimated better by the circulation of the Magazine." He offered many other tips on merchandising and production. He recommended that White not reprint an earlier issue, although distinguished, on the ground that editors of daily newspapers tended to notice none but the most recent publications. He suggested that the *Messenger's* appearance might be improved by using a lighter-faced type for the headings of articles. Beginning with the second volume, White bought a new font of type and did so; the magazine was much praised for its typography.

Nothing in Poe's literary experience entitled him to speak so confidently about the business of magazine publishing. But his air of expertise was well founded on a canny understanding of what interested the growing reading public. And much of his understanding, in turn, came from his eager effort to find an audience for his own work. Here too White found him useful. Beginning with his seventh issue, he started publishing tales and parts of an all-but-finished play by Poe and, even earlier, book reviews at the rate of eighty cents per column. He also tried to pay Poe to write notices of three successive issues of the *Messenger,* anonymously, in a Baltimore newspaper. Poe said he simply wished to aid the magazine's circulation, and insisted that White not send him "any remuneration for services of this nature. They are a pleasure to me & no trouble whatever." In composing these puffs he tried seriously not to compromise his own literary standards, allowing many individual pieces in the issues only guarded praise and damning some as "exceedingly insipid" or "crude." But he declared the *Messenger* as a whole equal to any other American magazine, and joined White in saluting it as the vanguard of a reborn Southern literary culture: "It is indeed a subject of general congratulations that the South has at length aroused herself from her lethargy in these matters, and ventured to erect a periodical literature of her own."

The dealings between Baltimore and Richmond were no less timely for Poe than for White. For Poe now felt more vulnerable than ever, "thrown entirely upon my own resources," he said, "with no profession, and very few friends." His difficulty showed. To several acquaintances he seemed a somber figure, his large gray eyes and dark brown, nearly black, hair befitting an expression that one recalled as "thoughtful, melancholy, and rather stern." Very slender, even delicate, he carried himself with military erectness, his bearing registering something of his army career but also of an inner pride that would forbid the appearance of indigence. He even dressed with some flair, emphasizing black—in Byronic collars and a black neckerchief, by one account, or, by another, habitually in a black frock coat buttoned up, a black cravat tied in a loose knot. Yet his poverty was not to be hidden. "Coat, hat, boots and gloves had very evidently seen their best days," an acquaintance recalled, "but so far as mending and brushing go, everything had been done apparently, to make them presentable."

Staying presentable, however, was proving more than Poe could manage. Through Kennedy he tried to draw a small advance for his "Tales of the Folio Club" from Carey and Lea, who were still considering the manuscript, and he enlisted Kennedy also in helping him get a teaching position in a Baltimore public school. But he obtained neither, and had nothing left, was "at length penniless." He even lost some little money that had been sent to him, he said, owing to thefts at the post office, where a boy had been "purloining letters." Once when Kennedy invited him to dinner, he replied with "deep mortification" that he must refuse because he lacked proper clothing; he asked Kennedy to lend him twenty dollars so that he could dress himself decently enough to accept. Kennedy later recalled that he found Poe in "a state of starvation." Not only that, but in welcoming him to his table, supplying him with clothing, and giving him the use of a horse for exercise, Kennedy felt that he "brought him up from the very verge of despair." He probably did not exaggerate, for in the spring Poe reported feeling too unwell to leave the house, moreover "so ill as to be hardly able to see the paper on which I wrote." A physician assured him, he said, that nothing but a sea voyage would save him.

But White's interest promised more than temporary financial relief. Poe had long found magazine publishing a mysterious and appealing realm, and tried to find a place in it. And Kennedy had suggested that in addition to publishing some of his works, White might be willing to give him some "permanent employ." A dependable income mattered more than ever, for Poe had fallen in love with his cousin Virginia, "my own darling," as he called her. In fact he wished to marry her, even though she was now only two weeks past the age of thirteen. The incidents through which their closeness evolved are unknown, although during his three years in Baltimore he had not merely found a temporary shelter with her and her mother, but had established with them a permanent family and a permanent home. Muddy, as his Aunt Maria was familiarly known, had become for him an unfailing source of affection and nurturing care. She considered him her own and in effect adopted him, acknowledging that he had become "indeed a son to me & has always been so." He returned her concern. Through the death of her paralyzed seventy-eight-year-old mother, she lost the use of a $240 annual pension that the Maryland assembly had granted to General David Poe's widow for life, leaving her more than usually pressed for funds. Poe could offer no money, but he tried to raise some from his cousin William Poe, as "*immediate* relief," he said, for "one who well deserves every kindness and attention."

A real chance for Poe to support Virginia as his wife and to care for Muddy came when White wrote to him in June. He asked, as Poe paraphrased his words, "if I would be willing to come on to Richmond if you should have occasion for my services during the coming winter." The iffy offer has the note of White's self-protectiveness, but Poe seized on it as a possible deliverance. He replied that nothing would please him more than to visit Richmond, as he had wanted to do for some time, and where he was now "anxious to settle myself." Still he understood that White had promised him nothing. While sending his wish that "possibly you might find something for me to do in your office" he also expressed hope that White might help him find some other suitable situation in Richmond, "were the salary even the merest trifle." For White, the correctness of his noncommittal treatment of Poe was perhaps confirmed later the same month, when a friend warned him that Poe's appearances in his magazine would rather injure than improve it, as his works were obscure and seemed designed mainly to display his erudition: "That he may be a scholar of the very highest grade I will not question," the friend said, "but it is not always the best scholars that write best, or have the best taste & judgment."

Poe went to Richmond anyway in August. He may have done so not to work for the magazine, but hoping to fill an advertised vacancy in the English department of the Richmond Academy, as he failed to do. Whatever his main reason for going to Richmond, he did within a few days join White at the *Messenger* offices. In person, his correspondent and new employer turned out to be a short, stocky middle-aged man with curly hair who offered him a salary of sixty dollars a month.

Whatever pleasure Poe found in his new situation can have lasted no more than two weeks, for at the end of August he received a disjointingly shaking letter from Muddy. She had been hard put, "struggling without friends," he said, "without money, and without health to support [herself] and 2 children." In the letter she sought his advice about an invitation extended to her by his cousin Neilson, the lawyer and newspaper editor. During Poe's few weeks' absence from Baltimore, Neilson had offered to take in Virginia to live with him and to educate her, and perhaps to take in Muddy as well. Presumably Neilson meant to rescue Muddy from her poverty, but he reportedly also hoped to prevent Virginia from marrying at so young an age, keeping open the possibility of her marriage to Poe a few years later, if they both still desired it.

To Poe the offer meant the certain loss of his cousin, of someone he loved. More than that, it threatened the new home he had made and the dependable presence of people who looked after him. He replied with hysterical supplication: "It is useless to disguise the truth that when Virginia goes with N.P. that I shall never behold her again—that is absolutely sure. Pity me, my dear Aunty, pity me. I have no one now to fly to . . . my wretchedness is more than I can bear." The uproar of his emotions and likely, so his long letter sounds, his alcoholic blur, told in the letter's many exclamation points, understrokes, misspellings, repetitions, lurching fresh starts. Writing while "blinded with tears," he said, he tried to drive home the actuality and intensity of his feeling: "I love, *you know* I love Virginia passionately devotedly. I cannot express in words the fervent devotion I feel towards my dear little cousin." To consent to Neilson's plan would be to resign his very life, yet there was no doubting that Neilson could make Virginia comfortable, even perhaps happy. The dilemma left him too bewildered to offer advice. "Oh," he wrote, taking Muddy's own tone of plaintive exclamation, "think for me for I am incapable of thinking. . . . Oh God have mercy on me! . . . . . . Oh Aunty, Aunty you loved me once—how can you be so cruel now?" All the same, he suggested that Muddy let Virginia decide herself whether to accept Neilson's offer. If she did, and wrote to him to say goodbye, forever, he said he would say no more.

But Poe left Muddy and Virginia little real choice. In a postscript he addressed his cousin herself: "My love, my own sweetest Sissy, my darling little wifey, th[ink w]ell before you break the heart of your cousin. Eddy." The request contained his usual warning, and actually he had made it clear throughout his letter that he felt betrayed. The offer to go with Neilson had come, he said, when his own arrangements for Muddy's and Sissy's welfare were far advanced. He had already "procured" a "sweet little house," newly redecorated, with a large garden. He had dreamt with "rapture" of bringing his aunt and cousin, "all I love on Earth," to live with him there, and of the pride he would feel in making them comfortable "& in calling her my wife." He felt betrayed too in his love for Virginia, who if she loved him would have scorned Neilson's offer, and in his belief that Muddy, like him, cherished their family intimacy as a bastion against the harshness of the world outside. "The tone of your letter wounds me to the soul," he told Muddy. "You speak of Virginia acquiring accomplishments, and entering into society—you speak in so *worldly* a tone." He let Muddy know not only that he considered Neilson's offered comforts crass, but also that his spirit could not survive the acceptance of them. "You have both [sic] tender hearts—and you will always have the reflection that my agony is more than I can bear—that you have driven me to the grave." He even warned that, faced with having to exist on his own again, he was thinking of killing himself, or at least letting himself die: "My last my last my only hold on life is cruelly torn away," he said, "I have no desire to live and *will not.*"

Adding a fillip of discouragement to its news of catastrophe, Muddy's letter arrived when Poe was already enjoying some success on the *Messenger.* White not only provided a salary, but also offered (improbably) to issue his still-circulating "Tales of the Folio Club" under the imprint of Carey and Lea, which had first accepted the manuscript, then delayed publication and finally declined it. And finding Poe's disposition "quite amiable," White took a fatherly interest in him, his own son having died of cholera three years before, at the age of nineteen. Poe also became friendly with White's eighteen-year-old daughter, said to have been an intelligent and graceful blonde with blue eyes, whose name was Eliza. Presented with the possibility of losing Virginia, he may for a time have become romantically involved with her. Evidently he was delighted to have attained what seemed to him some position in the literary world. White was careful to say that Poe was "now in my employ—not as Editor." Poe knew where he stood, for he told Kennedy he had been hired by White as a junior staff member, "in assisting him with the Editorial duties." But ever yearning for authority and a name, he described his position to several others quite differently, bearing out White's worst fears of being usurped. "I have lately obtained the Editorship of the Southern Messenger," he informed his cousin William Poe, "and may probably yet do well."

However he exaggerated his situation at the magazine, Poe was justified in regarding it as a "great improvement in my circumstances." But Neilson's menacing offer left him unable to take any pleasure in his success. Instead by early September he felt desperate, "suffering under a depression of spirits," he said, "such as I have never felt before." That he had begun drinking was apparent to White, who in addition to finding him amiable also soon found him a problem, "unfortunately rather dissipated,—and therefore I can place very little reliance upon him." Worse, Poe's mood remained self-destructive, as if without Virginia and Muddy he could no longer survive. He wrote urgently to Kennedy, in effect imploring him to prevent his ending his life: "Console me—for you can. But let it be quickly—or it will be too late. Write me immediately. Convince me that it is worth one's while—that it is at all necessary to live." Kennedy did reply quickly, only four days later, but hardly convincingly. "Rise early," he recommended, "live generously . . . take the air, and make cheerful acquaintances." Poe might reap a good profit, he said, by writing and trying to sell to New York theater managers some farces in the style of French vaudevilles.

But by the time Kennedy's letter reached Richmond, Poe was gone, "flew the track," as White put it. "His habits were not good.— He is in addition the victim of melancholy." Whether Poe quit or

White fired him is unknown, but the editor felt to some degree relieved, even as he recognized the seriousness of Poe's condition. "I should not be at all astonished," he wrote, "to hear that he had been guilty of suicide."

Poe had not simply flown the track, but returned to Baltimore, where, on September 22, he and Virginia took out a marriage license, and perhaps were privately married. On this point the records are unclear, and later accounts differ, although the likelihood is that they wed. They joined as blood relatives, Virginia being the daughter of his father's sister. First-cousin marriages were not unusual at the time; but Virginia's age was. Opinion about the appropriate marrying age for women differed, and women in the South married younger than those in other sections. Yet to marry at the age of thirteen was extremely rare and, as Neilson Poe did, most people would have considered Virginia far too young. For Poe, however, her age constituted part of her appeal. Even earlier he had flirted with his fourteen-year-old cousin Elizabeth. And his manner of addressing and referring to Virginia—usually as "Sissy," "Sis," or "my darling little wife"—itself suggests a preference for a childlike rather than a mature or even simply a young woman. Later events in his life make this preference more obvious, but in his present feelings of helplessness Poe rather experienced himself also as a child. In his claims to precocious genius he even emphasized his immaturity. Born in 1809, he several times gave the year of his birth as 1811 or even 1813, making himself seem two or four years younger than he was. His reaction to Neilson's offer also makes clear that he envisioned himself not only having Sissy but also retaining Muddy to care for him and, more generally, to maintain a warm and confiding domestic situation. The women provided him both a wife and a mother, and perhaps had the felt symbolic value of restoring his original family. Virginia's middle name was "Eliza," and as "Sis" she perhaps preserved for him some presence of his own sister Rose. (Muddy's eighteen-year-old son, it might be added, was named Henry.)

Whether married or only engaged, Poe hoped to return to Richmond, and wrote to White from Baltimore asking for his job back. White admired Poe's talents and genuinely liked him. Groping for language to convey the sincerity of his concern, he replied that he alone knew how much he had regretted their parting: "I was attached to you—and am still." But much as he desired Poe's return, he also anticipated a new and quick separation. "Edgar, when you once again tread these streets, I have my fears that your resolve would fall through,—and that you would again sip the juice, even till it stole away your senses." He lectured Poe sternly on his drinking: "No man is safe who drinks before breakfast! No man can do so, and attend to business properly." If Poe did return to Richmond and got drunk, he said, their relation would end immediately. He asked Poe in replying to say whether he would agree to forever separate himself from the bottle and from bottle companions. If Poe could promise that, he implied, then he would take him back: "Tell me if you can and will do so—and let me hear that it is your fixed purpose never to yield to temptation."

Poe returned to Richmond on Saturday evening, October 3, and by the new week was working once again for the *Messenger.* With him he brought Virginia and Muddy, although her son remained in Baltimore, working in the stone-cutting business. Poe's departure had created production problems for White, so that no October issue of the *Messenger* was published, and the November issue was delayed until December. Even so White remained wary, and decided to re-introduce Poe's name as that of a contributor, "taking care not to say as editor." Poe, incorrigible about proving to relatives that he would distinguish their name, nevertheless informed another cousin, George Poe, Jr., that he had now "undertaken the Editorship of the Southern Literary Messenger."

Poe's return with his family and with promises to reform produced satisfaction and high hopes all around. At Christmastime, White was able to "rejoice," as he put it, that Poe "still keeps from the Bottle." Poe himself, no longer asking to be convinced of the need for living, looked ahead optimistically to the new year. "My health is better than for years past, my mind is fully occupied, my pecuniary difficulties have vanished, I have a fair prospect of future success—in a word all is right." Muddy had come to Richmond in ill health, and Poe urged her not to try to undertake any business. She appreciated his concern, and his sacrifices in trying to house and feed the three of them, not in the "sweet little house" and large garden he had described to her, it turned out, but at any rate in a local boardinghouse, for nine dollars a week: "it takes nearly all he can make to answer that demand, but poor fellow he is willing to do all in his power for us." A religious woman, she believed that if God spared her family, Poe's salary would increase, allowing them to live still more comfortably. Meanwhile she was determined to be contented, and felt thankful. If she and Sissy brought her nephew, and now son-in-law, a steadying home life, the benefit was mutual: "myself & daughter know that we have some to love & care for us."

Writings
in the Southern Literary Messenger.

CA. MARCH 1835–JANUARY 1837

Whether or not called editor, Poe performed for White all the duties of one, and in a businesslike way. Among many other chores he advised White on articles submitted for publication, edited copy and checked proof, decided typographical matters, solicited manuscripts, kept track of the doings of other magazines, and wrote his own reviews, fillers, fiction, poetry, and editorial comments. The February 1836 number, he observed, contained no fewer than forty pages of editorial matter (perhaps, he confessed, "a little *de trop*"). Some business relations required letters painstakingly composed to avoid giving offense, as when he found himself fending off friends who wished to be published, suggesting substantial revisions to contributors, or turning down work by writers with some reputation. Such work called on him for unexpected reserves of diplomacy, which he mustered. Not only was he learning the magazine business, but his correspondence also brought him for the first time into wide contact with well-known literary figures of the day like Robert Montgomery Bird and James Kirke Paulding, peers with whom he could discuss versification, criticism, and other literary matters.

Poe's editorial duties kept him busy, to the neglect of his own imaginative writing: "having no time upon my hands," he lamented, "I can write nothing worth reading." Most of his own fiction that came out in the *Messenger* appeared before he took over its management, while he was advising White from Baltimore. Between March and November 1835 he published in the magazine six new tales and parts of an all-but-finished play. They kept faith with the guideline he recommended to White, that, "Virginia simplicity" to the contrary, the magazine-reading public wanted sensational subjects treated in a charged style, "the ludicrous heightened into the grotesque: the fearful coloured into the horrible: the witty exaggerated into the burlesque: the singular wrought out into the strange and mystical." They also fulfilled his promise to White that while preserving their sensational character, his tales would provide maximum variety, no two of them having, he said, "the slightest resemblance one to the other either in matter or manner." In fact, Poe's understanding of the demands of magazine readers for freshness and diversity led him to produce works that range in form and technique from three-page prose poems to forty-page voyage narratives packed with scientific observation, varying in mood from rising frenzy to chatty ridiculousness, works that might seem the creations of several different writers.

Among the strange and horrible, "Berenice—A Tale" came in the genteel pages of the *Messenger* with the effect of an affront, its air of madness and desecration violating the magazine's standard of propriety. Set in no defined time or place, it concerns the gloomily meditative Egæus, who plans to marry his once carefree cousin Berenice, now emaciated by disease. He grows ill himself, of a "monomania" in which he can think of nothing but her teeth. Before they can marry, Berenice is borne to her grave—"still alive!," it turns out—which Egæus in an amnesiac state digs open; using dental instruments he wrests her thirty-two teeth from her mouth. The unnamed narrator of "Morella" feels for his wife a "deep but most singular affection," singular in containing nothing erotic, deep in that he is her devoted "pupil," hour after hour learning from her lustrous melancholy eyes and musical voice the secrets of the "forbidden pages" she studies, especially the transcendental doctrine of Identity. He comes, however, to feel oppressed by everything in her he once loved; she languishes, and in dying gives birth to a daughter. With preternatural speed the child grows in size and intelligence, becoming more and more identical to her mother. The narrator has avoided giving her a name, but at last decides to have her baptized at the age of ten. Even at the baptismal font he hesitates for a name, then compulsively whispers that of his dead wife, Morella. Features convulsed, the child responds, "I am here!," collapses, and is borne to her mother's tomb, where no trace of the first Morella is found.

In a ludicrous or burlesque key, with rapid-fire dialogue, "Lion-izing. A Tale" satirizes the rage for literary lions and the ease of becoming one. For his large and grotesque nose, expanded each morning by dram drinking and by giving "my proboscis a couple of pulls," Thomas Smith of the city of Fum-Fudge wins applause in English literary reviews and gains entrance to aristocratic drawing rooms, where he and his pamphlet on "Nosology" are fawned upon by such as "Signor Tintontintino from Florence." He outwits himself, however, by shooting off the nose of Baron Bludenuff in a duel, bestowing on the baron the greater celebrity. In a still different mood and form, the lengthy "Hans Phaall—A Tale" tells through a letter, diary, and framing narrative how an indigent bellows maker from Rotterdam, scarcely two feet tall but with a nose "prodigiously long, crooked and inflammatory," escapes his creditors by flying by balloon to the moon, among whose inhabitants he remains for five years—or so he claims. In part a satire on a current enthusiasm for ballooning, and the high hopes for human progress seen in such technological feats, the imaginary voyage recounts with extensive astronomical, medical, and geographical detail such curiosities of Phaall's ascent as his unprecedented sighting of the North Pole.

Poe capped this diverse offering with the black-humorous "King Pest the First. A Tale containing an Allegory"; a brief prose dirge entitled "Shadow. A Fable"; and "Scenes from an Unpublished Drama," five sections from his incompleted blank verse tragedy, "Politian," laid in sixteenth-century Rome. In the tale, two drunken sailors stagger into a part of London quarantined because of plague, stumbling into an undertaker's shop. The shop has, however, a wine-cellar, where they join in the grisly carousing of six loathsome corpses who sit on coffin tressels, clad in shrouds, palls, and winding sheets, boisterously drinking from skulls. Condensed and as it were inverted, the same scene appears in the funereally lyric "Shadow." Here a company of seven attend the shrouded corpse of their young friend Zoilus during a pestilence in Egypt, dispelling their fears in drink, laughter, and song. From the black draperies enters a dark and undefined shadow that addresses them, its voice having not the tone of a single being but resonating with the voices of "a thousand departed friends"—another of Poe's shocking tale-tellers. Finally, the parts of his tragedy that Poe published concern the love of the English earl Politian for Lalage, an orphaned Roman beauty driven to near madness in being dishonored by the son of her foster father.

In creating "Berenice," "Morella," and stories like them, Poe drew

on a widely popular tradition of Gothic fiction. By the time he began treating the Gothic world in "Metzengerstein," it had been a
staple of British, American, and Continental writing for nearly half
a century. He particularly had in mind the so-called 'German tales'
featured in *Blackwood's* and other English magazines of the period.
These tales originated among German romantic writers who gave
English Gothicism their own twists and, disregarding probability,
greatly exaggerated elements of the horrible and the supernatural.
In its several varieties, Gothic fiction aimed at creating the presence
of something that suspends and calls into doubt the laws of the
universe. As in Morella's rebirth through her daughter or the appearance of the many-voiced shade in "Shadow," it implied that the
terrors of the world we know are driven by something unknown
and unknowable beyond them.

Poe derived many specific features of his tales from Gothic tradition. Among other devices he borrowed motifs of enclosure and
premature burial, animated portraits and tapestries, putrescence and
physical decay; the depiction of garishly lit dwellings, particularly
mansions and castles, as enclosing a nightmarish domain of the fantastic and irrational; the use of mirrors, interior decor, and external
landscape to reflect psychological states. Egæus and many of his
other protagonists also share with the Gothic hero their isolation
and extreme sensibility, their degenerated lineage from an ancient
family, and often an addiction to opium or alcohol. As tellers of
their own tales, they also follow their Gothic models in recounting
the past through a veil of illness, overexcitement, or memory, often
creating in the reader a sense of uncertainty about the correct interpretation of events. Poe particularly liked the kind of personal narration known as the 'tale of sensation,' featured by *Blackwood's* in
such tales as "The Man in the Bell" or "The Buried Alive." The
persons who relate them are usually solitary victims of a life-threat-
ening predicament, about to be hanged, trapped under a heavy iron
bell, locked in a copper boiler. Their minutely described sensations
in these terrifying circumstances constitute the narrative. In Poe's
"Loss of Breath" (a greatly expanded version of his earlier "A Decided Loss"), the often-killed narrator records for twenty-six paragraphs the swelling of veins in his wrists, the tolling noises in his
ears, and his other sensations while dying and being buried.

Poe did not merely imitate the popular Gothic or 'German' tales.
He enriched their texture, managing to preserve the narrative drive
of some central action while embroidering the whole with philo-

sophical speculation and lore that deepen the mood of dire awe, and with sense details that lend the improbable events a feeling of reality. With his essential concern for the craft of writing, he also refreshed the Gothic tales by exploring their technical possibilities. Deliberately deploying in his narrative prose the full range of English punctuation, calculating commas, semicolons, dashes for their variety and effect, he brought into play an arsenal of sentence structures and attention-getting devices—questions, exclamations, italics, inversions—to keep the prose surface moving and alive. He framed his narratives, too, between arresting openings and memorable endings, first inviting readers into the tale, then leaving them with a strong impression of it.

Once especially effective device that Poe began using frequently might be called the copulative ending. From the classical rhetorical figure of polysyndeton, a repetition of conjunctions, he devised a trick of composing the final sentence or two of his tale as a series of *and* clauses, retarded so as to call attention to each element. He used the device at the end of "Morella," "Shadow," and for instance "Berenice," after the awakening Egæus is unable to open the small surgeon's box:

> and, in my tremor, it slipped from out my hands, and fell heavily, and burst into pieces; and from it, with a rattling sound, there rolled out some instruments of dental surgery, intermingled with many white, and glistening substances that were scattered to and fro about the floor.

Although the sentence does not advertise its crafty construction, its punctuation and its compartmentalizing *and*'s are contrived to call attention individually to the tremor, the hands, the fall, and the breaking box, while the alliterative hissing *s*'s give the whole a sinister tonal unity. Poe often supported the mood and action of his tales by such rhythmic and sound effects. Again in "Berenice," heavy accents and prolonged vowel sounds reenforce a mood of crepuscular solemnity, as in the description of Egæus's "gloomy, gray, hereditary halls." Or, the reverse, a flurry of *t*'s points up a moment of quiet hesitance: "a light tap at the library door—and, pale as the tenant of a tomb, a menial entered upon tiptoe." In brief, Poe was becoming the first writer in English, or perhaps in any modern literature, to consistently apply to prose fiction some of the techniques of poetry.

Poe also found in the Gothic world a vocabulary for his own preoccupations. Corpses litter all of his tales in the *Messenger,* most of which concern the disabling effects of the loss of loved ones. "Berenice" and "Morella" are subtle psychological studies of the attempt to deal with such loss through avoidance and denial, told in eerie, disturbed tones by the traumatized survivors. The narrator of "Morella" has difficulty remembering his feelings about his wife, as he repeatedly insists: "In all this, if I think aright, my powers of thought predominated. My convictions, or I forget myself, were in no manner acted upon by my imagination; nor was any tincture of the mysticism which I read to be discovered, unless I greatly err, either in my meditations or my deeds." He calls Morella not his wife but his friend, lessening his loss by devaluing her. More extremely, Egæus in "Berenice" claims to have had no feeling for his wife-cousin at all: "During the brightest days of her unparalleled beauty, most surely I had never loved her."

Poe dramatizes how despite these and similar efforts to put at bay feelings of attachment, the bereaved characters are driven to express them. "Berenice" opens with Egæus talking about the rainbow, in which he comes to see an image of the manifold nature of misery: "How is it," he asks, "that from beauty I have derived a type of unloveliness?" His question is in fact the theme of the tale, as he is himself drawn to act against his will in ways that express the intensity of his feeling. When he pulls out Berenice's teeth he is unaware of doing so. On awakening he experiences some indecipherable memory; beside his bed lie a small box and an opened book underscored at a Latin sentence which means "My companions told me I might find some little alleviation of my misery, in visiting the grave of my beloved." But he has himself underscored the book and himself filled the box with Berenice's teeth, having all unknowingly wandered to her grave. Similarly, the narrator of "Morella" feels compelled, at the christening of his ten-year-old daughter, to blurt out the name of his dead wife, although many other names occur to him: "What prompted me, then, to disturb the memory of the buried dead? What demon urged me to breathe that sound, which, in its very recollection was wont to make ebb and flow the purple blood in tides from the temples to the heart?" The answer is that it is not so easy to put behind one objects that have inspired love or horror or both.

Not only does attachment to the dead refuse to be sundered or submerged, but death itself is treated as an illusion or mistake, the beginning of another life. "Here died my mother," Egæus remarks of his library. "Herein was I born." As he studies Berenice in her coffin—another one of many coffin-viewing scenes in Poe—he notices that her burial jawband has been broken, and thinks he sees her shrouded finger move. Morella and her husband study the German transcendental doctrine of personal identity, and he becomes engrossed in the problem of whether at death identity is lost for ever. During her illness, she promises him that "I am dying, yet shall I live," and is of course reborn in her daughter, who however dies once more after being named. But all of the tales contain similarly ambiguous fantasies of resurrection. The staring corpse of young Zoilus in "Shadow" appears alive: "his eyes in which Death had but half extinguished the fire of the pestilence, seemed to take such interest in our merriment as the dead may haply take in the merriment of those who are to die." The moon-voyager Hans Phaall is thought by his fellow villagers to be dead, but is not, and describes his adventurous trip as a sort of life in death: "I determined to depart, yet live—to leave the world, yet continue to exist."

This insistent questioning of the finality of death brings with it a network of already familiar related ideas. Eating and devouring pervade the tales, for instance in the feasting corpses of "King Pest," the mourners of "Shadow" who drink purple wine, and especially Egæus in his obsession with Berenice's teeth: "The teeth!—the teeth!—they were here, and there, and everywhere. . . . In the multiplied objects of the external world I had no thoughts but for the teeth." The hero of "Politian" proposes a suicide pact to the seduced and abandoned orphan Lalage, in the hope that they can be joined after death, can "Arise together, Lalage, and roam / The starry and quiet dwellings of the blest." The hope of a magical reunion with the dead casts light on Hans Phaall's statement that his distressed circumstances in Rotterdam "had at length driven me to the resolution of committing suicide," for the moon which he visits is itself rather like Heaven, "a shadowy and unstable land" that he finds populated with beings.

Other tales concern the quest for celebrity and success, especially "Lion-izing." This highly personal trifle revolves around one of many oedipal duels in Poe between two men, often an older and a younger, one powerful, the other weak, like Mr. Lackobreath and Mr. Windenough in the closely parallel "Loss of Breath." It asks whether adoration is to be had by being big or small, powerful or impotent, conqueror or cottager. The narrator's very large nose gains him celebrity in aristocratic drawing rooms and literary circles, but his prestige passes to Baron Bludenuff, for having no nose at all: "In Fum-Fudge," the tale concludes, "great is a Lion with a big probos-cis, but greater by far is a Lion with no proboscis at all." The funny moral makes an enlightening comment on Poe's constant recourse, despite his desire for authority, to postures of dependence and helplessness in order to gain attention or assistance. But it is also not so remote from his questionings about the fate of the self as might appear, since fame and success comfort the fear of death by the hope of immortality.

While editing the *Messenger,* Poe also contributed three extended prose pieces. In "Autography" he took from an English literary magazine the idea of printing a group of fictional letters by contem-porary literary figures, and appending to them facsimiles of the writers' actual signatures, one expression of a rage in the period for collecting autographs of the famous. He invented brief letters for, and gathered the signatures of, thirty-eight American writers. "Pi-nakidia" (roughly, "anthology") consists of some 173 items, usually only a sentence or two long, on the gender of Venus or Hebrew punctuation or Switzerland, but chiefly on literary plagiarism from the time of the Bible, a grab bag of curious observations on often arcane subjects that project a picture of Poe as a multilingual bib-liophile deeply read in the esoteric lore of several languages. This was, however, but a form of passing for editor of the *Messenger.* Much as he copied and paraphrased into "Hans Phaall" some dozen paragraphs from an astronomical treatise by J. F. W. Herschel, he lifted the quotations and surrounding commentary of "Pinakidia" nearly verbatim from various secondary sources.

In "Maelzel's Chess-Player" Poe began creating a public image of himself that he would greatly elaborate. His title refers to a pseu-domechanical marvel, built in 1769, that continued to be exhibited by its present owner, a traveling showman named Maelzel. The au-tomaton consisted of a costumed figure of a Turk seated at a wooden chest, on which lay a chessboard and pieces, with some candles for lighting. After Maelzel wound the figure with a key, it fitfully ma-nipulated pieces on the board and was able to play all comers, and usually win. Actually the Chess-Player was an ingenious stage illu-sion, originally built to conceal a Pole named Worousky, who had lost both his legs in battle. In its long history of exhibitions, the automaton became the subject of a large literature of exposé. That the figure concealed a human agent was widely agreed on; the basic means by which the inside of the chest could be shown to the audience while concealing an accomplice had been described in print a few years before Poe's essay. Poe in fact drew his own explanation of the automaton's workings largely from an earlier published account, which he not only failed to acknowledge but even went out of his way to disparage. To the credit of his powers of observation, however, it should be added that, as his source did not, he called attention to the fact that the chest was designed to look less roomy than it was.

Although Poe added little new to the subject then, and the issue has no meaning now, his essay has a continuing vitality, in part arising from his fascination with *Androides,* inanimate things seemingly imbued with spirit. More important, the essay remains readable for the cunning inquirer whose presence it creates. That a human mind regulated the automaton's operations, Poe wrote, was "susceptible of a mathematical demonstration, *a priori.*" In illustrating his purely deductive method, he detailed seventeen minute observations on which he based his conclusions, for instance that as Maelzel invariably arranged the six candles on the chest, those farthest from the spectators were the longest. He had begun sketching, that is, a new type of narrator, an investigator of the hidden activities that can be deduced from homely physical facts.

Constricted by White and largely dependent on his pool of regional contributors, Poe made no radical changes in the conduct of the *Messenger,* except in greatly enlarging the magazine's critical department. He devoted about fifteen double-columned pages each issue to reviews, most of which he likely wrote himself. Expanding his literary career into a new province, he surveyed not only recent fiction and poetry but also medical works, Latin grammars, dictionaries, almanacs, volumes of chancery reports, travel books, and speeches, as well as other magazines. Much as he looked to *Blackwood's* and other English magazines for models of his fiction, he saw in them also a congenial example of critical stance. They specialized in an often derisive style of reviewing, crackling with personal abuse and class antagonism. Bent on becoming noticed, Poe found this manner of extreme candor appealing and began building a reputation as a critic of blunt unshakable principle. The intellectual mood of at least some parts of America moreover welcomed displays of frankness. Many found the country lapsing into an insipid uniformity, succumbing to what Alexis de Tocqueville had called the tyranny of the majority. One traveler heard that in Boston, "the habit of conforming to each other's opinion, and the penalty set upon every transgression . . . are sufficient to prevent a man from wearing a coat cut in a different fashion, or a shirt-collar no longer a la mode, or, in fact, to do, say, or appear anything which would render him unpopular." Poe's older contemporary, Ralph Waldo Emerson, had begun denouncing what he soon called "our smooth times," times filled with "lying hospitality and lying affection." The remedy for this falsity, he said, was to speak the truth: "Your goodness must have some edge to it,—else it is none. The doctrine of hatred must be preached, as the counteraction of the doctrine of love, when that pules and whines."

Spurred by British example and a broader cultural hunger for forthrightness, Poe established himself immediately in the *Messenger* as a critic to be feared. In what may be his first reviews in the magazine, published anonymously in April 1835, he blasted one book as "a mere jumble of absurdities," attacked another (by Davy Crockett) for "the frequent vulgarity of its language," and began his review of a third by saying that "The most remarkable feature in this production is the bad paper on which it is printed." His capture of public attention as a critic and editor, however, can be dated from his review in the December 1835 issue of *Norman Leslie,* a much-heralded novel concerning murder charges brought against the son of a U.S. senator. Written by a New York lawyer, Theodore Fay, it became a best-seller. In his review, Poe facetiously summarized the improbable plot, called Fay's style "unworthy of a school-boy," and ridiculed the novel as "the most inestimable piece of balderdash with which the common sense of the good people of America was ever so openly or so villainously insulted." The harshness of his attack brought rejoinders in other magazines, creating a fuss. Poe took pride in having candidly shown the book's acclaim to be undeserved, and felt that the review, as he is reported to have said later, "introduced a new era in our critical literature."

One elementary critical standard that Poe often applied was simple correctness. Like other English and American critics of the time, he pointed out ambiguities of expression, errors in punctuation and grammar, questionable diction and syntax. He did so, however, with stabbing relentlessness, sometimes attacking not only the work but also the writer as vulgar or ill educated. One example can illustrate his customary practice, from a pulverizing review of William Gilmore Simms's novel *The Partisan*:

At page 136, vol. i, the hero, Singleton, concludes a soliloquy with the ungrammatical phrase, "And yet none love her like me!" At page 143, vol. i, we read—" 'That need not surprise you, Miss Walton; you remember that ours are British soldiers'—smiling, and with a bow was the response of the Colonel"—The present participle 'smiling' has no substantive to keep it company; and the 'bow,' as far as regards its syntatical [*sic*] disposition, may be referred with equal plausibility to the Colonel, or to Miss Walton, to the British soldiers, or to the author of "The Partisan". . . . At page 148, we hear "that the disease had not yet *shown* upon her system." Shown is here used as a neuter verb—shown *itself* Mr. S. meant to say. . . . At page 14, vol. ii, these words occur. "Cheerless quite, bald of home and habitation, they saw nothing throughout the melancholy waste more imposing than the plodding negro." The *"cheerless quite"* and the *"bald of home and habitation"* would refer in strict grammatical construction to the pronoun *"they"*—but the writer means them to agree with *"melancholy waste"*. . . .

The extract is long enough, although too short to convey the spirit of inquisitorial thoroughness in which Poe examined the text for errors: his savaging of Simms's "shockingly bad English" rips on for about two pages. In justification of his scrutiny, it should be said that the grammar and punctuation in much American writing at the time were astonishingly corrupt. And Poe had an eagle eye for mistakes. An editor who knew him later remarked that "he was a minute detector of slips of the pen, and, probably, was unequalled as a proof reader." Poe also weighed words carefully and savored the niceties of prose architecture, what he called "constructive accuracy." In some reviews he quoted a garbled sentence or two from a work, then rewrote it with an eye to greater clarity, conciseness, and grace, with often brilliant results, for he was in fact a superb editor of both prose and verse.

Poe's contempt for ignorant and slovenly writing was real, and a product of his refined aesthetic sense, but it was also self-protective. One New York newspaper pointed out that he often stumbled himself, his own works containing "blunders quite as gross as those on which it was his pleasure to descant." The charge was just, in that Poe often committed in his tales and poems the errors for which he excoriated others, particularly dangling modifiers. To cite only three:

Upon stepping over the threshold, the whole interior of the building presented itself to view. ("Bon-Bon")

Perceiving that I remained without motion, and made him no reply, (all my limbs were dislocated, and my head twisted on one
side) his apprehensions began to be excited. . . . ("A Decided
Loss")

> *On desperate seas long wont to roam,*
> *Thy hyacinth hair, thy classic face.* . . . *("To Helen")*

These and many other examples that might be given perhaps indicate no more than that Poe frequently wrote carelessly and hastily.
On the other hand, the image he projected in his reviews (and tales)
of the connoisseur-savant certainly did not reflect the mental furniture he had acquired in less than a year at the University of Virginia and a few months at West Point. As in "Pinakidia," much of
the learning he paraded as a critic came out of such secondary sources
as encyclopaedias.

Although Poe frequently quoted from other languages, too, his
knowledge of them was shallow. The nature of the occasional errors
in his Greek betrays ignorance of the language. In an 1837 review
he reproduced fourteen Hebrew words and phrases and discoursed
learnedly about their correct meaning in biblical times. He did not
bother to mention that he had merely copied the Hebrew as well
as his 'interpretations' verbatim from a letter to him by Charles
Anthon, a professor of classical languages at Columbia College. He
had a good reading knowledge of French but little feeling for the
language, and often inserted French-looking but false accent marks.
His Italian allowed him to read a little Dante, but he several times
used *in petto* (meaning "in reserve" or "in secret") to mean "in brief,"
probably confusing it with French *petit*. He regularly made serious
mistakes in German, a language he quoted but probably did not
know at all. Several times he misspelled as "Fitche" the name of the
German philosopher Fichte, and he referred to the authors of one
of his "Pinakidia" entries as Suard and André, having misread or
misinterpreted the German reference in his source to *Suard und
andere,* i.e., Suard and others.

Poe directed his critical wrath not only at particular works or
errors, but perhaps still more slashingly at the commercial institutions, literary politics, and ideological demands that shaped the production of literature in America. One of his chief targets was the
press, for overpraising poor and mediocre works. He began his re-

view of *Norman Leslie* by parodying the book's gassy prepublication publicity in newspapers such as the New York *Mirror,* of which its author was also an editor: "Well!—here we have it! This is *the* book— the book *par excellence*—the book bepuffed, beplastered, and be-*Mirrored.*" He also often derided works that had been talked up regardless of their literary value by self-interested literati and publishers, achieving acclaim "merely by keeping continually in the eye . . . of that great, over-grown, and majestical gander, the critical and bibliographical rabble." Even more fraudulent and damaging for Poe was the exaltation of works on purely nationalistic grounds. He reviewed at a time when Americans greatly worried about how their culture was perceived overseas, especially in England. The praises be-heaped on books like *Norman Leslie* could only, he felt, make American literature a laughing stock abroad, where it was already sneered at.

Poe made his fullest statement on the dangers of chauvinistic critical standards in reviewing *The Culprit Fay, and other Poems* by Joseph Rodman Drake, and *Alnwick Castle, with other Poems,* by Fitz-Greene Halleck. At the moment, he observed, perhaps "there are no American poems held in so high estimation by our countrymen, as the poems of Drake, and of Halleck." Nevertheless he gave a reasoned although entirely damning appraisal of the two poets' work, condemning Halleck's as often unintelligible and banal, and also refusing to consider as products of genuine Imagination Drake's fairy world of acorn-shell helmets and armored shrimp. He explained the discrepancy by sketching the history of literary judgment in America, which disclosed a perverse leap from excessive self-doubt to excessive self-confidence. At one time Americans read American works only after assurances from England that they were "not altogether contemptible." In this was some small degree of reason, he said, for in belles lettres America remains on a lower level than the "elder and riper climes of Europe." If the earlier timidity about valuing American works was absurd but understandable, more absurd but also baseless is the present swagger in glorifying them all, the belief that an American literature can be called into existence "by indiscriminate puffing of good, bad, and indifferent." Indeed the exaggerated praise given American writers, Poe said, far from encouraging a native literature has the reverse effect: "so far from deeply lamenting that these daily puerilities are of home manufacture, we adhere pertinaciously to our original blindly conceived idea, and thus find ourselves involved in the gross paradox of liking a stupid book the better, because, sure enough, its stupidity is American." He announced that it was his mission to reform the national habit of coddling American writers, with its debilitating effect on the health of American literature.

Poe's critical writing generated excitement and controversy, making him if not a lion at least a name. "Commend us to the literary notices of this Magazine for genius, spice and spirit," said the Cincinnati *Mirror*. "Those which are commendatory, are supported by the real merit of the books themselves; but woe seize on the luckless wights who feel the savage skill with which the editor uses his tomahawk and scalping knife." The images of Indian warfare clung to Poe and identified him to the magazine-reading public. While one or another periodical earnestly applauded his message that American literature had suffered for the praise lavished on mediocrity, many simply whooped over the body count: "a literal 'flaying alive!' a carving up into 'ten thousand atoms!' a complete literary annihilation!" Not everyone greeted his criticism so enthusiastically, of course. Many frowned on the "microscopic intensity" of his fault-finding, observed that he merely aped the manner of British periodical critics, accused him of publicity-seeking and overkill, "like the Indian, who cannot realize that an enemy is conquered till he is scalped." But even the many magazines that denounced the *Messenger*'s reviewing policies contributed to spreading interest in and curiosity about Poe.

Having yearned for fame, Poe did not hesitate to promote himself and found rich possibilities in the "golden age of periodicals." He retorted in print to some of the attacks on his criticism, creating more commotion through public quarrels with rivals like the editor of the New Bern, North Carolina, *Spectator,* who called often for his resignation or firing. In reviewing the *Messenger* for Baltimore newspapers, before joining White in Richmond, Poe also reviewed himself. Writing anonymously, he puffed his own "Lion-izing" as an "admirable piece of burlesque, which displays much reading, a lively humor, and an ability to afford amusement or instruction"; Poe's pen, he urged, "should not be suffered to lie unemployed, and will not, we trust, be neglected." The *Messenger* even helped him maintain the legend of his extraordinary athletic ability. After a reference appeared in the magazine to Poe's boyhood swim in the James River, White published part of a letter from him boasting, "I would not think much of attempting to swim the British Channel from Dover to Calais." Poe also remarked parenthetically, in the course of a book review, that he had once jumped twenty feet, six inches (a distance not reached in Olympic competition until 1952). Correctly, the later French critic Rémy de Gourmont sensed in Poe's work "the peculiarly American taste for notoriety, billboards, barbarous publicity, extravagant journalism."

While becoming a prominent magazinist himself, Poe made the *Messenger* popular and respected. Praised for the originality of its verse and fiction, the eminence of its contributors, the neatness of its typography, and the fearlessness of its reviews, the magazine came close to fulfilling White's dream of an important regional journal that would awaken Southern letters: "the Southern Literary Messenger," as one Boston magazine measured its impact, "is equal in interest and excellence to any Monthly Periodical in the country."

Second Marriage (?) to Virginia; Break with the Messenger.

CA. SPRING 1836–FEBRUARY 1837

Poe spent sixteen months or so in Richmond with Muddy and Virginia, his longest stay in the city since he had left it for the university at the age of seventeen. In many ways the place was unchanged since his childhood. There remained Thomas Jefferson's capitol building, housing Jean Antoine Houdon's marble statue of George Washington, taken from life, and of course the mild climate that usually made coats unnecessary, and brought the peach trees and magnolias into bloom by mid-March. But since 1810 the population had about doubled, approaching twenty thousand. And besides its continued importance in the tobacco trade, Richmond had gained manufactories for cutting nails and slitting iron, realizing in small part the industrial promise of its nearby mines. As early as 1824 travelers had remarked on the effects: "The atmosphere is impregned with the dense murky effluvia of coal smoke," one said, "which begrimes the pores of the skin, and affects respiration."

During much of his stay, Poe seems to have been contented to be back in the city. "My friends in Richmond," he said, "have received me with open arms." He remained with his family at a boardinghouse run by a Martha Yarrington, where on Monday, May 16, 1836, in the presence of Muddy and of T. W. White and his daughter, a Presbyterian minister openly married him to his cousin Virginia. This was probably a second ceremony, designed to make public in Richmond when Sissy was fourteen what had already been done in Baltimore when she was thirteen, and much too young. Even so, Poe cared about the public impression he might create by marrying a child. He sometimes handled the problem by simply misrepresenting her age. A few months before the marriage he told Kennedy that Virginia was fifteen. She appears on their marriage bond as being "of the full age of twenty-one years." The difficulty was not only her years, but also her cherubic appearance. One observer in Richmond recalled Sissy as "very *plump*" and also "small for her age," having as well a childlike gentleness and simplicity. After the marriage, Poe's sister, Rose, sometimes took her to the Mackenzies' school where she seemed "as much of a child as any of the pupils, joining in their sports of swinging and skipping rope." Virginia's immaturity mattered in a more personal way too. Reportedly, Poe later said that for two years he occupied a room alone and did not "assume the position of husband." The statement is secondhand, and ambiguous enough to leave it uncertain whether he had sexual relations with his wife even after the two years. As will appear, he emphasized that his attachments to women were ideal and spiritual.

Having brought Sissy and Muddy to Richmond, Poe regarded them as "residing under my protection." The expression apparently had some currency among them, for Muddy also told her cousin George Poe that "myself and daughter are under the protection of Edgar." To Poe, the words represented more than a catchphrase of family solidarity. He felt solemnly obliged to provide for Muddy and Virginia, the more so since for his sake they had resisted the comforts offered them by Neilson Poe. In his eighteen-month association with White, beginning with the sale of his first tales in March 1835 and including at least one raise in salary, he made altogether about $1,300, much more than he had ever earned before. Still, supplying his own and his family's needs was not easy. According to his friend Wilmer, he devoted much of his salary to Sissy's education, something Neilson Poe had also promised to provide for her. Already well-schooled in begging and borrowing, he tried to raise enough money for Muddy to open a boardinghouse of her own, and got a loan of one hundred dollars from cousin George, a banker in Mobile. That scheme came to nothing, and a similar one gained him only larger debts. As he explained the circumstances, White had bought a new home for ten thousand dollars, which he proposed renting out to Poe, if Muddy agreed to board himself and his family there. Poe thought the idea "highly advantageous to us," accepted the offer, and without having seen White's house bought two hundred dollars' worth of furniture on credit. But the place, he discovered, was scarcely large enough for one family, much less two. The plan collapsed, leaving him in debt for the furniture and asking Kennedy for a hundred dollars to pay what he owed.

Poe tried even more farfetched ways to raise extra income. He inquired after a lot of land bequeathed by the father of Maria's deceased husband, to which, he computed, Muddy's children were entitled to a 1/105th share. It turned out they had no claim on the land at all, and that even those who had some claim received no profit. Not much less unrealistic was his effort to compensate Muddy for her loss of the pension that had been granted her mother as the widow of General Poe. The annuity had only been an expedient, he believed, by which the state of Maryland for a while postponed paying his grandmother nearly forty thousand dollars, supposedly due her for loans her husband had made to the government during the Revolution. Poe wrote to Washington hoping to have the claim brought before Congress. Again nothing came of his efforts, try as he did to uplift his family "under my protection."

Poe's residence in Richmond enabled him to renew his tie with Rose, although little information remains about their reunion. She later wrote that she did not know she had a brother or brothers until "a good sized girl." Now in her mid-twenties, she worked at the female academy run by the Mackenzies, considered for its scholarship and social distinction one of the best in Richmond. She seems to have taught the class in penmanship, and to have made the pens. Owing to her fine hand, she also wrote out bills for the Mackenzies to send the parents of their pupils. Sometime or other she learned to play the piano, but it does not seem to have made her more appealing. It was said that she wept without cause, and some people thought her mentally defective. More probably she suffered so-called pseudoretardation, an unresponsiveness that, like her brother Henry's alcoholism, was an outcome of early disasters. The general impression of her is perhaps summed up in a later statement, derived from Neilson Poe, that she was "wholly unhandsome and unattractive."

However gratified to be working for White and to have Muddy and Virginia with him, Poe had reason to feel uncomfortable in Richmond. Disapproval of his behavior among partisans of the Allans had made him reluctant to show his face there, and stories of his misdeeds still circulated—that after returning to Richmond for Fanny Allan's funeral he stole silver spoons and table linens from the house; that when he returned to see John Allan during his illness, he so much insulted the new Mrs. Allan that she thereafter forbade him the house. And John Allan remained a presence. His legitimate sons and heirs still lived at Moldavia with Louisa Allan; the *Messenger* offices, at Main and Fifteenth streets, stood only a few doors from what had been the House of Ellis and Allan. Much implies that Allan's death gnawed at Poe: his illness in Baltimore (when a physician advised a sea voyage), his many tales of corpses, his frantic clinging to Muddy and Virginia, his threats of suicide, his very return to Richmond. Yet in describing his deceased guardian to Kennedy, he said that Allan "adopted me at the age of two years," gave him "an annuity sufficient for my support," and until nearly the end "always treated me with the affection of a father." It is a remarkably redrawn picture of the man he had long and bitterly depicted as unwilling to support him at the university, refusing to help release him from the army, failing to visit him at West Point, slandering him and his family, and worse. Concerning his disinheritance, he also told his cousin William Poe not that Allan had cut him out but that "No will was found among his papers."

Poe's falsifications seem aimed not so much at sparing John Allan's reputation as at putting to rest his own anger and thwarted longing. How much he had hoped to be John Allan's son appears in his at last acknowledging, or perhaps claiming, himself to be an Allan. In the first two letters he is known to have written following Allan's death, he signed himself "Edgar Allan Poe"—the only times in his correspondence, with a single exception, when he did not give his full name as "Edgar A. Poe" or "E. A. Poe," the names he used for his published works. But Poe's later tales and poems make it clear that what he suppressed in his public life repeatedly slipped into his writing. His brooding on the forbidden name already echoes in Al Aaraaf, Lalage, Phaall (with his "Unparralleled" [*sic*] adventures), and other characters and places formed on the letters double-a double-l.

Poe's return to Richmond in the aftermath of John Allan's death activated earlier memories as well. Muddy later recalled that she, Sissy, and Poe would drive out to Shockoe Hill Cemetery, where he pointed out the grave of Jane Stanard. He thought also of his parents, and of what it had meant to grow up without them. Speaking of himself and Rose, he told William Poe that "we were left orphans at an age when the hand of a parent is so peculiarly requisite." He felt moved, a few months later, to hear from the Virginia novelist Nathaniel Beverley Tucker, who years before had seen Eliza Poe perform on the stage. Tucker's speaking of her "touched a string to which my heart fully responds," he said. "To have known her is to be an object of great interest in my eyes." He seems to have retained no very clear, conscious picture of Eliza, still less of David, for he told Tucker that he "never knew her—and never knew the affection of a father." Yet the very dimness of his recollection weighed on him, a monumental absence. "I have many occasional dealings with Adversity," he said, "but the want of parental affection has been the heaviest of my trials."

Whatever else Richmond had come to mean to Poe, it now also figured as the place where he had begun to prove himself a first-rate editor, in large part responsible for the *Messenger*'s success. He later bragged that during his active management, subscriptions rose from fewer than one thousand to some five thousand. T. W. White counted things differently, however. A "nervous" man, as he several times refers to himself, White lived constantly with a sense that the magazine was a "Quixotic" venture that barely gave him a livelihood, and that his future losses might be great. He also retained some distrust of Poe. By at least the late summer of 1836 he publicly recognized Poe as editor, but he did so warily, calling him one "whom I employ to edit my paper." And although he always respected Poe's talents, he shrank from some of his methods, fretting over his sarcastic treatment of James Fenimore Cooper in "Autography," and cringing over his contemptuous review of *Norman Leslie* as possibly libelous.

By the late fall of 1836, White's worries became too much for him. The September issue was delayed and showed signs of slackening, being the first under Poe's editorship without a story or poem by him. Poe announced that he had been ill. The November issue contained only one review that can be certainly attributed to him, and he announced in an editorial that the "press of business" had prevented his paying the usual attention to the critical department.

Other pressures on White mounted atop the gaps and interruptions. The editor of the New Bern *Spectator,* who had campaigned for a year against the severity of Poe's criticism, observed in his editorial pages in mid-December that such literary scalp hunting was "discreditable to the South, promotive of bad taste, and ruinous to Mr. WHITE's laudable enterprise." White also looked anxiously on his accumulating debts, a public scarcity of money, a printer's strike, and the serious illness of his wife, who had developed uterine cancer.

By Christmastime White decided that in another week he would be "forced" to give Poe notice. He recalled that three months before he had felt similarly impelled but had allowed Poe to remain on "certain conditions," which Poe had now violated. White's "conditions" are unknown, although his phrase recalls the promise of sobriety he once extracted from Poe as the price for taking him back ("Let me hear that it is your fixed purpose never to yield to temptation"). Whether or not Poe was drinking again, White also wanted to regain his management of the magazine, to rely once again on his own judgment in selecting articles for publication, "let me even be a jackass," he added, "as I dare say I am in his estimation."

In the January number of the *Messenger,* White announced that as of the third, Poe had "retired" as editor. Nearly everything known about their breakup exists in a few comments by White, leaving it uncertain whether Poe also wished to quit the magazine. The New Year period was often a signal time for him, perhaps reflecting some restless resolve to change. It was in December that he left the University of Virginia, and in January that he was court-martialed at West Point. He seems to have departed the *Messenger* with amused disdain rather than rancor toward White, whom he later referred to as "Little Tom," an "illiterate and vulgar, although well-meaning man," a *"character* if ever one was." On the other hand he also seems to have clung to the job. A week after his 'retirement,' he was promising a former fellow cadet that the man's essay would appear in the *Messenger* the following month. Taking charge, White dismissed the piece as "bombast" and refused to print it. But he too let go reluctantly, at least at first. He wished to keep Poe as a contributor, still considered him a sort of son, and wanted to let him down easily. He tried to salve Poe's wounds with cash, agreeing to publish his new, long work-in-progress, "The Narrative of Arthur Gordon Pym." He paid Poe three dollars a page for the first installment, in the

January *Messenger,* and in addition advanced him at least twenty dollars. He promised besides to "do something more for you," even if he had to borrow the money from friends. But his rather guilty charity left him resentful, and he complained to others that "Pym" was costing him twenty dollars a page. Mostly he seems to have wanted Poe to leave Richmond, but to get the idea for himself; he told Beverley Tucker on January 19, with evident relief, that "Poe feels his situation at last."

Poe lingered in Richmond through January, however, perhaps trying to get reinstated. Feeling increasingly pestered by his presence, White spoke of him ever more caustically. He told Tucker that the *Messenger* would "outlive all the injury it has sustained from Mr. Poe's management." Since Poe had stopped acting as "Judge or Judge Advocate," he said, the magazine had received more contributions than ever before, "and all far better than his Gordon Pym." By month's end, continually put upon by Poe for money, he had had enough: "I am as sick of his writings, as I am of him." Disgusted now, he thought of returning Poe his manuscripts, with "another dozen dollars" to make him go away. How disenchanted he had become he revealed only after Poe and his family left Richmond, as they probably did in early February. "The truth is," White confessed, "Poe seldom or ever done [*sic*] what he knew was just to any book. He read few through—unless it were some trashy novels,—and his only object in reading even these, was to ridicule their authors. . . . But enough of this—this mortifying subject."

The Blank Period;
The Narrative of Arthur Gordon Pym *and "Ligeia."*

FEBRUARY 1837 – MAY 1839

Poe's break with the *Messenger* seems to have brought him a long period of unemployment, poverty, and disenchantment with literary life. Stress 'seems,' because for about twenty-nine months after he left Richmond Poe virtually disappears from biographical view.

There remain from these two and a half years only one note and two letters by him, and only one letter to him. Nor does anything of substance about him appear on public records. Knowledge of his life at this time again amounts to barely more than knowledge of the works he published.

After leaving White, Poe took Muddy and Sissy to live in New York City for perhaps fifteen months. He may have been drawn there by an offer to write for a new quarterly journal. The editor, a clergyman named Francis L. Hawks, invited him to commence some critical warfare in New York, "to fall in with your *broad-axe* amidst this miserable literary trash which surrounds us." Poe did review for Hawks's journal a book of Middle Eastern travels but apparently nothing else. Whatever attracted Poe and his family to the city, they settled in the Greenwich Village section, first at Sixth Avenue and Waverly Place, then a half-dozen blocks away, at 113½ Carmine Street. Another resident at the Waverly Place address was William Gowans, a well-read Scotsman who ran a sizable bookstore farther downtown. He later remembered Poe as highly intelligent and courteous, although he also felt kept at a certain distance by Poe's reserve. Virginia he recalled as being of "matchless beauty and loveliness," and very good-natured, having "a temper and disposition of surpassing sweetness." She and Muddy looked after all of Poe's "little wants" and in effect mothered him, "watched him as sedulously," Gowans observed, "as if he had been a child."

Poe always felt honor-bound to reward this succor by providing his family's food and shelter, and the *Messenger* had afforded a steady income. But how or whether he managed to maintain his household in New York is wholly unknown. He clearly tried to stay in touch with publishers and publishing, for on March 30 he attended the widely reported Booksellers' Dinner at the City Hotel. Given to promote the writing and sale of American books, the event brought to table Washington Irving, William Cullen Bryant, and many other literary celebrities. Poe perhaps hoped to arouse some interest in himself as a candidate for magazine work, for at the dinner he proposed a toast to "The *Monthlies* of Gotham—Their distinguished Editors, and their vigorous Collaborateurs." But his earlier struggle to get and keep money can only have been revived and worsened by the economic depression that began a few months later, centering in New York. Wild speculation in land and real estate during the 1830s, in part based on the country's real potential for economic growth, brought a piling up of credit, the creation and evaporation of huge fortunes on paper, and ultimately a financial panic. On May 10, after depositors began rapidly withdrawing their money, New York banks were forced to close, followed in a few days by banks all over the country.

Poe's writing cannot have improved his financial situation much, for he is known to have published little more during fifteen months in New York than two tales, "Von Jung, the Mystific," and "Siope. A Fable. (In the manner of the Psychological Autobiographists)." The first is a curiously self-referential comic anecdote about "the dominator Baron Ritzner Von Jung," a young put-on artist who controls others through their own smugness, especially their pretensions to learning. The transcendental prose poem "Siope" begins startlingly, as if in the middle of some other story, and with a cryptic gesture of possible menace: " 'Listen to *me*,' said the Demon, as he placed his hand upon my head." From the shadow of an open tomb, the Demon relates a fable that dramatizes the horror of devitalized being. He tells of once having observed a man in the Congo, seated on a rock, looking out on a landscape of poisonous flowers, sickly saffron-colored river water, and stagnant festering. At the sight of this infected world, the man trembled but remained seated. The Demon summoned up roaring hippopotamuses and elephants; the man trembled but still sat. The Demon then uttered "the curse of tumult," bringing thunder and tempest, but still the man sat, although trembling. In a final attempt to appall him, the Demon invoked the "curse of silence," commanding the water to remain level, the moon to stop climbing, the clouds to hang motionless. And this time the man fled, his face "wan with terror." The Malignity in the universe is not disease, decay, or destruction; what terrifies above all is human awareness of a derealized unworld of inexistence, the chill of unbeing. The Demon's successive efforts to scare the man also once again mirror Poe the storyteller, whose own relation to the reader is exactly the one dramatized in the tale's first sentence.

After about a year in New York, Poe left with Muddy and Sissy for Philadelphia, probably in the spring or early summer of 1838. At first they settled into a boardinghouse operated by a Mrs. C. Jones at 202 Mulberry (or Arch) Street, but around September moved to a small house on Sixteenth Street near Locust. Their existence was apparently aggravating and bleak, a comedown from Richmond, where Poe had earned a decent salary and a place on the literary scene. He tried to eke a living out of literary odd jobs, work he detested and that made him miserable. Probably a few

months after arriving in Philadelphia, he wrote to James Kirke
Paulding, a popular New York literary figure who had been appointed secretary of the navy. More than that, Paulding admired
and championed Poe's writing, and presumably was in a position to
distribute patronage. Poe asked, desperately, whether Paulding could
find him a job, even "the most unimportant Clerkship . . . *any
thing, by sea or land."* Rather the lowliest political appointment, he
said, than the hackwork he had been forced to take on, "the miserable life of literary drudgery to which I now, with a breaking
heart, submit, and for which neither my temper nor my abilities
have fitted me." Whatever precisely had happened to Poe since his
success on the *Messenger,* it left him seeking a name by some new
means, longing, he told Paulding, for a profession "beyond mere
literature." Poe's Baltimore friend Lambert Wilmer may have been
referring to this period when he recalled that Poe had tried to learn
lithography. Poe worked "long and painfully" to master the trade,
he said, so much so that the necessary confinement in a stooping
position affected his health. Virginia and Muddy persuaded him to
abandon the work, "which was hurrying him to the grave."

Poe also seems to have been fighting off a need for alcohol. His
letter to Paulding does not mention a time, and may refer to drinking problems in New York, or even earlier while with the *Messenger.* In any case he told Paulding that he had given up the bottle,
having become "fully awakened to the impolicy and degradation of
the course hitherto pursued." And he quit painlessly, he said, "without
a struggle." He explained that at its worst his drinking had never
been a habit. And if it had been, he added, he could have stopped
whenever he wanted: "it would have required scarcely an effort on
my part to shake it from me at once and forever." Clearly he hoped
to reassure Paulding that he was steady enough to undertake a government job. But, with the reverse effect, his offhand guarantee
that he could easily "shake it" rings with the typical denial of a
heavy drinker.

Ironically, less than two weeks after Poe implored Paulding to
help him into some other profession, Harper and Brothers in New
York published his first book of fiction, a clothbound volume of
two hundred pages entitled *The Narrative of Arthur Gordon Pym. Of
Nantucket.* Indirectly at least, his writing of a long narrative arose
from his failure to find a publisher for his complete "Tales of the
Folio Club," parts of which he had published in the *Messenger.* After
White's offer to print the manuscript under Carey and Lea's imprint

fell through, Paulding had tried to place the manuscript with Harper, his own publishers. They declined, explaining to Poe that many of the works had already appeared in print, that most were "too learned and mystical," and that the volume consisted of separate tales and pieces whereas their experience had taught them that American readers preferred works "in which a single and connected story occupies the whole volume." The last comment, reinforced by similar advice from Paulding, apparently convinced Poe to undertake a sustained fiction. He published two installments of *Pym* in the *Messenger* early in 1837 but revised them slightly and continued expanding the book after arriving in New York. In May, the Harpers announced that the book was nearly ready for publication, but the same month came the catastrophic bank panic, and they delayed publication more than a year, until July 1838. A pirated English edition appeared in London a few months later, unforgivably omitting the brilliant last paragraph.

The novella's lengthy subtitle accurately advertises its content, promising "Incredible Adventures," "Capture," "Massacre," "Mutiny and Atrocious Butchery," "Shipwreck and Subsequent Horrible Sufferings From Famine."† Getting his hero in trouble and keeping him there, Poe created in *Pym* a classic adventure story, through which he gave body to the classic theme of illusion. The deceit begins with the preface, a dizzying verbal hall of mirrors that confuses author and protagonist, fact and fiction. The narrative proper brings both Pym and the reader into a treacherous world of disguises, forgeries, and impersonations where appearances lie. Pym's friendly dog Tiger threatens to devour him, the natives who tell him *Mattee non we pa pa si* (there is no need of arms where all are brothers) try to murder him. Contrarily, the seemingly fiendish Dirk Peters befriends him, and the capsizing of his ship reveals not new perils but a keel encrusted with nutritious barnacles that save him from starvation. In the most jolting reversal of the book, the languishing Pym and Augustus spy a distant brig which they imagine to be their salvation. As it nears they can make out three sailors on deck, one a stout man with dark skin who "seemed by his manner to be encouraging us to have patience, nodding to us in a cheerful although rather odd way, and smiling constantly so as to display a set of the most brilliantly white teeth." But as the brig closes on

† A summary of the action of *Pym* appears in Appendix 1. Other works marked by a dagger in the text are similarly summarized or further discussed in subsequent appendices.

them they smell a hellish stench, see a deck full of putrefying corpses, and discover that the stout man is merely a human carcass draped over the rail. Its encouraging nods have been the motions, seen from afar, of a meat-eating sea gull that gorges on its back, seeking its liver: "The eyes were gone, and the whole flesh around the mouth, leaving the teeth utterly naked. This, then, was the smile which had cheered us on to hope!"

Not only in this episode does the theme of illusion take the characteristic form of life and death simulating each other. Acting as another of Poe's shock bearers, Pym at one point frightens one of the mutineers to death by impersonating the chalky and loathsomely bloated corpse of a poisoned crewmember. More ambiguously, the crate in which Pym stows away seems at first a welcoming place of sustenance but soon becomes for him a place of possible extinction. Stocked with blankets, food, and water for warmth and nourishment, it appears womblike, connected through the "intricate windings" of the hold to the deck above by a length of whipcord, one of the work's many ropes, lifelines, and other umbilicallike strands. Yet the crate seems at the same time a coffin, "nearly four feet high, and full six long, but very narrow," in which Pym remarks that he has been "buried" for three days and nights, horrified at being "thus entombed." Indeed although his adventures transpire over a gestational nine months, from June to March, he faces and manages to evade every conceivable form of death.

Through Pym's adventures, Poe also gave shape to his concern about the breakdown of order, the book's other marked theme. The problem of keeping things under control is epitomized in Pym's long discourse on "cautious stowage," on how to prevent a ship being rent by hard cargos shifting in violent seas, or burst by the expansion of compressed organic cargos like tobacco. In the corresponding human world, social barriers fail to hold. Pym opposes his family in going to sea, his dog defies its master, the mutineers overthrow their captain. As the narrative moves to acts of greater and greater violence, until the bay at Tsalal is strewn with "struggling and drowning wretches," psychological restraints also give way. Pym's journey moves backward in emotional time to early stages of society and of the self. The natives of Tsalal have barely emerged from a state of nature. The *ts* sounds in their language mimic the hissing of the bittern, and both men and birds on their island scream *"Tekeli-li!"* Their picturelike stone inscriptions seem contemporary with the origins of written human language itself. Living in a village called

Klock-Klock and having names like Nu-Nu, they speak a sort of baby-talk, shouting *"Anamoo-moo!"* and addressing their leaders as Wam-poo. The effect of regression is deepened by dozens of images and vignettes of oral attack. As already seen, scarcely a tale by Poe lacks something pecked, bit, gnawed, or chewed, but *Pym* is one long-drawn barbed wire of beaks, bills, "horrible teeth," and "ghastly fangs" that tear, mangle, and mutilate whatever they can.

Arthur Gordon Pym sails not only into the past, but specifically into the past of Edgar A. Poe. They have similar names and are fellow New Englanders, Pym born in Nantucket, Poe in Boston. From their place of birth both journey south, in Pym's case to a Tsalal that resembles the American South in its black population and in being marked by a singular rock ledge "bearing a strong resemblance to corded bales of cotton." To emphasize their kinship, the date on which Pym arrives in Tsalal is January 19, Poe's own birthday. Pym's account of his lineage closely follows Poe's version of his own history, emphasizing as it does his being the son of a "respectable trader in sea-stores," his education in private academies, and his growing up in expectation of inheriting most of his grandfather's property. And Pym's thirst for adventures had been Poe's Byronic own, perhaps explaining his middle name, Gordon.

Like some submerged elegy, *Pym* in fact memorializes many dead figures in Poe's past. Its world of shipping and tobacco cargos recalls the busy maritime trade of the House of Ellis and Allan. The name Tsalal, a Coptic word meaning "to be dark," again encapsulates the double *l* double *a* of *Allan,* and indeed during the narrative two different characters named Allen are put to death. Poe's grandfather, General David Poe, perhaps is summoned up in Pym's grandfather, a banker in "Edgarton," and perhaps also recalled in Dirk Peters, whose name shares the initials of both David Poes. Augustus in many ways resembles Poe's deceased brother William Henry Leonard. Like the roaming and alcoholic Henry, Augustus is associated with the sea, and a drinker. As Henry was to Poe, Augustus is also "nearly two years older" than Pym, whom he first meets at the academy of Mr. "E. Ronald," an anagram for "Leonard." Much as Poe took over his brother's accomplishments and merged with him in the fictional character "Edgar-Leonard," Pym and Augustus are presented as fused in sympathy and understanding: "Augustus thoroughly entered into my state of mind. It is probable, indeed, that our intimate communion had resulted in a partial interchange of character." Most pointedly, Augustus dies in the story on August 1, the date on which Henry Poe died in fact.

A deeper but also more elusive presence in the book is Eliza Poe. She seems most specifically recalled in the cry of *Tekeli-li* that resounds through its close. *Tekeli* was the surname of a Hungarian patriot who became the subject of a popular melodrama, *Tekeli; or, The Siege of Montgatz* (1806), in which Eliza acted several times. However dim Poe's recollection of her and her life, it stirred actively enough to fill his works with allusions to the stage and to singing and dancing. Among many other examples, his earliest surviving poem, "Oh, Tempora! Oh, Mores!," refers to the famed dancer Marie-Jean Auguste Vestris; Berenice has a "musical yet sad" voice; a tar in "King Pest" dismisses the devil as nothing but "Tim Hurlygurly the stage-player!"; and the hero of "Loss of Breath" memorizes two entire tragedies, hoping to fool his wife by using his "fine theatrical talent." But Eliza Poe's presence in the novella is more diffuse, to be sought rather in its maternal imagery. *Pym* is a book largely about hunger, and in its preoccupation with nutriment seems permeated by longings for some all-fulfilling Nourisher. The characters spend much of their time figuring out how to obtain food and drink, many kinds of which are described and consumed: cordials, liqueurs, Bologna sausages, a ham, a leg of mutton, a keg of sea biscuit, berries, Madeira, port, rabbits, goats, terrapin, olives, crabs, shrimp, birds' eggs, barnacles, bitterns, bêche-de-mer. Particularly maternal are the Galápagos tortoises, whom Pym describes for a page, carrying with them a constant supply of water in "a bag at the root of the neck." Pym's final journey, too, takes him through a warm ocean of "a milky consistency and hue."

Pym's desire is not only to feed but also to be consumed. His longings to destroy himself are evident throughout. "My visions were of shipwreck and famine; of death or captivity among barbarian hordes," he reveals early on. "Such visions or desires—for they amounted to desires—are common . . . to the whole numerous race of the melancholy among men." Later, as he is about to let himself down the steep precipice in Tsalal by handkerchief rope, he feels an "irrepressible desire" to look down into the abyss, until at last, the psychological stowage bursting its bonds, "my whole soul was pervaded with *a longing to fall;* a desire, a yearning, a passion utterly uncontrollable." The climax of the work, a fantasy of being swallowed and engulfed, reveals Pym's self-destructiveness to be driven by a desire to merge with the dead. As his boat rushes toward "the embraces of the cataract," a mysterious white presence appears, which he describes with wonder in the final words of his narrative, "a shrouded human figure, very far larger in its proportions than any dweller among men. And the hue of the skin of the figure was of the perfect whiteness of the snow." The shrouded figure radiates the ambivalence of all Poe's dead-alive presences, a being both human and superhuman, inviting and fearsome, perhaps protective perhaps destructive. In the end Pym gets what he seeks and dreads, for Poe's concluding, illusionistic note mentions that he has recently died in an accident.

Pym attracted perhaps two dozen reviews in New York, Philadelphia, and now also in London. A very few reviewers wrongly considered Poe to be perpetrating a hoax, and some others complained of an excess of preternatural and violent circumstances. But many praised him for creating entertaining adventures with a Defoe-like verisimilitude, and more reviewers than not inclined to the estimate of the *New-Yorker:* "a work of extraordinary, freezing interest beyond anything we ever read. . . . Those who delight in the wonderful and horrible have a feast before them." Ironically, Poe failed to receive much direct credit for *Pym*'s success. The title page did not contain his name, which appeared only in the deceptive preface, where Pym discusses Poe's editing of his manuscript. The reviewer in the New York *Gazette* was not alone in being confused: "It is hinted," he wrote, "that Mr. Poe, the accomplished Virginia writer, has something to do about the book."

Even after Poe published the novella, his financial condition evidently remained impossible. How much he made from the American edition is unknown, but for the two pirated English editions he of course received nothing. Settled in Philadelphia, he was again forced to borrow money for essentials. One loan of fifty dollars remained outstanding even after a year, and he managed to pay his landlady, he said, only by making "the most painful sacrifices." He also applied for money to Neilson Poe, but found his cousin "pushed himself" and unable to help. It may have been with this period in mind that a literary acquaintance, James Pedder, remembered Poe and his family as "literally suffering for want of food." He, Muddy, and Sissy were surviving, Pedder said, "on bread and molasses for weeks together." Poe's long familiarity with such need helps account for the famished atmosphere of *Pym*.

However soured on his writing, Poe still looked to it for a living. One friendly market he found in the first five months of 1839 was a new Baltimore magazine, the *American Museum of Science, Litera-*

ture and the Arts, edited by two of his friends. Some of what he published he merely cranked out, such as two installments of "Literary Small Talk" (anecdotes compiled largely from Gibbon's *Decline and Fall*) and a preface and introduction to *The Conchologist's First Book,* an illustrated school text on the subject by Thomas Wyatt, an English writer and lecturer. For his fifty dollars, Poe also allowed his name to be used as the book's author through two editions, probably to resolve a copyright problem for Wyatt, who later explained that Poe "needed money very sorely at the time." Poe called on his talents only a bit more strenuously in publishing "The Devil in the Belfry. An Extravaganza," where the devil creates havoc by setting clocks awry in the time-obsessed village of Vondervotteim-ittiss; jokey names and 'phunny' dialect are asked to generate much of the tale's little humor (" 'Vot is cum'd to mein kraut?' screamed all the vrows"). In "The Psyche Zenobia," also published in the *Museum,* Poe satirized the American rage for *Blackwood's*-type fiction. Using a literary recipe given her by Mr. Blackwood himself, Suky Snobbs of Philadelphia composes a (botched) *Blackwood's* tale, describing her sensations while the giant minute hand of a steeple clock severs her neck. Effectively burlesquing what are in fact the devices in many of his own serious tales—the desperate predicament, erudite French and German expressions—Poe sometimes sounds as if taking off himself.

During this blank period, the only two short works by Poe that evince continued literary ambition and force both appeared in the *Museum* early in 1839. In "The Haunted Palace" (an increasingly infrequent return to verse) he gave a psychological turn to the theme of rebellion recently treated in *Pym,* describing the development of a mind, as he put it, "haunted by phantoms—a disordered brain." Besieged by sorrow, the self that was once a "stately palace," filled with harmonious spirits moving to "a lute's well-tунéd law," recedes into an ungraspable past:

> . . . *evil things, in robes of sorrow,*
> *Assailed the monarch's high estate.* . . .
> *And round about his home the glory*
> *That blushed and bloomed,*
> *Is but a dim-remembered story*
> *Of the old-time entombed.*

The distinctive words that give the poem its particular pathos are "home" and "entombed." They identify the particular losses that explain the growth of "discordant melody," the slide into personal chaos.

In "Ligeia," the other notable work, Poe perfected the tale of the revenant, the person (usually woman) returned from the Other World. The tale begins in Germany, where the unnamed narrator has been married for several years to the beautiful, wealthy, and scholarly Ligeia. Devastated by her death, he wanders, becomes addicted to opium, and eventually moves to England, where he marries the utterly different Lady Rowena Trevanion, whom he loathes. She soon falls ill and dies, bringing about a familiar scene: "I sat alone, with her shrouded body." As the narrator watches, Rowena's corpse seems to shuttle between life and death, or between more life and more death, for after each return of increasing vitality she relapses into even more advanced signs of rigidity or decay. This "hideous drama of revivication" ends when "the thing that was enshrouded" finally arises and advances, seeming taller and darker-haired than in life, seeming to have the full, black, wild eyes, so the narrator cries at the end, not of Rowena but "of the lady—of the LADY LIGEIA!"

"Ligeia" is more than anything else a love story, a tale of the "unutterable wo" that follows from the loss of "the one only and supremely beloved." One reason the narrator finds the loss irremediable is that, although an adult, he depends on Ligeia as if he were a child. He looks to her with "child-like confidence" for guidance, awe-struck by her "gigantic volition" and "immense" learning. When she dies he immediately needs another caretaker. "Without Ligeia," he says, "I was but as a child groping benighted." (Arthur Gordon Pym also several times compares himself and his companions to children.) Driven into isolation by "feelings of utter abandonment," he regresses still further, indulging himself "with a child-like perversity." His remembrance of Ligeia preserves both her and his attachment to her, making him unwilling or unable to love Rowena: "I loathed her [Rowena] with a hatred belonging more to demon than to man. My memory flew back, (oh, with what intensity of regret!) to Ligeia, the beloved, the beautiful, the entombed."

The psychological complexity of the tale comes from the narrator's simultaneous wish to forget Ligeia. To some degree he succeeds. He begins his tale by remarking on his loss of memory: "I cannot, for my soul, remember how, when, or even precisely where I first became acquainted with the lady Ligeia." Ignorant even of Ligeia's family name, and unable to recall how he became so, he claims to remember only indistinctly many of the events he narrates and often repeats things as if he had not already said them. But his amnesia is superficial. After Ligeia's death he richly equips a new home and takes Rowena as his new wife, in the "faint hope" of relieving his sorrow. In furnishing the bridal chamber, however, he selects, among other funereal pieces, a "gigantic sarcophagus of black granite," revealing that his effort to forget conceals a stronger need to remember. Ligeia's ultimate rebirth only dramatizes more horrifyingly how those most deeply beloved live on within oneself, never dead and ever ready to return. And Poe's need to keep writing versions of the revenant plot indicates clearly enough his own difficulty in putting the past to rest.

Poe seems to have received ten dollars for "Ligeia," about fifty cents a page, the same as for the trifling "Devil in the Belfry." So far as is known, he earned during this difficult period less than a hundred and fifty dollars, roughly sixteen cents a day from the end of January 1837, when he left the *Messenger* for New York, to the early summer of 1839. After that the biographical record allows him once again to be seen in some detail in Philadelphia, thirty years old, and about to write much of his most lasting fiction and criticism.

Philadelphia; Billy Burton.

CA. SPRING 1839

Neat, clean, quiet, so most visitors described Philadelphia. Some spoke admiringly of the city's "perfect regularity," others disapprovingly of its "wearisome regularity." But everyone was struck by its long parallel streets, crossing each other at right angles, the gridiron design that its founder William Penn had been the first to impose on an American city. Viewed from on high, sandwiched some five miles between the rivers Delaware and Schuylkill, the city seemed a checkered rectangle. Water from the Schuylkill waterworks kept the treelined streets and the mostly red brick dwellings and their marble stoops "remarkably clean," one traveler observed;

every house splashed it on "from the attic to the basement." Tourists were impressed too by the quietness of the place. As one put it, "The first idea which strikes you when you arrive at Philadelphia is that it is Sunday."

The tranquillity was an effect of the city's Quaker traditions and the character of its inhabitants, having nothing to do with size. For Philadelphia distinctly was a city, to some the most imposing in the Republic. By 1850 its population would reach 340,000, and at the moment supported seven daily morning papers, two evening daily papers, and some weekly ones. Gas lighting had been introduced in 1836, at first into street lamps and shops and gradually into dwellings, and by day omnibuses moving in every direction crowded the narrow streets downtown. The city's markets were renowned for the variety and freshness of their provisions. Spread on snow-white napkins in Market Street or in the stalls of long covered buildings elsewhere, could be seen rockfish, shad, wagonloads of pigeon, excellent beef, vast supplies of peaches and flowers. The many public places contributed an impression of urban diversity: the immense Navy Yard shed towering over other buildings of the city; the Bank of the United States, designed as a Doric temple; the University of Pennsylvania and the Philadelphia Academy of Fine Arts; the three large theaters and Music Hall; the brick State House, where the Declaration of Independence had been signed some sixty years earlier; the massive castellated Moyamensing Prison, celebrated for its humane "separate system" of prison discipline, affording each criminal a private cell in which to follow work suited to his capacities. Most important for Poe, the city shared with New York the leadership of American book and periodical publishing. The Philadelphia firm of Carey and Lea especially patronized works by American writers and had issued Washington Irving's *Tales of a Traveller* and James Fenimore Cooper's *Last of the Mohicans*.

Poe, Sissy, and Muddy had settled at Sixteenth Street near Locust, on the outskirts of the city. The neighborhood was rural enough for Poe to consider accepting as a gift for Virginia a pet fawn, which he could imagine "nibbling the grass before our windows." He described their dwelling as a "small house" but it seems to have been only part of a house, the rest having been left unbuilt by the owner. Surrounded by a fence with entrance gate, it apparently contained a flower-bordered plot of grass, on which the rest of the house was to have been raised. A visitor described the place as "comfortable inside for one of the kind. The rooms looked neat and orderly, but everything . . . wore an air of pecuniary want." The tidiness was surely due to the ministrations of Muddy, who cleaned, shopped, ran errands, looked after getting Poe gloves and cravats and, an acquaintance said, "had more of the mother than the mother-in-law about her."

Not yet seventeen years old, Virginia remained plump-looking, with a round, childlike face. Yet she impressed one visitor also by her "air of refinement and good breeding," perhaps a result of Poe's instruction and encouragement. Keeping his promise to educate Virginia, he tutored her in languages and in algebra, subjects in which he had done well at school, and however hard-pressed he tried to provide a piano and apparently also a harp, to satisfy her taste for music. He particularly urged her to sing; the son of a singer and the creator of Ligeia and other women with hauntingly musical voices, he loved singing. When he ran into his former Baltimore flame Mary Starr, now married and visiting Philadelphia, he invited her home and asked her to render "Come rest in this bosom." As for Virginia, a visitor to the truncated house recalled that she had a voice "of wonderful sweetness, and was an exquisite singer."

After two and a half years of miserably hand-to-mouth freelance writing that left him seeking another profession, Poe found a source of steady if not sufficient income in William Evans Burton, a transplanted English actor and theater manager (Illus. 8). Billy Burton was some six and a half years older than Poe, heavyset, his broad face vivified by a cleft chin and dark eyebrows. In his five years on the American stage he had won an audience playing Irishmen, hypocrites, old tars, and other baggy-pants comic roles. A fellow actor thought him "an enterprising man but a vulgar indecent actor." Enterprising Burton was, not only touring American cities with his wife and children, but also writing fiction and plays, trying his hand at journalism, and later publishing collections of humor: "were I to detail my daily avocations," he told a friend, "I do not imagine that I should be believed." Divorced and twice married, he was also said to live fast and high. A Philadelphia editor described him as "a vagrant from England, who has left a wife and offspring behind him there, and plays the bigamist in 'this,' with another wife, and his whore besides."

Bluff, worldly, and money-minded, Burton made an unlikely colleague for Poe. What brought them together was the journal Burton had begun in 1837, known as *Burton's Gentleman's Magazine*, although it did not ideally suit Poe either. In addition to the standard menu of poems, fiction, and essays, it gave special attention to sporting life, offering articles on sailing, cricket, or hunting to appeal to men-about-town. Not only that, but the *Gentleman's* had given *Pym* its one entirely unfavorable review. The reviewer, whom Poe took to be Burton himself, deplored the excess of gruesome detail, the borrowed geographical descriptions, and the ignorant errors in nautical information; mistaking the work for a hoax, he put it down as an "impudent attempt at humbugging the public."

With whatever misgivings, Poe needed work and offered Burton his editorial services. Inevitably the two men misread each other from the start. Burton was reluctant to increase already "wofully heavy" production costs. The ever-increasing competition among magazines compelled him to buy expensive illustrations, and to use thicker paper and better printing than his competitors. Just the same he promised Poe ten dollars a week until the end of 1839, for editorial work he said would occupy only two hours a day. Poe would have time, he pointed out, for some other "light avocation," provided it did not conflict with the interests of the *Gentleman's*. Poe's reply is lost but was evidently badly miscalculated. As he had once done with John Allan, he presented himself as both invulnerable and helpless, offering both much too much and much too little. Seemingly for publication and as a sample of his wares, he sent Burton an imperious, liquidating review of the popular poet Rufus Dawes, concluding with the judgment that "no man in America has been more shamefully over-estimated." Burton, having been warned by friends about Poe's "uncalled-for severity in criticism," told him that the review was unfair and explained to him that as the *Gentleman's* was already noted for the independence of its book reviews, flogging was unnecessary.

But at the same time that he showed Burton his critical muscle, Poe evidently also bemoaned his pitiable situation. Burton had had to fight his way along, cheerfully admitted to "a very comfortable share of impudence," and scorned Poe's complaints. "The troubles of the world have given a morbid tone to your feelings which it is your duty to discourage," he said. "I have been as severely handled in the world as you can possibly have been, but my sufferings have not tinged my mind with a melancholy hue." Poe seemingly appealed for Burton's help as from a man of the world, but Burton replied that it was exactly his worldly experience that convinced him, emphatically, *"not"* to conciliate writers of whom he knew nothing and could expect nothing. He told Poe, as others had annoyingly done, to pull himself together: "rouse your energies, and conquer the insidious attacks of the foul fiend, care." To help Poe "regain a wholesome activity of mind," he also advised more exercise.

Irked or not, Burton wanted Poe's assistance and proposed a fresh start: "Let us meet as if we had not exchanged letters," he said. The two came to some agreement, for in the June 1839 issue Burton announced his pleasure in having "made arrangements with Edgar A. Poe, Esq., late Editor of the Southern Literary Messenger, to devote his abilities and experience to a portion of the Editorial duties of the Gentleman's Magazine." Poe was listed as "Assistant Editor," but his name appeared prominently beside Burton's on the frontispiece (Illus. 9).

Writing for Burton's;
"The Fall of the House of Usher" and "William Wilson"; Ciphering; Tales of the Grotesque and Arabesque.

CA. JUNE 1839–JUNE 1840

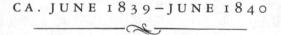

Poe's work for Burton plunged him, he said, into "a storm of business." Indeed it led off the most productive period of his career, immersing him in work for over the next six years. As he had done on the *Messenger,* he was once again reading proof and tending similar editorial chores, now also filling in for Burton while the actor played out of town. He wrote for the magazine on a hodgepodge of topics: an article on the use of parallel bars and other gymnastic equipment; another on the ruins of Stonehenge, printed on the front page but taken nearly verbatim from one of his favorite mines, Rees's *Encyclopedia;* some eighty-nine book reviews and cursory notices surveying not only novels and poems but also works on ornithology, housekeeping, advice to youth, flower painting, Paraguay.

Burton's cautions about harshness in reviews did not stop Poe from flicking his blade even in very brief notices. In fact whatever had happened to him during the previous two-and-a-half years had made him more combative than before. "I cannot bring himself to feel any goadings of conscience for undue severity," he wrote. "Indeed my remorse lies somewhat the other way." Sounding off about "these days of double dealing," he said he would not lie quiet if attacked for speaking the truth: "I intend to put up with nothing that I can *put down*." He wished to continue in *Burton's* what he had begun in his review of Halleck and Drake, a campaign of undermining the chief, but undeserved, American literary reputations, and some English as well. Only now he would desanctify such hallowed figures as Washington Irving and William Cullen Bryant.

For many Americans, Irving was the father and founder of American literature itself, beloved as the first native-born writer to achieve large success abroad. Poe considered him "much over-rated," and thought of making a flap by exposing him as head of the "school of the *quietists*," revealing his lack of originality and tame propriety. "A bold and *a priori* investigation of Irving's claims would strike home, take my word for it. The American literary world never saw anything of the kind yet." He did not write the essay, but for the front page of *Burton's* he did put together a biographical sketch of the also-beloved William Cullen Bryant, whose virtues he assessed as mainly negative: "In truth, a manly exemption from the prevalent poetical affectations of his time has done more for Mr. Bryant than any one positive excellence."

Poe also went after the rising fame of Henry Wadsworth Longfellow. Longfellow's best and his most popular verse still lay ahead, but in 1839 he had published his first volume of poems, *Voices of the Night*, containing "A Psalm of Life." In reviewing the volume Poe granted Longfellow imagination, but also declared him superficial, affected, disorganized, and otherwise "singularly deficient in all those important faculties which give artistical power." He ended the review with a "much more serious" charge, quoting the whole of Longfellow's "Midnight Mass for the Dying Year" and setting it beside Tennyson's "The Death of the Old Year." The poems resemble each other only very slightly, but Poe announced that the comparison disclosed a theft "too palpable to be mistaken; and which belongs to the most barbarous class of literary robbery." As he understood these extreme cases, the author's words are not used, but his most intangible property is "purloined," namely his underlying concept, what Poe called the "tournure" of the work. He charged Longfellow with having stolen Tennyson's conceit of personifying the old year as a dying old man. A few journals took up Longfellow's defense, denying that he had, as one put it, "imitated" anyone. Poe replied to them anonymously, speaking of himself as of another person and upping the stakes: "Mr. Poe does not say that Professor Longfellow's poem is 'imitated' from Tennyson. He calls it a bare-faced and barbarous plagiarism."

Poe was far from the last in his own time or later to call Irving, Bryant, and Longfellow tame and derivative. And he leavened even his most damning reviews with praises for a writer's particular virtues. Still, his efforts to de-nose these literary lions was unmistakably driven in part by a feeling that he himself had been misserved: "The laudation of the unworthy," as he put it later, "is to the worthy the most bitter of all wrong." And by contrast with the very small sales of his collected poems, Longfellow's *Voices of the Night* sold forty-three thousand copies. Burton perhaps sensed how much Poe's boasted candor served as an acceptable guise for his resentment, warning him that "you must get rid of your avowed ill-feelings toward your brother authors." Nor did Poe's envying will to power shrink from gross hypocrisy. Contempt for Washington Irving's "much over-rated" reputation did not prevent him from writing to Irving and begging his endorsement of some recent work: *"even a word or two,"* he pleaded, and *"my fortune would be made. . . .* would ensure me that public attention which would carry me on to fortune hereafter, by ensuring me fame at once." He wrote still more duplicitously to Longfellow, soliciting a magazine contribution. With cloying respect he conveyed what he called "the fervent admiration with which [your] genius has inspired me." He knew, he said, that "Professor Longfellow, writing and thinking as he does, will be at no loss to feel and to appreciate the honest *sincerity* of what I say." The statement is of a piece with Poe's declaration of principle to another correspondent at the time: "I have an inveterate habit of speaking the truth." Actually, he had fallen into a routine of easy lies and half truths since at least his adolescence. An early Richmond acquaintance later commented that under John Allan's nurture, "Dissimulation and evasion became habitual to him."

Poe did not exaggerate, however, when he claimed to be occupied by "a world of pressing engagements." He boosted his editorial salary by also contributing poems and tales to *Burton's,* for which he was paid separately. Several were revised versions of earlier pieces like "Morella," part of a continuous lifelong effort to rework and improve what he considered his best prose and verse. Of newer poems he published only a difficult fifteen-line sonnet entitled "Silence," contrasting the "corporate Silence" of the grave, which human ceremony and memory render "terrorless," with its truly terrifying *"shadow"*—perhaps a metaphysical silence, doubt of the very grounds of existence, or more simply the silence of spirits who live after death, ghosts literally, Silences within the Silence. His fiction in *Burton's,* some probably written before he joined the magazine, ranged from "The Conversation of Eiros and Charmion," a dialogue between two spirits in heaven on the destruction of the world, to "Peter Pendulum, The Business Man," a comic sketch of a petty swindler whose scams include "the Sham-Post," by which he delivers faked letters supposedly sent from far-off places like Bengal, and receives the expensive postage costs—as Poe may have once faked letters from St. Petersburg.

Between these extremes of high discourse and slapstick, Poe also published "The Philosophy of Furniture," on the interior decor of American homes; "The Man that was Used Up," a surreal encounter with the Indian fighter Brevet Brigadier General John A. B. C. Smith, who turns out to be constituted entirely of screw-in eyes and other prosthetic devices; and "The Journal of Julius Rodman," an uncompleted novella, serialized over six issues, purporting to be an authentic account of the first expedition of white men to cross the Rocky Mountains. It begins promisingly with a hypochondriacal hero in search of relief and *"the unknown,"* but peters out in trivial geographical detail, succeeding well enough as a hoax, however, to have been cited as factual in an 1840 U.S. Senate document on the Oregon Territory.

The appearance here of Poe's prized variety is in one sense superficial, for his kaleidoscopic imagination constantly redeployed the same narrative elements in new settings and rearranged them into new shapes. "Rodman," for instance, is but *Pym* transposed to the Rocky Mountains, with the same search for food and drink, the same protracted natural description (here not of penguins but of beavers), the same effect of progression to some Heart of Darkness, the black Tsalalians who shouted "Tekeli-li!" being replaced by Sioux Indians shouting "Ricaree!" The two works also contain, it should be added, the same surplus of grammatical blunders, of the sort that Poe continued to identify and chastise in other writers, and the same wholesale pilfering of long stretches of descriptive material from other books, at the same time that he was shaming Longfellow for copying Tennyson. Through Poe's many shifts from one vein of popular prose fiction to another, his characteristic images and motifs recur often: the theater, male rivalry, card games, loyalty to the past, unmerited acclaim, things being dismembered and returning to wholeness, the wishful fear of being devoured, the yearning for a home.

For all this remodeling of familiar material, Poe's fiction in *Burton's* also draws on new or at least untapped interests. The Indian warfare in "Rodman" and the Indian-fighting general of "The Man that was Used Up," for example, reflect widely reported conflict in Florida in 1839. Poe wrote at a time of tumultuous social change that supplied the daily fare of journalism and popular literature. In April 1838, about when he came to Philadelphia, a steam packet arrived in New York from Liverpool after a voyage of fifteen days, despite bad weather, promising regular, swift steam travel between the United States and the Continent. "The commercial, moral and political effects of this increased intercourse, to Europe & to this country, must be immense," one newspaper observed. The new ties would expand commerce, diffuse knowledge, and by reducing prejudice make *"war* a thing almost impossible." Communities and individual lives throughout the country were being transformed not only by new marvels in technology, communication, and transportation, but also by continuous migration, monetary instability, and ideological combat over issues that touched every level of society: women's rights, temperance, the abolition of slavery, the ending of capital punishment, the annexation of Texas. The effect was dizzying. It seemed to one foreign visitor that ten years in America passed like a century in Spain. How could people endure feeling, he wondered, "as if tied to the wing of a windmill?"

Poe for the most part lived and wrote apart from the whirl, preoccupied with feeding himself and family, imagining a ghostly afterlife. At a time when railroads were a national obsession, the characters in his tales still ride horses. Perhaps owing to the influence of Dickens's social realism, however, his writing of the late 1830s does at least glance at the state of American society, never without cringing. General A. B. C. Smith rolls out the clichés of the day in which Americans boasted their presumed progress: "we are a wonderful people, and live in a wonderful age. Parachutes and railroads—man-traps and spring-guns [security devices for the home]. Our steam-boats are upon every sea. . . . And who shall calculate the immense influence upon social life—upon arts—upon commerce—upon literature—which will be the immediate result of the application of the great principles of electro magnetics!" Turning to the modern city for his scene, Poe particularly lashed out at the all-powerful business culture. In "Peter Pendulum" he satirized businessmen as ledger keepers who oppose genius and practice fraud. Having long attacked a national lack of aesthetic discrimination, he now connected corruption of taste with pursuit of the dollar. In "The Philosophy of Furniture" he attributed the glaring lighting and excess glitter in American homes to a debasement of values among the economic herd: "It is an evil growing out of our republican institutions, that here a man of large purse has usually a very little soul which he keeps in it. The corruption of taste is a portion and a pendant of the dollar-manufacture." Democratic capitalism he saw as mere social climbing and hunger for rank. Having no "aristocracy of blood," Americans had "therefore as a natural, and indeed as an inevitable thing, fashioned for ourselves an aristocracy of dollars." So far as he remarked on the American scene, Poe had only scorn for what he saw as its foolish millennial enthusiasm for the products of technology, and its money-grubbing democratic rabble.

Poe also contributed to *Burton's* what became two of his most famous tales, matching the quality of "Ligeia." In "The Fall of the House of Usher"† he created the definitive tale of horror. He did so out of stealthy servants, subterranean passages, the grating sounds of massive iron doors, a building collapsing in storm, and similar elements that were already outworn conventions of Gothicism. Echoing many episodes and key phrases from Poe's earlier tales as well, "Usher" is in effect a re-imagining of the whole content of his imagination, seen as in some way doomed. The force of the tale comes not from any novelty of subject but from the treatment. To mention but one of many effective technical devices: beginning with the opening alliterative clause ("During the whole of a dull, dark, and soundless day"), Poe marshaled sibilant *s*'s and muffled *d*'s, as well as an abundance of dashes and other pauses, to create a mood of somber menace, an effect helped out by the elevated language, as when he gravely describes Madeline's illness as the "transient affections of a partially cataleptical character."

In "William Wilson"† Poe fashioned a classic psychological thriller out of the irritation one feels in learning that someone else has the same name, a wound to one's feelings of uniqueness. The idea for the plot was not original with him. As he acknowledged, he based his tale on a brief article by (note well) Washington Irving. It concerned an impulsive young man who finds himself followed everywhere by a masked figure who tries to thwart his intrigues; in the end, as likewise happens in Poe's tale, the young man stabs the figure with his sword, only to find beneath the mask, as Irving wrote, "his own image—the spectre of himself." Poe followed Irving's outline closely, but elaborated it into a tale with several levels. As an allegory of the operation of conscience, the tale is notable for its complex delineation of Wilson's habits of thought, which Thomas Mann admiringly compared to the "psychological lyricism" of Dostoyevsky. As a study of youth, it depicts Wilson's first school as a self-involved, enclosed world, turned in on itself in a profusion of levels, corridors, and subdivisions, and painful as well, its walls topped with broken glass embedded in mortar, its gates surmounted by "jagged iron spikes," a place of potential mutilation that foreshadows the bloody and climactic stabbing. As a very Poe-esque protest against death, too, it treats of a man who kills himself yet lives.

Although the depiction of English school life in "Wilson" extends Poe's new vein of social realism, while "Usher" reshapes much older Gothic conventions, the two stories have much in common. Both deal with the impossibility of restraining troublesome aspects of the self. For Roderick Usher and William Wilson, as for most of Poe's characters, nothing stays buried. Like the teeth of Berenice, painful objects, memories, and persons keep returning in defiance of the characters' conscious control. To distract himself from thoughts of his sister, Usher listens to music, hears a story, paints, but she comes back to fall upon him as "the shrouded figure of the lady Madeline of Usher." Wilson tries desperately to get away from his rival but is left repeating *"I fled in vain."* In Poe even more than in his contemporary Nathaniel Hawthorne, the past endures with smothering weight, often fatally.

It endures in part because of the characters' enamorment with it. After Madeline's seeming death, Usher does not dispose of her body but retains it in his house. Wilson cannot bring himself to fully hate the other Wilson but instead feels an unwilling affection toward him as at once "the namesake, the companion, the rival." In the startling presto-chango finale of the tale, he stabs the other Wilson, only to find himself facing not a corpse but his own reflection in a mirror, which he next realizes is not his reflection but the other Wilson after all, who, as appearance and reality change place bewilderingly, is really himself. *"In me didst thou exist,"* his dying duplicate tells him, *"and, in my death, see by this image, which is thine, how utterly thou hast murdered thyself."* Usher, in taking the life of his twin sister, also murders himself, as if the problems that haunt the self are inscribed in consciousness and can be overcome only by self-annihilation.

Wilson cannot escape his 'image' nor Usher his twin, that is, because these figures are also parts of themselves, doubles of them. Doubling is extensive in Poe's tales, many of whose heroes and heroines are hard to distinguish from each other and often have the physical and mental traits of Poe himself. It appears in many elements of the narrative. Roderick resembles his house, whose sentience has influenced and is duplicated in his own "morbid acuteness of the senses": local peasants use the name "The House of Usher" to mean "both the family and the family mansion." The house in turn is mirrored in the "lurid tarn" outside: the narrator gazes into it hoping to escape the oppressive effect of the house, only to meet there its "remodelled and inverted images." The tale's main action is repeated in the story of Ethelred, which the narrator tells to Usher and in doing so doubles Poe's relation to the reader. Although such doubling is common in romantic literature and essential to Gothic fiction, where criminals resemble victims, it has a special gravity in Poe's tales. To have twins, doubles, and twos means that, like William Wilson, one can be here and not here, can die and still survive.

The past is also doubled in the present, including Poe's past. The first William Wilson experiences through the second "dim visions of my earliest infancy—wild, confused and thronging memories of a time when memory herself was yet unborn." Both tales offer those familiar with Poe's early life a similar sense of déjà vu, abounding with associations to it. The two Wilsons have his own birthdate, January 19; in various revised versions of the tale he gave Wilson the correct year of his birth, 1809, as well as the fabricated years 1811 and 1813, which he sometimes presented as correct. He placed Wilson in the school of "Dr. Bransby," using the name of the actual schoolmaster under whom he had studied while living with the Allans in England. (He apparently had that period much in mind; in the dialect sketch "Why the Little Frenchman Wears His Hand in a Sling," written at around this time, he settled his narrator at "39 Southampton Row, Russell Square," the Allans' actual address in London.) *House* was of course for Poe a vibrant word, taking in the richness of Moldavia, reaching back to the House of Ellis and Allan, and perhaps extending to the house, or audience, for a play. At any rate, he named his hero after Noble Luke Usher and Harriet L'Es-

trange Usher, who had very often performed opposite David and
Eliza Poe. Not surprisingly, enveloped in the reek of its decayed
trees and black tarns, the fungi overspreading its gray walls, the
House of Usher is itself a corpse.

For his ninety-five pages of reviews and articles in *Burton's* Poe
received only his salary of ten dollars a week, while earning three
dollars a page extra for his tales, including "Usher," and five dollars
for each of his seven reprinted poems. Despite the extent and quality of his writing he found himself having to borrow money from
Burton and others, and he took on outside work. One freelance
project moved him further along on a new kind of reputation. He
began writing for *Alexander's Weekly Messenger,* one of the inexpensive "family newspapers" that promoted morality and religion. He
contributed light articles on such subjects as beet sugar, taking advantage of his anonymous article on swimming to make known yet
once more that "Mr. Poe," as he put it, had once swum the James
River, "a distance of seven miles and a half [raised from the earlier
six], in a hot June sun, and *against a tide of three miles per hour.* He
was then but 15 years of age." More creditably, he published over
four months a series on what he variously called hieroglyphical
writings, ciphers, puzzles, or posers. Advancing what he had begun
in "Maelzel's Chess-Player," these fifteen articles on cryptography
brought him a reputation as an ingenious analyst.

Poe invited readers to invent their own ciphers, instructing them
to replace the letter A with say a dagger, the letter B with an aster-
isk, using whatever characters they pleased to contrive in this fashion an entire alphabet. They were to use this alphabet in composing
brief pieces of prose, which he promised to be able to decode immediately. His gambit elicited ciphers written in hands, numbers,
and typographical devices, or printed upside down in an effort to
fool him. Some he reprinted, together with his solution, stressing
that the poser "gave us *no trouble whatever"* and offering to take on
all comers. Exploiting the excitement he had again managed to create, he protested that he had become inundated with challenges:
"Do people really think that we have nothing in the world to do
but to read hieroglyphics?"

Although boasting his infallibility, Poe at the same time insisted
that the ciphers be formed according to his instruction, and he rejected some entries as belonging rather to "Cryptography." In fact
what he solved were elementary substitution ciphers, of the sort
still printed on the comic-strip pages of newspapers as "crypto-

grams." Their difficulty remains the same whether the inventor merely replaces one letter of the alphabet with another or translates the alphabet into squiggles and blips. Poe seems to have read a bit on the subject, likely the articles on "Cipher" in Rees's *Encyclopedia* and the *Encyclopaedia Britannica*. But he was entirely a novice, as the still more naive readers of *Alexander's* failed to realize. Some made his simple task simpler by applying their invented alphabets to giveaway texts like the Lord's Prayer, and even so his solutions sometimes contained errors.

While working for *Burton's*, Poe also at last managed to bring out a collection of his tales, with the Philadelphia firm of Lea and Blanchard. The publication promised no financial relief, however. As the partners considered the project "not immediately pecuniary," they offered Poe only the copyright to his book and twenty free copies for friends, otherwise retaining all profits for themselves, if any were realized. Even these arrangements were optimistic, for as the publication date approached it coincided with new economic problems in the country, and the firm apparently reduced the size of the edition to only 750 copies—which took three years to sell out.

Poe had been trying for years to publish his book as "Tales of the Folio Club," but by now had abandoned the framing device of a group of litterateurs who meet to discuss each other's writing. The collection appeared in December 1839 as *Tales of the Grotesque and Arabesque,* making a substantial work of five hundred pages in two volumes. Its twenty-five varied tales included both older narratives like "Berenice" and "Hans Phaall," and more recent ones like "Ligeia" and "William Wilson." Poe's understanding of *grotesque* and *arabesque* remains uncertain. Historically the terms refer to different sorts of decoration, the first combining plant, animal, and human motifs, the other using only flowers and calligraphy. But in Poe's time *grotesque* and *arabesque* were often confounded and used synonymously. Given the nature of the tales he included, where an other world often intrudes on this one, he seems to have taken the terms to mean something close to the critic Geoffrey Harpham's definition of the grotesque. Harpham calls it a "transcategorical hybrid," a copresence of the normal and the abnormal, the archaic and the modern, the individual and a commonality that unites all orders of being.

In his peculiar preface, Poe attributed to this affinity-antagonism in his tales the often-repeated criticism of them as too "German," "too full," as one newspaper put it, "of the wild, mysterious, horrible, and improbable." The charge incensed him, probably because it implied some lack of invention and originality: "those little critics," he railed, "who would endeavor to put me down by raising the hue & cry . . . of *Germanism* and such twaddle." He may not have convinced his critics otherwise by printing an epigraph from Goethe, in German, on his title page, and describing his tales in the preface as "phantasy-pieces," a tag derived from E. T. A. Hoffmann's *Fantasiestücke.* Just the same he used his preface to argue that the charge failed to recognize his ability to write in many keys: "To morrow I may be anything but German," he said, "as yesterday I was everything else." But that Poe wrote in the "grotesque" purely from choice and could abandon it at will seems doubtful. In fact his next argument undermined the claim, for it suggested that the vein he worked was deeply expressive of his own life, grown out of his own experience however shaped and reinforced by his reading. "If in many of my productions terror has been the thesis, I maintain that terror is not of Germany, but of the soul,—that I have deduced this terror only from its legitimate sources, and urged it only to its legitimate results."

In the prefaces to his earlier volumes of poetry, Poe had asked readers to indulge his works as products of youth, written in adverse circumstances. Now, however, he ended by remarking that although he considered a few pieces in the volumes trifling, he expected to be judged on the others as representing his best efforts, as "the results of matured purpose and very careful elaboration." In fact, except Nathaniel Hawthorne's *Twice-Told Tales* two years earlier, *Tales of the Grotesque and Arabesque* was in 1839 the most powerfully imagined and technically adroit collection of short fiction ever published by an American writer.

While Poe's productive work on *Burton's* and *Alexander's* and the publication of his tales brought him little money, they enriched and magnified his reputation. His magazine writing was praised in dozens of periodicals, mostly in New York and Philadelphia but also in Richmond, Baltimore, and Boston, and occasionally in such distant places as St. Louis: "unusually excellent"; "some of the most popular tales of American origin"; "one of the most extraordinary narratives ever penned." The *Tales* received some twenty reviews, a few objecting to "the gloomy German mysticism," the worst coming from Boston, where the *Morning Post* concluded that "A greater amount of trash within the same compass it would be difficult to find." Most reviewers, however, praised the collection as at once serious and entertaining, and for some it established Poe on the national literary scene: "To say we have *read* this production attentively is not enough. We have *studied* it. . . . He has placed himself in the foremost rank of American writers."

Poe awaited his reviews hungrily. "The Philadelphians have given me the *very highest possible* praise," he told one correspondent. "The Star and the Evening Post have both capital notices. There is also a promise of one in the New-World." Several persons who knew Poe commented on his enormous desire to be admired for his work: "no man living loved the praises of others better than he did," one wrote; "whenever I happened to communicate to him anything touching his abilities as a writer, his bosom would heave like a troubled sea." A natural and skillful publicist, Poe continued to drum up applause for himself as well. In the second volume of the *Tales* he printed several pages of old and new plugs for his work, testifying to his "master-hand," or that he "puts us in mind of no less a writer than Shelley." Writing anonymously in *Alexander's,* he commended his simultaneous work in *Burton's,* his self-praises often reading like the razzle-dazzle framing devices of *Pym.* "Mr. Poe has a clever Sonnet," he remarked at one time. "Mr. Poe has a very singular story," he observed at another. He even honored Mr. Poe, anonymously again, with a conundrum:

> Why ought the author of the "Grotesque and Arabesque" to be a good writer of verses?
> Because he's a poet to a *t.* Add *t* to Poe makes it a Poet.

Break with Burton; The "Penn" Magazine.

JUNE 1840–FEBRUARY 1841

Despite his success through *Burton's Gentleman's Magazine,* Poe left it in June 1840, having again remained just one year at the job. He had not found his role as assistant editor profitable or comfortable. Among other dissatisfactions, he had little respect for the magazine and even advised a friend not to subscribe, as the "criticisms are not worthy your notice. Of course, I pay no attention to them." Among the unsigned reviews, too, his own mingled indistinguishably with those by Burton, and he found it "not pleasant to be taxed with the twaddle of other people." Burton also became financially pinched and stopped paying contributors for their works.

More, Poe particularly disliked the contest Burton had advertised, for the best works written expressly for his magazine. The several prizes and categories included $250 for a series of five tales dealing with American history and $200 for the best tale of pathos, the awards totaling one thousand dollars, a huge sum for such contests. Poe thought Burton's announcement of the rules not explicit enough, wished to have it known that he was not their author, and indeed objected to the premium scheme "in toto," he said, regarding it as strictly a matter of *"business."* After four months Burton canceled the contest on the ground that too few manuscripts had been submitted, in some categories none at all. He may have considered that explanation fair, although his original advertisements had not made a sufficiency of entries in all categories a condition for the awarding of prizes in some. Poe confided his own view of Burton's tactics to J. E. Snodgrass, a Baltimore editor and physician who had published "Ligeia," and would figure importantly in Poe's later life. Burton plainly intimated to him, "personally and directly," he said, that he never intended to pay a dollar of prize money. Burton's skulduggery was the immediate reason for his quitting the magazine, he told Snodgrass, "cutting the connexion as abruptly as I did."

Once more dressing up reality to please himself, Poe did not mention that at the end of May Burton had sent him a blistering letter, now lost, perhaps demoting or even firing him, but at the least accusing him of negligence and betrayal. So far as the circumstances can be reconstructed, Burton learned that Poe, although still working for him, intended to issue a rival magazine of his own. Poe had had the idea in mind for a while, and its timeliness was probably impressed on him by an advertisement in a Philadelphia newspaper, offering for sale an unspecified "monthly magazine of great popularity and profit." Poe correctly believed that the ad had been placed by Burton, who was far from innocent in their quarrel. Still a busy actor and stage manager, he intended to get rid of the *Gentleman's* and devote his time and money to establishing a large new theater in Philadelphia.

In replying to Burton's lost but no doubt enraged letter, Poe coolly asked him to consider who started it all: "you advertised your magazine for sale without saying a word to me about it. I felt no anger at what you did—none in the world. Had I not firmly believed it your design to give up your Journal, with a view of attending to the Theatre, I should [never] have dreamed of attempting one of my own." Poe repeatedly assured Burton that he was rather amused than angered by "your attempts to bully me." But Burton had sprung a Pandora's box of undeclared grievances that now rushed to expression. Poe complained that Burton paid him nothing for displaying his name on the title page, and habitually spoke "disrespectfully" of him behind his back. For the past three weeks Burton had deducted three dollars from his salary as repayment of loans, "an indignity which I have felt deeply," Poe assured him, "but did not resent." (The loans amounted to a hundred dollars, according to Burton, to no more than sixty, according to Poe.)

Slights to himself stayed in Poe's memory as if gripped in a vise. He now reminded Burton of the unfavorable review that had appeared in the *Gentleman's,* nine months before he joined it, of his *Narrative of Arthur Gordon Pym.* The reviewer, whom he took to be Burton, had blasted the "faulty construction and poorness of style" and professed regret "to find Mr Poe's name in connexion with such a mass of ignorance and effrontery." Apparently Poe had never before mentioned the review to Burton, nursing in silence the wrath he felt toward him as its presumed author. But now he took his long-delayed revenge. He attributed most of the difficulty between himself and Burton to the guilt that Burton allegedly felt over the review: "[Had I written a simi]lar critici[sm] upon a book of yours, you feel that you would [have been] my enemy for life, and you therefore ima[gine in my] bosom a latent hostility towards yourself. This has been a mainspring in your whole conduct towards me since our first acquaintance." Together with its tortuous self-justification, Poe's remark shows a remarkable lack of self-knowledge, projecting onto Burton his own habit of projection. Others might feel resentment at receiving a bad review, he breezed, but as for himself he was above it: "In a general view of human nature your idea is just—but you will find yourself puzzled in judging me by ordinary motives." As he himself thought *Pym* a "very silly book," Burton's severe review of it left him unmoved: "it did not occasion in me one solitary emotion either of anger or dislike." Not one!

Much as it had begun, Poe's relation to Burton ended with hard feelings on both sides. Poe perhaps felt not "one solitary emotion" of anger, but to others he cursed Burton as "infamous," a "scoundrel," one of the "literary swindlers." Burton fed Poe's antagonism by publicly insinuating that he had botched his editorial duties because of drunkenness. In one of the last numbers of the *Gentleman's,* he printed a letter to a subscriber who had failed to receive his issues, explaining that the subscriber's name had been "erased from our list by the person whose 'infirmities' have caused us much annoyance." Stories also reached Poe from his friend Snodgrass in Baltimore that Burton was accusing "the person" of getting drunk on his own time as well. Poe began referring to Burton as "Billy Barlow"—the stage name of a low comedian who had committed suicide in Mississippi—and then as the "basest of calumniators," a "buffoon and a felon" from whose office he had retired "in uncontrollable disgust at his chicanery, arrogance, ignorance, and brutality."

Poe also vigorously denied Burton's hints and tales about his drinking. He pledged to Snodgrass that during his entire term on the *Gentleman's* "*nothing stronger than water ever passed my lips.*" Generally candid with Snodgrass, he owned that for a brief period while editing the *Messenger* he "certainly did give way, at long intervals, to the temptation held out on all sides by the spirit of Southern conviviality." Sensitive to drink, as his companions were not, he sometimes became "completely intoxicated" and in each case was confined to bed for several days after. But he assured Snodgrass he had never been what is called "intemperate," and for nearly the last four years had "abandoned every kind of alcoholic drink." Now, he said, "My sole drink is water."

The truth of the matter cannot be judged with any certainty. But the credibility of Poe's claim to have sustained a four-year-long dry spell is not enhanced by his admission to Snodgrass of a "single deviation." This, he emphasized, occurred "*after*" his leaving *Burton's,* when hoping to relieve a "nervous attack" he had been "induced to resort to the occasional use of *cider.*" Perhaps so, but the testimony of others is not reassuring either. Years later, a contributor to *Burton's* recalled seeing Poe at the magazine office "industrious as a beaver," but also remembered having to help him home after he became drunk, Poe explaining that "it was an unusual thing with him, and would never occur again." The publisher of *Alexander's Weekly Messenger,* who remained well disposed toward Poe, later recalled that his drinking never interfered with the publication of the *Gentleman's,* but that it "may have occasioned some disappointment in the preparation of a particular article expected from *him*." Poe nevertheless repeated to Snodgrass a sort of oath, "my solemn assurance that my habits are as far removed from intemperance as the day from the night."

As for Burton's defaming him, Poe told Snodgrass that his only recourse was to the law courts. There he could prove the charges false by bringing witnesses who had seen him sober at all hours, including Burton's own clerk and printers. But he added, not very convincingly, that he had himself freely condemned Burton to others as a "blackguard and a villain," so that if he brought a suit Burton could meet him with a "cross action." There was then not very much he could do. Burton's stories about his drunkenness were malicious and slanderous, he insisted, but if he sued Burton, Burton would sue him: "you see," he told Snodgrass, "how it is."

Poe no sooner parted with Burton than he set out to realize his plan for a magazine of his own. The idea had been in mind when he began working for the *Gentleman's,* as a project that might "kick up a dust." While expecting the magazine to call attention to himself and his work, he also looked to it to end his chronic financial misery, feeling that in this case "fortune & fame must go hand in hand." In addition he hoped to gain a new freedom in speaking his mind. Laboring in the past only for others, he had found himself painfully constrained, "forced to model my thoughts at the will of men whose imbecility was evident to all but themselves." Having his own journal would make him independent, "not so much as regards money, as in respect to my literary opinions and conduct." He well knew that among the many new magazines that kept appearing, many swiftly failed. Yet he felt certain his own would succeed: "if there is any impossibility about the matter, it is the impossibility of *not* succeeding."

Poe did not plan to begin publishing until the new year, giving him six months to collect the necessary capital. To call attention to his design, he sent around prospectuses for the magazine and inserted one as a paid advertisement in the Philadelphia *Saturday Evening Post* for June 6: "PROSPECTUS OF THE PENN MAGAZINE, A MONTHLY LITERARY JOURNAL, TO BE EDITED AND PUBLISHED IN THE CITY OF PHILADELPHIA, BY EDGAR A. POE." If not as striking as the inspired titles of his tales and poems, the magazine title of course aimed at a pun on the place and the writing instrument. Poe looked particularly for support to the South, where he was still best known, and relied on readers' favorable recollections of his work on the *Southern Literary Messenger*. He announced that the "Penn" would retain some of the *Messenger*'s best features while abandoning or modifying the others.

Poe would keep, first, the *Messenger*'s spirit of independent criticism, but in a more subdued tone. He observed that while his *Messenger* reviews had had a "somewhat overdone causticity," the intervening years had made him less petulant but no less contemptuous of puffery, had "not yet taught him to read through the medium of a publisher's will." Criticism in the "Penn" would be guided only by the rules of art. Unlike the *Messenger,* too, the "Penn" would serve not a particular region but the larger interests of the republic of letters, "regarding the world at large as the true audience of the author." And it would take for its domain literature alone. Poe here made an important declaration of his wish to separate literature from such matters as politics and morality: "Its aim chiefly shall be *to please;* and this through means of versatility, originality, and pungency." Always concerned about the physical look and feel of literary works, he also vowed that the magazine would far surpass the average in the fineness of its paper and embellishments, making a half-yearly volume of about five hundred pages at a cost of five dollars a year. He promised the first issue on the first of January 1841.

Sometimes using the reverse side of his prospectuses for letter paper, Poe also began writing to writers, editors, journalists, and publishers, especially in the South. He asked their help in putting together a list of subscribers, hoping to obtain five hundred names by December 1. Through them he also tried to raise some five hundred dollars for advertising and circulars, and to finance his business trips to other cities, a few of which he seems to have made. As he had done before, he sought assistance too from members of the numerous Poe family in the South. Their aid in securing subscribers, he told them, would enable him to act on behalf of "the honor of our family name." From these and others Poe did receive encouragement and help. Progress reports appeared in the press, the Philadelphia *Daily Chronicle* announcing in September, for instance, that "It gives us much pleasure to learn that the subscription list of this forthcoming periodical, is receiving rapidly a succession of names." By the end of November Poe already had some literary material in hand, which he predicted would go to press early the next month as part of his first issue.

But no "Penn" appeared on January 1, 1841. Poe had found the work of beginning a magazine "difficult and most arduous," and in December he succumbed to a "severe illness." It kept him in bed the entire month, he said, forcing him to postpone the first number until March, "when it will certainly appear." That at least is how he explained his failure to his friend Snodgrass, to whom he also explained that his illness was, "for various reasons, a benefit to my scheme, rather than a disadvantage." Prospects for the magazine remained *"glorious."*

So far as Poe's remarks indicated anything more than his need ever to show himself the conqueror, they perhaps reflected his intention of giving the magazine a new direction. What he needed for the "Penn," he came to think, was "caste . . . the countenance of those who stand well in the social not less than in the literary world." Living in Philadelphia had perhaps influenced his thinking, for "in no city," as one visitor observed, "is there so much fuss made about lineage and descent; in no city are there so many cliques and sets in society." In seeking *cachet* for his magazine, Poe tried to enlist the very wealthy and prominent Nicholas Biddle, a former president of the Second Bank of the United States. In his writing for *Alexander's,* Poe had made clear his contempt for the "aristocracy of dollars." In the fall, nevertheless, he called at Andalusia, Biddle's family estate near Philadelphia, apparently bringing with him an autographed copy of *Tales of the Grotesque and Arabesque.* Reminding Biddle of this visit, Poe wrote in January asking him to contribute a brief article to the first issue, now scheduled for March. He stressed what it would mean to his magazine to have it known "that you were not indifferent to my success." Given that Biddle's name, he said, "has an almost illimitable influence in the city, and a vast influence in all quarters of the country," its appearance in the "Penn" would be of more actual value than perhaps a thousand dollars. Instead, Biddle seems to have subscribed for four years in advance.

That was not enough, for March too arrived without the "Penn." On February 4, the United States Bank suspended payment in specie, producing a panic and a run on the other Philadelphia banks, most of whom also stopped payment, followed by banks in the South. At least temporarily, the new financial emergency ended Poe's plans for the magazine. What resources for it he had managed to gather is unknown, but his cousins in Georgia failed to enlist even a few

subscribers. According to him, however, when the bank panic erupted
he had been putting the first sheet to press. "It would have appeared under glorious auspices," he guaranteed Snodgrass, "and with
capital at command, in March, as advertised."

Graham's Magazine;
Important Critical Essays;
"The Murders in the Rue Morgue."

FEBRUARY 1841 – APRIL 1842

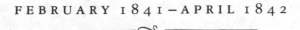

For $3,500, a dollar for each subscriber, Billy Burton sold the
Gentleman's Magazine to a twenty-seven-year-old Philadelphian named
George Rex Graham. Graham merged it with a magazine he already
published, the *Casket,* bringing his own subscription list to about
five thousand. With the commencement of 1841, he began issuing
the hybrid as *Graham's Lady's and Gentleman's Magazine (The Casket and Gentleman's United).*

Boyish-looking and clean-shaven save for a fringe of chin whiskers, George Rex Graham was amiable and generous, but also clever
and bold, and he knew what he was doing (Illus. 10). After no more
than a country school education and apprenticeship to a cabinet-
maker, he had studied law, been admitted to the bar, and developed a passion for publishing. Competing with nearly four hundred
monthlies, semimonthlies, and quarterlies now circulating in America, he aimed at and won a large popular readership. In its first year
of publication, *Graham's* jumped in circulation from five thousand
to twenty-five thousand. It owed its success to both innovation and
imitation. Graham hired the best American engraver of the day, the
Philadelphian John Sartain, to supply new illustrations for each issue, at a time when most monthlies re-used old plates cheaply acquired from other magazines. He insisted on original, that is, never-
before-printed, contributions. And he established an unheard-of
payscale, "at least as liberal," Poe said, "as that of any publisher in
America." Uniquely important in making magazine writing a

profession in America, Graham later boasted that in ten years he paid out to American writers more than eighty thousand dollars. In his time, a 'Graham page' became the standard of payment for magazine work.

At the same time, Graham adopted features of other periodicals that had proved commercially sound. He avoided controversial subjects. He provided pious verse entitled "Sabbath Bells" or "Little Children" (beginning, "I love those little happy things"), and mawkish fiction such as "The Blind Girl" or "The Father's Blessing," relieved by an occasional pirate thriller or Gothic tale like "The Alchymist" (beginning, "It was midnight. Darkness, deep as the sable of a funeral pall, hung over the streets of Madrid"). He printed syrupy music to be played and sung in the parlor: "Let me Rest in the Land of my Birth," "The Sweet Birds are Singing," "You Never Knew Annette." In seeking out the large female reading public, he also ran soft-focus illustrations of curly-locked children with their pets. And every issue featured a fashion plate depicting three or four men and women stiffly dressed in the latest European modes, "*collerette-fichû,* trimmed with Valenciennes lace," "*Corsage en gerbe,*" "*Douillette* . . . wadded, and lined with pink *gros de Naples.*"

The *Graham's* diet was hardly palatable to Poe, who came to detest what he later called "the contemptible pictures, fashion-plates, music and love tales." But after a layoff in salaried work of about eight months he needed employment, and Graham offered him eight hundred dollars a year, an amount he said he considered "liberal" and accepted with "great pleasure." He and Graham also liked each other. Impressed by both Graham's decency and his business enterprise, Poe considered him a "g[en]tlemanly personage" as well as "a man of capital." On his side, Graham had praised Poe's plans for the "Penn" in the newspaper which he also published, the *Saturday Evening Post*. In announcing Poe's arrival on the staff, in late February 1841, he remarked editorially that "Mr. POE is too well known in the literary world to require a word of commendation." So for only a few weeks more than his usual one year, Poe often found himself at Graham's top-floor office on Third and Chestnut streets, the hub of the city's newspaper and magazine publishing district.

Although listed as an editor, Poe did little editorial work. The magazine's tastes differed sharply from his, and the real editor was Graham, who knew his audience well, suffered none of T. W. White's reservations about his own judgment, and carefully chose material for the issues himself. Poe handled some correspondence and occasionally solicited contributions from important writers, but mostly he checked final proofs and wrote the reviews. For separate payment, usually four dollars a page, he also supplied tales. Graham issued from the same office both his magazine and his newspaper (with attendant *"confusion,"* Poe observed), and Poe occasionally contributed to the *Post* as well.

Although Poe's circumscribed role allowed him none of the personal editorial control he now sought through the "Penn," his writing for *Graham's* again created fascination and enjoyment, and surely helped boost the magazine's subscriptions. Through four issues he revived the popular cryptographical series he had begun in *Alexander's Weekly Messenger*. He later said that he became "absolutely overwhelmed" with challenges and requests, placing him in a dilemma: "I had either to devote my whole time to the solutions, or the correspondents would suppose me a mere boaster, incapable of fulfilling my promises. I had no alternative but to solve all." He estimated that, time being money to him, he spent more than a thousand dollars solving ciphers, to prove he could. His proud sense of personal power was obviously at stake, for he boasted to a friend (preposterously), "Nothing intelligible can be written which, with time, I cannot decipher."

As he had been hired to do, Poe also published several book reviews in each issue. Although he announced in his "Penn" prospectus that he had outgrown "causticity," his tomahawking style had earned him employment and was relished by many editors and readers who encouraged him to lay on. Graham perhaps was one of these, for he usually did not restrain Poe's bloodletting. In the pages of *Graham's,* Poe could thus print the review of Rufus Dawes that Burton had refused to publish, mangling Dawes's poems as "speciously bedizzened with a tinselly meaning well adapted to the eyes of the rabble"; could mutilate the author of *Powhatan,* who "never committed a greater mistake in his life than when he fancied himself a poct"; and could demolish Cornelius Mathews's *Wakondah; The Master of Life,* for having "*no* merit whatever; while its faults . . . are of that rampant class which, if any schoolboy *could* be found so uninformed as to commit them, any schoolboy should be remorselessly flogged for committing."

For every ten writers Poe cut up, it should be said in his favor, he fostered the reputations of two or three others. And most of what he had to review came nowhere near his high standard of stylistic clarity and precision. As a commercial reviewer of American books in 1840, he was usually annihilating gnats, which is what makes most of his criticism, although not his standards, uninstructive and tiresome. Beginning with his work for the *Southern Literary Messenger,* too, even his most slam-bang reviews contain in passing some thoughtful and original comment on literary art, making a piecemeal *ars poetica.* About style, for instance, he remarks here or there on how the transition from subject to subject "never fails to test the power of the writer," on adapting tone to fluctuations of the fictional action, on the importance of differentiating words that have "closely-approximating meanings." Many such by-the-way teachings brighten Poe's critical harangues. Viewed whole, his literary judgments are, as Henry James remarked, "pretentious, spiteful, vulgar; but they contain a great deal of sense and discrimination as well."

Far more important, Poe believed that one of the "leading errors" of American criticism was its "excessive *generalization.*" His casual remarks about specific matters like simile offered concrete standards of literary taste and judgment to his American audience. The country's arts indicated clearly enough an appreciation of its huge plains, boundless lakes, and immense territory. Poe however wished to bring a sense of beauty to a country that had so far conceived only sublimity. Despite his many-ways repeated contempt for the mob, and his own ambivalence over winning a popular success, he never wished to confine the experience of beauty to a social or intellectual elite. He understood his critical role to be in part pedagogical, that of explaining his refined and well-articulated aesthetic principles to his readers, so that they could form meaningful judgments of their own. The time was receptive, for all the leading American magazines were engaged in teaching Americans what to prefer in landscape, music, clothing, architecture, and decor, as he had done in his own "Philosophy of Furniture." Using *Graham's* as his forum, he now took it on himself to serve as the arbiter of American literary standards, a Tastemaker.

Within the first six months of 1842, Poe published amid the fichus and sentimental songs of *Graham's* three classic critical essays. They offered American readers a clear and sophisticated understanding of the function of criticism, and of the nature of fiction and poetry. In his "Exordium" he distinguished literary criticism from other literary forms and other exercises of judgment: "Criticism is *not,* we think, an essay, nor a sermon, nor an oration, nor a chapter in history, nor a philosophical speculation, nor a prose-poem, nor an art novel, nor a dialogue. In fact, it *can be* nothing in the world but—a criticism." He advised readers to look to criticism for an analysis not of the moral, political, or philosophical meaning of a work, but of its formal qualities: "we would wish, in a word, to limit literary criticism to comment upon *Art*. A book is written— and it is only *as the book* that we subject it to review. With the opinions of the work, considered otherwise than in their relation to the work itself, the critic has really nothing to do." True criticism was for Poe evaluative, not interpretive, an assessment of the work's "*mode* or vehicle" according to purely aesthetic criteria.

These included correctness—the precision of a writer's grammar, diction, and prosody—but more important the criterion he explained in reviewing Nathaniel Hawthorne's collection *Twice-Told Tales*. Poe valued the tale highly, considering it, next to the "rhymed poem," the literary form in which the "highest genius" might most advantageously exert its powers. Its compactness made possible both high excitement in the reader and maximum artistic control by the writer. Defined as a "short prose narrative, requiring from a half-hour to one or two hours in its perusal," the tale could be read in a single session, absorbing the reader until the end, without "external or extrinsic influences" to disturb its effect. (For the same reason, Poe argued that "a long poem is a paradox.") And the brevity of the tale allowed the writer to strive for that "unity of effect or impression" which Poe commended as a supreme criterion of aesthetic judgment.

Poe had touched on the idea in several earlier reviews. He drew on August Wilhelm Schlegel's often-invoked terms *Einheit des Interesse* (unity of interest) and *Gesammt Eindruck* (totality of impression). Following Schlegel's ideas closely, he wished to cultivate in American readers sensitivity to the adaptation of imagery, sentence rhythm, characterization, indeed every facet of the tale, to its single "preconceived effect" of horror, passion, sarcasm, or whatever. In his well-known formulation, if the writer's "very initial sentence tend not to the outbringing of this effect, then he has failed in his first step. In the whole composition there should be no word written, of which the tendency, direct or indirect, is not to the one pre-established design." Only works that aim at adapting each element to the other and subordinating them all to a single effect can produce, Poe observed, the "fullest satisfaction." Ignoring religious, political, or similar concerns, the discriminating reader should judge the work intrinsically and relationally, considering for instance whether its rhythm at a particular place enhances the action being narrated, and whether both promote the overall effect. "The true critic will but demand that the design intended be accomplished, to the fullest extent, by the means most advantageously applicable."

In a review of Longfellow's *Ballads and Other Poems,* Poe also attempted to clarify for his audience the nature of poetry, although here his instruction was more abstract, as well as highly personal. He used Longfellow as an example of the poet who, mistakenly, "regards the inculcation of a *moral* as essential." Beginning with the introduction to his 1831 volume of poems, Poe had often argued against the view that the end of literature is instruction, a misconception he associated with Wordsworth and the Lake poets. Now he told American readers not to look to poetry for discursive truth, including morality. Poetry can dramatize moral issues, but the poet is no essayist reasoning and preaching about virtue. Rather, and exclusively, poetry aims at representing Beauty. He had in mind not the lesser beauty of nature but what he called "supernal" beauty, "the beauty above." Poe's attempts to formulate this idea, and the related concept of Imagination, can also be traced back through many of his important reviews and poems to his earliest work. Some untitled stanzas in his 1827 volume already speak of earthly beauty as a foreshadow of the afterlife, "a symbol and a token, / Of what in other worlds shall be." Such a view of poetry as tied to the realm of spirits had of course intimate meaning for Poe, but was by no means exotic to his readers, so much environed by the hope of eternal life as to take for granted the depiction of heavenly rewards and reunions in countless engravings, tracts, and sermons. As he told his audience now, the poet attempts to express his anticipation of what eternity may be like. What inspires the poet, in his fine phrase, is "a prescient ecstasy of the beauty beyond the grave."

Belonging "solely to Eternity," this otherworldly beauty evades representation. The poet or artist can at most attempt to suggest it by combining forms of earthly beauty in novel ways, not all of them equal in truth or power. Tantalized by the differences, Poe tried in many essays and reviews to distinguish the merely entertaining combinations invented by the Fancy (such as Drake's armored shrimp) from the profounder combinings of the Imagination, which impart glimpses and echoes of deathlessness. He explained to his readers that the art which most nearly approaches the supernal is music, because the human attempt to combine beautiful sounds approximates the actual conditions of the afterworld: "In the soul's struggles at combination [of sound] it is . . . not impossible that a harp may strike notes not unfamiliar to the angels." It is because of this link between men and angels that rhyme and rhythm, verbal modifications of music, are essential to poetry, which Poe finally defines as the "Rhythmical Creation of Beauty." His definition casts light on his statement to a friend that "I am profoundly excited by music," for it is through the music of poetry that we reach out to the departed.

In these and in his other reviews, Poe treated criticism as a work of education. He did not talk down to readers of *Graham's,* but instead offered them real training in aesthetic judgment. His most thoughtful notices set a level of popular book reviewing that has remained unequalled in America, and that led George Bernard Shaw to call him "the greatest journalistic critic of his time."

Poe also stepped up his campaign to topple the ridiculous, billboard-size picture of the American literary scene dreamed or schemed up by "hyper-patriotic" readers and the corrupt critical-publishing establishment. As he travestied it, "Our fine writers are legion. Our very atmosphere is redolent of genius. . . . All our poets are Miltons." The reality was less glamorous: "it cannot be gainsaid that the greater number of those who hold high places in our poetical literature are absolute nincompoops." Poe felt that the moment was suited to righting the upside-down literary world, for by now America had actually gained some intellectual and artistic independence: "In fact we are now strong in our own resources. We have, at length, arrived at that epoch when our literature may and must stand on its own merits, or fall through its own defects."

Poe moved more systematically than before toward making a fair and comprehensive evaluation of American literary achievement past and present. He began clearing the ground in the fall of 1839, with an essay entitled "American Novel-Writing," conceived as the introduction to a series of articles surveying and rating the American novelists, beginning with Charles Brockden Brown. He got no further with the series, but over three issues of *Graham's* he published a lengthy article on "Autography," expanding his earlier, similar article in the *Messenger.* He reproduced in facsimile the signatures of 128 American writers, with a thumbnail evaluation of each, observing of Bryant, for instance, that "The *picturesque* . . . is equally deficient in his chirography and in his poetical productions." The piece created a minor sensation. E. P. Whipple, a well-read New England critic, berated Poe for setting up as a critical "censor general": "It is certainly a collossal [*sic*] piece of impertinence for Mr. Edgar A. Poe to exalt himself into a literary dictator, and under his own name deal out his opinions on American authors as authoritative." Whipple correctly divined Poe's long-range purpose, which was, Tamerlane-like, to subject the whole of American letters to his critical authority, ranking his contemporaries according to their deserts, establishing a native literary canon, and giving America a literary order.

Poe remained far better known as a critic than as a poet. He did, however, publish in *Graham's* slight revisions of "The Coliseum" and "To Helen," as well as a reworked version of "Israfel," whose seraphic lutanist illustrates the doctrine that poetry seeks, however despairingly, to emulate the ideal beauty of the afterworld and may be really linked to it through music. On the other hand Poe's reputation as a writer of fiction now nearly matched his reputation as a critic. Writing prolifically and sometimes at his best, he supplied a tale nearly every month to Graham, including one of surpassing novelty and influence. Again they differed greatly in manner and matter: "Never Bet Your Head," a spoof on moralistic fiction and critics who seek the moral out; "The Island of the Fay," a lyric fantasy on death as absorption into a universe which is a single sentient whole, thus allows nothing to die; "A Descent into the Maelström," a hair-raising tale of sensation that records the narrator's thoughts and feelings as he churns in an immense whirlpool, terrified of being swallowed in the maelstrom's "jaws," a variant of the omnipresent teeth and fangs.

Several of the tales draw directly on details of Poe's life. Uncle Rumgudgeon in "A Succession of Sundays" promises to award his nephew his portion of one hundred thousand pounds, but only when three Sundays come together in one week. With his hobby of being *"a man of my word,"* the bibulous and controlling uncle is a sharp caricature of John Allan—the John Allan, at least, whom Poe once accused of 'shuffling' him off for money and being "not very often sober." The nephew has been passed on to Rumgudgeon in childhood: "My parents had bequeathed me to him as a rich legacy, in dying." Like Allan too, the uncle disapproves the boy's literary pursuits: "my own inkling for the Muses excited his entire displeasure." Through the nephew Poe recalls his own long battles in squeezing money from Allan, when persistence usually paid off: "Against all attacks upon his purse he made the most sturdy defence; but the amount extorted from him, at last was always in exact

ratio with the length of the siege and the stubbornness of the resistance." Poe manages to show that three Sundays can indeed come
together in one week, but the slight joke provides less interest than
does the demonstration of his continued wrestling with feelings about
his foster father.

"Eleonora" (published in *The Gift,* an annual) forms with "Ligeia"
and "Morella" a trio of tales on fidelity to the deceased One Beloved. This time, however, Poe rendered the theme in terms of his
relation to Sissy and Muddy. The possibly mad narrator, Pyrros, has
married in youth his fifteen-year-old first cousin Eleonora, with whom
he dwells in intimate isolation from others, and not only with her:
"we lived all alone, knowing nothing of the world without the valley,—I, and my cousin, and her mother." When still a "child," Eleonora dies, grieved to think that Pyrros will transfer his love to
someone else. He vows never to do so, but later falls even more
deliriously in love with and weds "the angel Ermengarde." Like the
deceased Ligeia and Morella, Eleonora returns, but not in another
body or for revenge. Instead she revisits Pyrros, in a brief concluding paragraph, as a sweet nocturnal voice releasing him from his
promise of fidelity, "for reasons which shall be made known to thee
in Heaven." Justly enough, Poe considered the tale "not ended so
well as it might be." The problem may have been lack of conviction, for the miserably unconvincing ending suggests Poe's unwillingness even to imagine absolution from the duty of perpetual remembrance.

Poe combined the tale of sensation with the visionary fiction popular at the time to produce his remarkable "The Colloquy of Monos
and Una," one of what he called his "series of *post-mortem* reveries."
Its speakers are two lovers rejoined a century after their deaths.
The larger part of their discourse presents one of Poe's most elaborate imaginings of what it feels like to die, decay, and then survive
in an altered form of consciousness throughout eternity. Monos describes these processes to Una stage-by-stage and step-by-step,
without reference, however, to Christian ideas of immortality, a soul,
or heaven; as Poe remarked of the colloquy, "Its philosophy is
damnable."

Monos describes first a stage of synesthesia immediately after
bodily death, in which taste and smell are confounded, vision becomes sound, and consciousness is reduced to sensation, unme-
diated by the "deceased understanding." From this "wreck and chaos
of the usual senses" arises a new, sixth sense, which Monos de-

scribes as a "mental pendulous pulsation," a sense of duration independent of events, without effort or object. With the decay of the body the consciousness of being some-thing gives way to a sense of being some-where: "The narrow space immediately surrounding what had been the body, was now growing to be the body itself." In one of his strongest finales, Poe celebrates how the self is at last reconstituted as an itself-conscious portion of place and time:

> For *that* which *was not* [i.e., the mouldered body]—for that which had no form—for that which had no thought—for that which had no sentience—for that which was soulless, yet of which matter formed no portion—for all this nothingness, yet for all this immortality, the grave was still a home, and the corrosive hours, comates.

Poe's language vibrates with many dyings and separations in proclaiming how one can depart yet still have a "home" and "co-mates," how one can perish, yet remain. His erasure of the boundary between existence and inexistence appears also in the colloquists' names, Monos and Una, which insist that things are one, and illustrate the fact by expressing a distinction without a difference. The reassurance Poe hoped to gain from this and the other forced conceits of his colloquy, presented in defiance of his own "corrosive" experience, was that you can never lose yourself or your home or the people you love.

In the April 1841 issue of *Graham's,* its surprising title commanding attention amid verse on "An April Day" and music to "Oh! Gentle Love," appeared Poe's "The Murders in the Rue Morgue," inaugurating one of the most popular and entertaining forms of fiction ever conceived.† Poe had few if any precedents for such "tales of ratiocination," as he called what he attempted. The only near model was Voltaire's 1748 *Zadig,* whose hero performs a few similar prodigies of analysis, among them identifying some sand tracks as those of a lame bitch with pendent dugs and long ears who recently had puppies. But crime was much in the air, as its prevention became a pressing urban need. Following the establishment of the world's first professional police force in London, twelve years before Poe's story, American cities increased the number and pay of policemen and fostered scientific police work. The new and sensational "penny newspapers" printed records of criminal trials and reported bloody suicides and murders. Writing a story much concerned with newspapers, Poe picked up many hints from such articles—and from the several items in past and current American periodicals concerning razor-wielding apes.

Despite its thorough novelty, the story is also in many ways the natural continuation of Poe's earlier fiction, especially its Gothic element. As a scholarly recluse of "illustrious" descent inhabiting a gloomy mansion, Dupin is in effect a Parisian Roderick Usher. Literary historians point out that the inner logic of Gothicism demanded such a development, for all its fantasies of rotting houses and animate wall-hangings are mysteries, and Dupin is the hero the Gothic world needs to understand and oppose its evils. His mental processes in solving mysterious crimes, moreover, differ little from the kind of thinking by which Poe had often before made the impossible possible, showing readers how an empty chest might contain a chess player, how there might be three Sundays in one week, or how a thing might cease to exist, yet be. Only now Poe treated his inventions not as the stuff of narrative but as puzzles to be solved by a cunning intelligence. He was acutely aware that, since he knew the answer to the mystery in advance, the effect of analytic brilliance was illusory. Concerning "The Murders in the Rue Morgue" he asked: "where is the ingenuity of unravelling a web which you yourself . . . have woven for the express purpose of unravelling?" The story owes its brilliant effect, as he observed, to being "written backwards." His comment, incidentally, shows how deeply rooted was his concept of the tale of ratiocination in his theory of unity of effect. No other kind of fiction illustrated so clearly the writer's need to choose from the beginning some one outcome or effect, and to adapt every element of the narrative to it. In a larger sense all of Poe's tales are tales of ratiocination.

A 'short story' rather than a (less realistic) 'tale,' "The Murders in the Rue Morgue" also fully develops the urban note recurrent in Poe's fiction since his settlement in Philadelphia. Sallying forth at night into Paris, the narrator and Dupin seek matter for observation in "the wild lights and shadows of the populous city." Their roving recalls Poe's carefully written "The Man of the Crowd," published only months before, where one of his many recuperating invalids stalks an intriguing, down-at-heels old man through London's bazaars and slums, hoping to understand him and his activities—another urban analyst exploring the anonymous city to solve mysteries representative of urban life. (He finds that he cannot "read" the old man, figuring the uninterpretability of Poe's own enigmatic writing, and self.) The crime in the Rue Morgue is also a distinctly urban horror. "The face was fearfully discolored," a physician reports, "and the eye-balls protruded. The tongue had been partially bitten through. A large bruise was discovered upon the pit of the stomach, produced, apparently, by the pressure of a knee." Despite its page-one brutality, however, the story curiously reflects Poe's lifelong yearning for domesticity. The narrator and Dupin exist in cozy and exclusive seclusion, "within ourselves alone," an odd couple conforming to nineteenth-century ideas of the perfect marriage. Far from challenging cultural norms, Poe in many tales and poems delineated in a transmuted form the culturally-feminine values endorsed in the sickliest sentimental fiction of his day, upholding them much as he did in his own life.

For all its Parisian setting and ratiocinative plot, too, "The Murders in the Rue Morgue" is essentially one more of Poe's many works about the deaths of women, studded with associations and recollections. Like Muddy and Sissy, the murder victims are a mother and her young daughter who lead an "exceedingly retired life"; they are named "L'Espanaye," which contains Poe's initials twice and also nearly makes *Allan*. Dupin's situation and his long discourse on the subtleties of whist seem shadowed by much in John Allan's world— its own games of whist, business correspondence with Paris firms, advice that young employees learn the French language. In quoting the testimony of a laundress named Pauline Dubourg, and placing the sailor's orangutan in the "Rue Dubourg," Poe also fetched from memory the Misses Dubourg to whom he had gone to school while the Allans lived in London. He perhaps once more acknowledged William Henry Leonard Poe in creating still another Augustus character, this time C. Auguste Dupin himself. The most fascinating of these name bridges to the past appears when Dupin miraculously reconstructs the complex chain of personal associations that has led his companion to think of Chantilly, a cobbler who became "stage-mad," turned actor, and was lampooned for his attempts. *Chantilly* echoes *Dan Dilly,* the name once mockingly bestowed on another stage-mad actor, David Poe (a name that perhaps echoes in *Dupin* as well).

Poe understatedly called "Murders in the Rue Morgue" "something in a new key." In fact, few other works can claim its authority in giving rise to a new popular genre and setting its conventions. At the time Poe wrote, the word *detective* did not exist in English, and for many readers his story had the delight of profound novelty:

"it proves Mr Poe to be a man of genius," said the Pennsylvania *Inquirer*. "At every step it whets the curiosity of the reader, until the interest is heightened to a point from which the mind shrinks with something like incredulity; when with an inventive power and skill, of which we know no parallel, he reconciles every difficulty, and with the most winning *vraisemblance* brings the mind to admit the truth of every marvel related." Since Poe wrote, it would almost seem from their incalculable numbers that detective stories, novels, and films have been read or seen by nearly everyone. Poe's successors took over many large and small features of his work: the depiction of the detective as a detached gentlemanly amateur not associated with the police; the use of a first-person narrator who is not the detective (such as Dr. Watson or Archie Goodwin); the formulaic opening intrusion of the outside world on the detective's comfortable bachelor quarters or office; the general investigative pattern and presentation of clues to the reader; and not least the crime committed in a locked room, of which the first example is "The Murders in the Rue Morgue" itself.

Resignation from Graham's; *F. W. Thomas; Virginia's Illness; "The Mask of the Red Death."*

FALL 1841 – SPRING 1842

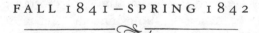

Graham's prospered from Poe's association with it. By March 1842, a year after he joined the staff, the magazine announced that it was issuing 40,000 copies monthly and planned soon to issue 50,000. The sevenfold increase over the initial 5,500 subscribers reflects the development of a new mass reading market that was reshaping American publishing. The leap seemed "astounding" to Poe, and surprised Graham himself. Poe in a little more than the same time earned around $1,200, more per month than he had ever earned before. The publication of such ingenious works as his cryptography series and "The Murders in the Rue Morgue" also brought him, atop his acclaim as a fearless critic and master of German horror, a popular reputation as a literary wizard. Pleased with the image, he several times compared himself to a magician.

Still, Poe's work left him dissatisfied. After only four months on the magazine he confided that "notwithstanding Graham's unceasing civility, and real kindness, I feel more & more disgusted with my situation." Among other disappointments, he learned that his popularity did not translate into literary power. When he tried to persuade Lea and Blanchard to bring out an updated collection of his tales, to include "The Murders in the Rue Morgue" and seven other recent works, they replied that the economic climate remained discouraging and that the firm had yet to earn back its expenses in publishing *Tales of the Grotesque and Arabesque*. He also still disdained the vapid tone of *Graham's* and grumbled over his salary, which, given the magazine's huge success, he considered "paltry." And Graham paid him less for his freelance work than he paid other well-known contributors. The cost of being a hired hand had also become clear to him when at Graham's behest he softened several critical judgments in "Autography" and regretfully ended up praising some "ninnies." In his writing, as nowhere else in his life, Poe could have things on his own terms, and he chafed at having to write under supervision. "To coin one's brain into silver, at the nod of a master," he complained, "is to my thinking, the hardest task in the world."

Even while seeing to his editorial chores and supplying tales to the magazine, Poe looked to other sources of income and satisfaction. Although he had put aside the "Penn" when he joined Graham, the hope of having his own periodical stayed alive. It occurred to him to issue his magazine in partnership with Graham, even while remaining with him as an editor. His employer, he observed, was a lawyer, an experienced magazine publisher, and a gentleman of social standing with "ample pecuniary means." Graham would furnish the means of production, he for his editorial work and list of subscribers to the "Penn" would receive a half interest in the magazine, provided he could enlist the contributors he sought. In meeting this condition he began writing to Irving, Cooper, Bryant, Longfellow, and a few other prominent writers, most of whom he had publicly or privately lambasted, describing his plans for the "Penn" and asking them to write for it regularly. He invited them to submit one piece a month for a year, pledging themselves to write for no other American magazine during that period, for a fee they might suggest themselves.

Poe intended to launch the magazine in January 1842. But by the fall Graham had lost interest in the project and dropped it, holding out some possibility of reviving it the following summer. Poe partly blamed himself for Graham's change of heart: "I was continually laboring against myself. Every exertion made by myself for the benefit of 'Graham['s],' by rendering that Mag[azine] a greater source of profit, rendered its owner, at the same time, less willing to keep his word with me." Considering the spectacular rise in subscriptions, he said, it was no wonder Graham had been "tempted to leave me in the lurch." Urging patience on himself, he began thinking of publishing the "Penn" elsewhere, perhaps in Baltimore, Washington, or even out West. But he felt certain of one day having a journal under his own control. "*If I live,* I will accomplish it, and in triumph."

The hope of a different sort of escape from literary drudgery arose for Poe through his friend Frederick W. Thomas, one of the most popular novelists and songwriters of the 1830s and 1840s. They seem to have first met in Philadelphia in the late spring of 1840, at a time when Poe was beginning to attract ardent admirers, persons deeply affected by his works and by what they glimpsed or imagined of his personality. Years earlier, however, Thomas had become "intimate," he said, with Poe's brother Henry in Baltimore, "and rather rivals in a love affair." There he probably also met Muddy and Virginia, with whom he maintained an affectionate relationship. He hankered after literary fame such as Poe had achieved, often declared his "profound respect for your genius and acquirements," and sometimes wrote to him three or four times a month. A bachelor who doted on his sisters, Thomas had a dark side. He had been injured by a childhood fall, grew up using crutches, and as an adult walked with the aid of what he called a "contrivance," by one account an "iron leg" that screwed on. He often joked about his lameness, however, and even presented himself as a *bon vivant,* someone who liked "the smack of a pair of rosy lips" as well as "the smack of wine." The latter at least may be believed, for perhaps at this time and surely a few years later, Thomas fought a sizable drinking problem, alternately lecturing on temperance and falling off the wagon.

The way out of literary toiling that Thomas offered to Poe was through politics. A student of human nature with serious political involvements, Thomas had traveled around Louisville, St. Louis, and New Orleans speechifying on behalf of the Whig party and recently had obtained a clerkship in Washington under the new Tyler administration, sifting applicants to the secretary of the treasury. The post allowed him time to begin writing a novel of current events. He suggested that Poe might enjoy such a sinecure himself, at the handsome annual salary of $1,500: "How would you like it," Thomas wrote to him in the spring of 1841. "You stroll to your office a little after nine in the morning leisurely and you stroll from it a little after two in the afternoon—homeward to dinner and return no more that day." More than that, the situation even pampered a literary man: "You have on your desk every thing in the writing line in apple-pie order—and if you choose to lucubrate in a literary way why you can lucubrate."

Poe felt, as he said, "*really* serious about the office." But he also wondered whether an application from himself to the president would succeed. He counted up his assets. He had "some slight personal acquaintance" with Tyler, probably through his work on the *Messenger*. Like Tyler, he was also a Virginian (at least, he noted, he called himself one, having lived most of his life in Richmond). And as a writer he saw an inclination in the new government to "cherish letters." Although his connection with politics was minimal to say the least, he also told Thomas that he was ideologically correct and had "battled with right good will" for Tyler's predecessor, President Harrison, "when opportunity offered," as it could hardly often have done. He apparently did not convince himself of his power to sway the president, for in his postscript he suggested that Thomas might be able to get him the job by showing Tyler his letter, and speaking of him as editor of the *Messenger*.

But Thomas doubted his own power as well. He recommended instead that Poe "slip on here" to Washington and see Tyler in person, or else appeal to him through someone prominent, such as J. P. Kennedy, then serving in Congress. Thomas's suggestion brought to Poe's mind how Kennedy had fostered his career and tried to lift him from his depression during hard times in Baltimore: "the first true friend I ever had—I am indebted to him *for life itself*." He asked Thomas to see Kennedy for him, and urge Kennedy in turn to speak with the secretary of war (considering his stay at West Point) or some other cabinet member, or even Tyler himself. But he impressed on Thomas how desperate he had again become to get around the chancy wages of literary work: "I would be glad to get almost any appointment—even a $500 one—so that I have something independent of letters for a subsistence." Fond and admiring of Poe, Thomas considered it unthinkable that he might not win a place. A man with Poe's "merits," asking "only for a clerkship," he said, must eventually succeed, though competing with "thousands of applicants." But in July Thomas tried twice to speak to Kennedy, without success. He discovered that the hurlyburly of a new administration so much busied public men that they became unavailable. It worked against applicants, too, that President Tyler was opposed to removing those currently in office.

Thomas's efforts for Poe dragged on through the fall and winter, and into the New Year. Late in August he did manage to see Kennedy, who expressed willingness to help Poe any way he could. But by the end of November, not having heard from his former patron a long while, Poe all but gave up on him: "he has treated me somewhat cavalierly," he decided, "professing to be *a friend*." Thomas persevered, promising to speak with Tyler (who occasionally invited Thomas for dinner), and meanwhile sending news that Washington was buzzing over Poe's cryptography, "really you have no idea of the talk it makes here." He did get to speak about Poe to Tyler's son Robert, who wrote poetry and valued Poe's critical opinions, Thomas said, more than those of any other critic in the country. But no job came of this either. Poe took the opportunity to ask Thomas whether he might at least interest Robert Tyler in the "Penn." Like *Blackwood's,* he fancied, the magazine "might be made to play even an important part in the politics of the day." But Thomas replied that Rob could do no more for Poe's projected magazine than write for it. At least for the moment, Poe gave up the hope of resettling himself in Washington.

Neither the "Penn" nor a government clerkship rescued Poe from *Graham's,* but in the beginning of April 1842, after about thirteen months on the staff, he resigned. He at last did so, he told Thomas, in "disgust with the namby-pamby character of the Magazine," and because the salary "did not pay me for the labor which I was forced to bestow." He nevertheless thought he would contribute occasionally in the future, and parted on fairly good terms with Graham, whom he now characterized as "very gentlemanly, although . . . exceedingly weak." It annoyed him, however, that Graham failed to print a notice of his resignation, leaving readers to assume that material in the spring issues had been written by him. A Boston newspaper attributed to Poe and drubbed one such poorly written review, a mistake the more insufferable as the reviewer had imitated Poe's manner. Incensed, Poe composed an anonymous reply which he asked his friend Snodgrass to run editorially in his Baltimore newspaper. As if speaking for himself, Snodgrass would assert that Poe did not, indeed could not, have written the review; among other things, he could not spell "liaison" as "liason" or commit the "grammatical blunders" that stamped the review as another's, "the handiwork of some underling . . . imbued with th[e] fancy of *aping* Mr Poe's peculiarities of diction." He also asked Snodgrass to denounce, again as if speaking for himself, Graham's failure to make known his resignation as "an act of the rankest injustice."

Graham at last made public Poe's resignation in his July issue, with "warmest wishes for success in whatever he may undertake." By then Poe felt that although he had no quarrel with Graham, neither did he have for him any "especial respect" nor wish to communicate with him "in any way." Graham became a cautionary tale. With the enormous success of his magazine while he was still under thirty years old, he moved to a large house, drove a fine team of horses, and with a fortune estimated at one hundred thousand dollars bought up other magazines and newspapers, then ventured into stock speculation and copper mining, began neglecting his publishing business, and by the age of thirty-five lost most of what he had owned.

One other event fed into Poe's dissatisfaction, and probably into his break, with Graham. The son of a celebrated singer, Poe always encouraged Virginia's own taste for singing, even providing a piano for her. Muddy claimed that she became a "perfect musician." Around the middle of January 1842, some two months before Poe quit *Graham's,* Virginia while singing began to bleed from her mouth. As Poe described the incident, she had "ruptured a blood-vessel." More accurately, she was hemorrhaging from her lungs, in an early stage of "death-in-life," as many people then referred to tuberculosis.

For nearly two weeks Sissy remained dangerously ill. A neighbor later remembered that the family's small house was ill-suited to caring for an invalid. Virginia lay in a cramped room, "a little place with the ceiling so low over the narrow bed that her head almost touched it." Except when fanned she was hardly able to breathe. Her condition frightened Poe. Graham, likely speaking of this time, later recalled visiting the family and noticing how Poe hovered watchfully about Virginia, reacting to her slightest cough with "a shudder, a heart-chill that was visible." However unpromising its beginnings, Poe's marriage to Sissy had brought him enough tranquillity to feed himself, stay for the most part sober, and come close to acquiring the name he wanted. Living cut off from the world with his cousin and aunt, as isolated and inbred as the Ushers and Dupins in his own tales, he also became, as he also greatly desired, the center of an exclusive and doting attention. With Virginia's hemorrhaging he therefore suffered "agony," as he told Thomas, "for you know how devotedly I love her." To Poe's neighbor it seemed that he meant to bar altogether from consciousness what the bleeding portended. He was so "sensitive and irritable," as she remembered the time, that no one in the sickroom dared speak. He allowed nothing to be said about the danger of Virginia's dying: "the mention of it drove him wild."

But Poe could not conceal from himself either his alarm or his attempt to deafen himself to it. Both penetrate two brief, intense Gothic tales he wrote in the wake of Sissy's hemorrhaging, published in *Graham's* just before and just after his resignation. "Life in Death" is told by a Virginia-like narrator, so "desperately wounded" as to forbid any attempt to reduce his fever by "letting blood." His tale concerns a painter and his also Virginia-like bride, "a young girl just ripened into womanhood" whom he has subjected to long, debilitating hours of posing in creating an oval portrait of appalling *"lifelikeliness."* The painter will not or cannot accept his bride's dying. He *"would* not see that the light which fell so ghastily in that lone turret withered the health and the spirits of his bride"; he *"would* not see that the tints which he spread upon the canvass were drawn from the cheeks of her who sate beside him." As he puts his last stroke on the painting, in the chillingly undercutting last sentence of the tale, the painter comes face to face with his bride's death but still cannot or will not recognize it: "And then the brush was given, and then the tint was placed; and, for one moment, the painter stood entranced before the work which he had wrought; but in the next, while yet he gazed, he grew tremulous and very pallid, and aghast, and crying with a loud voice, 'This is indeed *Life* itself!' turned himself suddenly round to his beloved—*who was dead*. The painter then added—'But is this indeed Death?' "

The painter's evasions and self-deluding questions are, however, scorned in "The Mask of the Red Death." Here the countryside is ensanguined by a devastating Virginia-like pestilence: "Blood was its Avatar and its seal—the redness and the horror of blood. There were sharp pains, and sudden dizziness, and then profuse bleedings at the pores." Like the painter, Prince Prospero (twice or thrice *Poe*) tries to banish the hemorrhaging doom that he sees. His country half wasted by disease, he retreats behind the welded doors of his luxurious castle with a thousand friends who like him consider it "folly to grieve, or to think." As the "brazen lungs" of a Virginia-like clock ominously toll, in a Virginia-like chamber with "blood-tinted panes," they frolic: "There were buffoons, there were improvisatori, there were ballet dancers, there were musicians." For all the barricade of lofty walls, iron gates, and welded doors, there appears among the masqueraders a "shrouded" figure, its grave-clothes "dabbled in *blood*." Prospero draws his dagger but falls dead. "And now," Poe writes, "was acknowledged the presence of the Red Death." The prince's death-denying friends drop one by one "in the blood-bedewed halls of their revel." Poe's strong copulative ending acknowledges, as he rarely did, that there can be no barrier against the fear of death, because none against death, that death knows no limit: "And Darkness and Decay and the Red Death held illimitable dominion over all."

Steeped in blood, disease, and injury, and concerned with the attempt to defend oneself against what is most feared and unwanted, both tales seem to play out Poe's refusal to hear anything about the danger of Sissy's condition. They perhaps also suggest why the mention of it, as his neighbor said, "drove him wild." For his depictions of the deaths of the painter's young bride and of the masked revelers seem infused with unforgettable shades, phantasms of a miniature portrait, of *The Tempest,* of a world of music, costume, and dancing. Like Prospero and moreso like the painter who refused to see that his painting depended on the death of a young woman, Poe too had insisted on the *"lifelikeliness"* of death, had tried to imagine how death might not exist, although it certainly did, and not only existed, but also made possible his art.

Virginia's Health;
The Custom House;
The "Stylus";
Washington.

SPRING 1842–JUNE 1843

Virginia's condition went up and down, and with it Poe's own spirits. The "white plague," as tuberculosis was sometimes called, accounted for up to a fourth of all deaths in nineteenth-century
America. It often seized the young, keeping anxious parents alert
to its symptoms in their children: the lassitude and coughing, the
blue-veined eyelids and rouged-looking cheeks. Although common,
debilitating, and dreaded, tuberculosis killed without disfiguring the
body or destroying the mind, even imparting to its frequently young
victims a bright-eyed flush that might be mistaken for loveliness.

Graceful, dark-haired and dark-eyed, Sissy at the age of nineteen
and a half retained her fleshy prettiness. But visitors noticed, as one
of them wrote, that "the rose-tint upon her cheek was too bright."
Continued night sweats also left her weakened. She found some
relief by drinking what Poe called "the Jew's Beer," evidently a
local brew also taken as a remedy. But after some unnamed domestic accident destroyed her supply of the beer, her perspiration and
cough returned. Poe managed to get some more, however, and she
immediately improved. By the middle of May 1842, he rejoiced in
her prospects: "my dear little wife is much better, and I have strong
hope of her ultimate recovery." But only a few weeks later he found
her suddenly worse, "again dangerously ill with hemorrhage from
the lungs," and he despaired: "It is folly to hope."

Poe watched closely and recorded the cycles of recovery and relapse. By the end of June he thought Sissy slightly improved, "and
my spirits have risen in proportion," he wrote. But by the end of
August she was much worse, leaving "scarcely a faint hope of her
recovery." Two weeks later she was a little better again, "slightly
improved," he said: "Perhaps all will yet go well." But only a week
or so after that, his friend Thomas visited and concluded from her
pale complexion, her deeply lined face, and her cough, or so he

recalled later, that she was "the victim for an early grave." Less is known of her condition during the new year, 1843, although "much better" that spring, Poe recorded, she went outdoors several times and took long walks. This improving turn may not have lasted long either, for in the early fall he seems to have put enough money together to visit Saratoga, presumably to see whether the mineral springs might provide long-term relief. After only a few days of "discouraging inquiry," by a later account, he learned only that even if Virginia could weather the move he could not afford it, and he returned to Philadelphia "utterly cast down in spirit."

It may have been hope of finding a more healthful environment for Virginia that also prompted Poe to leave his cramped portion of a house. The family moved once sometime before May 1842, then again sometime before September to Coates Street, in the rural outskirts of the city. They moved again sometime before June 1843, to 234 North Seventh Street, apparently a Quaker neighborhood in the suburban Spring Garden district. One visitor recalled the place as no more than a lean-to set against a wall of the four-story brick house of a neighbor, a wealthy Quaker plumber. Built of painted planks, it consisted of only three rooms, although there may have also been a garret with closet, and a garden. As always, whatever of neatness and refinement could be imposed on such dwellings came from Muddy. A neighbor recalled seeing her in the mornings clearing the front yard, washing the windows and stoop, even whitewashing the palings. Physically robust, she was also fortified by the religious faith that filled her talk and letters with pious expressions and led her to become a communicant of Trinity Church in Philadelphia.

Poe had disabling bouts of ill health himself. Perhaps referring to this period, he later commented that because of his suffering over domestic troubles he "nearly succumbed." And if he had indulged himself no further in four years than by a little cider to treat a "nervous attack," as he insisted, his dry period now ended. To medicate his grief over Virginia's illness and allay the anxiety raised by the threat of her death, he began seriously drinking. How much and how often he drank would become a controversial issue among the many persons who later commented on his habits, admirers as well as detractors. Some maintained that he drank in royal plenty, others that owing to his sensitivity to alcohol a single drink intoxicated him, a claim he often made himself. The truth most likely combines the two estimates: after one drink he could not stop. As his sympathetic friend Thomas put it, "if he took but one glass of weak wine or beer or cider the Rubicon of the cup was passed with him, and it almost always ended in excess and sickness." However much Poe drank it was more than he could manage. By one account, his binges brought on a weakening diarrhea, and he sometimes spent the next day or two in bed. Muddy herself later admitted that after a glass or two of wine "he was not responsible for either his words, or actions."

On a trip to New York in June 1842, a few months after Sissy's first hemorrhage, Poe drank himself into an alcoholic amnesia. He went to the city looking for work, and also hoping to get a new collection of his tales into print. He ended up giving a magazine publisher a review lacking half a page of the opening, and otherwise acting strangely enough to make him think the publisher must have formed "a *queer* idea of me." As he usually did, he explained that others had induced or forced him to drink, in this case the New York poet William Ross Wallace, who he said "would insist upon *the juleps,* and I knew not what I was either doing or saying." Probably during this trip to New York he also looked up Mary Starr, once his girlfriend in Baltimore and now a Mrs. Devereux, living across the river in Jersey City. She had spent a pleasant evening with Poe and his family in Philadelphia while he was working for *Graham's.* According to her later and perhaps exaggerated account, Poe went to her husband's place of business in New York to find out the couple's address. Being "on a spree," she said, he forgot the address and made several trips back and forth on the ferry, asking other passengers if they knew where she lived. He did locate her house, and when he arrived cursed her for her marriage and insisted that she did not love her husband, but loved him instead. She offered him a cup of tea, which he drank, but he ate nothing and became "excited in conversation." He also asked her to play and sing for him, and left after Mary sang his "favorite song." But he did not return to Philadelphia. A few days later, Muddy appeared at Mary Starr's house, worried, leaving Virginia at home, presumably, and "almost crazy with anxiety." A search was made, that found Poe wandering in the woods on the outskirts of Jersey City.

Poe tried more than once to laugh off the episode. Writing to his cousin Elizabeth Herring, he treated Sissy's concern as groundless and overprotective. Virginia began to "fret," as he said, because she had not heard from him "twice a day," until she became "nearly crazy," refusing to eat or sleep despite all Muddy could do. "What a thing it is," he commented, "to be pestered with a wife!" But like his drinking itself, the bemused sigh seems to shun the sight and deaden the meaning of Virginia's bleeding. Even leaving aside Mary Starr's account, which perhaps cannot be entirely believed, Poe's experiences in New York were chastening. "I am as straight as judges," he wrote in October, "and, what is more, I intend to keep straight."

Poe's October resolution was gone by May, however. "Poor fellow!," his friend Wilmer remarked to a mutual acquaintance, "he is not a teetotaller by any means, and I fear he is going headlong to destruction, moral physical and intellectual!" Poe learned of Wilmer's gossip, attributed it to envy, and denounced him as "a reprobate of the lowest class." But by the spring of 1843 his drinking was common knowledge around Philadelphia, even a matter for publicity. Writing from Baltimore, cousin William Poe cautioned him that many, "especially Literary Characters, have sought to drown their sorrows & disappointments," discovering worse misery in the bottle itself. William probably had in mind Poe's brother Henry, and perhaps David Poe as well, in reminding him that liquor had been "a great enemy to our family." By the end of the year Poe's drinking earned him an appearance in a temperance magazine. He was presented as a fictional character in one installment of *The Doom of the Drinker,* a serially published novel about a reformed drunk. Its author cast him as one inebriated member of a wine party, a writer and critic whose "fine analytical powers, together with his bitter and apparently candid style, made him the terror of dunces." As depicted, Poe seems out of place among his coarse fellows, a "gentlemanly looking personage . . . [who] would occasionally, under the excitement of the wine, utter some brilliant jests, which fell all unheeded on the ears of the majority of the drinkers."

Poe's drinking may also have been encouraged by his formidable money problems. He coupled Virginia's ill health and his "pecuniary embarrassments" as trials that had "nearly driven [me] to distraction." He was not alone, for the early summer of 1842 had brought widespread fear of an economic crash following an earlier run on the Bank of Pennsylvania. "Everybody has become poor," wrote one Philadelphian; "there is no business, there is no money . . . nobody can pay debts." Poe was determined to legally declare himself bankrupt, and only wished he had done so earlier, as the struggle to stay solvent, he said, had "entirely ruined me." Indeed it left him too broke even to file for bankruptcy, moaning the following month that he was still "*desperately* pushed for money." Out of work, he tried to sell off a lot still owned by Muddy in Baltimore. Wilder ideas for raising cash occurred to him too but went untried: returning to *Graham's,* renting out one of his family's three rooms in Spring Garden, even becoming trained as a lawyer. He could count for little on his writing, even though he published fairly actively in this period (see the next section). As far as can be determined, in the twenty months or so after leaving Graham's employ, he made only about four hundred dollars. And here too he seems to have been sometimes driven to desperate strategies. He offered a tale for publication at half or less the *Graham's* rate, and even tendered it to two publishers at the same time, a frowned-upon practice.

Poe saw the clearest way out of his financial straits in once more trying to obtain a government post. Thomas told him of a new possibility, which he said he had already discussed with President Tyler's son Robert. By now if not earlier, Thomas's proposals to Poe seem to have been solidly grounded; according to the musician John H. Hewitt, the president was "remarkably fond of poetry and music," and Thomas became "the White House poet-laureate." The new plan was to place Poe not in Washington, but in the Custom House in Philadelphia. In fact a dozen or more literary figures of the period found employment in the United States Customs Service, notably Hawthorne, Melville, and the historian George Bancroft. The post promised a subsistence and time for literary pursuits. And Rob Tyler felt confident, Thomas said, that Poe could have the job in two or three months, when vacancies would certainly occur.

Poe's hopes sprang at the prospect. It gave him "new life," he said: "Nothing could more precisely meet my views." In itself, the interest of the president's son in his situation so much pleased him that he boasted of owing his good fortune to "the personal friendship of Robert Tyler." All the same, his frustrations in seeking a government clerkship had made him cautious, and he also asked friends to say nothing about the matter, "for, after all, I may be disappointed." Over the next few months, alongside his alternating anxiety and relief about Sissy, he felt now down and now up about his prospects at the Custom House, telling Thomas in one sentence what he would do "If I do *not* get the app[ointmen]t," and in another sentence "of course I can no longer doubt that I shall obtain it."

Thomas's visit to Philadelphia in mid-September brought out reasons for both hope and doubt. Reassuringly, Thomas said that Rob Tyler genuinely wanted Poe to have the job. Thomas also apparently "hinted," as Poe put it after the visit, that he would be able to get more than enough government patronage to sustain the "Penn" if he published pieces supporting the administration. But even if such opportunities arose, Poe's behavior offered little evidence that he could take advantage of them. Thomas arrived late in the morning, but despite the hour found Muddy busy preparing Poe's breakfast. Several of Poe's acquaintances remarked that one could always tell he had been drinking from his dress: otherwise unfailingly neat, it became unkempt and dishevelled. When Poe appeared, Thomas remembered, "his dark hair hung carelessly over his high forehead, and his dress was a little slovenly." Poe complained of feeling unwell, but it was clear to Thomas that he had been at the bottle. When Thomas "ventured to remonstrate," Poe admitted that he had done some drinking recently, while in New York seeking employment, but "turned the subject off" by telling a dialogue of the Greek writer Lucian.

Thomas and Poe agreed to meet next day, a Sunday, at nine in the morning at the Congress Hall Hotel. The deeply admiring Thomas was a good friend, in Philadelphia on an infrequent visit of the sort the two often corresponded about but managed only rarely. Nevertheless, Poe got drunk, did not show up, and left Thomas waiting for him. Afterward he explained that he had been "taken with a severe chill and fever," too ill to go out, although he would have done so had Muddy and Virginia consented.

Poe now got a taste of useless waiting himself. About three weeks after Thomas's visit, following new municipal elections in Philadelphia, Poe called on the new collector of customs, a man named Smith. He seems at this point to have believed that his appointment was certain, even already arranged, for he came to claim a place for himself. As he recounted the events, he told Smith that as his own was not to be a political appointment, there needed no "political shuffling or lying." He was willing to postpone taking up his post in favor of the genuine "political claimants." Here he spoke more truthfully than in his self-serving earlier statement to Thomas that he had "battled with right good will" for the Whigs, and more candidly still in telling another friend that his own political views had "reference to no one of the present parties." But Poe's gesture of noble disinterest was politically naive. The Customs Service was based on patronage, and often manipulated by its employees for gain. Although President Tyler had opposed the spoils system on principle, when he found that offices were being dealt out to undermine his strength, he decided to cleanse the Philadelphia Custom House of appointees hostile to his adminstration, and directed the secretary of the treasury to make thirty-one changes there. The purge atmosphere made it highly unlikely that a claimant who put himself apart from "present parties" and above "political shuffling," such as Poe, could gain an appointment.

According to Poe, the new collector nevertheless told him to call again four days later, to be sworn in. He did so, but found Smith out. Next day he called again. Smith said he would send a messenger for him, when ready—although it occurred to Poe later that the collector did not think to ask him where he lived. Poe waited almost a month, and when it became clear that nearly all available positions in the Custom House had been filled, he called again. This time Smith did not ask him to be seated, in fact scarcely spoke, but muttered, "I will *send* for you Mr Poe."

Poe waited about another month, until mid-November, when his hopes again rose and again crashed. Philadelphia newspapers had been publishing lists of removals and replacements to the Custom House, in one of which Poe discovered the name of a new appointee, a man named "Pogue." He inquired about the name and learned, he said, that it was really his own, as heard at the Custom House and then garbled by some reporters. Since Smith had twice promised to send for him, he waited two days, expecting to be summoned for his swearing-in. When he heard nothing from Smith, Poe called on him and asked "if he had no good news for me yet." Smith's answer, as Poe reported it, was "No, I am instructed to make no more removals." After Thomas's many assurances that he had the endorsement of the president's son, Poe was astonished. He protested that he had heard from Robert Tyler, through a friend, that Smith had been asked to appoint him. Smith answered, "roughly" according to Poe, "From *whom* did you say?" Poe repeated Robert Tyler's name. "From *Robert* Tyler!" Smith said, "hem! I have received orders from *President* Tyler to make no more appts and shall make none." Yet the "scoundrel" collector then acknowledged, Poe said, that he had in fact made an appointment since the president's instructions.

The affair not only shut Poe out of a much-needed job that had seemed within reach. It also struck woundingly at his feeling of entitlement, his sense, as he put it, of "the station in society which is my due." As in the topsy-turvy literary world, and earlier in the home of John Allan, the recognition that belonged to his high-mindedness and superior abilities had gone instead to his inferiors. "You can have no idea of the low ruffians and boobies," he told Thomas, "who have received office over my head." His own motives in seeking the post had been uncorrupted by base considerations, since he had no political ambition and the job was a "gratuitous favor" from Robert Tyler. "If Smith had the feelings of a gentleman, he would have perceived that from the very character of my claim—by which I mean my *want* of claim—he should have made my appt. an early one." He decided that Smith was not really a Tyler man but a covert agent of Tyler's opponents. Smith's real offense was against the president's son, who had requested his appointment: "this insult," he assured Thomas, "is not *to me*."

But this seemingly final defeat left Poe even worse off than before. Hourly expecting employment in the Custom House, he had neglected his literary and other business. "You cannot imagine the trouble I am in," he told Thomas. Only one chance remained: if Thomas again put the matter before Robert Tyler, the president's son might possibly persuade his father to write a few lines ordering Smith to give him the place. As it happened, however, with the new year, 1843, Smith himself was removed from office. Poe then decided to go to Washington himself, to speak directly with Robert Tyler and with the president.

Here Poe's hopes of a government sinecure intersected with his plans for the "Penn." While anxiously eyeing the Custom House and the newspaper lists, he had all along been trying to launch his magazine, as an alternate or additional way of ending his money problems. Only a month after he spoke of declaring bankruptcy, he began anew trying to build a list of subscribers, looking especially toward the South and the West. He also explored the possibility of bringing the "Penn" into existence with the aid of a single, wealthy financial backer.

Poe believed he saw such an ally in one of his correspondents, the Georgia poet Thomas Holley Chivers. Chivers all but worshipped Poe. That seems a just description of someone who later called Poe "a god—an Exile from Heaven" and described his body as "a beautiful Myrrhine Fabric, clear as crystal, filigreed all around with *bazzi relievi* of Amaranth, full of Ambrosia." The two men were the same age, and had much else in common. Born into a wealthy, slave-owning family, Chivers at the age of nineteen married the sixteen-year-old daughter of his father's brother, who deserted him within the year. His remarriage was also to a sixteen-year-old girl, with whom he had a daughter whose birth he had foreseen eight years earlier in a vision: "she came down to me from Heaven in the form of an Angel. She bore a golden harp in her hand—of Heavenly Gold—on which she played most ravishingly." Chivers shared also with Poe a hatred for the herd, "the *No-Man,*" and a contempt for the world "because it is not only a sycophant, but a slave—feeling no sympathy for the Beautiful and the True."

Poe asked Chivers for his help, as "a gentleman of education & similarity of thought and feeling." He said he wished Chivers to "join" him in the "Penn," a word that left unsaid whether Chivers should consider himself partner, co-editor, or whatever, nicely chosen to invite interest while safeguarding his plan to retain exclusive control over the magazine. Poe was more definite in asking whether Chivers could, in helping him produce the first few issues, "command about $1000." The commercial prospects he held out were both stunning and fantastic. His initial 500 subscribers would mushroom before the end of the second year, he was certain, into 5,000. That would mean an income, for each of them, of some $10,000. And it was only a beginning: "there is no earthly reason why such a Magazine may not, eventually, reach a circulation as great as that of 'Graham's' at present—viz 50,000."

But Chivers was in no condition to think of the "Penn." He read the invitation, he later told Poe, while his three-year-old daughter sat smiling on his knee, the child whose birth he had foreseen. Her closeness and the expectation of joining Poe filled his heart with "joyful antisipations." But only a week or so later, the child died, "on the very hour of the very day on which she and I were born," Chivers said. He described the event for Poe in the distinctively Chiversian biblical-mystical-transcendental-typological-philosophical idiom that makes much of his writing seem stagey and insincere: "Hope, with her snowy wings, soared, beckoning me away, up to the gates of heaven. . . . the beautiful saintly winged dove which soared so high from the earth—luring my impatient soul to wander, delighted, from prospect to prospect—has been wounded in her midway flight to heaven by the keen icy arrows of Death."

Early in 1843 Poe did find someone to "join" him, Thomas C. Clarke, publisher of the Philadelphia *Saturday Museum*. By Poe's criteria Clarke made the ideally perfect partner, someone to finance the magazine and give him a half interest in it, without asking for a say. Poe was happily cynical about what he had achieved: *"at last . . .* the great object—a partner possessing ample capital, and, at the same time, so little self-esteem, as to allow me entire control of the editorial conduct." He now felt, however, that the "Penn" was "somewhat too local" a title, and decided to call the magazine the "Stylus." Under its new name it was to be no less ambitious than before. Poe and Clarke signed an agreement with the notable illustrator Felix O. C. Darley, who would thereby furnish no fewer than three illustrations a month. In a new printed prospectus, Poe assured potential readers that the illustrations would be in the "highest style of Art" and that for typography, paper, and binding the "Stylus" would "far surpass all American journals of its kind." Under his sole management it would differ from the *Messenger* and from *Graham's* in being "more *unique,*—more vigorous, more pungent, more original, more individual, and more independent." Guided only by "the purest rules of Art" it would ignore mere commercial reputation and instead employ only "the loftiest talent." Furthering his long-range plan to fix an American literary canon, he promised to begin with a series of sketches of American writers, investigating carefully and impartially the claims of each.

Poe went to Washington in March, on two missions. He intended to find additional subscribers and possibly government patronage for the "Stylus," and to speak with Robert Tyler and the president himself about a post at the Philadelphia Custom House. The city struck most foreign visitors as raw. Although many found the startlingly white marble Capitol building, elevated on a hill, magnificent, they also invariably criticized the flourishing slave trade, the copious tobacco-spitting, and above all the surreal environment of vacant spaces and waste ground that made Washington seem but a spectacular ghost town. Charles Dickens described the place he saw during his visit in 1842: "Spacious avenues, that begin in nothing, and lead nowhere; streets, mile-long, that only want houses, roads and inhabitants; public buildings that need but a public to be complete; and ornaments of great thoroughfares, which only lack great thoroughfares to ornament." To the English geologist Sir Charles

Lyell, the city had "the air of some projector's scheme which has failed."

Poe's trip to the Capitol City began in difficulty and ended in disgrace. In "sad need of means" simply to get there, he tried to call in thirty dollars owed him for his writing, and raised some money from Clarke. Arriving about March 8, he called on Thomas at his room in Fuller's Hotel. Although he "depended" on Thomas to achieve his ends, as he said, he found his friend in bed with a fever, covered with the marks of cupping and blistering treatment, unable to go out. Thomas had meant to present him in person to Robert Tyler, but instead gave him a letter of introduction. The delay caused by Thomas's illness, and greater expenses than he had foreseen, quickly exhausted Poe's funds. After only two or three days he was hastily writing back to Philadelphia, asking Clarke for ten dollars more and promising that "you will find your account in it—twice over." He based his prediction on having in a short time already managed to get some subscriptions, and a promise from Robert Tyler to give him an article for the "Stylus." "I believe," he wrote, "that I am making a *sensation* which will tend to the benefit of the Magazine."

Poe was making a sensation, but to no one's benefit. As he had once been drawn to the regulated life of a soldier and cadet, Poe had learned to thrive with some self-discipline under the supervising care of Muddy and Virginia. Away from them for any time he tended to flounder, as had happened during his New York trip the summer before, and happened again now. Thomas turned Poe over to a mutual friend, the Washington journalist and poet Jesse Dow, who had held a clerkship in the Post Office Department. Dow reported that Poe, on his first evening in Washington, became "overpersuaded to take some Port wine." The second day Poe stayed "pretty steady," but then became, off and on, "quite unreliable."

Just what Poe did is known only through his own later and somewhat obscure allusions to "peccadilloes" committed after too much port and bourbon. When drunk he seems to have worn his cloak inside out, left a barber shop without paying, and insulted, acted petulantly toward, or otherwise offended his friend Thomas, as well as Dow and his wife, Rob Tyler, and several other persons. Dow worried that Poe was not only making a fool of himself but also alienating people who could hurt him with the president and prevent his appointment. Poe suffered from his spree physically too. An old acquaintance who ran into him, and loaned him fifty cents for a meal, recalled that he seemed "*un homme blessé*—seedy in his appearance and woe-begone," trying to preserve a gentlemanly appearance but looking "used-up." Thomas said that his physician had to attend Poe for several days.

Like Thomas, Dow esteemed Poe as representing "the highest order of intellect," and wished to protect him. Feeling obliged to get Poe returned to Philadelphia, but tied up with business and family matters, he wrote to Clarke, urging Poe's new partner to come to Washington and see him safely back home. If Clarke could not come, Dow promised to see Poe on board a Philadelphia-bound train himself, although he feared Poe might stop off in Baltimore "and not be out of harm's way." He also urged Clarke to say nothing about Poe's condition to Virginia, given her "bad state of health."

After a week or so in Washington, Poe did manage to get back safely to Philadelphia, apparently on his own, indulging himself in Baltimore by no more than a shave and breakfast. He found Muddy waiting for him at the station and immediately went home. Virginia remained in about the same health as when he left but, as had happened during his New York escapade, deeply upset by his absence, "her distress of mind has been even more than I had anticipated." Although he had somehow succeeded in picking up a few subscribers for the "Stylus" in Washington, he was concerned that Dow's dire report on his condition may have undermined Clarke's confidence in him. After a warm bath and supper, he went on to see his publishing partner, ready with an excuse.

As Poe recorded their interview, Clarke was surprised to see him. From Dow's letter he had come to believe that "I must not only be dead but buried & [he] would as soon have thought of seeing his great-great-great grandmother." Poe offered Clarke a cover story he had schemed up before leaving Washington, with the compliance of Dow and Thomas. In reality, he explained, he had been "a little sick." Dow knew that in the past he had been "given to spreeing upon an extensive scale," and became "unduly alarmed." When he learned that Dow had sent out a needlessly disturbing call for help, the yarn went, he thought it best to return to Philadelphia, sound enough, as one could see. By Poe's account, Clarke swallowed this tale whole: "He said my trip had improved me & that he had never *seen me looking so well*!!!" However gleeful over bamboozling his partner, toward whom he felt little more than contempt, Poe still suffered from having been "a little sick." Next day he took medicine and stayed home.

Poe also tried to repair the damage done in Washington. In a jocular tone, he wrote to Dow and Thomas, asking them to transmit his apologies all around for the offense he had given, "to the Don, whose mustachios I *do* admire after all," to a "Mr Fuller" (perhaps the owner of the hotel) for "making such a fool of myself in his house," to Dow's wife, "for the vexation I must have occasioned her," and to Thomas himself, who should not believe that "I think all I said." As usual he depicted himself as having been coerced into drinking: "I should not have got half so drunk on [Mr. Fuller's] excellent Port wine but for the rummy coffee with which I was forced to wash it down." Half-jokingly he asked Dow and Thomas to tell the president's son that if he got the Custom House job he would join the Washingtonians, a temperance society: "I think it would be a feather in Mr. Tyler's cap to save [fr]om the perils of mint julap—& 'Port wines'—a young man of whom all the world thinks so well & thinks so remarkably well of himself." The lame Thomas enjoyed man-talk with Poe about drinking and women; he went along in laughing off the episode and denying that Poe, "as we say in the West, had 'broken for high timber.'" But Thomas was also keen enough to detect in Poe's jests, as he said later, "a great deal of heartache." As for his thinking well of himself, Poe spoke more penetratingly later in the year, in response to a comment that he must pride himself on solving ciphers: "I feel little pride," he said, "about anything."

Having patched things up as best he could, Poe renewed his twin quests for a dependable income. Set on propping Poe up after his fall, Thomas relayed news that President Tyler himself had spoken "kindly" of him, while the president's son John had urged his father to give Poe an office in Philadelphia. "John had heard of your frolic from a man who saw you in it," Thomas added, "but I made light of the matter when he mentioned it to me, and he seemed to think nothing of it himself." Encouraged, Poe wrote directly to Rob Tyler, requesting a formal recommendation. Trying to advance the "Stylus" at the same time, he wrote off to the son-in-law of the recently deceased T. W. White, hoping to buy the *Southern Literary Messenger*'s subscription list, although he felt the heirs might be prejudiced against him "on account of my quitting White"—as he described his having been let go, with relief. He also tried to get a contribution for the first issue, now scheduled for July 1843, from Nathaniel Hawthorne. Hawthorne respected Poe's writing and at first agreed to contribute at five dollars a page, promising even a drawing of his head, made by his wife, for Poe's projected series on American writers. But he had trouble working during the summer, and finally had his apologies sent to Poe with the explanation that at present he had "no more brains than a cabbage."

Whether Rob Tyler sent Poe a recommendation for the Custom House is unknown, but Poe's efforts for the "Stylus" were wasted on Clarke, who had had enough. Financially pinched himself, and likely put off by Poe's drinking, he withdrew from the partnership in May, wiping out Poe's financial support: "my Magazine scheme has exploded—or, at least, I have been deprived, through the imbecility, or rather through the idiocy of my partner, of all means of prosecuting it for the present." Still he thought he might resume the plan next year, under "better auspices."

Reputation after Leaving Graham's; *Charles Dickens and England; Lowell's* Pioneer *and Boston.*

CA. APRIL 1842–APRIL 1844

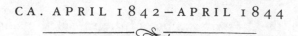

At the age of thirty-three Poe still made a slight figure, about five feet eight inches tall, slender, with black somewhat curly hair, rather fair complexion, gray eyes that he himself described as "restless." Many of those who knew him remarked on the thinness and delicacy of his lips and, particularly, on the extreme breadth of his forehead, so broad that in profile he seemed to be growing bald. The ordeal of witnessing Sissy's alternating progress and deterioration apparently intensified his customarily quiet, sad, and unsmiling manner. His somber state can be glimpsed in the daguerreotype probably taken in Philadelphia in 1842 or 1843 (Illus. 11). He was enthusiastic about the accurate representation afforded by the new process, then only three or four years old, which he acclaimed as "the most important, and perhaps the most extraordinary triumph of modern science." He appears clad in a greatcoat, rigidly posed while seated in a chair. His face is clean shaven except for side-whiskers. The darkness around his eyes and in the cleft may be owing to the state of the daguerreotype, known only in a magazine reproduction of 1905. But a tense sorrow seems apparent enough in the chevron of emerging furrows that track his cheeks, and in the lipless mouth, a crimped ridge of woe.

The face Poe presented his reading public, however, differed from that of the nearly bankrupt, office-seeking *"homme blessé"* on Pennsylvania Avenue. Despite worries, frustrations, and defeats following his resignation from *Graham's,* he worked hard at his writing and tried in different ways to advance his reputation. With literature in America losing its amateur character and becoming more and more a business, a writer's life and appearance proved effective in merchandising his works. Poe produced two biographical sketches of himself that helped to elaborate and fix the public's image of him. The first appeared in April 1842, as a headnote to three of his poems included in a popular anthology, *The Poets and Poetry of America.* The second appeared two weeks before his Washington fiasco, in a newspaper published by Clarke, the Philadelphia *Saturday Museum.* Clarke illustrated the article by a crude engraving of a husky and pompous-looking Poe, based on the daguerreotype. (Understandably, Poe complained that no one in his family recognized the "caricature": "I am ugly enough God knows, but not *quite* so bad as that.")

Although the *Museum* was one of the so-called mammoth newspapers, what Poe mocked as "giant hebdomadala," his biography covered the entire front page, measuring some two and a half feet long by two feet wide. It excited so much interest that Clarke reprinted it on the front page of a later issue, and announced plans for a separate edition on fine white paper. The edition never appeared, but abridged versions of the (auto)biography were published in Boston and Baltimore, familiarizing many readers with the story of Poe's life, as he wished them to perceive it.

Poe transformed his many abandonments, rejections, and postponements into a tale of personal distinction, glamour, and power. "EDGAR ALLAN POE," the *Museum* account begins, "is descended from one of the oldest and most respectable families in Baltimore." The distinguished ancestry of Edgar Allan Poe—one of extremely few contemporary appearances of his full name—begins with his great-grandmother's family, "noted in British naval history, and claiming kindred with many of the most illustrious houses of

Great Britain." It continues in his paternal grandfather, the intimate of Lafayette, "who, during his last visit to the United States, called personally upon the general's widow." It extends even to his marriage, for through Virginia Clemm, Edgar Allan Poe became "closely connected with many of the best families in Maryland." This account of distinguished heritage ignores the fact that General David Poe ran a dry goods store and appeared on the Baltimore court records in 1805 as an insolvent debtor, but that is only one of its dozens of distortions. In granting himself respectable birth and solid upbringing, Poe also informed his readers, among other fabrications, that his mother and father died "of consumption within a few weeks of each other, while on a visit to Richmond"; John Allan "adopted" him and "made a point of informing every one that he intended to make him his sole heir"; he "went to school for 5 years to the rev. Doctor Bransby" (in reality, two and a half years); studied at the University of Virginia for "3 years" (eight months); and afterward "found no difficulty in obtaining a letter of appointment" to West Point.

In having his readers know that he was not only high-born but also adventurous and many-ways accomplished, Poe gave the dignity and permanence of print to boasts or lies he had so far confined to conversation, correspondence, and daydreams. Born in 1811, the young Poe reaped "first honours" at the university, took the poetry *and* the prose prizes in the *Saturday Visiter* contest, " 'headed' every class" at West Point, leapt "the distance of twenty-one feet, six inches, on a dead level, with a run of twenty yards." Later, his *Pym* "ran through many English editions"—two, actually—and he produced "a work of fiction, in two volumes, under a *nom-de-plume,* never acknowledged;—also, two papers, on American topics, for a Parisian critical journal—with one or two anonymous articles in a British periodical." (No trace of such works has ever appeared, and it is unlikely that Poe ever wrote them.) As many friends and acquaintances already knew, a large reading public now learned how he swam the James River ("Byron's paddle across the Hellespont, was mere child's play in comparison") and after trying to join the Greek cause "made his way to St. Petersburg, in Russia, where he became involved in difficulties, from which he was extricated by . . . the American consul." (Fanny Allan, readers also learned, died "while POE was in Russia.") Poe's tales of his Byronic past entranced at least some readers, for one newspaper reviewer praised the *Museum* biography as an account of a "truly eventful life."

Poe sought other means of making himself and his name familiar to the public also. He looked to London, where he was little known, at a time when many readers measured the success of an American book by its reception in England. Aside from the English edition of *Pym,* only four of Poe's tales had been reprinted there, all by *Bentley's Miscellany* in 1840, without permission or payment. He saw a chance to bolster his transatlantic presence, in the visit to Philadelphia in March 1842 of Charles Dickens. Poe probably gave more space to reviewing the works of Dickens than to those of any other novelist. He saw Dickens as having achieved what he aimed at himself, securing a large popular audience without compromising his aesthetic standards. In reviewing Dickens he laid aside his tomahawk for the laurel wreath, calling one or another of his works "unequalled," "surpassingly fine," "supremely excellent," according him unique praise for his affecting pathos, technical brilliance, and profound originality. By his genius Dickens had, he said, "perfected a standard from which Art itself will derive its essence, in rules." In one instance he reinforced his own reputation as a logical wizard by reviewing the opening chapters of Dickens's serialized *Barnaby Rudge* and correctly forecasting the novel's outcome; he claimed to have known by page seven that later chapters would reveal the idiot Barnaby as the murderer's own son.

Poe's enthusiasm was of course nearly universally shared, for Dickens, at the age of thirty, was the most famous writer in the English-speaking world. When he visited America he received the most lavish and tumultuous reception the country had ever granted an English visitor, although to some it seemed an orgy of national self-reproach to the inferiority of American culture. "Let us dine Boz—let us feed Boz," one Philadelphia newspaper asked, "but do not let us lick his dish after he has eaten out of it." In fact, exhausted from an earlier "Boz Ball" in New York, attended by over two thousand persons in a pavilion laid out with tableaux of his novels, Dickens declined being honored at a public dinner in Philadelphia, explaining that his stay in the city would be short, and that he wished rather to see the people. Some local politicians, however, hoping to win votes by introducing their constituents to him, placed newspaper ads announcing that, on the morning of March 8, Dickens would shake hands publicly, for an hour. When the time arrived, Dickens was surprised to discover the offices and halls of his hotel, as well as the streets in front, mobbed with Philadelphians. He refused his advertised role, until convinced by the hotel owner and some others that his refusal would start a riot, then found himself shaking hands and exchanging words of introduction for several hours.

Moved by both admiration and the hope of becoming better known in England, Poe wrote to Dickens at the beginning of his visit, requesting a meeting. He sent along some books and papers, likely a copy of *Tales of the Grotesque and Arabesque* and perhaps some of his reviews of Dickens's works. Dickens suggested that Poe come to his hotel between half-past eleven and noon. According to Poe, they had "two long interviews," probably on March 7. He discussed with Dickens the backward state of American poetry and read to him Emerson's poem "To the Humble Bee." He also asked Dickens to use his influence to find an English publisher for a revised edition of the *Tales,* as Dickens promised and then tried to do. But the result for Poe was disappointment followed by resentment. Returned to England, Dickens mentioned Poe's work to several publishers he knew, including the noted Edward Moxon, who had issued poems by Wordsworth and Tennyson, but they all declined the republication. Dickens sent Poe Moxon's reply, adding that the only consolation he could offer was his belief that no "collection of detached pieces by an unknown writer," even an Englishman, would be likely to find a London publisher at the moment. He also assured Poe that he thought of him with "pleasant recollection" and remained ready "to forward your views in this country."

Poe may not have been entirely convinced. In January 1844, a few months before he left Philadelphia, the London *Foreign Quarterly Review* surveyed five books of American poetry, to demonstrate that "with two or three exceptions, there is not a poet of mark in the whole Union." The exceptions included Emerson and Longfellow, but otherwise the reviewer condemned American poets severely, provoking rebuttals in American periodicals and much speculation about the writer's identity. Poe was taken aback by the reviewer's comment about himself: "Poe is a capital artist after the manner of Tennyson; and approaches the spirit of his original more closely than any of them." Outraged by the not-to-be-borne charge of imitation, Poe also believed that he heard in the review echoes of the conversation about American poetry he had had with Dickens in Philadelphia, including its particular praise for Emerson's "The Humble Bee." He felt certain, as some others did also, that Dickens was the anonymous reviewer: "the article affords so strong internal evidence of his hand that I would as soon think of doubting my existence." He adjusted his estimate of the English writer accordingly, to include Dickens's "much ignorance and more spleen."

Poe made one other, also unsuccessful, attempt to get some tales published in London. This time he approached the English poet Richard Henry Horne, a friend of Elizabeth Barrett and author of an epic poem, *Orion.* Poe reviewed the work in *Graham's* in March 1844, calling it superior in its description of hell to *Paradise Lost,* and altogether "one of the noblest, if not the very noblest poetical work of the age." His reckless praise is the more surprising in view of his oft-repeated disapproval of long poems. But he perhaps simply meant to butter up Horne, to whom he wrote flatteringly the same month, sending a manuscript version of his tale "The Spectacles," revised for British readers. He asked Horne to help him sell the work in London. Horne thanked him for his "noble and generous" tribute, but explained that he was at the moment the subject of "attacks and jeers in magazines and newspapers." He believed he might be able to help Poe when the storm blew over, he said, and the manuscript was meanwhile "lodged in my iron chest." It never got much further. When he read Poe's tale, Horne revealed later, "my heart of hope sank within me." He realized that London publishers would find this tale of a young man's near marriage to his eighty-two-year-old great-great-grandmother repugnant. As he suspected, when he offered it to several editors he received nothing beyond "an uplifted eyebrow, or the ejaculations of a gentleman pretending to feel quite shocked." Poe ultimately had his wish, in a form not to be wished for; the following year, the American version of the tale appeared in London in the less squeamish *Lloyd's Entertaining Journal,* pirated and unpaid for.

Poe also sought to extend his reputation into New England. He had been rankled by what he and others considered the smugness of many New England writers and their claim to social, moral, and literary superiority over other regions of the country. He planned in the "Stylus," he said, to "make war to the knife against the New-England assumption of 'all the decency and all the talent.'" His indignation, however, was mixed with envy for the wealth, learning, and solid respectability New England represented, qualities that also made the region not a ready market for fiction such as his. Boston periodicals said little about his work and occasionally attacked him, and until 1843 none had undertaken to introduce one of his tales into print.

A chance for Poe to enter the New England literary world on

acceptable terms came through the announcement, in November 1842, of plans for a new Boston literary magazine. It would be published by James Russell Lowell, a bearded, long-haired twenty-three-year-old Harvard graduate who was planning to give up his law practice and devote himself to literature. Several of Lowell's poems had appeared earlier in *Graham's,* where Poe criticized qualities of clumsiness and conventional moralism in his work, but also credited him with imagination and prophesied that he would stand "*at the very head* of the poets of America." Poe also approved Lowell's plans for his magazine. They resembled his own design for the "Stylus" in promising care for typography and engravings, and in attempting to provide high-quality writing for a discriminating audience, "a rational substitute," as Lowell put it, "for the enormous quantity of thrice-diluted trash, in the shape of namby-pamby love tales and sketches, which is monthly poured out to them by many of our popular magazines."

Through Lowell's *Pioneer*, Poe registered his voice in Boston. Upon the announcement of the new magazine he offered to furnish a short piece each month on whatever terms Lowell could afford. Lowell already had him in mind as a possible contributor, for he admired Poe as "almost the only *fearless* American critic" and considered no other poet's early poems as good, Shelley's being "nearest, perhaps." He invited Poe to send anything he wanted, except harshly personal reviews, at ten dollars for each piece, with the promise to pay more later. He accepted from Poe a tale, a poem, and an essay for his first three issues, beginning in January 1843: "The Tell-Tale Heart" (which another Boston periodical had rejected), "Lenore," and "Notes Upon English Verse," Poe's first article on versification, later to be elaborated into a major essay on the subject. Poe boasted the accuracy of his ear and his close study of prosody; in a taste-making spirit, he offered working definitions of a few key terms, such as "rhythm," that might help readers identify and judge poetic achievement.

Poe's entry into Boston proved brief. The rapid multiplication of American magazines had brought a high mortality rate, and the *Pioneer's* third issue was its last. Lowell was left $1,800 in debt, and soon undergoing eye surgery as well. Sympathizing with Lowell's aims, Poe identified with his plight. When he thought of Lowell possibly going blind, he told the young man, "I grieved as if some dreadful misfortune were about happening to myself." He consoled him also for the death of the magazine, as "a most severe blow to the good cause—the cause of a Pure Taste." Poe's own reverence for "the cause" here brought out all his generosity and idealism. Although he had not been paid the badly needed thirty dollars due him for his work, he told Lowell to "give yourself not one moment's concern about *them*." Despite immersion in his own distress over Virginia's health, too, he sent Lowell long encouraging letters, praising his poetry and looking forward to sometime meeting him, as would, disenchantingly, happen.

In addition to its appearance in Lowell's Boston *Pioneer* and the New York *Ladies Companion*, Poe's work stayed before American readers through a variety of Philadelphia magazines, newspapers, and annuals, such as the *Saturday Museum*, the *Dollar Newspaper*, the *United States Saturday Post*, the *Saturday Courier, Godey's Lady's Book*, and *The Gift*. His poetry remained relatively little known and commented upon. "The truth is that the higher order of poetry is, and always will be," he told Chivers, "in this country, unsaleable." The long *Saturday Museum* biography included a reprinting of twenty of his poems, amounting to the first edition of his poetry in a dozen years. These revised texts of "Israfel," "The Sleeper," and other poems contain permanent versions of some of his most memorable lines. "To the beauty of fair Greece / And the grandeur of old Rome" (1831 edition) became:

> To the glory that was Greece,
> And the grandeur that was Rome.

Other famous lines in "To Helen" underwent similar transformations, from "Lo! in that shadowy window-niche" (1841 *Graham's* version) to "Lo! in yon brilliant window-niche," and from "The folded scroll within thy hand!" to "The agate lamp within thy hand!"

Poe included reprintings of two new poems, only recently published, both of which seem prompted by Virginia's illness. "Lenore" treats the question of appropriate response to the passing of a beloved young woman, "the most lovely dead / That ever died so young!" One speaker in the dialogue calls for customary ceremonies of mourning ("And let the burial rite be read— / The funeral song be sung"), and questions the other speaker's lack of emotion: "Guy de Vere, / Hast *thou* no tear? / Weep now or nevermore!" But de Vere explains that, in dying, his young fiancée has been delivered from the "damnéd earth," and he refuses to mourn: "tonight / My heart is light— / No dirge will I upraise." His light-heartedness, however, disowns the depth of his feeling, as the first speaker observes: "thou art wild / For the dear child." Guy de Vere exemplifies many figures in Poe who similarly shift or suppress their feelings, especially the need to mourn. The choice of the heroine's name perhaps evidences such displacement in Poe himself, resounding as it does with one of the middle names of William Henry Leonard, who often seems linked in Poe's mind with lost and grieved-for women.

"The Conqueror Worm" also seems to join present apprehension and past grief, by its sustained identification of death with the theater. Bitterly here, life is a musical "play of hopes and fears," the harsh but unmeaning destinies of its human actors plotted by voracious unbeings:

> . . . *vast formless things*
> *That shift the scenery to and fro,*
> *Flapping from out their Condor wings*
> *Invisible Wo!*

The real "hero" of the tragedy, however, is not metaphysical but physical, the "blood-red" worms that eat the "mimes" with their "vermin fangs." Poe's close contact with Virginia's illness was perhaps depriving him of long-accustomed ways of nullifying death, for the poem's heavy accents preclude the fearful consolations of the returned-from-the-grave or the half-alive, and proclaim an irresistible finality:

> *Out—out are the lights—out all!*
> *And, over each quivering form,*
> *The curtain, a funeral pall,*
> *Comes down with the rush of a storm. . . .*

Here, as rarely happens in Poe's work, dead means dead.

Although lacking a regular forum for his critical opinions, Poe managed to publish perhaps ten book reviews and miscellaneous pieces. They included two series of original but understandably unsigned conundrums in the *Saturday Museum,* about half of them simply repeated from his 1839 series in *Alexander's Weekly Messenger.* Such jokes seem to have been popular in Poe's household, for Muddy collected and wrote out specimens like "What was Eves [*sic*] bridal dress? A bear skin." Those Poe published were more pedantic, requiring his explanations, and oddly personal:

What difference is there between a regular sot and the purple convolvulus?

The one is drunk every day, and the other is blue only every other day.

Why is a bleeding cat like a question?

Because it's a catty gory. (category)

Why is the Pacific like an inhabitant of Languedoc?

Because it's a languid ocean (a Languedocian.)

With his proclaimed ability to write in a variety of styles, Poe prided himself on his humor, although it rarely found subtler expression than heavy-handed parody, slapstick with a brutal edge, and phunny phellow wordplay featuring flatulent names like Flatzplatz. He more convincingly remarked of himself that he was "not 'of the merry mood.' "

During the last two of his fertile years in Philadelphia, Poe published some important and popular fiction. In "The Pit and the Pendulum," an intense tale of sensation, the storyteller recalls his feelings in an airless unlit dungeon, where torturers from the modern Spanish Inquisition subject him to thirst and starvation, swarms of rats, closing walls of red-hot metal, and a razor-sharp pendulum that descends inch by inch threatening to slice him to death. In an entirely different mood, "Raising the Wind; or, Diddling Considered as One of the Exact Sciences" comically retails some deft swindles, or 'diddles,' by which con men collect nonexistent tolls or sell sofas that do not belong to them. The vain young hero of "The Spectacles," already mentioned, refuses to wear glasses while courting an exquisite young woman; when he is at last made to don them, he sees that she is in reality his octogenarian great-great-grandmother, padded, bewigged, and toothless. In an again contrary, supernatural key, "A Tale of the Ragged Mountains" tells how Augustus Bedloe, a young man who in this case has the vacant eyes of a "long-interred corpse," wanders during his morning ramble near Charlottesville into a deepening mist and soon finds himself among cocoa trees and sacred apes in the Indian city of Benares, trying as a British officer to quell an insurrection; during the frantic fighting he is shot in the right temple and slain by a poisoned arrow in the shape of a "creeping serpent." Returned to Charlottesville, Bedloe learns that such a battle historically happened in 1780, with the death of an officer named Augustus Oldeb, his own name reversed. A few days later, having caught cold, he is treated by the application to his right temple of a medicinal leech, which turns out to be of the poisonous black sangsue variety and kills him.

Poe also broadened his studies of crime and detection. The mad narrator of "The Tell-Tale Heart" describes how he murdered and dismembered an old man, but then, tormented by the louder and louder sound in his ears of a beating heart, frenziedly confesses his crime to the police. In a second psychological study of domestic violence and guilt, with supernatural overtones, the alcoholic narrator of "The Black Cat" fancies that his cat is avoiding his presence. He hangs the animal, first cutting one of its eyes out with a penknife. After a night of drinking, he takes into his home a second black cat closely resembling the first, but soon grows to hate, and dread, this animal as well. In attempting to kill it with an ax, he instead cleaves through the head of his wife, and bricks up her corpse in his cellar wall. When the police come to his house four days later, he leads them to the cellar and in a "phrenzy of bravado" raps on the brickwork, ostensibly to show its solid construction. A howl from inside leads the police to throw down the wall, revealing the wife's decayed corpse and, mistakenly immured with her, standing on her clotted head, the black cat, "with red extended mouth and solitary eye of fire."

In "The Mystery of Marie Rogêt," another story of a woman's murder, Poe brought back Chevalier C. Auguste Dupin, this time to solve the murder of a Parisian grisette whose corpse has been found floating in the Seine. Poe closely based the story on a sensational contemporary case, the actual slaying in 1841 of a New York "cigar girl" named Mary Rogers, whose bound body was found floating in the Hudson River. In having Dupin analyze the Paris murder, Poe intended at the same time to challenge current theories that Mary Rogers had been killed by a gang, and more generally delineate "the true principles which should direct inquiry in similar cases." Dupin ingeniously analyzes the available evidence and concludes that Marie-Mary was the victim of a single murderer, a sailor of some rank with a swarthy complexion who was her lover or close associate, and who transported her corpse in a boat, later removing its rudder. Ratiocination, cryptography, and (attempted) comedy combine in "The Gold-Bug," a tale that won Poe first prize of one hundred dollars in a story contest sponsored by the *Dollar Newspaper*. Here a reclusive, island-dwelling South Carolinian, William Legrand, accidentally discovers and then cleverly decodes a cipher written in invisible ink on parchment, which turns out to be an also cryptic set of directions. With the aid of his black servant and a heavy scarab, he succeeds after several comic missteps in locating and unearthing a huge chest of coins, jewels, and gold ornaments buried on the island by Captain Kidd.

Technically this group of tales and short stories is innovative and adventurous. For the most part Poe used simpler, more direct language than before. In conveying the considerable brutality of the action, an influential precursor to modern films of violence, he used chillingly flat declarative sentences: "I withdrew my arm from her grasp and buried the axe in her brain"; "I dismembered the corpse. I cut off the head and the arms and the legs." At the same time he retained his characteristic poetic effects. In his dark dungeon, for instance, the captive narrator of "The Pit and the Pendulum" experiences the descending blade by smell and sound, by how it "*hissed* as it swung through the air." Poe kept the menacing pendulum aurally present for the reader by deploying hissing words like "surcingle," "cessation," "crescent" and "scimitar," or in such sentences as "With a steady movement—cautious, sidelong, shrinking, and slow, I slid from the embrace of the bandage and beyond the sweep of the scimitar." As several of the stories are told by characters central to the action, whose manner of speaking reveals what they are like, Poe also fashioned syntax and rhythm to create an effect of speech. He dramatized the mental disorder of the narrator of "The Black Cat" by recurrent inversions and negatives, as in his opening statement: "mad am I not—and very surely do I not dream." Perhaps most daringly, in some of the works he banished story-telling for the sake of a different kind of fictive pleasure. Little happens in "The Mystery of Marie Rogêt," where Dupin and his colleague stay out of sight. Much of the narrative consists of discourses on body hair, mildew, the physics of drowning, elastic garters, whether criminals carry handkerchiefs, the growth rate of grass, and the shape of rips made in a fabric by thorns. Poe's concentration on the analysis of material clues represents another of his bequests to the classic detective story.

Poe took particular satisfaction in his characterization of Legrand's manumitted black servant Jupiter, which he considered a "perfect picture . . . no feature overshaded, or distorted." This meant depicting him as superstitious and stupid, unable to tell his left eye from his right ("tis my lef hand what I chops de wood wid"). Poe's brief characterizations of blacks in earlier works, to go back a moment, are no less denigrating. Describing the guffaw of a black servant in "The Man that was Used up," he wrote: " 'He! he! he! he-aw! he-aw! he-aw!' chachinnated that delectable specimen of the human family, with his mouth fairly extended from ear to ear." A black character in "The Journal of Julius Rodman" is even more repellent, "as ugly an old gentleman as ever spoke—having all the peculiar features of his race; the swollen lips, large white protruding eyes, flat nose, long ears, double head, pot-belly, and bow legs." Poe opposed abolition, and identified with slaveholding interests in the South, whom he felt Northern writers misrepresented. Although in no way consumed with racial hatred, he considered blacks less than human—as did many other Americans in the 1840s— therefore "utterly incompetent to feel the *moral* galling of [their] chain." His friend Mary Starr later remarked that he "didn't like dark-skinned people."

As usual, biting and oral mutilation are everywhere in the tales. Among a score of instances, the narrator of "The Black Cat" first becomes vexed with the pet when it "inflicted a slight wound upon my hand with his teeth"; the prisoner of "The Pit and the Pendulum" is eaten at by rats who "fastened their sharp fangs in my fingers"; the gold-bug, Jupiter says, "bite ebery ting what cum near him." In a variant of this imagery, eyes figure importantly in the tales, closely associated with teeth. After he is bitten by the black cat, the narrator cuts out its eye; to locate the pirate treasure, Legrand must pass the omnivorous gold-bug through the empty eye-socket of a skull; in explaining his hatred and murder of the old man, the narrator of "The Tell-Tale Heart" says: "I think it was his eye! yes, it was this! He had the eye of a vulture. . . . . . I grew furious as I gazed upon it." What relates eyes and teeth is their single capacity to take in, to incorporate objects. Poe frequently associates eyes with pits, tarns, whirlpools and other depths that can engulf, as when he writes in "Morella": "I met the glance of her meaning eyes, and then my soul sickened and became giddy with the giddiness of one who gazes downward into some dreary and unfathomable abyss." Like teeth, eyes in Poe's works arouse the dread of being consumed.

As often before, too, Poe drew much of his narrative vocabulary from his own experience past and present. In "A Tale of the Ragged Mountains" he returned to the countryside around Charlottesville, where he had lived as a student at the University of Virginia, and in "The Gold-Bug" to Sullivan's Island, where he had served in the army at Fort Moultrie for a year in 1827–28. He also again recycled the stock of preoccupying names, persons, places, and occasions which his imagination constantly reset in new habitations and constantly rearranged into new patterns. To point out only a few: the place where the narrator of "The Spectacles" first sees the woman he wants to marry is a theater; later he attends a soiree where (he believes) he hears her singing, and is smitten by her "miracles of vocal execution." Her name might be Eliza or Virginia but is Madame Lalande, a name borrowed from that of a famed opera singer but which also harbors *Allan*. (The prisoner in "The Pit and the Pendulum" is rescued by a General Lasalle.) "Raising the Wind; or, Diddling Considered as One of the Exact Sciences" also recurs to the theater, taking its title from a popular English farce called "Raising the Wind," in which David Poe acted at least three times. William Henry Leonard Poe seems commemorated again in a new Augustus, the Augustus Bedloe in "Tale of the Ragged Mountains," the reversibility of whose names suggests the closeness the orphaned brothers expressed in the character "Edgar-Leonard." Sailor and author of "The Pirate," Henry also looms amidst the sailors and Captain Kidd of "The Gold-Bug." Its hero, William Legrand, has Henry's first name, while "Legrand" lacks only an 'o' in otherwise perfectly superimposing the two names Edgar and Leonard upon each other.

A need to unearth the past seems to animate the main themes of the stories and tales as well. Several of the works concern revelation, and inversely the failure to keep something hidden. The decayed ancestor emerges from the pretty young singer, the real murderer of Marie Rogêt is disclosed, the corpses of the old man and the butchered wife are brought to light, Legrand deciphers the coded message and digs up the buried coffer. The revelations are not very different from each other, for the treasure-hunt in "The Gold-Bug" much resembles the exhumation of a corpse. The chest is located by means of a bug that looks like "a death's-head," which has to be lowered through the eyeholes of a skull, which rests on the *"dead limb"* of a tree, which leads to a pit containing a "mass of human bones," beneath which is an "oblong chest of wood." The thing buried within such a chest is of great value, a treasure indeed.

What has been hidden within the self will not stay concealed either. "The Tell-Tale Heart" begins with the narrator revealing his madness in the very attempt to deny it: "TRUE!—nervous—very, very dreadfully nervous I had been and am; but why *will* you say that I am mad? . . . Hearken! and observe how healthily—how calmly I can tell you the whole story." Nor can he hide his crime. He seats the police in the room under whose floorboards he has buried the old man, placing his own chair in "wild audacity" upon the very spot, until the suspicion grows on him that the police have uncovered his secret, and he shrieks "dissemble no more! I admit the deed!—tear up the planks—here, here!—it is the beating of his hideous heart!" To consider such revelations in psychological terms, tales like "The Spectacles," "The Black Cat," and "The Tell-Tale Heart" dramatize failures of various defenses, the protagonists' futile attempts to conceal from themselves and others what they feel. They and many other characters in Poe have little self-knowledge and suffer extreme conflicts. The alcoholic murderer in "The Black Cat" hangs the animal "with the tears streaming from my eyes, and with the bitterest remorse at my heart;—hung it *because* I knew that it had loved me." The narrator of "The Tell-Tale Heart" says that "I loved the old man. He had never wronged me." Yet he drags the old man out of his bed and smothers him with it. As if Poe were pondering his own tenuous self-control, what his characters deny or repress or project uncontrollably erupts.

If not a financial success, Poe's tales were again at least a popular success, especially the prize-winning "Gold-Bug," which one newspaper reviewer called the most remarkable American work of fiction published in the last fifteen years. The publishers of the *Dollar Newspaper* ran extra printings to meet the audience demand and took out a copyright on the story, although smaller newspapers pirated it just the same. Poe estimated that less than a year after publication, more than three hundred thousand copies had been circulated. It was also made into a short play that was produced at Philadelphia's Walnut Street Theatre. Eventually "The Gold-Bug" became, worldwide, one of the most popular stories ever written.

While living in Philadelphia Poe published thirty-one tales and stories, among them "Ligeia," "The Fall of the House of Usher," "William Wilson," "The Murders in the Rue Morgue," "The Gold-Bug," "The Tell-Tale Heart," "The Pit and the Pendulum," and "The Black Cat." It would seem that only by some defiantly willed self-transcendence could he produce so many works of such vast popularity and influence in between his hard-up wanderings from home to home and job to job, insulting friends or not paying the barber when lost in bourbon and port, so distressed by Virginia's hemorrhaging that he could not speak of it, not to mention the wave of disaster and affront that began practically with his birth.

Yet the enduring popular appeal of Poe's work represents no overcoming of his personal history, but in a specific sense his entrapment in it. The shocks of a past that he still mourned continued to shape his literary expression, leading him to create a Bedloe-Oldeb, a young man with "the eyes of a long-interred corpse" who is killed once by a serpent-shaped poisoned arrow in eighteenth-century Benares, and reborn in nineteenth-century Virginia, to be killed there again by a snakelike poisonous leech. In depicting eerie coincidences, doubles, confinements in dark places, amputated limbs, rat swarms whose "cold lips sought my own," Poe's works invite readers to feel once more that eyes and teeth can eat one up, as nearly happened to Hansel and Gretel or to Little Red Riding Hood, to once more experience the world in childlike ways.

In varying degrees such thinking still operates for most people. It returns, for instance, when something happens in waking life that has been dreamt, or when suddenly seeing a person one has been thinking of. Freud gave the name of The Uncanny to this quality of an event to support old beliefs that have been discredited but remain dormant in the self, to revive early, magical forms of thinking. As he explained:

> We—or our primitive forefathers—once believed in the possibility of these things and were convinced that they really happened. Nowadays we no longer believe in them, we have *surmounted* such ways of thought; but we do not feel quite sure of our new set of beliefs, and the old ones still exist within us ready to seize upon any confirmation. As soon as something actually happens in our lives which seems to support the old, discarded beliefs we get a feeling of the uncanny; and it is as though we were making a judgement something like this: 'So, after all, it is true that one can kill a person by merely desiring his death!' or, 'Then the dead do continue to live and appear before our eyes on the scene of their former activities!' and so on.

The continuing popular appeal of Poe's works is owing to their power to confirm once-real beliefs from which most people have never entirely freed themselves, and which his own past kept particularly alive in him: that one can be devoured and annihilated, that the darkness is astir, that the dead in some form survive and return.

Rufus Griswold;
Last Days in Philadelphia.

CA. MAY 1 8 4 1 – MARCH 1 8 4 4

However busy during his six years in Philadelphia, Poe found time for friends and drinking partners, especially among the city's clan of quasi-Bohemian journalists. Most were men in their twenties, such as Mayne Reid, an Irish novelist and soldier of fortune whose fanciful tales of adventures in Mexico and elsewhere Poe enjoyed hearing, and Henry Beck Hirst, a lawyer, sportsman, poet, and part owner of a seed store, remembered for smoking cigars, spouting verse, drinking absinthe, cultivating his alleged resemblance to Shakespeare, and saying "Eau reservoir" when taking leave. Poe's circle also included "Colonel" John Stephenson Du Solle, reputedly dissipated editor of *Spirit of the Times,* a lively penny newspaper which under the slogan "Democratic and Fearless" attacked banks, rich merchants, and railroad magnates. Poe was often at Du Solle's office, across the street from *Graham's,* and consorted with his firebrand young reporter, George Lippard. He liked Lippard's brawling, confrontational newspaper satire, and Lippard admired him as "perhaps, the most original writer that ever existed in America." A novelist as well, Lippard combined Gothic thrills, near-pornographic titillation, and a socialistic critique of the establishment, becoming famous for his lurid exposé of the underside of Philadelphia life, *Quaker City; Or, The Monks of Monk Hall* (1844), the best-selling American novel before *Uncle Tom's Cabin.*

Poe's work brought him in touch with many more writers, journalists, actors, engravers. But no association he made in Philadelphia was as tangled or fateful as that with a staff member of the Philadelphia *Daily Standard,* Rufus Wilmot Griswold. They first met around May 1841, while Poe still worked for Graham. By Griswold's later account, Poe called at his hotel, and not finding him home left two letters of introduction. Griswold visited him the next day, and they had a long talk about the literary scene, relating to the anthology Griswold was then compiling, *The Poets and Poetry of America.* Both men stood to gain from the meeting, Poe by having his poems included in the collection, Griswold by access to the most thoughtful and provocative critic in America. Six years Poe's junior, Griswold was at the time twenty-six years old, a slender, sharp-nosed, fashionably dressed young man with a self-confident manner, who discoursed engagingly about what he had read and seen (Illus. 12).

The effect of suavity cannot have come easily, for Griswold was hardly at ease with himself or the world. He had grown up in the hamlet of Benson, Vermont, twelfth of fourteen children of a pious mother and a father who was a shoemaker and farmer. Restless and rebellious as a youth, he formed a habit of close but short-lived attachments, some of them with men slightly older than himself. After running away from his brother's home in Troy, New York, where he had been sent to learn the printing business, he joined up in Albany with George Foster, a twenty-year-old flute-playing journalist who later became known as "Gaslight" Foster for his sensationalistic *New-York by Gas-Light,* and was jailed for signing Billy Burton's name on four checks. The two young men shared a room and argued about literature for three years, until Griswold became restless again and left. By that time, however, Foster had become enamored of him, and beseeched him to return:

> I have loved often and deeply. My heart has burned itself almost to a charred cinder by the flames of passion which have glowed within it—and yet I have never felt towards any human being— man or woman—so strong and absorbing an affection as I bear to you.

Foster ended, "Farewell—Farewell—come to me if you love me." Griswold preserved the letter until his death.

For several years after this, Griswold wandered restlessly in the East as a journeyman printer and editor, in part under the guidance of Horace Greeley, another of the several older-brother figures in his life. Then and later, he considered himself a loner, a "chimney corner man" Greeley called him. Two important things happened to him at the age of twenty-two: he was licensed as a Baptist minister, and he married. The conjunction does not seem accidental but rather suggests uneasiness in Griswold over his worldliness, a way of answering such questions as his mother posed to him in her letters: "Rufus, are you a Christian? Are you prepared to meet your God?" At the time Poe met him in Philadelphia, Griswold had recently made another abrupt departure, this time from his job as an editor for Horace Greeley's New York *Tribune.* He also left behind his growing reputation among the New York literati, his library of several thousand volumes, his wife (who had just given birth to their second daughter), and his idolatrous relation to Charles Fenno Hoffman, a handsome, gentlemanly editor and poet nine years older than he who had remained a bachelor, it was believed, because a boyhood accident had cost him the loss of a leg.

Poe submitted to Griswold for his anthology what he considered at the time his three best poems ("Coliseum," "The Haunted Palace," and "The Sleeper"), together with the autobiographical sketch mentioned earlier. His poems came to occupy only two pages at the rear of the 476-page volume, sandwiched between verses by an Anna Peyre Dinnies and one Isaac McLellan, Jr. Inconspicuous as the poems looked, to be included was nevertheless to partake of a certain event. *The Poets and Poetry of America* was the most comprehensive collection of American poetry ever made. Appearing in April 1842, it went through an unprecedented three editions in six months; reissued every year during Griswold's lifetime, it generated years of lively controversy over the canon of American poets he laid down.

Griswold's reading and training fitted him for the job. The publishing world respected him as a good business man who paid promptly and well; in the details of editing, Greeley called him "unrivaled." As for his knowledge of American literary history, he boasted of owning the fullest collection of American books in the country. And he knew and corresponded with many literary people, who genially addressed him as "Rufe," "Gris," "Wilmot," or "Animal," although their friendliness to him, as an influential man, often seems forced, rather like ingratiation. Yet Griswold was no literary Tamerlane bent on establishing a new order of things. Graham's partner Charles Peterson remarked that Griswold "fears to lead the public taste." Griswold featured in his anthology the popular poets of the time, such as Bryant, Halleck, and Longfellow, emphasizing the poets of New England and affording one of the largest sections in the book to his bachelor friend Charles Fenno Hoffman.

Poe often proudly proclaimed that he never allowed his feelings about literary personalities to warp his critical judgments about their work. But his view of Griswold's anthology was unmistakably colored by what he thought of the anthologist, who was after all contesting his self-appointed role as Arbiter of American Taste. Besides, in the year between their first meeting and the publication of the book, Poe and Griswold had sparred, although at a distance. In two separate reviews in *Graham's,* Poe trashed a collection of poems by the Boston banker Charles Sprague, whom he called "merely a well-educated poetaster," and briefly praised a volume by the Philadelphia physician Pliny Earle, who had supported his "Penn" project. Griswold, on the contrary, was then intending to afford Sprague a major section of his anthology, indeed to include an engraving of him on the frontispiece as one of the five leading American poets, the "copperplate five," as he eventually did. Defying Poe's judgment, Griswold reviewed his review of Sprague. He wrote in the Boston *Notion,* having removed to that city from Philadelphia in still another of his sudden departures. He lauded Sprague's poems as "inimitable," observing that the same critic who had ridiculed them had also praised Earle, of whose poetry he remarked: "We have been called upon in our time to examine vast quantities of rant and puerility, with which inexperienced boys or weakminded men have attempted to win popular admiration; but we never saw anything more ineffably senseless and bombastic, than these verses so lauded by the editor of *Graham's Magazine.*"

It is uncertain whether Poe saw this sharp slap at his taste. But later in the year he included a sketch and facsimile signature of Griswold in his "Autography" series. Perhaps simply because he still hoped to be represented in *Poets and Poetry of America,* he praised Griswold's taste. But in interpreting Griswold's signature he concluded that it "vacillates" and reveals "a certain unsteadiness of purpose," not an inappropriate comment considering that after three and a half months as an editor in Boston, Griswold returned again to Philadelphia, his wife and daughters remaining in New York. Whether or not Poe meant his remark as a counterpunch, his relation to Griswold had by this time become fouled. As a Boston critic noted to Griswold, "You are no particular friend of his, I believe."

The actual publication of *Poets and Poetry of America,* in April 1842, deepened the enmity. Privately Poe considered the anthology "a most outrageous humbug" and encouraged his friend Snodgrass to "use it up." In part he scorned the book because Griswold, a New Englander himself, had featured New England poets, giving fewer pages and less prominence to those from other parts of the country. For Poe the parts may of course have included Philadelphia, and he may have felt aggrieved at his minor representation in the book. He may have been wounded to find his own few poems cubbyholed in back of the volume, and resented Griswold's challenge to his role as tastemaker. Just the same, he offered to review the anthology, in circumstances that only increased his contempt for Griswold. As Poe recounted the episode, around July he told Griswold that he had thought of discussing the book fully in the New York *Democratic Review* but found it already reviewed there, and knew no other magazine where his essay might be accepted. According to Poe, Griswold said: "You need not trouble yourself about the publication of the review, should you decide upon writing it; for I will attend to all that." Then, he said, Griswold made him a lowdown proposition: "I will get it in some reputable work, and look to it for the usual pay; in the meantime handing you whatever your charge would be." As Poe interpreted this offer of advance payment it amounted to trying to buy a favorable review from him, "an ingenious insinuation of a *bribe* to puff his book."

Poe may have reported Griswold's actions accurately, and correctly interpreted his intentions. But Griswold may not have greatly cared about Poe's, or anyone else's opinion at this time. Only months before his anthology appeared, he experienced weakened eyesight, bleeding at the lungs, and other symptoms of tuberculosis. He was twenty-seven years old, and afraid: "to have so long a death," he said, "and feel its slow, constant, and sure approach!" The sense of a bleak future may have made him the more ready to indulge an older cynicism about the literary marketplace. He freely admitted that he believed a good review from Poe "might be of some consequence." And minister or no, Griswold was a florid instance of the puffing system Poe had often denounced from his own pulpit. Griswold blithely told his friend James T. Fields, a Boston publisher whose edition of Tennyson he had just reviewed, "I puff your books, you know, without any regard to their quality." Poe said that after writing the review of *Poets and Poetry* he handed it to Griswold, who paid him but did not dare look over the manuscript in his presence: "a pretty fellow," he added, "to set himself up as an *honest* judge."

Having paid Poe to review his anthology, Griswold was disappointed by the result. He felt that Poe failed to praise the book enough, something he laid to their uneasy relationship, "the author and myself not being on the best terms." He apparently even considered not using the review, although he had paid for it, and placed it in a Boston periodical only to avoid humiliating himself, "lest Poe should think I had prevented its publication." But Griswold was disappointed only because he expected too much for his money; a friend who read Poe's review more disinterestedly congratulated Griswold on having received a "good puff." For if Griswold had been willing to buy himself a good press, Poe's pen had also been for hire. In his review Poe faulted Griswold for overrepresenting New England poets, but at greater length praised him for correctly conceiving poetry as the metrical creation of beauty, satisfying both critical and popular taste, and writing "with judgment, with dignity and candor." However much he privately thought the book an "outrageous humbug," his paid verdict was emphatically favorable: *"the most important addition which our literature has for many years received."*

An overlapping event further vexed these crosscurrents of respect, sympathy, mutual fear, and bad blood. Only days after publication of the anthology, Griswold was invited by George Rex Graham to take over as book review editor of his magazine. Graham offered a salary of one thousand dollars, two hundred more than he had paid Poe. He also seems to have allowed Griswold a larger part than Poe in determining the magazine's content and policies. Griswold scored some notable successes, among them winning Longfellow's willingness to write for *Graham's* exclusively. Poe now added Griswold to his long list of inferiors who had been preferred to him. He told Thomas that Graham and everyone else was dissatisfied with Griswold, "with the exception of the Rev. gentleman himself." He likely also conveyed his view of Griswold's performance to his friends, or at any rate several joined him in razzing Griswold, and comparing him as editor to Poe. Jesse Dow, Poe's rescuer in Washington, snapped in print that "We would give more for Edgar A. Poe's toe nail, than we would for Rueful Grizzle's soul." George Lippard published a burlesque skit in which one character asks Rumpus Grizzle: " 'ye've a wholesome fear of this same poor author—Misther Poe?' 'He doesn't think I'm a great man,' quoth Rumpus." Who baited whom first is by no means clear, for Griswold at the same time was apparently making known his opinion of Poe. A letter writer to a Washington newspaper decried how Griswold used his editorial office to sponsor "malignant, unjust, and disgraceful attacks" on Poe's "literary character."

In the sniping, Poe came to speak of Griswold with insouciant disdain, as a "precious fellow." But Griswold was inwardly a troubled and chaotic soul, not to be taken lightly. The prolific New York novelist Ann Sophia Stephens observed that his "soft manners and cringing habits" concealed a double-dealer, someone "constitutionally incapable of speaking the truth." Acutely, she viewed Griswold as "a dangerous person to be connected with." Griswold also felt slights keenly and agonized over being taken for granted. A friendly acquaintance later recalled that for all his many acts of kindness he was also "one of the most irritable and vindictive men I ever met, if he fancied he was in any way familiarly treated,—when he became savage." Poe himself believed that he witnessed Griswold's petty vengefulness in the omission of F. W. Thomas from *Poets and Poetry of America.* Griswold had asked Thomas for biographical information about a certain poet; Poe explained to Thomas that Griswold excluded him from the anthology because "you gave him personal offence by *delay* in replying to his demand for information." With whatever dislike and misgiving, Poe maintained professional ties to Griswold, and to some extent a friendship, for at least once Griswold visited him and his family at home. But there were risks. George Lippard put tersely what many others felt about Griswold's sleek manner, calling him "a respectable jackal."

What happened to Griswold in early November 1842 dramatically hints his depths, and the ground of the turbulent affinity he felt with Poe. Seeing portents of approaching death in his wearying coughs and sweats, he had "trained" his wife, Caroline, to prepare for it, and even had dreams of her bending over his coffin. Like much else in Griswold, his feelings about his wife seem awry. He credited her with saving him from his lonely tendency to stand apart from others, a "chimney corner man." Nevertheless he remained in Philadelphia while she and their children lived in New York. On November 6 he traveled to New York, where she had given birth to their first son. Three days later, returned to Philadelphia, he was informed by a messenger who appeared in his dining hall that both Caroline and his son were dead. By night train he rushed back to New York, where he sat near and embraced her dead body for thirty hours. "I speak to her but she does not hear me," he wrote after midnight, "I kiss her cold lips, but their fervor is gone." After the funeral, he would not leave the cemetery until a relative commanded him to depart. Refusing to believe she was dead he dreamt night after night of their reunion.

Forty days after the funeral, Griswold returned to New York and journeyed the nine miles beyond to Greenwood Cemetery in Brooklyn, where, by his account, he got the sexton to open Caroline's vault. He entered the chamber and prayed. Then he unfastened the lid of her coffin. He turned aside her shroud. The decomposition of the body shocked him, but he kissed her "cold black forehead." He cut off locks, "damp with the death dews," of her hair. Then he collapsed, lying unconscious in the vault until a friend from the city found him that evening, his face still resting on his wife's.

The two men's troubled embroilment continued to the end of Poe's stay in Philadelphia, when it intensified. Griswold remained as editor of *Graham's* for about eight months after his wife's death, resigning in mid-August 1843. Still ill, and becoming in November "nearly blind," he considered going abroad to die. At just the same time, Poe looked into a new and still-needed source of income. Although he decried the "present absurd rage for lecturing," he began writing to committeemen and heads of societies, hoping to arrange a series of lectures for himself. Through James Russell Lowell he tried unsuccessfully to get an engagement at the Boston Lyceum. But he did line up six and perhaps seven appearances between November 21, 1843, and March 13, 1844, in various Mechanics' Institutes, Temperance Halls, and Odd Fellows' Halls in Philadelphia (twice); Wilmington and Newark, Delaware; Baltimore and possibly Elkton, Maryland; and Reading, Pennsylvania. Hundreds were unable to gain admission to his first lecture in Philadelphia. Nor were the listeners disappointed. Whatever he felt about lecturing, Poe clearly extended himself. The many favorable reviews spoke of him as a "correct and graceful reader," praised his "command of language and strength of voice," acclaimed the evening "an eloquent production eloquently delivered." For nearly two hours he delivered his opinions on American literary politics, the function of criticism, and the province of poetry, sometimes reciting poems.

The title of Poe's lecture, as given in several newspapers, was "The Poetry of America." The Baltimore *Sun,* however, gave the title more accurately, in spirit if not in fact, as "Poets and Poetry of America." For Poe's main subject was, as much as anything else, Rufus Griswold. He revealed to his listeners what he had kept from readers of his bought review, that his rival claimant to the attention of the literary world was a tasteless New Englander, unashamed puffer, and follower of the herd. Graham later characterized Poe's treatment of *Poets and Poetry* as "scathing," and said that he "gave Mr. Griswold some raps over the knuckles of force sufficient to be remembered." As a Delaware newspaper summarized this part of the lecture, Poe charged that Griswold put in many poets who should have been left out, and the reverse, and made his selections with "miserable want of judgment," often picking the "worst specimens" of a poet's work instead of the best. Griswold also devoted an "extravagant proportion of space" to inferior poets who were his friends, such as Charles Fenno Hoffman, at the same time shuffling off "superior merit . . . with a single page." As newspapers in other places reported Poe's comments, they were "witheringly severe" on Griswold or put him "to the blush."

Although still ill and still grieving over his wife's death, Griswold seems to have been aware of the horsewhipping, and later remarked that Poe handled him "very sharply." He tried spreading some poison of his own. At the end of the year he wrote to Longfellow, informing him that Poe had recently written a harsh review of his work, if anything "a little more personal and malignant than usual." Poe tried to sell the review to Graham, Griswold said, and has since given it to him free, "so anxious is the poor critic for its appearance." (Actually Graham gave Poe thirty dollars for the savage review but did not print it, presumably buying the manuscript only to prevent its publication anywhere.) Griswold warned Longfellow to beware of Poe's insincerity and wiles. Having unsuccessfully maligned Longfellow, he said, Poe would "attempt again to win your friendship with his praise." Such slithering describes the ongoing contest Poe and Griswold waged between themselves, positioning and repositioning as sycophant or serpent.

The Brennan Farm; Willis's Mirror; *"The Purloined Letter."*

CA. APRIL – DECEMBER 1 8 4 4

During the first week in April 1844, Poe and Virginia left their suburban Spring Garden house and arrived at a quarter past six in the morning at the Walnut Street station, there to begin their journey to New York. The decision to move seems to have been made abruptly, but New York was the place, Poe said, "where I intend living for the future." The coachman who drove them to the station demanded a dollar for the fare, but Poe refused to pay that much;

even so, he had to tip a boy for putting their trunks in the baggage car. With forty-five minutes to wait, he took Sissy to the hotel at the depot, where they looked through three Philadelphia newspapers, finding nothing of interest. At seven o'clock, feeling in good spirits, they boarded a train for the trip to Perth Amboy, New Jersey. The remaining forty or so miles to New York they went by steam boat, arriving at three in the afternoon, during a hard rain.

Poe left Virginia aboard the boat, putting their trunks in the "Ladies' Cabin" while he set out to find an umbrella and an inexpensive boardinghouse. He found the first, for sixty-two cents, and the second, on Greenwich Street, well-located in lower New York, near the Hudson River, the heart of the city. Knowing how anxious his absences made Sissy, he managed to make the arrangements quickly and to be gone from her not longer than half an hour, returning to the boat in a hack to save time. She had expected him to be away an hour, so was "quite astonished," he said, to see him back so soon. And as two other ladies were also waiting on board, "she was'nt [sic] very lonely."

Probably the day after arriving in New York, Poe sat down to write to Muddy, who had remained in Philadelphia together with Catterina, their cat (also called Kate). He told Muddy about their trip and described such details of their domestic arrangements as he knew she would enjoy hearing. They were staying in an old house, "buggy" looking, with brown stone steps and a porch with brown pillars, run by a "nice chatty" landlady and her husband, a "fat good-natured old soul." The care and hospitality the couple offered obviously stirred old longings for domestic comfort: "it is impossible," he told Muddy, "we could be more comfortable or more at home than we are." At the moment Sissy was busy mending his pants, he said, which he had torn against a nail. He had gone out the previous night to buy for the repair a skein of silk, a skein of thread, and two buttons, as well as a tin pan for the stove, which had kept its fire all night. The landlady couldn't regale them enough, and it made them feel "at home directly."

Best of all was the food: "I wish Kate could see it—she would faint." Sounding like the starved Arthur Gordon Pym, he described their previous night's supper: "the nicest tea you ever drank, strong & hot—wheat bread & rye bread—cheese—tea-cakes (elegant) a great dish (2 dishes) of elegant ham, and 2 of cold veal, piled up like a mountain and large slices—3 dishes of the cakes, and every thing in the greatest profusion. No fear of starving here." With a gusto that records years of scrounging scarcity, he also described for Muddy their plentiful breakfast: "excellent-flavored coffe [*sic*], hot & strong—not very clear & no great deal of cream—veal cutlets, elegant ham & eggs & nice bread and butter. . . . I wish you could have seen the eggs—and the great dishes of meat."

In all Poe could report hopefully on their situation: "Sis is delighted, and we are both in excellent spirits." There were some nagging worries, of course. The night before Virginia had had a "hearty cry," he said, because Muddy and Catterina weren't there. And he and Virginia had only four and a half dollars left. But he felt he could make a fresh and more prosperous start in New York. "To-morrow I am going to try," he said, as if referring to a routine practice, "& borrow 3 $—so that I may have a fortnight to go upon." The instant he could scrape together enough, too, he would send it on to Muddy to help her out, and he was resolved to find a place with two rooms so she could join them. And he was staying sober: "I . . . have'nt drank [*sic*] a drop," he said, leading him to hope that he could "get out of trouble." There was another, even greater reason for hope. Throughout their eight-hour trip to New York by train and steamboat, "Sissy coughed none at all." She continued to do as well, or nearly so. Since they had been in New York, he could report, she had "coughed hardly any and had no night sweat."

The elegant hams and stacks of tea cakes in New York boardinghouses did not nourish Poe long. Six weeks later he was feeling poorly, "ill in health," he said, "and wretchedly depressed in spirits." His earlier plan to live in New York "for the future" became reduced to living there "the next year or two." And after staying in the city proper only about two months he moved in the late spring or early summer to a farm some five miles outside town, now joined by Muddy and Catterina. The reasons for Poe's change of mood are unknown, but in Philadelphia too he had sought out homes on the outskirts of the city. He loved rambling in the woods, and as everyone else did he found the city's streets, with few exceptions, "insufferably dirty." He no more liked the din of immense charcoal wagons, traffic rumbling over the round paving stones, cries from the "leathern throats of the clam-and-cat-fish venders." Most important, he very probably also hoped to find more salubrious surroundings for Sissy, whose health soon again became, he said, "excessively precarious."

The setting of Poe's new home was distinctly rural, on a two-hundred-acre working farm adjoining the Hudson River, perhaps a hundred paces from the Bloomingdale Road leading into the city. Run by a family named Brennan, the farm was a supply depot for crops, fruit, and cattle. The place abounded in ponds, streams, and vernal nooks, offering also extensive views of the surrounding countryside and across the river into New Jersey. Poe, Muddy, and Virginia occupied part of a farmhouse that consisted of two connected buildings, one two-stories high, the other taller by a spare room and storage attic. The trio lived at the farm during the rest of 1844 and probably into the first two months of 1845. Poe stayed in seclusion, "playing hermit in earnest," he said, "nor have I seen a living soul out of my family."

But like his Prince Prospero, Poe could not shut out the world. He was all but broke, *as usual,* exceedingly in need of a little money," his money problems bringing on others that left him complaining of a "host of small troubles growing from the *one* trouble of poverty." Among other pressures he owed Graham about sixty dollars, in part for a direct loan to Muddy. To bring in a livelihood he churned out loads of hackwork, becoming for the first time in his career more a commercial journalist than an imaginative writer. He became New York correspondent of a small-town Pennsylvania newspaper called the *Columbia Spy,* producing a series of letters meant to give country people an impression of life in the metropolis; he probably prepared for the Philadelphia *Public Ledger* slight pieces on omnibuses, cabs, and cats, with lame quips like "You can get into a difficulty gratis, at any time, but it requires twenty-five cents to get into a cab." Despite his abhorrence of sentimental engravings he whipped up for the *Columbian Magazine* a so-called plate article entitled "Byron and Miss Chaworth," designed to accompany an engraving of a boy and girl in a garden, representing Byron and his first love (and of interest as illustrating the ideal of sexless passion he had celebrated at least since the time of writing "To Helen"). He even got off a campaign song, for a New York political organization called the White Eagle Club. The club's president, a New York artist and merchant named Gabriel Harrison, recalled that Poe dropped into his shop and during fifteen minutes wrote out five stanzas and a chorus, to the tune of the national anthem. Harrison later could remember only several lines, and those imperfectly: "See the White Eagle soaring aloft to the sky, / Wakening the broad welkin with his loud battle cry."

In November and December 1844, Poe also assembled in the *Democratic Review* the first two installments, 116 items, of a series entitled "Marginalia." During his career he would eventually publish fifteen more installments, and probably intended at some point to publish the whole as a book. In the introduction to this *"farrago,"* as he called it, he explained that the comments represented his own jottings in the volumes of his library, not a large one, but "I flatter myself, not a little *recherché."* The comments had been attached to the leaves of his books by slips of paper or written in the margins, spontaneously, and therefore "freshly—boldly—originally—with *abandonnement*—without conceit." This was all fiction, since his library was scanty at best, and he lifted many items from his earlier reviews and from "Pinakidia." Unhappy, impoverished, and sequestered on a farm, he portrayed himself as a comfortable bibliophile pencilling into his Persian compendia of natural history his leisured reflections on everything from synaesthesia and speed-reading to the calculus of probabilities and utilitarianism, with quotations from Hebrew, Greek, German, and even Danish. The comments are often striking, however, and as will appear they make an index to his views on a broad range of subjects.

Poe's only steady outlet for this ephemeral journalism was a New York newspaper entitled the *Evening Mirror,* which also published a *Weekly Mirror.* Its editors were the genial versifier and songwriter George Pope Morris, author of the well-known lyric "Woodman, Spare that Tree!" and his close friend, Nathaniel Parker Willis, one of the best-known literary figures of the period (Illus. 13). A joke of the day had it that Goethe was the N. P. Willis of Germany. As an essayist, Willis chronicled events in a precious, slightly mocking style—all puns, peculiar expressions, and outrageous distortions of words. His verbal trifling was widely imitated and parodied. By the early 1840s he had become the first successful professional magazine writer in America, commanding one hundred dollars for an article and earning nearly five thousand dollars a year. He succeeded socially too. His good nature attracted many friends, and fashionable drawing rooms welcomed him as a lively, clever, and well-traveled man of striking appearance, six feet tall, slender, dressed with dainty elegance, his deeply rosy cheeks framed by silky light-brown hair that fell, as "Gaslight" Foster described them, in "long, clustering, glossy ringlets." Willis's many detractors, however, saw him as Europeanized by his five-year stay abroad, and effeminate. One editor referred to him as "an impersonal passive verb—a pronoun of the feminine gender"; another spoke of his "Miss Nancy-ism"; a third described him *"chassaing* or *minuetting* up Pine Street in a white hat which he shakes as if to the music of the *minuet.* . . . gay as any gondola or gondolier."

However maligned as fluffy, Willis was a gritty practical journalist. He toiled, as he said, "under whip and spur," had no qualms about the puffing system, and looked on his career unsentimentally, "obliged to turn to account every trumpery thought I can lay my wits to. My rubbish, such as it is, brings me a very high price." Willis knew trouble too. He had become deeply estranged from his sister, the popular novelist who wrote as "Fanny Fern," and his brother was in an Ohio jail, imprisoned for "an outrage . . . on a young woman." During scarcely more than a year in this same 1844–45 period he also experienced the deaths of his youngest sister, his mother, and his twenty-nine-year-old wife, who died in childbirth together with their child.

Exactly when and how Poe came to work for Willis is uncertain. About six weeks after arriving in New York, he sent him a tale and an essay for consideration, saying he would be honored to have them appear in the *Mirror,* and had long been "exceedingly anxious" to meet him, as the author of the poem "Unseen Spirits." He may have visited the *Mirror* office, but according to Willis the job came about when Muddy, probably in the early fall, called on him seeking employment for Poe. She excused her errand by mentioning that Virginia was a "confirmed invalid" and that Poe himself was ill, compelling her to take on the job hunt for him. Poe began contributing to the *Mirror* in October; just when he began working in the newspaper's offices on Nassau and Ann streets, as he seems to have done, is again uncertain, since it meant a five-mile trip from the Brennan farm, and in his circumstances probably a walk.

Poe badly needed the salary of fifteen dollars a week, and also liked Willis. Over the years he had corresponded with him and often reviewed and spoken about his works, rather erratically, sometimes praising his sense of humor and his taste, at other times dismissing him as "a graceful trifler—no more," sometimes caustically defending him against ad hominem attacks, at other times himself tweaking Willis for the persona conveyed by his prose, "a pen in one hand, and a bottle of eau de Cologne in the other." Whatever he ultimately thought of Willis's writing, however, he respected his decency: "A more estimable man, in his private relations, never existed."

Willis in turn genuinely liked Poe. When later reflecting on Poe's term at the *Mirror,* he recalled that Poe "never smiled," but was otherwise a model office hand—punctual, reliable, cooperative in the business of getting out a newspaper, "any vanity of his own, so utterly put aside." Poe's absorption in the work seemed the more remarkable given his past experience. Willis well knew that Poe had edited several monthly journals, and that his position as a scribbler mostly of anonymous fillers, a "mechanical paragraphist," represented a step down: "It was his business to sit at a desk, in a corner of the editorial room, ready to be called upon for any of the miscellaneous work of the moment—announcing news, condensing statements, answering correspondents, noticing amusements—everything but the writing of a 'leader,' or constructing any article upon which his peculiar idiosyncrasy of mind could be impressed." Poe, he said, speaking for himself and his partner Morris, "was one of our 'boys.' We both loved him."

Willis was correct in thinking Poe was out of his element at the *Mirror*. When the periodical had reached a circulation of ten thousand, Willis labeled it the organ of the "upper ten thousand," reflecting his intention of speaking to and for the social world, those whom Poe regarded sourly as "the frivolous and fashionable." The *Mirror* offered almost no chance to write what he valued. One of his anonymous 'mechanical paragraphs,' probably representative of many others he got up, consists of two colorless sentences introducing the reprint of an anecdote concerning Sir Walter Scott: "A SILLY GIRL OF A NUMEROUS KIND.—Scott's printer's wife, Mrs. Ballantyne, has been induced to record her recollections of the great novelist. She begins by confessing to the following *Niaiserie:*—," after which follows the anecdote. No articles appeared under Poe's name, although he is also known to have written a humorous piece on some beplumed Swiss bell ringers then performing in New York. In his last month or two with the newspaper, he did write more substantially on the need for an international copyright law, and on didacticism in poetry. Such infrequent opportunities aside, the *Mirror* offered Poe only the sort of hateful literary work that had sent him looking for government employment as an alternative.

Even while finding something like a living in lightweight journalism, Poe wrote and kept trying to place new fiction, although some of this too has a journalistic cast. Probably only days after arriving in New York, likely hoping to mark his arrival with a fanfare, he sold to the New York *Sun* a hoax announcing the crossing of the Atlantic Ocean in three days by balloon. At the time there was much talk of the possibility of such a flight, together with books and articles on the subject from which Poe drew the details and language for perhaps a fourth of his hoax. The *Sun* printed his account with exclamatory headlines in a special one-page broadside edition, preceded by a stop-press announcement in the morning edition: "ASTOUNDING INTELLIGENCE BY PRIVATE EXPRESS FROM CHARLESTON VIA NORFOLK!—THE ATLANTIC OCEAN CROSSED IN THREE DAYS!!" Poe prided himself on the verisimilitude of his shocker and later wrote that the *Sun* office was "besieged" by people buying up copies of the "Extra" at any price: "I never witnessed more intense excitement to get possession of a newspaper." But in reality the hoax does not seem to have been a frantic success. Other newspapers put it down as "blunderingly got up" or compared it unfavorably to a moon hoax published by the *Sun* a decade before. The comment galled Poe as once more disparaging him in comparison to some lesser being. Replying in the *Columbia Spy,* he observed that the public's acceptance of the earlier moon hoax, "even for an instant, merely proves the prevalent ignorance of Astronomy."

Poe also turned out three comic tales, just as evidently for popular consumption. The spirit of "The Angel of the Odd. An Extravaganza" has a canteen for head, wine-pipe for body, kegs for legs, and speaks a phunny German-Dutch dialect ("mus pe so dronk as de pig, den, for not zee me as I zit her at your zide"). In "The Literary Life of Thingum Bob, Esq.," Poe satirically traced the literary career, often paralleling his own, of a barber's son who aspires to be an editor and poet. After beating up and ridding himself of his father, "the old bore," he succeeds in buying up and merging several journals, uniting all the literature of the country in "one magnificent Magazine" known as the "Rowdy-Dow, Lollipop, Hum-Drum, and Goosetherumfoodle." "The Thousand-and-Second Tale of Scheherazade" again mocks the belief that technological progress can cure the human condition, surveying such recent wonders as trains, steamboats, and telegraphs as they might be undeservingly marveled over in some Arabian Night's tale. Even in these negligible comic tales Poe's imagination dwelt on such preoccupations as devourable dead-alive persons and father-son rivalries.

Poe did produce some more substantial works at this time but wrote almost all of them before the end of May 1844, that is, either while still in Philadelphia or during his first eight weeks or so in New York. They appeared in print intermittently amid the stream of his shoddier journalism, including a fine new poem, "Dream-Land." Its speaker, like the narrators of many of Poe's tales, is a traumatized survivor returned to tell what has shaken him:

> *I have reached these lands but newly*
> *From an ultimate dim Thule—*
> *From a wild weird clime that lieth, sublime,*
> *Out of Space—out of Time.*

He has "wandered home" from the phantasmagoric world of dreams, a place of "Bottomless vales and boundless floods" whose archaic strangeness is emphasized by novel line arrangements, older grammatical forms ("lieth," "hath"), and arcane diction ("Eidolon," "Thule"). Here dreams are a path to Memory, and through it to a past that is otherwise literally buried. For like the voyage of Arthur Gordon Pym, the journey of the poem's speaker culminates in a shroud:

> *There the traveller meets aghast*
> *Sheeted Memories of the Past—*
> *Shrouded forms that start and sigh*
> *As they pass the wanderer by—*

A parable of Poe's art, the poem dramatizes how dream and memory lead invariably back to specters, "forms of friends long given, / In agony, to the worms—and Heaven." Especially because of its trancelike refrain, and the many repetitions and retards within the long verse sentences, "Dream-Land" conveys better than any other of Poe's poems the sense of feeling haunted.

The unnamed narrator of "The Premature Burial" is differently haunted. Susceptible to profound swoons, he dreads being mistaken for dead and then coffined. Here Poe addressed a widespread anxiety in the period, in part owing to uncertainty over the physiology of dying. Fontenelle's often reprinted *On the Signs of Death* (1834) showed how such grievous conditions as tetanus and asphyxia could simulate death. Books and pamphlets like Joseph Taylor's *The Dangers of Premature Burial* (1816) discussed lethal errors in medical diagnosis and funerary practice, giving rise as well to many fictional accounts that made the treatment of the subject something of a cliché by the time Poe's tale appeared. The year before, in fact, Willis had discussed in the *Mirror* a new "life-preserving coffin" that automatically opened if the occupant stirred.

Fearful of being prematurely buried, the narrator of Poe's tale places in his family vault receptacles for food and water, and makes himself a warm padded coffin built to fly open at the feeblest body movement. He even leaves a hole in the lid so that one of his hands can be linked to an alarm bell outside the tomb by a long rope. The setup resembles the womblike crate and guide rope in *Pym,* and illustrates Freud's view that the fear of being buried alive, for many people the most uncanny thought of all, derives from an earlier, pleasurable fantasy of intrauterine existence. The title itself captures the equation of tomb and womb, 'premature' of course often being coupled with 'birth.' (As applied to births, the word first appeared in the English language in 1838.) Or as Poe himself writes in the tale, "The boundaries which divide Life from Death, are at best shadowy and vague." "The Premature Burial" ultimately warns against too much concern with the grave. But in this it is virtually alone among Poe's works. At a time when James Fenimore Cooper, Ralph Waldo Emerson, and many other American writers and painters were creating a feeling of space and self-reliant freedom, he was creating in his many accounts of persons bricked up in walls, hidden under floorboards, or jammed in chimneys a mythology of enclosure, constriction, and victimization.

Biographically, "The Oblong Box" is one of Poe's most revealing tales, probably written within two or three weeks after he arrived in New York. It re-imagines his journey there with Sissy by train and steamboat, while Muddy remained in Philadelphia. In the tale, a morose young artist named Cornelius Wyatt sails from Charleston to New York with his wife and his two sisters. Oddly, he and his wife occupy separate staterooms. More oddly still, he retains in his room an oblong box some six feet long and two and a half feet wide, on whose lid is painted the name and address of his wife's mother. The narrator of the tale speculates that the box (one of many in Poe's fiction) contains a copy of Leonardo's *Last Supper.* He believes his suspicion confirmed when he hears the artist at night prying open the box by a chisel and muffled mallet, followed by a "low sobbing, or murmuring sound." This he attributes to the artist's passion: "He had opened his oblong box, in order to feast his eyes upon the pictorial treasure within."

The denouement of the tale invites little comment, it so starkly enacts Poe's feelings about Virginia. In a storm the ship breaks up and the passengers abandon it for lifeboats, in which they are rescued. The artist, however, refuses to save himself unless the oblong box goes with him. With what seems superhuman strength he drags it from his cabin up the companionway onto the deck of the sinking ship. He turns a three-inch rope several times first around the box and then around his body, and lashed to the box he disappears into the sea and drowns. As his suicide is later explained, on the day of departure his "adored" wife suddenly sickened and died. The captain knew that the other passengers would sooner cancel their trip than sail with a corpse. He arranged for a maid to act as the artist's wife, occupying a separate stateroom, and for the dead body to be partly embalmed, and transported on the ship as cargo. On his voyage to New York the morose artist had not only closed himself in his cabin with his wife's coffin, addressed to her mother, but as if he were some Rufus Griswold, he had hammered open the lid to sob all night over her corpse, and in the end killed himself rather than give up his tie to the thing so easily mistaken for the treasure of his art.

Sometime in his transition from Philadelphia to New York, Poe also wrote his two last detective stories. His ability to concentrate a narrative in a singular detail or perfectly chosen word served him again in the wonderfully titled "The Purloined Letter," which he considered "perhaps, the best of my tales of ratiocination." C. Auguste Dupin returns to recover a letter stolen from the French queen by one of her ministers, for which the police search in vain. Familiar persons, concerns, and symbolic objects return also. Auguste Dupin and the thieving minister are brothers under the skin: the minister also is named "D—" (and has a brother himself); he lives at the "Hotel D—," Dupin on rue Dunôt; both write verses and purloin letters. Indeed this story of the theft of language ends with a classical quotation concerning the fatal competition between the brothers Atreus and Thyestes. "Thou Art the Man," which treats a puzzling small-town murder, ends with the unpacking of a large box of wine, in what is called "the ceremony of disinterring the treasure." As would not surprise readers of "The Gold-Bug" and "The Oblong Box," or others attuned to Poe's meaning of "treasure," from the crate springs up the murder victim's "bruised, bloody and nearly putrid corpse," and says in the presence of his killer, "Thou art the Man!" This spirited cadaver is really a Maelzel-like human automaton powered by a length of whalebone in its esophagus and a bit of ventriloquism. But its reappearance, and the discovery of the purloined letter, make two more cases in Poe where precious hidden and buried things come back or are reclaimed. Both stories also introduce further innovations that later writers of detective fiction would explore: the frame-up; cloak-and-dagger political in-trigue; postmortem examination and ballistic evidence; the 'least-likely murderer.' Of no little importance for his successors too, Poe now outfitted Dupin with a pipe.

The last of these in-transit works, a dialogue entitled "Mesmeric Revelation," represents a new direction in Poe's career, but also a sign of exhaustion.† He had dramatized survival after death dozens of times in the returned, reincarnated, or reborn figures in his imag-inative works. Now, however, he began trying to explain it discur-sively, in physical and metaphysical terms. He presented his philo-sophical ideas as if elicited from a dying man who has been placed in a trance, in effect hypnotized, by a mesmerist. Poe perhaps hoped through the dignity of philosophy to lift his work above the jour-nalistic level to which it had recently often sunk. By thinking out the certainty of eternal life, too, he perhaps tried to steel himself against the meaning of Virginia's continued illness: the dying mes-merized subject, although named Vankirk, appears in the dialogue as "V.," while the therapeutic mesmerist appears as "P." Whatever Poe's hope, as he ventured into philosophical argument he also now began turning away from the writing of fiction.

Poe tried in brief space to develop mighty ideas that greatly mat-tered to him, but he was no philosopher. He did not trouble to define his key terms, sometimes used the same terms to refer to different things, and often argued disconnectedly and by mere as-sertion. A summary of his idiosyncratic arguments appears in Ap-pendix 5, but it would be folly to seek from "Mesmeric Revelation" a coherent exposition on matter, spirit, and the immortality of the soul. In essence, Poe affirmed the survival of the self in a second state after death, but not as spirit, not as a Christian soul. It exists rather as a material entity, an "unorganized" brainlike congerie of "unparticled" matter, lacking the particled form of "rudimentary" beings and imperceptible to them, but itself able to perceive other substances where in its "rudimentary" state it perceived nothing. Nor does the "complete" self survive in some Christian paradise. Able as part of the divine mind to will itself, it goes not to heaven, but rather, as he told Chivers, "every where." He philosophized his living-dead Madeline Ushers and Irenes into an unimpeded and nearly omniscient supersensitive cluster of unparticles.

Poe continued to ponder these ideas and would later elaborate them in a far more ambitious treatise. Meanwhile the dialogue had an effect he did not intend. As a medical therapy, mesmerism had a respectable scientific lineage, going back to Newton's concept of an electromagnetic ether. By the time mesmerism became popular in America during the 1830s, however, believers had invested the mesmerist with occult powers, granting him the ability not only to redress magnetic imbalances in the patient's afflicted areas, but also to control minds, enjoy clairvoyant visions, and dispense the comforts of pop psychology to many who no longer looked to churches for spiritual guidance. To Poe's chagrin, the dialogue was received not for its ideas, but as the authentic report of an actual mesmeric experiment in which a dying subject had brought back transcendant knowledge from the Other Side. For a year or more the piece was republished and commented on in such mesmeric, religious, or pseudoscientific periodicals as *The Regenerator, The Star of Bethlehem,* and *The American Phrenological Journal.* Poe called the misapprehensions of his intent "excruciatingly and unsurpassably funny." But they more deeply disappointed him. He had used the narrative framework of the mesmeric experiment, he explained, merely to vivify and arouse interest in his own "philosophy," in order to "introduce it to the world in a manner that should insure for it attention."

Poe's "Crisis"; Attack on Longfellow; "The Raven."

CA. OCTOBER 1844 – FEBRUARY 1845

Working hard at the Brennan farm, Poe felt low. Whatever flush of optimism had come with his move to New York in the spring, had faded by fall. "I have reached," he wrote in October, "a crisis of my life." A visitor to the *Mirror* office the same month found him looking ahead rather hopelessly, "very dejected and with apparent forebodings as to his future." He seems to have felt lonely also, lamenting that he had "few friends," meanwhile letting his personal correspondence lapse. "Why my old friend, have you not written to me," Thomas complained several times. Some of his silence was alienating. Chivers had written two unanswered letters, effusively lamenting the death of his young daughter. "I presume you did not trouble yourself to take them out of the [Post] Office," he wrote to Poe with some bitterness. "They, no doubt, contained a great deal of nonsense, and it is well, perhaps, that you did not pay any attention to them. They contained not only the information of the death of my little Angel-child, but the kindest expression of my regard for you."

Poe's self-absorbed unhappiness had many sources: Virginia, the accumulation of past woes, a settled instability in him, perhaps his age, for he was nearing thirty-six, time for reassessment. His dissatisfaction with his career had if anything grown. Aside from his work on the *Mirror,* begun late in the year, his earnings for the abundant writing he did in 1844 have been estimated at about $425—in a country where it was said people never conversed without pronouncing the word "DOLLAR." Poe keenly felt the difference to be demeaning. He had had to bear cheerfully, he said, the "sad poverty & the thousand consequent [ill]s & contumelies which the condition of the mere Magazinist entails upon him in America.— where more than in any other region upon the face of the globe to be poor is to be despised." Not only the poor pay for his work weighed on Poe, but also its captivity to the American equivalent of Grub Street. Conundrums and "mechanical paragraphs" were hardly what he had foreseen for himself when he declared to John Allan that ambition commanded him to seek the world for his theater. Out of step with the nation's busy commercial life, he also felt more than ever rootless and disinherited, lacking a family network that might otherwise help support him. He brooded on his aloneness, the "long & desperate struggle with the ills attendant upon orphanage, the total want of relatives."

Swimmer of the longest swim and jumper of the longest jump, however, Poe still indelibly wished for a name to be respected. He told Chivers that while in seclusion at the farm he was harboring his energies for a new assault on Parnassus, "busied with books and [ambiti]ous thoughts," he said, "until the hour shall arrive when I may come forth with a certainty of success." One such thought concerned his often-abandoned "Stylus." His fantasies about the rewards for having such a magazine had expanded with each defeat of his hopes, and by this time he envisioned a profit of $60,000, perhaps $70,000, even perhaps $200,000. What blocked him, he now believed, was his reputation, which had suffered from the scattered publication of his works in various periodicals. Because of the piecemeal appearance, his ability had been "misconceived & misjudged," estimated by one piece or another here or there. He did not distort the situation, for readers knew him as a critic or a writer of tales, a few as a poet, but fewer still as a versatile man of letters. He judged less accurately in estimating that, even leaving aside his criticism, poems, and miscellaneous pieces, his sixty-six tales might make five volumes the size of ordinary novels. Getting his tales published in book form, he thought, would increase his renown and lead "forthwith . . . to the establishment of the journal."

In this certainty, or yearning hope, Poe sent off a pleading letter in the late fall to Charles Anthon, a professor of classical languages at Columbia College whom he credited with "unbounde[d] influence" at the firm of Harper and Brothers, publishers of *Pym.* By the mid-1840s this uniquely successful New York house was purveying literature to the entire nation, each year issuing about a hundred new books, its bulging warehouses stocked with nearly a thousand titles, the brothers' wealth estimated at a million dollars. Since Poe's aim was not money but larger fame followed by realization of the "Stylus," he told Anthon that "I seek *no* pecuniary remuneration." But he made it clear that his welfare was at stake, "much if not all of the prosperity and even comfort of my future life." Anthon did call on the Harpers, but found them ill-disposed toward Poe: "They have *complaints* against you," he wrote back, "grounded on certain movements of yours, when they acted as your publishers some years ago." The Harpers' distrust does not necessarily speak badly for Poe. James Harper read little of what he published, and his three rules for achieving happiness reportedly were "Trust in God, pay your bills, and keep your bowels open." Anthon advised Poe to see the brothers himself and try to talk things out.

Ironically, Poe's ten-month stay at the Brennan farm ended, and his return to New York City commenced, with several events that vastly expanded his reputation. For one, early in December the Paris newspaper *La Quotidienne* published in two installments an adaptation of "William Wilson," marking Poe's introduction to French readers, and the first publication of his work in a foreign language. For another, James Russell Lowell published in the February 1845 *Graham's* the first serious, substantial essay on Poe's career. Considering Poe a "Dear Friend," Lowell sent a draft for his suggestions or approval, and wrote the essay with him much in mind, wishing it "to please you rather than the public." He included a biographical sketch, based on the earlier fanciful one in the mammoth *Saturday Museum,* and a new engraving of Poe that gets something of his curiously sloping forehead and the dark caterpillarlike heaviness of his long eyebrows, but also seems ideally wide-eyed, placid, and hopeful-looking. (Poe told Lowell, "It scarcely resembles me at all.")

More important, Lowell gave for the first time a view, laudatory but judicious, of Poe's literary life in the round. He depicted him as at once a discriminating critic, a technically skilled poet, and a prolific writer of fiction: "Among contemporary authors," he said, "we know of *none* who has displayed more varied and striking abilities." He characterized Poe's work as flowing from two of the main qualities of genius, "a faculty of vigorous yet minute analysis, and a wonderful fecundity of imagination." The second allowed Poe in his fiction to create "impalpable shadows of mystery" while the first gave him at the same time the "patience to be minute," thus to "throw a wonderful reality into his most unreal fancies," a formulation that aligns Poe's work with the dreamlike facticity of the later surrealists. Lowell discussed particular works also, and included a list of thirty tales Poe had written since the publication of *Tales of the Grotesque and Arabesque.* Reprinted in two parts on the front pages of the *Mirror,* his essay offered readers a way of viewing Poe's sensibility and experiencing the cumulative richness of his career. "Few knew precisely what he had written," one New York newspaper commented, "his name was not on Library catalogues or any of his books on the shelves. . . . Lowell's article removes the anonymous and exhibits the author of some of the most peculiar and characteristic productions in our literature."

Poe himself created the two other, more sensational events, both of which seem simultaneously to defy and confirm his "crisis." On January 13 and 14, the *Mirror* published his review of *The Waif,* an anthology of allegedly neglected poems edited by Henry Wadsworth Longfellow. Poe paid a backhand compliment in calling Longfellow's prefatory poem the "worthiest" poem in the volume, as its rhythmic defects suited its subject: "its particular excellence arises from what is, generally, a gross demerit." Then offering the back of his hand alone, he accused Longfellow of having written the anonymous poems in the collection himself, gathering the anthology specifically in order to salvage a group of his poems that were too few to make a volume of their own. He found more to suspect. For all its beauties, he said, the anthology was "infected with a *moral taint*." The moral taint sounds much like a frailty for omitting Edgar A. Poe from the selections: "there *does* appear, in this exquisite little volume, a very careful avoidance of all American poets who may be supposed especially to interfere with the claims of Mr. Longfellow." Having implied that Longfellow enviously excluded his rivals, Poe insinuated that he also plagiarized them: "These men Mr. Longfellow can continuously *imitate* (*is* that the word?) and yet never even incidentally commend."

Poe's slaps and clips did not go unanswered. The following week Willis published a reply to his review, by Longfellow's friend George Stillman Hillard. Hillard pointed out that Poe's ambiguously demeaning praise of Longfellow's introductory poem seemed unaware of the distinction between rhythm and meter—a direct hit at Poe's lessons to American readers on the fundamentals of prosody. Hillard also denied that Longfellow had written any of the anonymous poems in the volume and challenged Poe's reading of Longfellow's character. Longfellow was remarkable in lacking feelings of rivalry, he said, and on the contrary well known for "his warm and generous commendation of the poetical efforts of his contemporaries." Together with Hillard's reply, Willis published a mocking rejoinder from Poe: "I may know nothing about rhythm," it went, "for I remember (with regret) that it was precisely the *rhythm* of Mr. Longfellow in the proem, which elicited my unqualified applause." Ridiculing Hillard's comments one by one in brusque one-or-two-sentence paragraphs, he explained that Hillard had bumblingly set out to spare Longfellow criticism and wound up denying him praise, defending him not only against the one-tenth of "very moderate disapproval" in the review but also, as he put it later, "from the nine-tenths of my enthusiastic admiration into the bargain."

Such were the first lunges in what would end as arguably the longest, strangest, and most-publicized personal war in American literary history. Ultimately Poe would devote several times as many pages to Longfellow as to any other writer, fully a hundred in one modern edition of his criticism. Knives flashed again on January 25, when the Buffalo *Western Literary Messenger* published a letter that seemed to support Poe's charges. The pseudonymous writer compared Longfellow's "The Good George Campbell," a translation from the German of O. L. B. Wolff, with the Scots ballad "Bonnie George Campbell." He denounced Longfellow not only for "gross plagiarism" but also for impudence in supposing he could "undetected, palm off" an ancient Scottish song as his own translation from the

German. The two poems were in fact very close, and no wonder. While abroad, Longfellow had been given an anthology containing the German poem, which he translated and published; he had no idea, however, that the German was itself a translation of the original Scots ballad. Skillfully retranslating a translation, he had simply rendered the German back into something close to its original, which he was now accused of plagiarizing. New York newspapers exploited the new charge; one printed the poems side by side and nudged, "Singular *coincidence,* eh?"

Poe had his say on February 28, when he redelivered at the New York Society Library his lecture "Poets and Poetry of America." As given the year before, this lecture had of course been a vehicle for his rancor at Rufus Griswold. But among their several other similarities, both Poe and Griswold usually tried in their professional lives to work around personal antagonisms, especially where they stood to gain. Just as Poe's dispute with Longfellow erupted, Griswold wrote to him asking for some material to include in a new anthology of American prose. Griswold acknowledged past enmities: "I have some cause of personal quarrel with you, which you will easily enough remember." But he added that he did not allow private grievances to influence his literary judgment and retained "the early formed and well founded favorable opinion of your works." To Griswold's credit, maybe, it might be remarked that he said nothing of liking Poe, only of wanting to reprint his works; the week before, a New York publisher reported a conversation in which Griswold spoke of Poe, and "told me shocking bad stories about him." No novice in smarminess himself, Poe avowed to Griswold his pain in thinking "that I had lost, through my own folly, an honorable friend." He assured Griswold that he had erroneously based his criticisms of *Poets and Poetry of America* on "the malignant slanders of a mischief-maker," and that his new version of the lecture "left out *all* that was offensive to yourself."

Poe did not do the same for Longfellow. The *Mirror* played up his forthcoming talk, promising exquisite literary cannibalism, "divisions of sensitive membrane" by Poe's tomahawk of taste: "the feast will be Epicurean to all but the sufferers." Speaking for almost two hours before two to three hundred persons, Poe did slice away. Newspaper reviews contain a fairly full account of the lecture, otherwise known only from a surviving manuscript fragment. Going after the puffing system first, Poe singled out the "Dunderheaded critics of Boston" and slashed away at the huckster-made canon of

American poets, taking fully fifteen minutes to mince the Davidson sisters of New York, popular sentimental poets whose acclaim he attributed to their both having died in their teens. Longfellow he treated in relation to the rest of Griswold's "copperplate five"— Bryant, Halleck, Sprague, and Dana—the pantheon whose engravings adorned the frontispiece of *Poets and Poetry.* As the *Mirror* reported his comments he granted more talent to Longfellow than to the others, but remarked that "his fatal alacrity at imitation made him borrow, when he had better at home." The accounts in less friendly newspapers, however, indicate that Poe struck even harder than this. The *Tribune* objected to his "broad assertion that Longfellow is a plagiarist. Of all critical cant," it added, "this hunting after coincidence of idea or phrase, often unavoidable, between authors, is the least endurable." The 'dunderheaded critic' for the Boston *Atlas* came up with the same pun on Poe's name to which Boston theater reviewers had treated David Poe nearly forty years earlier: he said he would have preferred a "dancing dog or sommerseting monkey, to the man who could utter such remarks . . . in reference to the poetry of Sprague and Longfellow. If he was to come before a Boston audience with such stuff, they would *poh* at him at once."

As the opening of Poe's crusade against Longfellow brought him back to New York City with new notoriety, another event brought him an entirely new level of celebrity. In the January 29 issue of the *Mirror,* in a single long column running nearly the length of the back page, Willis published for the first time one of the most famous poems ever written. In introducing "The Raven" he called it "unsurpassed in English poetry for subtle conception, masterly ingenuity of versification, and consistent, sustaining of imaginative lift. . . . It will stick to the memory of everybody who reads it." †

The reception of "The Raven" might be compared to that of some uproariously successful hit song today. "Everybody reads the Poem and praises it," said the *New World,* two weeks after its appearance, "justly we think, for it seems to us full of originality and power." Readers thrilled to the poem's inevitable-seeming novelty, as of something unimaginable but entirely within reach. They became, one New Yorker said, "electrified by the weird cry of Nevermore." The *Pennsylvania Inquirer* reprinted "The Raven" under the heading "A BEAUTIFUL POEM"; the *New World* called it "wild and *shivery,*" written in "a Stanza unknown before to gods, men, and booksellers"; the *Morning Express* said it "may well defy competi-

tion in its way from the whole circle of cotemporary verse writers."
Within a month after its appearance "The Raven" was reprinted at
least ten times. Its sound effects made it ideal for reading aloud,
and in *A Plain System of Elocution* (2d ed., New York, 1845) it soon
found a place it still occupies, among the "Poetical Recitations" of
a school text.

Excitement over the catchy poem broke out in a rash of parodies.
Periodicals in Boston, New York, and Philadelphia comically turned
the famous bird into other creatures, "The Black Cat," "The Cra-
ven" (by "Poh!"), "The Gazelle," "The Whippoorwill," "The Tur-
key," "The Mammoth Squash" ("Green and specked with spots of
golden"). The poem became a vehicle for treating many other subjects. "Sarles" substituted a temperance owl, offered a thimble-full
of whisky:

> *I invited him to drink of, saying there was plenty more—*
> *But the owl he shook his head, he threw the whiskey on the floor,*
> *Plainly saying, "nevermore!"*

"Snarles," author of "THE VETO," commented on local politics:
"Once upon an evening dreary, the Council pondered weak and
weary, / Over many a long petition which was voted down a bore."
The resourceful Dr. F. Felix Gouraud of New York, manufacturer
of an "Italian" soap, lampooned his imitators in an advertisement:
"my mind's eye saw a scheming fellow counterfeiting Soap— / Yes!
counterfeiting GOURAUD'S matchless *Medicated Soap*."

Poe's own fame rose with that of "The Raven," and many readers
identified poet and poem. *The Town* published an illustration of a
humanized raven, presenting it tongue-in-cheek as the "portrait of
a distinguished poet, critic and writer of tales." According to a later
account, Dr. John Francis of New York invited Poe to his home
and introduced him to his wife and guests by saying, "Eliza, my
dear—'The Raven'!" These and many similar gestures offered for
once some large gratification of Poe's lifelong desire for approbation and victory. The writer Elizabeth Oakes Smith, a New York
acquaintance, recalled his telling her that the poem was "being talked
about a great deal." He said he had been at a theater last night,
when an actor inserted into the play the word *nevermore,* and the
audience "evidently took up the allusion." Poe told her this, Mrs.
Smith said, with "an unearthly look of pleasure." An English publisher named Frederick Saunders later reported that Poe thought of

going to England to read the poem before Queen Victoria, and of presenting her a copy, bound sumptuously.

The countless admirers also pleased Poe as confirming the soundness of his artistic aims. He had long thought it possible to satisfy both the many and the few, and contrived "The Raven," he said, to "suit at once the popular and the critical taste." All the same, he made effective small revisions in successive reprints of the poem throughout his life, was finicky about the typographical setup of the long lines, and regarded "The Raven" as in many ways a stylistic experiment, to be appreciated most by connoisseurs of technical niceties. He pointed out, for example, that the poem could be split down the midline breaks and printed in short lines, a "not uncommon form," except that the second line of each stanza had no such break, but rather "an aspirate pause in the middle, like that before the short line in the Sapphic Adonic," while at the pause of the fifth line alliteration is abandoned. By his later account, he also sought to give the "Nevermore" refrain a subtly different meaning with each reappearance, and to steer between straightforward narrative and the poetic "suggestiveness" he valued. He conceived the poem essentially as the tale of a student, desolated by the death of his beloved, visited on a stormy "bleak December" night by an "ominous bird." His problem, at least as he described his intent in retrospect, was how to avoid the "hardness or nakedness" of mere narrative, without veering into didacticism or allegory, to enrich the implications of the tale without pointing a moral. To do so, he explained, he added the two concluding stanzas, in which for the first time he introduced a metaphor, leading the reader to begin regarding the raven and what has come before as "emblematical," but even then withholding "until the very last line of the very last stanza" the meaning of the emblem.

How commendably Poe realized his craftsmanlike aims is something else. To a cold critical eye the dance-craze rhythms and technicolor alliteration can seem pointlessly deft, verbal equivalents of rolling a half-dollar across one's knuckles. William Butler Yeats, for one, thought the poem "insincere and vulgar." "Analyse the Raven" he said, "and you find that its subject is a commonplace and its execution a rhythmical trick. Its rhythm never lives for a moment, never once moves with an emotional life." For many the most discriminating critics, Poe succeeded all too well in suiting the popular taste, producing a work fatally destined to be Beloved, a poem for people who don't like poetry.

In his later comments on "The Raven," Poe explained that the emblematic meaning of the bird was *"Mournful and Never-ending Remembrance."* No doubt, for the phrase can stand as the motto of almost everything he ever wrote. But it seems more precise to call the dramatic situation in the poem a conflict between Remembrance and Forgetting. The student has done what he can to put the lost Lenore out of mind. He drowses, tries to find "surcease from sorrow" in study, vows not to repeat her name but leave her "Nameless *here* for evermore." Yet like all other submerged things in Poe, thoughts of Lenore refuse to stay down. When the student opens the door at the first mysterious tapping outside, he whispers, half-believing she still lives and has returned, "Lenore!" Despite his vow to leave her nameless, in the course of the tale he repeats "Lenore" four more times. He rests his head on a velvet cushion, only to be reminded that it is something *"She* shall press, ah, nevermore!" As unhealed memory thrusts itself into the student's consciousness, Poe subtly keeps the past present through other elements of the poem: in the quaint figure of the raven, come from "days of yore"; the antique bust of Pallas; the book of "forgotten lore"; archaic words like *Quoth, methought,* and *surcease.* He dramatizes the student's enthrallment to the past by using every conceivable device of repetition, not only the "nevermore" refrain but reiterated key words, lines, sounds, rhythms, even exact doublets like "rapping, rapping," "tell me—tell me," "still is sitting, *still* is sitting." The throbbing repetitions not only help to render the student's obsession with his loss and abandonment, and his struggle to keep sane. They also inflict on the reader the sensation of oppressively unrelenting recurrence which the student experiences himself: as Willis astutely observed, the poem "will stick in the memory of everybody who reads it."

Obscurely, Poe himself viewed the student's hopeless inability to forget as pleasurable. In his later comments on the poem, he explained that the student's continued questioning of the bird is in part impelled by "that species of despair which delights in self-torture." The student asks not because he believes the raven has an answer, but in order to elicit the expected word *Nevermore* and so receive "the most delicious because the most intolerable of sorrow." Aside from an element of conventional Romantic Agony, Poe's understanding of the poem perhaps reflects his notion, expressed earlier in "Irenë" ("The Sleeper"), that the dead rest only as long as they remain in living memory; when forgotten they return to the world in anger. To forget is to incur the guilt of disloyalty and risk reprisal from the betrayed departed. From this point of view the student suffers not only from an inability to stop remembering, but also from a fear of forgetting. Another, no more comforting reason for his need to commemorate without stop is that the poem offers no hope of reunion in heaven. When the student asks the raven to tell him, "by that God we both adore," whether he shall again clasp Lenore in "the distant Aidenn," the bird responds as it does invariably. However persecuting and impalpable, memory may be the only means of preserving the dead.

In several details "The Raven" seems to illustrate Poe's own irrepressible need to remember. There is no telling just how much Virginia's progressive illness and his anticipation of her death figured in the poem, but the "bleak December" perhaps recalls the other December when Eliza Poe died, as *Pallas* again invokes *Allan,* and *Lenore,* like the earlier tale "Eleonora" and the poem "Lenore," touches on the name of William Henry Leonard. In fact in 1826, Henry himself had published a poem with the refrain "I'll ne'er forget—no—never!" Suggestively too, one source for Poe's poem was a ballad published five years earlier in an English magazine, entitled "The Raven; or, The Power of Conscience." Unlike Poe's raven "croaking 'nevermore,'" although perhaps with one underlying element of Poe's meaning, its raven reiterates the name of the narrator's dead brother: *"He croaks of my dead brother still!"*

Although the student at last screams at the raven to "Take thy beak from out my heart, and take thy form from off my door," at the end of the poem the ominous bird remains on the bust of Pallas, and "still is sitting, *still* is sitting." As he will always, for in recollection the dead in some form endure, and the raven, a devourer with its beak in the heart, is still a link with the past. Indeed the hated-welcome bird of *"Mournful and Never-ending Remembrance"* is Poe himself, beak in the reader's heart, evermore repeating that those we have loved and who become lost to us can never return, that we can never clasp them in Aidenn, that they can never be forgotten, and that however painful it may be to remember them, it is still more painful to give them up.

Return to the City;
The Broadway Journal;
The Longfellow War.

CA. JANUARY—APRIL 1845

Poe, Muddy, and Virginia returned to New York City at the end of January or sometime in February 1845. Built on a narrow island, Manhattan rose from its harbor like Venice from the sea, its shoreline fringed by wharves and great thickets of masts and rigging. Already a booming port, New York was on its way to becoming a major world city, now often nicknamed the "Great Metropolis," the "Empire City," "the Tyre of the western world." During the 1840s the number of its inhabitants grew from just over three hundred thousand to more than half a million, more than half of whom had been born abroad, mostly in Ireland or Germany. Long confined to the southern tip of the island, the city was fast extending northward, spreading its massy ornate palazzi up Fifth Avenue, trailed by a swelling jam of carriages, coaches, wagons, and transportation of all sorts. By one estimate in 1848, New York's 350 omnibuses, the democratic "Carriage for the Million," collected seventy thousand fares a day. All was eagerness and activity, nonstop change. Philip Hone, a mayor of New York, decided that the city's motto was "Overturn, overturn, overturn!"

Many felt that New York had also taken the lead from Boston and Philadelphia as the nation's literary and publishing center. "No man well acquainted with the history of Literature and Art in our country during the last ten years," Horace Greeley remarked in 1839, "can refuse to acknowledge that New York has towered above her sister cities." The major writers of the older literary generation in America—Irving, Cooper, and Bryant—remained closely identified with New York. But the city was nourishing a younger, still more gifted and daring generation as well. In 1846 the New York publishers Wiley and Putnam issued the American edition of *Typee,* the first novel of twenty-six-year-old Herman Melville, himself a native of the city. The book was reviewed in the Brooklyn *Eagle* by twenty-seven-year-old Walt Whitman, then a resident of Brooklyn and beginning his literary career as a journalist and fiction writer. Dozens of lesser literary figures lived and wrote in New York in the 1840s, profiting from the rise there of great American publishing houses that began to dominate the book and magazine market, enduring firms with such family names as Harper, Van Nostrand, Scribner, Wiley, Putnam, and Dodd, Mead.

During the year (again) that Poe and his family spent in the heart of New York, they lived in three different places. No more is known about their dwellings than the street names and house numbers. The trio moved from the Brennan farm to 154 Greenwich Street, where they stayed about four months. Around May they moved to the second floor of 195 East Broadway, a boardinghouse. Not only strangers and bachelors lived in boardinghouses but often whole families, who took meals with fellow lodgers at a public table and joined them in the drawing room. Likely at the end of the summer Poe moved again, to a three-story house at 85 Amity Street. He correctly described the area as one of the city's "more fashionable quarters," for the house stood only two streets from Washington Square. Center of the city's wealthiest ward, the square was enclosed on the east by the neo-Gothic main building of New York University, and on the north by the red-brick row houses of prominent merchants.

What brought Poe back to the city from the suburbs he preferred was almost certainly his decision to leave Willis's *Mirror* and work for a new weekly, the *Broadway Journal*. This magazine was operated in partnership by a former schoolteacher named John Bisco, who looked after the publishing and financial end, and Charles Frederick Briggs, who controlled the editorial department and solicited contributions. Poe dealt mostly with Briggs, a small rather slight man with a thin face who walked, in Poe's description of him, with a "quick, nervous step" and, being interested in art, inclined in his dress to "affect the artist" (Illus. 14). Like the preening Willis and the suave Griswold, he came by his appearance through several metamorphoses, having been a Nantucket sailor, later a wholesale grocer, then the author of a novel entitled *The Adventures of Harry Franco,* whose sudden success led him to abandon mercantile pursuits to earn a living in journalism. His father had been imprisoned for debt; he could recall, when a child, touching his father's hand through the bars of a jail cell. He too had failed in several business ventures, felt little confidence about his business ability, and saw himself as a commercial jinx.

Around the middle of December 1844, Poe had called on Briggs, bringing a letter of introduction from James Russell Lowell, a close friend with whom Briggs shared a hostility to slavery. Lowell described Briggs as someone Poe would like, who desired his aid. For a month or so Poe wrote for Briggs's new magazine at the rate of a dollar a column. He evidently thought the *Broadway Journal* promising, for early in January he published a brief piece in the *Mirror* entitled "WHY HAVE THE NEW YORKERS NO REVIEW?" He called for a magazine distinctive of the city, a "proper indigenous vehicle" for the literary opinions of New York's many writers, a rallying point against assaults on the city's intellectual life launched from the magazines of Boston.

Poe got what he called for, and more. On February 21, 1845, he signed an agreement, binding for a year, to "assist" Briggs in editing the *Journal* and furnish every week at least a page of original matter. So far the contract offered only the same journalistic grind he had bemoaned since leaving *Graham's*. But the contract offered something else too. During a trial period of one year, he would receive in exchange for his work one third of the magazine's profits, payable as often as every four weeks. To ascertain what the profits were, he would also be allowed to inspect the account books whenever he wished. The terms made him if not exactly an owner of a magazine, not simply a salaried hack either. In exchange for his work he would receive a financial stake in the *Journal* itself. In the tenth issue, his name appeared on the masthead as one of the magazine's three editors. "I have taken," he let several people know, "a 3d pecuniary interest." What this meant for his personal history he confided to his cousin George Poe: "you will appreciate my efforts to elevate the family name."

Briggs was pleased with his new editor but hardly saw Poe as his partner. After their first meetings he found that he liked Poe "exceedingly well," despite "abominable lies," he added, told about him by Rufus Griswold, "which his whole demeanor contradicts." Poe evidently spoke of his artistic aims, for Briggs had originally thought him "one of the Graham and Godey species" but now began to understand what Poe was striving for in his work, his wish to be, as Briggs recorded what he said, "entirely free from didacticism and sentiment." But however sympathetic to Poe, Briggs regarded him as "only an assistant to me," a hired hand working under his control who might boost circulation. He took on Poe, he explained, because of his own "liability" to be distracted from business, because

1. Miniature portrait of ELIZA POE
(Rare Book Department, Free Library
of Philadelphia)

2. Boston playbill of a performance by the Poes and Noble Usher
(Harvard Theatre Collection)

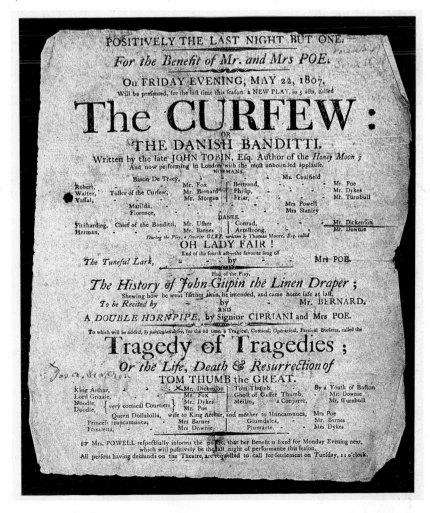

3. JOHN ALLAN
(Edgar Allan Poe Museum of
the Poe Foundation, Inc.,
Richmond, Virginia)

4. FRANCES VALENTINE ALLAN
(Edgar Allan Poe Museum of
the Poe Foundation, Inc.,
Richmond, Virginia)

5. Moldavia (The Valentine Museum, Richmond, Virginia)

6. Carte de visite of MARIA CLEMM
(Ingram-Poe Collection, University of
Virginia Library)

7. THOMAS WILLIS WHITE
(Harry Ransom Humanities Research
Center, University of Texas at Austin)

8. WILLIAM EVANS BURTON, oil portrait by Henry Peters Gay (Courtesy of The New-York Historical Society, New York City)

BURTON'S

GENTLEMAN'S MAGAZINE.

EDITED BY

WILLIAM E. BURTON AND EDGAR A. POE.

VOLUME V.

FROM JULY TO DECEMBER.

By a gentleman, we mean not to draw a line that would be invidious between high and low, rank and subordination, riches and poverty. No. *The distinction is in the mind.* Whoever is open, just, and true; whoever is of a humane and affable demeanour; whoever is honorable in himself, and in his judgment of others, and requires no law but his word to make him fulfil an engagement;—such a man is a gentleman;—and such a man may be found among the tillers of the earth as well as in the drawing rooms of the high born and the rich.

DE VERE.

PHILADELPHIA.
PUBLISHED BY WILLIAM E. BURTON,
DOCK STREET, OPPOSITA THE EXCHANGE.

1839.

9. Frontispiece of *Burton's Gentleman's Magazine* (Fales Library, New York University)

10. GEORGE REX GRAHAM
(Free Library of Philadelphia Picture
Department)

11. POE at about age thirty-three,
reproduced from *The Critic*, April,
1905

12. RUFUS W. GRISWOLD, oil portrait by Charles L. Elliott (Courtesy of The New-York Historical Society, New York City)

13. NATHANIEL P. WILLIS, pastel portrait by Samuel Laurence (Courtesy of The New-York Historical Society, New York City)

14. CHARLES FREDERICK BRIGGS
(Fales Library, New York University)

University of the City of New=York.

ORATION AND POEM,

BEFORE THE

PHILOMATHEAN AND EUCLEIAN SOCIETIES,

Tuesday ~~MONDAY~~, 1st JULY, 1845, 7½ P. M.

AT

UNIVERSITY PLACE CHURCH, DR. POTTS.

Orator, Hon. D. D. BARNARD.   Poet, EDGAR A. POE.

15. Ticket of admission for Poe's
cancelled reading at New York
University (New York University
Archives)

16. THOMAS DUNN ENGLISH,
engraving by John Sartain
(Courtesy of The New-York
Historical Society, New York City)

17. Watercolor miniature of POE at about age thirty-seven, by John A. McDougall (Henry E. Huntington Library and Art Gallery)

18. FRANCES SARGENT OSGOOD, miniature by George P. A. Healy (Courtesy of The New-York Historical Society, New York City)

19. Oil portrait of Poe, ca. 1845, by Samuel S. Osgood (Courtesy of The New York Historical Society, New York City)

20. The Fordham cottage in 1884 (The Bronx County Historical Society)

21. ROSALIE POE
(Edgar Allan Poe Museum of the Poe
Foundation, Inc., Richmond, Virginia)

22. Carte de visite made from a
daguerreotype of POE, perhaps taken
in New York about 1847 (Harvard
College Library)

23. NANCY RICHMOND
in later life (University of Lowell)

24. Oil portrait of SARAH
HELEN WHITMAN at age
thirty-five, by C. Giovanni
Thompson (The Providence
Athenaeum)

25. Photograph of SARAH HELEN
WHITMAN at a later age (Fales
Library, New York University)

26. Daguerreotype of POE taken in Providence on November 9, 1848
(Courtesy of The George Eastman House and the American
Antiquarian Society)

27. Daguerreotype of POE taken shortly before he left Providence on November 13 (Brown University Library; photography by John Miller)

28. SARAH ANNA LEWIS ("STELLA"), oil portrait by Charles L. Elliott (Courtesy of The New-York Historical Society, New York City)

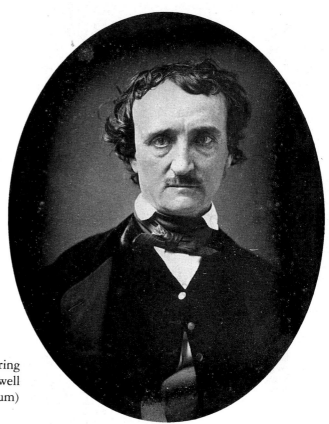

29. POE as he appeared during
his final visit to Lowell
(The J. Paul Getty Museum)

30. ELMIRA SHELTON (The
Valentine Museum, Richmond,
Virginia)

31. Elmira Shelton's house in Richmond (The Valentine Museum, Richmond, Virginia)

32. One of Poe's last letters, written to Muddy from Richmond on August 5, 1849 (Fales Library, New York University)

Richmond — August 5.

My own dearest Muddy — What can be the reason that you have not written to me? Here I have been a whole fortnight & not one line from you yet. I did not think you would treat your poor Eddy in such a way as that. Be sure & write the moment you get this and, if possible, send the "article". Mr Thompson has accepted it. I gave him, also, the article about Mrs Lewis & he will publish it. Of course, I could not ask him anything for it — as it was a great favor to get him to insert it at any rate. I am still out at John's — although I have been to Mrs —'s. & am going back in a day or two to stay some time. Mrs M. was very cordial — but Louisa still more so. I think she is the sweetest creature in the world and makes John the best of wives. She is hardly changed in the least. You know how often I have spoken to you of her heavenly smile. — Be sure & enclose any notices of "Eureka". I write this in the greatest hurry, as John is getting ready to go to town. God bless you, my own dearest mother. Write immediately.

Your own Eddy.

33. The last known daguerreotype of POE,
taken about a week before he left Richmond
(Rare Book and Manuscript Library, Columbia University)

Poe's name had "some authority," and because it would be particularly helpful to have a full-time reviewer. Advertisements provided a reliable income for the *Journal,* book advertising especially,
and to secure such ads meant publishing more than "squibs" of recent books. Having Poe's services as a critic, Briggs believed, would
help to attract advertising from publishers.

It was not unreasonable for Poe to present himself as a one-third
'proprietor' of the *Journal,* considering his written agreement with
Briggs. But the lifelong fantasy of transforming his existence by
having his own magazine led him in some degree to replay the
struggle he had waged years earlier with T. W. White of the *Messen-*
ger. In fact Briggs had hesitated even to post Poe's name on the
masthead as editor. He agreed to do so, and then reluctantly, only
after Poe persuaded him its appearance would immediately attract
new subscribers. "I did not much like the plan," Briggs said, "but
he had more experience than myself in such matters, so I consented."

Whatever Poe's misconception about his standing with Briggs in
business, he was well attuned to Briggs's literary intentions. As Briggs
envisioned the *Broadway Journal,* it matched in some important features the ever-elusive "Stylus." Briggs publicized his determination
to offer only original contributions, not reprints, and to favor "the
whole brood of unfortunates, called American authors," although
treating them candidly and without puffing. Following his own bent
rather than Poe's, he also promised to feature discussion of American art, notice concert and theatrical life, and now and then comment on current issues. In its earlier numbers the *Journal* editori-
alized extensively on the town, describing in a light, satirical tone
the paying of New Year's calls, a recent snowstorm, rumors of the
imminent arrival of Franz Liszt. Through sixteen double-columned
pages of fine print, the magazine offered lots to read, for 6¼ cents
a copy, three dollars a year.

In his first months as editor (or one-third proprietor) Poe served
the *Journal* vigorously, "working 14 or 15 hours a day," he said,
"hard at it all the time. . . . I never knew what it was to be a slave
before." He contributed no new fiction to the magazine but instead
reprinted there or published in revised versions some forty of his
tales, including "Ligeia," "William Wilson," and "The Tell-Tale Heart."
Most of the revisions were small, although given his pleasure in
refinements of language, not slight: altered capitals and italics, re-
ductions of phrases to single words, changes in punctuation to achieve

a certain cadence. A few tales appeared under new and permanent titles, "The Mask of the Red Death" becoming "The Masque of the Red Death." This extraordinary republication of more than half his tales, virtually a new edition of his fiction, grossly violated the *Journal*'s advertised policy of offering only original work: a dozen of the tales were appearing for the third time, another half-dozen the fourth time, "MS. Found in a Bottle" the fifth time. The wholesale recycling arose partly from the pressure to fill up issues, partly from Poe's situation. As a proprietor he could not be at the same time a paid contributor without paying himself out of his own pocket.

Poe also wrote long reviews, some of them featured on the front page, and drummed up many short articles and squibs. He often used these scraps to comment on topics that seriously concerned him, especially the literary marketplace. His financial interest in the *Journal* perhaps made him more than ever aware of literature as a business, but he had also entered an arena of fiercer and more competitive literary trading than he had known in Richmond, Baltimore, or Philadelphia. Willis called New York "the most over-stocked market in the country, for writers. . . . all the country flock and send here for fame." Poe particularly addressed such commercial matters as the nature of magazines, the growth of 'cheap literature,' the need for a copyright law, and the economics of literary nationalism.

Writing here and there in the *Journal,* Poe defended magazines against a widespread belief that they represented a degeneration of taste. "The whole tendency of the age," he said "is Magazine-ward." In fact, the 'golden age of periodicals' was approaching a fulfillment; the number of American periodicals, not including newspapers, had risen from fewer than a hundred in 1825 to about six hundred in 1850, and New York alone in 1849 turned out fifty-four monthlies with some half-million readers. The opportunities and limitations of Poe's own career had been inseparable from that growth, and he wrote as an experienced professional magazinist, his views matured by the prolific work of more than a decade. He told his readers that the magazine's province and power were "illimitable," its supremacy inevitable: "in the end (not far distant) [it] will be the *most* influential of all the departments of Letters." Unlike the older, more dignified quarterly reviews, with their long torpid articles on conventional subjects, aimed at an elite audience, the magazine suited the mid-nineteenth-century's condensed style of thinking and its pace, what he called "the rush of the age," dealing out "the condensed, the pointed, the readily diffused." Far from viewing commercial magazines as literary trash heaps, he rated the artistic possibilities of the "true Magazine spirit" highly. At least as practiced in England and France, magazine writing afforded a wealth of subject matter in diverse tones, presented with invention and skill; magazine writers in those countries both wrote well and earned a living. That few American writers had followed their lead, Poe attributed less to immaturity than to the economics of American publishing. "The few American Magazinists who ever think of this elaboration at all," he observed, "cannot afford to carry it into practice for the paltry prices offered them by our periodical publishers."

Poe traced this economic problem to what many others considered the source of the proliferation of magazines itself: lack of an international copyright. Under existing law, American works could be copyrighted but English (and European) works could not. In the literary marketplace this meant that American publishers had to pay American but not English writers for their work, encouraging them to pirate English books rather than publish American. Many held that it was this lack of economic protection for American books that reduced their number and drove writers into the magazines. But there the situation was even worse, for American publishers of periodicals pirated not only English magazine pieces but American as well.

"Without an international copyright law," Poe wrote, "American authors may as well cut their throats." Not surprisingly, he approved the decision of George Rex Graham, against much protest, to copyright each issue of his magazine, and he joined the American Copyright Club organized in New York in 1843 under the presidency of William Cullen Bryant. The group denounced literary piracy as a crime and promoted enactment of laws against it. Many publishers opposed such laws, arguing that their very absence made a vast amount of literature affordable to a vast American public, especially in the form of so-called cheap literature. Poe, however, denounced this flood of inexpensive books shabbily printed on flimsy paper as a "quagmire of . . . yellow-backed pamphleteering." He believed too that advances in print technology only intensified the need for a copyright. In an article for the *Journal* on "Anastatic Printing," a transfer process by which facsimiles of writings and drawings could be produced from zinc plates, he predicted that publishers would be able to turn out unlimited copies at minimal cost. The result would be to greatly reduce the material value of a book or magazine and proportionally raise the value of its literary content, "and since it is the latter value alone which the copy-right laws are needed to protect, the necessity of the protection will be only the more urgent and more obvious than ever."

Because the lack of an international copyright crowded American writers out of competition and flooded America with English reprints, the issue gave a focus to Poe's thinking on literary nationalism. In 1845, the United States was still an expanding, undefined place; that year, the New-York Historical Society appointed a committee to consider whether some effort should not at last be made to give the country a "PROPER NAME." (The candidates included America, Columbia, and Appalachia, but the committee recommended Allegania.) In most minds the country remained as much unformed culturally as geographically. Calls for a distinctively American literature had been issued since just after the American Revolution; taken up by Emerson and others, they had converged with romantic ideals of the preciousness of self-development in individuals and nations alike, becoming philosophically-grounded and passionate.

Poe had of course long challenged this demand for a literature not only by Americans but also about and for them, and often reasserted his cosmopolitan view that not one nation but the world itself was the stage for the "literary histrio." In his own fiction and poetry he rarely used pointedly American settings and characters, and never in a celebratory, nationalistic way. His removal to New York from Philadelphia, however, brought him in touch with the strenuous literary nationalists, centered around the city's *Democratic Review,* known as "Young America." They not only wished to free American writing from English influence, but also demanded that it become a literature for 'the people' and help in achieving radically democratic social and political goals. Several unsigned editorial articles in the *Broadway Journal* endorsed the movement, professing for example "the most earnest sympathy in all the hopes, and the firmest faith in the capabilities of 'Young America.' We look upon its interests as our own, and shall uniformly uphold them in this Journal." But it is not at all certain that Poe wrote this or the other *Journal* articles that championed the movement. Although he kept on cordial terms with several New York members of Young America, such as Evert Duyckinck, he does not at any time seem to have sponsored its main views.

But in being nearby, the Young Americans did move Poe to for-

mulate his ideas about nativism more fully and precisely than before. He observed in the *Journal* that the talk of cultivating nationality in American literature was conceived in confusion and
propagated unthinkingly: "what this nationality *is,* or what is to be
gained by it, has never been distinctly understood. That an American should confine himself to American themes, or even prefer them,
is rather a political than a literary idea—and at best is a questionable
point." In fact for purely literary reasons, he added, foreign themes
are to be preferred for providing an element of strangeness. (He
put the matter still more strongly a year or so later, denying to
American literature anything "very distinctive" and calling the country
a "continuation of England.")

Poe articulated in the *Journal* a contrasting literary nationalism,
centered on a copyright law, which he called "the nationality of self-
respect." It involved not looking to English critical opinion to establish the worth of American writers, a habit both he and Young
America condemned as servile and also irrational, the British bearing America little but ill will. More personally, he also proposed
taking American literature away from unimaginative men of wealth.
As he formulated the matter around 1846, an "aristocracy of dollars" governed American literary life; wealth or social position "determines an author's success here *very* emphatically." The imitative-
ness of American writing, so much deplored by Young America,
itself grew out of an economic situation that consigned the production of literature to leisured gentlemen, "a class proverbial for conservatism." A true literary nationalism would advocate international
copyright and thereby afford American writers a living, putting them
in this important sense on a par with English writers. It would af-
firm Americanness not through the use of native subjects and themes
but by exercising "that nationality wh.[ich] will do all it can to procure our authors fair play."

Living in New York and writing for a New York magazine made
it natural for Poe to venture into theater reviewing. New Yorkers
boasted of having more public places of amusement than any city
in Europe of like extent, among them six theaters and a circus open
nightly and two museums offering "dramatic entertainments." Poe
remained aware of his heritage, too. "The writer of this article," he
pointed out in one theater review, "is himself the son of an actress—has invariably made it his boast." But his boast, however also
loving, seems to have been of the same order as his saga of aristocratic lineage, a way of emphatically denying the shame he felt over

his socially questionable birth. Omitting his scapegrace, abandoning father altogether, he paid public tribute to Eliza Poe's theatrical talent and comeliness: "no earl was ever prouder of his earldom," he wrote, "than he of his descent from a woman who, although well-born, hesitated not to consecrate to the drama her brief career of genius and of beauty."

Poe flung his tomahawks as unflinchingly through the theatrical world as through the literary, calling some actor "intolerable," pronouncing some production of *Taming of the Shrew* "a mere jumble of unmeaning rant," describing the rats that infested New York's leading theater, "scouring the pit for chance peanuts and orange-peel." One theater manager withdrew Poe's name from the free-list for having lambasted his production of *Antigone.* Poe got back in the *Journal,* where he rapped the free-list as a gimmick of the puffing system and needled the manager for living at the fashionable Astor House, supposedly writing from "his suite of *boudoirs"* and maintaining "a style (no doubt) of luxurious elegance and ease." As his remarks about copyright also make evident, Poe was growing more and more embittered toward the rich. Among broader theatrical issues, he took up the alleged and much-discussed decline of playwriting in his time. In an article entitled "Does the Drama of the Day Deserve Support?" he argued that drama has suffered from its own inner dynamic as an "essentially imitative" art, and not so much declined as stood still, mired in soliloquies, asides, and other "absurd conventionalities." He foresaw the possibility however of its renewal, perhaps through the abandonment of past models and the conception of a play in some mixed mode, "neither tragedy, comedy, farce, opera, pantomime, melodrama, or spectacle . . . but which may retain some portion of the idiosyncratic excellences of each."

Having created a sensation with "The Raven," Poe expanded in the *Journal* his recent assault on Longfellow, and became more talked about than ever. The Longfellow War, as it got to be known, began in earnest on March 1, when Willis's newspaper published a lengthy letter by a purported acquaintance of Longfellow who signed himself Outis, the Greek word for "Nobody." With mild-mannered reasonableness, Outis turned aside Poe's charges of plagiarism against Longfellow. He argued that the existence of very similar elements in two literary works does not prove literary theft. The closer the resemblances, indeed, the less likely the possibility of plagiarism, for no one seeking literary reputation would blatantly lift another writer's best thoughts and claim them as his own, knowing that the pilferage could be instantly exposed. Any two literary works can also exhibit many "identities," Outis said, which are not "imitations" but rather the "common property of all bards" or the result of two people having similar thoughts. Outis illustrated by comparing "The Raven" with an anonymous poem called "The Bird of the Dream." He pointed out fifteen distinct "identities," such as the existence in both poems of a broken-hearted lover and of a bird at the poet's window. He made it clear at the same time that no "imitation" by Poe was involved.

Over the next month Poe published in the *Journal* no fewer than five rejoinders to Outis's letter, mounting a siege of Longfellow that in modern editions runs to some fifty pages. Still more remarkably, the great likelihood is that with Willis's aid Poe himself concocted the entire exchange. Having blasted Longfellow in the *Mirror* and in his lecture, Poe could hardly keep doing so in the *Broadway Journal* without fresh cause, which Outis's letter provided. In fact, Outis was likely Poe himself, attacking himself under a pseudonym. Among many reasons for thinking so, although Outis claimed to be an acquaintance of Longfellow, Longfellow did not know who Outis was. In defending Longfellow, too, Outis was oddly complimentary to Poe, speaking of him as "one of our finest *poets*" and remarking of the name Edgar A. Poe, "Write it rather EDGAR, a *Poet,* and then it is right to a T." Here Outis quoted the conundrum on Poe's name that Poe himself had invented and published while working in Philadelphia. It seems most unlikely that anyone but Poe would have remembered the slight personal joke he had given to *Alexander's Weekly Messenger* a half-dozen years before. Moreover, Poe was not unused to carrying out anonymous dialogues with himself in print. While editing *Burton's,* he had accused Longfellow of plagiarizing Tennyson; when the Philadelphia *Gazette* rejected his statement as "Preposterous!," he replied anonymously in *Alexander's,* supporting the charges against Longfellow made by the writer of the anonymous article in *Burton's,* i.e. himself, to whom he referred as "a Mr. Poe, one of the editors of that very excellent and very popular journal." The hoax-loving Poe had played a similar game in the illusionistic preface of *Pym.*

Some of Poe's essay-length replies to himself monopolized half the issue of the *Broadway Journal.* For page after page, with a condescending show of elaborate patience, he ridiculed Outis's "labyrinth of impertinences," belaboring both the obvious and the improbable in unscrambling his arguments. He scoffed at Outis's view that, in effect, plagiarism does not exist, remarking that if a plagiarist knew he would be caught he would not plagiarize, and that most plagiarists are established writers who pilfer from some "poverty-stricken, and therefore neglected man of genius." With loony meticulousness, he examined and dismissed one by one the fifteen "identities" that "Outis" found between "The Raven" and the "Bird of the Dream," showing for instance that in the anonymous poem the poet only asks the bird to come to the window. For pages more he exposed Longfellow's numerous thefts from Sidney, Milton, Tennyson, Bryant, Scots ballads, and others, most particularly himself. He set a quotation from Longfellow's *Spanish Student,* nearly two pages long, beside an even longer one from his own verse drama "Politian," pointing out that the comparison established "at least the *imitation* beyond all doubt"—despite the fact that the two works are plainly unlike each other. He had moreover suffered for Longfellow's crimes, he added, being subjected to accusations of plagiarism "for the very sins of this gentleman against myself."

The ongoing "Longfellow War" distressed Poe's partner-employer Briggs. In allowing Poe to undertake his campaign, he had expected him to write no more than one article. But Poe was becoming, he said, "a monomaniac on the subject of plagiarism." Poe's fervor seems to have intimidated him, for he felt unable or unwilling to stop him: "I could not cut it off until he had made a finish of it in his own way." Briggs understood too that Poe's "fol de rol" called attention to the *Journal* and gained it readers. But he also had close ties with New England, especially among abolitionists there, and he worried over the response of Boston and Cambridge: "I hope that Longfellow is too good a fellow to take it much to heart." He also fretted that Longfellow might turn against Lowell (the two were becoming friendly), who after all had introduced Poe to the *Journal*.

Longfellow, although by now much battered by Poe, did not answer him in print. He considered life, he said, "too precious to be wasted in street brawls." Lowell was irritated by Poe's remarks, especially an irrelevant swipe in one essay at Longfellow's young wife. Poe had said that no doubt he was considered a fool by not only Outis and Longfellow, but also by "Mrs. Outis and her seven children . . . and by Mrs. Longfellow and hers—including the grandchildren and great grand-children, if any." Lowell had a high-minded idea of marriage and thought the remark vulgar. He complained of

it to Briggs, who wrote it off as only "a playful allusion to an abstract Mrs. L," since Poe did not even know that Longfellow was
married. He also told Lowell that however offensive Poe's comments about Longfellow, they did not seem to him "half as bad as
I have heard you say." In one respect Briggs's reminder should be
emphasized. Lowell himself considered Longfellow's talents to be
exaggerated by his admirers, and many others thought his poetry
derivative. William Gilmore Simms called Longfellow a "clever imitator" and declared Poe's views about him "more than half right."

But Poe's scorn for Longfellow encompassed more than his poetry. In April he published in the New York *Aristidean* a review of
four volumes of Longfellow's poems—three of which he had reviewed before. When writing pseudonymously as Outis, he had
presented himself as a defender of Longfellow; writing anonymously now, he presented himself as a defender of Poe. The review
can be identified as his, however, or at the least written in very
close collaboration with him, on the basis of its many Poe-isms (such
as the words *purloin* and *purloining*), and on its specific criticisms,
some of which repeat nearly verbatim his remarks in other essays
on Longfellow.

Whether considered to be entirely or only largely by Poe, the
review is probably the cruelest he ever wrote. Incredibly, he commented briefly on each poem in each of Longfellow's four volumes,
intermittently praising but generally ripping one after another as
"exceedingly feeble," "singularly silly," "utterly worthless," "mere
prose," "mere common place," "scarcely worth the page it occupies," "nothing," "pure inanity," "We never saw a more sickening
thing in a book." He also lengthened the list of those plagiarized
by "the GREAT MOGUL of the Imitators," which now included
Shakespeare, Pope, Coleridge, and others, accompanying each exposure of Longfellow's larceny with an evaluation of its degree: "one
of the most palpable plagiarisms ever perpetrated," "A more palpable plagiarism was never committed," "altogether contemptible
imitation."

Poe did not of course forget himself. Speaking ventriloquially he
observed that "Mr. POE, in his late *exposé,* has given some very
decisive instances of what he too modestly calls *imitations* on the
part of Mr. LONGFELLOW from himself (Mr. Poe)." Baring what
the too-discreet "Poe" would not, he unveiled Longfellow's previously undetected looting of Poe's "The Sleeper," and identified the
Southern Literary Messenger as "the great store-house whence the

Professor has derived most of his contraband goods." In his ignorant envy, Longfellow had excluded "Poe" from his anthology, *The
Waif,* even though he had so admiringly flattered Poe's "The Haunted
Palace" as to "purloin everything that was worth purloining about
it." Only Longfellow's "little clique" could fail to see him for what
he was, "not only a servile imitator, but a most insolent literary
thief."

Poe clubbed Longfellow not only for his poetry but also for his
life. A Harvard professor of distinguished ancestry, well-traveled
abroad, Longfellow had married the daughter of a wealthy Boston
merchant, who bought the couple Craigie House as a wedding present. Longfellow could not have won his reputation, Poe said, "without the adventitious influence of his social position as Professor of
Modern Languages and Belles Lettres at HARVARD, and an access
of this influence by marriage with an heiress." Forgetting his own
often-announced contempt for cheap-looking books, he added that
Longfellow owed the success of his collected poems not to their
quality but to their cost, "the luxurious manner in which, as merely
physical books, they have been presented to the public." Keeping
in view this vision of Longfellow as a pampered pedant by referring
to him as "the Professor," he also pounded Longfellow's abolitionist
principles as threadbare, incendiary, and hypocritical. Whether Poe
wrote this part of the anonymous indictment is a little less certain,
but he (or conceivably another) revealed that Longfellow intended
his *Poems on Slavery* "for the especial use of those negrophilic old
ladies of the north, who form so large a part of Mr. LONGFEL
LOW'S friends."

Whether in editorial squibs, reviews of other writers, or notices
of current magazines, Poe found some occasion to hack Longfellow
in nearly every issue of the *Broadway Journal:* "We hear that the
professor receives three thousand dollars for editing the work";
"throughout is obvious a suggestion from 'The Evening Wind' of
Bryant, to which we refer our readers"; "If this is *not* a plagiarism,
and a very bold one, on the part of Professor Longfellow, will any
body be kind enough to tell us what it *is?*" The vicious relentlessness of Poe's onslaught, and his tactics of masquerade, self-debate,
and ventriloquism, seem queer enough. Still more unaccountably,
as Briggs assured Lowell, "Poe has, indeed, a very high admiration
for Longfellow." In fact, Poe insisted that he was "if not his warmest admirer and most steadfast defender, at least *one* of his warmest
and most steadfast." The next year he named Longfellow as the

"principal" American poet. Poe did usually make it clear in his reviews that he admired particular lines or images of Longfellow, and considered him talented. His reviews of other writers too, however gashing, often contain elaborate praise, reminiscent of the alternating postures of insolence and cravenness he often had adopted in his youth, conqueror and cottager.

But by this time Poe's mix of pats and wallops was becoming extreme, and noticeable. The satirical New York *Town* parodied a typical Poe review, describing the fictitious book as on the one hand "a mass of insufferable trash, without one redeeming quality," and on the other "one of the most delightful books . . . printed in a beautiful arabesque style." Such incompatible judgments suggest inner stress, some "crisis," as Elizabeth Barrett noticed. Poe gave her *Drama of Exile* his most important review in the *Journal,* in two substantial, strangely equivocal parts. He faulted her for repetition, inadmissible rhymes, rhythmic deficiencies, and pet words, for being "contaminated by pedantic study of false models," mouthing transcendentalist cant, and committing "the sin of imitation." At the very same time he pronounced her, "unhesitatingly, the greatest—the most glorious of her sex." Nonplussed at being both flogged and caressed, Barrett marveled at how Poe's review embraced "the two extremes of laudation and reprehension, folded in on one another. You would have thought it had been written by a friend and foe, each stark mad with love and hate, and writing the alternate passages."

'Mad with love and hate' is apt, for Poe's treatment of Longfellow seems deeply personal, which did not escape George Rex Graham. "I do not know what your crime may be in the eyes of Poe," he told Longfellow, "but suppose it may be a better, and more widely established reputation. Or if you have wealth . . . that is sufficient to settle your damnation so far as Mr. Poe may be presumed capable of effecting it." In fact, as no one else in America had done before, and few since, Longfellow made poetry financially profitable. Through such aggressive business strategies as paying for and owning the stereotype plates of his works, which he then leased to different publishers for reprinting, he became the first American to make a living as a poet. Poe perhaps still smarted, too, from the notorious English review that had tweaked him as a "capital artist after the manner of Tennyson," while praising Longfellow as an exception to the imitation rampant among American poets. And Lowell had written to him that the review was not by Dickens, as Poe believed, but by a man named Forster, "a friend of some of the Longfellow clique."

In itself, the idea of plagiarism had a charged personal meaning for Poe. He railed at Longfellow for snatching literary goods even as he robbed them himself. To cite only one brief example, in a new tale entitled "Some Words with a Mummy" he described the mummy's grave windings as:

> a sort of sheath, made of papyrus, and coated with a layer of plaster, thickly gilt and painted. The paintings represented subjects connected with the various supposed duties of the soul, and its presentation to different divinities. . . . Extending from head to foot, was a columnar, or perpendicular inscription in phonetic hieroglyphics, giving again his name and titles, and the names and titles of his relations.

While raving about Longfellow's storehouses of "contraband goods," Poe took this from the *Encyclopedia Americana,* where it reads:

> a sort of sheath, made of paper or linen, and coated with a layer of plaster, on which are paintings and gilding. These paintings represent subjects relating to the duties of the soul, its presentation to the different divinities; and a perpendicular hieroglyphical inscription in the centre gives the name of the deceased, and of his relations, his titles, &c.

As Poe also accused Longfellow of doing, he frequently stole from himself, shifting sentences or whole paragraphs from one of his hundreds of reviews and notices to another. Only two months after his final exchange with Outis he published a review in the *Journal* containing three double-columned pages of plot summary, lifted from a review he had written nearly ten years earlier.

Yet in the face of such thieving of his own, Poe proposed the compilation of a *"Chapter on American Cribbage."* In its duplicity, his devotion to detecting purloined letters and capturing plagiarists recalls his zeal in hunting out and denouncing grammatical errors in other works that he often committed in his own. Like the protagonist of "The Tell-Tale Heart," who in the presence of the police plants his chair on the floorboards where his victim lies buried, he in effect proclaimed, 'I who feel the most profound repugnance toward plagiarism and wish to expose it wherever it exists, I could never be guilty of such a thing myself.' ("A poem, in my opinion, is opposed to a work of science by having, for its immediate object, pleasure, not truth.") In this way he perhaps kept from himself the envious admiration he had long felt toward older and more gifted men, expressed in his many imitations and pilferings of Coleridge, Byron, and others, and most strikingly in his continuing to borrow a life history from his brother William Henry Leonard, whose name echoes eerily in that of Henry Wadsworth Longfellow.

And Poe found his financial situation unchanged by his fourteen-hour day and the fame of "The Raven." "I have made no money," he complained in May. "I am as poor now as ever I was in my life." Longfellow, with his heiress-wife and luxuriously produced books, in many ways represented what a son of John Allan might have become had he received the educational opportunities and inheritance to which he was entitled, a figure of station and wealth, "the Professor," an Elector of Cambridge. Longfellow himself detected in Poe's severity toward him some more enveloping and diffuse complaint, "the irritation of a sensitive nature," he later called it, "chafed by some indefinite sense of wrong." In fact Longfellow embodied for Poe a catalog of grievances he had suffered, beginning when fate chose to orphan him. By making war against "the GREAT MOGUL of the Imitators," as in his larger struggle to tear down the old and unjust literary order, Poe sought to assume his rightful place in the world and avenge himself against his destiny.

Poe's Condition;
The Lyceum War.

CA. APRIL–NOVEMBER 1845

In the wake of the Longfellow War, Poe's behavior grew more confused and excessive, a worsening of his "crisis." To the publisher Frederick Saunders, who knew him at the time, he seemed to be fighting the world, or at least the literary world. "His jealousy of other writers amounted to a mania," Saunders recalled, "and he labored under the delusion that every one was trying to slight him and underrate the value of his work." Poe was drinking, too. On

April 17, he was scheduled to deliver for a second time in the city his lecture on American poetry. Owing to a night of hail and sleet only thirty or forty people showed up. Poe appeared on the platform to announce that the lecture would be postponed, and the ticket-money refunded. Next morning he arrived at the *Journal* "helpless with drink," the office boy recalled, "leaning on the arm of a friend."

Many others noticed Poe's condition, among them James Russell Lowell, who visited New York in May. So far the two men had only corresponded—with mutual admiration, although early in the year Lowell had become irked by some of Poe's remarks about him in the *Mirror,* and more recently by Poe's manhandling of Longfellow. His visit did not improve the deteriorating relationship. He found Poe at home, recovering from a binge, "a little soggy with drink," as Lowell recalled it, "not tipsy—but as if he had been holding his head under a pump to cool it." As Poe tried to pull himself together for Lowell's visit his manner became stilted. To Lowell he seemed to be straining for the solemnity "with which men in such cases try to convince you of their sobriety." Lowell particularly remembered, for it pained him, Virginia's "anxious expression." Poe may well have been in a fog. Years later, Muddy explained to Lowell that on the day of the visit Poe was *"not himself"* and suffered when she told him so: "Oh if you only knew his bitter sorrow when I told him how unlike himself he was."

By June Poe was badly depressed, "dreadfully unwell," he said, "and fear that I shall be very seriously ill." In explaining his state he mentioned no more than some "matters of domestic affliction," certainly Virginia's health and the family's poverty—"The Devil himself was never so poor," he said the month before. As had happened in Richmond after he learned of his cousin Neilson's offer to take in Sissy, he may again have been feeling suicidal. Replying to a letter from him, now lost but plainly grim, the New York poet Anne Lynch said she was "exceedingly pained at the desponding tone in which you write. . . . Tell me what you see, & ten to one I can prove to you it is a chimera of your own vivid imagination." She offered to come talk with him and meanwhile urged him, "do not give up." At the least, Poe had decided to leave the *Journal* and retire to the country for six months or a year, "as the sole means of recruiting my health and spirits." Briggs, on his part, felt no less ready to "haul down Poe's name" from the masthead. He believed that Poe had not drunk anything for more than eighteen months, but since had glaringly relapsed into his "old habits," Briggs said, and been "very frequently carried home in a wretched condition."

At about this time, June or July 1845, Poe also met for the first time his correspondent Thomas Holley Chivers, who visited at his East Broadway lodgings. The wealthy and ill-fated seeker-after-truth, who bought bacon by the half-ton for his many slaves, and by now had experienced the deaths of four of his children, had come to New York from Georgia to arrange publication of a volume of his poems. He found Poe in bed, apparently ill, and giving instructions that callers should be told he could not see them. Virginia was there, and struck Chivers as "very tender-hearted and affectionate," especially to Poe, whom she addressed as *"My Dear!"* The seriousness of her condition struck him also. Coughing fits seized her now and then, with "spasmodic convulsions" that he said seemed "almost to rend asunder her very body." The violence of her paroxysms seemed to threaten to strangle her.

Like Lowell, Chivers had happened on the wrong time for meeting Poe in the flesh. The two men exchanged views on poetry, Poe's voice rolling, as Chivers inimitably put it, "like the soft tones of an Aeolian Harp when the music that has been sleeping in the strings is awakened by the Breezes of Eden laden with sweet Spices from the Mountains of the Lord." Chivers's own poetry at this time dwelt on shrouds, coffins, angels, and celestial reunion with lost loved ones, his *The Lost Pleiad* (1845) featuring sonnets with such titles as "Death," "The Grave," and "On Hearing of the Death of my Mother." Not surprisingly, Poe praised the volume as "the honest and fervent utterance of an exquisitely sensitive heart," and particularly admired a poem of Chivers whose refrain was "She came from heaven to tell me she was blest." (He often recited it, with tears in his eyes, according to Muddy.) After Chivers quoted some lines from Shelley's *Prometheus Unbound,* beginning "Drink to the nectar circling in your veins," Poe looked at him, he said, with "a suspiciously apprehensive owllike stare." Only much later did he realize why Poe had glared at him: Poe had taken the quotation as a taunt about his drinking.

Chivers found Poe volatile on the subject, by turns sensitive, denying, and explosive. Seemingly only a few days after this visit, he ran into Poe on Nassau Street. Now at least out of bed, Poe was however weaving along the pavement, "tottering from side to side," Chivers said. Chivers asked, "What under Heaven, could have put you in this fix." Poe frowned impatiently and asked back, "What fix?" As Chivers tried to steer Poe home they ran into Lewis Gaylord Clark, editor of the *Knickerbocker,* one of the most popular magazines of the period. Poe and Clark had been feuding for several years, most recently over a review by Poe published anonymously in the *Journal.* Clark criticized the reviewer for praising an English work while at the same time taking "an indiscriminate fling at American periodicals." The moment Poe saw Clark, Chivers said, he vowed to get him, and tried to break away from Chivers's hold. As they approached Clark, Poe asked "belligerently" what right he had to abuse him in the last number of the *Knickerbocker.* Clark moved off, Chivers recalled, explaining that as the review was unsigned he had no way of knowing that Poe wrote it. Backing away, he managed to bow himself out of the tense scene.

Chivers maneuvered Poe back to East Broadway, Poe so much staggering, Chivers said, "that it was with the greatest of difficulty I could keep him from falling prostrate in the Street." Virginia had been watching from an upstairs window but drew back her head as they approached the house and locked herself in her room. Muddy met them at the door and took off Poe's coat, saying, as Chivers nicely caught her whining, exclamatory tone, "Oh! Eddy! Eddy! Eddy come here, my dear boy! Let me put you to bed!" Once Poe was settled and covered with a counterpane, she told Chivers tearfully that she had prayed Poe would not "get in this way" during his visit, but feared the worst. "Oh!" she said, "I do believe that the poor boy is deranged!" And Virginia could not bear to see him in this condition. Virginia was "at the point of death with Bronchitis" and "wasting away, day by day," the doctors unable to help her. And if they could help, Muddy added, "seeing this continually in poor Eddy, would kill her—for she doats upon him! Oh! She is devoted to him!"

Muddy revealed something else to Chivers. The illness that had confined Poe to bed, as Chivers found him during his first visit, was feigned. He had been in bed an entire week, only pretending to be sick. In this way he got out of a commitment to write and recite a new poem before the Philomathean and Eucleian Societies, a student literary club of New York University. The ceremony had been scheduled for the evening of July 1, at a fine new Gothic church in University Place; printed invitations announced the delivery of "the Annual Poem by Edgar A. Poe, Esq." (Illus. 15). But Poe was in a "deranged state again," Muddy said. He had another reason for ducking the event, serious also. For perhaps the first time in his career, he was finding it difficult to write. According to Thomas Dunn English, editor of the *Aristidean,* Poe called on him, "much troubled," saying he could not compose the poem and asking for advice about what to do. English suggested he be frank with his sponsors; instead, English said, he stayed drunk during the week of the ceremony. Those who attended it, including some part of New York society and the student body of the university, were informed that "Mr. Poe had been severely ill for a week past, and it had not been judged prudent for him to exert himself."

Chivers too much admired Poe to be turned against him by their first meeting. But others had less tolerance for his increasingly erratic ruses and affronts. Poe further antagonized James Russell Lowell by discussing in an August issue of the *Journal* a new poem by him called "To the Future." Poe granted it a "noble commencement" but accused Lowell of having stolen from a poem by Wordsworth his image of an "ancestral buckler . . . Self-clanging from the walls." Poe confirmed this "palpable plagiarism" by quoting, from memory, Wordsworth's line, "Armor rustling on the walls." Understandably the charge rankled Lowell, especially as he had not long ago written a laudatory biography and critical notice of Poe. He pointed out moreover that Poe had *mis*quoted Wordsworth, whose line read "Armour *rusting* on the walls," not "rustling" as Poe had quoted it—apparently to conform it to "clanging" for the sake of turning Lowell into a new Longfellow. Soured on Poe, Lowell wrote him off as a vulgar seeker after "a newspaper reputation" and "wholly lacking in that element of manhood which, for want of a better name, we call character."

In his misery Poe managed to estrange several others also. Richard Henry Stoddard, a twenty-year-old self-educated poet, submitted to the *Journal* a poem entitled "Ode on a Grecian Flute." Poe perhaps paid little attention to it, for he addressed a notice to Stoddard in the magazine announcing, "We fear that we have mislaid the poem." In the next issue, apparently having recovered the poem, he printed a follow-up notice saying he suspected plagiarism: *"We doubt the originality of the 'Grecian Flute,' . . . Unless the author can re-assure us, we decline it."* Hoping to assure Poe of his integrity, Stoddard called on him at home. He was "very gracious," Stoddard recalled, expressed confidence in the poem's originality and promised to print it. After waiting a few weeks for his work to appear, Stoddard confronted Poe at the *Journal* office. He found him drowsing uneasily in a chair, this time not gracious but "irascible, surly, and in his cups." As Stoddard began reminding him of the circumstances involving his poem, Poe started up "wildly" and said, "You never wrote the Ode." Stoddard left quickly. Poe's rashness in this instance was if not justified at least not groundless. Stoddard later acknowledged that his "Ode on a Grecian Flute" was modeled not only on Keats, as the title makes clear, but also on a Major David Richardson's "Ode to a Grecian Flute." The episode anyway left him with lifelong bitterness toward Poe.

The same month, Poe also received a home visit from Laughton Osborn, a poet just his age. Like Chivers and some others, Osborn responded passionately to the quality of longing in Poe's work and did not so much admire as adore him. He confided to Poe that he had an unloving mother, one "who *cannot* sympathize with me," and revealed himself as a man "Absolutely and terribly alone." Poe's friendship "would be all in all" to him, he said, "while to you mine could only be the overflowing of a cup already full to the brim." Osborn forgot a package at Poe's lodging, came to retrieve it the next morning, and was mistakenly given a parcel of *Broadway Journals*. In one issue he discovered a review by Poe of his satirical poem, *The Vision of Rubeta.* Poe had characterized it as "an illimitable gilded swill-trough." The rough review had appeared anonymously, and Osborn rather blamed Poe for publishing than accused him of writing it, even though he correctly understood Poe had done so. Crushed, he wrote Poe a long anguished letter, bewailing that he had imagined Poe saw him as a "brother-bard," only to find that a journal published under Poe's "sanctions" depicted him as swinish, "but a hog in letters and the mere pilferer . . . of swill."

Poe felt bad enough about the incident to reply the next day. He said he could not afford to give up Osborn's friendship and would therefore overstep "editorial decorum." This meant retailing a cock-and-bull story to the effect that despite the posting of his name on the masthead, his connection with the *Journal* at the time the review appeared was simply that of contributor. "The article to which you refer," he said, "had never been seen by me until you pointed it out." The statement was an outright lie, but for good measure he told Osborn, spitefully, that he had also been accused of writing a malevolent anonymous attack on Fitz-Greene Halleck, which had actually been written *"by a brother poet, Lowell."* Lowell had in fact written the review, but surely not in the knowledge that, as Poe insisted, "the odium would inevitably fall upon myself." Pacified, Osborn sent back a long missive full of overheated forgiveness and appreciation, characterizing the sentiments Poe had expressed to him as those "the noblest Greek might be proud to have written. . . . I cannot even conceive how, for the occasion, the moral sublime could ever rise higher." But the moral sublime had not risen high enough to spare the poor man another rebuff. In fulfilling a promise to Poe, Osborn gave him for the *Journal* his translation of some Italian sonnets. When the poems failed to appear after several weeks, he solicited their return from Poe by a formal, pained note, "forced to conclude," he said, "that they are not so important as my vanity had led me to believe."

In others less emotionally entangled with Poe, his behavior aroused not resentment but concern. News and gossip about him distressed William Gilmore Simms, for instance, although he doubted the chances of helping. He suggested that members of Poe's New York literary circle might try to provide guidance, but it would need a delicate tact: "for such a man it is difficult to devise anything," he told Evert Duyckinck, "unless it be to control his infirmities with a moral countenance which coerces while it soothes & seems to solicit." That Poe had some awareness of hurting not only others but himself as well is suggested by his "The Imp of the Perverse," published in the July *Graham's*. Surprisingly constructed, it reads at first as a thoughtfully argued essay on human impulse; but two-thirds through it begins to reveal itself as, all along, a monologue spoken from his jail cell by a condemned poisoner. He considers the human need to act contrarily, "for the reason that we should *not*." As examples he offers the varyingly 'perverse' wishes of a speaker to tantalize his listeners by circumlocution, provoking their anger; of a procrastinator to put off some urgent action, although delay will ruin him; and of someone on a precipice tempted to leap, although he will be shattered. Poe of course had often dealt incidentally with people propelled to act against their conscious desires. But his making into an independent subject the suffocating power of temptations to provoke others and harm oneself, implies concern about controlling his own Imp.

The concern took other forms also. Poe struck some observers at the time as overcontrolled, "rather formal," as Lowell thought him, or "under restraint," as he seemed to Briggs, "as though guarding against a half-subdued passion." In addition to keeping watch on himself, Poe contained the Imp by the same means he used in answering Chivers: "What fix?" As if to deny any drift toward unreason, he presented himself as a champion of order, analysis, mind.

It was of course not a new stance for Poe, debunker of Maelzel's automaton, cryptographer, inventor of the ratiocinative Dupin. But he now gave greater and more intense attention than before to the importance of Reason, his language laden with mathematical and mechanical imagery, as if to demonstrate not the power of thought but his allegiance to sanity. "This is emphatically the thinking age," he declared in January, "indeed it may very well be questioned whether mankind ever substantially thought before." He began registering a new disdain for German literature as vague and disorderly, "one indistinguishable chaos of froth," commending instead the literature of intellect: "I am not ashamed to say that I prefer even Voltaire to Goethe." In his reviews he reverted often to the critic's obligation to construct his work on philosophical principles and to make clear "the machinery of his own thoughts." Genius, he said, required "the faculty of analysis," and for himself, he would write "a lyric on the Quadrature of Curves—or the Arithmetic of Infinites." Repeatedly proclaiming the supremacy of thinking, mental rigor, and rational 'machinery,' he meanwhile accused all in sight of plagiarism, tottered down the street, stayed in bed to back out of a speaking engagement.

But Poe's fix would not be denied. While still in Philadelphia he had tried through Lowell to arrange a lecture before the Boston Lyceum, a literary association. At the time he applied, the lectures for the year had concluded, but he had been offered an engagement for the following October, which now arrived. Even without the resentment he had stirred in Boston literary circles for his war on Longfellow, and more generally on them, his appearance in the city might offend. The literary magazines of Boston and New York contended for preeminence in American letters and often carped at each other. Briggs reported the existence in New York of "a little squad of Literati . . . who have sworn to exterminate the whole race of Yankee authors."

Poe ranked himself in this squad, although his turbulent feelings about Boston involved more than literature. It was the city his mother had instructed him to love as his place of birth, to which he had fled John Allan to publish his first volume of poems, "By a Bostonian." At the same time, Boston drew some of the anger he felt about the luckless circumstances of his beginnings and, as a sort of Longfellow writ large, some of the class resentment he felt toward well-off litterateurs of genteel taste, as he saw them, elegant men of leisure. He also viewed Boston as the headquarters of what he derided as "the Humanity *clique,*" the New England Transcendentalists. This informal group of writers, ministers, and educators revolved around Ralph Waldo Emerson, whose *Nature* (1836) declared that a single spiritual law of Becoming underlay and united all forms of being; decried social institutions and traditions for distorting the individual's very perception of reality; and called for a revolution in consciousness, a new trust in intuition and personal desire that would free the self's power and capacity for growth. The moral and ethical preoccupations of Transcendentalist thinking, with its long roots in Puritan New England, had little appeal to Poe, who had been raised as a southerner, and within the lax religious atmosphere of the Allan home. He disliked what he understood to be the Transcendentalists' optimism, their belief in social progress, their obscurantism ("quips, quirks, and curt oracularities"), and their moralistic aesthetic views. Transcendentalist taste, he said later, was "Taste on her death-bed." (On their side, the Transcendentalists did not think much of Poe either; Emerson reportedly remarked of "The Raven," "I see nothing in it.")

But much of Poe's thinking about Transcendentalism only reflects the tumult of his feelings about Boston. He used the terms *Humanity party of Boston, Transcendentalists,* and *Socialists* loosely and interchangeably, and tried to justify his inconsistency by explaining that the "party's" chief trait was confusion: "They could not define their own position & it cannot be expected that I can define them exactly." He either had little first-hand acquaintance with major Transcendentalist writings like *Nature,* or else failed to grasp their meaning. Otherwise he could not have lumped together as Transcendentalists Emerson, Lowell, Hawthorne, and Whittier, or attributed to them all a faith in mesmerism, phrenology, feminism, Progress, Swedenborgianism, Fourierism, and water-cures. To compound the confusion, when not blasting the "party" he sometimes praised it. "You mistake me in supposing I dislike the transcendentalists," he told Chivers; "it is only the pretenders and sophists among them." His desire to distinguish true from false transcendentalists perhaps arose from the fact that many critics spoke of his own work as 'transcendental,' a correct judgment in the limited sense that he too dealt with matters beyond the senses. But his confounding of quite different writers and of not necessarily related ideas suggests again that his grievance against Boston took in more than specific literary, social, or philosophical issues. However loudly he denounced the city, he envied much of what he thought it represented, and had sought and still desired its acclaim. Going there to perform meant venturing into a maelstrom of ill-comprehended emotion.

The trouble began even before Poe left New York. For his Boston presentation too, scheduled to open the Lyceum season on October 16, he had promised to write and deliver a new poem. The invitation to do so signaled his new prominence as a poet since the publication of "The Raven." But he could not write this poem either. Once again, a week before the lecture, he sought out T. D. English, editor of the *Aristidean* (Illus. 16). Like others, English had observed that Poe was neat by nature; slovenly dress meant he was on or getting over a spree. And he now looked, English said, "dilapidated." A strong temperance advocate, English lectured him on his drinking, which may have been a relapse set off by mounting anxiety over the Boston trip. Only about six weeks earlier, Poe had written to Chivers promising "not to touch a drop as long as I live." He pledged himself again to English, but explained that he had been in no condition to write the poem, and now no longer had time. English advised him to have the talk postponed two weeks, but Poe said he needed the fifty-dollar fee. According to English, Poe then said he had thought of a plan, and went off.

Poe was slated to read his new poem at the Odeon, on a program that included an address by Caleb Cushing, the American commissioner to China. Among several newspapers that advertised the event, the Boston *Daily Times* called for a full house, to "testify the public appreciation of these distinguish-ed writers." Several members of the program committee called on Poe at his hotel just before the lecture. One of them later recalled that Poe asked the group to accompany him to his room while he got his manuscript, as they did, sitting on his bed while he opened his trunk. He began taking out the articles in the lower part, until he had emptied it. Looking hopeless, he said he feared he had left his manuscript behind. The others knelt on the floor beside him and again began going through his wardrobe. In the top of the trunk they turned up the manuscript, or at least a manuscript.

Cushing opened the program with a spread-eagle address, two and a half hours long. Only then, after this filibustering solo, did an officer of the Lyceum introduce Poe. Dressed in black, he faced an audience whose hometown he had long and recently abused, with a 'plan' designed to cover his lack of preparation. By his own account, he began with fifteen minutes consisting largely of apologies for the "indefinitiveness" and "general imbecility" of the poem he was about to deliver, "so unworthy a *Bostonian* audience." As Poe's self-abasement was recorded by the young Harvard student Thomas Wentworth Higginson (later the mentor of Emily Dickinson), he stood on the platform "with a sort of shrinking" and began to speak in a "thin, tremulous, hardly musical voice." He repeated his apology for the poem and his "sycophantic" deference to the Boston audience, Higginson said, "in a sort of persistent, querulous way, which . . . impressed me at the time as nauseous flattery." In his prologue Poe also gave his reasons for not delivering a didactic poem, as is usual on such occasions, a didactic poem being in his view no poem at all. Then he enacted his 'plan.'

Poe began to read the whole of "Al Aaraaf," retitled "The Messenger Star" for the occasion. His choice recalls the case in "The Imp of the Perverse," of someone who wishes to please his listeners but also perversely to irritate them, and "the thought strikes him, that by certain involutions and parentheses, this anger may be engendered." Probably written when he was twenty years old and in the army, in two parts and more than 260 lines of verse, the poem still taxes even practiced readers by its obscurities, much less an audience that had already sat through a two-and-a-half hour oration and was now being asked to digest the equivalent of nearly twenty sonnets. The admiring Higginson found it "rather perplexing," but the audience, he said, looked "thoroughly mystified." He remembered too that when Poe reached the song in Part Two ("Ligeia! Ligeia! / My beautiful one!") his listeners warmed to him and became entranced. According to the program manager, however, Poe had not recited fifty lines before their attention was "irrecoverably gone." By most other accounts the audience fidgeted and quickly, noisily, began thinning out. Someone suggested that to save the evening Poe be asked to read "The Raven," as he consented to do, "and did it well," the manager recalled, "thus enabling us to make some show of front after a most lamentable defeat."

How much Poe saved is questionable, however. One Boston newspaper reported the next day that despite the announcement that he would read "The Raven," most of the audience already felt fatigued by "Al Aaraaf" and "could not be detained." Other papers gleefully carved up his performance, reporting his didactic introductory remarks condemning didacticism, his confession of doubt about his ability to write a poem for Bostonians, and the ticketholders' flight. Poe gave his detractors more ammunition by telling a social gathering after the lecture that "The Messenger Star" was not a new poem prepared for the occasion, but a "juvenile poem" he had written before the age of twelve. His remarks were taken up and flung back by Cornelia Wells Walter, the young editor of the *Boston Evening Transcript,* who had earlier dismissed him as *"poh"* for tromping Longfellow. "A poem delivered before a literary association of adults, as written by *a boy!"* she wrote. "Only think of it! Poh! Poh!"

Having devised one 'plan' to conceal his writing problems in New York, Poe devised another to cover his debacle in Boston. It was to pretend that he had meant to mock his Lyceum audience, that his performance had been a deliberate put-on. "We have been quizzing the Bostonians," he announced in the *Journal* upon his return, "and one or two of the more stupid of their editors and editresses have taken it in high dudgeon." The new plan quickly embroiled him in a new war of words that spread around the country. Walter responded over several issues of the *Transcript,* twitting him as a "poe-ser," alluding to his drinking habits, observing that "the quizzer sometimes turns out to be the *quizzee."* The oddity of Poe's plan raised eyebrows as far off as St. Louis, where the *Daily Reveille* wondered, "Does he mean . . . that his late Boston poem, was intended by him as a *hoax?"*

To try to make his 'plan' clear, Poe printed a full explanation of his intentions in the *Journal* on November 1, occupying nearly two columns. He had however maneuvered himself into a position that left not much room for clarity. There seems no doubt that although unable to compose a poem for the occasion, he had hoped to impress the Boston audience by reading "Al Aaraaf" and had expected to be praised. Just eight months before the Lyceum appearance, after all, James Russell Lowell had publicly praised Poe's juvenile verse as "the most remarkable boyish poems that we have ever read," and supported his judgment by quoting the "exquisite" section of "Al Aaraaf" that entranced Thomas Wentworth Higginson. Poe's announcement that he had schemed all along to "quiz" the Bostonians followed his usual pattern of disregarding reality. T. D. English remarked, with some accuracy, that "everything he said for a purpose was true to him, however false it might be." This time Poe sought to deny that he had made a fool of himself, even at the cost of claiming that he had wished to make himself one.

In his bizarre clarification in the *Journal,* Poe consequently blasted the newspapers of Boston for misrepresenting his successful reading as a failure, and the Boston audience for stupidly thinking his failed reading a success. The "facts of the case," or really the first case, were the following: his audience was "large and distinguished"; when he rose to speak he was "most cordially received"; he read the poem with "many interruptions of applause"; by the time he finished only about a tenth of the audience had departed; and when he recited "The Raven" he was "very cordially applauded again." Having shown that he gave an earnest reading that was earnestly well received, however, Poe reversed himself to show that he had been ignorantly applauded while perpetrating a hoax. The facts in this second case were that he had agreed to deliver a poem in Boston "simply and solely, because we had a curiosity to know how it felt to be publicly hissed." The motive lay in his aversion to Boston: "We were born there," he said, "and perhaps it is just as well not to mention that we are heartily ashamed of the fact." As he listed the deficiencies of the place and its inhabitants they included bad hotels, dullness masking as mannerliness, hostility to himself for "enlightening them about the originality of Mr. Longfellow," and a boasted duck pond whose ducks could not be heard for the frogs. He could hardly be expected, he said, to put himself out by composing anything like an original poem, but had "lying by" him one published when he was ten years old (apparently revised from the earlier twelve) and "quite as good as new—one, at all events, that we considered would answer sufficiently well for an audience of Transcendentalists." So, much to his own amusement, he had deliciously hoodwinked a Boston audience, "who evinced characteristic discrimination in understanding, and especially applauding, all those knotty passages which we ourselves have not yet been able to understand."

Poe's zany arguings clearly arose from the torment he felt over his inability to write a poem for the event and having a Boston audience walk out on him. Some such connection was apparent to his contemporaries as well. "The circumstances must indeed be exceedingly unhappy and distressing," Lewis Gaylord Clark wrote in the *Knickerbocker,* "which would cause a poet . . . to read a rhapsody composed and published in his tenth year, and afterward bring forward, as a proof of the stupidity of his audience, that they listened to him with civil attention." Poe entangled himself further in self-condemning logic by trying to explain his explanation. Writing in the November 22 *Journal,* this time over nearly four columns, he revealed that he had had prior knowledge of a plot against him, that "among a certain *clique* of the Frogpondians, there existed a predetermination to abuse us under *any* circumstances." Knowing that this clique would criticize whatever he did, he preferred pleasing himself and thus presented what the Boston newspapers correctly said was a bad poem. "It *is* bad—it is wretched—and what then? We wrote it at ten years of age—had it been worth even a pumpkin-pie undoubtedly we should not have 'delivered' it to *them.*"

Poe's attempt to blame a knot of literary conspirators for his presentation of a ludicrous poem left unexplained his insistence that the poem had been well received during a serious evening of poetry. He had come up with an answer. The larger part of the audience did not belong to the "ridiculous little cabal": "the *clique* (contemptible in numbers as in every thing else) were overruled by the rest of the assembly. These malignants did not *dare* to interrupt by their preconcerted hisses, the respectful and profound attention of the majority." This pseudoexplanation of a pseudoexplanation, however, only raised the question of what the "profound attention of the majority" might be worth, having been paid to a poem not worth a pumpkin-pie. Just the same, Poe pursued his desperate logic in a tone of cackling triumph: "and thus the Frogpondians were *had*—were delivered up to the enemy bound hand and foot. Never were a set of people more completely demolished."

The venom released by Poe's Lyceum appearance spurted through the spring of 1846. He was himself unwilling to let it subside, for instance gloating in the *Journal* at the end of November: "The Frog-Pond seems to be dried up—and the Frogs are, beyond doubt, all dead—as we hear no more croaking from that quarter." More croakings of course came. The *Harbinger,* a Transcendentalist periodical, remarked the following week on the notoriety Poe had gained from waging war against New England, a war "which it would be most charitable," they said, "to impute to insanity."

Ownership and Loss
of the Broadway Journal.

OCTOBER 1845–JANUARY 1846

A new defeat followed quickly on Poe's Lyceum disaster, although it first appeared in the guise of victory. On October 24, only a week after his reading in Boston, he entered into an agreement to take over the exclusive publishing and management of the *Broadway Journal.* After years of hoping and planning, he now owned and controlled his own magazine.

The *Journal* came into Poe's hands through an intricate confluence of the problems that beset it: ideological clashes, difficulties in distribution and in raising subscribers, Briggs's disgruntlement and indifference, legal technicalities. Financially, the magazine had from the beginning barely survived; Poe's position as 'one-third proprietor' amounted to little more than Briggs's securing his services without having to pay for them. Well aware that the *Journal* squeaked by, issue-to-issue, Briggs tried not to offend potential sources of revenue and subscription: he avoided comment on controversial issues of social reform, and such consuming matters of public concern as the annexation of Texas. As a New Englander, however, he had been expected by his friends to use the *Journal* to serve the cause of abolition. Just after the magazine began publication, he explained to Lowell that while "unqualifiedly opposed to slavery in every shape," he held that wrath belongs only to God, and found many abolitionists sanctimonious. Besides, as he admitted, the *Journal* had already won favor in the South, and to take a strong antislavery stand would turn Southern readers against it.

But Briggs's pragmatism, and Poe's Southern loyalties, probably cost him readers in the North. In the spring, the *Journal*'s other proprietor, John Bisco, agreed to act as a New York agent for the *Southern Literary Messenger.* He asked Poe, as a former editor of that magazine, to write something favorable about it to run in the *Journal.* Poe produced a puff, praising the *Messenger* for catering to "the *élite,* both as regards wealth and intellectual culture, of the Southern aristocracy" and exerting its influence "in behalf of the chivalrous, the tasteful and the true." His blurb outraged some Northern reformers. The Boston *Liberator,* an abolitionist weekly, published an angry letter observing that the *Journal* tried to win new subscribers for the *Messenger* by calling attention to its support by the Southern gentry and its role as the main organ of Southern opinion, "Precious inducements, truly, to Northern democratic freemen!" The writer denounced the *Messenger* as a "miserable magazine" of the vilest principles that sought to "uphold the 'peculiar institution,' to decry the colored race, to libel the abolitionists."

Briggs saw nothing wrong with Poe's puff, but by the summer had become disenchanted with him anyway. He was put off by Poe's drinking, and had come to think his critical writing grudging and mechanical, a hunt for grammatical and prosodic errors little different from mere proofreading. "I was rather taken at first with a certain appearance of independence and learning in his criticisms," he said, "but they are so verbal, and so purely selfish, that I can no longer have any sympathy with him." To reorganize the magazine and give it "a fresh start," he planned to dissolve his partnership with Bisco and to drop Poe. Poe's initial reaction, typically, was the announcement that he had "resolved to give up the B. Journal." He also proposed to Chivers that they join as coeditors of the "Stylus."

But what followed instead was a whirl of bargainings and intrigues by which Poe shut out Briggs and formed his own partnership with Bisco. Briggs gave several differing versions of the complex events. To distill what seems the most reliable of them: in making his new start, Briggs arranged terms with Bisco for buying out his interest in the *Journal.* But when they came to close the deal, Bisco asked for more than they had agreed on. During this deadlock between the partners, the *Journal* suspended publication for a week. At the same time, Briggs said, Poe "got into a drunken spree, and conceived an idea that I had not treated him well, for which he had no other ground than my having loaned him money, and persuaded Bisco to carry on the Journal himself." Poe may or may not have been drunk and irrationally miffed at the time. But Briggs's account is reliable at least to the extent that on July 14 Poe drew up and signed a contract with Bisco. It provided that Bisco would continue to publish the *Journal* at his own expense, and receive half the net profits, while Poe would be the "sole editor" and receive half the profits above the costs of publication.

From 'one-third proprietor' Poe was suddenly 'sole editor' and something like half owner. His promotion rested, however, on shaky legal ground. Although Bisco had contracted with Poe to issue the *Journal,* his original partnership agreement with Briggs remained in force. Briggs understood his prerogative in the situation and, he said, laughed at the folly of Bisco and Poe and told them to go ahead: "I still hold the same right that I ever did, and could displace them both if I wished to do so." By this time his regard for Poe had dwindled to where Poe seemed "badly made up," "the merest shell of a man," "a drunken sot, and the most purely selfish of human beings." ("He makes quotations from the German," Briggs added, "but he can't read a word of that language.") While certain that he could put an injunction on the magazine and recover it whenever he wanted, Briggs also felt worn and disgusted by the petty power-brokering. Turning his attention to writing a comedy for the theater, to be called the "Literati," he decided to leave Poe and Bisco alone, certain their attempt to continue the magazine would fail.

In fact only a month after Poe signed his contract with Bisco, the *Journal* was sinking in deep financial trouble. Poe wrote to Chivers asking a loan of fifty dollars, which he said would put the publication "out of all difficulty." Like his language, Chivers promised much and delivered little. He offered to send the money, but as it failed to arrive, Poe wrote him again pleadingly: "For Heaven's sake do— as soon as you get this—for almost everything (as concerns the paper) depends upon it." This time Chivers lectured him on his drinking, claimed a temporary cash shortage, and enclosed five dollars. Poe tried to raise money through the *Journal* itself, in an advertisement headed "A RARE OPPORTUNITY." Having contrived the alias Edward S. T. Grey, he asked any "gentleman of enterprise and respectable education" who had seven hundred or a thousand dollars at hand and was looking for "an excellent opportunity for its investment," to address a note at the *Journal* to "E. S. T. G." He also planned a trip to Ohio, to elicit support there from influential individuals. Some of these fund-raising efforts likely concerned not the *Journal* but the "Stylus." Poe's experience had taught him the importance of having a replacement to fall back on, and under Bisco the *Journal* was floundering in more ways than financial. In Baltimore it sometimes arrived a week behind, creating the impression that it had ceased publication, while no issues had reached Washington for months. Characteristically, even as "sole editor" and part owner Poe was keeping the possibility of the other magazine alive.

As the *Journal* limped along during the early fall, Poe took advantage of his editorial control to gash Briggs. Commenting on an essay about "American Humor" that had appeared in another magazine, he described his ex-partner as a "vulgar driveller . . . the whole of whose point, as far as we can understand it, consists in being unable to pen a sentence of even decent English." Briggs felt he had given Poe no cause for ill feeling; on the contrary, he said, he had tried compassionately to conceal Poe's "ill habits" from others, and loaned him money, still unrepaid, to pay his board "and keep him from being turned into the street." Poe hated him, he explained, for knowing "the secret of his real character" and was jealous because the essay on American humor had mentioned Briggs but not himself, "for he has an inconceivably extravagant idea of his capacities as a humorist." And in private, according to Briggs, Poe also spread lies about him, for instance that Briggs had told him Lowell was "crazy." "I cannot conceive of such wanton malice," Briggs said, "as Poe has been guilty of towards me."

By October, Bisco had given up on the *Journal*. On the twenty-fourth, eight days after his disgrace at the Lyceum, Poe signed the agreement that gave him "entire right and title" to the magazine. In scraping together an initial payment to Bisco of fifty dollars, he borrowed thirty dollars from T. D. English, promising him an interest in return in the *Journal*. He also gave Bisco a note promising to pay an additional one hundred dollars three months later, to reimburse him for outstanding debts to the magazine—payable whether or not Poe succeeded in collecting the debts himself, as he would now have to do. Although the agreement loaded Poe with financial obligations, it gave him tangible possession of the elusive object that would allow him to speak as he pleased, distinguish his name, and make a fortune. But how much he had won the prize himself and how much it had only fallen to him is arguable, and perhaps puzzled him also. As he put the situation, "By a series of manoeuvres almost incomprehensible to myself, I have succeeded in getting rid, one by one, of all my associates . . . [and] have now become sole editor and owner." However the Electorship came to him he left no doubt that he had at last attained it. In the *Journal* for October 25, he placed his name alone on the masthead as "Editor and Proprietor." Lest anyone fail to understand that he was at last in control of his fate, he announced: "With this number, it will be seen, [*sic*] that we assume the sole control (proprietary as well as editorial) of the 'Broadway Journal'."

The comma error that Poe failed to catch was ominous. He had envisioned a magazine of his own as an aesthetically appealing seat of judgment, a five-dollar monthly wherein the best American writers would be honored, the worst exposed without respect to personal influence, according to standards of judgment that would be laid bare with a consequent elevation of popular taste. But to realize these intentions, his new situation also demanded large, steady, sure-handed attention to the mechanics and financing of publication, as he soon discovered. "I have to do *everything* myself," he told Chivers, "edit the paper—get it to press—and attend to the multitudinous *business* besides." And much was against him: as usual lacking money for food and rent (his earnings for all of 1845 amounted to about $699), he had in hand a business that was failing, his wife was dying, and his grip on himself was slipping.

Only two days after signing the agreement with Bisco, Poe was scrambling for loans to carry the *Journal*. Sounding again like the adolescent begging money from John Allan to keep him alive, he asked Rufus Griswold for fifty dollars: "*Will* you aid me at a pinch— at one of the greatest pinches conceivable? If you will, I will be indebted to you, for life." Griswold seems to have lent Poe twenty-five dollars, promising an equal amount at the end of November if needed. The same day Poe asked another fifty dollars from his old mentor John Pendleton Kennedy, who sent good wishes, as being "pretty nearly all the capital I have for such speculations." He borrowed fifty dollars from Horace Greeley and, miraculously perhaps, managed to increase the advertising in the magazine from about two pages under Bisco to more than four pages. But whatever money he managed to bring in or borrow in his first few days as publisher was not enough. He remained "dreadfully" behind, although confident that could he hold on a little while, buy "time in which to look about me," the *Journal* would thrive: "I will make a fortune of it yet." Feverishly, he tried in November to raise money from his publishers Wiley and Putnam, pressed Chivers for the rest of his promised fifty dollars ("If you *can* send me the $45, for Heaven's sake do it, *by return of mail*"), asked cousin George Poe for two hundred dollars, with the ritual assurance that he would "appreciate my efforts to elevate the family name."

The unassisted office work alone proved a full-time labor. It was "utterly impossibly to conceive how busy I have been," he told Chivers, "editing the paper, without aid from any one, all the time." He did not mention, however, that he was making an undistinguished, even a botched job of it. To the detriment of the magazine's rounded coverage of New York cultural life, he curtailed music, drama, and art criticism. Hardly using the magazine to establish a new American literary order independent of personalities, he published mostly himself and his friends, more often than not leading off with one of his own already-published tales, together with a poem or poems by women poets whose interest in him, as will appear, he had begun to cultivate. Too overburdened to write much for the magazine himself, and unable to pay for contributions by other important writers, he apologized in print for the "insufficient variety" of an issue or the brevity of the book notices.

To fill up pages, Poe sometimes padded his critical comments with long excerpts from the work at hand or passages cribbed from his earlier reviews. And he often reviewed books he surely had not had time to read. He thus pronounced *The History of Silk, Cotton, Linen, Wool, and other Fibrous Substances* an "able work," and claimed that a Lewis Durlacher's *Treatise on Corns, Bunions, the Diseases of Nails, and the General Management of the Feet* "cannot fail to do a great deal of good." Under his ownership and editorship, the *Journal* also sprouted more errors than before. Normally, as Briggs remarked, "even a typographical error, threw him into an ecstasy of passion." But now he was forced to run errata notices apologizing for editing and proofreading blunders that had occurred in "the hurry of getting to press." These occasionally mattered, as when he omitted an entire line from a published poem or the name of a contributing poet.

However oppressive the work and worry, Poe seems to have felt that it settled him, cleared his mind from the preceding chaos of the Lyceum affair. "For the first time during two months," he told Duyckinck in mid-November, "I find myself entirely myself— dreadfully sick and depressed, but still myself. I seem to have just awakened from some horrible dream, in which all was confusion." The more lucid hindsight showed him what some others had thought also of his peculiar 'plans' and peculiar explanations of them: "I really believe," he said, "that I have been mad."

But how much Poe had become "entirely myself" can be doubted. In the *Journal* at least, he presented himself as even more embattled than before. "Every body is at us," he wrote editorially in December, "little dogs and all." Skirmishing on all fronts against enemies old and new, he yet again insisted in print that the notorious *Foreign Quarterly* article came from "nobody in the world but Charles Dickens," again slapped Longfellow for his "palpable imitation of the

German spirit," promised soon to revisit "Frogpondium," as he had "a fine poem that we wrote at seven months. . . . They want it immediately—they can't wait." He repaid Griswold's twenty-five dollar loan by remarking in a review that if *Poets and Poetry of America* were "to be received as a fair representation of our poetical literature, then are we in a very lamentable—or rather in a very ridiculous condition indeed."

By the first of December, after scarcely five weeks in control, Poe felt the walls closing in. As he described his predicament, "On the part of one or two persons who are much imbittered against me, there is a deliberate attempt now being made to involve me in ruin, by destroying *The Broadway Journal.*" Who or what cabal he now had in mind is unknown. But two days later, with the magazine's circulation falling, he was unable to go on as "Editor and Proprietor." He signed over half his interest in the magazine to Thomas H. Lane, a Custom House employee he had known in Philadelphia. Lane agreed to publish the magazine, handle its business affairs, and pay off its recent debts. The editing remained Poe's responsibility.

Poe's new partnership lasted one month. According to T. D. English, whose flat adjoined Lane's, Poe "went off on one of his fits of drunkenness," leaving the December 27 issue incomplete. Lane tried to sober him up, English said, but failed, and decided to close down the magazine with the issue of January 3. The collapse of the *Journal* may have left Poe destitute. On January 2 he witnessed an indenture by which Muddy sold her "dower right" to a piece of Baltimore real estate that had been owned by her deceased husband, in this way managing to get hold of twenty-five dollars. She had tried to make a similar sale a few years before in Philadelphia, while Poe was unemployed, the piecemeal signing-over of her meager holdings clearly being a last resort. Luckily, on the other hand, Poe had a partner to stand between himself and reality. As he wished to understand the death of his golden opportunity, it was the fault of Thomas Lane, "to whom I transferred the Journal," he said, "and in whose hands it perished."

The Salons;
Fanny Osgood and Elizabeth Ellet.

CA. FEBRUARY–JUNE 1845

Poe's "crisis" heralded not only his defeats at the Boston Lyceum and the *Broadway Journal,* but also a romantic scandal that unfolded simultaneously alongside them. Its setting was the literary salons of New York City, where he had been a welcome guest since returning from the Brennan farm.

Some rewards of New York's frenetic commercial activity could be seen in the richness of the city's dark brown upper-class residences, their drawing rooms aglow with satin upholstery, abundances of porcelain and ormolu, marble-topped or inlaid tables strewn with silk-bound volumes of verse. Some wealthy New Yorkers, conscious of literary salons abroad, wished to offset the city's reputation for crass ostentation by bringing together in such tasteful surroundings what Willis called "the two Aristocracies of Brain and Pocket." On the one side were musicians, artists, poets, and myriad other people of talent, seeking an intellectual society where they could mingle for an evening and enjoy the advantages of money without stooping to possess it. On the other side were gracious, intelligent, and usually affluent women (and some men), often correctly typed as "Mrs. Leo Hunters." The two groups satisfied their desires by coming together in the salons, or conversaziones, as many called these high-toned parties.

Poe found himself invited to salons hosted by several different people, New York offering three or four a week. The most respected and talked-about were those given by the leader of New York literary society, Anne Charlotte Lynch. A slender, dark-haired young woman of thirty, simply but attractively dressed, she taught English at the Brooklyn Female Academy, living with and caring for her mother, publishing verses, and ambitiously planning what became her *Universal Handbook of World Literature* (1860). To her many friends she seemed the perfect literary hostess. "Lynchie," as Willis fondly called her, was not only articulate and artistic but also modest and sincere. Friendship, she told Poe, "is my mental sustenance—as absolutely necessary as the material & infinitely higher."

Her delight in personal relations made her guests feel comfortable, encouraging them to converse and socialize.

The tone of Lynch's Saturday-evening conversaziones matched her unassuming character. The perhaps thirty-five persons who came to her home at 116 Waverly Place, adjoining Washington Square, assembled at seven o'clock in two simply furnished drawing rooms. For refreshments they were offered tea and cookies. After two or three hours of rational pleasure they departed. However seemingly meager, the evenings sometime drew eighty or ninety people and became so crowded that guests had to sit on the staircase. Lynch's formula for success was simple too: "I give no entertainment except what they find in each other." There was much to find, for at one time or another she received Washington Irving, William Cullen Bryant, Ralph Waldo Emerson, Margaret Fuller, Herman Melville, Matthew Arnold, and the great violinist Ole Bull, not to mention, as a friend of Lynch put it, "scores and scores of delightful people who were not even well known, but simply delightful." The musicians among them played, the poets read, and all joined in dancing quadrilles and polkas. To be invited to Lynch's salons signified distinction.

During 1845 and at least the early part of 1846, Poe could frequently be seen at the salons, particularly at the home of Anne Lynch. His entrée was insured by the recent fame of his poem, which he seems to have read impressively at several gatherings: "to hear him repeat the Raven," one guest remarked, "which he does very quietly, is an event in one's life." Together with his reputation for such eerie tales as "Mesmeric Revelation," his mournful bird made Poe a magnetic figure to the other guests. "People seem to think there is something uncanny about him," one reported, "and the strangest stories are told, and, what is more, *believed*, about his mesmeric experiences, at the mention of which he always smiles. His smile is captivating!" He became a literary lion of the New York drawing rooms, "the observed of all observers," a contemporary said. "Everybody wants to know him; but only a very few people seem to get well acquainted with him."

Anne Lynch found Poe an ideal guest for the polite atmosphere of her salon. He "had always the bearing and manners of a gentleman," she wrote later, "interesting in conversation, but not monopolising; polite and engaging. . . . quiet and unaffected, unpretentious, in his manner." Many others confirmed her sense that, in contrast to the insurrectionary air of his criticism, Poe's drawing-room manner was courteous and amiable, forthcoming but in no way quarrelsome. When in genteel company he evidently also managed to stay sober and on his best behavior. Evert Duyckinck was struck by the contrast: "Poe with coolness, immaculate personal cleanliness, sensitiveness, the gentleman, continually putting himself on a level with the lowest blackguard through a combination of moral, mental and physical drunkenness." At the salons Poe not only acted the gentleman, but despite his financial straits also looked it. Slim, neatly dressed, he was always, Lynch said, "elegant in his toilet." The general impression of breeding is confirmed in a fine watercolor of Poe painted during this period by the New York miniaturist Alexander McDougall, showing him in a high, rounded collar and cravat knotted tight and low, clean-shaven except for his muttonchoplike sideburns (Illus. 17).

Poe delighted in the company of women, and many of those at the salons, Anne Lynch noted, became "personally attached, and some *devoted,* to him." It was in the milieu of the salons that he carried on a flirtation with Frances Sargent Osgood, then nearly thirty-four years old (Illus. 18). A Bostonian by birth, she evoked several figures from his past and present. She shared her familiar name, Fanny, with that of Fanny Allan. More important and revealing, she replicated Virginia and Eliza in having a childlike personality and physique. She was small in stature, perhaps just over five feet. To her many friends she seemed a sprite. Her admirer Rufus Griswold remarked on her "almost infantile gaiety and vivacity." George Foster described her at a New York conversazione, "clapping her hands and crowing like a baby." Others called her a child of nature, or an angel. Poe's choice of her suggests in retrospect how much of Virginia's own appeal for him had come from her being a child of thirteen, suggesting as well an unwillingness or inability to join himself to women with emotionally and sexually developed personalities. With her very black, glossy hair and unusually pallid complexion, Fanny may at the time have had something else in common with Virginia, and perhaps Eliza. She may have been in an early stage of tuberculosis.

Fanny Osgood was also a woman of intelligence, with a talent for facile literary composition. She spun out poems, Griswold said, "with almost the fluency of conversation." Anne Lynch told of riding with her down Broadway, when Osgood realized she had forgotten her purse; on the spot she wrote off a two-stanza poem, took it into a publisher, and came out with ten dollars. The story may not be much exaggerated, for Osgood was one of the best-known female poets of the period, in a literary market that sought and respected writing by American women, dozens of whom sold works on every subject and in every form. (The Connecticut poet and novelist Lydia Huntley Sigourney altogether published about sixty books and, by her estimate, more than two thousand articles.) Osgood kept up a sizable businesslike correspondence with editors, and contributed to most of the leading periodicals of the time, under her own name and several pseudonyms. Poe himself had published a story and a poem by her while working for *Graham's,* and had followed her career. Altogether she wrote or edited some dozen volumes of prose and verse, including *The Poetry of Flowers* (1841, often reprinted), *The Snowdrop, a New Year Gift for Children* (1842), and *Puss in Boots* (1844). As the titles suggest, in keeping with her personality she wrote many poems for children.

However immature she appeared, Fanny Osgood was also the mother of two young daughters, offspring of her ten-year marriage to Samuel Stillman Osgood. A craggy-faced, adventurous man, he had spent time at sea and undergone shipwreck, but was by profession a fashionable portrait painter, trained at the Royal Academy in London. His commissions often took him to other places, leaving Fanny alone. His few surviving letters to her during these trips are very affectionate; but he also became involved with other women, stirring gossip. With her spontaneity and warmth Fanny did not lack admirers either. Several men engaged her in literary flirtations. Delighted by flattery, as she acknowledged, she invited their praises, and sent rather coquettish poems in return. It is unlikely that she took lovers, but perhaps felt disposed to do so. The doves, fairies, and flowers of her poetry pulsate with gentle eroticism. In one poem, "The Dying Rosebud's Lament," she portrayed herself as a floral Sleeping Beauty, waiting to be aroused:

> *My leaves, instinct with glowing life,*
> *Were quivering to unclose;*
> *My happy heart with love was rife—*
> *I was almost a rose.*

At the time she met Poe, she seems still to have felt "almost a rose." Her marriage had apparently become strained once more, and the couple may even have been living apart.

Poe's acquaintance with Fanny Osgood came about through his February lecture at the New York Society Library, in which he had battered several American poets, having at Longfellow and chopping up the Davidson sisters. In the same talk, however, he prophesied for Osgood "a rosy future of increasing power and renown." Fanny missed the lecture, but learned about his remarks and was immensely pleased. "Did you see how beautifully Mr Edgar Poe spoke of me in his lecture on the Poets—the other night?" she wrote to a friend. "He recited a long poem of mine exquisitely, they said—& praised me very highly—He is called the severest critic of the day—so it was a real compliment." What happened next is uncertain, as is much else about their relationship. By Osgood's account, Poe asked for an introduction and sent through Willis a copy of "The Raven." But here and in all of her later recollections of the events, she consistently presented Poe as the initiator of them. Most of the solid evidence, however, indicates that she more freely and actively considered the possibility of a serious liaison, while his feelings were more conflicted and his behavior accordingly changeable.

Whoever made the approach, Poe and Osgood met in early March, as he first settled into his editorial position on the *Broadway Journal.* Poe may have felt some reluctance, for he broke their first appointment, due he explained to an "unlucky *contretemps"* in getting out the magazine. But they spoke a few days later in the drawing room of the Astor House (a hotel whose fashionable character he detested), apparently in the company of Willis. Poe seemed to her haughty but feeling, attractive despite or through his reserve: "he greeted me, calmly, gravely, almost coldly," as she recalled the meeting, "yet with so marked an earnestness that I could not help being deeply impressed by it." These were afterthoughts. At the time she summed up her reaction more directly: "I was introduced to him . . . & like him very much."

For two months following their meeting, Poe and Osgood intimated their feelings to each other through exchanges of verse. As the dubious 'one-third proprietor' of the *Journal,* he printed two poems submitted by Fanny under the names Kate Carol and Violet Vane. That he identified them as hers seems clear from his coy editorial remark that "We might *guess* who is the fair author of the following lines." That she meant them for him is also clear from their many echoes of the language and imagery of his own poetry. The pained female speaker of the first poem complains of the coldness of her married male friend, a coldness Osgood remarked in her first meeting with Poe. In what seems an allusion to Virginia

Poe, the speaker tells her friend that his wife would surely not deny them a companionship:

> *The fair, fond girl, who at your side,*
> *Within your soul's dear light, doth live,*
> *Could hardly have the heart to chide*
> *The ray that Friendship well might give.*

In the second poem, on the Sleeping Beauty theme, a rivulet sings the praises of a star that shines upon it with "heavenly looks of light." The rivulet longs to dwell with the star; but as morning comes, the star fades, and the rivulet realizes on second thought that its vision of a "star-love" has been merely a "sweet dream." Poe perhaps found the conclusion a relief, for in commenting on this poem in the *Journal*, he made a point of saying that he preferred the rivulet's " 'sober second thought'."

Poe printed several other poems by Fanny and himself that seem gambits in a hands-off, but interested, courting game. So far as they may be interpreted as obliquely raising the possibility of a serious romance, they show Fanny as genteelly seductive and Poe hesitant to the point of appearing indifferent, preoccupied, or guilt-ridden. He reprinted a poem by Fanny that depicted a woman who is innocent-seeming but seductive, and bound to triumph:

> *Her eyes are too modest*
> *To dazzle; but oh!*
> *They win you to love her,*
> *If you will or no!*

As if in answer, Poe published in the following issue a new poem of his own, unrevealingly entitled "To—" and signed "M." It put the question of his availability beyond doubt. In the first stanza he held out the prospect of friendship, but alluded to both his chaotic existence and to their spouses:

> *I would not lord it o'er thy heart,*
> *Alas! I cannot rule my own,*
> *Nor would I rob one loyal thought,*
> *From him who there should reign alone;*
> *We both have found a life-long love*
> *Wherein our weary souls may rest,*
> *Yet may we not, my gentle friend*
> *Be each to each the second best?*

Poe's reluctance was obviously mixed with strong attraction. Writing under his own name, he praised her in the *Journal* as "the most truly graceful, delicate, and yet impassioned of American poetesses." If not abandoning, at least trifling with, his role as the fearlessly disinterested critic, he would ultimately publish twelve of her poems in the magazine, where her name appeared more than thirty times.

Not much is known of the other means by which Poe and Osgood stayed in touch. She apparently wrote to him often, and he wrote to her. Their letters have been destroyed or lost, but a friend of Fanny's reported that she described his letters as noncommittal, "mere notes filled with expressions of devoted friendship & admiration, but very brief." The New York publisher John Russell Bartlett frequently entertained Osgood as a houseguest, and said that "when she was with my family, Poe called every day and generally spent the evening remaining invariably until midnight." And the couple frequently saw each other at the conversaziones, mingling among the rich, the celebrated, and the delightful. The writer Elizabeth Oakes Smith recalled seeing them there, "the childlike face of Fannie Osgood suffused with tears under [Poe's] wizard spell." They made an effect, for Poe's friend English also recalled an evening at Anne Lynch's home when Poe held stage center, opining and reading passages from poems. There was "little Mrs. Osgood," as he too remembered, "doing the infantile act . . . her face upturned to Poe."

The dalliance did not stay confined to long looks at the salons or poems by M and Violet Vane. Probably in the later part of June, a New York merchant named Edward Thomas heard a rumor that Poe had committed forgery. So far as can be known in this murky episode, Thomas himself was taken by Fanny Osgood, saw Poe as a rival, and repeated the rumor to her. One way or another Poe learned of Thomas's attempt to discredit him. He called on Thomas at his business office in Broad Street, denied the charge, and asked him to retract it. Thomas promised to trace the rumor to its source. But T. D. English, who had a law degree in addition to a medical degree, counseled Poe to sue Thomas for libel. Poe wrote Thomas a brusque letter, hand-delivered by English, calling on him to state distinctly whether he had himself originated "the charge of *forgery* urged by you against myself." English brought back a verbal reply that Poe considered "somewhat vague."

Poe considered commencing a suit. To gather evidence in his

defense, he went to see Fanny Osgood. That at least was his later explanation of how he came to visit her in Providence, Rhode Island. At the time, however, he explained the unusual trip differently to Chivers, during their tottering walk on Nassau Street. "I am now going to reveal to you the very secrets of my heart,"—as Chivers remembered his words—"I am in the d—dst amour you ever knew a fellow to be in in all your life." Without naming the woman, Poe confided that he had received a letter from her, asking him to come to Providence that afternoon on the four o'clock boat. He revealed that the woman's husband was a painter, "always from home—and a d—d fool at that!" Next day Chivers took Poe for a ride in a rented carriage and asked the name of the lady "with whom he was so in love?" Poe looked abashed, Chivers recalled, and vigorously denied being involved with any woman. But the day after that, he said he was off to Providence because "Some body" had obliged him to go there, and borrowed ten dollars from Chivers for expenses. He asked him, also, to say nothing to Muddy or Sissy about his going.

Chivers's account of Poe's clandestine visit to Providence may be exaggerated or misremembered in details. But other evidence confirms its essential meaning, that by the summer Poe had broken through his conflicted feelings about Osgood and begun to woo her. According to Fanny herself, he now in fact beamed more "star-love" than she sought. "I went to Albany, and afterwards to Boston and Providence to avoid him," she recalled, "and he followed me to each of those places and wrote to me, imploring me to love him." Further evidence of Poe's pursuit perhaps appears in her story "Ida Grey," published in the August *Graham's*. The name of the heroine may well allude to Poe's pseudonym, Edward S. T. Grey. And Osgood marked in a personal copy of the magazine a passage in which her heroine says, "He bids me tell him that I love him, as proudly as if he had a right . . . a divine right to demand my love." In what seems a reply to this, Poe published in the October *Graham's* a poem called "The Divine Right of Kings," signed "P." He presented himself as not wanting to rule by divine right, but rather to be enthralled: "were she mine / I'd strive for liberty no more, / But hug the glorious chains I wore."

Whatever the motives and results of Poe's trip to Providence, he was back in New York the next day. He found on his return a letter from Edward Thomas retracting the charge of forgery. Thomas explained that the person from whom he had heard the rumor now denied knowing it, much less repeating it: some word he had used in speaking to Thomas, he said, must have been misunderstood. Thomas assured Poe he was delighted to find the story "destitute of foundation" and promised to tell the results of his inquiry to Osgood. Poe decided not to proceed with his suit.

Once Poe took over the *Journal* as editor and owner, he began publicizing Osgood's work, and his relation to her, more boldly than before. He gave nearly five columns of a December issue to reviewing a new volume of her poems. He praised her for versatility in experimenting with different poetic forms, correct grammar, and originality, although to the credit of his integrity he also gently criticized her tame imagination, deficient rhythmic sense, and sometimes affected diction. A stroke-and-sting pattern of course identifies most of Poe's criticism, and in this respect he treated Osgood more or less as he treated other writers. Yet parts of the essay seem as much to compliment her person as her verse: "it is in that indescribable something which, for want of a more definite term, we are accustomed to call *grace* . . . it is in this charm of charms . . . that Mrs. Osgood pre-eminently excels. It is in this that she has no equal among her countrywomen." He also asked Fanny, as well as T. D. English, to compose the new poem he felt incapable of writing for his October appearance at the Lyceum. Aware of her "astonishing facility," he reasoned she could easily and quickly give him "a poem that shall be equal to my reputation." This remark too bespeaks infatuation rather than aesthetic judgment, and what Fanny produced for him was "Lulin, or the Diamond Fay," a lengthy narrative that echoed Drake's *The Culprit Fay,* which he loathed.

Once in control of the *Journal,* Poe not only printed Fanny's verses to him under her own name, but also usually placed them beside his own also-signed tales. More brazenly still, two of her poems speak very directly of and to him. One begins with a quote from his "Israfel," using it as the point of departure for an expression of deep personal sympathy:

To———
"*In Heaven a spirit doth dwell,*
Whose heart-strings are a lute."

I cannot tell the world *how thrills my heart*
To every touch that flies thy lyre along;

> *How the wild Nature and the wondrous Art*
> *Blend into Beauty in thy passionate song—*

The second poem, printed as the lead item on the *Journal*'s front page, quotes "Israfel" again and also alludes to "The Raven" in hinting at some privileged knowledge of Poe's passions:

> *I know a noble heart that beats*
> *For one it loves how "wildly well!"*
> *I only know for whom it beats;*
> *But I must never tell!*
> *Never tell!*

Osgood associated the word "wild," occurring in both selections, with Poe. It was worth a trip to New York, she told Elizabeth Barrett, to see Poe's "wild eyes flash through tears" when he read Barrett's poems.

Such public praises for each other's grace, nobility, and wildness could not fail to attract attention. According to T. D. English, "The supposed intrigue became town talk." Fanny may have alluded to the gossip in two more of her poems, both published in the *Journal*. One, called "Slander," concerns whispers "barbed with shame." Another, seemingly addressed to Poe, reproves the scandal-mongers who "dare accuse *thee* of flirtation"; they may as well castigate the stars, she wrote, for kindling light in the "wild wave." Apparently neither Samuel Osgood nor Virginia Poe joined the accusers. The worldly painter himself had some reputation as a philanderer, and even did a portrait of Poe, the only one known from life (Illus. 19). It conveys Poe's hazel-colored eyes, blackish brown curling hair, and fringe of chin whiskers. But it also makes him seem, as people who knew Poe commented, bland and characterless.

Fanny Osgood even visited Poe at home, sometimes, she said, at Virginia's own invitation. She also said that, far from expressing distrust, Virginia asked her to maintain a correspondence with Poe, imagining she would have a "restraining" effect on him. (That happened, Fanny added; Poe promised her to "give up the use of stimulants," and was never drunk in her presence.) Fanny's remarks may be believed, for Sissy was aware of the seriousness of her condition and concerned about Poe's welfare as he tried to withstand her dying and death. She had occasionally accompanied him to the conversaziones, where one guest recalled that she displayed "the greatest

admiration for her husband's genius, and fairly worshipped him."
The worship was mutual, for even when Poe came by himself her
presence was felt: "he was fond of naming her, and dwelling upon
her loveliness of character." But Virginia now went out rarely. Aged
twenty-three, she retained her sweetness and gentleness, but a visitor to the East Broadway flat found her no longer plump, as in
girlhood. She looked "pale and wasted," and he came away thinking, "she is dying of consumption." Poe at once denied and recognized the fact. In speaking of Sissy to others, he often attributed
her invalided state not to tuberculosis, but to the rupture of a blood
vessel during what he persisted in describing as her singing "accident." At the same time he could scarcely fail to acknowledge that
she had not recovered from the "accident," and, he admitted, "I
fear that she never will." In Frances Osgood he sought more than
anything else a replacement for Virginia's steadying love and care.

Combined with the other stormy products of Poe's "crisis" and
the gossipy atmosphere of the salons, his romantic situation required not much else to bring forth a new disaster. The needed
ingredient came as the wealthy and imposing Mrs. Elizabeth Ellet.
Then twenty-seven years old, she was married to a professor of
chemistry at South Carolina College but spent much time in New
York City. As a busy professional writer she made a familiar presence at the city's literary evenings, where she encountered among
others Poe and Fanny Osgood. In addition to publishing verse, novels, plays, anthologies, reviews, and children's books, she had a wide
acquaintance with European literature in the original languages and
produced translations from French, German, Spanish, and Italian,
as well as essays on Schiller and on Italian drama. Proudly independent, she refused to be identified with the feminist movement, "that
club of female seekers after notoriety," although notable among her
works was the multi-volume *Women of the American Revolution* (1848;
4th ed., 1850). She later became the first white female to make the
hazardous northwest trip to Lake Minnetonka in Minnesota.

This formidable and knowledgeable woman was also a zealous
Christian. She boasted what she called her heritage of "strict religious faith and observances, unblemished moral training and conservative ideas." However righteous she felt herself to be, many
contemporaries thought her meddlesome, thieving, and vindictive.
They charged that among other misdeeds she ransacked the desk
of the writer Sarah Anna Lewis, while being entertained at her home;
sold a story to *Putnam's* and resold it under another title to *Harper's*

fifteen years later; and repaid Rufus Griswold for some unfavorable comments about her by sending anonymous letters to his wife, accusing him of bigamy.

Yet as 1845 ended, Poe began to feature Elizabeth Ellet's work in the expiring *Journal*. During the magazine's last two months he praised her as "one of the most accomplished of our countrywomen," and published her stilted poems—all "terrors of the deep" and "golden glory of the sun"—on the front page four times, including the last issue he edited. In the same period he allowed Fanny Osgood the starring position only once, otherwise assigning her poems to inner pages. He did other literary favors for Ellet as well, for instance asking Evert Duyckinck to print an unsigned article by her in his newspaper.

The meaning of Poe's sudden attention to Mrs. Ellet and seeming withdrawal from Fanny Osgood can be divined, if at all, only through meager evidence. With her husband teaching in South Carolina, Ellet may have tried to interest Poe in a romantic friendship. That is vaguely suggested by her bantering invitation to him, written in German, to send for a letter she was holding or else "heute abend . . . bei mir entnehmen" (call for it at her residence that evening). Her meaning may have been seductive but seems to have been lost on Poe, who she discovered "would not decipher my German." The most revealing fact in the situation may be that Fanny Osgood was at this time pregnant with her third child, who would be born in June. Her condition implies a reconciliation with her husband, but no information survives about this either, and it has even been suggested that the child's father was Poe. That is possible but most unlikely. The air of dangerous fascination that attached to Poe at the salons arose in large part from his burning need to be taken care of. His moral primness and complex aversion to at least undomesticated sexual feeling led him to deny passion a place in poetry and to most often depict women as far-off statues, fearful revenants, or pimply hags.

While Poe's exact relation to Osgood and Ellet at this time remains obscure, it seems he had again become hesitant about Fanny, or she had become less available, moving him to replace her by some less fervent attention to Elizabeth Ellet. That Fanny Osgood felt some jealousy in the situation is suggested by her later curt remark that Mrs. Ellet "asked an introduction to him and followed him everywhere."

To be under the eye of Elizabeth Ellet called for staying on guard, as Poe discovered. Probably in January, she visited Poe at his Amity Street lodgings and somehow saw a letter sent him by Fanny Osgood. Again the events are known through later, conflicting, and mostly second-hand accounts: in Ellet's version, the (supposed) love letter to Poe was shown to her by Virginia, who even pointed out and repeated "fearful paragraphs" in it. Whether Ellet learned about the letter by accident, by snooping, or through Virginia, she chided Fanny Osgood for her indiscretion, and persuaded her to get the letter back. A demand for its return was presented to Poe at his home by Margaret Fuller and Anne Lynch. Angered by the interference in his private life, Poe denounced them as "Busy-bodies" and answered their demand by saying that Mrs. Ellet had better come and "look after her *own* letters." The statement dramatically insinuated that Mrs. Ellet too had written him indiscreet letters.

In Poe's account of what followed, given about three years later, he no sooner made his remark than he regretted it. He believed Mrs. Ellet had acted maliciously, out of jealousy. But he nevertheless regretted having spoken in "the heat of passion," and felt she would have been justified in reproaching him as a cad, for "having betrayed, under *any* circumstances, her confidence." In this frame of mind, he said, he retrieved her letters from his desk, made a package of them, and personally left them at her door. With "diabolical malignity," however, instead of feeling grateful for the return of her compromising letters, Ellet urged her brother "to *demand of me* [Poe] *the letters,*" letters he actually had given back and of course no longer had.

Poe's account was probably a lie. T. D. English retold the same events quite differently. In his version, Mrs. Ellet had not written any letters to Poe. When her brother learned of Poe's menacing statement—"look after her *own* letters"—the man angrily sent word to him to either produce the letters or recant and apologize for his insinuation that she had written them. According to English, Poe then came to his rooms to borrow a pistol. He explained that Ellet's brother had threatened his life unless he showed him the letters. When English asked why he did not simply produce them, Poe replied that he refused to do so under compulsion. English told Poe that he believed "he had no such letters in his possession." The best thing Poe could do, he said, would be to acknowledge that he had spoken in vexation, and to apologize. The two men argued, then fought.

It was a lopsided match. Ten years younger than Poe, the mustachioed English had been trained early as a carpenter, and his tough speech-making had given him some reputation as a political brawler, and a prominent place in torchlight processions. Poe rushed toward him menacingly, he said: "I threw out my fist to stop him, and the impetus of his rush, rather than any force of mine, made the extension of my arm a blow. He grasped me while falling backward over a lounge, and I on top of him." The scuffle lasted a few moments. English said that he hit Poe in the face, unintentionally and badly cutting it with the heavy seal ring he wore on his pinky. The racket attracted someone in a neighboring room who separated them and led Poe away. Poe, in his own account of the fracas, did not contradict English's version of the preliminaries. Rather, he said he remembered nothing that happened, except for having "wearied and degraded myself, to little purpose" by fighting. His version of the outcome, however, was his own: "I gave E.[nglish] a flogging which he will remember to the day of his death."

The beating, whoever took it, gave a disturbingly violent turn to Poe's antics over the last year. As Horace Greeley summed up current gossip, Poe "scandalized two eminent literary ladies, and came near getting horsewhipped or pistoled." As a result of the fight, English said, Poe was confined to bed. But he had his physician bring a letter of regret to Ellet's brother. It explained that if he had accused her of sending him indiscreet letters, he had no recollection of it, and "was labouring," as English reported his words, "under a fit of insanity to which he was periodically subject." The doctor added that Poe was "suffering under great fear" and warned Ellet's brother that unless he accepted the retraction and relented, Poe's mind might be affected seriously.

No such letter from Poe survives, but English's summary of it is corroborated by a later statement of Elizabeth Ellet. Insisting she had not written compromisingly to Poe, she remarked that she had evidence of her innocence in a letter from him; it apologized for slandering her "as he alleged, in a fit of lunacy." English's account gains further credibility from Poe's several remarks during the year that he felt he had become "mad." The available evidence indicates that Poe simply concocted the story of having, gathering, and returning Ellet's 'letters.' All but admitting as much, he said of his part in the mess, "there was much—very much—there was everything—to be offered in extenuation."

On the circle of literary women from whom Poe had sought relief and reassurance, the letters affair had varying effects. Ellet wrote to Fanny Osgood, asking pardon for her earlier reproofs to Fanny's "indiscretion"; her own experience with Poe, she said, had convinced her that the "fearful paragraphs" read to her by Virginia *"must have* been a forgery." She conceived an enduring hatred for Poe, decrying him to others as "intemperate, and subject to attacks of lunacy." Although Osgood later made light of her own relationship to Poe, she apparently did so to protect both their reputations; she earnestly cared for him, as he did for her. In a poem written several years later, she spoke of remembering his voice and his praise for her work, and the difficulty of forgetting him: "He haunts me forever, I worship him yet; / O! idle endeavor, I cannot forget!"

By Valentine's Day, 1846, Fanny Osgood was reunited with her husband, about halfway through her pregnancy, feeling ill in mind and body. Poe composed a puzzle poem for her of twenty-one lines, in which the first letter of the first line, the second letter of the second line, and so on, spelled out her "sweet name," as he called it in the poem. Recklessly or perhaps insolently, he sent it to the Valentine's Day party given by Anne Lynch, the leader of New York literary society who had come with Margaret Fuller to demand the return of Fanny's letter. Poe's Valentine poem may have been read aloud at the party, as the best entries were, but it is unlikely that he attended. Anne Lynch had stopped inviting him to her conversaziones: "with all his genius he has no moral sense," she decided, "& he said & did a great many things that were very abominable." He had come into such "bad odour" with people who visited her, she said, "that if I were to recieve [*sic*] him, I should lose the company of many whom I value more."

But Poe was remembered on February 14 anyway. He received a Valentine poem himself. It came from Sissy, from Virginia Eliza, the only verse she is known to have written. He perhaps showed her his poem to Fanny, for hers formed, less ambitiously, an acrostic whose initial letters spelled out EDGAR ALLAN POE. It spoke of her desire to lead a sequestered and tranquil life with him, perhaps in the country:

> *Ever with thee I wish to roam—*
> *Dearest my life is thine.*
> *Give me a cottage for my home*
> *And a rich old cypress vine,*

Under the double *LL*'s of his guardian's name she explained how a leafy cottage would shelter them from the gossip that more and more beset their life in the city, and ventured the hope that his love for her might repair the worrisome damage done by her singing "accident":

> *Removed from the world with its sin and care*
> *And the tattling of many tongues.*
> *Love alone shall guide us when we are there—*
> *Love shall heal my weakened lungs. . . .*

Quite as Poe thought of his escapades, there was much to be offered in extenuation.

Other Writing and Editions in 1845; "The Philosophy of Composition."

1845

Poe's "crisis" in the fall of 1844 had brought in a frenzied year. Except the triumph of "The Raven," he spent most of 1845 in an uproar, displeased with his work, falling out with friends and business associates, skipping engagements, conniving to keep his magazine, cutting up Longfellow, "quizzing" the Bostonians, ventriloquizing "Outis," pursuing Fanny Osgood, "flogging" T. D. English, drinking, recurrently depressed, always without money, ever more frightened as he saw Virginia failing. His writing and editorial labor for the *Broadway Journal* were both ground and outlet for many of his woes. But his agitation also shows through much of his other literary employment during the year, apart from the magazine.

As already noted, Poe contributed no unpublished fiction to the *Journal,* but only revisions of earlier works, selling his few new tales elsewhere. "The System of Doctor Tarr and Professor Fether," published in *Graham's,* relates a visit to a madhouse in southern France, run according to a 'new system.' During a lavish but oddly raucous dinner at the place, the narrator gradually realizes that his richly dressed table companions, presumably the superintendent and keepers, are actually the insane inmates. They have overthrown, tarred and feathered, and locked in cells the real staff, usurping their clothing and jewels and making free with the chateau's kitchen and wine cellars. This is the 'new system.'

Hinting some concern in Poe about his own mental health, the tale stands apart from most of his antically comic attempts by its affecting realism and undercurrent of irrational ferocity. It conveys something of the sad dilapidation of an asylum, and of the inmates' distress. Mostly it consists of vignettes in which the mad dinner guests, posing as keepers, make fun of various inmates at the place, who are in reality themselves. One after the other 'keeper' abusively describes some 'inmate' who mistook himself for a champagne bottle, frog, top, or rooster, then starts hissing, croaking, spinning, or crowing. The broad comedy comes uncomfortably near to representing the Poe who scathingly mocked puffers, plagiarists, and errant grammarians, and then anonymously praised himself, lifted the work of others, and mispunctuated. The asylum is superintended, it might be added, by a Monsieur Maillard, a name in which *Allan* again nearly resurfaces, as it also does in keeper-inmates named Laplace, Boullard, and Gaillard (and in Allamistakeo, the prematurely embalmed hero of "Some Words with a Mummy," published in the *American Review: A Whig Journal*).

Concern about Virginia overlies "The Facts of M. Valdemar's Case," also published in the *Review*. Poe's most gruesome tale, it is narrated as an authentic case history by a mesmerist, "P—," who wants to learn whether his science can arrest the approach of death. He finds an ideal subject in his dying friend Ernest Valdemar, whom he puts into a trance. When the mesmerist asks whether he is asleep, Valdemar, showing no vital signs, replies *"I am dead."* He remains in a dead-alive state nearly seven months, until the mesmerist and several physicians try to awaken him. Then he dies forever. As the mesmerist makes passes, Valdemar's eyes begin moving. From his eyelids seeps a "profuse outflowing of a yellowish ichor." His black tongue jerks in his mouth to make the words "dead! dead!" Instead of returning to life his body shrinks to a stinking mush. He "absolutely *rotted* away beneath my hands," the mesmerist says in the final words of the tale. "Upon the bed, before that whole company, there lay a nearly liquid mass of loathsome—of detestable putrescence."

Poe's disgusting ending greatly influenced later fiction and films of the supernatural, especially by followers of H. P. Lovecraft. And as happened with "Mesmeric Revelation," many magnetic healers took the tale as a factual report. Robert Collyer, an English mesmerist then lecturing in Boston, wrote to Poe saying that he had himself restored to "active animation" a man who had been pronounced dead and lay encoffined, readied for interment. (Actually he had revived no more than a dead-drunk sailor by means of a hot bath and prolonged massage.) Another English expert, Thomas South, writing in his *Early Magnetism in its Higher Relations to Humanity* (London, 1846), confidently identified the mesmerist "P—" as Poe himself and praised his "demagnetising passes." In one sense he may not have been far wrong. As in "Mesmeric Revelation," not only is the mesmerist of the tale identified as "P—", but the name of the dying patient also begins with a *V*. Valdemar suffers moreover from a "confirmed phthisis," that is, from pulmonary consumption. Poe describes his condition in disturbingly objective detail:

> The left lung had been for eighteen months in a semi-osseous or cartilaginous state. . . . The right, in its upper portion, was also partially, if not thoroughly, ossified, while the lower region was merely a mass of purulent tubercles, running into one another. Several extensive perforations existed; and, at one point, permanent adhesion to the ribs had taken place.

While Poe often maintained that Virginia was suffering the effects of a singing accident, he was hardly ignorant of what the ravages of tuberculosis might be like.

Similar currents of meaning circulate through one of Poe's most consequential essays, "The Philosophy of Composition." Probably written early in the new year, it appeared in *Graham's* for April 1846. Here Poe undertook to describe the deliberate steps by which he composed "The Raven." In doing so he also formulated more compactly than anywhere else his major dicta about poetry and fiction: originality as an essential "source of interest"; the shaping of every element according to a predetermined single effect; the antagonism of Beauty to Passion and Truth; the direct relation between intensity and brevity. In the essay he wholly devaluated inspiration and empathy in art, and correspondingly emphasized technique and artistic detachment. His determined separation of the man who suffers and the artist who creates has long been recognized as a preliminary manifesto of literary modernism and postmodernism, and has had enormous influence, especially in France.

To cite only two of many audacious French writers for whom Poe became an adored master, Stéphane Mallarmé said that Poe taught him to exclude chance from poetry and to calculate the semantic and aural impact of every word. In a part of *Tel Quel,* Paul Valéry made Poe's theories not only a practice but also the content:

> *I seek a word (says the poet) a word which is*
> *feminine,*
> *has two syllables,*
> *contains p or f,*
> *ends in a mute vowel. . . .*

In his essay Poe dramatized the making of a depersonalized art indifferent to political and moral considerations, its subject being its own dynamic inner relationships. From the point of view of later literary history, his true contemporary was Gustave Flaubert, who wished to write a novel about a blade of grass, able to stand on the strength of its style alone.

From the point of view of Poe's life, however, "The Philosophy of Composition" seems but a larger and more fortified hedge against his increasing irrationality. Patiently, lengthily, minutely dissecting "The Raven," he showed that he wrote the poem by exercising a methodical, total control. He contended, for example, that he deliberately made the night tempestuous in order to account for the raven's seeking entrance to the room; deliberately made the bird alight on a bust in order to contrast its plumage with the marble; deliberately chose a bust of Pallas in order to evoke the scholarship of the mournful student, and so on through every feature of the poem's plot, imagery, and language. Far from having worked in "a species of fine frenzy," he said, he wrote in a state of hyperanalytic lucidity: "no one point in its composition is referrible either to accident or intuition . . . the work proceeded, step by step, to its completion with the precision and rigid consequence of a mathematical problem."

Many readers have wondered how seriously Poe meant them to take "The Philosophy of Composition" as a description of his creative processes, some even suspecting a hoax. The source of their uncertainty is evident. Like the mutilated corpses uselessly hidden under floorboards, the Red Death vainly held at bay by Prospero's nested rooms, the thoughts of lost Lenore futilely kept from mind by the bereaved lover, Poe's fearful preoccupations and anxious state repeatedly emerge through the philosophical reasonings meant to master and conceal them. To suggest his detached condition while writing the poem he chose the highly charged example of the actor, his seeming emotion on stage but a product of theatrical mechanics, "the tackle for scene-shifting—the step-ladders and demon-traps— the cock's feathers, the red paint and the black patches, which, in ninety-nine cases out of the hundred, constitute the properties of the literary *histrio*." He in effect also returned to the world of the theater in describing the poet's search for a subject:

> . . . I asked myself—"Of all melancholy topics, what, according to the *universal* understanding of mankind, is the *most* melancholy?" Death—was the obvious reply. "And when," I said, "is this most melancholy of topics most poetical?" . . . the answer, here also, is obvious— "When it most closely allies itself to *Beauty:* The death, then, of a beautiful woman is, unquestionably, the most poetical topic in the world. . . ."

The voice that speaks here and throughout "The Philosophy of Composition" recalls that of the crazed narrators in some of Poe's tales, whose tone of eerie calm is intended to demonstrate their lucidity and self-control, but arouses only the reader's fear and pity.

Amid the tumult of 1845, Poe also published new editions of his tales and of his poems. Both came out in the Library of American Books issued by the New York publisher Wiley and Putnam. Meant to appeal to a middle-class reading and buying public, these rather drably manufactured volumes aimed at striking a tasteful and affordable balance between expensive books and the 'cheap literature' of the day, to sell extensively but maintain, Poe said, "a sufficiently standard character to warrant their preservation in our book-cases." Poe's inclusion in the series was arranged by Evert Duyckinck, who admired his work, negotiated the contract, and as Wiley and Putnam's reader also selected the twelve works to appear in the *Tales*.

Duyckinck chose brilliantly well. Perhaps as a concession to Poe's unfounded sense of himself as a humorist, he included "Lionizing," but otherwise emphasized Poe's subtle psychologizing ("The Black Cat," "The Fall of the House of Usher") and philosophical fancies ("Mesmeric Revelation," "The Colloquy of Monos and Una"). He featured, however, tales of ratiocination, including "The Gold-Bug," "The Murders in the Rue Morgue," "The Mystery of Marie Rogêt," and "The Purloined Letter." New evidence about the murder of

Mary Rogers had turned up since the first publication of "Marie Rogêt," refuting Poe's theory that Mary-Marie had been murdered by a naval officer. To account for the new likelihood that her death had been due to a bungled abortion, he made some fifteen small changes in his tale for the 1845 edition. He had written, for example: "We have attained the idea of a murder perpetrated in the thicket"; it became, "We have attained the idea either of a fatal accident under the roof of Madame Deluc, or of a murder perpetrated, in the thicket." He also added detailed footnotes to make it seem that his analysis of the murder had been correct from the start.

The 1845 *Tales* was Poe's only volume to achieve some commercial success. He claimed that after four months of publication more than 1,500 copies of the fifty-cent book had been sold, at a royalty of eight cents each, which meant that he earned $120. The edition succeeded critically as well, receiving some forty reviews and notices, mostly favorable, in periodicals from Boston to New Orleans to Paris, Edinburgh, and London. Rufus Griswold generously ranked Poe with "the first class of tale writers who have appeared since the marvel-loving Arabian first attempted fabulous history." In France the *Magasin pittoresque* published an adaptation of "The Purloined Letter" as "Une lettre volée," "The Gold-Bug" appearing in the *Revue brittanique* as "Le Scarabée d'Or." The half-dozen English and Scottish reviews generally applauded the tales for their novelty and strangeness, but usually also faulted them as ordinary in style, magazinish, grisly, or simply too American. Americans, for many in England since the founding of the country, meant Indians. And among the several English reviewers who called attention to Poe's "microscopic power of analysis," one remarked, "Put him on any trail, and he traces it as keenly as a Blackfoot or Ojibbeway." Another even attributed Poe's skill in detection to the influence of native Americans and their ability to track a foe: "He has learned from the dwellers in the American woods a marked acuteness." The remark annoyed Poe, who shot back in the *Journal:* "The only objection to this theory is that we never go into the woods . . . and are quite sure that we never saw a live Indian in our lives."

Poe was nettled as well by the selection of tales in the volume, despite its critical success. Duyckinck's emphasis on ratiocinative works, he felt, left his virtuosity undisplayed. To set matters straight, he or a collaborator reviewed the *Tales* in the New York *Aristidean,* objecting that "Mr. P. should never have consented to so brief a selection. . . . He has made a point of versatility of invention. But it is obvious that this point is entirely lost in a selection of merely twelve stories from eighty [as he counted the sixty or so he had written]. Most of the pieces in the present volume, too, are of one kind—analytical." Aside from illustrating again Poe's failure to join his own crusade against puffers, the remarks are valuable for recording how he viewed his accomplishment as a writer of short fiction. He had given such works a new dignity, he or his accomplice observed, and "elevated the mere 'tale,' in this country, over the larger 'novel.' "

In their Library of American Books, Wiley and Putnam also issued Poe's *The Raven and Other Poems*, a one-hundred page volume dedicated to Elizabeth Barrett. The thirty-one-cent selling price was in keeping with the self-deflating remarks in Poe's preface. He described the poems as "trifles," published only because they were being reprinted here and there with unauthorized changes, and he wished them to be known, if at all, through their correct texts. "Events not to be controlled," he explained, had kept him from treating his poetry seriously, although in happier circumstances he would have devoted to it his best efforts. Indeed the preface reveals that Poe had come to think of his verse as above and apart from his fiction and criticism. For him, he said, "poetry has been not a purpose, but a passion," and like all passions "should be held in reverence." It had nothing to do with—as if he did not yearn for them—"the paltry compensations, or the more paltry commendations, of mankind."

Paltry commendation and worse were what Poe received. Willis, Simms, and a few other friends or supporters praised his "inventive genius so brilliant and vigorous," and several other reviewers expressed renewed admiration for "The Raven." But his self-critical preface beckoned to ill-wishers, not to mention his recent follies and his many years of dismembering other poets. As Margaret Fuller supposed in the *Daily Tribune*, "A large band . . . must be on the watch for a volume of 'Poems by Edgar A. Poe,' ready to cut, rend and slash in turn." Among this band, Lewis Gaylord Clark of the *Knickerbocker* ridiculed Poe's preface, commenting that the mysterious uncontrollable events he lamented could hardly have been more disabling than Milton's blindness or Dante's exile, and that Poe's disregard for compensation or commendation was fortunate, since "the amount of either likely to be bestowed upon him as a poet by the 'mankind' he esteems so lightly we fear will be small." Knives gleamed in Boston, whose reviewers condemned the poems as coldly studied: "Poe does not write for Humanity; he has more of the art than the soul of poetry," said the *Harbinger*. The *Boston Post* rated the volume "a parcel of current trash."

English reviewers and readers lashed the most sensitive places. Several pointed to Poe as an example of the Americans' inability to create a literature out of native materials, in a native style. The London *Critic* likened his manner in various poems to that of Tennyson or Coleridge, concluding that American poets "echo the ideas wafted to them from England, and with the feebleness of echoes. The characteristic of American literature is, the absence of a character." Elizabeth Barrett, already perplexed by Poe's friend-and-foe review of her, was bewildered to find him both "dedicating a book to one and abusing one." When she later received a copy of "The Facts of M. Valdemar's Case," she forwarded it to Robert Browning, asking him to decide whether the tale or Poe's "outrageous compliment" to her "goes furthest to prove him mad."

Turtle Bay; Fordham; The "Literati" War.

CA. MARCH – JULY 1846

Poe and his family left New York around the beginning of March. He perhaps hoped to flee rumor and gossip, and surely to find a more healthful environment for Sissy. Many people thought the city unwholesomely filthy; a writer in the *Journal* observed that those who moved from New York to Long Island made "a very great savings in their doctor's bills." Poe may have returned to the Brennan farm a short while, but then boarded at a house in Turtle Bay, on the East River, owned by a family named Miller. As the son and daughter later described their home, it was an attractive place of large airy rooms, fresh eggs and milk, fruit trees and riverfront, the closest neighbor a quarter-mile off. They recalled that Muddy told their mother about her poverty and want, often crying as she spoke. Virginia treated them gently, but was housebound, pale, delicate, "very ill." They heard her tell Poe that after she was "gone," she would be his guardian angel.

Poe stayed with the Millers a month or two, only long enough to find somewhere for his family to set up housekeeping on their own. Occasionally he rowed out in his landlord's boat to islets in the East River for an afternoon swim, but by his own account he generally felt "quite sick," so ill as to be unable to leave his room. Probably in March, he for some reason visited Baltimore. A printer named DeUnger saw him there, having a whisky with a newspaperman at a coffeehouse bar, nervous, downcast, talking of Virginia's illness, broke but borrowing. At one point Poe advised DeUnger not to hurry into marriage. "It has its joys," as DeUnger recalled his words, "but its sorrows overbalance those." Poe became ill in Baltimore also, enough so to delay his return.

Poe's continued sickness and his seclusion at Turtle Bay raised speculations about what ailed him. On April 12, the St. Louis *Reveille* printed a rumor that he had lost his sanity: "[he] has become deranged," the newspaper said, "and his friends are about to place him under the charge of Dr. Brigham, of the Insane Retreat at Utica." The story may have had some foundation, for Poe's friend J. E. Snodgrass repeated it the following week in the Baltimore *Saturday Visiter,* adding that the news of his "mental derangement. . . . will be a painful piece of intelligence to thousands." Ten days later Poe turned down an invitation from the University of Vermont literary societies to serve as their commencement poet. He perhaps wished to avoid a repetition of the New York University and Lyceum fiascoes; but in his reply, thanking them for the honor, he explained that he had to decline because of other engagements and, as he put it, "serious and, I fear, permanent ill health." Snodgrass reported his withdrawal and informed readers that Poe was living in retirement, "still severely suffering from an attack of 'brain fever.' "

Around May, Poe and his family moved still farther from New York, to the village of Fordham, about thirteen miles away. Although recently connected to the city by a railroad, the area had a rural character, its towering hills offering broad views of the countryside, with glimpses, through the heavy foliage, of the Bronx River, groves of fruit trees, gabled cottages, swatches of dusty road.

For a hundred dollars a year, Poe rented a small, one and a half story frame house, built about twenty-five years earlier (Illus. 20). It stood on the top of a hill. The place had a ground-level porch or piazza with cherry trees close by, and was surrounded by about an acre of fenced-in land and greensward "as smooth as velvet," one visitor remembered, "and as clean as the best kept carpet." The interior of the house consisted of a small kitchen, bedroom, and square sitting room, the parlor barely five paces across, the bedroom not three. The half-story attic, up a narrow staircase, was divided into three rooms, through the largest of which passed a chimney, affording a fireplace. The furnishings evidently were minimal. By one account, they included two small pine tables made by Poe himself, neatly covered with green baize fastened by brass-head nails. A hanging shelf in the parlor displayed his few books. There were also the cat, Catterina, and by several accounts one or more caged birds. Like Poe's other residences, the Fordham house gave an impression of resolute keeping-up. "The cottage was very humble," one visitor said; "you wouldn't have thought decent people could have lived in it; but there was an air of refinement about everything."

The Fordham house uniquely suited Poe and his family. Although cramped, it stood in a peaceful and pretty spot, conducive to helping him compose himself. It was said that he enjoyed going to a rocky elevation nearby, from which could be seen the distant blue of Long Island, and to the grassy walkway atop the Croton Aqueduct, leading to High Bridge and its distant view of New York City. He also became friendly with Jesuit faculty members of neighboring St. John's College, and visited the campus. To Virginia, Fordham offered the retreat from gossip she had wished for in her Valentine's poem, and notably pure, delicious air. To Muddy, setting up housekeeping again meant offspring she could cherish within a close-knit family, shut from the world. According to her, Poe rarely left the little house but rather spent most of the morning in his "study," then worked in the flower garden or read and recited poetry to her and Sissy. "Oh, how supremely happy we were in our dear cottage home!" she wrote later. "We three lived only for each other." She probably did not exaggerate the trio's clinging closeness, for she had even come to resemble Poe. At times her handwriting was hard to tell from his, and friends believed they looked alike, and when speaking earnestly even sounded alike. The powerful mutual dependence seems to have affected even Catterina, who reportedly would not eat when Poe was away.

But neither the intimate privacy nor the bucolic locale brought relief. "We are in a snug little cottage, keeping house," Poe wrote from Fordham, "and would be very comfortable, but that I have been for a long time dreadfully ill." He felt sick and depressed throughout the summer, scarcely able to write a letter, even asking Muddy to write for him. He vowed that he had "done forever with drink," as he often had before, but spoke often of being "ground into the very dust with poverty." His desperate lack of money came in part from his continued problems in working. Although "The Philosophy of Composition" broadcast his complete control of the writing process, he was immobilized. "I have not been able to write one line for the Magazines in more than 5 months," he told Chivers in July; "you can then form some idea of the dreadful extremity to which I have been reduced." Rather as the family resolutely kept their cottage presentable, he determinedly maintained some optimism for the future, "a sweet *hope* in the bottom of my soul." But expressions of it often came with afterthoughts that he might not be able to survive, allusions to his possibly impending death: "I have *magnificent* objects in view—may I but live to accomplish them!" And as far off as New Orleans, stories persisted that he had gone mad.

Poe's deteriorating condition was but the image and result of Virginia's. Her complexion now seemed pearly, the intense pallor alarming. Poe habitually addressed her with such pet phrases as "my dear Heart," and signed his one brief, extant letter to her "Your devoted Edgar." Although he had treated many others abrasively, falsely, or manipulatively, with Virginia he seems always to have been soft, concerned, nearly reverential, his manner as much that of a devoted older brother as a husband, living with her under the care of "our Mother." Yet despite Sissy's youth, he had also looked to her for his own well being, feeling in fact that his survival depended upon her. "I should have lost my courage *but for you*," he wrote to her during an overnight trip, "my little darling wife you are my *greatest* and *only* stimulus now, to battle with this uncongenial, unsatisfactory and ungrateful life."

But Virginia could no longer be counted on to help. To one visitor at Fordham she looked ethereal, "almost a disrobed spirit, and when she coughed it was made certain that she was rapidly passing away."

In the late spring or early summer Poe likely had a visit from Rosalie, the first since she spent several weeks with him in Philadelphia some five years earlier (Illus. 21). She still lived with the Mackenzie family in Richmond, teaching penmanship in Jane Mackenzie's school. A student later remembered her collecting the quill pens after class, wiping them on her apron, and resharpening them for the next day's exercises. Then she would stand a long time by the window, gazing at the world outside, combing her hair with her fingers. She was proud of Poe's literary fame and made it known that she was his sister. Just the same, her stay at Fordham may have been uncomfortable. She is said to have remarked that her brother and Muddy "petted" Virginia "like a baby," while Muddy and Virginia "cared for nobody but themselves and Edgar." The exclusiveness of Poe's family circle makes the note of envy understandable, the more so since those closest to Rosalie had long ignored her existence. Muddy rarely mentioned her niece, and then with distrust and dislike, perhaps because of the suspicions about Rose's birth. Poe saw and wrote to her rarely. After a visit of a month or more Rose returned to Richmond, carrying a letter from Muddy soliciting money for Poe because of his ill health.

As Poe's move to Fordham did nothing to restore Virginia's health, neither did it allay the anxiety and frustration he felt, some of which he let out in new and more vengeful literary warfare. Despite his writing block he managed to publish thirty-eight sketches entitled "The Literati of New York City." The series appeared between May and October in *Godey's Lady's Book,* published in Philadelphia. Claiming a readership of one hundred thousand, *Godey's* was the most successful journal of the period, largely owing to its combination of sentimental verse and fiction with hand-colored fashion plates and excellent engravings. Poe of course despised such magazines, but Louis Godey was known for paying well, and Poe apparently received five dollars a printed page. Although the essays continued his long campaign to set America's literary house in order, they were also the bitter fruit of his circulation, now discontinued, among the literary salons of New York.

Poe offered the "Literati" as a sort of exposé. He began by explaining that the printed, public estimates of American writers differed from the more candid estimates privately expressed in literary circles. These he would now reveal. He would disclose what "conversational society" in New York said about various local literary figures, presenting as well his own offhand opinion of them, rather than his formal critical judgments. Generally he gave a brief review of the writer's career and works, his comments coming in a familiar alternation of caresses and slaps to make a pattern either of narrowly focused but superlative praise amid general censure, or of general praise with devastating restrictions. Here as elsewhere, he used material from earlier reviews and often interjected valuable remarks on Fancy, style, and other aesthetic matters, mixed with peevish digs at New England, denunciations of Griswold's *Poets & Poetry,* obligatory hits at Longfellow as "a dexterous adopter of the ideas of other people."

The praise-blames and filleting were of course no novelty in Poe's criticism. The sensational element of the "Literati" lay rather in its concern for the characterology and physiology of literary reputation-making. Of Anna Cora Mowatt's play *Fashion,* for example, Poe remarked that it "owes what it had of success to its being the work of a lovely woman who had already excited interest." In the same spirit of divulging the gossip of the conversaziones, he evaluated not only the writer's work but also his or her personal beauty and personality, or lack of them. In each case he discussed the subject's age, hair and eye color, height and weight, physique and dress, smiles and gestures, as well as matters of particular significance to himself: family background and education, wealth, command of languages, use of grammar, marital state. Many of his remarks seem guided by the hope of curing his misery through new conquest, as if having outjumped his contemporaries in the literary world, he now needed to believe and to demonstrate that he also surpassed them in personal appeal.

Poe's thumbnail character sketches are too brief and formulaic to bring the subjects to life, but were spiteful enough to waken resentment. Even his favorable notices of various New York writers contain some offensive comment about their appearance or idiosyncrasies. Willis's face is "somewhat too full, or rather heavy, in its lower portions. Neither his nose nor his forehead can be defended"; Margaret Fuller's overlip, "as if impelled by the action of involuntary muscles, habitually uplifts itself, conveying the impression of a sneer"; the "fidgety" editor William M. Gillespie "never knows how to sit or to stand, or what to do with his hands and feet, or his hat. In the street walks irregularly, mutters to himself." The most unfavorable sketches offer double- or triple-barreled affronts, first abusing the writer's works, then his resort to underhanded means of achieving reputation, and finally his looks and physique.

Even before the "Literati" began appearing in *Godey's,* Poe's well-known banishment from New York literary circles had created excited anticipation of what he might say. The *Tribune* forecast that "the uproar which attended Pope's Dunciad was nothing to the stormy confusion of the literary elements which will war and rage." With the first installments Poe created still another literary tempest. Horace Greeley reported that he had twice tried to buy a *Godey's* in New York but found every copy bought up. Such was the demand that magazine agents in the city took out advertisements promising that copies would soon be available; Godey, unable to supply hundreds of copies sought in Boston and New York, reprinted Poe's first number in the same issue that contained his second.

Inevitably, even the first installment sparked controversy. A few newspapers defended Poe for providing an insider's look at New York literary life, instead of relying on self-promoting material furnished by the writers. But many others questioned his "minute description of personal appearance, height, figure, age, foreheads, noses," or condemned his intrusions into the private lives of living people as impertinent and even slanderous. Mindful of reports about his emotional condition, one newspaper observed that he was presently "in a state of health which renders him not completely accountable for all his peculiarities." Godey defended Poe against the murmuring, and promised shows of strength to come: "Mr. Poe has been ill," he announced in his magazine, "but we have letters from him of very recent dates, also a new batch of the Literati, which show anything but feebleness either of body or mind."

Had Poe contented himself with satirizing some New York literary lights, the "Literati" might have generated no more than a newspaper squabble. But he also used the series to settle scores. In several cases he turned from casual critical comment and satire to personal tribute and vendetta. To Fanny Osgood he afforded the longest of the sketches, radiantly depicting her as "ardent, sensitive, impulsive; the very soul of truth and honor; a worshiper of the beautiful." Repaying a different debt, he prepared a sketch of Elizabeth Ellet portraying her as "short and much inclined to *embonpoint.*" He reconsidered, however, and omitted it from the series, as he toned down for publication the first drafts of some other sketches. He cancelled for instance some howls at Lewis Gaylord Clark's confusing verbs with prepositions, "if indeed he has any idea what 'verb' and 'preposition' mean." Clark nevertheless appeared with a " 'bullety' " forehead and vacuous personality, having "no determinateness, no distinctiveness, no saliency of point;—an apple, in fact, or a pumpkin, has more angles. . . . he is noticeable for nothing in the world except for the markedness by which he is noticeable for nothing."

Two sketches in particular turned the "Literati" from a sensation

into another painfully self-revealing scandal. Poe mockingly drew
his former employer and partner Charles F. Briggs as affected and
vulgar, attributing to him among other disfiguring limitations a pre-
tense of knowing French ("of which he is profoundly ignorant"), an
inability to judge literature ("Mr. Briggs has never composed in his
life three consecutive sentences of grammatical English"), and "eyes
not so good, gray and small." Briggs replied by publishing anonymously in the *Mirror* a decent parody of a "Literati" sketch, making
Poe himself the shrimpy subject:

> Mr. Poe is about 39. . . . In height he is about 5 feet 1 or two
> inches, perhaps 2 inches and a half. His face is pale and rather
> thin; eyes gray, watery, and always dull; nose rather prominent
> . . . hair thin and cropped short; mouth not very well chiselled,
> nor very sweet; his tongue shows itself unpleasantly when he speaks
> earnestly, and seems too large for his mouth; teeth indifferent;
> forehead rather broad . . . chin narrow and pointed, which gives
> his head, upon the whole, a balloonish appearance, which may
> account for his supposed light-headedness. . . .

Briggs also reported that some students had made a pilgrimage "to
gaze upon the asylum where Mr. Poe was reported to be confined."
   Briggs scored. Now thirty-seven and a half years old, and five
foot eight, Poe writhed under Briggs's cartoon, which outraged his
pride in his precociousness and his physique. He asked the editor
of the St. Louis *Reveille,* Joseph M. Field, to condemn Briggs's portrait of him "and to do away with the false impression of my personal appearance it *may* convey, in those parts of the country where
I am not individually known. You have seen me and can describe
me as I am" ("I am 33 years of age," he added, "height 5 ft. 8").
Field complied, pointing out in his newspaper that "Instead of being
'five foot one,' &c., the poet is a figure to compare with any in
manliness, while his features are not only intellectual, but handsome." Poe made similar requests of other friends and editors. The
Philadelphia *Saturday Courier* corrected Briggs's picture by remarking that Poe was "about thirty-three years of age, slight make, sharp
features, with very broad forehead"; William Gilmore Simms reported in the Charleston *Southern Patriot* that Poe was "probably
thirty three or four years old, some five feet eight inches in height,
of rather slender person, with a good eye, and a broad intelligent
forehead." Poe's need to rebut Briggs's sneers at his person of course

reflects his habitual touchiness; being "like an exposed nerve," one acquaintance said, he "could not but suffer at the slightest touch." But the urgency of his need suggests rather his emotionally fragile condition at the moment, a demoralized sense that he might in fact be unpresentable and worth little.

Full-scale war over the "Literati" broke out with the third install-ment, featuring a sketch of T. D. English. Poe's animosity toward English did not begin with their recent fistfight ("I have given him a flogging which he will remember to the day of his death"). They had known each other earlier in Philadelphia, when English was an eighteen-year-old medical student publishing verse in *Burton's* and *Graham's,* admiring Poe's "undoubted genius." In his sketch, Poe drew on their shared knowledge of each other, aiming many of his darts at English very particularly. He charged him, for example, with "downright plagiarism" from the Philadelphia poet Henry B. Hirst, knowing that English considered Hirst's poetry hilariously bad. He also well knew that in ridiculing English's understanding of grammar, as he did, he struck the jugular. English read some Latin and Greek, had a substantial knowledge of French, Spanish, and Polish, and later took up the etymological study of Romany dialect and Celtic speech. Despite his facility with languages, however, his grammar was weak. The first version of his famous poem "Ben Bolt" contained the line "There is only you and I." He and Poe had ar-gued about grammar in the past. Poe once explained to him, En-glish recalled, that suppressed auxiliaries accounted for subjunctive verb forms: the form "if it be" omitted a 'could,' 'should,' or 'would.' If that were true, English asked Poe, where would he place the auxiliaries in "if it were"? Poe grew red in the face, called him an ass, and left the room: "I believe," English said, "that this was the beginning of Poe's dislike of me."

Now it was Poe's turn to show up English, whose grammar he made the centerpiece of his sketch. He attributed the demise of English's magazine, the *Aristidean,* to his lacking "the commonest school education." But what made English ridiculous, he said, was less his ignorance of grammar than his attempt to conceal it:

> [English] was not laughed at so much on account of writing "lay" for "lie," etc. etc., and coupling nouns in the plural with verbs in the singular . . . as that, in the hope of disguising such deficiency, he was perpetually lamenting the "typographical blunders" that "in the most unaccountable manner" *would* creep into his work.

Nobody was so stupid as to suppose for a moment there existed in New York a single proof-reader—or even a single printer's devil—who would have permitted *such* errors to escape. By the excuses offered, therefore, the errors were only the more obviously nailed to the counter as Mr. English's own.

Poe concluded his sketch by characteristically turning against English an insult recently leveled at himself. He offered hope that English might be able to improve his defects, since he was "young— certainly not more than thirty-five."

English was actually a virile twenty-seven, seasoned in local political infighting, and not a punching bag, as several newspapers indicated in noting that Poe had "waked up the wrong passenger." In fact Poe had jolted him. English wrote a long sneering reply to his "exhibition of impotent malice" that was printed by the New York *Evening Mirror,* the same newspaper where Poe had worked as a "mechanical paragraphist" when it was run by Willis. English's opening remarks bore out his reputation for coarse invective. Others had already handled Poe's "Literati" appropriately, he said, having "converted the paper on which his sketches are printed to its legitimate use—like to like." This was only the beginning. Poe had made himself vulnerable by calling on English for advice during several desperate moments of his chaotic life over the past year. English now dragged into print and before a sizeable public many embarrassing details of Poe's already well-publicized disgraces. He debunked reports that Poe had been "indisposed" the evening of the New York University reading, revealing that he had been powerless to write a poem for the occasion and "remained in a state of intoxication during the week." He disclosed Poe's visit to him before the Boston Lyceum engagement, again unable to write but wanting the fee and determined to " 'cook up something.' " Omitting the names of Fanny Osgood and Elizabeth Ellet, he exposed Poe's behavior during the letters affair, his request for a gun, his plea that he had been "laboring under a fit of insanity to which he was periodically subject," his having been "confined to his bed from the effect of fright and the blows he had received from me."

In publicly unmasking Poe as duplicitous, impotent, and cowardly, English alluded often to his drinking. "The kennels of Philadelphia streets, from which I once kindly raised him," he said, "have frequently had the pleasure of his acquaintance." He also laid bare Poe's "frequent quotations from languages of which he is entirely

ignorant . . . his cool plagiarisms from known or forgotten writers," intimated that Poe had spent time in jail, and hinted that only
a sense of honor restrained him from uncovering still nastier depths.
English also made two charges that had legal implications. He had
loaned Poe thirty dollars to help him buy the *Broadway Journal,*
allegedly on the understanding that he would have an interest in
the magazine. He now claimed that Poe had obtained the money
from him "under false pretences." The second charge was that Poe
had committed forgery, the victim, English alleged later, being Poe's
own uncle.

The violence of English's assault surprised many. "Mr. English is
a disbeliever in Capital Punishment," Horace Greeley wrote, "but
you would hardly have suspected the fact from the tenor of this
retort acidulous upon Poe." The *National Press* declined requests to
publish the piece, calling it "one of the most savage and bitter things
we ever read." Even Rufus Griswold was shocked. "I, who have as
much cause as any man to quarrel with Poe," he told Duyckinck,
"would sooner have cut off my hand than used it to write such an
ungentlemanly card, though every word were true." Some newspapers alerted their readers to the unfolding of a major war. "This is
the first brush between the literary combatants," said the *Public Ledger,*
predicting that Poe would "muster his intellectual forces, and give
his adversary another battle."

How much 'intellectual force' Poe could muster at this time may
be questioned, but the prediction was otherwise correct. From his
seclusion at Fordham he wrote off a counterattack within a week,
arising from a sickbed, he said, so ill that he could scarcely stand or
see. Much concerned about his manliness in this time of failing self-
confidence, he particularly resented English's claims to have given
him a "sound cuffing." He wrote to Philadelphia asking for details
of fights there in which English had taken a beating of his own.
Early in July he sent the piece off to Godey for publication in the
Lady's Book. But friends advised Godey not to use it, and Godey
turned it over to the Philadelphia *Spirit of the Times,* a political daily
newspaper. He further infuriated Poe by having it printed as a personal advertisement or "Card" and paying ten dollars for its inser-
tion, charging Poe with the cost.

"I have never written an article," Poe proclaimed, "upon which I
more confidently depend for *literary* reputation than that Reply."
"Mr. Poe's Reply to Mr. English and Others," filling some ten pages
in modern editions, is to be sure polished, the sentences carefully

built to throw maximum weight on the most insolent words or phrases. But the Billingsgate lacks the sting of wit and never surmounts its occasion, expending its cold fury on English's speaking with "filthy lips," wallowing in "hog-puddles," befriending "dock-loafers and wharf-rats," resembling "the best-looking but most unprincipled of Mr. Barnum's baboons," and being *"very* generally reviled, hated, and despised." Poe did acknowledge that his own recent behavior had been erratic, an expression of "errors and frailties which I deplore," and explained that behind it lay a "terrible evil." This he did not name, although later he privately confided that he had in mind the impending death of Virginia. Beyond this abstract although touchingly frank confession, he said nothing of the Lyceum affair or the other wreckage English had picked through, but instead raked over the scavenger's own cowardice.

Still aching from English's published vaunt of having manhandled him, Poe devoted nearly a third of his "Reply" to a history of the shellackings English had absorbed himself. They included a "thrashing" by a publisher for having read through some private manuscripts; a confrontation with a Philadelphian's bowie knife for an "insult to ladies at a private house"; a twenty-minute pummeling by H. B. Hirst, who also threw a pack of cards in his face; and of course the beating from Poe, who had to be "dragged from his prostrate and rascally carcase." More than that, Poe attributed to English a sordid pleasure in being knocked about and degraded. English received the publisher's thrashing "as a sort of favor"; when a politician failed to respond to his printed attack, English was disappointed that "he could not get himself kicked." English *"accepts* everything," Poe jeered, "from a kick to a piece of gingerbread—the smallest favors thankfully received." While he himself worked on the *Broadway Journal,* English "was always in my office for the purpose of doing himself honor in running my errands."

Nothing in English's known behavior justifies Poe's picture of him as pathologically masochistic. How much of his own imp of self-destruction he invested in it is arguable. But in answering English's denunciation of him for cowardice, he remarked explicitly on the human tendency to criticize others for what one disapproves in oneself: "A poltroon charges his foe, by instinct, with precisely that vice or meanness which the pricking of his (the poltroon's) conscience, assures him would furnish the most stable and therefore the most terrible ground of accusation against himself." Poe's wrath at English seems to have fed on some ancient grievances also.

Denied a rightful middle name, he taunted his tormentor for signing himself "Thomas Dunn English," mocking " 'the magic of his name'—his three names," holding up for ridicule "the animalcula with moustaches for antenna that is in the capital habit of signing itself in full, 'Thomas Dunn English.' "

Poe saved what he considered his coup de grâce for the end. Here he dramatically denied English's allegation that he had criminally obtained money under false pretenses and committed forgery. He declared that on the contrary English owed money to him. And he reprinted the letter from Fanny Osgood's admirer Edward Thomas, the merchant who had first leveled the charge of forgery against him, saying that after investigation he had found the charge baseless. "These are the facts which," Poe forewarned in conclusion, "in a court of justice, I propose to demonstrate." He hardly needed a legal battle to extend his notoriety and deepen his confusion, but this was no idle threat. English responded promptly in the *Mirror:* "Let him institute a suit, if he dare, and I pledge myself to make my charges good by the most ample and satisfactory evidence."

The Libel Suit;
"The Cask of Amontillado";
"The Domain of Arnheim."

CA. JULY—DECEMBER 1846

On July 23, Poe's lawyer, Enoch L. Fancher, presented to the New York Superior Court a declaration of grievances, commencing on his behalf a civil suit for libel. He stated that Poe's "good name, fame and credit" had maliciously been brought into "public scandal, infamy and disgrace with and amongst all his neighbors," specifically by causing it to be "suspected and believed" that Poe had obtained money "under false pretenses" and had "virtually admitted" the crime of forgery. As Poe's attorney, Fancher asked damages of five thousand dollars.

Poe did not bring his suit against T. D. English but against the then owners of the New York *Mirror,* Hiram Fuller and Augustus W. Clason, Jr. They had taken over the newspaper from Willis and therein published English's charges. Poe's lawyer presumably advised him on technical legal grounds to present his suit in this form, but Poe also had grievances against Fuller, who had blasted the "Literati" as "insane riff-raff" and published the sketch by Briggs that unforgivably shrank Poe's height to five feet. Poe had already retaliated in his "Reply to Mr. English" by likening Fuller to "a fat sheep in reverie." Privately he had also compiled and revealed to friends an English-like dossier on Fuller's supposed swindling and lack of manhood. It included a story of his standing by impotently at a New York theater while his wife was beaten up by her father. The man was enraged, Poe said, over "the disgrace inflicted upon his family" by his daughter's marriage to Fuller. The weakling Fuller looked on as his wife was repeatedly punched in the face, "not even attempting to interfere."

At a preliminary hearing, Fuller and Clason pleaded not guilty to the libel charge, arguing that the statements they had printed were true. The court ordered the trial set for the first Monday in September. News of the suit, amid the continuing appearance of the "Literati," brought Poe a new wave of derision and disapproval. Some newspapers snickered that he was better able to dish out than take. "This is rather small business," wrote the New York *Morning News,* "for a man who has reviled nearly every literary man of eminence in the United States." Others regretted the whole business as tasteless, trivial, and a misuse of the press, especially considering that America and Mexico were actively at war. Poe took his most vehement pounding in the *Mirror* itself, where Fuller kept at him despite the suit. In an editorial piece called "A SAD SIGHT," he recounted a visit that Poe made to his office in order to berate him. Poe probably did appear at the *Mirror,* perhaps in such a state of mental disequilibrium and physical depletion as Fuller drew:

> A poor creature . . . called at our office the other day, in a condition of sad, wretched imbecility, bearing in his feeble body the evidences of evil living, and betraying by his talk, such radical obliquity of sense, that every spark of harsh feeling towards him was extinguished, and we could not even entertain a feeling of contempt for one who was evidently committing a suicide upon his body, as he had already done upon his character.

According to Fuller, Muddy accompanied Poe, worn out by trying to protect him from himself—"an aged female relative, who was going a weary round in the hot streets, following his steps to prevent his indulging in a love of drink; but he had eluded her watchful eye by some means, and was already far gone in a state of inebriation." He also continued riding Poe for the ongoing "Literati," commenting dryly that "In scanning the verses of Mrs. Osgood he is quite at home."

Poe was in no condition to fight off the verbal battering. However firm he seemed in bringing a suit, it was an appearance. Like one of his own characters he felt eaten at, as he told Chivers, exposed to "flocks of little birds of prey that always take the opportunity of illness to peck at a sick fowl of larger dimensions." And living in effect in exile he felt he had nowhere to turn for help, "not even *one* friend, out of my family, with whom to advise." His sense of abandonment was probably little eased by what advice is known to have come to him. William Gilmore Simms, replying to what he called a "very desponding" letter from Poe, preached the need to rejoin the "moral province in society" and to reform: "trample those temptations under foot, which degrade your person, and make it familiar to the mouth of vulgar jest." Well-intentioned bromides had nothing to say to Poe's condition, being written in a different language. As Poe put it himself, he was being "driven to the very gates of death, and a despair more dreadful than death."

Those who would devour him, Poe felt, found another advantage in his "dreadful poverty." If not working much, he was trying to. He planned to expand "The Literati of New York City" into a book treating the entire American literary scene, a culmination of his work as a critic, aesthetician, and tastemaker. In offering what he called "a full view of our Literature" for English and American readers, he intended to remark on how social position in America determines a writer's success; the depreciation of southern and western writers, owing to sectional animosities; "cliquism" and its effect on the magazines; the falsity of notions about the "distinctiveness" of American literature; and the harm done from want of a copyright law. Somewhere along he also planned to newly analyze the nature of poetry, drama, criticism, "without reference to previous opinions by *anybody*." He envisioned the bulk of the book, however, as consisting of frank "Literati"-like sketches of American writers, including but now no longer limited to those of New York. He would work on this volume over the next three years under a variety of possible titles, including "American Parnassus," "Literary America," and "The Living Writers of America. Some Honest Opinions about their Literary Merits, with occasional Words of Personality."

Poe remained under siege and athirst for revenge through the fall and early winter. Lawyers for him and Fuller appeared at New York's City Hall on September 7 for the opening of the libel trial. As it turned out, however, the court calendar was full, putting off Poe's suit to February first in the new year. The delay provided no lull in his turmoil. William Cullen Bryant reported that Muddy approached him in the city evidently to ask for money, saying "her son-in-law is crazy, his wife dying, and the whole family starving." The postponement of the trial also coincided with the launching of the most protracted and probably the most vicious of all the attacks yet made upon Poe. After blurbs promising "an excitement, perhaps not surpassed by any American book," Fuller published in over sixteen issues of the *Mirror,* on the front page, a novel entitled *1844, or, The Power of the S. F.* Basically a story of political intrigue, it concerns a plot by a secret organization called the "S. F." ("Startled Falcons") to swing a presidential election. Along the way it introduces many New York literary personalities in fictional guise, including Fanny Osgood, who appears as a "would-be-juvenile lady" named "Mrs. Flighty."

The anonymous author stood in a position to know, for he was Thomas Dunn English. He drew with extended and brutal concern one Marmaduke Hammerhead, a hack journalist with "broad, low, receding, and deformed forehead," author of the "Black Crow." The five episodes where Hammerhead figures follow his downward course from the literary salons of New York, illustrating in the process his philandering, petty larceny, pretensions to know foreign languages, relentless sponging, and especially his drinking. In his cups he accosts one and all with the question "Did you see my re-re-view upon L-L-L-ongfellow?," gives in to "an irresistible inclination to fight with some one," and winds up flat on the sidewalk offering to take on six at a time and discoursing on English meter. Drinking wastes Hammerhead's body and mind, and he soon develops "Mania-à-potu," madness through intemperance. It first appears in paranoid delusions, e.g., in the "Literati": "He deemed himself the object of persecution on the part of the combined literati of the country, and commenced writing criticisms upon their character." Hammerhead ends in a cell of the Utica Insane Asylum, babbling about Thomas Carlyle:

I am prepared to prove that in less than ten pages of his book, I have discovered no less than one hundred and ten dashes, instead of parentheses. Can any man who uses the dash instead of the mark of parenthesis, be considered a man of genius? . . . I have settled him, as I have settled Pope and Burns, and Longfellow. . . . No one can withstand me. I am the great mogul of all the critics.

Threatening to kill everyone, Hammerhead is impounded in a part of the asylum reserved for "confirmed madmen."

If English was a bare-knuckled foe, Poe had weapons of greater refinement and more enduring effect. Late in October, *Godey's* printed a tale that took up in fictional form where his "Literati" had left off, the first tale he had published in almost a year, and only the second in nearly two years of stalled effort, illness, and conflict. The opening sentence of "The Cask of Amontillado," spoken by the wealthy Montresor, is well known: "The thousand injuries of Fortunato I had borne as I best could; but when he ventured upon insult, I vowed revenge." Indeed the tale is a meditation on the art and passion of revenge. Montresor's family has taken for its motto *Nemo me impune lacessit:* No one insults me with impunity. On a carnival night in an unnamed European city, he has lured the drunken Fortunato to his wine cellar and walled his screaming victim up alive. He describes the event long after, in an afterglow of exultation that has endured for fifty years.

In Montresor, Poe now figured the writer not as a ghost but an avenger, and storytelling as a means of getting even with the world. Read in the setting of the last year of Poe's life, the tale of course brings to mind English, Fuller, Briggs, Clark, and the host of other enemies he had attracted. Current woes seem present as well in Fortunato's repeated coughing, so violently that for several minutes he cannot speak but at last says, "the cough is a mere nothing; it will not kill me. I shall not die of a cough." As yet another tale of the inability to forget, the tale also echoes the past. Its key words first appear in a letter Poe wrote to an earlier foe, Billy Burton, five years before. He scolded Burton for flying into a passion over an imagined wrong, "for no real injury, or attempt at injury, have you ever received at my hands." And he quoted at him what became the motto of the Montresor family: "If by accident you have taken it into your head . . . that I am to be insulted with impunity I can only assume that you are an ass." It happens that *Nemo me impune lacessit* is also the national motto of Scotland, one of whose sons, "Scotch" John Allan, much resembled Fortunato in being a man "rich, respected, admired, beloved," interested in wines, and a member of the Masons. (His name is also contained in "Amontillado.") Pointing still further back, the carnival costumes and masks create a theatrical ambiance, here as in "The Masque of the Red Death" associated with dying. In these and its many other deeper reverberations, the tale lives up to the toast proposed by Fortunato: " 'I drink,' he said, 'to the buried dead that repose around us.' "

With a memory no less tenacious than Montresor's, Poe repaid some other insults in his strange essay on Nathaniel Hawthorne's *Mosses from an Old Manse*. He sold it to *Godey's* around late November, but to his puzzlement and then anger, it did not appear for nearly a year. Godey may well have been reluctant to publish the piece, for nearly a fourth of it comes from Poe's earlier review of Hawthorne's *Twice-Told Tales*. The new material includes an incisive condemnation of allegory, but is marred by an overall incoherence that bespeaks much conflict and even a difficulty in thinking clearly: hairsplitting distinctions, double negatives, shifts of direction, overelaborate syntax, praise bestowed with so many grudging qualifications as to be indistinguishable from condemnation. In fact Poe seems to have entirely changed his estimate of Hawthorne's work. In the earlier review, and again as recently as ten months ago, he had praised Hawthorne above all for "originality—a trait which, in the literature of fiction, is positively worth all the rest." Reversing himself, he now traced Hawthorne's tone and choice of subjects to the German writer Ludwig Tieck, and condemned him on the same ground: "He is peculiar and *not* original."

The key to Poe's change of mind and to the odd manner of the essay probably lies in its concluding sentence, calling on Hawthorne to forsake allegory:

> Let him mend his pen, get a bottle of visible ink, come out from the Old Manse, cut Mr. Alcott, hang (if possible) the editor of "The Dial," and throw out of the window to the pigs all his odd numbers of "The North American Review."

For more than three years, Hawthorne and his wife had been living at the Old Manse in Concord, Massachusetts, the home of Ralph Waldo Emerson. Their situation clearly allied Hawthorne in Poe's mind with the hated Boston-Cambridge-Concord axis, including the

Transcendentalist Bronson Alcott, the Transcendentalist periodical *The Dial,* and the chief organ of New England literary life, the *North American Review.* He frequently berated Hawthorne in his essay for having "imbibed . . . the phalanx and phalanstery atmosphere in which he has been so long struggling for breath." But Poe took out on Hawthorne even longer-suffered insult and injury. His concluding sentence virtually replicates what a hostile Philadelphia reviewer had said of his own *Tales of the Grotesque and Arabesque:*

> Let him [i.e., Poe] give up his imitation of German mysticism, throw away his extravagance, think and write in good sound sober English, and leave all touches of profanity to the bar room. . . .

Not only the rhythm and syntax are the same, but in accusing Hawthorne of following Ludwig Tieck, Poe also taxed him for the same "imitation of German mysticism" that the reviewer had levied against *Tales of the Grotesque and Arabesque.* His turning back his own hurt on Hawthorne is the more remarkable in that the Philadelphia review appeared in 1839; for seven years, Montresor-like, he had retained its cadences and language in vengeful memory. As he once confided to his friend F. W. Thomas, his "resentments" were "implacable."

Poe exacted still more bizarre revenge in "A Reviewer Reviewed," probably written in early December. He signed the essay by the pseudonym Walter G. Bowen, left it unfinished, and never published it, probably wisely, for it confirms the suspicion that in depicting English as self-demeaning, he was in some degree speaking of himself. Writing as "Bowen," he reviewed his own works, playing both the assassin Montresor and the victim Fortunato. "Bowen" remarks that Poe's criticisms seem to him "captious, faultfinding, and unnecessarily severe." He therefore feels justified in teaching him a lesson, "showing him that he is far from being immaculate himself." He exposes numerous errors in Poe's own diction, misuses of *drop* for *fall, except* for *unless, upon* for *on,* and in his grammar and syntax:

> For example—"If what I have written is to circulate at all, I am naturally anxious that it should circulate as I wrote it." Now here the sentence should obviously be—"I am naturally anxious that

what I have written should circulate as I wrote it, if it circulate at all."

"Bowen" also observes that although Poe has become notorious for catching plagiarists, he has himself been guilty of *"wilful and deliberate literary theft."* Here Poe played "Poe" to himself as Longfellow. He set passages from his own works beside those from other poets they closely resembled, revealing what he had cribbed from Thomas Moore, Pope, and others:

> One of Mr Poe's most admired passages is this, forming the conclusion of the poem called "The City in the Sea". . . .
>
> > *Hell rising from a thousand thrones*
> > *Shall do it reverence.*
>
> But unfortunately Mrs Sigourney, in a little poem called "Musing Thoughts," first published in "The Token," for 1829, has the lines,
>
> > *Earth slowly rising from her thousand thrones*
> > *Did homage* to the Corsican.

Poe planned to add a self-exposé of the borrowings in his tales as well, but broke off the manuscript before uncovering the other literary crimes under his floorboards.

Ironically, as Poe was doing himself in, his reputation abroad suddenly surged. At the end of December he learned that Paris newspapers had been writing about his "Murders in the Rue Morgue." Twice ironically, the tale had become the subject of a newspaper war and libel suit that brought his name prominently before the French reading public. The affair began when the Paris newspaper *La Quotidienne* published an adaptation of the tale as a "Histoire trouvée dans les papiers d'un Américain." A second newspaper, *Le Commerce,* published a different version, entitled "Une sanglante énigme," by the critic E. D. Forgues. Neither version mentioned Poe's name. Forgues was accused by a third Paris newspaper, *La Presse,* of having plagiarized the tale earlier printed in *La Quotidienne.* In defending himself, he explained that both works depended on the same source: "les Contes d'E. Poe, littérateur américain." When the editor who had accused him of plagiarism refused to publish the explanation, Forgues sued him for libel.

Other Paris journals reported on the controversy and in the process began noticing Poe: "ce Poë est un gaillard bien fin, bien spirituel," one wrote, this Poe is a fellow of great acuteness and spirituality. Early in December, as Poe at Fordham awaited the reopening of his libel suit against Fuller, Forgues's libel suit opened in Paris. He testified at the trial that he had taken his tale not from the other newspaper, but from the American writer Poe. "Avez-vous lu Edgar Poe?" he bristled. "Lisez Edgar Poe." The defense counsel bristled back: "Grâce à M. Forgues, tout le monde va savoir que M. E. Poe fait des contes en Amérique."

Forgues's libel suit was thrown out. But he had made sure that French readers knew that Poe "wrote stories in America." Before the trial he published in the prestigious *Revue des Deux Mondes* the first discussion of Poe's work to appear in France. He devoted his twenty-page critical article to the 1845 *Tales,* in which to Poe's chagrin Duyckinck had emphasized the stories of ratiocination. In retrospect the decision was fortunate. To Forgues, Poe's novelty and importance consisted precisely in the philosophic, analytic attitude he brought to fiction. Poe seems, he wrote, "to have only one faculty of inspiration, reason; only one muse, logic." The controversy stirred interest in Poe's other work. Paris periodicals published a new translation of "A Descent into the Maelström," and first translations of "Eiros and Charmion" and "The Black Cat," the last as the work of a writer "connu au delà de l'Atlantique et dont on commence à s'occuper en France." The 1845 French translation of "The Gold-Bug" became the basis, in 1847, of Poe's literary debut in Russia, in a Russian translation. Most important, the Paris versions of "Murders in the Rue Morgue" and "The Black Cat" caught the attention of the French poet Charles Baudelaire, who read them, he said, with "singular excitement" and "incredible sympathy" and began to collect and translate Poe's works in a spirit of worship.

According to Evert Duyckinck, Poe always looked out for "the smallest paragraph in a newspaper touching himself or his writings," and in his low mood he found some encouragement in the clippings from Paris. He asked Duyckinck to write a brief article about them for one of the New York papers. Published anonymously as "An Author in Europe and America," it pointed out that while French journals were translating and praising Poe's work, in his own country he was being pestered by literary grubs, "penny-a-liners whom his iron pen has cut into too deeply." The international celebrity also played into Poe's lifelong idealization of his ancestry, his orphan's longing for a distinguished family name. In sending a genealogy several years earlier to his cousin George, he had claimed, with no basis in fact, that the original Poes were not Irish but, more respectably, German. The name occurred often in German books on natural history, he assured his cousin, adducing a well-known naturalist named Poe who currently lived in Vienna. "The name there is spelt with an accent thus, Poé, and is pronounced, in two syllables, Poe-a." His French fame inspired him to give this reassuring fable a Gallic twist. The Philadelphia *Spirit of the Times,* which had published the "Reply to Mr. English," ran an item about the French dispute, informing its readers—surely at Poe's behest—that the correct spelling of Poe's name required a diaeresis, Poë: "Mr. P. is descended," it observed, "from the French naturalist of that name."

Taking what satisfaction and revenge he could, Poe remained overborne by what propelled in all directions his need to get back at the world. A visitor to Fordham during Virginia's last month or two found him numbed, "lost in a stupor, not living or suffering, but existing merely." He offered some comfort to himself in "The Domain of Arnheim," an expansion of a piece he had published earlier as "The Landscape Garden." Both new and old versions are hybrids, part narrative, part essay. The narrative concerns one of Poe's many Inheritor figures, "young Ellison," who has come into an ancestral fortune of four hundred and fifty million dollars. A poet by temperament, he decides to devote his stupendous wealth to producing novel forms of beauty through the medium of the landscape garden. The essay half of the piece relates his unusual aesthetic ideas. These take off from the "enigma" that Nature is unmatchable in the beauty of its individual parts, but blemished in its larger aesthetic organization. "In the most enchanting of natural landscapes," he holds, "there will always be found a defect or an excess—many excesses and defects." Invariably some gully, fallen tree, or boulder in the natural scene makes for a defective composition, which the artist can correct, improving on nature.

This is only a partial view, however. Ellison speculates that what seem defects in the landscape to human eyes, may, to a quite different eye, "a class of beings, human once, but now invisible to humanity," fill a perfect place in a profound larger design. He plans to realize this superior beauty by creating a vast landscape whose formal unity can be glimpsed only macroscopically, achieving a deep formal perfection with no apparent contrivance, an artlessness that shall seem, on reflection, the Art of superhuman intelligence.

"The Domain of Arnheim," Poe's expanded version of the tale-

essay, reexamines these ideas under the shadow of Virginia's dissolution. It uses them to glorify death as the only means to full
aesthetic enjoyment. In the new version Ellison is, at the time of
the telling, deceased. But in his lifetime he has reached some understanding of why nature's organization of its individual parts seems
blemished, why gullies and boulders exist to discompose the form
and color-harmony of the landscape. They are "prognostic of *death.*"
As in the earlier version, these seeming disturbances vanish in the
perspective of superior beings. But Poe now speaks of such perception as the "death-refined appreciation of the beautiful." This powerful formulation of his own artistic aims extends his habit of denial
into the aesthetic realm. It amounts to viewing death as a privilege,
to declaring that only the dead know beauty, to imagining Virginia's
pleasure in her transfiguration.

In the new version, Ellison travels four years in search of a suitable place to create, on a God-like scale, his world of magically
sombrous or glittering rivers, gorges, and mountains. For this Master Builder, as for Poe, art aims at sampling paradise, and what his
angelic version of Nature embodies is the journey from life into
death into the life beyond death. Poe's lyrical description of the trip
to Arnheim is a stylistic *tour de force,* rapturously sustained for five
pages. The traveller is at first borne through the mazy river of a
towering chasm, whose overhanging plumes of moss impart "an art
of funereal gloom." After several hours in this deathlike place, as if
"dropped from heaven," he reaches a bay that seems fed by treasures, a cataract of rubies and sapphires rolling silently from the
sky. Here he reembarks in a delicate ivory canoe, apparently self-
borne, that presses forward to the strains of soothing but melancholy music.

Ultimately the traveler's craft glides through a fretted gate of
burnished gold, passing into what is clearly Poe's vision of the Afterworld:

> . . . the whole Paradise of Arnheim bursts upon the view. There
> is a gush of entrancing melody; there is an oppressive sense of
> strange sweet odor;—there is a dream-like intermingling to the
> eye of tall slender Eastern trees—bosky shrubberies—flocks of
> golden and crimson birds—lily-fringed lakes—meadows of violets,
> tulips, poppies, hyacinths and tuberoses—long intertangled lines
> of silver streamlets—and, upspringing confusedly from amid all, a
> mass of semi-Gothic, semi-Saracenic architecture, sustaining itself

as if by miracle in mid air; glittering in the red sunlight with a hundred oriels, minarets, and pinnacles. . . .

It may be doubted whether Poe found much reassurance in imagining that death, Virginia's death, meant gliding into the domain of supernal life, there to enjoy the "death-refined appreciation of the beautiful." Like his many other visions of Aidenn, Arnheim seems dead as well as alive, suffused with in-betweenness. Ellison hopes to achieve an "intermedium" between human and divine art, something appealing to "earth-angels," and his Paradise contains "semi-Gothic, semi-Saracenic architecture . . . in mid air." Even its scentedness and brilliant color seem funereal, as Marie Bonaparte noticed, resembling a rouged corpse in a flower-filled death chamber. In this respect too "The Domain of Arnheim," as Poe felt, "expresses *much of my soul.*"

Virginia's Death;
The Libel Suit Won; Loui Shew.

CA. NOVEMBER 1846–MAY 1847

By November, Virginia's condition was hopeless. Visitors to the cottage found her in her neat, scanty room, lying on a straw mattress with snow-white sheets, often covered, as the cold of winter approached, with Poe's old military cloak, shivering in the hectic fever of consumption.

Reports reached the city that the whole family was living in "the greatest wretchedness." Muddy, now nearly fifty-seven years old, remained tall, hale, large-featured, tending to Poe's and Virginia's needs in her black dress, a patterned widow's cap over her white hair. However stalwart-looking, she had lost a two-year-old child, also named Virginia, some twenty-five years earlier, and fewer than ten years earlier her young unmarried son Henry. Virginia Eliza was her one surviving child, and, a visitor said, Muddy's "distress on account of her illness and poverty and misery, was dreadful to see." Poe himself admitted that Sissy's illness had been "hopeless from the first." His money problems were hopeless too, since he was publishing little. The artist Gabriel Harrison recalled meeting him in the city late one day, when Poe swayed and complained of feeling faint. After they had a glass of wine and a biscuit in a cafe, Poe revealed that he had not eaten since early morning. It was said in New York that Muddy often appeared at a publisher's office to borrow a shilling.

News of the family's plight got into print. On December 15, the New York *Morning Express* carried an item headed "ILLNESS OF EDGAR A. POE":

> We regret to learn that this gentleman and his wife are both dan-
> gerously ill with the consumption, and that the hand of misfortune
> lies heavy upon their temporal affairs.—We are sorry to mention
> the fact that they are so far reduced as to be barely able to obtain
> the necessaries of life.

The newspaper called on Poe's friends and readers to come to his aid. Several other papers reprinted the item, some elaborating it, describing Poe and his family as unable to feed or clothe themselves. "Great God!" one exclaimed, "is it possible, that the literary people of the Union, will let poor Poe perish by starvation and lean faced beggary in New York? For so we are led to believe, from frequent notices in the papers, stating that Poe and his wife are both down upon a bed of misery, death and disease, with not a ducat in the world." With the Christmas season arrived, even the target of Poe's libel suit, Hiram Fuller of the *Mirror,* ran an appeal calling Poe "a man of fine talents" and urging his admirers to take up contributions, otherwise "we, whom he has quarrelled with, will take the lead."

The longest and most personal of these pleas came from Poe's dandyish, good-natured friend Willis. They had not seen each other or corresponded for two years, but their mutual affection remained. Poe had been pained to learn, the year before, about the death of Willis's wife in childbirth; Willis, as Virginia lay dying, sent Poe for a Christmas gift an inspirational book called *The Marriage Ring; or How to Make a Home Happy*. He also published in his *Home Journal* a lengthy editorial asking aid for Poe: "Here is one of the finest scholars, one of the most original men of genius, and one of the most industrious of the literary profession of our country, whose temporary suspension of labour, from bodily illness, drops him im-

mediately to a level with the common objects of public charity."
Willis took the occasion also to counter crass gossip about Poe's
sanity, explaining that he suffered from an unusual sensitivity to the
slightest stimulus: even a single glass of wine might on rare occasions rob him of control of his brain and tongue, so that he "talked
like a man insane," even while being "perfectly self-possessed in all
other respects." Mentioning that he had received an anonymous
donation for Poe, with a request that it be passed on to him, Willis
offered to forward any other such "tribute of sympathy with genius."

Poe felt buoyed by the concern shown him as a result of the
various appeals. One newspaper editor collected fifty or sixty dollars for him and his family at New York's Metropolitan Club; a
Brooklyn lawyer collected a like amount during a court appearance;
John Jacob Astor's grandson sent ten dollars. Much as Poe appreciated the generosity, the publicity troubled him. Someone sent
Virginia the original appeal in the *Express*—maliciously, he felt, for
it "heightened" her illness. It also offended his pride to become in
effect a charity case, "pitilessly thrust before the public," and cheered
his enemies. On December 30 he sent Willis a letter to print in his
Journal, making it known to the reading public that he was down
but not defeated. That his long illness had left him in need of money
was true enough, he said, but not that he had suffered deprivation
"beyond the extent of my capacity for suffering." Nor was he, as
the appeals described him, "without friends." "Even in the city of
New York I could have no difficulty in naming a hundred persons,
to each of whom . . . I could and would have applied for aid and
with unbounded confidence." In fact he was getting better, "if it be
any comfort to my enemies." He still had a future, and a great deal
to do, "and I have made up my mind not to die till it is done."

But little of this public testament represented Poe's actual condition or feelings. As he admitted several months later, he thought
it prudent to disavow the reports of his abject poverty, "since the
world regards wretchedness as a crime." And at the time that he
wrote the letter he expected his own illness to "soon terminate in
death." These considerations persuaded him to parade a brave front,
he said, and put him to the "expense of truth at denying those
necessities which were but too real."

Friends came to Fordham offering personal aid, mostly women
from the New York conversaziones, or friends from the past. They
included the poet Sarah Lewis ("Stella"), who had a salon in Brooklyn; Poe's Baltimore cousin, Elizabeth Herring; Eliza White, the

daughter of his former employer on the *Messenger;* and Mary Starr, his almost fiancée in Baltimore, who had known Virginia there as well. None brought as much relief as did twenty-five-year-old Marie Louise Shew. A resident of Greenwich Village, she had some talent for watercolors, but was not a literary person. Having a practical medical education from her father, and a sympathy, grounded in religious belief, for the poor and miserable, she described herself as "a country Doctor's only daughter, with a taste for painting and a heart for loving all the world." In addition to medical knowledge and compassion, she brought to the cottage some money she had raised by subscription, and a down comforter from her own room to replace Poe's military cloak as a cover for Virginia. She also sent Virginia a few boxes of wine. They had a "cheering and tonic influ-ence," Muddy noted, and Virginia always drank the wine "smiling, even when difficult to get it down." Visiting Fordham often from the city, "Loui" ministered not only to Virginia but to Muddy and Poe as well.

Loui Shew and Mary Starr were at the cottage on January 29, the day before Virginia died. They later recalled that she was much concerned for Poe's future welfare. She took a picture of him from under her pillow, kissed it, and gave it to Loui. With Muddy out of the room, she placed Mary's hand in Poe's and said, "Mary, be a friend to Eddie, and don't forsake him; he always loved you—didn't you, Eddie?" Inevitably Virginia's now certain death prompted thoughts of other close ones who had died. Virginia showed Poe a worn letter she had kept in a portfolio. It was from John Allan's second wife. The letter expressed her desire to see Poe and ac-knowledged that, out of jealousy, she had caused John Allan to neglect him. Poe had not seen the letter in years, for Virginia had apparently saved it from the flames, where he had thrown it scorn-fully. As he read it, Loui recalled, he began "weeping heavy tears." Sissy made him promise to preserve the letter, and he replaced the portfolio in his desk. Loui apparently returned to the city, but later in the day or at night Poe also made a promise to her, in a letter. He said he would act as Loui wished him to: "Yes," he wrote to her, "I *will* be calm."

On February 1, the New York *Daily Tribune* and the *Herald* car-ried an obituary notice: "On Saturday, the 30th ult., of pulmonary consumption, in the 25th year of her age, VIRGINIA ELIZA, wife of EDGAR A. POE." In the next few days several other newspa-pers in New York and Richmond also reported her death, which does not seem to have come easily. According to Muddy, she "ceased to speak (from weakness) but with her beautiful eyes!" Poe remarked that the night before her death Sissy failed quickly, "suffering much pain."

Loui helped with the funeral arrangements. She sprinkled Virginia's room with cologne and bought her a coffin and linen grave clothes. Muddy felt especially grateful for the cerements. "If it had not been for her," she reportedly said, "my darling Virginia would have been laid in her grave in cotton. I can never tell my gratitude that my darling was entombed in lovely linen." Loui also made a watercolor painting of Virginia in death, propped up on the death bed, and together with Mary Starr furnished suitable mourning clothes for Poe.

Virginia's funeral took place on the afternoon of February 2, 1847. The day was so cold that Mary did not go to the gravesite. Virginia was interred in the vault of the Valentine family, who owned the Fordham cottage, located in the graveyard of a Dutch Reformed Church about a half mile away. Several New York literary people attended, including Willis, and some neighbors. Poe seems to have draped himself in the cloak that had served Sissy for a blanket. Loui had kept it out of his sight, presumably thinking it an unsuitable garment for the funeral.

To add to Poe's distress, his postponed libel suit against Hiram Fuller reopened at the New York Superior Court the day before Virginia's funeral. The court appointed a commission to take testimony in Washington from T. D. English, serving there as a newspaper correspondent during the session of Congress. In his deposition, English described Poe's character as "that of a notorious liar, a common drunkard and of one utterly lost to all the obligations of honor." But his allegation that Poe had obtained thirty dollars from him under false pretenses was undermined when he revealed, under cross-examination, that he conveyed the money not to Poe directly but to Poe's then partner in the *Broadway Journal,* and claimed to have mislaid Poe's receipt for it. A twelve-man jury heard the case in New York on February 17. To clear Poe of the forgery charge, his lawyer, Enoch Fancher, called Edward Thomas, the New York merchant who had first made the charge, then traced it to a verbal misunderstanding and retracted it. Lacking evidence to support the allegations against Poe, Fuller's lawyer tried to prejudice the jury, arguing in his summation that Poe's disreputable character made him unfit for consideration. The jurors disregarded this and convicted Fuller of libel. They awarded Poe $225.06 in damages, and court costs of $101.42.

Poe sent Muddy to the city with a note authorizing her to receive the spoils, but he did not attend the trial. As Fancher explained, he had "recently buried his wife, and his own health was such as to prevent him being present." His victory also brought him much further criticism in the press, with re-rehashings of the Ellet letters and the "Literati" scandals, and new kinds of condemnation. Fuller contemplated a countersuit, and having contributed to the dole gathered for the Poes at Christmastime, asked pointedly in the *Mirror:* "WHAT HAS BECOME OF THE FUNDS?" He also began serializing a novel entitled *The Trippings of Tom Pepper,* the work of C. F. Briggs, who caricatured Poe as the "drunken critic" Austin Wicks, "a small man, with a very pale, small face" who reduces himself and his family "into a starving condition by his irregularities." The heavy fine demanded of Fuller for a libel he did not write made him a sympathetic figure to other editors and publishers. In his New York *Tribune,* Horace Greeley called Poe's suit "mistaken and silly," as he had punished not his libeler but "the harmless publisher." The new shouting match continued through the summer as Poe's attorney, irate over comments about him in the *Mirror,* began bringing his own suit against Fuller.

Poe was aware of the uproar, but otherwise feverish, too unwell even to leave his room, deprived, he said, "of all power of thought or action." Something of his prostrating desolation appears in a couplet he composed. Three years earlier he had written a minor poem called "Eulalie," seemingly an expression of his feeling that Sissy lifted him from a state of stifled energy and barren aloneness:

> *I dwelt alone*
> *In a world of moan,*
> *And my soul was a stagnant tide*
> *Till the fair and gentle Eulalie became my blushing bride—*

In the wake of Virginia's death, he took a manuscript copy of the poem and penciled on it, as if to say that he had returned to the state from which she had rescued him:

> *Deep in earth my love is lying*
> *And I must weep alone.*

Muddy, having lost her only surviving child, was devastated too; she "wished to die," she said later, "but *had* to live to take care of

. . . poor disconsolate Eddie." Reportedly she had to keep a watch on him, for he sometimes visited Virginia's burial vault late at night, even in snow, stealing from the house in his stockinged feet so she would not hear him.

Poe now spoke of his "Very serious illness," but in Loui Shew's opinion, informed by her medical training, his state was moribund: she did not expect him to live long. She found that his pulse beat, at best, only ten regular beats, then stopped, "intermitted." Even before Virginia's death, she believed, he suffered from a lesion on one side of the brain, now worsened by a "brain fever" resulting from the hunger, cold, and want he had borne in supplying food and medicine for his wife. To confirm her diagnosis that Poe's brain was *"diseased,"* she took him by closed carriage to a well-known New York physician, Dr. Valentine Mott. Apparently Mott agreed with her on the gravity of Poe's illness, for she embarked on a regime of cure with some confidence. She taught him to sit away from the stove, with a soapstone at his feet, and she revised his diet. To replenish the phosphates lost by his mental exertions, she got him to eat fish, clams, and oysters, and had Muddy make bread with "Hosfords yeast," to preserve the phosphates in the wheat. She also tried to reduce his "brain fever"—likely a condition of powerful anxiety. Owing to its severity and to his organic lesion, however, even sedatives had to be administered carefully, she said, lest they "excite him to madness." She also cautioned him to lead a more prudent and settled life, supervised by a competent and caring woman, someone "fond enough—and strong enough to manage his work and its remunerations for his best good."

Loui recalled that Poe received her lectures with "irony," as they came from a woman unintellectual and unworldly. Just the same, he and Muddy both felt deeply grateful to her: "what we should do without you," Muddy said, "is fearful to think of." Loui had promised Virginia to visit Fordham every other day for a long time, or until Poe was able to begin work again. Loui did come to the cottage often, and when she did not she sent flowers by train, or cooling applications for his head and other medications for Muddy to administer. Poe also spoke of his "great debt" to her and called her the "most unselfish of all who ever loved me." He may even have seen her, as he earlier saw Fanny Osgood, as a possible replacement for Virginia. He wrote a Valentine's Day poem for Loui, likening his gratitude to worship, and indeed treating her as a divinity, a "sacred sun" that restores faith in truth and virtue, bringing "the resurrection of deep-buried faith." In a second, now lost poem, known only through Loui's account of it, he depicted his own over-excited state, every stanza containing the line "The pulse beats ten and intermits." He described Loui holding her watch and counting as she took his pulse, looking for the moment when she might risk giving him a sedative.

As Loui tried to calm and strengthen Poe in his panicky bereavement, she also found him confiding in her. By her account, he related a bizarre version of his earlier stories of Russian and European adventure, in which Loui, Fanny Allan, Muddy, Henry, T. D. English, as well as several recent and past events, seem present in transmogrified forms. He told her that after leaving West Point he fought a duel over a woman in France, and was wounded by his antagonist, leaving him ill, in a fever, and for a time insane. A cultivated Scotswoman of noble birth brought him food and water, and came to see him daily for thirteen weeks, accompanied by her brother, who had taken to gambling and other evil ways. The "angelic" Scotswoman, a cross between Muddy and Loui, was "a plain looking large featured maiden Lady," although her trusting faith in God was so intense that he wrote a poem for her called "Holy Eyes." While in France he also wrote an autobiographical novel called "Life of an Unfortunate Artist," later falsely attributed to Eugene Sue, which the lady and her brother helped him translate, earning him his hundred-dollar passage home.

Poe confided to Loui not only his fancies but also his history, which she recorded in her journal. In the way that mourning dissolves time, superimposing one loss on another, leading the mind to wander through its suite of griefs, Poe, she said, "talked to me *incessently* [*sic*] of the past." As if in and through Virginia, dead at twenty-five, he returned to the deceased William Henry Leonard, adventurous and admired, dead at twenty-four, "a Secretary to some foreigner," Loui recalled him saying, a "dashing gay cavalier" unsuited by his tastes to the time he was born to or bred in, and with more of the Poe nature than himself, *"coárser* rougher."

Especially Virginia's death led Poe back to his mother, also dead at twenty-four, to Eliza Poe. She had already visited the scene. The day before dying, Virginia had removed from her workbox and presented to Loui a small jewel case given her by Poe, and to him by Eliza. He apparently showed Loui what other effects of his mother had come to him. In addition to a miniature portrait of her, Loui recalled, he owned two sketches by his mother, one the watercolor of Boston harbor ("For my little son Edgar"), the other in pencil or ink. He also had a bundle of her letters, written in a round hand that Loui found "very like" Poe's own. He told her that his "beautiful mother" had been born at sea. He said that he owed to her everything that he wished to think he was, "every good gift of his intellect, & his heart."

Poe told her this "privately," Loui noted, clearly so that Muddy would not hear him. Caution was needed, for Muddy overheard some of his remarks and objected, "reproved me," Loui said, "for indulging *him in his fancies,* about his mother." Loui learned that Muddy did not value Eliza Poe's sketches, in fact dismissed them as "antiquated specimens of art." This was more than Muddy's resentment of whatever intruded on the closeness and exclusivity of her household. Eliza had after all been only Eliza Arnold, had been only her brother's wife; yet Poe never mentioned his father, and spoke as if everything good in his nature had come from his mother, from outside the Poe family. Poe was well aware of ill feeling among his several Poe cousins toward Eliza, who had after all also been an actress, had led David Poe away from a career in law, and was suspected of having betrayed him with some other man. He told Loui that he had burned "the sweetest poem he ever wrote, *or conceived,"* evidently about his mother, in order to please Muddy and conciliate his father's family.

In fashioning a proud ancestry for himself, Poe had always portrayed the Poe family in an idealized light, celebrating in particular his blood relation to the "Zealous Republican" and friend of Lafayette, General David Poe. But Virginia's death brought out a shame he felt in relation to his mother he had apparently kept hidden. He told Loui, she recalled, that "it was the regret of his life, that he had not vindicated his mother to the world," vindicated Eliza Arnold for what she was, or at least for what he now remembered her to be, perhaps had always remembered her to be, "as pure, as angelic and altogether lovely, as any woman could be on earth."

Attempted Recovery; "Ulalume"; Eureka; Parting from Loui Shew.

CA. SUMMER 1847 – JUNE 1848

In trying to repair his existence, Poe came even more closely to resemble characters in his own tales whose efforts to suppress past woes impel and disfigure their lives. Callers at rural Fordham during the summer and fall were often surprised at what they saw. When Evert Duyckinck arrived with some others in June, they found the floor of the bandbox cottage graced by a brand-new rag carpet. Muddy presided over a supper table laden with delicacies, decanting amber coffee from a new silver-plated urn—the fruits of Poe's victorious libel suit. Likely the same month, an Episcopal minister named Cotesworth P. Bronson came with his young daughter, Mary. She expected a grave and melancholy Poe, but he welcomed the group cordially, with an amused look. As they walked the banks of the Bronx River after dinner, he discussed the "science of composition" and pointed out his favorite ramble. A visitor around October recalled that the company had "a very cheerful time." Two or three of the men tried to surpass Poe in a game of leaping. In his great jump he burst his long-worn and carefully kept gaiters, but nevertheless outdistanced them all.

By summertime, Poe could be seen in the city again as well, after a long absence. Having missed the libel trial, he paid what seems a gloating visit in June to the offices of the *Mirror,* the newspaper he had vanquished. His booty apparently furnished not only a groaning board but also new clothes, for Hiram Fuller reported that he wore "a decent suit of black, which had doubtless been purchased by the money so infamously obtained." Poe's mood as well as his clothing seemed improved. Rufus Griswold recorded meeting him in the street later the same month and finding him "extremely civil." Sometimes Poe called at the home of Loui Shew, near Washington Square. Having done what she could to improve his physical health, she tried to foster his emotional and spiritual recovery. As he admired the "classic" taste shown in the softly lit crimsons and gold of her home, she invited him to select furnishings for the library and music room in her uncle's new house several streets away. Poe had always disliked formal worship and was at best indifferent to traditional Christianity: C. F. Briggs reported that he once called the Bible "all rigmarole." But Loui, a devout Episcopalian, tried to awaken his religious belief, and won from him the healthy-minded admission that she had "renewed my hopes and faith in God."

Poe's appearance at this time is perhaps caught in a daguerreotype (Illus. 22). The picture cannot be dated certainly, but may be the portrait he sat for during a visit to the Reverend Bronson and his daughter in New York. He looks thin-lipped, but nevertheless fit, and groomed to an approximation of elegance. He retains his heavy sideburns but, strikingly, now sports a small mustache, twirled or perhaps waxed at the ends.

The amber coffee, broad jumping, and civility were deceptive, however, not signs but gestures of recovery. Around July Poe decided to venture a trip away from Muddy, Fordham, and New York, on his own. He may have traveled as far south as Washington, visiting his old friend F. W. Thomas and attending a high-school commencement where he was unexpectedly asked to recite "The Raven." He stopped in Philadelphia, calling on George Rex Graham in the hope of contracting for some magazine articles. But by his own account he became "exceedingly ill," near death, he believed, and felt he had no hope but to return home immediately. In September, the Reverend Bronson and his daughter returned to Fordham and found him "grown thin," agitated, exhibiting "a degree of nervousness unusual." Around Christmas, Loui took Poe to a midnight Episcopal service at the Church of the Holy Communion in New York. In her recollection, he observed the first part of the service "like a 'churchman,'" holding one side of her prayer book and singing the psalms. But when the priest several times repeated the text "He was a man of sorrows and acquainted with grief," Poe asked her to remain quiet and said he would wait for her outside. With that, he "rushed out, *too excited to stay.*"

By the New Year, although jittery within, Poe declared himself healed. On January fourth, two weeks before his thirty-ninth birthday, he wrote that he now felt "better—best. I have never been so well." He intended to stay well, also, and follow an abstemious health regime: "I rise early, eat moderately, drink nothing but water, and take abundant and regular exercise in the open air." He considered himself recovered not only from Sissy's death but also from the emotional riot that had preceded it. Much of his new insight about this earlier period he imparted to a recent correspondent named

George W. Eveleth, a young medical student in Maine. Eveleth regarded himself as "a poor, unlettered, unknown backwoods youngster," but he responded to the otherworldliness of Poe's writing and made him *"my favorite one."* Just the same, he did not approach Poe with the hunger for personal closeness of his other most devoted admirers. On the contrary, he spoke his mind, criticizing what he disliked in Poe's work and behavior.

As Poe told Eveleth, he now understood that what had led him to act chaotically was his alarm over the prospect of losing Virginia. The unceasing threat of it brought on overmastering anxiety that only alcohol could subdue. "Six years ago," he said, "a wife, whom I loved as no man ever loved before, ruptured a blood-vessel in singing. Her life was despaired of. I took leave of her forever & underwent all the agonies of her death." But the torture was repeated over and over. "She recovered partially and I again hoped. At the end of a year the vessel broke again—I went through precisely the same scene. Again in about a year afterward. Then again—again—again & even once again at varying intervals." With each new cycle of restoration and breakdown he reexperienced her loss and at the same time more urgently desired her to live. The strain toppled him. "I became insane," he explained to Eveleth, "with long intervals of horrible sanity." It was during these fits, and to pacify them lest they destroy his mind, that he drank, Poe said, "God only knows how often or how much." His enemies crucified him for drinking himself into insanity, when in fact he drank because crazed by Virginia's struggle, "the horrible never-ending oscillation between hope & despair which I could *not* longer have endured without the total loss of reason." Its cause removed, his drinking problem was over. "I had indeed, nearly abandoned all hope of a permanent cure when I found one in the *death* of my wife."

Feeling or at least professing to feel cured now, "better—best," Poe told several people in January that he planned to revive his career, "re-establish myself in the literary world." A comeback would not be easy: over the past year his already diminishing output had practically stopped, earning him little more in 1847 than what he recovered from his libel suit; he remained excommunicated from the New York literary salons; and many of the writers, editors, and publishers he had antagonized kept him under fire. Just two weeks after Virginia's death, a Philadelphia newspaper had arraigned him for committing one of "the most remarkable plagiarisms." This empty charge concerned Thomas Wyatt's *Conchologist's First-Book,* the textbook to which his name had been attached as a copyright convenience eight years earlier. (Poe planned to prosecute but decided the matter was not actionable.) T. D. English had begun a new satirical magazine, *The John-Donkey,* where he depicted Poe lying in prison, undersized and dowdy, "a melancholy-looking little man, in a rusty suit of black." But others were glad to have Poe back. The *Southern Literary Messenger* announced in January that he was "returning to his literary labours. The public will doubtless welcome the return of so favorite an author to pursuits in which heretofore he has done so much and so well."

Poe saw his best hope of regaining a literary foothold in at last issuing the "Stylus." "To be controlled," he had learned, "is to be ruined." But his already oversized plans for the magazine had grown boundless. "If I succeed, I put myself (within 2 years)," he said, "in possession of a fortune & infinitely more." He decided to make a "Magazine expedition" to the South and West in order to interest personal and literary friends, hoping to begin with a list of *"at least 500 subscribers."* He also prepared a new prospectus, promising that the first number would contain the initial installment of his "Literary America," and that to keep readers in touch with literature, fine arts, and drama "throughout the civilized world," he had made "accurate arrangements" in London, Paris, Rome, and Vienna—a fantastic claim.

Another chance to make an entrance on the literary scene arose through the Reverend Bronson. Also known as "Professor" Bronson for his talks and textbook on public speaking, he had asked Poe to write a poem suitable for reciting in his elocution lectures, something embodying "thoughts that would admit of vocal variety and expression." His creative power no longer locked, Poe brought to Bronson's home in the city a poem beautifully handwritten on one of his wafered-together scrolls, "almost like engraving," Bronson's daughter said. Bronson decided not to use the poem, however, which was also rejected by the *Union Magazine,* whose reader said he could not fathom Poe's meaning. Others had the same complaint, even though, according to Muddy, Poe at the time considered the poem "his best," as it may well be. She brought the poem to the *American Review,* which published it in December. To excite interest, Poe had the poem appear anonymously in the *Review* and asked Willis to reprint it in his *Home Journal,* with an inquiry about the writer. Willis complied, praising the poem's "rarity and niceness of language," asking "Who is the author?," and answering that "Ulalume—A Ballad," "although published anonymously in the 'American Review,' is known to be the composition of EDGAR A. POE."

Poe evidently shaped "Ulalume" to suit Bronson's needs as a lecturer on elocution. With its euphonious philological oddities, chantlike rhythm, symmetrical patterns of syntax, and incessant sibilants, it often seems straining to escape referential language into some astral music. Indeed, with its weird geography of wolds, Mount Yaanek, and the tarns of Auber, populated no less weirdly by Astarte, Dian, and Ulalume, it seems a poem from outer space. Its action occurs at night, "in the lonesome October / Of my most immemorial year." As much as any one word can, *immemorial* sums up the poem, embracing, as Poe uses it here, both what most richly deserves remembrance and what cannot be remembered. Having buried his beloved Ulalume, the storyteller paradoxically suffers from both amnesia and obsession. On the one hand, he is unaware that the present night marks the anniversary of Ulalume's death and that the funereal Poescape through which he wanders, discoursing with himself, is the route to her grave:

> *. . . . our thoughts they were palsied and sere—*
> *Our memories were treacherous and sere;*
> *For we knew not the month was October,*
> *And we marked not the night of the year—*

Part of himself, however, recognizes the route and warns him away from it: "Ah, fly!—let us fly!—for we must." But characteristically he tries to devalue what he in some sense knows: "This is nothing but dreaming. / Let us on. . . ." Knowing-unknowingly he gravitates to Ulalume's burial vault.

Deterioration and decay permeate the poem. The anniversary of Ulalume's death is a "senescent" night in October, a time of autumnal dying, when the leaves are "withering and sere." With his "palsied" thoughts and his cheeks "where the worm never dies," the narrator himself seems used up, and looks back on a more vital stage of his life, "days when my heart was volcanic." His weakening betokens a larger cosmic exhaustion, symbolized by Astarte, a heavenly body associated with the planet Venus. The narrator (or part of him) wishes to believe that Astarte's light points the way toward inner peace and forgetfulness, but discovers that it brings him to Ulalume's grave. This planetary deception is explained in the obscure last stanza, where he asks, still discoursing with himself:

> *"Ah, can it*
> *Have been that the woodlandish ghouls—*
> *The pitiful, the merciful ghouls,*
> *To bar up our way and to ban it*
> *From the secret that lies in these wolds—*
> *From the thing that lies hidden in these wolds—*
> *Have drawn up the spectre of a planet*
> *From the limbo of lunary souls—*
> *This sinfully scintillant planet*
> *From the Hell of the planetary souls?"*

Poe's meaning seems to be that the serviceable-threatening ghouls, in trying to lead the speaker away from his preoccupation with death, may have fetched not the genuine Astarte, representing hope and peace, but Astarte's ghost, "the spectre of a planet." Daringly, Poe imagines a universe in which not only human beings and the rest of organic life succumb to death, but where stars and planets also expire, their spirits, as it were, being consigned to humanlike otherworlds, a "limbo of lunary souls" or a "Hell of the planetary souls"—a cosmos of total death.

Still more distressingly, the ghostly Astarte appears with "love in her luminous eyes," and "point[s] us the path to the skies." But her promise of hope and faith, healing and forgetfulness—recalling Loui Shew—proves an illusion. The way of positive thinking leads to "the thing" hidden in the woods. Unexpectedly arrived at the grave of his lover, the journeyer cries, "Ah, what demon hath tempted me here?" The demon is of course himself, his Imp of the Immemorial, whose voice is the strange new music Poe contrived in "Ulalume," the music of Hell.

"Ulalume—A Ballad" evinces undiminished even heightened skill and imaginative force. But neither its double-*l* double-*a* configurations, its renewed dramatization of the failure to insulate oneself against troubling feelings and memories, nor its vision of ghost-planets encourages confidence in Poe's assurance that he felt "better—best." Still less does the grandiosity of what he attempted next. According to Muddy, during the cold nights of January he had been walking up and down the porch at Fordham, an overcoat across his shoulders, "contemplating the stars until long after midnight." His mind was shaping something of *"moment,"* he said, a treatise that in good time would transform human thought, "revolutionize the world of Physical & Metaphysical Science. I say this calmly—but I say it."

He would describe and explain the birth, evolution, and destiny of the Creation. Now that he was well, his powers restored and then some, "better—best," he would unveil the mysteries of Being and Nothingness, baring nothing less than the secret of Eternity.

On February 3, Poe delivered his new work as a lecture entitled "The Universe." The timing may have mattered, the date being a few days after the first anniversary of Virginia's death. Poe also connected the event with his dreams for the "Stylus," since public lectures remained a major form of entertainment during the period, and he hoped to take in enough money to begin his search for subscribers in the South and West. He believed he could count on an audience of three or four hundred, "and if even 300 are present, I shall be enabled to proceed with my plans." But although he spoke at the prestigious Society Library, on Broadway and Leonard Streets, no more than sixty people came, certainly in part because of the stormy night.

His coat tightly buttoned across his slender chest, as one spectator recalled the occasion, Poe lectured for fully two and a half hours. Some listeners praised the profundity of his argument and his rhapsodic delivery, one judging the performance "a nobler effort than any other Mr. Poe has yet given to the world." Not everyone agreed. To Duyckinck, who seems to have attended, the evening came off as "a mountainous piece of absurdity for a popular lecture and moreover an introduction to his projected magazine." Others found the talk imaginative but not persuasive, or simply too long: "At the end of an hour and a half . . . no end was visible; the thin leaves, one after another, of the neat manuscript, were gracefully turned over; yet, oh, a plenty more were evidently left behind." Either way Poe was miffed. "All praised it," he said, "and all absurdly misrepresented it." Their reactions only illustrated what he meant in telling a friend he did not expect the present generation to appreciate the work, which would be read, if ever, two thousand years later.

By the end of May Poe revised and expanded the lecture into a monograph of nearly 150 pages. He called it *Eureka: A Prose Poem*, from the remark of Archimedes when he discovered specific gravity: "I have found it."† G. P. Putnam agreed to publish the book in an edition of about five hundred copies, priced at seventy-five cents. It sold poorly, even though *Eureka* can claim some scientific and philosophic respectability, and much aesthetic interest. Expecting to be misunderstood, Poe addressed himself, he said, "To the few who love me and whom I love." Yet he promised that since what he offered was true, it was immortal: "it cannot die:—or if by any means it be now trodden down so that it die, it will 'rise again to the Life Everlasting.' " He dedicated the work to Alexander von Humboldt, then considered the last universal genius, who had traveled the world gathering scientific evidence for his panorama of heaven and earth in *Kosmos* (1845–62). Bidding for similar standing, Poe notified readers of *Eureka* that he intended to "challenge the conclusions, and thus, in effect, to question the sagacity, of many of the greatest and most justly reverenced of men." In that spirit he jeered at Aristotle and Bacon as "Aries Tottle" and "Hog," the idols of logicians, fact collectors, and other "intellectual grovellers," and pointed out—"with no unwarranted fear of being taken for a madman"—that in explaining the operation of gravity he had gone beyond Newton.

What Poe revealed, to capsulize his treatise, was that in the beginning, Divine Volition willed into being a "primordial Particle" and diffused it as atoms into a limited part of Space, the Universe of Stars. Owing to a tendency to regain their original oneness (gravity), the atoms began to agglomerate, forming clusters of nebulous matter. The condensation and rotation of one such cluster gave rise to the solar system, whose planets represent the coalescings of ring after ring of matter whirled off by the shrinking sun at the center. The planets have continued the same revolutionary movements (orbits) around the sun that characterized them as rings. Innumerable similar systems exist. In a necessary reaction to the originating divine diffusion of atoms, they will one day draw together into an almost infinitely less number of vast spheres, the "ingathering of the orbs" proceeding until the spheres themselves collapse into "the final globe of globes." Being rather nonmatter than matter, this ultimate globe will instantaneously disappear, leaving God to remain "all in all." The entire process is likely repeated forever and forever, "a novel Universe swelling into existence, and then subsiding into nothingness, at every throb of the Heart Divine."

Newton, Leibniz, Laplace and other scientists thus pointed Poe's way past the cosmic thanatos of "Ulalume" to a new and ultimate theory of deathlessness. In essence, the cosmos of *Eureka* presents a stupendous spectacle of rejuvenescence, an infinitude of pulsating universes alternately willed into orbic systems and reactively condensed into primary particles by an infinitude of gods. After the original diffusion, every atom of every body attracts every other atom, both of its own and of every other body, the fragments of detached godhead yearningly seeking reunion with each other and with their creator: "Does not so evident a brotherhood among the atoms point to a common parentage? Does not a sympathy so omniprevalent, so ineradicable, and so thoroughly irrespective, suggest a common paternity as its source?" ("There can be no tie more strong than that of brother to brother," he had written years before to John Neal, "it is not so much that they love one another as that they both love the same parent—their affections are always running in the same direction.") Dissolved in its own embraces, the universe springs to life again, an eternal revenant eternally returning to fullness from Material Nihility.

Most meaningful to Poe, the self does not perish in this drama of cosmic annihilation and rebirth, but instead grows exalted. The evidence that we survive and conquer death is our own sense of greatness. "No thinking being lives," Poe wrote in *Eureka,* "who, at some luminous point of his life of thought, has not felt himself lost amid the surges of futile efforts at understanding, or believing, that anything exists *greater than his own soul.*" Our feeling of personal infinitude is but the residue of an original identity between ourselves and God, for the universe consists simply of fragments of diffused godhead, "infinite individualizations of Himself." The "Heart Divine" that gives birth to the universe is *"our own";* each soul is "in part, its own God—its own Creator." God presently exists as the Universe of Stars, whose reunion is but his reconstitution as Individual. As the clusters ingather, we will become more conscious of our identity with Him and at last blend into the one God. Then our awareness of individual identity will gradually be merged in the "general consciousness." Our distress in considering that we shall lose our person-ality dissolves in the realization that at the epoch of final condensation our consciousness will be identical with Divinity. Then the self knows: "he shall recognize his existence as that of Jehovah." After dying, we eventually become God.

Inflamed anew by Virginia's death, Poe's need to confirm a Life Everlasting thus brought him to the conclusion that God, as all of *Eureka* seems to imply, is Poe. "My whole nature," he reportedly said of the work, "utterly *revolts* at the idea that there is any Being in the Universe superior to *myself!*"

Whatever consolation Poe found in his ideas, they offended the religious belief of Loui Shew and ended their intimate friendship. The implications of *Eureka* were brought to her attention by her confidant, a young theological student named John Henry Hopkins,

Jr. Son of the Episcopal bishop of Vermont, Hopkins had attended Poe's lecture "The Universe" and reviewed it in the *Evening Express* as an "extraordinary work of Art." Poe thought his summary of the talk full of inaccuracies, like all the others, but nevertheless the "only report of it which approaches the truth." He met Hopkins at Loui's home in the city and received them both at Fordham when preparing *Eureka* for publication. It may have been during this visit that Hopkins got a taste of Poe's cynicism toward formal Christianity; he later recalled hearing Poe praise the "highly cultivated" Jesuit fathers at nearby St. John's College, because they "smoked, drank, and played cards like gentlemen, and never said a word about religion."

In May, Hopkins saw the manuscript copy of *Eureka* at the office of Poe's publisher, G. P. Putnam. Poe's additions to the lecture appalled him. Instead of closing with the sublime thought of a new universe coming into existence at each Divine Heart-throb, Poe had added his vision of a never-dying self coextensive and identical with God, "a system of complete and pure pantheism," Hopkins called it. He wrote to Poe about the new ending, emphasizing his admiration for the lecture, but wishing Poe to see the change as "*scientifically*" unsound and in contradiction to other parts of his theory. Hopkins pointed out, for instance, that Poe made the primary irradiation of matter limited in extent. Yet since God is infinite, and the whole of God now exists only as irradiated matter, the irradiation must have been infinite also. To equate God pantheistically with the created universe as Poe described it was therefore "scientific *suicide*." He also pointed out that most Christians deemed pantheism a damnable heresy and would consign Poe's "great discovery" to "the empty chimaeras of infidelity." If Poe published the book as it stood, he added, conscience would compel him to denounce it.

About two weeks after the publication of *Eureka*, a long, anonymous critique appeared in the *Literary World*, which Poe attributed to Hopkins, probably correctly. Reviews of the book tended to extremes, the most ecstatic predicting it would shed "unfailing lustre upon the American name," as it demonstrated "a degree of logical acumen which has certainly not been equalled since the days of Sir Isaac Newton." But the reviewer in the *Literary World* lumped Poe with the Transcendentalists (accurately, in this case), rated his account of planet formation a rehash of Laplace, and generally junked *Eureka* as "*arrant fudge*." He attacked the pervasive pantheism and derided Poe's statement that nothing exists greater than his own soul, calling it "extraordinary nonsense, if not blasphemy; and it may very possibly be *both.*"

Poe wrote off a long retort, something of a "Reply to Mr. Hopkins," repeatedly referring to his assailant as "the Student of Theology." Incensed by the belittling charge that he had merely copied Laplace, he made clear his actual scientific stature: "The *ground* covered by the great French astronomer compares with that covered by my theory," he said, "as a bubble compares with the ocean on which it floats." He also belabored "the Student of Theology's" misquotations, faulty grammar, and tone of *"turn-down-shirt-collar-ness."* As to being branded a pantheist—or indeed polytheist, pagan, or "God knows what"—he cared very little what he was called "so it be not a 'Student of Theology.' "

Whether or not young Hopkins wrote the critique, he did counsel Loui Shew to distance herself from Poe. He told her that on the question of pantheism he considered Poe "either insane or a hopeless infadel [*sic*]." Being "a childish undeveloped loving woman," as she described herself, Loui was susceptible to influence, and came to regard Poe as *"lost, either way."* She could see too that for all her advice and warnings, Poe was drinking again and acting erratically. Later accounts leave the exact chronology of events confused, but on one occasion in the spring Poe dined out with Rufus Griswold. According to Loui, Poe said that he counted Griswold an enemy but had promised Muddy to treat him courteously in order to keep receiving his financial and literary "favors." Griswold moved now in the same literary salons that had exiled Poe, gathering around him the same women, especially after he announced plans to publish a new anthology of *The Female Poets of America.* He had remarried since the shocking death of his first wife, although disastrously. As a twenty-nine-year-old Baptist minister from Vermont, he had wed a forty-two-year-old Jewish woman from South Carolina. Their wedding night brought the surprise, he alleged, that she was incapable of having sex: as he suggestively but puzzlingly described the problem, no more marriage existed than had the ceremony taken place "between parties of the same sex, or where the sex of one was doubtful or ambiguous." Since then he had conceived a romantic interest in Fanny Osgood, "the most admirable woman I ever knew," he felt.

Something apparently stirred in Poe during dinner with Griswold, deep perhaps calling unto deep. He got drunk, according to Loui, and became "insane and unmanageble [*sic*]." He gave someone her New York address, and when notified of his condition she sent Hopkins and her husband to look for him. The men found Poe, Hopkins said, "crazy-drunk in the hands of the police." They took him back to Fordham, and finding the household penniless left five dollars for necessities.

A visit from Poe around May reinforced Loui's dismay. He came to her home one evening, saying he had to write a poem but lacked inspiration. Between them they playfully worked out some lines, in fact the germ of what would become "The Bells." But it all became a sort of blank for Poe. Word was sent to Muddy that he would stay the night with Loui and her brother; in the morning, after a twelve-hour sleep, he could hardly recall the evening's events. Loui again noticed that his pulse beat irregularly, and called in the prominent physician Dr. John Francis, her neighbor. He concluded that Poe suffered from "heart disease" (a diagnosis Poe later rejected) and would die early in life. Loui drove Poe back to Fordham, his eyes heavy, step unsteady. He did not seem to realize he had been ill, she recalled, and wondered why she had brought him home.

Loui's growing estrangement hurt Poe, and upset him. She seems to have begun curtailing her trips to Fordham at least by the end of March, when he wrote her in some impatience, "What *is* the reason that you have not been out?" But her visits no longer brought solace or, if they ever had, faith. Always sensitive to slights, he detected in her looks and gestures a desire to drop him. Perhaps in May, she came to the cottage dressed in a white robe, he recalled, and greeted him with the words "Good morning Edgar." Her manner struck him as hurried, formal, strained by a "conventional coldness." Her smile pained him also, a smile he felt of *"sorrow."* Still more woundingly, she arrived in the company of the "Student of Theology," whose presence gored him. Young Hopkins stood, he said, "smiling and bowing at the madman Poe!" When they sat down for dinner and Hopkins said grace, Loui gave an amen that Poe described as "low." The faintness of her response registered with him as hopelessness or resignation. "I felt my heart stop," he said, "and I was sure I was then to die before your eyes."

Around June, Loui sent Poe a letter of farewell. He read it over and over, in disbelief although it only confirmed what he already sensed. "You did not say so," he wrote back to her, "but for months I have known you were deserting me, not willingly but none the less surely . . . I have had premonitions of this for months." The time for protest was past, and he made no recriminations. He even offered what seems an apology for his sacrilegious views in *Eureka,* sending "my *regret,* my *sorrow,* if aught I have ever written has hurt you! My *heart* never *wronged you.*" He owed much to Loui, who had bought Virginia's coffin and grave clothes, then watched over him, medicated him, listened to his fancies. He now consigned her "loyal unselfish and womanly heart" to his lifelong history of desertions, something, he said, "to vanish like all I love, or desire." He recalled to her what he had revealed of his past, promising that in his esteem she remained beside "the friend of my boyhood, the mother of my school fellow, of whom I told you"—Jane Stanard, the maternal confidante of his youth, who had died deranged at about the age of thirty. With Loui Shew he had for a while been the "school fellow," she the "mother," a nurturer from beyond the collapsing Universe, "an angel to my forlorn and darkened nature."

Poe understood that Loui still wished him well, and vowed for her sake to overcome his grief. But the loss of her care was "not a common trial," he said; "it is a fearful one to me." She had told him candidly that nothing could prevent his sudden death but a calmly prudent life, with a woman fond and strong enough to manage his affairs in his best interest. He felt so himself, for he intimated to Loui that her withdrawal was a sort of death warrant: "unless some true and tender and pure womanly love saves me, I shall hardly last a year longer, alone!"

Jane Locke; Nancy Richmond;
Sarah Helen Whitman; Elmira Royster.

SUMMER 1848

During July and August 1848, immediately after his parting with Loui Shew, Poe looked into possibilities of marriage north and south, becoming more or less involved with four different women.

Virginia's approaching death had itself introduced the first prospect. In response to newspaper accounts of his family's destitution, Poe had received an idolatrous poem entitled "An Invocation for Suffering Genius." On its heels, about a month after Virginia's death, came a letter expressing sympathy and admiration, sent from Lowell, Massachusetts, by a poet named Jane Locke. Born Ermina, she had assumed the name Jane and published a book of vapid poems. Her invocation to Poe began: "Oh, Charity, where hast thou fled with heavenly-lustred wing, / While on a low and sorrow bed Genius lies suffering?" The early course of their interest in each other is difficult to map. Parts of their correspondence have not survived, including all of Jane Locke's letters to Poe, known only through quotations from them in Poe's letters to her. And what remains is difficult to interpret because its language is veiled, hinting, roundabout. Poe and Locke communicated in an exploratory language of elevated sentiment—"noble," he called it—meant to feel out each other's intentions and suggest possible interest while avoiding self-exposure. Writing in the dark, worried about saying too much or too little, each tried to get the other to show an emotional hand first. Their "noble" circumlocutions about the holiness of Friendship conveyed the message, If you tell me what you really think of me, then I'll tell you what I really think of you.

A further uncertainty compounded Poe's need for delicate expression. He thought Jane Locke a widow but was not sure. Hoping to prompt a clarification of her marital status, he remarked in one letter that he knew "nothing" about her. But she took the statement to mean that he questioned her ancestry and social station. "Can it be that because you absolutely know 'nothing' of me," she wrote back, "because of what seems to you my obscurity there may be something wrong that makes you secretly hesitate to call me friend." In replying this time he became more explicit, rather: "will you still refuse to tell me at least *one* particular of your personal history? . . . Tell me only of the ties—if any exist—that bind you to the world." And cautiously he suggested that he raised the question with marriage in mind, possibly: "now that I have asked it, it seems to me the maddest of questions, involving, possibly, the most visionary of hopes."

What might or might not be possible between Jane Locke and Poe became clearer in early July 1848, when Poe went to Lowell. Then populous and aspiring, the city was famous for its several factories and the Lowell girls who ran them. Dickens when he visited six years earlier, however, found it muddy and frontierlike: the new wooden church, as yet unpainted, lacked a steeple; the rickety walls of a large hotel were so thin and slight, he said, that "I was careful not to draw my breath as we passed." Jane Locke had arranged for Poe to lecture at the local Wentworth's Hall, where he spoke once more on the poets and poetry of America, paying special attention to the work of Fanny Osgood and some other women poets and also reading "The Raven."

If he had not known so before, Poe certainly learned at Wamesit—Locke's Gothic cottage on the Concord River—that she was not a very likely prospect. Forty-three years old, she was married to the attorney John G. Locke, and the mother of five children. The information seems to have come as a shock. Its effect was described by a resident of nearby Westford who understood why Poe had come to Lowell: "she has a husband and three or four children!! [*sic*]" He asked his correspondent to keep the story secret: "Do not ever say in the hearing of a mortal man, and especially *woman,* that Mr. P. ever thought Mrs. L. a widow. 'Twould be so mortifying to him if he supposed any one out of Heaven knew it." Poe's frustrating revelation may explain why, after his lecture, he spent the evening and part of the next day not with the Lockes but at the home of their relatives, the Richmonds, to whom Jane Locke introduced him.

At the Richmonds' substantial stone house, about a mile away from the Lockes' fanciful wood cottage, Poe found another woman to interest him. Mrs. Nancy Richmond was twenty-eight years old, the wife of a well-to-do paper manufacturer and mother of a three-year-old girl (Illus. 23). Tall, handsome, trusting, she busied herself in local charities and affairs of the Unitarian Church, but enjoyed poetry and music; a relative described her house as "full of works of art, pictures, books." Poe liked her light-chestnut-colored hair and gracefulness, and a quality he detected in her of ethereal inner vitality: "So intense an expression of romance, perhaps I should call it," he wrote in a fictionalized account of their meeting, "or of unworldliness, as that which gleamed from her deep-set eyes, had never so sunk into my heart of hearts before." Nancy Richmond was equally taken by his uniqueness. As she recalled her first impression, "He seemed so *unlike* any other person, I had ever known, that I could not think of him in the same way—he was incomparable—not to be measured by any ordinary standard."

Poe spent a sociable evening at the Richmonds' home, lionized by a few persons who came to meet him after his talk, helped to ice cream, entertained by a waltz played on the piano. He may even have spent the night, at the cost of offending Jane Locke. He also held forth, expressing a hope that *Eureka* would "hand down his name to posterity" and provocatively remarking that males ought never to sing, since females alone could make real harmony. Nancy Richmond's brother, Bardwell, recorded the comments Poe also made about his own history (whether to Bardwell alone or to the whole company is unclear). With minor variations Poe told his tale of orphanage, adoption, and disinheritance, often-repeated but to him always poignant and fraught with explanatory power. He also spoke of Virginia: "tears running down his cheek in torrents," Bardwell reported, he described her as "beautiful beyond discription [*sic*]— lovely beyond conception." He explained that when living with Muddy in Baltimore he developed a "great intimacy" with his young cousin. They came to regard each other "as *brother* and *sister.*" Poe may have stressed the point, for Bardwell underscored it: "notice that was the kind of affection—a brotherly and sisterly affection and *nothing more or less.*" But many others thought they should marry, Poe continued, and he at last acquiesced, "yealded to the solicitations of friends and married her at the early age of *thirteen.*"

In describing his detachment from Sissy and reluctance to marry her, Poe of course completely revised the past. Thirteen years before, in the fall of 1835, he had even threatened suicide in imploring Muddy and Virginia to refuse Neilson Poe's offer that they reside with him. "I have no desire to live and *will not,*" he had warned; "I have been dreaming [manuscript torn] every day & night since of . . . the pride I would take in making you both comfor[table] & in calling her my wife." Given Poe's complex sense of loyalty to deceased loved ones, his present version of events perhaps helped ease his guilt in searching for a new wife, at the same time assuring Nancy Richmond that she had no ground for jealousy of his past. But in speaking of Sissy he also recalls several characters in his tales who deny the depth of their attachment, such as Egæus in "Berenice," who claims to have had no feeling at all for his wife-cousin: "During the brightest days of her unparalleled beauty, most surely I had never loved her." To reduce his sense of loss, Poe too now devalued what he had loved.

Even as he explored possible ties to two different women in Lowell, Massachusetts, Poe had begun cultivating a third romantic involvement some seventy miles away, in Providence, Rhode Island.

Unlike Jane Locke and Nancy Richmond, Sarah Helen Whitman was a woman with sophisticated philosophical and literary interests—after her friend Margaret Fuller, perhaps the leading female literary critic in America. Since childhood she had read Shakespeare and attended the theater. A friend to new ideas, she scorned what she called in one poem "the vassal throng, / Slaves to custom, serfs to wrong," and wrote a defense of Shelley's right to unbelief. Schooling herself in German culture, she translated some of Goethe's poetry and took, she said, "a profound plunge into the fathomless waters of the Hegelian philosophy." But the decisive influence on her intellectual life was the Transcendentalism of Emerson. She heard him lecture in Boston and Providence, published an article on him "By a Disciple," got to know other members of the New England group, and became in effect a Transcendentalist herself, with an Emersonian belief in the Unity of Being. She also studied mesmerism and magnetic science, of which Providence was a center. Convinced that an Other World existed, she went beyond both Emerson and Mesmer in the pursuit of occult knowledge.

Helen, as she preferred to call herself, had been aware of Poe for several years. The reading of one of his stories overpowered her, she wrote later, gave her "a sensation of such intense horror that I dared neither look at anything he had written nor even utter his name." Horror gave way to fascination, and she soon "devoured with half-reluctant and fearful avidity every line that fell from his pen." At the height of Poe's celebrity in New York as author of "The Raven," she had learned much about him through friends in the city: Fanny Osgood had described to Helen her first meeting with Poe, the salon leader Anne Lynch had told her about the "electrifying" effect of his recitation. Curious to know more, Helen had written to Lynch asking whether Poe's "Mesmeric Revelation" were based on fact, requesting a copy of his review of Elizabeth Barrett ("discriminating," she thought it, "but rather hypercritical"). From her New York friends she later received accounts of Virginia's last days and of Poe's own illness and poverty at Fordham.

Through Anne Lynch, Helen had also made her first contact with Poe. In January 1848, Lynch had solicited some verses from her, to be read at the Valentine's Day party she planned at a conversazione, addressed to guests who would be attending. Helen and her sister complied, sending several valentine poems for the occasion. Believing that Poe would be among the guests, she included one "To Edgar A. Poe." After the party, however, she learned from Lynch that Poe had deliberately not been invited, as several guests would have found his presence offensive. But the brilliant soiree made news; a few weeks later, Willis's *Home Journal* published forty-two short poems that had been read during the evening, furnished at the editors' request by Anne Lynch. Helen's poem to Poe was not among them.

Helen evidently wanted Poe to know she had saluted him, without too boldly sending him a copy of the poem herself. She asked Lynch to try to get the poem printed, but Lynch discouraged her. "I really do not think it would be any advantage to you to publish the Valentine to Poe," she said, "not because it is not beautiful in itself but their [*sic*] is a deeply rooted prejudice against him." Lynch added, however, that if Helen still wished the poem to appear, she would ask someone to "have it done." Apparently Helen persisted, for a week later her "To Edgar A. Poe" also appeared in the *Home Journal*. That Helen had meant to make herself known to Poe was evident to Fanny Osgood. "I see by the Home Journal," Fanny wrote to her, "that your beautiful invocation has reached the Raven in his eyrie and I suppose, ere this, he has *swooped* upon your little *dove cote* in Providence." For all her playfulness, Osgood in fact still felt affectionate toward Poe, and the possibility of a liaison between him and a close friend of hers aroused some jealousy. Although playfully too, she added a caution: "May Providence protect you . . . for his croak [is] the most eloquent imaginable. He is in truth 'A glorious devil, with large heart & brain.' "

As it happened, Poe had seen Helen's poem before its publication. Anne Lynch, apparently, had sent him an anonymous manuscript copy. In whichever version, the valentine poem was probably his first indication that Helen knew of his existence. The news was gratifying, for he had long been aware of her, and through the same channels. Anne Lynch had spoken to him about Helen, "not very kindly," he said later, alluding to what she called Helen's " 'eccentricities' " and hinting at her "sorrows." She apparently did not mention that Helen was a widow, for Poe believed her happily married, an impression, he afterward thought, that Lynch might have created purposely. More than that, before seeing Helen's valentine he had once seen Helen, or so he later told her. During his overnight trip to Providence in July 1845, Fanny Osgood had described Helen and invited him to accompany her to Helen's house. Believing Helen to be married, his story went, he refused. Because of the sultry heat, he spent the evening wandering the hills overlooking the city. Late at night, he passed Helen's house. He recognized it from Fanny's description, which also enabled him to identify the woman he saw walking down a lime-shaded walk in the neighborhood—a Pym-like apparition dressed in white, with a thin white shawl or scarf thrown over her head.

Whatever interest Poe took in Helen before receiving her valentine, can only have been quickened by the poem itself. Beginning with the first stanza, where the Raven's shadow appears in her moonlit bedroom, Helen unbared her fascination with his writing and the personality revealed in it:

> Oh, thou grim and ancient Raven,
>   From the Night's Plutonian shore,
> Oft, in dreams, thy ghastly pinions
>   Wave and flutter round my door—
> Oft thy shadow dims the moonlight
>   Sleeping on my chamber floor!

The poem's slightly kidding tone, appropriate to a social valentine, does not diminish its similarly appropriate note of romance, its seductive air of refined eroticism. In the other nine stanzas, Helen told Poe that she heard the raven's "sullen storm-cry" come to her in "the lonely midnight hour," that its "dark wing," swooping down to "swans and dovelets," was to her a sight "nobler" than Romeo. Could the Raven be true to her, she could promise in return a love lofty and exclusive: "Not a bird that roams the forest / Shall our lofty eyrie share!"

Poe answered immediately. From a copy of his 1845 *The Raven and other Poems,* he cut out "To Helen," the now-famous poem he had first published in 1831, inspired by Jane Stanard. He pasted the clipping on a sheet of stationery, which he folded into the form of an envelope, addressed, and sent to Helen. The envelope contained no enclosure; opened out, it disclosed the pasted-on poem. In not transcribing the poem, he hoped to leave some doubt in Helen's mind as to who sent it and why. He clearly expected her to identify the sender, however, for her failure over the next three months to respond distressed him. Very likely she felt cautious; she did know the poem had come from Poe, a New Yorker then in Providence having identified for her the handwriting on the envelope.

Poe's need to find a helpmate left him little patience for waiting. In May, even while trying to tease out the intentions of Jane Locke in Lowell, he sent to Helen in Providence the manuscript of a poem entitled "To Helen." This was not his earlier fifteen lines for Jane Stanard but a new poem more than four times as long. It described his nighttime glimpse of Helen in her white dress, and recounted the events in a dream he had shortly after. Beginning "I saw thee once—once only—years ago," it left no doubt about the intensity of his feelings:

> . . . *the hated world all slept,*
> *Save only thee and me. (Oh, Heaven!—oh, God!*
> *How my heart beats in coupling those two words!)*

Poe presented himself to Helen as haunted, since that initial vision, by her eyes:

> *They follow me—They lead me through the years.*
> *They are my ministers—yet I their slave.*
> *Their office is to illumine and enkindle—*
> *My duty, to be saved by their bright light.* . . .

'Haunted' is no exaggeration, for in the morbid dream recorded by the poem, the moon, paths, rose garden, and trees die away one by one, leaving Helen's eyes the only living things:

> . . . *the very roses' odors*
> *Died in the arms of the adoring airs.*
> *All—all expired save thee—save less than thou:*
> *Save only the divine light in thine eyes—*

Poe makes it sound as if the salvation he sought from his so-far imagined Helen was to be achieved not in life but in death, as though in gaining her his deeper longing was to reach the Other World. For the Helen with whom he wishes to merge exists beyond the grave, a shrouded figure "all in white," indeed returned from Deathland, "a ghost, amid the entombing trees."

Whether for here, hereafter, or both, Helen by now seriously tempted Poe. In mid-June, probably amid preparations for his lecture in Lowell, he wrote to an ailing English poet named Anna Blackwell, who had visited with him and Muddy. Blackwell had recently been to Providence to receive magnetic therapy, and Poe prodded her for information about Helen: "Can you not tell me something about her—anything—every thing you know—and . . . let no one know that I have asked you to do so?" His interest was no secret to Helen, however: although he sent the poem anonymously, she again identified it as his, this time simply by comparing the handwriting with that on the letter-envelope enclosing his earlier "To Helen."

So Poe returned to Fordham from Lowell, in mid-July, with three possible romances afoot. Only about a week later he visited Richmond and started a fourth.

Poe had planned the trip for a while, hoping to find subscribers for the "Stylus." Probably around this time, he began entering in a notebook the names of possible patrons, listing some 250 persons from as far south as Georgia and Tennessee. Borrowing money to get to Richmond—financial straits were again "pressing me to death"—he seems to have stayed there a month or longer. He apparently visited with Rosalie at the Mackenzies, and may have lodged with the family. She presumably no longer worked as a teacher of penmanship, for their school had ceased operation. Becoming acquainted with the current editor of the *Southern Literary Messenger,* John R. Thompson, he proposed doing some writing for the magazine, and sold it his essay "The Rationale of Verse" (see pages 394–95). He probably made little progress in winning subscribers, however, since according to Thompson he stayed drunk for two or three weeks, losing his coat among the wharves of the disreputable shipping district, "and discoursing 'Eureka' every night to the audiences of the Bar Rooms." Thompson perhaps exaggerated Poe's condition, but he did not imagine it. Others also recorded Poe's alcoholic declamations from *Eureka,* large portions of which he evidently knew by heart. A commercial clerk remembered seeing him in a Richmond tavern, late at night: "his talk ran wild concerning a new work which he had just finished, and which he declared would explain the mystery of the beginning and ending of all earthly things." Poe even came near fighting a duel. He arrived at the *Messenger* office one day "in a great state of excitement," asking Thompson to bear a challenge to John M. Daniel, young editor of the Richmond *Semi-Weekly Examiner.* The circumstances are obscure, but seemingly involved a slur about Poe that appeared in Daniel's newspaper. After Thompson refused to transmit the challenge, Poe went to confront Daniel face-to-face. They must have settled the point of honor, for the duel never happened. But the affair left on Daniel too the impression that during his Richmond visit Poe was overwrought, in "a state approaching mania."

Late in July, Poe called on Elmira Royster. When about fifteen years old, to recall, she had "engaged myself" to Poe. But Elmira's father disapproved the match and intercepted Poe's letters to her from the university, breaking the engagement. Poe had retold his bitter story in the narrative he coauthored with his brother, Henry, recasting Elmira as the fiancée of "Edgar Leonard," who on coming to her house learns that she is to be married in half an hour, and stabs her to death. The woman Poe called on in Richmond, however, was now a well-to-do widow known as Mrs. Shelton. Although amazed by his turning up she knew him instantly. And Poe, as she remembered the moment, seemed buoyed at finding her: "He came up to me in the most enthusiastic manner and said: 'Oh! Elmira, is this you?'" Poe's first shock of pleasure came rather from reencountering Elmira Royster than meeting Elmira Shelton, for he reportedly soon found that years of separation had changed her tastes and idiosyncrasies, and his own too. Just the same, he felt kindly received by Elmira, and considered proposing marriage to her.

Poe came close to doing so, except that his search for a wife had kept three women in the North thinking about him. During his absence Muddy had received a call at Fordham from Nancy Richmond, as well as a poem for Poe from Jane Ermina Locke. No more is known of Mrs. Richmond's visit than that Muddy, perhaps sensing an interest in Poe, described Virginia to her as "almost an angel on earth." But Mrs. Locke, although a middle-aged mother of five, had found Poe's presence in Lowell enflaming, and relived it in a thirty-one stanza poem entitled "Ermina's Tale." With the poem she sent a love-struck covering letter directing him to *"acknowledge the receipt of this immediately."* After months of intentions half-revealed and inquiries half-hidden, she all at once disburdened her feelings in a swooning reprise of their meeting, heated by the language of religious ecstasy:

> *I felt as in the presence of a god!*
> *My heart awe-struck, sent up a censer flame*
> *With fingers clasped. . . .*

In Mrs. Locke's consuming vision Poe sulphurously glows as her *"soul's ideal,"* forlorn strains issuing from his harpstrings of fire, a serpent wreathing his brow, his dark eyes flashing like Jove's. Anything beyond a mere acknowledgment of her poem, Mrs. Locke said, she left to Poe's feelings: *"mine* are written out, and you cannot mistake them."

What stalled Poe's marriage proposal to Elmira Royster, however, was a communication from Sarah Helen Whitman in Providence. She had put off responding to his second poem "To Helen," but several friends confirmed the seriousness of his interest in her, Rufus Griswold among them. She had known Griswold several years,

and seen his Charleston-born wife, from whom he now lived apart—
"the little Jewess," Helen pronounced her. He visited Helen around
mid-July, looking not more than thirty, she remembered, and "very
handsome," although in fact his health at about this time had taken
a bad turn: rarely leaving his rooms at New York University, he
suffered attacks of vertigo, sometimes crying, exhausted, scarcely
caring to live, taking opium for energy to write. He told Helen that
Poe had highly praised her work in his lecture at Lowell, and generously defended Poe's character. When Helen asked why so many
of the New York literati disliked Poe, he said Poe had done nothing "exceptionably wrong" and was less blameable than his enemies
for his literary embroilments. Soon after Griswold's visit Helen received other flattering and reassuring news of Poe. Some came from
the English poet Anna Blackwell, to whom Poe had written for
"everything you know" about Helen. He had asked Blackwell to
keep his request confidential, but she told Helen about it. With
Blackwell was Maria Jane McIntosh, a popular Georgia-born novelist who had recently met Poe at the house of one of his Fordham
neighbors. She told Helen that Poe's "whole talk" had been about
her.

Emboldened, Helen wrote two six-line stanzas of verse for Poe,
without title or signature, which she sent to Fordham. From there,
Muddy forwarded the poem to Richmond, where Poe could judge
the impression he had made on her:

> A low bewildering melody
> Is murmuring in my ear—
> Tones such as in the twilight wood
> The aspen thrills to hear
> When Faunus slumbers on the hill
> And all the entranced boughs are still.

Helen later said that she wrote the lines only as a "playful acknowledgment" of Poe's second "To Helen." But with their hint that his
poem had brought her a deliciously confusing, delicate sensual delight, the lines clearly enough also beckoned. To make certain he
would identify the writer, she quoted in the second stanza the phrase
"Beauty which is Hope," lifted from his poem to her.

Poe took Helen's meaning as she probably intended it. Although
on the verge of proposing to Mrs. Shelton, and planning to extend
his magazine expedition farther south, he immediately left Rich-

mond and returned to New York. He now intended to meet Helen
in the flesh. To make certain she was in Providence and not traveling somewhere outside it, he first sent a request for her autograph—posing as "Edward S. T. Grey," a collector of the autographs of distinguished American writers. Helen apparently answered,
for in mid-September Poe obtained a letter of introduction from
his acquaintance and her friend, Maria Jane McIntosh. McIntosh
enjoyed the matchmaking. She wrote in the note—meant for Poe
to hand Helen in person—"I feel much obliged to Mr Poe for per-
mitting me thus to associate myself with an incident so agreeable to
both of you, as I feel persuaded your first meeting will prove."

Benefit Street

SEPTEMBER 21–24, 1848

Poe arrived at Helen's house on the twenty-first of September. 76
Benefit typified the ambiance of Providence, a pleasant town of neatly
painted white houses set on quiet streets interspersed with elms,
built on steep hills overlooking Providence Bay. Helen's home stood
on a hilly corner, a two-story frame building higher by a one-story
basement in the rear due to the slope. Wooden shutters, a substantial attic under the peaked roof, and a pedimented doorway facing
the tree-shaded street contributed to a look of unostentatious but
ample comfort.

In person, Helen first struck Poe by her physical and spiritual
delicacy. She entered the room, he said, "pale, timid, hesitating,
and evidently oppressed at heart." She looked at him squarely, "ap-
pealingly," he thought, but only for "one brief moment." Her hand
resting in his in greeting, she spoke "falteringly," seeming scarce
conscious of what she said. Something of this fluttering, wary sensitivity appears in the portrait of Helen that hung in Benefit Street,
painted about ten years before Poe's visit (Illus. 24, 25). The pale
face is rather long and narrow but wide-jawed, framed in a narrow-
ing cascade of carefully coifed brown curls, bunched at the fore-

head, that partly conceal the deep-set blue eyes. The wide lips repeat the handsome but dainty effect, fleshy but tapering to pencil-line thinness. The expression seems serious, vulnerable.

Like himself, in fact, the woman Poe had come running to was inwardly disquieted. She had been born on January 19, the same date as Poe. And like him too, she gave the year variously, in her case because the obscured date in her family Bible, she claimed, left her uncertain whether it was 1800, 1803, or 1808. At different times she believed herself to be a few or at least ten years older than Poe. In actuality, born in 1803, at the time of their meeting she was forty-five years old, his senior by six years.

Whatever her birth date, Helen regarded it with grim irony. It was a time when "oblique Saturn," she said, "sat in the house of Agonies." When she was ten, her roguish, handsome father, Nicholas Power, failed in business and left Providence to look after some property in the South. When she was thirty, he suddenly reappeared after a nineteen years' absence, to the family's astonishment. As her sister Anna put it in some doggerel:

> Nicholas Power left home in a sailing vessel for St. Kitts,
> When he returned, he frightened his family out of their wits.

Miraculously come back to Providence, Power boarded at the hotel and spent his time, Helen added, "taken up with actresses." Something of the rage she felt toward this man—whom she had adored—can be glimpsed in the name that, at the age of eleven, she gave to her doll: Gulnare, the harem slave in Byron's *Corsair* who kills the Turkish pasha with a dagger, in his sleep. Her feelings perhaps also expressed themselves in the heart ailment she believed afflicted her, reflected in Poe's observation that upon their meeting she seemed "oppressed at heart." Beset with notions that she might soon die, she eased her attacks with ether, recommended at the time for angina pectoris. Its odor was said to waft about her.

Nicholas Power played his part in Helen's poetic imagination too. By accident or design, her poems again and again drift to the word *power*. Invariably, too, the proper and the abstract nouns seem fused, as if declaring at once longing for her father and for his boldness and strength. (She later pasted a coronet over the bonnet she wore in a photograph, crowning herself, she said, after the examples of King Charles of Sweden and Napoleon Bonaparte.) To cite three of many instances:

I dared not listen to thy words, nor turn
　To meet the mystic language of thine eyes,
I only felt their power. . . . ("The Last Flowers")

. . . in that gorgeous world, I fondly deem,
Dwells the freed soul of one whose earthly dream
Was full of beauty, majesty and wo;
One who, in that pure realm of thine, doth grow
Into a power serene. . . . ("Arcturus")

Vainly my heart had with thy sorceries striven
It had no refuge from thy love—no heaven
But in thy fatal presence;—from afar
It owned thy power. . . . ("To—")

All the above quotations, moreover, come from poems Helen later addressed to Poe, on whom her longing evidently sought to stamp the incongruous lineaments of her father. While Poe hoped to find at 76 Benefit Street a replacement for his own vanished protectors, Helen looked to him to restore her lost "Power" and his "power."

The House of Agonies had presided over Helen's marriage also. At the age of twenty-five she married a zestful young lawyer named John Winslow Whitman, a graduate of Brown University. He fell ill the next year, then became ill often, and left her a widow at the age of thirty. During their marriage he was also arrested for what Helen called "an endorsement"—perhaps guaranteeing, then failing, to cover someone else's debt—and confined a while in a Boston jail. She considered his death "a relief," she said; throughout the five-year marriage she had lived "in a great state of anxiety."

The years since Helen's marriage had brought several suitors. But she refused them, either because her mother objected, she explained, or because of her sister Anna's condition. Helen's mother, with whom she lived in Benefit Street, was an intrusive, grasping woman who controlled her financially and morally. Anna, Helen's younger sister, had been born around the time Nicholas Power left his family, and perhaps suffered the long-range effects of his desertion. She lived on an emotional edge, finding all constraint unbearable, "warped through & through by a naturally haughty and dominant temper," as Helen described her. At some time she was hospitalized for "acute mania." Helen felt obliged to care for Anna, indeed saw herself as a guardian of her sister's sanity.

No doubt the two women did stand in the way of Helen's remarriage. But she had also grown wary of entrusting real affection to men, as is suggested by the nature of the men on whom she bestowed its semblance. One of her suitors at the time Poe arrived was a Rhode Island lawyer—vigorous, but in his early sixties and the father of twelve children. She also favored younger men, with whom she formed attachments of flirtatious discipleship, such as the young Transcendentalist George William Curtis. In the "happiest marriages," she wrote, "the woman was the senior." The statement might seem to qualify Poe, but it also disqualified him by erecting unconventional standards that Helen could not risk in actuality. In a quite sensuous poem about Michelangelo's statue of David, she celebrated the figure as both a paternal "prophet, king" and a childlike "slight stripling." Compact of her wishes and fears, the ambivalent figure of the "bold and gentle boy" promises both sensual gratification and the prevention of it.

Poe remained in Providence from Thursday, September 21 until Sunday, September 24. He recalled Helen moving restlessly around the room during the evenings they spent together, now sitting by his side, now far away, her hand sometimes resting on the back of his chair. He met her mother and sister, and during one of the evenings Helen gathered a party of her Providence friends to meet him. They talked much. Among other personal matters, Poe revealed the history of his awareness of her, beginning with a few words about her spoken "not very kindly" by Anne Lynch, and including his nighttime sight of her in Providence while visiting Fanny Osgood. He reminisced about his early years, describing Fanny Allan with "the tenderest affection," Helen recalled, and John Allan as sometimes lavish in giving him money, at other times penurious, withal a man of "gross & brutal temperament." He told her he had seen little of Rose; they were "of very opposite temperaments." It may have been on this first visit that he also spoke to Helen of Virginia, again in a disparaging way that minimized the convulsive importance to him of her death. As Helen recounted his comments, he regarded Virginia as a sister and a child who "could not enrich his life," with whom he could experience "little reciprocity of thought," whom he had married solely for her own happiness. He no sooner said as much, Helen added, than he condemned himself for the admission.

Much of their conversation apparently turned to literature. Helen's love of beauty, what Poe afterward called her "poet-nature," made an essential part of her appeal to him. Now or later she kept among the pressed flowers in her scrapbook a pansy from the grave of Keats and a bit of "Heart's Ease" from the tomb of Shelley. Hoping that his own works might help to argue his desirability, Poe brought Helen gift copies of his *Tales* and of *The Raven and Other Poems,* bound in a single cloth volume with the inscription "To Mrs Sarah Helen Whitman—from the most devoted of her friends. Edgar A Poe." He also gave her a bound set of the *Broadway Journal,* and in her presence paged through it initialing as his own the more important of his unsigned contributions and making some marginal comments.

Some luck helped out Poe's literary wooing. As they sat one morning in an alcove within the Atheneum Library, she asked whether he knew "Ulalume," whose "weird imagery" captivated her. The poem had appeared anonymously in the *American Review,* and she had failed to identify the author although she questioned "everybody likely to have heard of it." Poe not only revealed the author to have been himself—to "my infinite surprise," she said— but also took a volume of the *Review* from the alcove and added his signature to the poem. He may have also read it to her during his visit, for she later remarked that he seemed to prefer it to "The Raven" and recited it more impressively, "with a look as if he were filled with its solemn splendor."

However much the literary talk excited feelings of kinship, it also exposed a possible source of strain. A New Englander by birth and temperament, active in female literary circles, Helen counted among her closest friends many people Poe detested, including Elizabeth Ellet, Margaret Fuller and the other New England Transcendentalists, and the Boston circle around Longfellow. The fact must have been known to him before, but now became oppressive. At some moment he said to her—with a deep sigh, she recalled—"My heart is heavy, Helen, for I see that *your* friends are not my own." The remark was truer than he knew. Anna Blackwell was in Providence during his visit, and warning Helen away from him as from someone "incapable of taking care of himself," a sizing-up unfeeling but correct.

Conflicts and kinship both came into dramatic relief during an excursion. Probably on the second day of his visit, Poe and Helen walked the four or five miles from her house, through fields and woods, to the Swan Point Cemetery. Cemeteries were popular resorts for romantic couples in the period, although for Poe more than for most the resort also of his imagination of the past. At Swan

Point he spoke of Jane Stanard, who in the wake of Sissy's death often came to his mind as a woman who had been "very kind" to him, exemplifying in his orphanhood what motherly affection might be like. Like most of the women since Eliza Poe who had figured importantly in his life, now including Helen, Jane Stanard had been ill, overborne by what she described as a "death-like sickness." ("I could not love," he had written, "except where Death / Was mingling his with Beauty's breath.") Poe recalled for Helen how Mrs. Stanard had taken his hand, when they first met, welcoming him so kindly and gently as to leave him speechless. When she died suddenly a few weeks later he felt "overwhelmed with sorrow," as Helen recorded what he said: "he could not endure to think of her lying there forsaken & forgotten." Every night he visited the cemetery where she was buried.

As they sat together, Helen showed Poe a poem she had written concerning some early loss of her own, containing the lines "I think on thee and on thy lone grave / On the green hillside far away." Whether she presented it before or after Poe told her of Jane Stanard is unknown. According to her, the poem had been accepted by a magazine, whose editor had asked her to alter one line, and she showed it to Poe only for his opinion of the editor's criticism, which he called valueless. Whatever the timing and Helen's reasons, the poem annoyed Poe. He wondered whether in showing it to him she had had some "very especial" purpose.

As they stood by an unmarked grave, Helen's poem "yet ringing in my ears," Poe said, he declared his love. As he reported his own words they were: "Helen, I love now—now—for the first and only time." The avowal took up from his admission that he had married Virginia for her happiness alone, and a sense of betrayal, or perhaps simply of loss and waste, or more simply still of crying need, may have shaken him, for as he spoke, he said, "bitter, bitter tears sprang into my eyes." He may have kissed Helen, for he also said that at one moment during the cemetery visit his arm "tremblingly encircled" her waist.

Having known Helen only a day or two, Poe now proposed marriage. He stressed that she would inspire his literary gifts to larger achievement, of which he had as yet given no sign, and would end the miserable confusion that had overtaken him. His suddenness and zeal may have flustered Helen, for she felt that she "dared not respond." That marriage to her would energize his literary ambitions and resuscitate his spirits seemed less certain to her than to him. "I knew too well that I could not hope to exercise over him the power"—as she said—"which he ascribed to me." She felt, also, not really free to do what she wished, but instead "wholly dependent on my mother, & her life was bound up in mine." She told him she could not, at present, say she loved him or accept his proposal. She needed time to decide.

Although the outing to Swan Point Cemetery left Poe still far from the altar, Helen was developing a deep feeling of affinity with him. If a poem she later wrote about their trip accurately recounts her feelings at the time, even while putting him off she inwardly consented, "My heart according to thy murmured prayer / The full, sweet answers that my lips denied thee." Her fascination in first reading Poe's works had prepared her to perceive him Ideally, in terms of her beliefs in Transcendentalism, occult science, Universal Redeeming Love, spiritual counterparts. And his physical presence at Benefit Street confirmed and swelled her sense of mystical kinship with him. She recalled a conversation between them, on this visit or a later one, in which Poe commented that they markedly resembled each other in some tastes and habits of thought that otherwise seemed idiosyncratic. She agreed, and added that they might even have descended from distant branches of the same family. The name Power and the name Poe, she told him, were variants of an original name, Poer. Poe looked up with surprise and pleasure, and revealed that some members of General David Poe's family spelled their name that way; some of his grandfather's papers, he said, referred to a certain Chevalier Le Poer, a relative. Helen traced her own father's family to a Sir Roger Le Poer, Norman chaplain of Henry the First, a " 'high & mighty Baron,' " as she characterized him, "founder of a race connected with some of the most romantic and chivalrous incidents of Irish history." Helen believed that in Sir Roger Le Poer, she and Poe had a single root.

Actually the two families were entirely unrelated. Like Poe's illustrious representations of General Poe, Helen's claimed descent from a "Mighty Baron" seems the attempt of a deserted child to dignify her past, while her view of Poe as a lost "Poer" illustrates again her picture of him as the living likeness of romantic Nicholas Power. Convinced of her hereditary oneness with Poe, she wrote some doggerel noting that the family tree made him "Another cousin or 'twin star'; / (We drop the W, he the R)." She discovered in her name, written Sarah Helen Poer, the anagram "Ah, Seraph Lenore." She later ascertained that the features and expression of

George Poe, brother of the general, resembled those of Nicholas Power "as closely as if he had been his twin brother." She even masqueraded as Poe. Dressing for a tableau in the costume of an Albanian chief as described by Byron, she applied burnt cork to her face to create Poe-like eyebrows and mustache.

In his similar craving for some interpenetrating union, Poe did nothing to discourage Helen's fantasies about him. On the contrary, he fostered his own version of their mystical twinship, featuring his surrogate mother Jane Stanard as Nicholas Power. He opened one of his presentation volumes of the *Broadway Journal* at "Morella," the tale of a mother reborn in her daughter. Beside it he wrote, for Helen's enlightenment: "Robert Stannard Helen Stannard Helen Whitman—Helen Ellen Elenore Lenore!" The genealogy made Helen the present incarnation of the loved and lost figure of his youth who had inspired his later poetry and fiction. Helen also recalled that during a later visit to Providence, Poe sat dreamily musing by the fireside. Her portrait hung in a dim corner of the room. When she entered, he told her he had been uncertain whether he woke or slept, and in his drowsy state the face in her portrait seemed to him the face of Robert Stanard, his boyhood friend, Jane's son. "And then," Poe went on, the impression changed: "it seemed to be *herself* that looked at me from that dark corner." Helen Whitman's face became not the face of Robert but of Jane Stanard, of the first Helen.

Poe's first meeting with Helen ended on Sunday, September 24. As the steamboat for New York did not operate on Sundays, he had to stay the night in Providence, and most of the next day, when he revisited the Swan Point Cemetery. His failure to win from Helen a declaration of love, much less an agreement to marry, discouraged him. But in saying good-bye she promised to write to him and explain many things she had been unable to say in their conversations.

An Exchange of Letters;
Return to Lowell.

OCTOBER 1 – CA. NOVEMBER 4, 1848

Poe returned to Fordham churning with hopes of marrying Helen, and only three or four days later received a letter from her. Like her other five or six letters to him, it is known only through his references to it in reply. But these reveal that, disappointingly, she still failed to acknowledge love for him, and moreover said that despite her farewell promise, she could not explain all that had gone unspoken during their meeting. She also brought up possible obstacles to their marriage. Although his intellect and genius made her feel a child in his presence, she was "many years older than yourself." A heart condition threatened to cut short her life and, she implied, made the sexual demands of marriage intolerable: "were I to allow myself to love you, I could only enjoy a bright, brief hour of rapture and die."

To overcome Helen's resistance, Poe felt he must somehow make his ardor tangible to her. A treasure within reach, could he make her experience the force of his own emotion, she would surely love him in return. In replying to her letter he recalled his statement at the cemetery that he loved now for the first time. Obviously his saying so had failed to convey what he felt. He could make it mean what it meant, he said, only if "throughout some long, dark summer night, I could but have held you close, close to my heart and whispered to you the strange secrets of its passionate history." To give his feelings a palpable weight and potency, he enclosed twelve closely written pages—the longest letter he had ever written, he assured her. It made a rapturous monologue of dashes, underlinings, questions, exclamations, groaned out with prayerful, heart-throbbing fervency, a confession of pressing her letter again and again to his lips, "bathing it in tears of joy," of wishing to kneel before her, fall at her feet in worship ("at your feet—at your feet, Helen"), of shivering ecstasy enveloped in scintillant vitalness, an "electric light, illumining and enkindling my whole nature—filling my soul with glory, with wonder, and with awe."

Particularly Poe impressed on Helen that their profound mutual sympathy was fated. Going over the entire early history of their relation, he recast it as a tale of psychic magnetism. He had fallen in love with her not in Providence, but from the moment, years before, when Anne Lynch first described her to him, and an extra-sensory transaction bestirred his soul: "your unknown heart seemed to pass into my bosom—there to dwell forever—while mine, I thought, was translated into your own. From that hour I loved you." Thereafter, inexplicable workings had brought to pass one after another pregnant coincidence. While enraptured by the thought of her, he unexpectedly received her valentine poem, with "unbelieving joy"; when desperate to know how to answer it, his eyes "fell upon a volume of my own poems"; while "accidentally" paging through the book, he found his earlier "To Helen" "*happening* to be the last," blank on one side, miraculously ready to be cut out and pasted. When Helen sent her poem in reply, it too engaged the wheels of destiny: "you happened to address your lines to Fordham in place of New-York—by which my aunt *happened* to get notice of their being in the West-Farms Post Office." And her lines reached him in Richmond, he pointed out, "*on the very day* in which I was about to depart on a tour and an enterprize which would have . . . borne me 'far, far away' and forever, from *you,* sweet, sweet Helen, and from this divine dream of your Love."

In his twelve pages Poe also gave Helen in retrospect his passionate impression of her in Providence. Here, too, what he said exposed the management of their affairs by spiritual influences. From his first glimpse of her, he recognized, come to life, the vision on which his imagination had forever doted:

> I saw that you were *Helen—my* Helen—the Helen of a thousand dreams—she whose visionary lips had so often lingered upon my own in the divine trance of passion—she whom the great Giver of all Good had prëordained to be mine—mine only. . . . I heard no words—only the soft voice, more familiar to me than my own, and more melodious than the songs of the angels. Your hand rested within mine, and my whole soul shook with a tremulous ecstasy. . . . And when, afterwards, on those two successive evenings of all-Heavenly delight, you passed to and fro about the room—now sitting by my side, now far away, now standing with your hand resting on the back of my chair, while the praeternatural thrill of your touch vibrated even through the senseless wood into my heart—while you moved thus restlessly about the room—as if a deep sorrow or a more profound Joy haunted your bosom—my

brain reeled beneath the intoxicating spell of your presence, and it was with no merely human senses that I either saw or heard you. It was my soul only that distinguished you there.

It was his belief, Poe said, "that my Destiny, for good or for evil, either here or hereafter, is in some measure interwoven with your own."

Poe tried also to counter Helen's objections to their marrying. He vigorously denied that she lacked, as she had protested, "youth and health and beauty." He had heard the "more than melody" of her voice, seen the "magic" of her smile. In reality his tribulations and disappointments made him older than she, he said. And illness and sorrow had made her seem older than she was, which argued only the duty of loving her the more: "Cannot my patient cares— my watchful, earnest attention—cannot the magic which lies in such devotion as I feel for you, win back for you much—oh, very much of the freshness of your youth?" Besides, his love for her looked past and beyond the body, ill or not, being the love of his soul for her soul: "do you not perceive that it is my diviner nature—my spiritual being—which burns and pants to commingle with your own?" He realized now that in proposing marriage he had, to her mind, been endangering her life. Speaking circumspectly, but clearly in reference to lovemaking, he promised that if she consented to marry him, he would ask nothing of her sexually: "I would cast from me, forever, all merely human desire, and clothe myself in the glory of a pure, calm, and *unexacting* affection."

Altogether, Helen's objections seemed "so groundless," Poe said, as to make him wonder whether they masked other objections, "more real, and which you hesitate—perhaps in pity—to confide to me." He did not expand on the matter, but obviously had in mind his personal reputation and financial circumstances, for he alluded to his "late errors and reckless excesses" and observed that she must take some of the initiative herself, as he felt that his poverty deprived him of the right to urge his love upon her: "were I wealthy, or could I offer you worldly honors—ah then—then—how proud would I be to persevere—to sue—to plead—to kneel—to pray—to beseech you for your love." Although his passion certainly fixed on the ethereal and preternaturally sensitive person he conceived Helen to be, the material well-being at 76 Benefit Street no doubt appealed to him. Asking Helen to write soon, but not so much as to weary or agitate herself, he begged her for what alone could satisfy him: "Say to me those coveted words which would turn Earth into Heaven."

Poe waited anxiously for Helen's answer, cursing the "inexorable *distance*" between them. Her letter, when it arrived, offered the solace that his own had in some measure overcome their physical separation and succeeded in transporting his presence to Providence. She said that in pressing it between her hands "there passed into [my] spirit a sense of the *Love* that glowed within those pages." But otherwise what Helen sent left Poe, he said, in "passionate agony." She had taken eight days to reply to his twelve-page rhapsody of exalted love—and still made no profession of her own, much less accepted his marriage offer. The meaning of her delay and of her silence was wrackingly clear: " *'You do not love me'*:—in this brief sentence lies all I can conceive of despair. . . . You do not love me; or you could not have imposed upon me the torture of eight days' silence—of eight days' terrible suspense. You do not love me—or, responding to my prayers, you would have cried to me—*'Edgar, I do'*."

Jolted by what Helen had taken so long not to say, Poe found what she did say crushing. Her letter included the complaint that she had heard disturbing criticisms of his character:

> But ah,—again, and most especially,—you do *not* love me, or you would have felt too thorough a sympathy with the sensitiveness of my nature, to have so wounded me as you have done with this terrible passage of your letter:—"How often I have heard men and even women say of you—'He has great intellectual power, but *no* principle—*no* moral sense'."

Helen's complaint contained a power of disenchantment, fracturing Poe's vision of her as the replica of himself in sensitivity and tenderheartedness, his spiritual twin: "That our souls are one, every line which you have ever written asserts—but our hearts do *not* beat in unison." And for her to entertain the idea that he had *"no* principle—*no* moral sense"! His career rested entirely on principle, a superior moral sense, the exposure of fraudulence and imbecility. He felt duped, self-deluded: "Is it possible that such expressions as these could have been *repeated* to me—to me—by one whom I loved—ah, whom I *love*—by one at whose feet I knelt—I *still* kneel—in deeper worship than ever man offered to God?"

However offended, Poe tried to convince Helen that the gossip about him amounted to envying drivel, producing a letter barely shorter than his first one, and no less fiery. Without mentioning his drinking he admitted moral lapses, "occasional follies and excesses which I bitterly lament, but to which I have been driven by intolerable sorrow." But otherwise, he said, he had erred only on the side of overmuch chivalry. It was from a sense of honor that "in early youth, I deliberately threw away from me a large fortune, rather than endure a trivial wrong." It was a too-exacting sense of self-sacrifice that had tied him to Virginia: "I did violence to my own heart, and married, for another's happiness, where I knew that no possibility of my own existed." He expressed surprise that Helen could ask *"why* men so *mis*judge me—*why* I have enemies." They resented and opposed him because he had chosen to remain poor, so that as a critic he could preserve his independence, freely express his outrage, and be scrupulously honest ("unscrupulously honest," he wrote, in a most revealing slip). Pointing out that he had a hundred friends for every enemy, he picked at a sore point touched on during his visit: "has it never occurred to you that you do not live *among* my friends? Miss Lynch, Miss Fuller, Miss Blackwell, Mrs Ellet—neither these nor any within their influence, are my friends. Had you read my criticisms generally, you would see, too, how and why it is that the Channings—the Emerson and Hudson coterie—the Longfellow clique, one and all—the cabal of the 'N. American Review'—you would see why all these, whom *you* know best, know *me* least and are my enemies."

Feeling threatened and angry, Poe replied in kind to Helen's account of what she had heard about him. "I have lately heard that of you," he said, "which . . . puts it forever out of my power to ask you—*again* to ask you—to become my wife." An "informant" had revealed to him a fact about Helen that he *"dreaded":* she owned some property and had some money. Having often seen affection bartered, he explained, he had resolved never to wed where financial "interest" could be suspected as his object. He had been relieved to see in Providence that she depended financially on her mother. Together with her ill health and past domestic sorrows the knowledge brought thoughts of tenderly devoting himself to her comfort, perhaps in some magnolia-surrounded cottage on a quiet river, a place of "strange, wierd [*sic*], and incomprehensible yet most simple beauty." But the news of Helen's prosperity, Poe said, dispelled his "sweet dreams." Dealing her blow for blow, he announced the end of their affair: "That *many* persons, in your presence, have declared me wanting in honor . . . forbids me, under such circumstances, to insult you with my love:—but that you are quite independent in your worldly position (as I have just heard)—in a word that *you are comparatively rich while I am poor,* opens between us *a gulf*—a gulf, alas! which the sorrow and the slander of the World have rendered forever impassable—by *me.*"

But while punishing Helen for wounding him—*Nemo me impune lacessit*—Poe had no thought of relinquishing her. He repeatedly recalled the love he had borne her, and even enclosed in the letter a lock of his hair. Perhaps unknown to Helen, he had also accepted an invitation to lecture in Providence in mid-December. Still, in their posturing and unreality the two letters seem ill calculated to persuade and ultimately win her. In their great length—nearly fifteen printed pages in modern editions—they also seem driven by the hectic longing of his despair, only in part avowals of hopelessly deep love and more largely cries for help. Indeed both letters contain intimations of suicide, even subtle invitations to a suicide pact. In the first letter, after suggesting that his calm care might overcome her heart ailment, Poe added that if the cure failed and Helen died, "then at least would I clasp your dear hand in death, and willingly—*oh, joyfully—joyfully—joyfully*—go down *with* you into the night of the Grave." Both letters recur to such thoughts of his "deadly grief," of his having "absolutely no wish but to die," his wanting Helen to be "mine only—if not now, alas! then at least hereafter and *forever,* in the Heavens."

How Helen responded to the undercurrent of violence in Poe's letters, if at all, is unknown. But her ways of thinking and feeling differed in many respects from those of the Helen he prayed to and adored. For one thing, despite her mystical streak, she had a whimsical side that enjoyed writing doggerel, watching fires, and eating candy. More important, Poe ignored or failed to see a trait remarked on, acutely, by one of Helen's friends: she was "very cautious and prudent, with all her amiability and generosity." The conservatism shows in her writing, all of which has an air of formal correctness, at once tasteful, elevated, and reserved—"high-born," in her phrase—a playing out of the myth of Poer. Aloof and elevated, she felt too much a lady ever to accommodate herself to Poe's ideal of a weird cottage, much less the hand-to-mouth actuality of his life with Muddy. The excesses of Shelley, Byron, and Goethe that she defended in her writings, charmed her little in a potential suitor. (She later found Walt Whitman's poetry repugnant and resented any implication that he belonged to her husband's family.) And for all her transcendental philosophizing, her allegiance to the cause of sincerity and personal liberation, her advanced beliefs in clairvoyance and spiritual twinship, she was under her mother's thumb, afraid of seeming a fool, and at bottom rather timid and conventional.

In turmoil over Helen's "horrible words,"—"great intellectual power, but *no* principle"—Poe lunged in two directions at once. Only a few days after writing to her, and without waiting for a reply, he went to Providence to see her. He was en route, however, to Lowell, to repeat his lecture "The Poets and Poetry of America." What happened this time at Benefit Street is known only through Helen's two later, brief accounts. Apparently feeling guilty over his harsh remarks, Poe begged her to forgive his "waywardness & his reproaches." Perhaps as a peace offering he showed or read her a page from the manuscript of his Lowell lecture, comparing her poetry favorably to that of Fanny Osgood and Anne Lynch. When she asked if she could obtain a copy, he tore out the leaf and gave it to her, promising to replace it with "a more elaborate notice." Although he had sworn in his letter that he would never propose to her again, he did, requesting that she weigh the reasons he had given her for marrying him, "for entrusting to him my future welfare & happiness." He asked her to consider for a week, and send her answer in a letter addressed to the Lowell post office, as she promised to do.

In Lowell, Poe put up once more at the wooden Gothic cottage of the Lockes. Unlike Helen, Mrs. Jane Ermina Locke had left no doubt about her regard for him: "I felt as in the presence of a god!" But if he had ever seriously cared for her, he did no longer. He stayed with the Lockes out of gratitude for past favors, and because he thought it in his interest to "keep in with them." The visit anyway turned out to be short. He found the couple not only hospitable to him but also boastful of it, "blazoning their favors to the world." And Jane Locke perhaps recognized his indifference to her for, he said, she insulted him. He also quarreled with the Lockes over their distant relatives, the Richmonds, where his affections were more deeply engaged. In his rapt encounter with Helen he had not forgotten Mrs. Nancy Richmond, with her chestnut-colored hair. Fifteen years Helen's junior, tall, graceful, she in turn cared enough about him to have visited Muddy at Fordham. The Lockes outraged him, Poe said, by asserting that only through their patronage had

Nancy been admitted to society, and that it would ruin Muddy to have her even enter the door. At this he got up and left their house.

Incurring Jane Locke's wrath, Poe went to stay with the Richmonds. He transferred not only his person but, in the wake of Helen's balky responses, his longing as well. Nancy Richmond's younger sister later recalled him sitting before an open wood fire, gazing into the coals, as he held Mrs. Richmond's hand: "for a long time no one spoke," she said, "and the only sound was the ticking of the tall old clock in the corner of the room." What the quiet handholding meant to Poe can be judged from the letter he sent Nancy Richmond about two weeks later, looking back on his visit. "Why am I not *with* you now *darling,*" he wrote, "that I might sit by your side, press your dear hand in mine, & look deep down into the clear Heaven of your eyes . . . *all* that I wish to say—all that my soul pines to express at this instant, is included in the one word, *love.*" On her part, Mrs. Richmond felt deeply enough about Poe to alter her name at his suggestion. As Helen's name revived the Helen of his boyhood, Virginia's the place of his growing up, Nancy Richmond's rang of his hometown and of Fanny Allan's sister, Miss Nancy. Perhaps disliking the association he called her Annie, and convinced her the name better suited her than Nancy. She tried to get her relatives and friends also to call her Annie.

Poe's romance with Annie developed in the presence of her husband Charles, a prosperous manufacturer. He liked Poe and indulged the relationship, perhaps flattered by the presence of a famous writer in his house, perhaps not caring. The couple's marriage seems to have been tolerant but cold. Quiet and fond of his wife, a niece explained, Charles was "devoted to making money, of which she had all she wanted; but he enjoyed sitting by himself evenings, reading his paper, then going to bed." His lack of "home sympathy" may have been agreeable to Annie, who was active in various causes and, as her brother described her, "not particularly domestic."

In fact Charles had no reason to fear an interruption of his evening newspaper reading and early retirement. Poe's love for Annie threatened neither adultery nor divorce, being childlike and desperate. He saw her as a caretaking angelic sibling, a replacement for Virginia as Sissy: *"sweet sister Annie,"* he called her, "my *pure, virtuous, generous, beautiful, beautiful sister* Annie." In another sense too Charles Richmond had little need to worry that Poe was sitting by his fire holding hands with his wife. Part of the attraction Poe felt toward Annie, and toward the also-married Fanny Osgood, Loui

Shew, and Jane Locke before her, surely lay in the impossibility of being more than attracted to them. Much as he wished to remarry in order to restore his balance, it was apparent to several people who knew him that he also did not wish to remarry. The writer Elizabeth Oakes Smith, for one, said that Poe at around this time "gave me the impression that he dreaded marriage. . . . generally the bent of his feelings so far as women were concerned were totally of an ideal kind." It may have been, as Smith's remark suggests, that Poe's fear involved the carnality of marriage. In his early tale "A Decided Loss," the protagonist finds on the morning after his wedding that he has lost his breath, and soon becomes horribly mutilated. A flight from sexual danger seems present in Poe's eager willingness to offer Helen *"unexacting* affection," a lifetime together without sex.

But Poe's 'dread' of remarriage clearly involved much else in his experience, and many other features of his personality. That may need no saying, for in other contexts the sources of his 'dread' have been emphasized here often. There was of course his reluctance or inability to bury the dead, endlessly dramatized in his tales and poems, and recently reenacted in his proclaiming Helen Whitman the dead Jane Stanard and Annie the dead Sissy, experiencing them all, although he did not say so, as the dead Eliza Poe. To marry also of course meant betraying the dead and wakening their wrath. Remarking on the "propriety of second marriages" in reviewing *Undine,* one of his favorite works, Poe pointed out that the knight's remarriage and gradual forgetting of the sprite causes her "deep grief, in consequence, beneath the waters." And more than grief of course wells up in Irene, the dead young woman of his early poem "The Sleeper"; when those left on earth cease mourning for her, she rises "Indignant from the tomb." Helen herself, a most insightful critic of Poe's work, remarked on its note of shamed and anxious commemoration, "a lingering pity and sorrow for the dead;— an ever-recurring pang of remorse in the fear of having grieved them by some involuntary wrong of desertion or forgetfulness." In Helen's particular case, her supposedly precarious heart also harbored the possibility of new and again devastating loss. Holding hands by the fire with a married woman offered calm, without inviting new trauma, loss of breath, reprisal, and the guilt of disloyalty.

Although Poe had found in Annie a possible replacement for the uneager Helen, should one be needed, as he stayed on in Lowell he still expectantly awaited a letter from Providence. He did not get to deliver his lecture, for in the excitement attending the upcoming presidential election, arrangements for it fell apart. He spent about three days at the farm of Annie's parents in nearby Westford, where he spoke informally to a local reading circle, reciting "The Raven," "Ulalume," and some short poems by Byron, and matching wits with a young Unitarian minister in discussing *Eureka*. He rode, walked, and climbed the rugged local hills, sometimes in company, sometimes alone. He seems not quite to have known what to do with himself. Annie's sister recalled him patiently unwinding from a nail a piece of twine that had been twisted and knotted around it, then hanging the string back again on the nail in long straight loops. While staying with the Lockes, and likely also with the Richmonds, he went to the post office every day, returning nervous and abstracted, explaining that he awaited an important letter, which had failed to arrive.

Despite her promise to write Poe at Lowell, Helen had put off doing so from day to day. She felt grossly torn, "unwilling to say the word which might separate us forever," she explained later, "& unable to give him the answer which he besought me to accord him." In a rather different version of her confusion, she also later explained that she was "unwilling to give him pain by my refusal, yet fearing to mislead him & compromise myself by any word of friendly sympathy & encouragement." Whether she more feared hurting or losing Poe, what she finally sent, around November 2, was a brief note that she herself thought unsatisfactory, and likely to perplex and agitate him. It must have agitated him indeed, for he wrote back immediately, saying he would be in Providence the following evening.

Before leaving Lowell, Poe consulted Annie on the course he should take with Helen. While drawn to Poe, she felt it in his best interest to marry Helen, encouraged him, for her sake, to continue his suit, and suggested what he might say. Her advice, however helpful in one direction, contained in another the sting of rejection: "*Can* you, *my* Annie," he wrote later, "*bear* to think I am another's?" Poe's distressed disbelief in receiving what he sought in the hope of happiness illustrates his larger situation. His this-way-and-that pursuit of tranquillity had coiled him in a strangling emotional tangle. From an attractive young married woman around whom he had woven fantasies of recuperative closeness, he was accepting unwanted advice on how to court an older woman—in delicate health, tied to her mother and father, and much conflicted herself—to whom he had pledged that he would never again propose a marriage he may never have wanted anyway.

Poe found the pulling and hauling nearly rending. He parted from Annie in a frazzled pent-up state, an "agony of grief," he said. With nervous foreboding, he looked on his journey to Benefit Street as preposterous and futile, feeling in dreadful fact that he might not be able to withstand the emotions it aroused. Before leaving Lowell, he got from Annie what he described as a "holy promise"—her vow that if he found that he could not do what he had to do, she would, under all circumstances, "come to me on my bed of death."

Suicide Attempt; "Conditional" Engagement.

NOVEMBER 4 – DECEMBER 18, 1848

By the time he reached Providence, on November 4, Poe was out of control. He had promised to call on Helen immediately. But according to his later account, he retreated to his hotel room, weeping through a "long, long, hideous night of despair." At daybreak he went out and tried to quiet himself by a rapid walk in the cold air. It did not help, he said: "the demon tormented me still."

Instead of returning to his hotel, Poe bought two ounces of laudanum. Then he took a train to Boston. When he arrived he wrote a confessional letter to Annie, "whom I so madly, so distractedly love," saying that not even for her sake could he make himself propose marriage to Helen again. He also said he had reached the end; his struggles were "more than I could bear." Reminding her that she promised to come to him on his deathbed, he implored her to come to him now, mentioning the place where he would be found in Boston—"the place of his birth, and where his mother found her *best,* and *most sympathetic* friends."

As if to curse the one and embrace the other, Poe then swallowed about half the laudanum. It is a solution of powdered opium in alcohol, weaker in opium content than morphine or heroin. In

Poe's time it was administered through cotton earplugs to hallucinating patients in mental hospitals, but was easily obtained and also widely used as a tranquillizer. The drug works quickly, producing maximum respiratory depression in ten minutes, and its peak effect in twenty minutes. The ounce or so that Poe said he took, equivalent to about 300 milligrams of morphine, represents some thirty times the average dose. The quantity is by itself enough to be fatal, although he intended, after Annie arrived, to swallow the remaining ounce or more as well.

Whatever his plan, Poe miscalculated. He hurried to the post office with his letter for Annie, but never mailed it. Before he reached the place, he said, "my reason was entirely gone."

What happened then and over the next two days cannot have been pleasant. But Poe, in recounting the events, passed over what he called "the awful horrors which succeeded." He reported only that he retched up some of the laudanum. An unidentified friend was nearby, too, who he said saved him, "if it can be called saving." It took him several weeks to remember that after vomiting he became calm, and "to a casual observer, sane." Having recovered himself at least so far, he decided to return, or as he put it "was suffered to go back," to Providence to complete his mission.

Poe arrived at Benefit Street early on the morning of November 7, a Tuesday. As he had promised to appear three days before, Helen was distressed and, having passed a restless night, felt unable to see him. Later in the morning she sent word by a servant that she would receive him at noon. Angered at being turned away from her door, Poe told the servant that he had an engagement and must see her immediately. But he also wrote out a note, addressed *"Dearest Helen,"* in which he said otherwise: "I have *no* engagements but am *very* ill—so much so that I must go home, if possible—but if you say 'stay,' I will try & do so." He explained that he would have kept his promise to appear on Saturday, but that it had not been in his "power." He asked her to see him if only for a few moments, and if not to send some message that might uplift him: "write me *one word* to say that you *do* love me and that, *under all circumstances, you will be mine.*" She replied in writing that she would meet him in half an hour at the Providence Athenaeum, farther along Benefit Street. Only about six weeks earlier, he had sat in an alcove at the same Greek Revival building, autographing his "Ulalume" for her.

When they met this time, Poe reproached Helen for so long delaying to write him at Lowell, and then sending a letter so vague and elusive. He also gave her a much revised account of his last few days. As Helen recalled it, on first arriving in Providence he had "taken something at a druggists" for his nerves, which had not composed but bewildered him. Confused, he boarded the next train for Boston and stayed there several days "ill & depressed" before returning to Providence. She apparently distrusted his tale and believed instead that he had become drunk, "fallen under the old temptation, which he vainly endeavored to persuade me was caused only by the restless anxiety my silence had occasioned him." During the meeting, too, Poe tried vigorously to persuade her to marry him at once and return with him to New York.

Poe kept up his appeal at Helen's house the following day. He pleaded that his happiness and welfare—"in time & in eternity," Helen said—depended on her. But Helen had again been harkening to friends, who told her such a marriage seemed "full of evil portents." To persuade him it should at least be postponed, she read passages from letters she had recently received, criticizing him, including a letter from "one of his New York associates." (She did not identify the correspondents, but one certainly was Mrs. Elizabeth Ellet, and the "associate" may have been Rufus Griswold.) Helen's willingness to hear out his enemies' slander had infuriated and even unhinged Poe before. And his long conversation with her now, she thought, left him "deeply pained & wounded." When some casual visitors turned up, he abruptly rose to depart. As he held Helen's hand for a moment in saying good-bye it seemed to her that "something had strangely moved him." She said, "We shall see you this evening?" He bowed without answering.

Poe spent the evening in the bar of his hotel. At some point he wrote and sent Helen a note, now lost, which struck her as "wild, incoherent." It renounced their relationship, bid her farewell, and said that if they met again it would be as strangers. Like his earlier letter of renunciation, however, it contained a lock of his hair. Poe's state can still be seen in the daguerreotype taken of him the next morning, November 9, at the request of a "Mr. MacFarlane," otherwise unidentified, whom he had met in Providence. The gaze alone makes it one of the great photographic images of the nineteenth century, comparable to some self-portraits of van Gogh in the intensity of its forlornness (Illus. 26).

Since the last known portrait of him, after Virginia's death, Poe has altered his facial hair. The jaunty upturned mustache-ends are gone, together with the muttonchop sideburns he had worn throughout life, leaving his cheeks clean shaven. He is not changed but deteriorated. His features seem asymmetrical and askew, his lower lip somehow not centered with his nose and slanted right, left eyebrow slanted left, one cheek swollen the other not, one side of the mustache shorter than the other, a vein bulging on the bulging forehead. Surely no longer capable of swimming six miles of the James River under a hot June sun against a strong tide, he looks dead ahead, his blackly-browed shadowed eyes darkly pouched, his black-furrowed nostrils flaring, his black frock-coat and the black aureole of tangly hair merging into the funereally black background, someone emotionally electrocuted.

Reportedly in his shirt sleeves, Poe appeared early the same morning at Helen's house, where her mother received him. He was beside himself, "in a state of wild & delirious excitement," Helen recalled. Apparently shouting, he called on her to save him from impending doom. "The tones of his voice were appalling," she said, "& rang through the house. Never have I heard anything so awful." She seems to have been upstairs when he arrived, and surprised by his return to the house. Supposing he had taken the evening train for New York, she had spent a worried night, thinking what might happen to him traveling alone. As Poe ranted, she stayed in seclusion, unable to nerve herself to see him. Meanwhile her mother remained with him, for more than two hours, apparently upbraiding him, as did Helen's sister Anna. When Helen at last had enough collected and steeled herself to face him, Poe exclaimed that his fate for good or evil rested entirely with her. He hailed her, she said, "as an angel sent to save him from perdition."

As Poe grew more composed during the afternoon, Helen's mother sent for a well-known local physician, Dr. Abraham H. Okie. Okie spent an hour with Poe and discerned symptoms of "cerebral congestion." He recommended that Poe be taken to the house of William J. Pabodie, a friend, lawyer, and local litterateur, and in addition one of Helen's admirers. Attentively nursed there for several days, Poe seems to have regained some hold on himself.

Surprisingly perhaps, Poe's eruption of raging panic did not end the courtship. An overriding hope for a married life evidently persuaded him and Helen to continue their willing-reluctant shuffle of retreating advance and advancing retreat. On Poe's side, the latest evidence of how he fared in the world when alone, proved even more sternly than before the truth of Loui Shew's remark that he needed a woman to regulate his existence. On her side, Helen retained her occult sense of twinship with his *"unearthliness,"* and admiration for what she considered his sincerity, his being "passionately genuine," not to mention his fantasized resemblance to Nicholas Power. She found Poe comely too, and spoke later of the "unrivalled beauty & nobility of his face." And she felt, at least in retrospect, that he could be redeemed, perhaps by herself, that he had "a reserved power of self-control that needed only favoring circumstances to bring his fine qualities of heart & mind into perfect equipoise."

Whatever other motives encouraged Poe and Helen to keep stumbling toward each other, a few days after the harrowing scene at Benefit Street he at last obtained her consent to a *"conditional"* engagement, as Helen called it. The conditions were that he completely stop drinking—"never again to taste wine"—and that her mother consent. Neither condition would be easily met. At least in the last few years, Poe had not been able to stay sober for long. And Helen's mother stridently opposed the marriage. She more than once said in Poe's presence, Helen recalled, "that my death would not be regarded by her so great an evil as my marriage under circumstances of such ominous import."

Understandably, neither Poe nor Helen seems to have been much uplifted by having arrived at this *"conditional"* engagement. Herself a troubled mix of New England Puritanism and Byronism, prude and femme fatale, Helen later admitted that she acted amid "terrible mental conflicts" and felt "many misgivings." Moreover, at the time of Poe's visit she seems to have been ailing, and she firmly believed that they would soon be separated by her death. "I had *no* fears about the results of such an imprudent union," she explained later, "because I believed that its earthly tenure would be of very brief duration." Poe seems no more elated in the daguerreotypes he took for Helen shortly before leaving Providence (Illus. 27). He wears the same wide-lapelled greatcoat he wore for the picture taken six years earlier, possibly the military coat that had been used to warm Virginia. He no longer appears shocked into a tense, apprehensive disgust, as in the daguerreotype four days earlier. But he does not seem a successful suitor either: hair stringy and unwashed-looking, chin slightly tremulous, he looks not at peace but pacified, wrung out.

The joyless engagement became immediately threatened. Only an hour or two after Poe left Providence, on the evening of November 13, someone sent Helen more unsettling information about him. The "painful rumors," Helen said, raised her mother's opposition to the match "almost to phrenzy" and brought on a scene. As they quarreled excitedly, everything seemed to Helen "a portent or an omen." At one point she saw through the window Poe's favorite star, Arcturus, shining brightly through a rift in the clouds, while the Serpent and other nearby constellations were in deep shadow. Dutiful as Helen felt toward her mother, the woman's violent opposition apparently rekindled her sympathy for Poe, and perhaps some spark of resistance. For at one o'clock in the morning, feeling she said a "strange accession of prophetic exaltation," she wrote a poem entitled "To Arcturus." It alluded to how their tentative engagement had quickly given way to the quarrel, and asserted comfortingly that memories of Poe outlasted and outshone the malicious new rumors that had come to Benefit Street:

> Star of resplendent front! thy glorious eye
> Shines on me still from out yon clouded sky—
> Shines on me through the horrors of a night—
> More drear than ever fell oer day so bright—
> Shines till the envious Serpent slinks away
> And pales and trembles at thy steadfast ray.

In poetic fancy at least, Helen held out something like hope for the engagement, perceiving far off through the stormy sky "the dawn of a diviner day."

Poe returned to New York at around five A.M., after traveling by train and steamer ten hours or more. He wrote to Helen as soon as the ship docked, before taking the 7 A.M. train to Fordham. By writing immediately he hoped to demonstrate that he was in command of himself and also sober, "that I have not *dared* to break my promise to you." He made plain too that he felt immensely grateful to her, not only for at last favoring his offer of marriage, but also for having put up with his behavior in Providence, remaining "unmoved by all that would have moved one who had been less than angel:—beloved of my heart of my imagination of my intellect—life of my life—soul of my soul—dear, dearest Helen." But whatever pleasure Helen may have taken in Poe's reassurances, gratitude, and ardor may well have been undermined by his forebodings and dejection. In his mind their engagement was not only conditional but also precarious, for he sensed, he told her, "a strange shadow of coming evil." Nor, he admitted, had he found delight in his new situation. "That I am not supremely happy, even when I feel your dear love at my heart, terrifies me. What can this mean?" Perhaps his downcast mood, he speculated, was the aftermath of his recent "terrible excitements." Or perhaps, he said bleakly, he and Helen needed a more "refined" word than *happiness* to express what they felt, something to convey at once "all . . . of hope & fear, of sorrow & of h[appiness]."

However dismally qualified, the solace Poe offered to Helen came far from expressing the frantic bewilderment he felt. Actually, her tentative acceptance had unnerved him no less than her earlier rejection. He returned from Providence much as he went there, shaken by a nameless dangerous upwell, in "fearful agitation," he said, "which if continued, will either destroy my life or, drive me hopelessly mad." His appearance alarmed Muddy: *"how changed!"* she exclaimed. "I scarcely knew him." He had failed to write her from Lowell or Providence, leaving her "nearly distracted," certain that *"something* dreadful had occurred." On his return he apparently told her that he had tried to poison himself, confirming her forebodings as well as her Christian faith. "God has heard my prayers and once more returned my poor, darling Eddy to me," she wrote. "And oh! how near I was losing him!"

Two days after returning from Providence, more or less engaged to Helen, Poe wrote to Annie as the one he loved, he said, "as no man ever loved woman." He told of his need to again sit beside her in Lowell pressing her hand, of his willingness to die for her or with her, to *"joyfully* abandon this world," to have her as "mine hereafter & *forever in the Heavens."* Recounting the trials of the previous ten days, he stressed that he had inwardly revolted against his mission to Helen, had forced himself to tell her what Annie urged him to, and now had fatally trapped himself into an engagement: "I feel I must die if I persist, & yet, how can I now retract with honor?" Helpless to act for himself, he implored Annie to interrupt the course he had set in motion: *"think* for me—before the words—the vows are spoken, which put yet another terrible *bar* between us." As if putting from his mind the middle-class solidities of Benefit Street, he held out for her a vision of the bowered life they might spend together in a small cottage at Westford, near Lowell, "oh *so* small—so *very* humble." He did not mention Annie's husband Charles, nor did he suggest that they live together as husband and wife. Instead they might exist as soul-entwined and cared-for brother and sister, attended by Muddy: "I could see some of your beloved family *every* day, & you often—oh VERY often—I would hear from you continually—regularly & *our* dear mother would be with us & love us both." But he also needed Annie now, in his distress, and implored her to come to Fordham for his relief. "I am so ill—so terribly, hopelessly ILL in body and mind, that I feel I CANNOT live, unless I feel your sweet, gentle, loving hand pressed upon my forehead."

During the next month, with at least half of his mind and feelings visiting the delicious cottage at Westford ("oh *so* small—so *very* humble"), Poe nevertheless worked confusedly at transforming his *"conditional"* engagement to Helen into a marriage. He arranged to return to Providence sometime after the first week in December, and again about two weeks later for a lecture in the city. Meanwhile, writing at first every other day, he tried to assure Helen that he could be trusted. He set forth hopeful, even regal prospects for their future together. His excitement had subsided, he told her, and he exhibited the restoration of his self-control by seasoning his letters with formulaic courtesies expressive of normalcy: "My mother was delighted with your wish to be remembered. . . . My kindest regards to Mr Pabodie." Indeed his ordeal, he said, had made him conscious of his personal power as never before: "the terrible agony which I have so lately endured—an agony known only to my God and to myself—seems to have passed my soul through fire and purified it from all that is weak. Henceforward I am strong:—this those who love me shall see." His artistic power also renewed, he held out Tamerlanian-Powersian visions of the literary heights they might scale together. "Would it *not* be 'glorious,' *darling,* to establish, in America, the sole unquestionable aristocracy—that of intellect—to secure its supremacy—to lead & to control it?" He said he dared not trust his plans to a letter, but would disclose what he had in view when he saw her, perhaps envisioning joint editorship as husband and wife of the "Stylus."

In trying to gain Helen's trust, Poe particularly sought to counter stories about his past follies that continued to reach her. Mostly they concerned his threat to show the world the (likely phantasmal) letters to him from Mrs. Elizabeth Ellet. The episode had of course been much publicized, but he believed Helen was hearing about it anew from Ellet herself. Although he had given Helen his version of the events before, he went over it again in greater detail, correctly detecting her concern. With her reserve and propriety, Helen feared scandal, and after all Poe had letters from her also, and highly personal. He denounced Ellet as a "fiend" whose "persecutions" had not stopped at himself but reached out cruelly to his wife, whom she so continuously "tortured" by anonymous letters that Virginia on her deathbed, Poe claimed, "declared that Mrs. E. had been her murderer." That seems unlikely, but otherwise Poe did not much exaggerate Ellet's habit of repaying real and fancied injuries by vindictive rumor-mongering. After allegedly being cussed at by Rufus Griswold, she wrote to his wife informing her that her husband had used obscene language in public. Advising Helen that she might receive anonymous letters from Mrs. Ellet defaming him, Poe warned her: "If you value your happiness, Helen, beware of this woman!"

Whatever the truth in Poe's warnings, his vow to revenge himself on talebearers hardly sustained his pretensions to restored self-command. "I will rest neither by night nor day until I bring those who have slandered me into the light of day," he swore to Helen, "I *have* the means and I will ruthlessly employ them." Helen cannot have relished this prospect of public exposures. And Poe's attempted display of calm, as he prepared his return to Providence, rippled throughout with old disquiet, dank rage, threats. For every sober assurance he offered Helen, he offered some ranting doubt as well. Affirming in one place that he had reformed his drinking, he demanded in another that she must accept him as he was: "all does *not* depend, dear Helen, upon my firmness—all depends upon the sincerity of your love." Extending here the hope of marital harmony and high literary attainment, he pointed there to possible sources of discontent: "the [intolerable insults of your mother & sister still rankle at] my heart—but for your dear sake I will endeavor to be calm." Quick to sense rejection, too, he searched Helen's replies for clues that might augur abandonment. In one letter she enclosed a version of her poem "To Arcturus," minus the hopeful lines about seeing amid clouds "the dawn of a diviner day." Why had she omitted the lines, he wanted to know: "is that dawn no longer perceptible?"

Poe was taking no chances on the answer. While trying to hearten *"dear dear* Helen" during the month, he stayed in passionate communication with Annie. Having not received a letter from Annie for a week, only, he became panicky. "If I do not hear from her soon, I shall surely die—I fancy everything evil—sometimes I even think that I have offended her, & that she no longer loves or cares for me." The intimidating possibility of a real marriage to an unattached adult made Annie seem an even more ideal and necessary figure than before. "In my wildest dreams, I have never fancied any being so totally lovely—so *good*—so *true*—so *noble* so *pure*—so *virtuous,*" he wrote to Annie's younger sister, Sarah; "her silence fills my whole soul with terror." Only proximity to the younger and married Annie could afford what he called "the *purest* & most exacting love"—a close intimacy, clearly, undisfigured by sexual contact. He asked Sarah to relay to Annie the message that if he had somehow angered her he begged pardon—literally, "on my knees": "tell her that I am her *slave* in all things—that whatever she bids me do, I will do."

So far as Poe had any real choice between Helen and Annie, Muddy directed him toward Lowell. Although she felt "very sick" herself at this time, she worried about his health, remained determined to do "all I can to cheer and comfort him," and stayed well-informed about his courting. She welcomed his estrangement from Jane Locke: "I never liked her, and said so from the first." Annie, by contrast, filled something of the place in her affections once occupied by Virginia; indeed in her gratitude for Annie's kindness to Poe, Muddy addressed her as "my darling child." Whether Muddy shared Poe's reverie of a cottaged life in Annie's vicinity is unknown, but the arrangement had the advantage of preserving the prized intimacy of Fordham. Writing to Annie around early December, Muddy thanked her "a thousand times" for her steadying influence on *"our* Eddy." She also revealed her fear that she would be unable to wholeheartedly accept Helen as a daughter-in-law. "I *know* I shall never love her as I do *you,* my own darling," she added. "I hope at all events they will not marry for some time."

Not much, probably, could be expected of a marriage that both bewildered the participants and displeased their friends and relatives. Poe's incandescent spirituality evoked a proprietary care that left others also feeling they had some stake in the match. Fanny Osgood, Helen's longtime friend, came to Providence from New York as soon as she heard rumors of the engagement. According to Helen, Fanny confessed the "enthusiasm" she herself had felt for Poe and questioned her about the relationship, covering her hands with tears and kisses. When Helen mentioned Poe's letters of ten or twelve pages, Fanny was "almost incredulous," Helen said, and remarked that Poe's letters to her had all been "very brief." Proud of her unworldliness, Helen later professed hurt surprise over Fanny's silence after the visit: "She . . . manifested so much affectionate interest in me, that I was deeply grieved to receive no answers to the many letters which I wrote to her." But she can hardly have failed to notice that her friend was jealous. Fanny cherished to the end of her life the memory of Poe's "irresistible charm," and later admitted that she regarded his engagement with "mingled joy & sorrow." Helen, too, later acknowledged concern that the result of her conversation with Fanny might be, as she said, "to increase her influence over him & consequently to weaken my own."

The marriage plans moved another troubled step forward during Poe's brief trip to Providence around December 10. Insultingly, he was made to submit to the wishes of Helen's mother. Seeing that she might not be able to prevent the marriage, she tried at the very least to make her daughter and Poe pay for it. She drew up legal papers transferring to herself the sole control of her sister's estate, part of which had been left to Helen. The amount seems to have been substantial, as the inheritance included owning stock shares in six banks and unclaimed loans to private parties of more than five thousand dollars, secured by mortgages. On December 15, Helen signed over her stake in the bequest to her mother, thereby also putting it out of the reach of Poe. The legal transfer demeaningly expressed suspicion of his motives, even though he had made a show of disdaining Helen's wealth. Still more galling, he was asked or forced to sign his name to the documents as a witness. Mrs. Power's stratagem for thwarting his supposed fortune-hunting vexed him, likely giving a fresh bitterness to his much chewed-over disinheritance by John Allan. When he returned briefly to New York, before setting out again for his lecture in Providence, he wrote Helen a note, passing along Muddy's promise to "return good for evil & treat you *much* better than *your* mother has treated me." He nevertheless advised her to keep up heart, *"for all will go well."*

Poe probably thought all would go well, and also probably did not think so. Before leaving New York, he called at the home of the poet Mrs. Mary Hewitt. She mentioned having heard that he was about to be married. Standing with his hand on the knob of the parlor door, she said, he drew himself up and replied: "that marriage will never take place." Preparing to be married and not to be married, he returned to Providence on Wednesday morning, December 20, putting up at a large hotel on Main Street called the Earl House. He planned to get some sleep, and to see Helen early in the afternoon before his lecture at 7:30 that evening.

Lyceum Lecture;
Marriage Announced and Called Off;
Repercussions in Lowell.

DECEMBER 20, 1848 – SPRING 1849

Poe spoke before the Franklin Lyceum at Howard's Hall, in a series of talks that had already presented Daniel Webster. Providence newspapers reported lively anticipation of his performance, "our readers being so familiar with his numerous productions." Local gossip about his interest in Helen may have drawn the curious as well, for he attracted an audience estimated at two thousand persons.

Poe had written little over the last year (see the next section), but he specially composed for the occasion a lecture entitled "The Poetic Principle." Mostly it reiterated the aesthetic ideas he had been fostering for a decade, such as the origin of true poetry in the human thirst for Supernal Beauty, "the glories beyond the grave." Years of defining and redefining these ideas endow "The Poetic Principle," however, with a distinguishing assurance, clarity, and coherence in the expression of them. Poe memorably formulated his vision of uniquely aesthetic pleasure in speaking of "this poem which is a poem and nothing more—this poem written solely for the poem's sake," and permanently impaled the contrasting confusion between poetry and Truth as "the heresy of *The Didactic.*" He gave perhaps half his time on the platform to illustrative readings of about a dozen poems by himself and others, including "The Raven." Over the years he seems to have developed a quietly lyrical, legato way of speaking poetry; Chivers commented that he read "rather monotonously and flute-like," indeed "rather *cantilated* than read."

Poe fashioned his lecture as an act of wooing, using his remarks and recitations to address Helen, who sat directly in front of him. Looking down at her, one spectator recalled, he gave dramatic emphasis to the opening of Edward Coote Pinkney's "A Health": "I fill this cup to one made up / Of loveliness alone." Assuring Helen that her friends among New England's literary cliques had no reason to oppose him, he spoke pointedly of "we Bostonians," and meaningfully read an eleven-stanza poem by Longfellow, praising its "delicacy of expression." Appealing to Helen to scorn the gossip about him, he also read Byron's "Stanzas to Augusta," beginning:

> *Though the day of my destiny's over,*
> *And the star of my fate hath declined,*
> *Thy soft heart refused to discover*
> *The faults which so many could find. . . .*

Poe also clearly meant for Helen's ears his concluding remarks on women's beauty and faithfulness as sources of poetic feeling, and his closing recitation of the popular "Song of the Cavalier." A rousing call to arms, commanding "brave gallants" to "don your helmes amaine," it made a covert tribute to her tale of high descent from the mighty Sir Roger Le Poer.

Poe thought the lecture went off "much better" than the one five months earlier at Lowell, and he delighted in the large audience— "and such applause!" His success and his veiled messages to Helen may have influenced what happened a day or two later. He had often cautioned her that their marriage, if delayed, would never take place—and she now at last agreed to marry him.

Helen's consent to the marriage came with no more joy and no fewer encumbrances, however, than her earlier agreement to a *"conditional"* engagement. As she later characterized their decision to unite, Poe "prevailed upon me, not without the reluctant concurrance of my friends & family." The approval of Helen's mother cost Poe further humiliation. On his last trip to Providence he had merely witnessed the document in which Helen transferred her potential estate. But now Mrs. Power had a new document prepared, by which he would legally acknowledge his acceptance of the transfer as well. "Whereas a Marriage is intended between the above named Sarah H. Whitman and the subscriber, Edgar A. Poe," it read, "I hereby approve of and assent to the transfer of the property in the manner proposed." The document required him, after a lifetime of begging and poverty, to sign away such amenities as Helen might have brought to the marriage. On December 22, he signed it.

The same night Poe came to Benefit Street tipsy. Among those at the house was Helen's thirty-three-year old admirer William J. Pabodie, who had nursed Poe during his raving attack of "cerebral congestion" the month before. Pabodie too opposed the marriage, perhaps self-interestedly, but he liked Poe and felt a bond with him. Being, as Helen described him, "rather *super*fine in dress and manners, witty & sarcastic in conversation . . . & *very* indolent," he had abandoned the profession of law to write literary criticism and high-minded verse. According to Pabodie, Poe in his "partial intoxication" said little and was very quiet. Partial or not, his drinking violated the chief condition of his engagement to Helen, as he recognized in returning to Benefit Street the next morning to apologize. He expressed "the most profound contrition and regret," Pabodie recalled, "and was profuse in his promises of amendment." But the strain in the situation affected his regrets too. Before leaving his hotel to apologize, he had braced himself with a glass of wine.

For the rest of this long day, Saturday, December 23, Poe needed whatever strength he could muster. Helen evidently accepted his excuses and failed to notice that he had fortified himself for making them. She agreed to his contacting a local Episcopal clergyman, the Reverend Nathan Crocker, to initiate the nuptials. Rhode Island law required an engaged couple to announce publicly their intention to marry, and Poe asked Crocker to publish these banns on Sunday and on Monday. Promising to inform the minister when a wedding date had been picked, he also asked Pabodie to deliver the note in person. Perhaps only an hour or two later, however, he and Helen agreed to schedule the wedding for Monday, after the second publication of the banns. Poe wrote to Muddy, to announce that they would be arriving by the first train on Tuesday, as man and wife. Later in the morning, he and Helen went out for a ride, and then began making preparations for her move to Fordham.

What happened that afternoon is known from three later descriptions by Helen, so from her viewpoint alone. While with Poe at a library, she received another of those anonymous 'communications' which seem, in her accounts, to have followed her everywhere around Providence. It disclosed "many things in Mr. Poe's recent career" she had not known, and warned her afresh against the marriage. She did not identify the sender, beyond saying that his or her authority was "not to be questioned." Nor did she divulge the nature of the "things," although they included Poe's tipple to bolster himself the same morning. With the news that he had *"already* violated the solemn promises that he had made," as often before, she thought first of what others might think and say to her. Even could she overlook his latest errors, her friends would learn about them "within hours," and confront her. And the fact that he had broken his promise for the second time in two days left her feeling inept, "utterly hopeless," she said, "of being able to exercise any permanent influence over his life."

Helen said nothing of this to Poe until they returned to Benefit Street, when she told him the substance of the communication. She also told Pabodie, who was present, not to deliver Poe's note instructing the Reverend Crocker to publish the marriage banns. Gathering some papers Poe had entrusted to her, she handed them to him without explanation. Poe tried to persuade her that she had been misinformed, especially about his morning drink. She listened without reproach, although her quietude was deceptive. The seesaw of exaltations and defeats, confirmations and suspicions over the past few days had left her not placid but numb, and not only hardened into "marble stillness of despair" but also drained, "utterly worn out & exhausted." Given as well the guilt-provoking presence on the scene of her grimly disapproving mother and her emotionally fragile sister, she may also have felt trapped.

Seeking some way out, and now having violent chills, Helen drenched her handkerchief in ether, breathed the vapors, and threw herself on a sofa. Although she frequently used the drug to relieve her 'heart condition,' she now hoped merely, she said, "to lose myself in utter unconsciousness." Poe sank to his knee beside her. Seemingly both alarmed and frustrated, he entreated her to speak one word, *"but one word."* As she later remembered the exchange, she at last responded, almost inaudibly, "What *can* I say." He replied, "Say that you love me, Helen." She said, *"I love you."* Poe continued explaining and complaining, but she had fallen into a stupor. He covered her with some shawls and carried her to another sofa, near the fire, where kneeling as before he chafed her hands trying to get her to speak.

But Helen said nothing. Remaining lifeless-looking, she could hear vaguely what others said in the room. Her mother and Pabodie argued with Poe and tried to get him to leave, and at last Mrs. Power insisted. Poe started up, Helen said, and in departing declaimed with angry hauteur, "Mr. Pabodie, you hear how I am insulted." That evening, Pabodie accompanied him to the train to Connecticut, where he could connect with the steamboat bound for New York.

In the spirit of its many other contradictions, the affair between Poe and Helen came to an end without finishing. In January of the new year, 1849, one day after Poe left Providence, a newspaper in nearby New London, Connecticut, heralded their wedding: "Edgar A. Poe, Esq., the celebrated poet and critic, is about to lead to the Hymenial altar, Mrs. Sarah H. Whitman, of Providence, a well known and popular authoress." Newspapers in New York, Lowell, and perhaps elsewhere, repeated the notice, while still later in the month the Richmond *Examiner* wished the couple (most improbably) "a house-full of very fat babies." Literary circles assessed the wedding-to-be. "Now I know a widow of doubtful age will marry almost any sort of a white man," Horace Greeley wrote to Rufus Griswold, "but this seems to me a terrible conjunction. Has Mrs. Whitman no friend within your knowledge that can faithfully explain Poe to her?" Attracted to Helen himself, Griswold needed no telling: as a New York poet characterized his view of the wedding, he saw Helen as ready to embark trustingly "upon what a wreck."

Nothing had been said in Providence about ending the match— Helen's last, stupefied words to Poe had been "I love you"—but both understood that it was over. While others discussed the supposedly upcoming wedding, they reeled from the effects of its collapse. Helen suffered chills and fever for weeks after, brought on she said by "exposure and anxiety." Poe staggered under a two-week-long headache, during which he passed his fortieth birthday. With the pain of body and mind, however, came a sense of relief. What had ended was a pursuit no less anguished than heady, over-laden with quandaries in the present and entwinements in the past, leading, both now realized, to a too-complicated future. For Helen, even the "bitter moment" when she told Pabodie not to request the banns brought easement, a feeling, she recalled, of being light-ened, "freed from the intolerable burden of responsibility which he had sought to impose upon me, by persuading me that his fate for good or for evil, depended upon *me*." Poe too, so long unsettled by oscillations of attraction and repulsion, felt relieved. "I need not tell you, Annie," he wrote to Mrs. Richmond, "how great a burden is taken off my heart by my rupture with Mrs. W."

It was of course to Annie that Poe returned. If events close up in Providence revealed Helen as an attractive woman in rustling gowns who had a penetrating mind and difficult family and friends, in short as flesh and blood, Annie far off in Lowell remained an angelic ideal, desirable because always disembodied. "Indeed, in-deed, Annie, there is *nothing* in this world worth living for except love," he wrote to her now, "love *not* such as I once thought I felt for Mrs. —— but such as burns in my very soul for *you*—so pure—so unworldly." Within three months of his breakup with Helen, he repeated this message in ten or more letters, saluting Annie as his "own *dear sister,*" enclosing the wishes of "Our dear mother," swearing that his future depended on her alone: "I do not believe *that any one in this whole world fully understands me except your own dear self.*"

Poe could no longer fall back to Lowell, however, in retreat from his confusions and failures in Providence. News of the broken engagement disturbed Annie, in part because he had promised her to seek the marriage though it meant abandoning his vision of nestling in her vicinity. He reassured her that his promise had been genuine: "*no* sacrifice would have seemed to me too great, I felt so burning—so *intensely passionate* a longing to show you that I loved you." But even more damagingly, Annie's husband, Charles, was from Providence; the disgraceful news that reached Lowell came from his family there, who sympathized with Helen, blamed Poe for the damage, and emphasized that he had acted dishonorably. Although Charles trusted Poe, Annie said, the letters bothered him, and for a while his displeasure made her feel "that our acquaintance *must* end." Trusting and innocent herself, Annie had seen Poe only at his most gentle and chivalrous, never when drunk or stampeding. She thought him "the very personification of high mindedness & true nobility." Just the same, feeling the aftershock of his wreck within her own family, she wrote him a letter, now lost, that evidently repeated and asked him to account for the gossip her husband's family had sent from Providence. It mentioned his drinking there and referred to "vile and slanderous" comments allegedly made about him by Helen.

"I felt *deeply* wounded by the cruel statements of your letter," Poe wrote back, stunned that his all-understanding "own dear sister" could entertain such charges. However offended, he thought up a strategy for clearing himself with Annie, typically roundabout. He composed a coldly formal letter to Helen, which he sent to Annie first, inviting her to read it, then seal and forward it to Helen. The letter contained scandalous remarks about his behavior in Providence quoted from Annie's letter to him, especially to the effect that although the wedding banns had been published, Helen felt compelled to call on the Reverend Crocker in person, ask him to stop the proceedings, and state her reasons for doing so. In fact the banns had not been published and Helen had not called on Crocker. The tale implied that in order to have driven her to this extreme, Poe must have acted monstrously. "That *you* Mrs. W—have uttered, promulgated or in any way countenanced this pitiable falsehood," Poe wrote to Helen, "I do not & cannot believe . . . what I beg of you is, to write me at once a few lines in explanation." He promised Annie to send her Helen's reply, so she could see the falsity of the rumors. Meanwhile, he told Annie, he had learned a lesson about bluestockings: "from this day forth I shun the pestilential society of *literary women.* They are a heartless, unnatural, venomous, dishonorable *set,* with no guiding principle but inordinate self-esteem." Fanny Osgood, he added, was the *"only* exception."

But a second set of rumors menaced Poe's dream of cottaging near Annie. Annie's husband had also become alarmed by reports about Poe coming to him from his neighbors the Lockes. Poe attributed their "malignant misrepresentations" to his having fled their house when they insulted Annie, and to Jane Locke's jealousy. On the second point he may have been correct, for according to Annie the rejected Mrs. Locke had fallen "deeply in love" with him—dark eyes flashing like Jove's—and she had also probably heard of his intended marriage to Helen, whom she knew. "In the name of God," Poe protested to Annie, "what else had I to anticipate, in return for the offence which I offered to Mrs Locke's insane vanity & self-esteem, than that she would spend the rest of her days in ransacking the world for scandal against me." He threatened to sue the Lockes if they said anything actionable: "they may provoke me a little too far."

Poe blamed not only the Lockes for bad-mouthing him but also Annie's husband for listening to these "unmentionable nobodies." Charles had tolerated Poe's fireside attentions to his wife, but the Lockes' tales about him, atop those from family and friends in Providence, may have finally offended his sense of propriety and awakened him to the possibility of personal humiliation. Poe may also have communicated to Charles the pleasure he took in belittling him by openly alluring his wife. The pleasure seems plain in his remarks about Charles's willingness to hear out Jane Locke: "the most unaccountable instance of weakness," Poe told Annie, "that ever I knew a *man* to be guilty of:—women are more easily misled in such matters." His mockery of Charles's manhood rings with old rage at accounts of his own thrashing by T. D. English, caricatures of him as watery-eyed and five-feet-one. He rubbed it in: "that any man *in his senses,* would ever *listen* to accusations, from so suspicious a source. That any man could be really *influenced* by them surpasses my belief." The real cause of Charles's "prejudices" against him, he let Annie know, was not the Lockes' scandal-mongering but her husband's oafish insensitivity: "I much fear that he has mistaken the nature—the purity of that affection which I feel for you. . . . God knows dear *dear* Annie, with what horror I would have shrunk from insulting a nature so *divine* as yours, with any impure or earthly love—But . . . it is clear that Mr R. cannot enter into my feelings on this topic."

The situation in Lowell was becoming disillusioning and humbling to the point where Poe considered ending it too. He had planned a visit there, probably in February, and even considered giving up the Fordham house and asking Annie to board Muddy while he made a trip south, perhaps a first step in moving to the neighborhood of Lowell himself. But he scrapped both plans. His presence might divide Annie and her husband, he explained, and given Charles's distrust he could not feel at ease in *"his* house." Assuring Annie that he was staying sober and would sooner or later marry, as she wished him to, he said they must stop writing to each other.

Like much else that Poe rashly vowed or threatened, that did not happen. Far from it, he persisted in trying to regain his standing with the Richmonds. He asked Annie to find out from Charles's relatives exactly who in Providence had "slandered" him, "for I find that it will not do to permit such reports to go unpunished." He also prevailed over the Lockes. They had denied insulting Annie behind her back, and as no witnesses had been present, Poe could not prove they had. Nor could he prove that Jane Locke, as he claimed, had sent him letters "filled with abuse" against the Richmonds, for he also claimed to have returned the letters to her. Cut suspiciously close to the pattern of the Ellet affair, the story seems fabricated. But in March, according to Poe, Mrs. Locke wrote to Muddy and admitted at least that she had warned him against Annie. Poe sent her presumably self-incriminating letter back to Lowell: "Read it!" he told Annie. "You will find it thoroughly *corroborative of all I said."* The Richmonds seem to have been convinced, for Charles denounced the Lockes "in the *strongest terms,"* Annie said, ending the friendship between their families. He also invited Muddy to Lowell, to stay as long as she wanted.

If Poe also succeeded in debunking rumors coming from Providence, he did so unaided by Sarah Helen Whitman. His letter asking her to deny that she had called off the marriage went unan-

swered. He believed it never reached her, having been intercepted
by her mother, "who is an old devil." In reality Helen did receive
the letter, but it hardly encouraged an answer; like many of Poe's
other pleas and offers to her, it rather created the conditions in
which he must be refused. Together with the high-minded promise
that gossip by others would not provoke him into speaking ill of
her, he sent lofty intimation as well: "You will of course write me
immediately on receipt of this," he said, "only in the event of my
not hearing from you within a few days, will I proceed to take more
definite steps." He also presented their failed courtship as a matter,
simply, of "my declining to fulfill our engagement"—a fancy drawn
after his earlier fables of having quit, not been fired from, some
job, although in a deeper sense than he perhaps realized he did
'decline' being married. (Helen's version centered on Poe's truthfulness and reliability: "had he kept his promise never again to taste
wine," she said, "I should never have broken the engagement.") To
appease the many onlookers who seemed to care what happened,
he now planned, if Helen agreed, to say that the marriage had been
postponed on account of her ill health. After a while people would
lose interest and "thus," he told Helen cuttingly, "this unhappy matter
will die quietly away."

Poe's letter contained much else to hurt or exasperate Helen, and
make it difficult to reply. But what persuaded her not to answer
had little to do with what he said. She "did not dare" reply, she
explained, because she feared that any contact with him would bring
on more bickering with her friends and family, from which she had
already "suffered so much." She believed that she did manage to
convey her feelings to Poe, however, without even intending to.
Before their parting, she had promised a poem for a new magazine,
and he had advised her to submit "Lines to Arcturus." When their
engagement ended she withheld the poem, thinking that others would
readily detect the tribute to Poe in her address to the "Star of re-
splendent front!" Too ill to write something else, she sent the magazine a song she had written several years earlier for guitar accom-
paniment, entitled "Our Island of Dreams." But the choice dissatisfied
her, and she thought of recalling it—until Poe's letter arrived. Then
it occurred to her that he would read the song symbolically, taking
its tale of lost love as being the reply she dared not write:

> *Tell him I lingered alone on the shore,*
> *Where we parted, in sorrow, to meet never more;*

The night wind blew cold on my desolate heart,
But colder those wild words of doom "Ye must part!"
. . . .
When the clouds that now veil from us heaven's fair light,
Their soft, silver lining turn forth on the night;
When time shall the vapors of falsehood dispel,
He shall know if I loved him; but never how well. . . .

Helen said that she derived a particular, "secret pleasure" from thinking that Poe would read the last lines as an avowal that she had never betrayed their intimacy by spreading stories about him.

Helen maintained her silence, although by an effort. She parted from Poe, she revealed later, in "intense sorrow," and it troubled her to think that he believed her affection for him had turned to disgust. Her reasons for thinking so included a review in the February *Southern Literary Messenger* of Griswold's *Female Poets of America*. The previous summer, Poe had shown her a manuscript of his Lowell lecture, containing laudatory comments about her work; he had promised to rewrite the comments when Griswold's book appeared, and then say "very much more." But the review in the *Messenger* allowed her poems only, she said, a "cold & incidental allusion." However chilled by this fancied slight from Poe (who was probably not the reviewer), she wrote several times to Fanny Osgood, asking after his health and welfare. Receiving no reply, she hoped that he at least knew of her inquiries. But she also wondered whether, to repay her silence, he had asked Osgood not to answer.

As the time of their separation lengthened, Helen began to reckon more precisely what she had lost and gained by her separation from Poe. She had rid herself of the mistrust between them, and the feeling of being overwhelmed by the past griefs he carried. On the other hand, Poe brought to her "desolate and lonely" existence, as she called it, the companionship of a gentle, deeply spiritual being of extraordinary intellect and literary gift, "one whose sweet and gracious nature had endeared him to me beyond expression, and whose rare and peculiar intellect had given a new charm to my life."

Helen put her wrenched feelings about Poe most forcefully in a later sonnet. She depicted him as providing the personal elevation and distinction to which she felt entitled, but which the House of Agonies had denied her:

. . . thy song, thy fame,
The wild enchantments clustering round thy name,

> *Were my soul's heritage, its royal dower;*
> *Its glory and its kingdom and its power!*

And yet, Poe's "power," as Helen recognized also, sprang from depths that emerged all too fearsomely in his behavior, unbearable:

> *. . . ah! no human heart could brook*
> *The darkness of thy doom to share,*
> *And not a living eye could look*
> *Unscathed upon thy dread despair.*

Poe had made restitution for her deserting and disappointing father, her disappointing husband dead in young manhood, her unbalanced sister, grasping mother, complaining friends. He had allowed her briefly to be what she was, a Poer. But his majesty also closed in as a pit, entombed her. Her heart

> *. . . had no refuge from thy love,—no Heaven*
> *But in thy fatal presence. . . .*

New Attempts to Resume a Literary Career; "The Bells," "Hop-Frog," and Other Writings.

SPRING 1848–SPRING 1849

During eight months or so of courting Helen, Poe wrote and published little. Romantic involvements of course drained some of his time and vigor, but he perhaps again found his literary energies recurrently closed off. Considering that he agreed to serve as New York correspondent for the *Miner's Journal,* a weekly newspaper in Pottsville, Pennsylvania, he may also have had difficulty finding a market. In the whole of 1848 he seems to have earned only about $166. Except for *Eureka,* completed in the spring, he published but one consequential article, "The Rationale of Verse," and had written it nearly two years earlier, elaborating the still earlier "Notes Upon English Verse."

Poe had a hard time placing the long essay. He sold it first to the *American Whig Review,* which decided not to print it—because, Poe believed, he had "come down too heavily" on the editor's "personal friends in Frogpondium." He took the piece back in exchange for "Ulalume" and resold it to *Graham's,* which however also failed to publish it. At last "The Rationale of Verse" appeared in the *Southern Literary Messenger* in October 1848. The editor, John Reuben Thompson, said that he bought the essay "more as an act of charity than anything else," and correctly explained its misadventures: "it is altogether too *bizarre* and too technical for the general reader." In fact, Poe departed from his usual critical practice of addressing a large general public on basic principles of literary judgment. Dismissing the existing studies of English prosody as inadequate—"It may be said, indeed, that we are without a treatise on our own verse"—he produced an exotic account of the genesis of verse, and a highly technical method of scansion. The essay prickles with invented or oddly defined terms like *bastard iambuses,* the *quick trochee,* and *caesura* (defined not as a pause but as "a single *long* syllable; *but the length of this syllable varies*"). †

In this lean period Poe also turned out the futuristic satire "Mellonta Tauta." Appearing in February 1849, it was the first work of fiction he had published for two whole years, and slight even so. Set in the year 2848, it records a present where mile-high balloons transport three or four hundred passengers at 150 miles per hour, and looks back satirically on a past where the ancient "Amriccans" built what they called churches—"a kind of pagoda instituted for the worship of two idols that went by the names of Wealth and Fashion." What attention the piece merits comes from its containing Poe's most absolute repudiation of democracy. The narrator learns that "Amriccans" lived in egalitarian chaos,

> a sort of every-man-for-himself confederacy, after the fashion of the "prairie dogs" that we read of in fable. . . . they started with the queerest idea conceivable, viz: that all men are born free and equal—this in the very teeth of the laws of *gradation* so visibly impressed upon all things both in the moral and physical universe. Every man "voted," as they called it—that is to say, meddled with public affairs—until, at length, it was discovered that what is everybody's business is nobody's, and that the "Republic" (so the absurd thing was called) was without a government at all. . . . . . democracy is a very admirable form of government—for dogs.

Poe was looking at threats to social hierarchy abroad as well, for he also bitterly appraised *"Mob,"* a foreign giant "said to have been the most odious of all men that ever encumbered the earth. . . . insolent, rapacious, filthy; had the gall of a bullock with the heart of an hyena and the brains of a peacock." Although Poe rarely wrote about current political affairs, in this case he had been repulsed by the violent popular revolutions in France, Italy, Germany, Denmark, and Hungary during 1848, the year that also brought *The Communist Manifesto.*

With his parting from Helen, Poe felt his stagnant literary career moved by a fresh wind. "I am about to bestir myself in the world of Letters rather more busily than I have done for three or four years past," he wrote at the beginning of the new year. In the six weeks since his final trip to Providence, he said, he had allowed no day to pass without writing one to three pages, and felt reinvigorated, too, "in better health than I ever knew myself to be—full of energy and bent upon success." He described his prospects to Annie: "Engagements to write are pouring in upon me every day. I had two proposals within the last week *from Boston."* Not only from, of all places, Boston: he had also sent articles to the *American Review,* the *Metropolitan,* and the *Southern Literary Messenger,* had received offers from a Cincinnati magazine, and indeed, he said, had "made permanent engagements with every magazine in America (except *Peterson's National*)." And so active a literary life meant money. "The *least* price I get is $5 per 'Graham page,' and I can easily average 1 1/2 per day—that is $7 1/2." He saw himself not just easing his financial pinch, but also amassing wealth, thereby making himself invulnerable. "I am resolved to *get rich,"* he told Annie; "I must get rich—rich. Then all will go well." Pulling out of his deepening discouragement about the literary life in America, he discovered new satisfaction in being a writer. "Depend upon it, after all . . . Literature is the most noble of professions. In fact, it is about the only one fit for a man. For my own part, there is no seducing me from the path."

But there turned out to be little to keep Poe in the path either. Like his illusory artistic and personal resurgence the year before ("better—best"), this one sputtered. By early spring he was telling Annie he had met "one disappointment after another," frustrating his hopes for new success and wealth: "The *Columbian Magazine,* in the first place, failed—then Post's *Union* (taking with it my principal dependence); then the *Whig Review* was forced to stop paying for contributions—then the *Democratic* . . . More than this, the *S.L. Messenger,* which owes me a good deal, cannot pay just yet." He found himself back where he started, borrowing money, in one case signing a promissory note for sixty-seven dollars, due in sixty days, possibly to help pay the annual rent at Fordham. The steady N. P. Willis again tried to raise charitable contributions for him, telling *Home Journal* readers that "Money . . . could not be better laid out for the honor of this period of American literature . . . than in giving EDGAR POE a competent annuity."

In his renewed drive for serenity and wealth, Poe published much that was warmed-over, flimsy, or cribbed. In January he proposed to J. R. Thompson a continuation of his popular "Marginalia," to run in the *Messenger* through the year at the rate of five pages a month, for two dollars a page. Making ninety-one items, the new series appeared from April through September, complemented by a gathering of briefer jottings printed in *Graham's* as "Fifty Suggestions." As always, Poe's best aperçus are at once informal, pithy, and surprising, whether they concern women's purses, vengeance, insanity, or the good sense of Chinese romance writers in beginning their books at the end. On the other hand he also refashioned much or lifted it verbatim from his own earlier essays and reviews, including nearly all ten items for May. His thirty-four June "Marginalia," for instance, include some piercing aphorisms:

> Pure diabolism is but Absolute Insanity. Lucifer was merely unfortunate in having been created without brains.
>
> It is only the philosophical lynxeye that, through the indignitymist of Man's life, can still discern the dignity of Man.
>
> To be *thoroughly* conversant with Man's heart, is to take our final lesson in the iron-clasped volume of Despair.

The larger group of comments compose an Ecclesiastes-like Book of Woes, a personal testament of despair.

But not only the pessimism is remarkable. The bitterness Poe vented was surely his own, yet he adapted or filched about half these entries from some "Mems for Memory" published in *Burton's Gentleman's Magazine* nearly a decade earlier. Their author was Horace Binney Wallace, a gifted Philadelphia lawyer who wrote as "William Landor" before committing suicide in Paris at the age of thirty-five. Landor inspired the first two of the sayings quoted above, and served as a literary prey for some of Poe's other nay-saying meditations, including:

> There are moments when, even to the sober eye of Reason, the world of our sad humanity must assume the aspect of Hell; but the Imagination of Man is no Carathis, to explore with impunity its every cavern. Alas! the grim legion of sepulchral terrors can*not* be regarded as altogether fanciful; but, like the Demons in whose company Afrasiab made his voyage down the Oxus, they must sleep, or they will devour us—they must be suffered to slumber, or we perish. (Poe)
>
> . . . he sounded passion to its depths, and raked the bottom of the gulf of sin; he explored, with the indomitable spirit of Carathis, every chamber and cavern of the earthly hell of bad delights. . . . . . The passions are like those demons with whom Afrasiab sailed down the river Oxus, our safety consists in keeping them asleep; if they wake we are lost. (Landor, from his novel *Stanley*)

To perhaps make matters worse, Poe had used this passage before, as the (effective) concluding paragraph of his tale "Premature Burial." In republishing it now as a "Marginalia" entry, he was stealing his own plagiarism.

The deterioration of Poe's literary morals also appears in his service to Sarah Anna Robinson Lewis, a most minor poet, but well-off (Illus. 28). In effect he became her paid press agent. Twenty-four years old but jowly looking, she began one of her poems with the line "I wish I had a pretty name." She settled on "Stella," a name change that suited her starry-eyed and self-dramatizing aspirations. "I crave," as she put it, "with all the fervor of a soul that has sounded its own depth . . . to be understood by lofty, generous, intelligent and appreciable beings." She played not only the Literary Dreamer but also the Literary Temptress, startling a visitor to her salon by her "dishevelled ringlets" and "low-necked dress of flaming crimson tarlatan."

Poe had known Stella and her husband, the attorney Sylvanus Lewis, since about 1846, and often profited from their hospitality and charity. He frequently spent the evening at their three-story brick home in Brooklyn, dining, playing whist, reading aloud his latest work; the Lewises visited in Fordham during Virginia's final illness, too, and attended her funeral; after Virginia's death, Muddy and Poe sometimes sojourned at the Lewises' home several days at a time; Sylvanus Lewis helped in Poe's libel suit, and by his own account also gave Poe and Muddy some money. Poe appreciated the largesse, but found it hard to take. Loui Shew said that during her visits to Fordham she often found Stella, a "fat gaudily dressed woman," waiting in the cottage to see Poe, who had escaped to the fields or the nearby college. Mrs. Shew recalled that Muddy once sent her to look for Poe, and she found him sitting on a rock, muttering "his desire to die, and get rid of *Literary bores.*"

Poe in part repaid the Lewises' beneficence by advancing Stella's writing career. He gave her literary coaching, extensively revising one (and probably more) of her poems, which she published under her own name without acknowledging his help. He puffed her shamelessly, joining the worst of the claques he had spent his professional life reviling. And her view of her accomplishment was considerable. Sending some newspaper clippings to a friend, later in life, she observed that "the British press has placed me on a plane with Shakespeare—the highest position accorded to a woman since the Greeks seated Sappho by the Side of Homer on the pinnacle of fame." As a critic for hire, Poe praised Stella hardly less. In one of his several blurbs for her *Child of the Sea and Other Poems,* he remarked: "If we err not greatly, [it] will confer immortality on its author." In the same review he flattered her hefty figure too, "finely turned—full, without being too much so." Enlisting others to make a chorus of praise for Stella, he asked F. W. Thomas to insert some prepared comments about her in his new periodical, "editorially."

Poe may have badly needed the Lewises' favors. For his boast of having made "permanent engagements with every magazine in America" came down to writing mostly for a single journal, the *Flag of the Union.* More degrading still, in its every feature the *Flag* inverted his ideal of the substantial, well-printed, tasteful five-dollar journal, purged of New England influence. A weekly printed in the jam-packed style of the mammoth newspapers, each page holding eight broad columns, the *Flag* sold for two dollars a year and was published in Boston. It paid, however, five dollars a 'Graham's page,' and Poe agreed to become a regular contributor, out of "sheer necessity," he said. Still the association distressed him. The *Flag* misprinted his work, and he felt anyway that whatever he published there would go unnoticed. "It pays well as times go," he told Willis, "but unquestionably it ought to pay ten prices; for whatever I send it I feel I am consigning to the tomb of the Capulets."

Ironically, the *Flag* served to bring readers several of Poe's most distinctive poems and one of his strongest tales. In one sense he had not been wrong in proclaiming a new impetus to his literary career. At whatever personal cost, the careening of the preceding year had given him much to say of loss, disillusionment, and especially of rage, and it asked expression. The poems he published in the *Flag* are unusually autobiographical, directly reflecting his recent life. Shunning his usual dreamscape and aural magic, the sonnet "To My Mother" hails Muddy for filling the place both of Eliza Poe and of Virginia:

> *You who are more than mother unto me,*
> *And fill my heart of hearts, where Death installed you*
> *In setting my Virginia's spirit free.*
> *My mother—my own mother, who died early,*
> *Was but the mother of myself; but you*
> *Are mother to the dead I loved so dearly,*
> *And thus are dearer than the mother I knew. . . .*

Poe also memorialized Annie, creating a character of the same name in "Landor's Cottage." (The title perhaps registers some awareness of his debt to Landor.) The Annie of this verbal landscape painting, at once maternal and girlish, presides over a "fairy-like" and immaculately kept rustic home, outside all velvety turf and crystal springs, within all snowy muslin curtains and delicate French wallpaper, the place Poe had idealized since *Tamerlane*—and likely long before, for the cottage impresses the narrator "very much as I have been impressed when a boy, by the concluding scene of some well-arranged theatrical spectacle or melodrama."

Poe drew the connection between Annie and his mother even more directly in "For Annie." This quietly savage poem alludes to his self-poisoning in Boston, and Annie's promise to come to his deathbed. It treats death, or at least the attempt to die, as a return to infantile bliss by drinking "a water that flows, / With a lullaby sound," suggesting both mother's milk and the laudanum Poe swallowed. The mood of maternal tenderness lapses into and out of a crepuscular fright, rendering a state of restful horror that is simultaneously an infant's slumber and the repose of a corpse:

> *She tenderly kissed me,*
> *She fondly caressed,*
> *And then I fell gently*

> *To sleep on her breast—*
> *Deeply to sleep*
> *From the heaven of her breast.*
>
> . . . .
>
> *And I lie so composedly,*
>   *Now, in my bed,*
>   *(Knowing her love)*
>   *That you fancy me dead—*
> *And I rest so contentedly,*
>   *Now in my bed,*
>   *(With her love at my breast)*
>   *That you fancy me dead—*
>   *That you shudder to look at me,*
>   *Thinking me dead:—*

The many identical rhymes and broken-off rhythms create an effect of explosive emotion stifled but all-mastering, a loop playing and replaying a crescendo of anguish to no conclusion.

The identity of the woman commemorated in "Annabel Lee" is less certain. Completed around May (and published in the New York *Tribune* in October), the ballad seems to have had a special poignancy for Poe: Muddy reportedly said that when he read it to her, "oh! how he cried!" Here again he celebrated a nonsexual, childlike attachment:

> *I was a child and she was a child,*
>   *In this kingdom by the sea;*
> *But we loved with a love that was more than love—*
>   *I and my Annabel Lee—*

Such surpassing love stirs the envy of others—"high born kinsmen," angels in heaven, "demons down under the sea"—who bear Annabel Lee away, and ultimately kill her. (The struggle for possession against older or more powerful figures perhaps explains the scrambling of *Allan* in the title.) The heroine's name suggests that in depicting this innocent love, Poe had in mind Annie Richmond. But Sarah Helen Whitman believed that he intended the poem for her; Muddy later told Mrs. Lewis that Poe meant it for her, Stella; and Fanny Osgood said he wrote it for Virginia. Fanny was a candidate herself, and Poe clearly knew her closely-akin ballad "The Life-Voyage," which begins: "Once in the olden time there dwelt / Beside the sounding sea." But except for Muddy's self-serving later statement to Stella, all of the claimants and identifications were correct:

> . . . *the moon never beams, without bringing me dreams*
>   *Of the beautiful Annabel Lee;*
> *And the stars never rise, but I feel the bright eyes*
>   *Of the beautiful Annabel Lee:—*
> *And so, all the night-tide, I lie down by the side*
> *Of my darling—my darling—my life and my bride,*
>   *In her sepulchre there by the sea—*
>   *In her tomb by the sounding sea.*

In Poe's promise of never-ending remembrance of her girlish beauty, and his pleasure in joining her in early death, Annabel Lee represents all of the women he loved and lost.

Poe's powerfully recharged poetic energy produced three more-generalized poems, treating not specific circumstances and persons but his whole feeling about his life at the time. "A Dream within a Dream" quietly dramatizes his furious bewilderment in helplessly watching the little that he holds precious sift away:

> *I stand amid the roar*
> *Of a surf-tormented shore,*
> *And I hold within my hand*
> *Grains of the golden sand—*
> *How few! yet how they creep*
> *Through my fingers to the deep,*
> *While I weep—while I weep!*
> *O God! can I not grasp*
> *Them with a tighter clasp?*
> *O God! can I not save*
> *One from the pitiless wave?*

The image of "golden sand" derives from the discovery of gold fields in California in 1848, with the rush there within two years of more than forty thousand prospectors. Poe disdained the clamor, and also published in the *Flag* a hoax entitled "Von Kempelen and His Discovery," in which an acquaintance of the supposedly noted chemist reports Von Kempelen's discovery of a method for creating gold from lead, making the precious metal of no more than industrial value and reducing the gold rush to a fool's errand.

The prospecting returns with darker personal meaning, however, in the elegant "Eldorado":

> *Gaily bedight,*
> *A gallant knight,*
> *In sunshine and in shadow,*
> *Had journeyed long,*
> *Singing a song,*
> *In search of Eldorado.*

Poe's image of the poet as a questing knight or troubadour gives a grim turn to Helen's vision of him as a chivalric Poet. For the knight's fate is inglorious, a long journey nowhere, overtaken by the failing strength and awareness of aging that weigh on all of Poe's poems in this period. Borrowing a device from "The Raven," he compressed the significance of the knight's career into the changing meanings of "shadow." Prominently set at the turning point of each stanza, the word first means simply the lack of sunshine, then gloom, then a ghost; its deepest sense is revealed to the knight in the final stanza by the "pilgrim shadow":

> *"Over the Mountains*
> *Of the Moon,*
> *Down the Valley of the Shadow,*
> *Ride, boldly ride,"*
> *The shade replied,—*
> *"If you seek for Eldorado!"*

The pilgrim imparts what Poe had always known about Eldorado, that the way to the golden treasure lies through the valley of death.

The most literary-seeming of these distinguished poems is also perhaps the most despairing. In its virtuoso onomatopoetic effects, "The Bells" aspires to the condition of nonverbal sound, although its structure closely resembles that of "Eldorado." Like the four evolving meanings of "shadow" there, here the sounds of sleigh bells, wedding bells, fire-alarm bells, and finally funeral bells make a similar succession from youthful gaiety to death and disillusionment. But Poe greatly emphasized the faith-destroying horror of the transformation. In mounting frenzy and verbal discord, the happiness foretold by the sleigh bells and wedding bells is revealed as a cheat, the insignificant preliminary to an onslaught of annihilation. The hideously frolicsome bell ringers who toll the final bells

> *Feel a glory in so rolling*
> *On the human heart a stone—*

> *They are neither man nor woman—*
> *They are neither brute nor human,*
> *They are Ghouls:—*
> *And their king it is who tolls:—*
> *And he rolls, rolls, rolls*
> *A Pæan from the bells!*
> *And his merry bosom swells*
> *With the Pæan of the bells!*
> *And he dances and he yells. . . .*

Poe depicted existence as the plaything of a lying, sadistic Overlord of Life, the banquet of a Ghoul-God.

Something of this rage for extinction animates Poe's criticism and fiction at this time also. His three years or so "out of the literary world," he told F. W. Thomas, had left him ornery: "The fact is . . . living buried in the country makes a man savage—wolfish." And he was ready to pounce: "I have *some* old scores to settle," he said. "I am just in the humor for a fight." Although the quantity of his book reviewing, like that of his fiction, had fallen off, his notoriety for literary massacres remained. Early in the year the *Dollar Magazine* published a silhouette by F. O. C. Darley, caricaturing Poe as an Indian brandishing hatchet and scalping knife: "With tomahawk upraised for deadly blow, / Behold our literary Mowhawk, Poe!" Lacking an editorial position, Poe did not write much criticism now either, although what he did produce also seems animated by rage, and trigger-happy.

In "About Critics and Criticism," an essay he did not manage to get published, Poe proposed forthrightly that the critic's *"legitimate task"* is condemnation, a matter of "pointing out and analyzing defects and showing how the work might have been improved." He illustrated by exposing affectations and absurdities in some lines by Elizabeth Barrett Browning (as she now was), whom he had earlier ranked second to Tennyson among poets of the period. For lesser literary women, the growing number of bluestockings, he proposed deadlier handling. They "should be decimated, at the very least," he wrote in his "Marginalia." "Have we no critic with nerve enough to hang a dozen or two of them, *in terrorem?*"

The particular 'blue' Poe imagined leading to the gallows may of course have been Helen, and her ties to Emerson and to Boston may also have made him more than ever contemptuous of New England literary life. Parodying Longfellow's foolish (he thought) attempt to imitate Greek hexameters in English verse, he jeered at New England writers as incorrigibly arrogant bumpkins:

Do *tell me* / *when shall we* / *make common* / *sense men* / *out of the* / *pundits*
Out of the / *stupid old* / *God-born* / *Pundits who* / *lost in a* / *fog-bank*
Strut about / *all along* / *shore there* / *somewhere* / *close by the* / *Down East*
Frog Pond / *munching of* / *pea nuts and* / *pumpkins and* / *buried in* / *bigwigs*/
Why ask / *who ever* / *yet saw* / *money made* / *out of a* / *fat old*
Jew or / *downright* / *upright* / *nutmegs* / *out of a* / *pine-knot* /

(Poe's equation of Jews and moneylenders was conventional; his relation with individual Jews seems to have been friendly.) Just thinking about New Englanders put him "into a passion," Poe said. Margaret Fuller was a "detestable old maid," James Russell Lowell "a ranting abolitionist and *deserves* a good using up."

Poe's chance to award such deserts came when he reviewed, for the March *Messenger*, Lowell's recent *A Fable for Critics*. In this satirical survey of American letters, Lowell had portrayed Poe as inspired but eccentric, given to pedantry and overanalysis:

> There comes Poe, with his raven, like Barnaby Rudge,
> Three-fifths of him genius and two-fifths sheer fudge,
> Who talks like a book of iambs and pentameters,
> In a way to make people of common sense damn metres,
> Who has written some things quite the best of their kind,
> But the heart somehow seems all squeezed out by the mind.

Poe had once prophesied in print that Lowell would stand *"at the very head* of the poets of America," and the remarks left him gnashing his teeth. Writing anonymously, he savaged Lowell's *Fable* as badly constructed, imitative, and ignorant, concluding that "no failure was ever more complete or more pitiable." Writing also in a Southern journal for Southern readers, he bludgeoned Lowell as a Northern abolitionist. Lowell's critical standards, he said, cannot be fathomed apart from the knowledge that he is "one of the most rabid of the Abolition fanatics" and representative of them all, a "fanatic for the sake of fanaticism." Such Northerners, he explained, are fanatical in every circumstance: if they owned slaves, they would ill-treat them; if an abolitionist tried to free their slaves, they would murder him. Given the politics that shaped Lowell's judgments, Poe proscribed the reading of him: "no Southerner who does not wish to be insulted, and at the same time revolted by a bigotry the most obstinately blind and deaf, should ever touch a volume by this author."

Retaliation also dominates the two pieces of fiction Poe wrote for the *Flag,* "X-ing a Paragrab," and "Hop-Frog: or, The Eight Chained Orang-Outangs." The first is scarcely more than a humorous bagatelle, Poe's version of popular anecdotes about bizarre-looking prose that has resulted when printers, lacking type for a particular letter, have perforce substituted *X*'s. The biographical interest of the piece lies in its explosive-sounding protagonist, the "fiery" editor "Mr. Touch-and-go Bullet-head." Driven to "desperation" by a sneer at his style, he composes a reply, which however appears in print with *X*'s in place of *o*'s, after which he disappears from town. Inhabitants of the place offer various explanations of the cabalistical-looking article and of his vanishing. But in the concluding words of the piece the printer's helper attributes both to his drinking: "Mr. Bullet-head . . . vas *con*tinually a-svigging o' that ere blessed XXX ale, and, as a naiteral consekvence, it jist puffed him up savage, and made him X (cross) in the X-treme." Disappearing forever, the angry Bullethead crosses himself out of existence.

Poe's mood following his failed courtship of Helen seems most fully recorded in "Hop-Frog," a briskly narrated tale of revenge, written about a month after his final trip to Providence. Here the also touchy and explosive protagonist is a court jester, doubly plagued in being both a dwarf and a cripple. He and his companion Trippetta, "a young girl very little less dwarfish than himself," have been kidnapped from their homes and sent as presents to the king. This sadistic practical joker enjoys commanding Hop-Frog to drink, although even a little wine befuddles him. Wishing to host a masquerade, the king summons Hop-Frog and orders him to invent some novel sport for it. He also forces the dwarf to drink, which Hop-Frog does, looking around with a "half-insane stare." Trippetta tries to intervene, but the king pushes her away and dashes wine in her face. Seething, Hop-Frog drinks some more, and vengefully suggests that the king entertain his guests with a costumed skit.

On the evening of the masquerade, the king and his seven ministers gleefully consent to be coated with tar and flax, to look like escaped orangutans. They rush into the grand salon, hoping to frighten the company, as they do. Apparently aiding their jest, Hop-Frog hoists them to the ceiling, chained together. A grating sound is heard: "it came from the fang-like teeth of the dwarf, who ground them and gnashed them as he foamed at the mouth, and glared, with an expression of maniacal rage." Then Hop-Frog torches the combustible costumes, cremating the men in a sheet of flame that leaves a "fetid, blackened, hideous, and indistinguishable mass." Having murdered the king, Hop-Frog runs off with Trippetta, neither of them to be seen again.

The conflict between the mighty king and the crippled jester dramatizes years of accumulated gripes and griefs. In the king's indifference to the suffering of others, his callous affronts, his demands to be entertained, Poe summoned up a small army of people by whom he had come to feel abused and misled—the Elector of Moldavia, cronies who induced him to drink, editors ("We want characters—*characters,* man," the jaded king tells Hop-Frog, "something novel—out of the way"), friends of Helen. In the jester Poe portrayed much of himself, kidnapped from home and presented to the king, bearing a name not given in baptism but "conferred upon him," protective of the girlish Trippetta, and susceptible to wine, which "excited the poor cripple almost to madness"—a touch-and-go bullethead who when insulted and forced to drink becomes insane with rage. Over the conflict between these characters, too, hangs a sense of the future. X-ing himself, the murderous dwarf announces to the masqueraders, at the end of the tale, his own disappearance. "I am simply Hop-Frog the jester," he declares, prophetically for Poe, "and *this is my last jest.*"

New Revival of the "Stylus"; Final Trip to Lowell; Journey to Philadelphia.

APRIL–JULY 1849

Alone together at Fordham, Poe and Muddy spent a dismal spring. He seemed to her seriously ill: "I thought he would *die* several times," she said. Poe however believed that in her concern for him, Muddy often became alarmed without cause. He felt not so much physically ill as depressed, although now deeply so. "I cannot express," he wrote, "how terribly I have been suffering from gloom."

And no merely worldly consideration had the power to so dispirit him. "No," he said, "my sadness is *unaccountable,* and this makes me the more sad. *Nothing* cheers or comforts me. My life seems wasted—the future looks a dreary blank." He said he felt determined to struggle on, to hope against hope. But Muddy felt hopeless: "God knows I wish we were both in our graves," she wrote; "it would, I am sure, be far better."

Some possible relief arrived, from a surprising source—Edward Horton Norton Patterson, a writer and editor who had just turned twenty-one years of age, and who lived in northern Illinois. His coming-of-age had proved meaningful to him: the same year, he became apparently the first person in Illinois to write and publish a novel, and received a large interest in his father's weekly newspaper, the Oquawka *Spectator.* Perhaps owing to the young man's enthusiasm for Poe's writing, the paper had praised Poe editorially, republished a few of his stories and poems, and even informed citizens of remote Oquawka that "the celebrated poet and critic, is about to lead to the hymenial altar, Mrs. Sarah H. Whitman of Providence, a well known and popular authoress."

In April, Poe received a letter from Patterson, offering the most solid promise of support he had ever received for a magazine of his own. Patterson proposed that Poe would have complete editorial control, while he would pay the costs of editing, printing, and distribution. They would share equally in the receipts, payable to Poe monthly. Poe had wasted many hopes on the "Stylus," and seeing them now depend on a twenty-one-year-old in Illinois made him both cautious and uncompromising. "If we attempt it we *must* succeed," he replied to Patterson, "for, so far as concerns myself individually, all my prospects, pecuniary as well as literary, are involved in the project—but I shrink from making any attempt which *may* fail."

Poe found several features of Patterson's proposal disagreeable or doubtful. He disliked the title Patterson devised, and held out for the "Stylus," sending him a possible title page he had drawn himself. Patterson also envisioned a low- or middle-priced journal, but as always Poe argued that no *"cheap"* magazine could prosper. "We must aim high—address the intellect—the higher classes—of the country . . . and put the work at $5:—giving about 112 pp. (or perhaps 128)." As he had done to others, Poe held out to Patterson a rosy future for such a magazine, foreseeing that after five years it might well circulate twenty thousand copies, producing "a clear income of 70 or 80,000 dollars." Poe also doubted Patterson's plan to publish the magazine at Oquawka. Lying up the Mississippi River from St. Louis, the town had commercial possibilities, but was hardly a literary center like Philadelphia or New York. A decade earlier, a guide to Illinois described the place as having a fine river for milling, crossed by a substantial bridge, but otherwise consisting of two warehouses, one store, one grocery, two taverns, and "several dwelling houses." A local judge later called Oquawka "godforsaken." Poe suggested that the title page of the magazine might say something like "Published simultaneously at New-York & *St Louis*."

Having collected Poe's works, Patterson understood and valued his literary opinions, and was anxious to accommodate him. He agreed to publish a monthly magazine of 96 pages at the annual rate of $5; if circulation after the first year justified a change, he would then consider enlarging the magazine to 112 or even 128 pages. He was willing to begin when a thousand subscribers had been secured in advance—as they could be, Poe assured him. Concerned about publishing expenses, however, he maintained that he could produce the magazine as neatly in Oquawka as in St. Louis or elsewhere, but at less cost. He argued, too, that subscribers would be drawn not by the place of publication, but by Poe's name on the masthead, and the contributors.

Details remained to be worked out, but the "Stylus" again seemed a real possibility, and Poe agreed to meet with Patterson out West. He proposed resuming his subscription tour of the principal states, certain that in three or four months he could round up the thousand subscribers, pledged to pay with the first issue. When he wrote to Patterson on May 23, he said he would begin his tour at once, so that the first issue might appear in January 1850. He planned to go to Boston and to Lowell for a week, then to Richmond, where he would wait for Patterson's reply—and for the fifty dollars he asked the young man to send him there, as he was "not overstocked with money (what poor-devil author *is?*)." If the reply brought news that Patterson still favored the project, he would go on to St. Louis to discuss matters with him in person. But as for himself, Poe said, Patterson could announce their agreement to his friends and go forward "as if all was signed & sealed."

Poe went to Lowell in late May or early June, visiting for a week or more. He may have hoped to find subscribers there, but he had not at all abandoned his fantasy of living nearby with Muddy, and surely the main purpose of his visit was to see Annie. He perhaps

hoped to lift his depression, too, for by now the uncompleted-look-
ing factory town had a homelike feeling for him; containing Annie
and her husband, Annie's Westford relatives, Annie's brother Bardwell, sister Sarah, and daughter "Caddy," it seemed a place of family and friends. They in return enjoyed his company. Annie's pas-
tor, the Reverend Warren H. Cudworth, challenged Poe with a
cryptogram that he readily broke into "The patient was severely
attacked with spasms and acute pain in the hypogastric region; re-
medial agents were employed, but without effect, and death soon
ensued." Although the simple substitution code gave up its meaning easily, Cudworth was impressed and remarked that Poe solved
the cipher in a fifth the time it had taken him to compose it.

Annie's brother Bardwell spent in Poe's company every moment
he could spare from his job as principal of a grammar school, anxious not to lose, he said, "the benefit of his original thoughts, which
were continually dripping from his lips." Poe visited Bardwell's school
twice, the second time to speak again with a twenty-one-year-old
teacher he had met during his first visit, Eliza Jane Butterfield. Although nearly twice her age, he evidently saw in her a candidate for
the mate he still hoped to find. Bardwell understood Poe's interest,
took him into her classroom, and left them alone. He could not tell
whether Poe proposed to the young woman, but thought something
had transpired: "I . . . noticed an uncommon flush upon her cheek
when they came out." Whatever the nature of Poe's interest in Eliza
Butterfield, it left him feeling guilty, believing that his overtures to
her made Annie jealous, as perhaps they did. After telling Bardwell
to "remember me to Miss B.," he felt obliged to reassure Annie
that he sent the regards "in jest"—"darling Annie, no one in this
whole world except your sweet self, is *more than a friend* to me."

Poe apparently arrived in Lowell with little or no money, for in
order to raise some cash he wrote a bad check. It was very likely
Annie who paid for the two nearly identical daguerreotypes of him
taken during this visit. She kept (or was given) one; Poe gave the
other to Stella when he returned to New York (Illus. 29). Annie
insisted that the image made Poe's thin face seem heavy. All the
same, because of its unusual clarity the daguerreotype defines several features of Poe's mien more clearly than any other, such as the
receding hairline (some curling hair brushed forward, perhaps to
cover it), the light-hazel-colored eyes, and a small scar near the left
eye, conceivably a record of the time T. D. English punched his
face, cutting it with a large seal ring. The picture also seems to

record Poe's statements that "My life seems wasted—the future looks a dreary blank," for he appears pained and apprehensive.

Unknown to Poe, his stay in Lowell prompted a tense little drama. Jane Ermina Locke had not forgotten Poe's rejection of her passionately offered companionship. Earlier in the year she had published a poem called "The Broken Charm," expressing a disenchantment with him comparable to that of a pagan realizing her god is a clay idol:

> *Not that I thought to clasp thee as mine own.—*
> *But I had robed thee with such holiness,*
> *And round thy form a veil of glory thrown,*
> *I can but weep before the false impress.*

Mrs. Locke also wrote to Poe in New York, professedly to show goodwill, but obviously hoping to alarm him. She asked his advice about a book she intended to publish soon—a fictionalized account of all that had happened between them. She would make him appear, as he summarized her letter, "noble, generous, &c. &c.—nothing bad." But while requesting his comments about this flattering portrait of himself, she also served notice and gave him a scare: if he did not reply in two weeks she would publish her book as is; and, as Poe put it, "she is coming on immediately *to see me at Fordham.*"

Poe does not seem to have replied, nor does "Ermina" seem to have carried out her threats. But she schemed up a vengeful entertainment in their place. She wrote several times to Sarah Whitman, asking Helen to visit her for a week in Lowell. Since Jane Locke was a stranger, Helen declined. But Locke pressed the invitation, promising to impart important information that could not be trusted to a letter. Helen at last agreed to spend a week with her. But once Helen was settled in Lowell, in May, Locke prodded her to stay a day or two longer. She had reason to believe, she explained, that Poe would be coming. As Helen recalled her reaction at the time, she "thrilled" at the thought of seeing Poe again, but also understood that Locke felt "deeply wronged" by him. She suspected that Locke hoped to manipulate the visit in order to "pique" Poe, or even to bring about her own reconciliation with him. Helen decided not to prolong her stay. In this way it happened that she left Lowell on the same day that Poe arrived. Their trains in and out of town, she believed, passed each other. At the moment the cars met, she said later, a "singular thing" happened, which she did not describe beyond alluding to "spiritual or magnetic phenomena."

Poe's trip to Lowell probably got him few or no subscribers and did nothing to overcome his gloom. The novelist Elizabeth Oakes Smith, who apparently saw him in New York early in June, thought he looked ill at ease and "emaciated." Whatever his condition, with the "Stylus" in reach he intended to continue his subscription tour. He had planned to be in Richmond by June 1 but put off his journey until June 11, then postponed it again, being, he said, *on the point of* starting every day." Part of the difficulty was that he lacked money to get there. He requested a loan of ten dollars from J. R. Thompson of the *Messenger,* also asking him to forward the letter from young Edward Patterson that should by now have reached Richmond, containing fifty dollars of start-up money for their partnership. No money arrived, but Muddy said that she sold off "everything I could," evidently personal and household belongings, to get enough for Poe's travel expenses and a few essential "articles."

Poe's delay involved more than want of money, however, much as his tour involved more than subscribers. He had apparently been feeling some need to revisit the place of his growing up, and he had kept in mind the possibility of marriage to Elmira Royster. But to think of leaving Fordham and traveling to Richmond troubled him. According to Muddy, he feared that the trip might be his last, that "he might be called suddenly from the world." In his apprehensive mood he told her—or so she later claimed (and still later denied)—that he wished Rufus Griswold to act as his literary executor, should he die. Except in appointing an executor at all, Poe did nothing surprising in choosing Griswold, who acted as a literary agent for several writers, including Fanny Osgood. Around May, too, Griswold had invited him to contribute some new poems to *Poets and Poetry of America,* soon to appear in its tenth edition. Well aware of the publicity value of appearing in Griswold's popular anthologies, he sent "Lenore," "For Annie," and "Annabel Lee." Poe's solo excursions had of course often ended in embarrassment or illness, but his premonitions may also have been stirred by the epidemic of cholera that had been reaching across the United States, carried by gold prospectors all the way to California. It was virulent in New York, where over five thousand people died between May and August.

Feelings of foreboding are the subject of an extraordinary, untitled tale that Poe likely wrote at about this time, but did not publish. Only two pages long in modern editions, it consists of entries in a journal between the first and the third of January 1796. The last words of the tale, as if to begin a new entry, are "Jan. 4." But here the journal, and the tale, end. Nothing follows the date but the blankness of the page—perhaps because Poe left the tale incomplete, perhaps because he so meant to indicate the death of the narrator, a lighthouse keeper. In his journal, the man sets down his thoughts and feelings during his first (and maybe last) three days on the job. He does not identify himself, but his meditations reveal him as a "noble of the realm" who has come to shun society, having sought the appointment in order to be alone, and to finish a book. Alone he is, separated from land by two hundred miles of high, rough sea. He seems protected from their menacing force, however, by the monumentality of the lighthouse, whose iron-riveted walls are over four feet thick, and whose huge cylindrical shaft he estimates to be at least 180 feet high, 20 feet of it lying below the sea's surface.

The journal entries record the insidious swelling of the lighthouse keeper's anxiety, despite his attempts to stifle it. He no sooner arrives at the isolated spot than he begins to fear for his bodily health and emotional stability: "there is no telling what may happen to a man all alone as I am—I may get sick, or worse. . . . but why dwell on that, since I am *here,* all safe? . . . I do believe I am going to get nervous about my insulation. *That* will never do." By the third and last day, he has begun to sense danger not only within himself but also without, doubting whether the lighthouse, however monumental, can protect him from the raging sea. He explores the interior and at first decides that the lighthouse is invulnerable: "A structure such as this is safe enough under any circumstances." Moments later, however, he begins to fret that the shaft would have been stronger had it not been left hollow below sea level, but filled with masonry. In the concluding sentence of the tale (fragment?), he decides: "The basis on which the structure rests seems to me to be chalk." His grim conclusion is followed by the date of the next day's entry, and then by nothing.

In the lighthouse keeper trying to finish a book, Poe figured his current situation as a writer, disaffected, menaced, doubting his ability to "manage the light." But the tale speaks still more intimately to his personal life, in the narrator's uncertainty about whether he can survive *"alone"* without falling ill, succumbing to anxiety, or being overwhelmed from outside: "The basis on which the structure rests seems to me to be chalk." Titleless and endingless, told in gaps, pauses, and cut-off sentences, the tale is likely the last that Poe wrote. With the blank for January 4, recalling Hop-Frog's *"this is my last jest,"* he vanished himself off the page. Remarkably, he timed his existence to end on January 3, 1796, the same day and the same year that the young actress Eliza Poe, after a voyage from her native England, arrived with her mother for the first time in America, in Boston.

Poe finally left for Richmond on June 29, having delayed another week hoping for a letter from Annie, which did not arrive. He and Muddy spent the afternoon and dined at the Brooklyn home of the Lewises. He had continued his press-agentry on Mrs. Lewis's behalf, most recently by suggesting to Griswold that the anthologist had "not *quite* done justice" to her in his *Female Poets of America.* Claiming that Stella had no part in the request, he asked Griswold to include a revised biographical sketch of her in his next edition, "a somewhat longer one prepared by myself. . . . I would reciprocate the favor when, where, and *as* you please." Before leaving for Richmond, he exacted from Stella the sort of payment that lured him into this sort of work, her promise to see Muddy often, and be sure she did not suffer in his absence. Muddy understood the bargainings of the literary marketplace, too, and did her part. She wrote to Griswold herself, offering compensation if he included Poe's piece on Stella. "If you will do so I will promise you a favorable review of your books as they appear," she said. "You know the influence I have with Mr. Poe."

Muddy saw Poe aboard the steamboat to Perth Amboy, New Jersey, there to connect with the Philadelphia train. He seemed to her "dejected," although he tried to cheer her. As she recorded his words, he said, "God bless my own darling muddy do not fear for your Eddy see how good I will be while I am away from you, and will come back to love and comfort you." Intending a tour of a few months, likely to take him as far as St. Louis, he brought a valise of clothing and probably a trunk of books and manuscripts, needed for dealing with editors and potential subscribers. He also carried with him, so it was reported to Loui Shew, the miniature portrait of Eliza Poe. To the back of it he had pasted a piece of paper containing the date of his departure and the words, "My adored Mother! E. A. Poe, New York."

Poe probably arrived in Philadelphia on the last day of June. As a writer he had spent his most productive years amid its long, tree-lined avenues and fine markets. But the city's celebrated atmosphere of order and tranquillity was broken by the cholera epidemic. With little if any warning, a comma-shaped bacterium invaded the digestive tract, producing diarrhea, spasmodic vomiting, and cramps that quickly led to dehydration, often with cyanosis, leaving the victim with darkened hands and feet, blue-faced. Those infected might be well in the morning and buried before night. Pressed for hospital beds, the local government of Philadelphia had to take over the public schools, tear out desks, and replace them with cots.

Poe probably intended only to pass through the city on his way to Richmond, but became sick and ended up staying there almost two weeks. "My *dear, dear* Mother," he began a letter to Muddy about a week after his arrival, "I have been *so* ill—have had the cholera, or spasms quite as bad, and can now hardly hold the pen." That day, in fact, forty-four new cases of the disease had been reported in Philadelphia, with nine deaths, following thirty-four new cases with twelve deaths the day before. Poe said that to fight his illness he took calomel, a chalky mercury compound often prescribed for cholera in large doses. It could make the gums suppurate as in mercury poisoning, but Poe contended that its effect on him was "worse than death," a prolonged confusion, "congestion of the brain." Among other things, he had lost his valise, containing the lectures he was to deliver on his tour.

Poe's diagnosis of his 'brain congestion' may have been correct, but sounds as though he made it himself: he had had "cholera, or spasms quite as bad"; his confusion "possibly" sprang from calomel. Other evidence suggests that during his two weeks in Philadelphia, Poe was not in the grip of cholera but pumped to a psychic bursting point by an all but uncontainable anxiety. He apparently tried to medicate his condition with alcohol, only to experience for the first time some derealizing effects both of intoxication and of 'withdrawal. The matter is beyond proving, but when telling Muddy of his mental state, he also revealed that he had been taken to Philadelphia's massive Moyamensing Prison for being drunk, unjustifiably, he said: "I was not. It was about Virginia." Whether from calomel, alcohol, or withdrawal, the devastating severity of what he underwent he was able to indicate only two weeks later, when he had regained some quiet. "For more than ten days I was totally deranged," he then told Muddy of his time in Philadelphia, "although I was not drinking one drop; and during this interval I imagined the most horrible calamities. . . . All was hallucination, arising from an attack which I had never before experienced—an attack of *mania-à-potu.*"

Poe spared Muddy the details of his hallucinations, which are known mostly through his descriptions of them to the Philadelphia publisher and engraver, John Sartain. A handsome cockney about Poe's age, born in London, Sartain had bought and would publish "The Bells." In explaining Poe's condition, Sartain claimed to know that on arriving in Philadelphia, Poe had gotten in touch with old friends, and with their encouragement started drinking heavily, "to the verge of madness." Early on Monday afternoon (seemingly July 2), Poe came to the engraving studio in his home. He looked "pale and haggard," Sartain recalled, "with a wild and frightened expression in his eyes." Poe said that he had come for refuge and protection. When Sartain asked why he needed them, Poe said that on the train he had overheard some men, a few seats behind him, plotting to kill him and throw him off. They whispered so low that he could not have understood them except for his acute sense of hearing. He escaped by leaving the train at Bordentown, New Jersey, then taking another train to Philadelphia. Sartain asked why these men wanted to kill him. Poe said it was for revenge over "a woman trouble."

While engraving, Sartain conversed with Poe off and on. Poe's talk moved from ideas of being murdered to thoughts of suicide: "his words clearly indicated this tendency," Sartain said. After a long silence, Poe remarked that if his mustache were removed he would not be so easily recognized. He asked Sartain for a razor, so he could shave it off. Worried that Poe might try to kill himself, Sartain answered that he had no razor but, if Poe wanted, would cut off the mustache himself with scissors. He took Poe into the bathroom and did the job, leaving him "absolutely barefaced." The change "satisfied him somewhat," Sartain said, and calmed him down.

But that evening, Poe announced that he was going off to the Fairmount district, on the Schuylkill River. Sartain insisted on accompanying him. Poe wore a borrowed pair of Sartain's slippers, his own shoes having become so much worn down that they chafed. As the two men waited for an omnibus, Poe asked a favor concerning the portrait of him painted by Fanny Osgood's husband: that after his death, Sartain would see to it that the picture went to Muddy. By bus and foot they got to Fairmount district, whose waterworks supplied the city and whose cascades and fountains made it a favored place for relaxation or exercise. All was "pitchy dark,"

Sartain recalled, but Poe pressed on, talking again and rapidly about the conspiracy to kill him, steadied by Sartain, who kept trying to distract him. The talking stopped as Poe began climbing the breakneck flight of wooden steps that led nearly to the summit of the reservoir. Breathless, they rested on a bench at the top landing. "The night was black, without a star," Sartain recalled, "and I felt somewhat nervous alone with Poe in the condition he was in."

Sitting on the highest point in Fairmount, overlooking the river, the stillness broken only by the sound of the waterfall, Poe began talking of his experiences since arriving in Philadelphia. Sartain later felt inadequate to recording these hallucinations, unable he said to give "even a faint idea of his wild descriptions." Although he published the following details many years after the events, in slightly differing accounts, they seem generally reliable. Poe spoke of having been confined in a cell at Moyamensing Prison, suspected of trying to pass a fifty-dollar counterfeit note. (Sartain added that Poe had actually been brought to the prison charged with drunkenness, but was identified as "Poe, the poet," and dismissed without the customary fine.) From his cell window, Poe could see the prison's granite tower, and discerned a woman standing there against the dark sky, "a young female brightly radiant, like silver dipped in light, either in herself or in her environment." From her distant perch this luminous woman asked him a series of questions, which he dared not fail to answer, for the consequences would have been terrible. His acute sense of hearing again enabled him to understand what she said and to pass the ordeal, which he said was "a snare to catch me." But a worse snare awaited. One of the prison attendants invited him to a stroll about the prison. In walking the ramparts they came to a boiling cauldron. The guard invited him to take a drink, but he declined—fortunately again. For the drink was part of another plot to kill him. Had he taken it, Poe said, "I should have been lifted over the brim and dipped into the hot liquid up to the lip."

The conspirators at Moyamensing were however set on torturing him, Poe said. To do so they now brought out his mother. "When he alluded to his mother, which was always with feelings of affectionate devotion," Sartain explained, "it was not his own natural mother, who died when he was in his infancy, but Mrs. Clemm, his mother-in-law." His tormenters now tried, Poe said, "to blast my sight." They did so by forcing him to watch while they mutilated his mother. First they sawed off her feet at the ankles, then they sawed off her legs to the knees, then they sawed off her thighs at the hips.

Describing this scene threw Poe, Sartain recalled, "into a sort of convulsion." He thought that Poe might leap into the darkness below, dragging him along. He suggested that they leave, as they did, descending slowly and holding the handrails. "All the way down the steep steps I trembled," Sartain said, "lest he should remember his resolve of suicide." Sartain managed to get Poe back to his home, and gave him the dining-room sofa to sleep on, Sartain sleeping close by him on three chairs, still in his clothing. Poe stayed with Sartain the following day and evening also, apparently benefiting from the rest and the regular meals. The next morning he seemed enough recovered to go out, Sartain recalled, although not entirely free of his dread. He napped in the grass on the fresh earth, whose smell, he said when he returned, cleared his mind. He remembered nothing distinctly of what had happened at the waterworks, but agreed with Sartain that he had experienced "delusions."

Poe borrowed some money from Sartain to continue his journey, although far from well. Writing to Muddy on July 7, he entered the place of writing as New York instead of Philadelphia, as if feeling or wishing himself to be there with her. Indeed he asked Muddy, the instant she received his letter, to come to him. She had been, he said, "all in all to me, darling, ever beloved mother, and dearest, truest friend." The joy of seeing his mother again would almost make up for their sorrows, and he longed now to rejoin her. He indeed proposed a higher form of joy: "We can but die together. It is no use to reason with me *now;* I must die." He explained that since writing *Eureka,* he had no desire to go on, and could accomplish nothing more. "For your sake it would be sweet to live," he said, "but we must die together."

On July 12, still in Philadelphia, Poe climbed four flights of stairs to the offices of the *Quaker City,* a weekly paper. He sought out the twenty-seven-year-old newspaperman and novelist George Lippard, with whom he had spent time in Philadelphia years before. Hating the upper classes, Lippard sympathized with Poe and championed his attacks on the literary business establishment. He recalled that Poe arrived poorly dressed and wearing only one shoe, having managed to lose the other, as he had lost his valise. Poe revealed that he had nothing to eat, nowhere to sleep, and no friends. "You are my last hope," he said. "If you fail me, I can do nothing but die." Lippard had no money to spare, having just paid his rent, but he decided to try raising some from local publishers. "Tell them that I am sick," Poe said. "That I only want enough to get me out of Philadelphia." When Lippard went out into the hot summer streets, however, he found them half-deserted, the doors of other newspaper offices displaying cholera bulletins. Feeling ill himself, he went home, but hurried back to his printing office the next morning. Poe was still there, sitting at a table in a corner, his head between his hands. As Lippard reported his words, Poe said, tearfully, "I thought you had deserted me." He begged Lippard to help him get out of Philadelphia. "I am heart-sick for Virginia," he said. If he could only get to Virginia he would be a new man.

Lippard went out soliciting again. This time he came back with contributions of one to five dollars from five different people, including John Sartain, Louis Godey, and the editor-clergyman Charles Chauncey Burr, who also invited Poe to his home and bought him a ticket as far as Baltimore. Lippard and Burr stayed with Poe during the day, a Friday, awaiting the ten P.M. train, trying to bring down his anxiety. Poe said later that the two men "comforted me and aided me in coming to my senses." Lippard and Burr also accompanied him to the depot where, now or earlier, his lost valise somehow turned up. Lippard remembered that at their parting that night, Poe's voice, look, and manner conveyed "something of a Presentiment." Poe held his hand a long time, he said, and seemed unwilling to leave.

Richmond

JULY 14–CA. EARLY SEPTEMBER 1849

Poe reached Richmond on Saturday, July 14, and took a room at the new American Hotel on Main Street. Before going to bed on his first night back in the city, he wrote to Muddy, knowing she must be worried about him. "Oh, my darling Mother," he began, "it is now more than three [actually two] weeks since I saw you, and in all that time your poor Eddy has scarcely drawn a breath except of intense agony." He told her that his valise had been lost for ten days in Philadelphia and then recovered. But—she would "scarcely credit it"—when he opened the case this evening he discovered that it had been rifled, by the conspirators: "they had opened it and stolen *both lectures.*" As he had planned to use the talks to finance his expedition for subscribers, his purpose in coming to Richmond was defeated unless he could recover the lectures or rewrite one of them. "Oh, Mother, think of the blow to me . . . when on examining the valise, these lectures were gone."

But his mother herself had been the worst part of his trials in Philadelphia, Poe wrote, "that terrible idea which I could not get rid of—the idea that you were dead." He still feared she had fallen ill, or left Fordham in despair, or died. "If you are but alive, and if I but *see you again,* all the rest is nothing. . . . . . I never wanted to see any one half so bad as I want to see my own darling mother." In fact he regretted having made his trip. His experiences in Philadelphia had shown him more powerfully than ever that he could bear anything when with his mother, but without her became too miserable to live. In part he blamed her: "it is cruel in you to let me leave you; nothing but sorrow *ever* comes of it." He had also learned a lesson, however, and believed now that no circumstances would ever again tempt him to leave her. Having two dollars left over from the money Lippard and the others had collected for him, he sent one dollar with his letter, imploring Muddy to write instantly. Better yet, he begged her to come on to Richmond. "If possible, oh COME! My clothes are *so horrible,* and I am *so ill.* Oh, if you *could* come to me, *my mother.*"

Muddy had been more than worried about Poe—*"distracted"* she said. He had written to her from Philadelphia on July 7, but enclosed the letter in a note to Mrs. Lewis, who failed to pass it on until two weeks later. Stella may have meant to spare Muddy Poe's news that he had contracted cholera and his call for them to die together. But whether she caringly suppressed the letter or simply forgot about it, Poe's silence left Muddy imagining everything, aware that he had no one to comfort him but herself, "no one to nurse him and take care of him when he is sick and helpless!" In his absence the request of her daughter had come to mind: "so tranquil, so pale," Virginia had looked at her and said, "Darling, darling Muddy, you will console and take care of my poor Eddy—you will *never never* leave him? Promise me, my dear Muddy, and then I can die in peace." She had wanted to accompany Poe to Richmond, but was unable to scrounge up the money. His trip, with its chance of success for the "Stylus" and perhaps his engagement to Elmira Royster, might have real benefits for them, but she recognized its dangers too. "If Eddy gets to Richmond safely and can succeed in what he intends doing, we will be relieved of part of our difficulties," she wrote to Annie, "but if he comes home in trouble and sick, I know not what is to become of us."

When Muddy at last received Poe's letter, on a visit to Stella's Brooklyn home, she was incredulous and angry: "would you believe it?" she told Annie. "She had a letter from Eddy to me begging her for Gods sake to send it to me without a moment's delay." Had his letter reached her in time, she would have gone on immediately to Philadelphia, "if I had to have *begged* my way, and then how much misery my darling Eddy would have been saved." Instead she wrote off to Philadelphia and got "all the particulars" of what Poe had undergone. In writing to her son in Richmond, she said nothing of Stella's failure to deliver his letter. Presumably she hoped to avoid upsetting him further, for she knew that before leaving New York he had gotten Stella's promise to see her often and be sure she "did not suffer." On the contrary, she told Poe that Stella had been *"very kind"* to her and that she wanted for nothing.

Assuring him that his mother still lived, Muddy's letter "acted like magic," Poe said. But by the time he replied to it, some five days after arriving in Richmond, he felt in much better health and spirits anyway. He had not taken a drink in nearly a week, he told Muddy (and before that "only a little Port wine"). And he had begun to think he might be able to regain his balance. *"If possible,* dearest Mother, I *will* extricate myself from this difficulty for your *dear, dear sake."* He would at least give it his best effort, and would try to do some writing, "When I get my mind a little more composed." Muddy's attempt to deceive him about Mrs. Lewis worked, for he also sent fondest love to Stella: "Tell her that *never, while I live,* will I forget her kindness to my darling mother." (The deception was twofold, for Muddy understood that Poe disdained Mrs. Lewis: "he cares nothing about her indeed less than about any one I know—He would devotedly love any one that is kind to me." The deception was actually threefold, for according to Muddy, Stella also understood how Poe regarded her: "she says she knows Eddie does not *like her."*)

Feeling more himself again, Poe began to stir in Richmond. The cholera epidemic had come but was abating, restoring the city to its hills above the bright islands of the James River, its flesh dealers setting out with gangs of manacled slaves, newly purchased, across the mountains to the Ohio River. Poe's feelings about Richmond had always wavered. It was the site of the deaths of Eliza Poe, Jane Stanard, and Fanny Allan, the home of the wealthy sons and widow of John Allan, after whose second marriage he had written, "I no longer look upon Richmond as my place of residence." However bitter, such associations formed at the same time time a bond to what was also, after all, the place of his growing up, and where he had first gained a literary reputation, lived as for the first time a married man. Despite a professional life spent mostly in Northern cities, too, his attachment to the South and its ideology had remained strong. Southern and western literary talent seemed to him superior to that of the North, "more vivid fresher . . . less conventional, less conservative." And although he had been raised in a merchant family, his profound and sensitive pride owed something to the planter-elite's ideal of the gentleman, as did his fastidiousness of dress and speech, and his gallantry with women, at least when sober. He could with equal truth tell his cousin George Poe, several years earlier, "Richmond is my home, and a letter to that City will always reach me in whatever part of the world I may be."

Poe roomed at the Swan Tavern, built in the 1780s near Thomas Jefferson's capitol building, in his youth a fashionable hotel but now an inexpensive framed boardinghouse, respectable but antiquated. He visited former Richmond haunts, old acquaintances—Sanxay's book store, friends of Fanny Allan, relatives of his old boss T. W. White, Jane Stanard's son Robert, his boyhood friend. He found himself often invited out but not often able to go, "on account of not having a dress coat." The Swan stood on Broad Street, a wide road leading east to Church Hill, where Elmira Royster lived, and west to the Richmond suburbs, where he might visit the Mackenzies. He sometimes stayed with them, and called at nearby Talavera, the fine home of a twenty-seven-year-old relative of Fanny Allan's, Susan Archer Talley. She recalled that once Poe's health improved he "became the fashion." People were invited to meet him at evening entertainments, expecting that he would recite "The Raven," as he apparently often did (although finding it, she added, "an unwelcome task"). She remembered him as dressed habitually in black, despite the heat of a southern summer, and quietly dignified in manner, "even at times unconsciously approaching *hauteur*." Although he joined the social conversation and seemed amused by the young people's chatter, he preferred sitting quietly or strolling about the lawn or garden with a friend.

At the Mackenzies' handsome brick house, Duncan Lodge, Poe renewed his tie to Rosalie. Evidently they had fallen out of touch, for two years earlier, she had written to Willis in New York asking if he knew Poe's whereabouts; not having heard from him in a long time she supposed he had moved. A small woman with dark brown hair and hazel eyes, of drab personality, she was now thirty-nine, but wrinkled; it was remarked in Richmond that she looked much older than her forty-year-old brother. Proud of what he had done for the Poe name, by several accounts she followed him around the city during his stay, to his annoyance. Susan Talley said that he often teased her about her dress and hair, playfully, but also vexed by her lack of taste and carelessness about her appearance. She submitted, and told others, as Talley quoted her words, "Edgar could never love me as I do him, *because he is so far above me.*" In the process of taking Poe's trunk from Talavera after one of his stays, a lamp got broken; Rose commented that nothing should be said about the mishap, for the lamp was broken by a poet.

Poe also began seeing about the matters that had taken him to Richmond. On his arrival he had found two letters from Edward H. N. Patterson at Oquawka, one containing the fifty dollars he had awaited in New York, seed money for the "Stylus." Apparently too ill at first to reply, he waited two weeks before acknowledging the money, fibbing that he had just reached Richmond and promising to write in a few days. But he waited two weeks more, this time explaining that he remained debilitated by calomel. He may simply have wanted time to consider Patterson's latest proposal, which on an essential point differed from their earlier understanding. Patterson had gone along with Poe's insistence on a five-dollar magazine, but now held out for an annual subscription price of three dollars. Poe gave the idea "full consideration," and was left hesitant. To fail in this life-long goal would be ruinous to him, as such a magazine surely would under his supervision. He told Patterson that he could not edit a run-of-the-mill journal whole-heartedly, *"con amore."* The class of people to whom he looked for sympathy and subscriptions would see the venture as second-rate in its aspirations, doomed to "namby-pamby-ism & frivolity."

Poe got his way. Patterson wrote to him toward the end of August, again agreeing to a five-dollar magazine, although he proposed setting some of it in a smaller typeface than they had agreed on. Wary of the financial risk involved, too, he asked Poe for some assurance that the initial printing costs could be met through his subscription campaign. By Patterson's estimate, inaugurating the magazine required him to lay out at least $1,100, including the cost of paper for three months' run of two thousand copies. If Poe could secure the promised thousand subscribers, pledged to pay on receipt of the first number, then he would go ahead. And if Poe approved these terms, Patterson said, he might begin his trek to St. Louis, taking Southern subscriptions along the way, and planning to reach the city by October 15, when they could meet. He thought the time had passed for bringing out the first issue in January; as it was commercially unsound to begin at any other time than the beginning or middle of the year, he suggested commencing in July. The yet-again reborn hopes for the "Stylus" also seem to have composed Poe. Susan Talley recalled that he was absorbed in thinking about the journal, told her he had been guaranteed the capital to launch it, and said he meant to succeed.

Poe also began his lectures. He spoke first at the Concert Room of the Exchange Hotel on Friday evening, August 17, tickets twenty-five cents. Richmond newspapers played up the talk as an event, a chance to hear a famous native son whose works had been praised as far off as France. "Mr. Poe is a native of this city and was reared in our midst," one reported. "After a sojourn of many years in a distant part of the land, he reappears among us with increased reputation, and a strong claim upon public attention." No less good a theater town than in the time of Eliza Poe, Richmond brought its citizens the same year the singing of Jenny Lind and the acting of Junius Brutus and Edwin Booth. The announcement that Poe would conclude the evening by reading "The Raven" brought the further newspaper comment that his recitations were thought "very fine, and would do no discredit to any, even the most finished actor."

Standing in "a graceful attitude," as it seemed to one spectator, "leaning one hand on a small table beside him," Poe gave the lecture on "The Poetic Principle" he had delivered eight months earlier in Providence, with Helen seated before him. How or whether he had recovered his manuscript is unknown; he may have spoken from memory, as by one account he did when he repeated the lecture a month later. Although the oppressive heat of late summer drove many residents of the city into the country, the concert room was filled. And except some objections to Poe's "sing song" recitation by John Daniel, the editor he had nearly dueled during his previous visit, the reviews were superlative, describing the evening as "full of strong, manly sense," "one of the richest intellectual treats we have ever had the good fortune to hear." Pleased by his reception, Poe wrote Muddy that if he lectured again and put the tickets at fifty cents, he would clear a hundred dollars. "I *never* was received with so much enthusiasm," he said.

Setting about his second important project, Poe sought out Elmira Royster. Since the breaking of their engagement more than twenty years earlier, she had gained social prominence and wealth from marrying into an established Virginia family, the Sheltons. Her industrious husband, Alexander Shelton, went into the transportation business, eventually conducting his own cartage firm and owning in partnership a boat line on the James River. He died at the age of thirty-six, leaving her with three children and an estate estimated at $100,000, enough to keep a comfortable home, dress handsomely, and drive a double team of horses in a fashionable carriage.

Widowed some five years, and about two years younger than Poe, Elmira Shelton is said to have been a sprightly, intelligent, and well-read woman with dark brown hair, full cheeks, and a thin, patrician nose. A surviving daguerreotype of her, severely coiffed and tight-lipped, also leaves an impression of primness (Illus. 30). Baptized in adulthood at St. John's Episcopal Church, and a devout churchgoer, she seems indeed to have been troubled by a sense of personal sin. "I often ask myself," she wrote in one letter, "can this heart which seems so full of corruption be a dwelling place for the 'Holy Spirit'? Will He live where there are so many unholy thoughts & desires?" To judge from this same letter, written about nine months before she reencountered Poe, she confronted her situation in life with conflicted feelings of resolve and resignation. Her religious beliefs called on her to act: "it is but a short journey to eternity," she wrote, "therefore it behoves [*sic*] me to be up and doing." But she looked out at the same time on a "world of troubles & disappointments" that promised little reward: "I am fearful . . . that I never shall be a happy woman again," she said, "time will certainly do a great deal in obliterating past events from my feelings, but I am certain that I shall never feel like myself again."

On a Sunday, probably early during his stay in Richmond, Poe turned up at Elmira Shelton's tall brick house, appropriately located on Grace Street, facing the rear of St. John's Church (Illus. 31). He had been on the point of proposing to her the year before, to recall, but returned to New York after receiving the alluring poem from Helen. When he came to Elmira's house this time, he found her dressed for church. She said she never let anything interfere with her worship, but told him to call on her again. He did so, apparently trying at first, as he had done with Helen, to implore and sweep her into a marriage. By her account, she laughed at his rushing, but he said he was serious and had long thought of marrying her. Finding him in earnest, she became so herself and asked for time to consider. He said that "a love that hesitated, was not a love for him." Nevertheless, he may have learned something in Providence, and did not react impulsively to her delay. Instead he remained pleasant and cheerful, according to Elmira, and visited her frequently, sometimes accompanied by Rose (to his chagrin, it was said). Shelton later remembered that he spoke affectionately of Fanny Allan, Muddy, Virginia, and "his parents" (whether the Allans or the Poes is uncertain); by other accounts, he also often read "The Raven" to Elmira—with assurances that its "lost Lenore," and his "Annabel Lee," represented her.

By the end of August, rumors circulated in Richmond that Poe and Elmira Shelton were to be married. The match offered both of them some obvious consolations and advantages, and some problems. Like many other women, Elmira found Poe fascinating and admired him ("more than any man I ever knew," she remarked later), and looked to him for some relief of her malaise, her sorry sense that she would never again be "a happy woman." Her affection for Poe during their shared youth, when he was "a beautiful boy," had lingered into her marriage. She confessed that a chance encounter with Poe and Virginia, shortly after their wedding, stirred "agonizing" feelings of jealousy, that she fought off: "I remembered that I was a married woman, and banished them from me, as I would a poisonous reptile." Although Poe did not share her religious beliefs, her sanctity met some response in his prudery. She recalled that after a visiting female friend said something coarse, Poe protested: "I am surprised you should associate with anyone who could make such a remark"—a comment she took as evidence of his refinement. A more problematic protest, on the other hand, came from her two surviving children, who apparently resented seeing their father replaced. They reportedly opposed their mother's interest in Poe, one mimicking him behind his back when he called.

For Poe too, Elmira Shelton was powerfully connected to the

past, but not only through the fondness that he likewise retained for her. Once he had trudged up the blocks-long slope to Church Hill to her house, in a quiet, respectable neighborhood, he stood directly opposite the small cemetery of St. John's Church, where Eliza Poe lay in an unmarked grave. Each visit to Elmira brought him within view of where his mother was buried. As a mature woman of means and a churchgoing Christian, Shelton did not fit the pattern of the girllike women, the ethereal little sisters who most attracted Poe. But marriage to her promised economic relief, and he deeply wished to repay Muddy for her loyalty by providing a home secure from the want she had long endured. On the other hand, Elmira's wealth would dwindle by her remarriage. Her husband had contrived his will to discourage gold-digging suitors and to keep his estate intact for his children. By its terms, she retained control of the estate only while widowed. If she remarried, she ceased to be the executrix, and thereafter received only one-fourth the net proceeds. As Poe understood the arrangement, Shelton's property would be secured to his ten-year-old son. And there was the existence of the boy himself, whose education he agreed to undertake.

As marriage to Elmira Shelton meant the prospect of serving as a father, it raised more acutely than any other problem the question of Poe's stability, and of his drinking. He apparently had stopped hallucinating, and was enough recovered from his breakdown to go about his affairs. But according to Susan Talley, he drank heavily on two occasions in Richmond, seemingly in August. The first time he was looked after by the Mackenzies in his room at the Swan Tavern, and when he appeared at Talavera a few days later seemed pale and tremulous. The second time he had to be taken by two physicians to Duncan Lodge, where for some days, Talley said, his life was in danger. The doctors diagnosed his condition as "mania à potu" and warned that another such attack would kill him. Talley's recollections are often unreliable, but her account of Poe's drinking gains support from the surprising fact that on August 27, he took a public pledge against alcohol by joining a Richmond branch of the Sons of Temperance. He perhaps did so because the effects of his drinking in Richmond and Philadelphia had frightened him, and perhaps also to impress Elmira Shelton with his sobriety. She cannot have been unaware of his formal entry into this temperance organization, for within three weeks a half-dozen newspapers in Richmond, Raleigh, Philadelphia, and Boston reported his membership. A local temperance journal urged him to write on behalf of the cause: "A vast amount of good might be accomplished by so pungent and forcible a writer."

Having heard from Poe only once or twice over six weeks or so, Muddy had become literally sick with apprehension, "entirely unable to make the least exertion," she said (Illus. 32). She suspected the worst, that he might be dead or deranged: "This I am perfectly sure of, if he were living and *in his senses,* he would write," she told Annie; "I cannot bear it much longer." Or he might be needing her in Richmond and expecting her to come to his aid. She wrote to Annie's husband, Charles, asking him to lend her enough for the trip. If he complied she would leave for Virginia immediately, but if not she could only submit to her helplessness: "all that I can do will be to pray for *him,* and give *myself* up to despair." Having also hoped and expected that Poe might be able to send some money, she found herself "without the necessaries of life for many days," lacking even the means for getting into New York to see whether a letter from him had come. She turned for a small loan to Rufus Griswold, adding "how distressing it is to my feelings to make this request."

When Muddy at last heard from Poe, probably at the beginning of September, what he disclosed was, unexpectedly, a relief. His description of his successful lectures, his welcome in Richmond society, and his "intended marriage" heartened her, left her supposing that "the dark dark clouds . . . are beginning to break." The uplifting news came with a request, and a question for her to consider. Evidently Poe told Elmira that he had long retained a pencil sketch of her, drawn by him during their youth. He wrote out for Muddy some language to confirm his lie and to include in a letter when she next wrote to him. Muddy was to say that she looked all over the Fordham cottage for the sketch, but without turning it up. "I took down all the books and shook them one by one," he told Muddy to write. "The one you spoilt with Indian Ink ought to be somewhere about the house. I will do my best to [fin]d it." He would then show her statement to Elmira as proof that the sketch existed, testimony to his unbroken years-long affection.

Now that the dark clouds were beginning to break, Poe also had a question for Muddy. He believed that once he married Elmira, the three of them could never be happy at Fordham; he even felt that he could no longer return there. The question was whether he, Elmira, and Muddy could be happy in Richmond either. For an essential element of his happiness remained in Lowell. "I *must* be somewhere where I can see Annie," he explained to Muddy. "I want to live *near Annie*." In this regard, Muddy's praise of Annie pained him to hear, for it called attention to what stood in the way of his happiness. "Do not tell me anything about Annie—I cannot bear to hear it now," he said, "unless you can tell me that Mr. R.[ichmond] is dead."

Poe ended on an affirmative note, however. "I have got the wedding ring.—and shall have no difficulty, I think, in getting a dress-coat." Except that Annie remained far off, not near him as he wished, and that Charles remained alive and by the fireside, not dead as he wished, things were going well, for he had a wedding ring and would likely get a dress coat.

Old Point Comfort, Norfolk, Richmond; Death and Burial in Baltimore.

EARLY SEPTEMBER—OCTOBER 8, 1849

Poe spent nearly four more weeks in Richmond, in September, moving from the Swan Tavern to similarly inexpensive lodgings at the Madison House. Early in the month he traveled to Norfolk to repeat his lecture on "The Poetic Principle," first spending several days at Old Point Comfort, an hour away by steamer. The popular resort offered delightful bathing, fishing, sailing, and dancing in the balmy off-season, as well as walks along the massive battlements of Fortress Monroe, on the tip of the point, with its several bastions and three hundred mounted cannon. Poe seems to have stayed there as the guest of some Norfolk friends, but his sidetrip may have also been prompted by nostalgia. As army recruit Edgar A. Perry, he had once disembarked at the fortress and been promoted there on New Year's Day to the rank of regimental sergeant major.

Poe passed at least one evening near the fort, on the moonlit veranda of the ample old Hygeia Hotel, facing the ocean. Here he recited "The Raven," "Annabel Lee," "Ulalume," and other poems to a group of adolescent girls in white dresses, among them Susan Ingram, the niece of his hosts. The day after telling him that she admired "Ulalume," she received a manuscript copy of the poem, in ten stanzas beautifully handwritten on one of Poe's scrolls, with a note saying, "I would do any thing else, at your bidding." The young woman apparently appealed to him, for he also commented on her fondness for orris root, whose violetlike odor clung to her clothing. He told her he enjoyed it also, and that it made him think of Fanny Allan. "Whenever the bureau drawers in her room were opened there came from them a whiff of orris root," he said, "and ever since when I smell it I go back to the time when I was a little boy and it brings back thoughts of my mother."

From Point Comfort, Poe wrote to Muddy, telling her to prepare for a possible move: "hold yourself in readiness as well as you can, my own darling mother." He had begun making serious plans now for his marriage to Elmira Shelton—or at least entertaining them, for he stated his expectations curiously: "I *think* . . . that it will certainly take place." Elmira had suggested going to live in her Richmond house immediately after the wedding. The couple would then send for Muddy to join them, giving themselves time to make more permanent arrangements for the future. For Poe, her plan meant quitting Fordham, and moving or selling off the furniture and household goods.

But Poe told Muddy to dispose of nothing yet, quoting to her the proverb that "there is many a slip between the cup and the lip." "I confess," he said, "that my heart sinks at the idea of this marriage."

Poe's lecture at the Norfolk Academy, on September 14, was a modest success, appreciated but not well attended. A local newspaper observed that his "recitations were exquisite, and elicited the warmest admiration," but regretted "there were so few to partake." Poe himself noted that Norfolk was a small town and that two other entertainments had been scheduled for the same evening. He felt satisfied in having had a fashionable audience, and making enough to settle his bill at the Madison House, with two dollars over.

The trip out of Richmond gave Poe time to think about the marriage, but he returned there, on September 17, only a little less gloomy and indefinite about it. An evening spent at Elmira's rallied his hopes, somewhat. "I think she loves me more devotedly than any one I ever knew," he said, "& I cannot help loving her in return." He was also lifted on his return to find a letter from Muddy, assuring him she was well—guilefully, however, since unstoppable worry about him had brought on what she called "a severe attack of nervous fever" that left her bedridden. He answered her letter the next day, unhappy he could not enclose some money, even a dollar, but offering the hope that with his approaching marriage "our troubles are nearly over." "Nearly" was an uncertain amount, however. "Nothing is yet definitely settled," he explained, "and it will not do to hurry matters." However nagged by uncertainty, he told Muddy he would set out for New York on the twenty-fifth, going to the home of the Lewises and sending for her when he got there. "It will be better for me not to go to Fordham—don't you think so?" So far as his fog of indecision allowed him to see ahead at all, he presumably planned a stay in New York to settle his affairs, before returning to Richmond for the eventual marriage, and soon after continuing his tour for the "Stylus." *"If possible* I will get married before I start," he added, "but there is no telling."

Concerned as ever that Muddy benefit from his choice of a mate, Poe induced Elmira Shelton to write to her. In fact Muddy already approved the marriage, at least in part for its prospect of financial well-being. And Elmira's letter gave added encouragement. "I am fully prepared to *love* you," she told Muddy, "and I do sincerely hope that our spirits may be congenial." The rest of what she said was similarly cordial if slightly high-toned. In speaking of Poe as "your dear Edgar" and showing her awareness of Sissy's importance in their lives, she demonstrated that she would not try to undo old bonds. She also discreetly indicated that she shared Muddy's hopes for keeping Poe steady: "it will be gratifying to you, to know," she said, "that he is all that you could desire him to be, sober, temperate, moral, & much beloved." Muddy had expressed concern that Rosalie, whom she disliked, might try to turn Elmira against her. Poe conveyed her concern to Elmira, who now assured Muddy that Rose had not spoken against her, and would anyway have accomplished nothing but "a very decided disapprobation of such a course." Elmira needed no coaxing to do so, but she also revealed herself throughout her letter as a pious Christian, a further recommendation to Muddy. She said she trusted in Providence to protect Poe, "and guide him in the way of truth, so that his feet slip not." Remarking that it was midnight and she must conclude, as "I am encroaching on the Sabbath," she wished Muddy a glorious and blissful eternity.

Some literary business called for Poe's attention before his return to New York. A Philadelphia piano manufacturer, nicely named John Loud, had offered him a hundred dollars to edit a volume of poems by Mrs. Loud. The task can have been only slightly less odious to Poe than his promotion of Mrs. Lewis, but he nevertheless planned to stop a few days in Philadelphia, en route, to do the job. He also made some arrangements with the *Messenger.* While in Richmond, he had visited and conversed with J. R. Thompson, talking about the "Stylus," reciting Tennyson (and Longfellow) to him. Thompson had invited him to do some writing for the magazine during his stay, but Poe's ability to work had evidently frozen again: "I am so anxious," he said, "that I cannot." Before leaving Richmond, however, he gave Thompson five new segments of his "Marginalia" and a manuscript copy of "Annabel Lee," the latter probably in return for a loan of five dollars to help cover travel expenses. Thompson said that he advanced Poe a "small sum" as well, for an article to be written later.

Thompson may also have paid for the new portrait taken of Poe in Richmond, likely about a week before departing (Illus. 33). By one account Thompson commissioned the two small, nearly identical pictures beforehand from a local daguerreotypist, who soon after, by coincidence, saw Poe passing in the street and called him into his studio for the sitting. The portrait does look impromptu: Poe's hair and clothing seem disheveled—the collar undone, the black cravat loosely tied, a white handkerchief thrust into the open waistcoat, its mournful black offset by a sprig of evergreen. A lover of flowers, Poe reportedly was rarely seen in Richmond without one in his buttonhole. Despite the touch of gaiety, he seems tired. His mustache is regrown from the time in Philadelphia, some three months earlier, when John Sartain clipped it with scissors to allay his fear that he would be recognized and murdered.

On September 24, three days before setting off, Poe repeated his lecture on "The Poetic Principle" at the Exchange Hotel. Speaking without a manuscript, he concluded as usual by reciting "The Raven." Rose and Elmira sat conspicuously in front of the platform, facing him. The audience was smaller than had been expected, but the local *Times* praised the boldness of his views and the "melodious modulations" of his voice, remarking that "the audience seemed almost to hear the evil bird ominously croaking his 'Never more!' "

On September 26, Poe again called on Thompson, who gave him a letter for Rufus Griswold. He seemed buoyant on this day before his departure, Thompson recalled, speaking "in the highest spirits of his resolves and prospects for the future." He did not leave the same impression, however, on Elmira Shelton, to whom he said good-bye that evening. "He was very sad," she said, "and complained of being quite sick." She took his pulse, discovered that he had fever, and felt he would not be able to start for New York. Exactly what understanding about their future now existed between them is unclear. He told Muddy he had bought a wedding ring, and others in Richmond understood they were to be married upon his return. Elmira claimed years later, however, that they were not engaged; rather, they had what she vaguely called a "partial understanding." She is also reported to have said that Poe pressed her before leaving: "He entreated me to marry him . . . it was distressing to see how he implored me—He was the most distressed man when he parted with me I ever saw." It may have been fever and distress that led Poe at about nine-thirty the same evening to the office of a young physician, Dr. John Carter, whose walking stick he reportedly took by mistake. He left behind his own, together with a copy of Thomas Moore's *Irish Melodies*—two new lost objects in a list that included his valise, his lectures, and his shoe. After seeing the doctor he reportedly had a late supper at Sadler's Restaurant, leaving at midnight.

In the early morning of September 27, a Thursday, Poe began the first leg of his return to the North, setting out from Richmond for Baltimore on the 4 A.M. steamer, with a trunk containing some clothing, books, and manuscripts.

No reliable evidence exists about what happened to or within Poe between that time and October 3, a week later, when a printer named Joseph Walker saw him at Gunner's Hall, a Baltimore tavern, strangely dressed and semiconscious.

It was Election Day for members of Congress, and like other local watering holes the tavern served as a polling place. Poe seemed to Walker "rather the worse for wear" and "in great distress." Apparently flooded with drink, he may also have been ill from exposure. Winds and soaking rains the day before had sent Baltimoreans prematurely hunting up overcoats and seeking charcoal fires for warmth—"a real breeder of suicides," one newspaper called the weather, "and a genuine precursor of Old Winter." Poe managed to tell Walker that he knew Joseph Evans Snodgrass, the Baltimore editor and physician with whom he had often corresponded while living in Philadelphia. As it happened, Walker had worked as a typesetter for Snodgrass's *Saturday Visiter*. He sent Snodgrass a dire note, warning that Poe needed "immediate assistance."

When Snodgrass arrived at Gunner's Hall he found Poe sitting in an armchair, surrounded by onlookers. Poe had a look of "vacant stupidity." He wore neither vest nor tie, his dingy trousers fit badly, his shirt was crumpled, his cheap hat soiled. Snodgrass thought he must be wearing castoff clothing, having been robbed or cheated of his own. He ordered a room for Poe at the tavern, where he might stay comfortably until his relatives in Baltimore could be notified. Just then, however, one of them arrived—Henry Herring, Poe's uncle by marriage, who somehow had also learned of his condition. A lumber dealer now nearly sixty years old, he had wed Muddy's sister, and spent time with Poe during his early days in Baltimore and later when both families lived in Philadelphia. But he refused now to take over his care, saying that on former occasions, when drunk, Poe had been abusive and ungrateful. Instead, he suggested sending Poe to a hospital. A carriage was called for. Poe had to be carried into it, Snodgrass said—insensible, muttering.

Through the chilly wet streets Poe was driven to the hospital of Washington Medical College, set on the highest ground of Baltimore. An imposing five-story building with vaulted gothic windows, it afforded both public wards and private rooms, advertised as being spacious, well ventilated, and directed by an experienced medical staff. Admitted at five in the afternoon, Poe was given a private room, reportedly in a section reserved for cases involving drunkenness. He was attended by the resident physician, Dr. John J. Moran, who apparently had living quarters in the hospital together with his wife. Moran had received his medical degree from the University of Maryland four years earlier and was now only about twenty-six years old. But he knew the identity of his patient—a *great* man," he wrote of Poe, to whose "rarely gifted mind are we indebted for many of the brightest thoughts that adorn our literature." He as well as the medical students, nurses, and other physicians—all considered Poe, he said, "an object of unusual regard."

According to Moran and his wife, Poe reached the hospital in a stupor, unaware of who or what had brought him there. He remained thus "unconscious" until three o'clock the next morning, when he developed a tremor of the limbs and what Moran called "a busy, but not violent or active delirium." His face was pale and he was drenched in sweat. He talked constantly, Moran said, addressing "spectral and imaginary objects on the walls." Apparently during Poe's delirium, his cousin Neilson Poe came to the hospital, having been contacted by Dr. Moran. A lawyer and journalist involved in Whig politics, Neilson was just Poe's age. In happier circumstances Poe would not have welcomed the visit. Not only had Neilson offered Virginia and Muddy a home apart from him; his cousin also, he believed, envied his literary reputation. Years before he had remarked that he considered "the little dog," as he called Neilson, the "bitterest enemy I have in the world." The physicians anyway thought it inadvisable for Neilson to see Poe at the moment, when "very excitable." Neilson sent some changes of linen and called again the next day, to find Poe's condition improved.

Poe being quieted, Moran began questioning him about his family and about where he lived, but found his answers mostly incoherent. Poe did not know what had become of his trunk or when he had left Richmond, but said he had a wife there, as Moran soon learned was untrue. He said that his "degradation," as Moran characterized it, made him feel like sinking into the ground. Trying to rouse Poe's spirits, Moran told him he wished to contribute in every way to his comfort, and hoped Poe would soon be enjoying the company of his friends. "At this he broke out with much energy," Moran remembered, "and said the best thing his best friend could do would be to blow out his brains with a pistol."

Then Poe seemed to doze, and Moran left him briefly. On returning he found Poe violently delirious, resisting the efforts of two nurses to keep him in bed. From Moran's description, Poe seems to have raved a full day or more, through Saturday evening, October 6, when he began repeatedly calling out someone's name. It may have been that of a Baltimore family named Reynolds or, more likely, the name of his uncle-in-law Henry Herring. Moran later said that he sent for the Herring family, but that only one of Herring's two daughters came to the hospital. Poe continued deliriously calling the name until three o'clock on Sunday morning. Then his condition changed. Feeble from his exertions he seemed to rest a short time and then, Moran reported, "quietly moving his head he said '*Lord help my poor Soul*' and expired!"

The cause of Poe's death remains in doubt. Moran's account of his profuse perspiration, trembling, and hallucinations indicates delirium tremens, *mania à potu*. Many others who had known Poe, including the professionally trained Dr. Snodgrass, also attributed his death to a lethal amount of alcohol. Moran later vigorously disputed this explanation, however, and some Baltimore newspapers gave the cause of death as "congestion of the brain" or "cerebral inflammation." Although the terms were sometimes used euphemistically in public announcements of deaths from disgraceful causes, such as alcoholism, they may in this case have come from the hospital staff itself. According to Moran, one of its senior physicians diagnosed Poe's condition as encephalitis, a brain inflammation, brought on by "exposure." This explanation is consistent with the prematurely wintry weather at the time, with Snodgrass's account of Poe's partly clad condition, and with Elmira Shelton's recollection that on leaving Richmond Poe already had a fever. Both explanations may have been correct: Poe may have become too drunk to care about protecting himself against the wind and rain. Whatever the cause, the poet who above all others worshipped Poe also keenly sensed how much his death at the age of forty was demanded of him. "This death was almost a suicide," Charles Baudelaire remarked, "a suicide prepared for a long time."

Dr. Moran seems to have looked after Poe's effects, and to have made many of the funeral arrangements. The trunk Poe brought with him from Richmond had become lost, containing among other things a manuscript copy of his lecture, a packet of letters from Elmira Shelton, and several books, including copies of his own works marked with corrections and revisions for a new edition. Moran later claimed that he located the trunk at a hotel on Pratt Street where Poe had stayed, and turned it over to Neilson Poe. (Loui Shew believed that Poe had with him at the hospital the miniature portrait of his mother, but if so, Moran did not mention it.) To conduct the funeral, Moran enlisted the Reverend W. T. D. Clemm, one of Virginia's cousins. Moran's wife said that she made a shroud for Poe and helped prepare his body for burial. The hands were placed one upon the other on the corpse, and the Reverend Clemm recalled that Poe's black hair was carefully adjusted in locks around his expansive forehead. The effect satisfied Dr. Moran. "Those who had previously known him," he observed, "pronounced his corpse the most natural they had ever seen."

With no display and little ceremony, Poe was buried on Monday afternoon, October 8, at about four o'clock. Some people may have viewed his corpse at the hospital, but only eight or so went to the small Presbyterian cemetery, crowded with above-ground vaults and obelisks, and the graves of many soldiers from the American Revolution and the War of 1812. Henry Herring said that he provided the mahogany coffin; Neilson Poe paid for the hearse that transported Poe's body, and for the single carriage that followed it. In addition to these two men the carriage brought the Reverend Clemm, a Baltimore lawyer named Z. Collins Lee (who had been Poe's classmate at the University of Virginia), and probably Dr. Snodgrass. At the cemetery they met up with Poe's first cousin Elizabeth Herring and her husband, and Joseph Clarke, one of Poe's early schoolmasters.

The scattering of mourners is not surprising, for the funeral was hastily arranged and held just one day after Poe's death, before news of it reached beyond Baltimore, without the knowledge of Poe's friends in Richmond and New York, unknown even to Elmira Shelton and to Muddy. The ceremony, scanty as well, lasted by one account no more than three minutes, perhaps in respect to the weather, reported to have been raw and cloudy. Poe was put into lot 27, a family burying place near the center of the graveyard, close to the treasures of William Henry Leonard Poe and of General David Poe.

Muddy

The news of Poe's death reached Muddy at Fordham on Tuesday morning, October 9, the day after his funeral. It came through one of the many newspapers that across the country and as far west as Oregon had begun to print lengthy obituaries of him, copying each other's brief and vague accounts of his delirious last days.

Having expected that Poe would soon return and soon bring her to Richmond and a new home, Muddy half-credited the reports. To verify them she wrote immediately to Neilson Poe, "I have heard this moment of the death of my dear son Edgar," she said; "I cannot believe it, and I have written to you, to try and ascertain the fact and particulars." In her bewilderment she misdated the letter 1845 instead of 1849. "If it is true," she added, "God have mercy on me, for he was the last I had to cling to and love." At the same time, she wrote for further information to Willis as well. "Can you give me any circumstances or particulars?" she asked. "Oh! do not desert your poor friend in this bitter affliction." She sent a third letter the same morning to Annie, to whom for the past three months she had confided her frantic concern for her son's condition. But this time she acknowledged what she knew could not be denied. "Annie my Eddy is dead," she began; "Annie my Annie pray for me your desolate friend. My senses *will leave me.*"

Muddy's hunger for the details of Poe's death could be only partly satisfied. When Neilson replied two days later he confirmed the worst. "I wish to God I could console you with the information that your Dear Son Edgar A. Poe is still among the living," he wrote. "The newspapers, in announcing his death, have only told a truth." He revealed to her that Poe had died early on Sunday morning at the Washington Medical College, where he had been since the previous Wednesday, and had been buried on Monday afternoon. But he did not know when Poe had arrived in Baltimore, or where he had spent his time there, or in what circumstances. From what Muddy was able to learn later through other sources, she came to believe that while awaiting the train from Baltimore to Philadelphia, Poe met some old West Point friends, who invited him to a champagne supper and encouraged him to break his temperance pledge, with the result that he got drunk and was robbed and severely beaten.

Immediately after receiving certain news of Poe's death, Muddy went to stay at the Lewises' home in Brooklyn. She reciprocated by writing to Poe's Philadelphia friend Henry Hirst, on black-bordered stationery, asking him to make good Poe's promise to write still another favorable review of Stella's work, this time for *Graham's*. After spending two weeks with the Lewises, she went to Lowell, where Annie had offered her a separate little room with a fire, imploring her not to part with anything she wished to keep, but to bring everything she cared for. Muddy packed up her family's belongings at Fordham, finding Catterina, Poe's cat, dead when she returned to the cottage for a last load of boxes.

Muddy remained in Lowell a year and a half or more. The Richmonds treated her well. Charles owned a pair of fine horses, and insisted on taking her for a ride every day. She went sleighing, too, made friends, and in the summer apparently accompanied Annie and her five-year-old daughter on a few weeks' vacation in Maine. She received many letters of condolence from literary figures, and a visit from Longfellow, who made her promise to spend time at his home in Cambridge. She said he spoke of Poe as the greatest man living, and sincerely mourned him.

Yet at least some of the time at Lowell, Muddy was physically ill, able to swallow only a little liquid. And it gnawed her to think that had she accompanied Poe to Richmond she would not have lost him. She said that although she had met many kind friends in Lowell, she could never be happy again. "Oh!" she wrote, "when my precious Virginia left us to dwell with the angels, I had my Eddie to *comfort* and *console* me. But now *I am alone.* I have the *kind*dest *best* friends of any one in the world, but that is not my dear Eddie."

Muddy even found herself assailed with new troubles. Less than a week after Poe's death, she gave Rufus Griswold a power of attorney, allowing him to contract for a uniform edition of Poe's prose and poetry. He said he undertook the work only to aid her; once the publishing costs were recovered, she would receive most of the profits. Wishing to include the manuscript material Poe had brought along on his last trip, he tried to retrieve Poe's trunk from Baltimore. But he discovered that Rosalie, with the legal advice of J. R. Thompson, was claiming to be her brother's sole heir, "his sister and the only one he has," she said. Rose not only insisted that Poe had given the trunk to her, but also challenged Muddy's right to any share in the profits of the new edition. Muddy responded with indignation. Rose had spoken nothing but ill of Poe, she said, and he had not written to her in more than two years: "what right has Rose to any thing belonging to *him.*" Legally, Rose probably had some interest in Poe's effects and estate, but she was naive and helpless. Counseled by Stella's husband, an attorney, Griswold and Muddy managed to discourage her from pressing her claims, easing Rose out of her one chance of gaining some independence.

But Muddy gained little from Poe's remains either. She wrote futilely several times to Neilson Poe trying to get him to return Poe's trunk to her, but received no reply. She also wrote to Dr. Moran, asking him to persuade Neilson to return it. After about five months it apparently reached her at Lowell through Rufus Griswold, to whose requests Neilson proved more responsive. But her hopes of profiting from Griswold's edition of Poe's works came to not much. The publishers were apparently able to offer her no more than some sets for her own use. These she tried to sell, at a cut rate of $3 instead of the $3.75 retail price. Usually she asked friends of Poe to try to sell the books for her: "oh! did you know the desolation of my heart," she told G. W. Eveleth, "you *could* not refuse to grant the request I make in asking you the great favor of disposing for me a few copies of his works." In exchange, she implied, she offered privileged information about Poe: "If you *do* write me, I will then tell you all about my *noble, generous* Eddie. . . . May God put it into your heart to listen to the request of a heart-broken and childless mother!"

In a different way, Griswold's edition proved to Muddy not just a disappointment but a grief. Griswold had no sooner learned of Poe's death than he hastily prepared an obituary article for the next

day's *Tribune,* which other newspapers reprinted. Writing pseudonymously as "Ludwig," he began by observing that few people would
mourn, as Poe had few or no friends. He praised Poe as a skilled
writer of faultless taste, but otherwise depicted him as erratic, cynical, and unprincipled, adding lurid vignettes of Poe mumbling curses
as he roamed the streets, or flailing his arms at the storming wind
and rain, speaking as if to spirits. Willis, Graham, Neal, and others
published articles defending Poe's reputation and memory against
Griswold's smears. In reply to them, Griswold prepared a lengthy
"Memoir" of Poe as the preface to the third and final volume of his
edition, published in September 1850. Among other rumors, false-
hoods, and deliberate inventions, he alleged or implied that Poe
had been expelled from the University of Virginia, had deserted
the army, had tried to seduce John Allan's second wife, and had
been hauled from Sarah Helen Whitman's house by the police. In
quoting several of Poe's letters to himself, he concocted and inserted passages in Poe's style, contrived to make Poe seem treacherous to Graham, Godey, Eveleth, and other friends. Griswold's
still more scabrous private comments included a story that Poe and
Muddy had been lovers.

In Lowell, Muddy was prostrated by Griswold's "Memoir." "I
nearly sunk under it," she said; "I was confined to bed for a long
time with a nervous fever." Having not seen Poe's letters to Griswold before Griswold printed the self-incriminating versions, she
unquestioningly accepted the forgeries as genuine, and was left feebly explaining that Poe wrote them at a time when he did not know
what he was saying. Even so, she felt outraged and despondent: "I
thought nothing could again distress *me,* but alas have I not reason
to be miserable," she said. "To think of that *villian* [*sic*] Griswold
dragging before the public all my poor poor Eddie's *faults* and not
to have the generosity of speaking one word of his *good qualities.*
. . . did you ever feel as if you wished *to die?* as if you wished to
shut out the world and all that concerns it? *It is thus I feel."*

Rufus Griswold had many reasons for disliking Poe: resentment
over his public derision of *Poets and Poetry of America,* their rivalry
as canonizers of American taste, their subtler rivalry for such women
writers as Fanny Osgood. Indeed he said that he wrote his "Memoir" with her spirit looking down on him; she had died of tuberculosis, eight months after Poe, at the age of thirty-nine. But the character assassin who signed himself Ludwig—the mad king of Bavaria—
wrote from the mazier depths of the backwoods Baptist minister

with large sensuous eyes who turned himself into a debonair New York, who spent the night in his wife's burial vault with his lips on the forehead of her corpse. As Muddy hoped, neither Griswold's character nor Fate allowed him to go unpunished. While taking the ferry to Brooklyn in 1849, he suffered an epileptic fit, fell in the water, and sank twice before being rescued. In 1853, his fifteen-year-old daughter was aboard a train in Connecticut that plunged from an open drawbridge into a river. Rushing there from New York, he viewed by lamplight forty-nine corpses in the temporary morgue, but found her nearby. She had been pinned underwater, pronounced dead, and revived by a physician who worked on her for hours. The same year, a gas leak in the large New York house he shared with his wealthy third wife set off an explosion that severely burned his face and took off seven of his fingernails. In 1857, his lingering tuberculosis became active. Wrapped about the throat, he looked unrecognizable, fell out with most of his friends, and died of the disease the same year, at the age of forty-two. His wife removed to Maine, he had been living alone in New York, in a small room decorated with portraits of himself, Fanny Osgood, and Poe.

Muddy had no reason to begrudge Rose Poe either, who outlived Griswold but fared perhaps worse. She lived in Richmond with the Mackenzies until after the Civil War, which impoverished and broke up the family, casting her, she said, "on the charities of this cold uncharitable world Homeless & Friendless." For a while she roamed restlessly in the vicinity of Richmond. By one account, she sometimes had hysterical fits—shrieking and screaming, then for a day or two afterward lying as if hardly alive. She made her way to Baltimore, but Neilson and the remaining Poes there found her objectionable and offered little more than advice. Then about sixty and homeless, she walked the city by day in the same thin calico dress, trying to support herself by selling postcard pictures of her brother, looking at night for a place to sleep. In her neat hand she wrote to his admirers asking a dole, adding to her signature the tag "Sister of Edgar A. Poe." Occasionally she managed to get herself taken in by some benevolent family, whom she rewarded by playing the piano and composing scraps of verse: "Tho we may never meet again / Thy image I will long retain."

At the age of sixty-four, in poor health, Rose was admitted to a charity shelter in Washington, the Epiphany Church Home. Although slovenly herself, she felt superior to the other indigent inmates and refused to sit with them in church. Sometimes flouting the rules, she slipped out and boarded the Washington streetcars to sell her pictures of Poe to the passengers: "everything I get I beg for it," she said. On the morning of July 21, 1874, she went to the front door of the home to sign for a registered letter. Although it contained a charitable gift to her of fifty dollars, she did not read it, for by the time she returned to her room she was somehow exhausted. The secretary of the home was surprised to find her lying on her bed unconscious. "Ladies," she said, turning to the employees standing around, "isn't this very sudden?" Rose had always wanted to be buried near Poe, but after awaiting burial in an ice-lined receptacle, her body was interred in a Washington cemetery, in a pauper's plot belonging to the home.

The Richmonds treated Muddy well, but she was about sixty-one, white-haired, bothered by the cold Massachusetts climate—and nothing really helped: "since he left me to dwell with the angels," she said, "I feel every hour more desolate." After leaving Lowell, she wandered for nearly a dozen years, living off the generosity or tolerance of others, moving from home to home, wherever she might be taken in. Still faithful to Poe, Willis publicized her destitution in his *Home Journal,* again called on readers for aid, and transmitted their contributions to her. But as she wandered she also begged, writing to a host of Poe's literary friends—writers, editors, publishers—asking not only money but also free copies of their works, free subscriptions to their magazines or newspapers, her requests bringing few replies.

During the first year or two of her life as an itinerant, Muddy stayed again with the Lewises in Brooklyn, then apparently for a while with Loui Shew, before returning to Lowell for a several months' visit in the spring of 1852, although suffering violent headaches, intense pain in her eye that made her almost blind, and such coughing as to suggest tuberculosis. "Oh how much I have missed my loved ones in this affliction!" she said. Still seeking a less harsh climate, she moved at the end of the year to Milford, Connecticut, putting up with some friends of Loui Shew, the Strongs, although the scarcely warmer weather here did nothing to alleviate the neuralgic pains in her head and hand. Other friends offered her a home in Louisiana, and she wished to go: "I have been so sadly tossed about since my beloved children left me forever," she said, "that I will hail with transport a haven where I can be at peace." Entirely without money, she tried to raise the cost of the long trip from Thomas Holley Chivers, even from Tennyson in England. Her embarrassment in writing to someone she did not know, she told him, was reduced by the realization that "a *Poets mother* is writing to a *Poet*."

Muddy's sojourns strained and damaged old friendships. She lingered with her hosts, stayed on, exploiting their charity: "She had no haste," as Loui Shew put it. Her jealous desire to have Poe as exclusively her own also grated and irked. She had burned a package of Loui's letters to Poe, as she revealed to Loui, and had intercepted and destroyed his long letters to Stella, as she told Stella. Indeed she said that after his death she destroyed hundreds of letters written to him by "literary ladies"—as she knew he wished her to do, she explained. Loui came to think her overbearing, manipulative, secretive, and materialistic; Stella spoke of her as "the woman Clemm," and complained she could not get rid of her. Even Nancy Richmond, the dearest of her friends, came to distrust her. She gave Muddy access to her letters and confided her secrets, only to find some of the letters, presumably from Poe, missing, and her confidences betrayed to others. Although Mrs. Richmond throughout her life corresponded with Muddy, her letters grew guarded and brief, and she perhaps wrote them at all only to honor the memory of Poe, whose superiority to other men became ever clearer to her over the years. She spoke of their relation as sacred, not to be understood by the world, and grew convinced that she would die in October, the same month as he. After her husband's death, in 1873, she legally changed her name to Annie, the name Poe had bestowed on her.

Several times Muddy slyly hinted to Sarah Helen Whitman that she would welcome a home, or at least a stopover, at 76 Benefit Street. In one ruse she said she desired Helen's opinion on how she might get to Louisiana: "Oh, if I could see you for a short time, I know for *his* sake you would advise me what to do." Inventing another pretext, she said she wished to visit Providence in order to personally thank Helen's friend William J. Pabodie, who had nursed Poe there during his drunken panic. (In 1870, shortly after coming into a hundred thousand dollars through the death of a brother, Pabodie committed suicide by swallowing prussic acid.) Like Annie, Helen for the rest of her life corresponded with Muddy, sometimes sending money. But her reserved and wary tone discouraged intimacy, and her news of sickness in the family, including the painful enlargement of her own heart, could not be mistaken for an invitation to come calling. The two women never met.

Helen was anyway engrossed in the Spiritualist phenomenon that swept over America, beginning around the time of Poe's death. That same fall she began hearing mysterious noises in her room, sometimes as if in response to a mental question—slight sounds from the center of a table, raps on the back of her chair. For six weeks a spiritually gifted young girl, dubbed "M," channeled daily messages to her from departed loved ones. A trance poet named Sarah Gould put her into communication with the spirit of Poe, who sent the message: "Pray for me, Helen; pray for me." She had of course not forgotten him. When she became a medium herself and held seances at home, she kept a portrait of him before her. Once after looking at it, she wrote some lines beginning:

> After long years I raised the folds concealing
> That face, magnetic as the morning's beam:
> While slumbering memory thrilled at its revealing. . . .

Many of those who began to write about Poe and to refute Griswold's slanders, sought Helen out for information. As she grew older, she concealed tell-tale lines of age with veils and subdued lighting. Sitting in her dimly lit parlor with her back to the light, she seemed to one visitor a person embalmed while still alive.

Wandering, spending time in Cambridge at the home of the forgiving Longfellow, still trying to get to Louisiana, Muddy found some respite from her transiency in Alexandria, Virginia, about a hundred miles from Richmond. By early 1859, ten years after Poe's death, she was living there in the family of a lawyer and journalist named Reuben Johnston. She seems to have stayed for about two years. In exchange for her board she taught the three Johnston children in the morning, and devoted the rest of the day to sewing. Ailing, she was confined to her room one winter by a vehement cough and later placed in a physician's care, forbidden to use her eyes in any way.

While in Alexandria Muddy also seems to have found some small relief from her poverty. Her few remaining resources included a land warrant that had been issued to her husband for his service during the War of 1812. With unlimited territory but little cash, the American government had paid its troops with titles to tracts of land, which often were later sold to speculators for cash. Muddy apparently succeeded in selling the warrant, and asked Neilson Poe to manage the money for her. For all her bit of good fortune, however, she remained alone. After her day of teaching the Johnston children and sewing, she would retire at about five o'clock to her room. "Oh how sad and lonely I am," she wrote on her seventieth birthday, "and with what rapture, I will hail the time when I will go to meet all my loved ones."

Around May 1861, Muddy left for Putnam, Ohio. The fall of Alexandria to Union troops, in one of the first military actions of the Civil War, dictated the timing of her move. But she had been offered a home in Putnam the year before by a family named Robins. In exchange, she was to provide information about Poe to young Sallie E. Robins, a daughter who planned to write a biography of him. The arrangement included an invitation to accompany the family to Europe, for a stay of two or three years, although she believed that she would not live long enough to return from abroad. As it happened, she never got to Europe, nor did Sallie Robins complete her biography of Poe. The young woman became insane and had to be carried to an asylum, "with little hope of a permanent recovery," Muddy said. Sallie's mother kept to her room, leaving Muddy feeling both dependent and alone. "How I wish I could get a home in some pleasant family," she lamented. "I want little else."

In the spring of 1863, with major battles about to erupt at Chancellorsville and Fredericksburg, Virginia, Muddy made her way to Baltimore, where Neilson Poe and her sister's children still lived. She wanted to be admitted to the Widows Home as her final residence on earth, but could not get the necessary $150. Instead she unwillingly entered the Church Home, a charitable Episcopal institution run by children and grandchildren of some of her old Baltimore friends. It was not what she had imagined for her last years: she wanted, she said, to "have some place to die in which I have not *now.*" From the home she kept in touch with Neilson and his family, grateful for small favors—a Christmas gift from his wife, ten dollars from the money he supervised for her, the freedom of asking him to look after her burial. Off and on she was ill, at one time in 1865 confined to her room for three months, making only more evident that she had nobody and nothing: "oh how much I did wish for some kind friend to get me a few little comforts," she said, "I often wonder why my existence is so prolonged."

The Church Home had perhaps one advantage, although it may have contributed to Muddy's uneasiness and discomfort, or even been the ground of them. The institution, as she knew, had once been the Washington Medical College. The five-story building with vaulted gothic windows, in which she lived as a charity case, was under another name the same place where Poe had died nearly twenty years before. The association perhaps brought him back to her more vividly than ever. In her roving she had often told others the details of his life and career, told and retold the particulars of their life together. But to one interviewer at the home she gave, near the end of her life, an especially minute picture of his appearance, his features making an artwork of porcelain delicacy and refinement:

> 5 feet 8¼ inches high, slightly, but elegantly formed, exceedingly graceful; no woman ever had more beautiful feet and hands; broad massive exquisitely white forehead; hair dark brown almost black, curly, & worn in graceful ringlets; eyes of dark grey, almond shaped long black lashes; most beautiful mouth & teeth; moustache, long but not heavy; most beautiful manners.

Muddy died at the Church Home on February 16, 1871, at the age of 81. Her funeral was attended by about a dozen of her friends and admirers of Poe. By her request, she was buried next to him.

Muddy had of course long looked forward to a heavenly reunion with those she had lost. "Oh Annie," she had written from Alexandria, "I do so long for the time to come, when I will go to my beloved ones." Alexandria was then a pretty eighteenth-century town of small brick houses and parallel streets, across the Potomac River from Washington. But it is unlikely that Muddy took much pleasure in the place, for she felt that she had few enjoyments left to her. The most beautiful among them, she told Annie, was to look at the beautiful stars. She looked at them and thought that her Father in heaven had made them, and made them for her too. "I can gaze upon them as I please," she said, "and think of my dear ones *there.*" It was in part her Christian faith that helped her envision the continued existence of her dear ones, but the picture owed something too to her son, who had all his life imagined a home for the departed, an Al Aaraaf where the dead defied death, owed something to the life of supernal expectations she had spent with him, evenings they had walked the porch at Fordham as he discoursed on *Eureka,* contemplating the stars.

And Muddy had also learned, and perhaps also from her son, that the dead survived in another form as well. That knowledge too had returned to her luminously in Alexandria, at a moment when she realized that she had but one autograph of him left. Over the years she had had countless requests for samples of his writing from friends who had loved and appreciated him. In answering them she had given away the letters he had written to her, and now had but the one autograph remaining, and refused to part with it. It was "closely imbedded" in her heart, she said, and *that* she could not give away even if she wanted to. With the sense that it was her son's signature but belonged also to her, was somehow *in* her, there came again but unexpectedly the knowledge that she still nurtured life, indeed his life, that the dead had always been alive, and not only in heaven, but with her on earth. The recognition, as she wrote of it to Annie, had come with sorrow, but also with such surprise as to seem almost pleasure, and it was this terrifying pleasure that made her exclaim, as if Eddie had come alive for her to see once more, "Oh memory, memory, how faithful it *still* is."

NOTES

In reproducing printed and manuscript sources I have retained the capitals, punctuation, and italics of the originals. I have indicated internal omissions from quoted material by points of ellipsis. But except for indented quotes, I have not included points of ellipsis for matter omitted from the end of a quotation. Obviously this affords possibilities for misrepresentation, but I believe that in no case in the text does the lack of final ellipsis points distort the meaning of the quotation. Where an omission has run over one or more sentences of the source, I have indicated the gap by a double set of ellipsis points (six dots).

In the notes below, I have used the first few words of each paragraph in the text, printed in bold face, to group citations for that paragraph. Individual citations are keyed to a prominent word from the relevant part of the text. The following abbreviations appear frequently.

BJ: Broadway Journal

BPB: John Carl Miller, ed., *Building Poe Biography* (Baton Rouge, 1977)

BREV: Burton R. Pollin, ed., *The Brevities,* vol. 2 of *Collected Writings of Edgar Allan Poe* (New York, 1985)

CR: Ellis and Allan Company Records, Library of Congress

GM: Graham's Magazine

GRIS: Rufus W. Griswold Collection, Boston Public Library

HARRISON: James A. Harrison, *The Complete Works of Edgar Allan Poe,* 17 vols. (New York, 1902)

HRC: Harry Ransom Humanities Research Center, University of Texas at Austin

INGRAM: John Henry Ingram Poe Collection, University of Virginia Library. The entry numbers, e.g., Ingram 134, are those assigned to individual items in the university's nine-roll microfilm edition of its collection.

IOWA: Thomas Ollive Mabbott Poe Collection, University of Iowa Libraries, Iowa City

JA: John Allan

LI, LII: John Ward Ostrom, ed., *The Letters of Edgar Allan Poe,* 2 vols. (rev. ed. New York, 1966)

LILLY: Sarah Helen Whitman Manuscripts, Lilly Library, Indiana University

LOG: Dwight Thomas and David K. Jackson, comps., *The Poe Log: A Documentary Life of Edgar Allan Poe 1809–1849* (Boston, 1987)

MI, MII, MIII: Thomas Ollive Mabbott, ed., *Collected Works of Edgar Allan Poe,* 3 vols. (Cambridge, Mass., 1969–78). Unless otherwise noted, all quotations of Poe's tales and poems are from this edition.

NYPL: Manuscripts and Archives Division, New York Public Library (Astor, Lenox, and Tilden Foundations)

PHR: John Carl Miller, ed., *Poe's Helen Remembers* (Charlottesville, 1979)

PL: William R. Perkins Library, Duke University

PMLA: Publications of the Modern Language Association of America

SHW: Sarah Helen Whitman

SLM: Southern Literary Messenger

T: G. R. Thompson, ed., *Edgar Allan Poe: Essays and Reviews* (New York, 1984)

THOMAS: Dwight Rembert Thomas, "Poe in Philadelphia, 1838–1844: A Documentary Record," Ph.D. diss., U. of Pennsylvania, 1978

VM: The Valentine Museum, Richmond, Virginia

WALKER: I. M. Walker, ed., *Edgar Allan Poe: The Critical Heritage* (London and New York, 1986)

WHITTY: J. H. Whitty, *The Complete Poems of Edgar Allan Poe . . . with Memoir, Textual Notes, and Bibliography* (Boston and New York, 1911)

WP: Sarah Helen Whitman Papers, Hay Library, Brown University

Eliza

To The Humane/ Log, 13. **So theatergoers/** David Poe, Jr.: Several traditions concerning David Poe's disappearance have grown up. The most likely account seems to me the contemporary statement of Samuel Mordecai, in Log, 13. It is supported by F. W. Thomas's statement that a lawyer intimate with the family told him that Edgar Poe's father had deserted Eliza in New York, and by the fact that New York newspapers at the time of Eliza's last performances there describe her as having been left alone. See Geddeth Smith, *The Brief Career of Eliza Poe* (Rutherford, 1988), 132–33. My treatment of Eliza Poe's career draws throughout on Smith's book. Children: On the birth dates of the Poe children see Ingram 414. **Help might be/** Three hundred: this and other figures for the number of Eliza's roles are computed in Smith, *passim*. Exceeded: Smith, q. 26. **For two years/** Salenka's: Eola Willis, *The Charleston Stage in the XVIII Century* (Columbia, 1924), q. 408. **Billed as/** Unequalled: *Philadelphia Repository and Weekly Register*, 28 Mar 1801. **Eliza resumed/** David Poe, Jr.: Poe's father was born 18 Jul 1784. See Delman-Heyward Files, Maryland Historical Society. He also appears on the Baltimore records taking subscriptions toward a billiard table, in Thomas Moale Account Book, 12 Jun 1797, Maryland Historical Society. Abyss: Eola Willis, "The Dramatic Careers of Poe's Parents," *The Bookman*, LXIV (Nov 1926), q. 291. Strathspey: Richmond *Enquirer*, 25 Dec 1804. According to Maria Clemm, David Poe became attracted to the stage from seeing a performance by Eliza Arnold, whom he married shortly after. See MS "Statements of Mrs. Maria Clemm. Noted in short-hand by E. L. D.[idier]," Harvard University Library. Her statement does not square, however, with extant records of David Poe's theatrical appearances, which show that he was acting a year or more before he joined Eliza's company, and knew her for about a year before they married. **Likely seeking/** Cantilevered: Brooks McNamara, *The American Playhouse in the Eighteenth Century* (Cambridge, Mass., 1969), 125. Edmund etc.: *The Repertory*, 18 Oct 1808 and 20 Feb 1807; *The Emerald*, 21 Feb 1807. **The Poes' frequent/** Hissed: *The Emerald*, 3 Oct 1807. Erroneous: *The Emerald*, 3 Jan 1807. Mutilated: *The Emerald*, 31 Oct 1807. Incorrect: *Ladies Afternoon Visitor*, 3 Jan 1807. Tamely: *The Emerald*, 20 Dec 1806. Improving: *The Emerald*, 16 Apr 1808. Appreciated: *The Emerald*, 8 Nov 1806. Obnoxious: *The Repertory*, 7 Apr 1807. Chastise: Joseph T. Buckingham, *Personal Memoirs and Recollections of Editorial Life*, I (Boston, 1852), q. 57. **By contrast, Eliza/** Marry: John M'Creery, *A Selection . . .* (Petersburg, 1824), 112–13. The version printed in this songbook is the one Eliza sang at the New York theater. But she also performed the song in Boston. See Boston *Independent Chronicle*, 13 Feb 1809. Ophelia etc.: *The Repertory*, 29 Jan and 18 Oct 1808, 7 Apr 1809. Sold: *The Repertory*, 18 Apr 1809. Mixed: *The Emerald*, 21 Mar 1807. **Otherwise reviewers/** Mogul etc.: *The Repertory*, 15 May 1807 and 18 Apr 1808; playbill of Federal Street Theater, 30 Oct 1809, Harvard Theater Collection. Supported: George E. Woodberry, *The Life of Edgar Allan Poe*, I (1909; rpt. New York, 1965), q. 11–12. Precedence: Smith, q. 106. **Especially for Eliza/** Lull: His misfortunes following him, David Poe appeared on the tax assessor's records as "David Poo." Mary E. Phillips, *Edgar Allan Poe the Man,* I (Chicago, 1926), 2. Sketch: Known only through information given to Ingram by Mrs. Shew. See PHR, 279. Usher: Eliza had acted with Noble Usher since she was a child, in Philadelphia in 1802; see the theater ads in the Philadelphia *Aurora.* David Poe, Jr., could have known him during Usher's earlier days as an umbrella merchant in Baltimore. See Charles R. Staples, *The History of Pioneer Lexington (Kentucky) 1779–1806* (Lexington, 1939), 238. Phillips, Allen, and other biographers of Poe have suggested that he knew the Ushers later himself. But West T. Hill, Jr., points out to me in a letter (28 May 1986) that both Usher and his wife died in 1814. It remains possible that Poe knew their children, including Agnes Pye Usher, who was just his age, and an actress. Odd-looking: *The Emerald,* 3 Oct and 14 Mar 1807. See also West T. Hill, Jr., *The Theatre in Early Kentucky 1790–1820* (Lexington, 1971), 73–95. Haymarket: Edward Valentine to Mary Phillips, als, Richmond, 3 Jul 1915, Boston Public Library, quoting from the Richmond *Enquirer,* 8 Jul 1808. **During their third/** Peasants: *New-England Palladium,* 3 Jan 1809. Storms: Phillips, I, 70–71. Acclaimed: *Independent Chronicle,* 13 Feb 1809. **The birth of/** Property, losses: Phillips, I, 2; *New-England Palladium,* 15 Apr 1808. Headed: According to Maria Clemm, only five weeks after Poe's birth, David and Eliza took him to Baltimore and left him for about six months with his paternal grandparents. Eliza cannot have made such a trip, however, for the records of the Boston stage show her to have been performing there at the time. Perhaps David went on his own, with the children. BPB, 48–49. Stockerton: Arthur H. Quinn, ed., *Edgar Allan Poe: Letters and Documents in the Enoch Pratt Free Library* (New York, 1941), 5–6. **Eliza's marriage/** Weightier: *The Rambler's Magazine and New-York Theatrical Register for the Season of 1809–10,* 19, 26, 106. Fared: Log, 7–8. A Boston critic defended David against the harsh New York reviews, insisting that "He *has* talents." See *Something,* 16 Dec 1809, 76. Drinking: Smith, q. 157, n. 17. **But David/** Quarreled: Log, 13. **On her own/** Misfortunes, support: *The Columbian,* 2 Jul 1810; Smith, q. 118–19. **By the following/** Gem: Smith, q. 122. Concertized: *Charleston Courier,* 21 Mar 1811. Murmur: Elena Zimmerman, "Tragic Ingenue: Memories of Elizabeth Arnold Poe," in J. Lesley Dameron and James W. Mathews, eds., *No Fairer Land: Studies in Southern Literature Before 1900* (Troy, 1986), q. 138–39. **Eliza's gaunt/** Manager: Log, 13. Buried: Ingram 1020. **Eliza's children/** Farewell: Hervey Allen and Thomas Ollive Mabbott, *Poe's Brother: The Poems of William Henry Leonard Poe* (New York, 1926), 41. Rumors: The widow of Charles Ellis, who had known the Allans well, reportedly said that "Mrs. Poe's husband had deserted her so long before her death, as to cast a doubt upon Rosalie's birth." See Mary L. Dixon to [R. H. Stoddard], als, Richmond, 9 Oct 1872, NYPL. Boston: BPB, 121.

Richmond; John and Fanny Allan

Built on several/ Richmond: Description based mostly on Agnes M. Bondurant, *Poe's Richmond* (1942; rpt. Richmond, 1978), *passim.* Liberal: Bondurant, q. 6–7. **Among them was/** Jack: See for instance Ingram 813, CR #5346, #5350. Lean: Killis Campbell, "Some Unpublished Documents Relating to Poe's Early Years," *Sewanee Review,* XX (Apr 1912), 205. Hawk: Susan Archer Weiss, *The Home Life of Poe* (New York, 1907), q. 22. House: See the MS "Articles of Agreement" between JA and Ellis, 14 Mar 1809, Virginia Historical Society. For reference to the business as "The House of Ellis & Allan" see, e.g., John Ellis to Charles Ellis, als, Pedlar Mills, 13 Feb 1810, CR, vol. 100. My picture of the operations of Ellis & Allan is mostly based on a search of about 150 of the 634 volumes of the company's records at the Library of Congress. This huge collection should be distinguished from the representative, but very limited, single reel of microfilm published by the library as the "Ellis and Allan Company Records." I have tried to detail the sources of important information within the complete records, but the large number of documents involved makes exhaustive annotation impossible. Office: Several writers about early Richmond and about Poe speak of the Ellis-Allan firm as if its whereabouts and physical dimensions were clearly known, although in fact they remain obscure. The most dependable information, based on extant insurance records, appears in Mary Wingfield Scott, "Richmond Buildings Associated with Poe" (TS notes, VM). Scott shows that the partners insured several buildings on Fifteenth Street In 1817 and 1822—a warehouse, a counting room, and what was likely their office. *The Richmond Directory, Register and Almanac, for the Year 1819* (Richmond, 1819) lists the firm as being on the "e[ast] s[ide] of 15 bt D and E sts. second from E st." Chains etc.: CR, *passim.* On the psyche specifically see CR, #26278, on the globes see St. George Tucker to JA, als, Williamsburg, 6 Feb 1816, Virginia Historical Society. Cavallo: CR, #5327. Employees: CR, #26613, #25761. **The commerce of/** Shipments: CR, #25342, #29677, #30265, #30113. Frog-land: JA had specially close ties with the Paris firm of Veuve Morliere. See among many other examples CR #34298. Napoleon: See Ellis's letters from Paris in CR, vol. 100, and JA to Ellis, als, Richmond, 20 Jun 1810, vol. 102. **John Allan had/** Benevolence: James Ellis to Charles Ellis, Jr., als, West Point, 15 Apr 1834, PL, and Ingram 320. The remark about the beggar comes from Edgar Poe himself, in LI, 48. Theatergoers: The surviving evidence includes Mary Allan to William Galt, Jr., als, London, 10 Nov 1818, PL, which shows that Allan attended the theater in London. Aid: Ingram 237. Rosalie: Jane Mackenzie Miller to J. H. Whitty, als, Cardinal, 16 Apr 1914, HRC. Opposed: Several later accounts by persons close to the Allan and Ellis families agree on this opposition. See, e.g., the testimony of Mrs. Charles Ellis recounted in the 1876 MS memoranda of T. H. Ellis, VM. Baltimore: That JA was in touch with the Baltimore Poes is clear from Poe's own later statements about this period, and corroborated in the account of Dr. John F. Carter, who reported that Allan corresponded with them "for weeks" but found their responses "not at all satisfactory." Meanwhile, Frances Allan had become strongly drawn to Poe and "begged her husband to keep him." See Charles Marshall Graves, "Landmarks of Poe in Richmond," *Century Magazine,* LXVII (Apr 1904), 914–15. Afford: These two very differing accounts of the circumstances—too poor, or won over by JA—were later given, four years apart, by Poe himself. See LI, 68, 39. Adopt: The evidence concerning Poe's adoption or the lack of it remains elusive. Writing to JA in 1815, his friend J. H. Cocke spoke of Edgar as "your little adopted boy" (als, Richmond, 10 Aug 1815, HRC. See also the 1813 letter to Frances Allan in Campbell). On the other hand, John Allan never called Edgar adopted, and Mrs. Dixon speaks of the Allans as the boy's "foster parents." Most other evidence suggests there was never a formal adoption. **The three-year-old/** Real estate etc.: CR, #25970, #28898, #26047–48. Comfort: Like the other houses in which biographers have confidently placed Eliza Poe and her son during his early life, the location and nature of this one are in fact unknown. Scott, above, points out that the houses described by Whitty, Allen, and Quinn as Poe's first home with the Allans, beginning in 1811, were in fact not built until 1817. Coachee, slaves, etc.: CR, #29188, #29025, among others. The furniture in the house can be glimpsed in the record of JA's 1815 auction of his household goods, CR #29977–78. **The furniture/** Galt: See G. Melvin Herndon, "From Scottish Orphan to Virginia Planter: *William Galt, Jr., 1801–1851,*" *Virginia Magazine of History and Biography,* LXXXVII (1979), 326–27; Ingram 817. On his smuggling see R. M. Hogg to "Dr. Chase," typescript letter, Stewarton, 18 Apr 1916, University of Iowa Library. Tight: JA to William Galt, Jr., als, London, 5 Oct 1816, PL. Ground: JA to William Galt, Jr., als, London, 8 Mar 1817, PL. Protégés: JA to William Galt, Jr., als, London, 28 Jan 1820, PL. **Allan's sense/** "Fortitude" etc.: All of these words and terms appear for instance in Allan's als on 8 Mar 1817, above. Creator: als of 5 Oct 1816. Addicted: JA to Charles Ellis, als, Richmond, 3 Jun 1813, CR, #26718. Safe: JA to Charles Ellis, als, Richmond, 28 May 1810, CR, vol. 102. Forgive, Poor Richard: JA to [unaddressed], als, London, 6 Mar 1817, VM. Maxims: als of 5 Oct 1816. **John Allan had promised/** Emphasized: William Galt to William Galt, Jr., als, Richmond, 30 Nov 1816 and 14 Jun 1815, PL. Elegant: als of 8 Mar 1817. Repaired: als of 28 Jan 1820. Pianoforte, Rees: CR, #29948, #21991, #22082, #33319. Cervantes etc.: CR, #27267; Log, 22. Journal: JA, MS journal, 1723–24, HRC. **John Allan's exacting/** Naturalized: JA took his oath of naturalization before Chief Justice John Marshall. Order Book 4, U.S. Circuit Court, Fifth Circuit, 469, VM. Blacks: JA to William Galt, Jr., als, London, 12 Nov 1818, PL. Hunting: als of 28 Jan 1820. Masons: JA's partner Charles Ellis was treasurer of the lodge. CR, #21867, and bill dated 6 Jul 1810, vol. 102. Pious: The letters of JA's sister speak continually of prayer, sabbath keeping, and Bible reading. Allan himself, however, had a pew in the Richmond Episcopal Church, the choice suggesting aspirations toward gentility. See CR, #37509. Chided: William Galt to JA, als, Richmond, 30 Dec 1817 and 17 Aug 1818, CR, vols. 186, 199. The Allans also owned a backgammon board (CR, #29977). Liquor: See, e.g., the receipts in CR, vol. 104. Belles: JA to Powhatan Ellis, als, Richmond, 5 Jan 1828, HRC; JA to William Galt, Jr., als, London, 23 Jun 1818, PL. Illegitimate: Hervey Allen and later biographers of Poe have presented this young man as JA's son on the evidence of the school bills (see, e.g., Log, 18). Although Allen said that he had additional evidence of JA's paternity, he did not provide it in his biography, and it remains possible that JA was supporting the boy out of charity. **The care of Edgar/** Guardian: The guardian was John Dixon, one of Virginia's earliest printers. See the handwritten note to Dixon's signature on a receipt in 1776, HRC. Slight: JA to Charles Ellis, als, London, 31 Aug 1816, CR, #34596. Strawberry: On Fanny's activities see JA to Charles Ellis, als, London, 20 Oct 1815, CR, #31009; receipt to Frances Allan, 14 Apr 1814, CR, #28238; Thomas Williamson to Frances Allan, als, 31 May 1813, CR, #26686. Economical: JA to Charles Ellis, als, London, 17 Jul 1819, CR, #45135. Endevour: Frances Allan to JA, als, [n. pl.], 11 Sep [1813?], CR, #28680. Nancy: JA to Mary Allan, Richmond, 27 Mar 1827, Ellis and Allan Company Records, Library of Congress microfilm. Beau: Log, 38. Fractured: Log, 24, 20, and later remarks below. **Edgar Poe's new/** Bible: See the transcription by Charles Ellis, Jr., Poe–Ellis Collection, VM. Measles: Log, 20. Ned: Charles Ellis to JA, als, Richmond, 12 Aug 1816, VM. Pets: Rosanna Dixon to JA, als, Richmond, 6 Sep 1812, VM. Sweetheart: Mary L. Dixon to "Mess. Editors," Richmond, 11 Sep 1872, NYPL. Suit: Receipt of 28 Mar 1814, CR, #29981. Spa: Log, 18. Educate: Log, 21, 35. T. O. Mabbott speculated that Clotilda Fisher was identical with the Elizabeth Fisher listed in the Richmond directory of 1819, who taught in the Sunday school of the Monumental Church, where the Allans had a pew. See his file of correspondence at VM, especially his als to the museum on 27 Mar 1963. **During this time/** Rosalie: Log, 18. Brother: Log, 19.

London; The Fall of the House of Allan and Ellis

At the age of/ Steamboat: JA to Charles Ellis, als, Richmond, 20 Jun 1815, CR, #30010. **Fanny Allan balked/** Trust: JA to Charles Ellis, als, London, 20 Nov 1815, CR, #31205. Auctioned: CR, #29977–79. Suit, Reader: CR, #29981; George E. Woodberry, *The Life of Edgar Allan Poe*, II (1909; rpt. New York, 1965), 360. Ned: Log, 24. **Niggardly accommodations/** Floor: JA to Charles Ellis, als, Liverpool, 29 Jul 1815, CR, #30318. Captain: JA to Moses Myers, als, Liverpool, 4 Aug 1815, CR, #30357. Sick: Als of 29 Jul 1815. Afraid: JA to Charles Ellis, Greenock, 21 Sep 1815, Ellis and Allan Company Records, Library of Congress microfilm. **Edgar began his/** Scotland: On the trip see Ingram 1027 and JA to Charles Ellis, als, Glasgow, 24 Aug 1815, CR, #30509. Southampton: JA to Charles Ellis, als, London, 10 Oct 1815 and 30 Oct 1815, CR, #30849, #31009; on the move from No. 47 see JA to George Dubourg, als, Cheltenham, 12 Sep 1817, HRC. Housekeeper: See the receipt to Elizabeth Martin for seven months' wages in 1817, CR, #37923; on the rest see miscellaneous bills in Poe–Allan Collection, Box 1, VM. Liquor: See, e.g., the following bills in CR: #33510, #32817, #31844, #37384, #35714. Parrot, clothing: JA to George Dubourg, als, Cheltenham, 6 Aug 1817, HRC; bills for 21 Aug 1816 and 8 Jun 1816, CR, #34488, #33592. Snug: Als of 30 Oct 1815. **The London House/** Basinghall, Dubourg: CR, #34050; C.S. Dubourg to JA, als, Sloane St., 30 Jan 1817, CR, #36323. Depressed: JA to Charles Ellis, als, London, 14 Mar 1816, CR, #32697. Credit: JA to Charles Ellis, als, London, 31 Jan 1816, CR, #32074. *Dash:* JA to Charles Ellis, als, London, 12 Feb 1816, CR, #32226. Bargains: JA to Charles Ellis, als, London, 26 Oct 1815, CR, #30972. Arranging: See, e.g., JA to Charles Ellis, als, London, 1 Nov 1815, CR, #31031. Worth: MS "List of all the real property belonging to Ellis & Allan," CR, #37121. Eminence: JA to Charles Ellis, als, London, 21 Jan 1818, #40028. Wardrobe, copy: Bills in CR, #39715, #40877. **While in London/** Known: See the remark by Dr. Bransby (q. Ingram 747), confirmed in the receipt to JA from George Dubourg, 6 Jul 1816, CR, #33947. School: School bill to JA from George Dubourg, 6 Jul 1816, CR, #33947. Reports: See, e.g., the als from C. S. Dubourg on 30 Jan 1817. **For part of/** Bransby: Ingram 747; Arthur Hobson Quinn, *Edgar Allan Poe: A Critical Biography* (New York, 1942), 73. Scholar: Log, 42, 36. Spoilt: Log, 36. Rasor: Log, 31. **However sharp/** Weekends: PHR, 237; Log, 39. Irvine: Ingram 1027. J. H. Whitty, the author of this account, did not specify his sources. He presumably found his information in unpublished papers of James Galt, who became the executor of JA's estate. Quinn doubted that Poe made the second trip to Irvine, or ever went to school there, but Whitty's account seems to me chronologically possible, and consonant with Poe's early and later character, and with his expressed feelings about his education in England. **Nor can the occasions/** Stranger: JA to [unaddressed], als, London, 6 Mar 1817, VM. Snipped: Mary Allan to William Galt, Jr., als, London, 10 Nov 1818, PL. Fine: Log, 36, 42, 32. Uncle: See, e.g., William Galt to JA, Richmond, 25 Aug and 12 Dec 1815, HRC. The only other real exception was an intimate friend of the Allans in London named Susan Rennolds or Reynolds. In one letter she writes, "pray tell me if Edgar be well," and in another, "Kiss Edgar for me"—the only such overtly affectionate entry in all the plentiful London correspondence of John Allan which I have seen. Susan Rennolds to JA, als, Buxton, 29 Aug and 7 Sep 1817, CR, #38421, #38486. Scores, brothers-in-law: CR, #33161, #33168, #33306, #33370. **Fanny Allan cannot/** Cursedly: Als of 10 Oct 1815. Dreamt: JA to Charles Ellis, als, London, 16 Nov 1816, CR, #35400; JA to Charles Ellis, als, London, 9 Aug 1816, CR, #34289. Ailments: See als of 10 Oct 1815; Allan Fowlds to JA, als, Kilmarnock, 25 Jul 1816, CR, #34163; JA to Charles Ellis, als, London, 10 Jan 1818, CR, #39803; JA to Charles Ellis, als, London, 23 Jun 1818, CR, #41427; Log, 29. Nursed: Als of 23 Jun 1818 and 10 Jan 1818. Knot: Log, 31. Complaining: Log, 32. Cheltenham: JA to Charles Ellis, als, London, 31 Aug 1816, CR, #34596; JA to Charles Ellis, als, Cheltenham, 9 Aug 1817, CR, #38270. Hearty: JA to Charles Ellis, als, London, 26 Sep 1817, CR, #38632. Wight: JA to Charles Ellis, als, London, 17 Aug 1818, CR, #42005. Devonshire, Dawlish: George Elwall to JA, als, [n. pl.], 7 Oct 1818, CR, #42488; Frances Allan to JA, als, Dawlish, 15 Oct 1818, VM. Frolic: JA to Charles Ellis, als, London, 25 Jun 1818, CR, #41443. **A settled home/** Spooked: George Elwall to JA, als, [n. pl.], 7 Oct 1818, CR, #42488. Spirits: George Elwall to JA, als, [n. pl.], 15 Oct 1818, CR, #42556. Bristled: Als of 15 Oct 1818. **Often ill and/** Desires: Log, 34. **With little warning/** Campbell: JA to Charles Ellis, als, London, 8 Jan 1819, CR, vol. 206. Inevitable: JA to Charles Ellis, als, London, 26 Feb 1819, CR, #43779. Failing: Marianne Sheldon, "Richmond, Virginia: The Town and Henrico County to 1820," Ph.D. diss., U. of Michigan, 1975, 198. Hurt: JA to William Murdoch, als, London, 17 Jul 1819, CR, vol. 527. Hanged: JA to Charles Ellis, als, London, 24 Apr 1819, CR, #44340. **John Allan's own/** *Exhausted,* rake: JA to Charles Ellis, als, London, 11 Mar and 24 Apr 1819, CR, #43868, #44340. Canvassing: JA to Charles Ellis, als, London, 15 May 1819, CR, #44539. Command: JA to Charles Ellis, als, London, 3 Jul 1819, CR, #45033. **The chain of/** Starving: JA to Charles Ellis, als, London, 17 Jul 1819, CR, #45135. Rent, owed: Unsigned dunning note to JA, 2 Oct 1819, CR, #45706; William Galt to JA, als, Richmond, 8 Oct 1819, CR, #45744. Indebtedness: Ellis and Allan to Arthur Saltmarsh, als, Richmond, 25 Jun [1822?], and to Nicholas Faulcon, als, Richmond, 29 Jun 1822, CR, vol. 526. Erred: Log, 43. **Luckily, John Allan/** Decided: William Galt als of 8 Oct 1819. Pleurisy: JA to Charles Ellis, als, London, 27 Mar 1820, CR, #46787. Fortitude: JA to William Galt, als, London, 17 Jul 1819, CR, vol. 527. Aversion: Log, 42. **On 21 July/** Portrait: Log, 49. Seasick: Woodberry, 360–61. Doctor: Log, 45.

Early Ambition; Jane Stanard; Moldavia

Unsettled and financially/ Moves: That the Allans moved in with the Ellises seems certain from several comments by T. H. Ellis and by a grandson of the family, Charles Talbott. See, e.g., Talbott to Arthur Hobson Quinn, als, [n. pl.], 22 Jan 1940, PL. How long Allan stayed with the Ellises remains unclear; Ellis claimed it was the better part of a year. The most thoroughly researched information on the Allans' housing before 1825 appears in Mary Wingfield Scott, "Richmond Buildings Associated with Poe" (TS notes, VM), on which I have relied. **During these moves/** Academics: Richard Beale Davis, *Intellectual Life in Jefferson's Virginia 1790–1830* (Chapel Hill, 1964), 29–69. Clarke, Burke: The academies may have been at the same location, Burke taking over from Clarke after Clarke resigned the school. Poe began Burke's school on 1 Apr 1823; the date is established by a payment of thirty dollars to Burke on that day "in advance" for five months' tuition, recorded in JA's MS journal, 1723–24, HRC. On Burke see J. T. L. Preston, "Some Reminiscences of Edgar A. Poe as a Schoolboy," in Sara Sigourney Rice, ed., *Edgar Allan Poe: A Memorial Volume* (Baltimore, 1877), 37. University: Log, 55. **Edgar's schooling/** Horace: Receipt of payment for 11 Jun to 11 Sep 1822, Ellis and Allan Company Records, Library of Congress microfilm. Writing in old age, Clarke claimed that at twelve Poe was reading the *Iliad* and had mastered Horace and Livy. But Clarke's memory was not very reliable. See David K. Jackson, "Two Notes: A Joseph H. Clarke Manuscript and Something about a Mr. Persico," *Poe Studies,* IX (Jun 1976), 22. Capping, verses: Preston, 38–39; Ingram 228. Fugitive: Eugene L. Didier, "Life of Edgar A. Poe," in Didier, ed., *Life and Poems of Edgar Allan Poe* (New York, 1882), 30–32. MI reports several later stories about poems that Poe supposedly wrote in his youth, but none seems to me well authenticated, resting on much later, and sometimes third-hand, evidence. **Edgar's accomplishments/** Competitive: Didier, q. 32, 31; Preston, 40–41. See also Ingram 855. Ruddy: MS "Statements of Mrs. Maria Clemm. Noted in short-hand by E. L. D.[idier]," Harvard University Library. The testimony in Ingram 236, probably from Mary Dixon, contradicts Maria Clemm's statement that upon his return Poe looked "fat." On his sinewy build see also Didier, 33–34. Ellis: Log, 47. Boxer: Preston, 38. Preston explained that the trick was to inflate one's lungs to the uttermost and exhale at the moment of receiving the blow. Swimmer: Didier, q. 34. For various accounts of Poe's swim on the James see Ingram 228, 332, 607. Poe's own account appears in LI, 57, and *SLM,* I (May 1835), 9. **Not only ambitious/** Ellis: Ingram 817. Lafayette: Agnes M. Bondurant, *Poe's Richmond* (1942; rpt. Richmond, 1978), 59–61; Samuel Mordecai, *Richmond in By-Gone Days* (Richmond, 1946), 338–39. Self-sacrificing: See, e.g., David Poe, Sr., to Thomas Lee, als, Baltimore, 18 Jul 1780 (Massachusetts Historical Society), and 24 Jan 1780 (HRC). Ally: Log, 61; Didier, 22–23. Cosigned: LI, 3–4. **In wanting to excel/** Orphans: See Marvin Eisenstadt et al., *Parental Loss and Achievement* (Madison, Conn., 1989), 26, 66. Status: See, e.g., the school receipts in Log, 50 and 52, where Poe is referred to as "Master Edgar Poe" and as "Edgar Poe." Christened: Rosanna Dixon to JA, als, Richmond, 6 Sep 1812, VM. Formally: James Galt accompanied the Allans on their return to America. When William Galt, Jr., arrived in Richmond from Scotland in 1817, 'Uncle' Galt welcomed him to what the older man called "his fathers house," and before several callers during the day deliberately "acknowledged him to be my adopted son." William Galt to JA, als, Richmond, 14 Nov 1817, CR, #39101. **At the same time/** Henry: Log, 65. Mackenzie: See Ingram 237. Several biographers have placed the Mackenzies' home very close to JA's various residences, but in fact the Mackenzies built several properties in Richmond to rent or sell, and it is uncertain in which one they lived. The location of their school remains similarly uncertain. See TS [by Mary Wingfield Scott?], "Where did the Mackenzies live during Rosalie Poe's childhood?," VM. Ten: Jane Mackenzie Miller to J. H. Whitty, als, Cardinal, 28 Apr 1914, HRC. Bible: Log, 10. Stunted: Flora Mackenzie to J. H. Whitty, als, Danville, 12 May 1914, HRC. Songs: Log, 35. **In fact, Edgar/** Affectionate: Poe also appreciated the kindness of Fanny's brother, Edward Valentine. See LII, 404. Orrisroot: Ingram 918. Ma: Susan Archer Weiss, *The Home Life of Poe* (New York, 1907), 21. Devotion: Ingram 66. Death-like: Robert Stanard to Jane Stanard, Fredericksburg, 26 Apr 1826, and Jane Stanard to Robert Stanard, Richmond, 18 May 1823, in *Papers of the Cazenove, Stanard, Craig, and Lee families,* Alderman Library microfilm. **Edgar frequently visited/** Pantaloons: Log, 52; for other items see the various payments in CR, vols. 460, 573. Sulky etc.: Log, 61–62. **Edgar's failure/** Sacrificing: Ellis and Allan to Arthur Saltmarsh, als, Richmond, 25 Jun 1822, and to Nicholas Faulcon, als, Richmond, 29 Jun 1822, CR, vol. 526. Bankruptcy: Marianne Sheldon, "Richmond, Virginia: The Town and Henrico County to 1820," Ph.D. diss., U. of Michigan, 1975, 199. Partner: Bondurant, 200–201, and JA's MS journal, entry for 23 Jan 1824. **On the morning/** Died: Untitled MS account, in JA's hand, dated Richmond, 26 Mar 1825, PL. **Said to be/** Bequeathed: Untitled TS concerning lands of William Galt, Virginia Historical Society (MSS 7-2/B9964). The estimate of Allan's inheritance was by Poe but does not seem exaggerated. See LI, 68. **The endless dunning/** Moldavia: Despite the Eastern European sound, the place had really been named for two of its previous owners, Molly and David Randolph. See Mordecai, 131–32. Eligible: Mary Wingfield Scott, *Houses of Old Richmond* (Richmond, 1941), q. 47. Interior: See Woodberry, 361–64; Mary E. Phillips, *Edgar Allan Poe the Man,* I (Chicago, 1926), 223–24; Bondurant. **Aunt Nancy was/** Oysters: Receipt on 22 Dec 1825, CR, vol. 573. Elector: Bondurant, q. 214.

Difficulties at the University of Virginia and Flight from Richmond

Edgar's conflicts/ Collegiate: LI, 7. Problems: See UVa Faculty Minutes 1825–1830, typed transcript, University of Virginia Library, 44. Progress: LI, 6. Enrolled: *A Catalogue of the Officers and Students of the University of Virginia, Second Session, Commencing February 1st, 1826* (Charlottesville, 1880); Log, 68. Blaetterman: MS Memoirs of George Walter (Clements) Blatterman, University of Virginia Library. Correct: Ingram 167. One student wrote that Blaetterman's way of teaching history was "all Fudge, for their is nothing to be learn'd from his lectures which are nothing more than a collection of facts jumbled together." John Munford to Sarah Munford, als, Charlottesville, 4 Oct 1828, PL. Competence: Log, 72. Tasso: Ingram 107. Studying: LI, 6. Excelled: Faculty Minutes, 146; Ingram 92. **Edgar sought to be/** Secretary: Jefferson Society MS Record Book, Estelle Doheny Collection, St. John's Seminary, Camarillo, California. Debater: Ingram 494. Snodgrass may well have had this remark from Poe himself. Exercises: Ingram 76; see also Ingram 855. Jump: Mary E. Phillips, *Edgar Allan Poe the Man,* I (Chicago, 1926), 245. Verse: Ingram 351; sketch, Ingram 76. Byron: Ingram 239. **For all Edgar's/** Moody: Ingram 351. Talkative: Ingram 261. Henry: "E[dward] V V[alentine]'s Conversation with Mrs. Shelton [19 Nov 1875]," MS notes, VM. Likeness, music: Ingram 263. Cultivated: Whitty, 188. Engaged: "E[dward] V V[alentine]'s Conversation." Intercepted: Ingram 261. **Having to live/** University: Charles Coleman Wall, Jr., "Students and Student Life at the University of Virginia, 1825 to 1861," Ph.D. diss., U. of Virginia, 1978, 148. Riot: Faculty Minutes, 27, 149. Trifling: LI, 5. Cards, besieged: Faculty Minutes, 69, 76, 106. Testified: Faculty Minutes, 160. **The violent and dissolute/** Unease, incidents: LI, 4–6. **Reporting this savage/** Whist: Phillips, I, 209. Harrowing: LI, 6. **What mostly fed/** Expensive: Wall, 48–75. Beggar: LI, 40. **A week after/** LI, 40. **The truthfulness of/** Trousers: LI, 4. Begrudged: JA to [unaddressed], als, London, 6 Mar 1817, VM. Card games: The Faculty Secretary, William Wertenbaker, claimed that Poe had "an ungovernable passion for card-playing." Ingram 92. Finery: Log, 73. **No matter whose fault/** In debt: The estimates vary. Wertenbaker recalled that Poe told him his debts were around two thousand dollars; Thomas Ellis said that James Galt told him they amounted to about twenty-five hundred. See Ingram 817. Fanny: Whitty, xxviii. Ostracized: LI, 14. Disgrace: Wall, 55. Clerk: Whitty, 188; Ingram 817. Engagement: Whitty, xxviii; MI, 65. **Most seriously/** Schoolmate: Log, 78; Bernard Peyton to John

Cochran and Co., als, Richmond, 3 Mar 1827, VM. Nonage: Bernard Peyton to John Cochran and Co., als, Richmond, 14 Mar 1827, VM. Warrant: LI, 41. **Barely two months/** Quotations in this and the next two paragraphs are from LI, 7–8. Those who have reprinted this letter have followed each other in solidifying into long paragraphs what in the holograph letter are clearly short paragraphs setting forth individual grievances, much as in the *Declaration*. **Allan wrote back/** Quotations in this and the next paragraph are from Mary Newton Stanard, ed., *Edgar Allan Poe Letters Till Now Unpublished* (Philadelphia, 1925), 67–68. Manipulate: It is evident that Poe recognized the streak of generosity and charitableness in JA and learned to play on it. Fanny Allan's brother, Edward Valentine, later remarked that he "quickly detected the weak points of his protectors; and took advantage of them." Ingram 236. **"The world" replied/** LI, 8–9 and n. **Edgar's tale of starvation/** Overseas: Whitty, xxix–xxxi; Ingram 958. The most elaborate account of these doings appears in Ingram's own biography of Poe, *Edgar Allan Poe: His Life, Letters, and Opinions* (1886; rpt. New York, 1965), which not only fully accepts the story of Poe's visit to England, but also involves him romantically with a "Scotch lady of position" in France and much else, perhaps on the authority of F. W. Thomas. The ultimate source for these tales may well have been Poe himself. But I accept the view of scholars beginning with G. E. Woodberry that the two months elapsed between Poe's known existence in Richmond and his known existence in Boston was too short a time to have included a trip back and forth to England and the Continent. Important confirmation of this view appears in a letter from G. W. Eveleth in 1869 (Ingram 105), reporting the testimony of James W. Davidson, according to whom "Mrs. Clemm told me, years ago, that E. A. Poe never was out of America, except while at Dr. B[ransby]'s school." Henry: Log, 77. Sea: Log, 78. Greeks: Bernard Peyton to John Cochran & Co., als, Richmond, 28 Sep 1827, VM. Russia: Whitty, xxxi. **The reality was less/** Struggling: On the imagery of travel in adolescent rebellion see H. Shmuel Erlich, "Denial in Adolescence: Some Paradoxical Aspects," *Psychoanalytic Study of the Child*, XLI, (1986), 331.

Boston; Tamerlane; *The Army; Death of Fanny Allan*

For a month or two/ Merchandise: Theodore Pease Stearns, "A Prohibitionist Shakes Dice with Poe," *Outlook*, CXXVI (Sep 1920), 25–26. I have refrained from using more than the bare bones of this account, which is at best thirdhand. Thomas: MI, 539. **With their concern/** Tamerlane: Tamerlane seems to have had a certain vogue in the period. An article called "Selection in Reading" speaks of people discussing topics of the day—Byron, canalling, chemistry, "the American Revolution, or the Conquests of Tamerlane." *SLM*, II (Feb 1836), 141. Imbued: Whitty, 189. **Edgar created this portrait/** Byron: See Katrina E. Bachinger, "Poe's Vote for Byron: The Problem of its Duration," in Erwin A. Stürzl and James Hogg, eds., *Byron: Poetry and Politics* (Salzburg, 1981), 301–22. **By the time Tamerlane/** Perry: "Enlistment Paper for Edgar A. Perry, May 26, 1827," *Selected Military Service Records Pertaining* *to Edgar Allan Poe,* National Archives and Records Administration microfilm, 1987. On Poe's aliases see Burton R. Pollin, *Discoveries in Poe* (Notre Dame, 1970), 215–18. Reduced: Col. James House to "General Commanding the E. Dept.," Fortress Monroe, 30 Mar 1829, *Military Service Records.* **With whatever complex** / Company: *Returns From Regular Army Artillery Regiments 1821– Jan. 1901,* National Archives microfilm M727, reel 1. Gales: Log, 84. Fortress: On the various forts see Francis Paul Prucha, *A Guide to the Military Posts of the United States 1789–1895* (Madison, Wis., 1964). On Fortress Monroe see also C. B. Dana to Elias Loomis, als, Baltimore, 6 Jan 1834, Yale University Library. **Details of Edgar**/ Housekeeping: J. Thomas Russell, *Edgar Allan Poe: The Army Years* (West Point, 1972). A.C.S.: "Company H, 1st U.S. Artillery . . . Muster Roll," *Military Service Records.* Reports: Several of these documents seem to be in Poe's hand. See the *Returns From Regular Army.* Promptly: Commendatory letters of Lt. J. Howard and Capt. H. W. Griswold, 20 Apr 1829, *Military Service Records.* **For all that**/ Inclination: LI, 9–10. News: *Military Service Records.* Col. James House, an officer in Poe's regiment, said that John Allan had not heard from Poe "for several years." See his letter of 30 Mar 1829. **Allan gave his reply**/ Termination: LI, 9. Cavalier: Mary Allan to JA, als, Irvine, 3 Mar 1828, PL. Evasively: Mary Allan to JA, als, Irvine, 23 Sep 1830, PL. **Edgar now wrote**/ LI, 9–11. **Edgar received no**/ LI, 11–12. **After six weeks**/ Quotations in this and the next paragraph from LI, 13–14. **Whether John Allan**/ Fanny: It remains possible that Poe kept in touch with Frances Allan while maintaining an illusion of overseas exile. See Whitty, xxxi. Fanny's sister, Nancy, reportedly said that Poe wrote home but somehow created the impression that his letters issued from Russia. See "E[dward] V V[alentine]'s Conversation with Mrs. Shelton [19 Nov 1875]," MS notes, VM. On the other hand, Thomas H. Ellis recollected that no one knew Poe's whereabouts. See Ingram 817. Absent: LI, 11. Improvement: Log, 78. Lingering: Log, 89. **Fanny had never**/ Desired: Unidentified MS, Gris 857. The correctness of the other information in this unsigned and undated document leads me also to credit its statement that Fanny expressed a wish to see Poe. Warning: LI, 15. **Fanny's death softened**/ Clothes: Log, 89. On JA's temporary softening toward Poe see also Ingram 494. Forgive: LI, 41. Happier: LI, 15.

Application to West Point; Renewed Quarrel with John Allan

Entering West Point/ Adopted: Col. James House to "General Commanding the E. Dept.," Fortress Monroe, 30 Mar 1829, *Selected Military Service Records Pertaining to Edgar Allan Poe,* National Archives and Records Administration microfilm, 1987. **None of this**/ Discharged: "Remarks, in Explanation of Alterations on the Face of the Return [for April 1829]," *Returns From Regular Army Artillery Regiments 1821–Jan. 1901,* National Archives microfilm M727, reel 1. Promised: Harrison, XVII, 371–72. **Back in Richmond**/ Applications: Edward Everett to [unaddressed, but perhaps to Poe or JA], als, Washington, 1 Apr 1830, Gris. Distinguished: James P. Preston to [John H.

Eaton], als, Richmond, 13 May 1829, *Military Service Records.* Acquisition: Andrew Stevenson to John H. Eaton, als, Richmond, 6 May 1829, *Military Service Records.* **John Allan himself/** Log, 91–92. **In May, Edgar/** Learned: LI, 23. Ranked: "Records Relating to the U.S. Military Academy . . . Register of Cadet Applicants, 1819–1830," *Military Service Records.* Certain: LI, 25. **The postponements/** Established: LI, 16. Arnold: LI, 22. **As the admission/** LI, 28. **New clashes over/** LI, 22. **New and still deeper/** Introduction: LI, 17. Marlow: Log, 94. Ignorance: William Wirt to Poe, als, Baltimore, 11 May 1829, Gris. **Disregarding John Allan's/** LI, 18–19. **Returned to Baltimore/** Quotations in this and the next paragraph from LI, 20. **What remains of/** Censuring: LI, 21 n. Beset: Log, 97. Wills: Log, 106. Anxious: LI, 26. **As Edgar interpreted/** Prohibition: LI, 26. Trouble: LI, 23–24. Pursue: LI, 28. Indignant: LI, 26. **As his brief trip/** Uncomfortable: LI, 29. Taunt: LI, 24. Baltimore: LI, 30. Material: LI, 34.

Al Aaraaf

Edgar did more/ Sickly: Log, 99. Neal: Benjamin Lease, *that wild fellow John Neal and the American Literary Revolution* (Chicago, 1972), 29–65. Nonsense: Walker, 66. **Coming amid his /** Impudence: LI, 27. Evaporated: LI, 32. **Edgar retained/** Overhauled: On the revisions see Dwayne Thorpe, "Poe and the Revision of 'Tamerlane,' " *Poe Studies,* XVIII (Jun 1985), 1–5. Fifteen: LI, 32. **With Tamerlanian ambition/** Extravagance: LI, 32. Intended: LI, 19. **But Edgar also carefully/** For extended discussion of "Al Aaraaf" see Floyd Stovall, *Edgar Poe the Poet: Essays New and Old on the Man and his Work* (Charlottesville, 1969), 102–25; Robert D. Jacobs, "The Self and the World: Poe's Early Poems," *Georgia Review,* XXXI (Fall 1977), 638–68; and Daniel Hoffman, *Poe Poe Poe Poe Poe Poe Poe* (New York, 1973), 35–47. **Unlike *Tamerlane/*** Sanxay: Log, 103–4. Reviewed: Walker, 69–73.

West Point

In the spring/ Powhatan Ellis to John H. Eaton, Washington, 13 Mar 1830, and JA to John H. Eaton, Richmond, 31 Mar 1830, "Records of the Adjutant General's office, 1798–1918," *Selected Military Service Records Pertaining to Edgar Allan Poe,* National Archives and Records Administration microfilm, 1987. **While awaiting his entrance/** Abused: LI, 42. Disclosure: JA's second wife later charged that Poe squandered the money. Whatever the truth of this complex matter, it seems clear to me from Poe's letter to Bully Graves that the money for the substitute remained unpaid. See Arthur Hobson Quinn, *Edgar Allan Poe: A Critical Biography* (New York, 1942), 167–68, 205–6. Sober: LI, 36. **Some sort of truce/** Blankets: Log, 105. Property: LI, 37. **The Academy's barracks/** Trollope: Frances Trollope, *Domestic Manners of the Americans* (New York, 1984), 325. Capacity: John H. Eaton to [JA?], als, Washington,

16 Dec 1830, HRC. **For the summer/** Rigid: LI, 37. Dwindling: Peter Force, *Register of the Army and Navy of the United States. No. 1 1830* (Washington, 1830), 84. Advantages: LI, 37. **At the end of/** Karl E. Oelke, "Poe at West Point—A Revaluation," *Poe Studies,* VI (Jun 1973), 1–6; J. Thomas Russell, *Edgar Allan Poe: The Army Years* (West Point, 1972). **Edgar found the study/** Incessant: LI, 38. Ranked: "Records Relating to the U.S. Military Academy, 1803–1917 . . . Consolidated Weekly Class Reports, 1819–1831" and "Merit Rolls, 1818–1866," *Military Service Records.* Scott: LI, 37–38; Scott may have helped Poe gain admission to the academy. See BPB, 98. **Like his boyhood/** Arnold: Russell, 13. Adopted: D. E. Hale to Sara Josepha Hale, als, West Point, 10 Feb [1831], Huntington Library. Whaler: George E. Woodberry, *The Life of Edgar Allan Poe,* I (1909; rpt. New York, 1965), q. 70. Hoax: T. W. Gibson, "Poe at West Point," *Harper's Monthly,* XXXV (Nov 1867), 754–56. Talent: D. E. Hale, als of 10 Feb [1831]; Sara Hale herself wrote to Poe at West Point, extending his growing network of literary connections. **In all, Edgar/** LI, 38. **But the fall brought/** Patterson: Ingram 813. Illegitimate: Hervey Allen, *Israfel: The Life and Times of Edgar Allan Poe,* rev. ed. (New York, 1934), 694. **Among its many/** LI, 38–39. **Edgar's unexpressed/** LI, 41–42. **Thrown out and away/** Quotations in this and the next two paragraphs from LI, 39–42. **No letter arrived/** Mary Newton Stanard, ed., *Edgar Allan Poe Letters Till Now Unpublished* (Philadelphia, 1925), 258. **Edgar did as he/** "Records Relating to the U.S. Military Academy, 1830–1917 . . . Conduct Rolls July 1830–January 1831," *Military Service Records.* **On January 28/** This and the next two paragraphs based on "Court Martial Case Files, 1809–1838," *Military Service Records.* **Edgar remained in/** Log, 117–18. **Edgar left West Point/** LI, 43–44. **From Moldavia/** Survived: Log, 116. Polish: LI, 44. **Edgar's plan/** LI, 45.

Poems by Edgar A. Poe; *Remarks on Childhood Mourning*

Still, the volume/ Reviews: See Walker, 175–76. Doggerel: PHR, 136. Cheap: Log, 118. Cheat: John W. Robertson, *Commentary on the Bibliography of Edgar A. Poe* (1934; rpt. New York, 1969), 84. **Many lines in Edgar's/** Poe's sources are identified in MI and here transcribed from that edition. Deficiency: On the part played in plagiarism by feelings of deprivation see Phyllis Greenacre, "The Nature of Plagiarism," *Journal of the Philadelphia Association for Psychoanalysis,* III (1976), 159–62. **American culture/** Emerson: "An Address Delivered Before the Senior Class in Divinity College," *The Works of Ralph Waldo Emerson,* I (Boston, 1909), 141. Mementoes: Michael McEachern McDowell, "American Attitudes Towards Death, 1825–1865," Ph.D. diss., Brandeis U., 1978, 89. Lieber: McDowell, q. 66. **For sentimentalists/** Irving: McDowell, q. 75. Orphans: McDowell, q. 314. **While this cult of memory/** Denial: See for instance Vamik D. Volkan, *Linking Objects and Linking Phenomena: A Study of the Forms, Symptoms, Metapsychology, and Therapy of Complicated Mourning* (New York, 1981), 42. **Other poems announce/** To emphasize my comment about Poe's need to kill off the past, I have given the first two lines of the final quotation as they appear in the next version of the poem. **The most persuasive/** Bereavement: Helpful brief reviews of current literature on the subject appear in Christina Sekaer and Sheri Katz, "On the Concept of Mourning in Childhood," *Psychoanalytic Study of the Child,* XLI (1986), 287–92, and in David R. Dietrich and Peter C. Shabad, eds., *The Problem of Loss and Mourning: Psychoanalytic Perspectives* (Madison, Conn., 1989), 1–23. The now-voluminous literature on prolonged mourning shapes this entire biography, and I am very grateful to Dr. Eugene L. Goldberg of New York City for having introduced me to it. The paragraphs that follow are particularly indebted to three classic papers by Martha Wolfenstein: "How is Mourning Possible?," *Psychoanalytic Study of the Child,* XXI (1966), 93–122; "Loss, Rage, and Repetition," *Psychoanalytic Study of the Child,* XXIV (1969), 432–60; and "The Image of the Lost Parent," *Psychoanalytic Study of the Child,* XXVIII (1973), 433–56. It should be mentioned that some psychoanalysts believe, contrary to Wolfenstein, that children are able to mourn even before adolescence (which by obliging the child to give up its opposite-sex parent offers practice in renouncing a loved object). This seems an appropriate place to acknowledge Marie Bonaparte's *The Life and Works of Edgar Allan Poe: A Psycho-Analytic Interpretation* (English ed. 1949; rpt. London, 1971). My interpretations of individual works and episodes often differ from hers. But on many points her book remains persuasive and revealing, and it was the first to perceive the pervasive effects of mourning on Poe's life and writing. Freud: Humberto Nagera, "Children's Reactions to the Death of Important Objects," *Psychoanalytic Study of the Child,* XXV (1970), q. 375. Demons: Harrison, XVII, 437. **The modern understanding/** Fear-and-longing: See Vamik Volkan, "Typical Findings in Pathological Grief," *Psychiatric Quarterly,* XLIV (1970), 231–50. Massive: On the monumentality of burial places see Volkan, *Linking Objects,* 61. Enshrined: David W. Krueger, "Childhood Parent Loss: Developmental Impact and Adult Psychopathology," *American Journal of Psychotherapy,* XXXVII (Oct 1983), 582–92. **Edgar's underlying denial/** Contradiction: MI, 148. **The inability of young/** Maugham: Quoted in William G. Niederland, "Trauma, Loss, Restoration, and Creativity," Dietrich and Shabad, 75. Brodkey: Dinitia Smith, "The Genius: Harold Brodkey and his Great (Unpublished) Novel," *New York,* 19 Sep 1988, 56. **Much of Edgar's/** Niederland remarks that Poe's works are "profoundly autobiographical . . . the expression of intense strivings for restoration in which memory and images, experience and perception, facts and fantasies coalesced in a consuming search for survival and truth" (77). On the very large amount of repetition in Poe's work, see especially the remark of the Finnish psychoanalyst T. B. Hägglund, that when "creativity replaces mourning work, it is manifested in compulsory repetition." Quoted in George H. Pollock, "The Mourning Process, the Creative Process, and the Creation," Dietrich and Shabad, 30. On the general relation between mourning and creativity see also George H. Pollock, "The Mourning-Liberation Process and Creativity: The Case of Käthe Kollwitz," in Sol Altschul, ed., *Childhood Bereavement and its Aftermath* (Madison, Conn., 1988), 391–419.

Baltimore; Maria Clemm; William Henry Leonard Poe

Citizens of Baltimore/ Description in this and the next paragraph based on Jared Sparks, "Baltimore," *North American Review*, XX (Jan 1825), 100; J. S. Buckingham, *America, Historical, Statistic, and Descriptive*, I (London, 1841), 401–38; Joseph John Gurney, *A Journey in North America* (1841; rpt. New York, 1973), 86–87; Frances Trollope, *Domestic Manners of the Americans* (New York, 1984), 171–74, 275; "Traits of a Summer Tourist," *SLM*, II (Oct 1836), 696. Cobden: Elizabeth Hoon Cawley, ed., *The American Diaries of Richard Cobden* (1952; rpt. New York, 1969), 93. **Edgar was the fourth**/ Branches: Ingram 220. Rope: Baltimore City Chancery Court Records B62, fol. 403, Maryland Hall of Records, Annapolis. Battle: Mary E. Phillips, *Edgar Allan Poe the Man*, I (Chicago, 1926), 29. Republican: Ingram 446. **It was to these**/ Infant: BPB, 47. Stranded: LI, 16. SHW told Eveleth that Poe did not see Mrs. Clemm from the time of his early childhood until after he left West Point. Her remark seems true in spirit, although applicable not to his stay at the academy but to his hitch in the army. BPB, 224. Worse: LI, 29. Slave: "Purloined Bill of Sale For Poe Slave Found," Baltimore *Evening Sun*, 16 Jan 1954; Log, 100. Dwelling: Log, 118. Wax: Augustus Van Cleef, "Poe's Mary," *Harper's New Monthly Magazine*, LXXVIII (Mar 1889), 635. **Forty-one when**/ Countenance: Ingram 546. Clemm is here described as she appeared in 1836. Single: Phillips, 29. Husband: Maria Clemm was married on 12 Jul 1817. See St. Paul's Parish Register, vol. 3, and Baltimore County Marriage Records, Maryland Hall of Records, Annapolis; but compare Log, 33. A William Clemm, Jr., seemingly her husband, advertised hardware, cutlery, and saddles in the Baltimore *American & Commercial Daily Advertiser*, 16 May 1805. Inbred: Francis Barnum Culver, "Lineage of Edgar Allan Poe and the Complex Pattern of the Family Genealogy," *Maryland Historical Magazine*, XXXVII (Dec 1942), 421–22. Quarreled: LI, 67. Loan: Land Records, Baltimore Court House, T. K. 257, folio 391. **An overburdened woman**/ Piecework: Log, 85, notes that an 1827 city directory lists a "Maria Clemm" as preceptress of a local school. This entry may refer to another Maria Clemm who lived in Baltimore at the same time and was related to William Clemm's family. Many documents in the Land Records at the Baltimore Court House refer to this second Maria Clemm, such as W. G. 215 (28 Nov 1831), concerning a large plot deeded to "Maria Clemm." Of course it may also be that the directory entry, and some of the land records do refer to Poe's aunt. Judge: BPB, 22. **The wax-neat rooms**/ Fortitude: LI, 67. Henry: Henry was born in September 1818. See Delman-Heyward Files, Maryland Historical Society. Virginia Maria was born 22 Aug 1820; Virginia Eliza was born 15 Aug 1822. See St. Paul's Parish Register. Complexion: Van Cleef, 635. **Whatever its trials**/ Georgia: Arthur H. Quinn, ed., *Edgar Allan Poe: Letters and Documents in the Enoch Pratt Free Library* (New York, 1941), 11. Relatives: See "The Poe Family of Maryland," TS, James Southall Wilson Poe Collection, University of Virginia Library; LI, 45. Mortified: Quinn, *Edgar Allan Poe*, 12. Great: Log, 104. **Edgar's settlement**/ Singular: George B. Coale to R. H. Stoddard, als, Baltimore, 26 Apr 1871, NYPL.

Feeble: Whitty, xxi. Much of the account of Henry that follows, including quotations from his verse and tales, is drawn from Hervey Allen and Thomas Ollive Mabbott, *Poe's Brother: The Poems of William Henry Leonard Poe* (New York, 1926), with additional material from Whitty. **Although fostered in/** Best: Log, 19. Burling: See Allen and Mabbott, and Susan Archer Weiss, *The Home Life of Poe* (New York, 1907), 43. Entirely: LI, 29. Discovered: LI, 43. Channel: LI, 32. **In fact, like other/** Orphaned: A moving personal memoir of the clinging between orphaned siblings is Eileen Simpson, *Orphans: Real and Imaginary* (New York, 1987). Symbiotically: Another of Henry's tales, "Recollections," concerns the narrator's search for his long-lost brother, "at the request of a loved parent whose eyes had been recently closed in death." **Edgar's cherished reunion/** Died: Log, 122. Intemperance: MS by editor of the *Minerva* [undated but after 1865], University of Virginia Library (#8795). See also LI, 23. Coincidental: George H. Pollock, "On Anniversary Suicide and Mourning," in E. James Anthony and Therese Benedek, eds., *Depression and Human Existence* (Boston, 1975), 369–93. Pollock writes that in some cases "it was the actual or feared attainment by the patient of the age the parent had reached at his or her death that set in motion suicidal activity" (390). Henry's sketch called "A Fragment" begins with its narrator contemplating suicide: "WELL! I have determined."

Marriage Hopes; Early Tales; The Saturday Visiter *Contest*

The picture of Edgar's/ Schoolteacher: Eugene L. Didier, "Life of Edgar A. Poe," in Didier, ed., *Life and Poems of Edgar Allan Poe* (New York, 1882), 50, 150. Editorial: Log, 127. Army: MI, 543. Objections: George E. Woodberry, *The Life of Edgar Allan Poe*, I (1909; rpt. New York, 1965), 90. **Edgar also had his/** Augustus Van Cleef, "Poe's Mary," *Harper's New Monthly Magazine*, LXXVIII (Mar 1889), 634–40. Following Mabbott, I have accepted in outline Mary Starr's account. Although probably misremembered or distorted in some details, her description of Poe's impulsiveness and explosive behavior at the time agrees with other accounts of his life in Baltimore, and later. See MI, 232–33. I warily omit the more melodramatic sequel, however, in which Poe allegedly also beat Mary's uncle with a cowhide, and angrily confronted her father with the news of having whipped his brother. **While Edgar's personal/** Stir: Lawrence C. Wroth, "Poe's Baltimore," *Johns Hopkins Alumni Magazine*, XVII (Jun 1929), 299–312. *Ninead:* Floyd Stovall, *Edgar Poe the Poet: Essays New and Old on the Man and His Work* (Charlottesville, 1969), q. 70. The poem could conceivably be referring to Henry Poe. Wilmer: Thomas Ollive Mabbott, ed., *Merlin: Baltimore, 1827* [by Lambert A. Wilmer] (New York, 1941), 9. **Out of work, Edgar/** Mabbott tentatively attributed "A Dream" to Poe. See MII, 5–6. Professor Burton R. Pollin, however, feels certain that Poe did not write it. Some of my own reasons for (tentatively) assigning the tale to Poe are given in the text, especially the insistent repetition of key words. I add here that "A Dream" shares with some later works by Poe the Jerusalem setting and apocalyptic atmosphere; the use of sound as a device of dramatization (here the creaking of bone hinges); and the driving of a nail or naillike object through the flesh. **Although only three pages/** Relieving: I owe this insight to Dr. Lenore C. Terr of San Francisco, who graciously shared with me her conclusions about Poe, derived from her work with traumatized children. See also her "Children Traumatized in Small Groups," in Spencer Eth and Robert S. Pynoos, eds., *Post-Traumatic Stress Disorder in Children* (Washington, 1985), 47–70. **If Edgar did write/** TALE: Log, 120. Berlifitzing: The name may also recall Poe's boyhood friend Ebenezer Burling, who died of cholera the same year, although after the story was published. See Log, 127. For the view that "Metzengerstein" satirizes the unwholesomeness of the Byronic personality, see George H. Soule, Jr., "Byronism in Poe's 'Metzengerstein' and 'William Wilson'," *Emerson Society Quarterly*, n. s., XXIV (1978), 152–62. I cannot agree with this view, nor with the more general line of interpretation of Poe that inspires it, begun in G. R. Thompson's intelligent and influential *Poe's Fiction: Romantic Irony in the Gothic Tales* (Madison, Wis., 1973). In nearly all its features "Metzengerstein" seems to me similar to other popular Gothic fiction of the period. **This concern with survival/** Incorporating: I put oversimply here what is complexly discussed in Vamik Volkan, "Typical Findings in Pathological Grief," *Psychiatric Quarterly*, XLIV (1970), 231–50. Volkan remarks that in cases of pathological grief, the lost one represents a source of narcissistic supplies for the mourner, and incorporation of him is also an attempt to restore the self. According to Sidney Tarachow, love of the dead—necrophilia—contains intense oral aspects: "The cadaver is equated with the orally giving mother who never frustrates." See his "Judas, the Beloved Executioner," in Joseph T. Coltrera, ed., *Lives, Events, and other Players: Directions in Psychobiography* (New York, 1981), 93. **Edgar was writing other/** Place: LI, 53. *Visiter:* Log, 129–30. *Printing:* BPB, 207. **The judges received/** Hundred: Log, 135. Distinguished: Walker, 78–79. **On the same day/** Raciness: Walker, 79. Probably around this time Poe composed a comic preface for the collection, explaining the Folio Club's purposes and listing its eleven members, including Mr. Convolvulus Gondola and De Rerum Naturâ, Esqr, elements in what he seems to have intended as a satiric look at the contemporary literary scene. Several scholars have tried to identify the specific writers he had in mind, and to trace the evolution of the never-published volume. See for instance MII, 200–206, and Alexander Hammond, "Edgar Allan Poe's *Tales of the Folio Club:* The Evolution of a Lost Book," in Benjamin Franklin Fisher IV, ed., *Poe at Work: Seven Textual Studies* (Baltimore, 1978), 13–43. Inspiration: Walker, 72. See also the eight letters from "M. Hewitt" to an unidentified book dealer, Berg Collection, NYPL. Underhanded: John Hill Hewitt, *Recollections of Poe* (Atlanta, 1949), 18–19. **Probably because of/** Log, 135.

John Allan

Edgar likely had not/ LI, 46. **Edgar's "May God/** LI, 47. **No evidence of Edgar's/** Misfortune: LI, 48. Extricate: Mary Newton Stanard, ed., *Edgar Allan Poe Letters Till Now Unpublished* (Philadelphia and London, 1925), 295. **With**

Allan's aid/ Amity: Log, 128. Careworn: Jay B. Hubbell, "Charles Chauncey Burr: Friend of Poe," *PMLA*, LXIX (Sep 1954), 839. Destruction: LI, 49–50. **John Allan's reaction/** LII, 472. The violence of JA's reaction to Poe's letter may have sprung from a prior conflict recorded in some now-lost previous communication between them. If so, the missing evidence may have been the letter referred to by Phillips, in which they quarrelled over some money that JA sent to Poe for a schoolbook, which Poe diverted to his living expenses. In this letter, Poe allegedly upbraided Allan for his relations with women, and for humiliating him by sending him to a school in Richmond where he had to sit in the same class with JA's illegitimate son. Mary E. Phillips, *Edgar Allan Poe the Man*, II (Chicago, 1926), 1617–18. T. O. Mabbott spoke with a "gentleman" who claimed to have heard the letter read before it was destroyed. The man told him that Poe also referred to Fanny Allan's childlessness as in some way JA's fault. "Letters" file, Box 7, Material Under Seal, Iowa. Lacking the letter, and distrusting Phillips's retelling of things, I have avoided mentioning this supposed correspondence in the text. I add here that I am very grateful to Mrs. Maureen C. Mabbott for allowing me to study the reserved papers of her late husband, deposited at the University of Iowa as "Material Under Seal." **The man with whom/** Tottering: Agnes M. Bondurant, *Poe's Richmond* (1942; rpt. Richmond, 1978), 208. Spa: Log, 127. Cavalcade: Phillips, I, 456–57. **Just when Edgar/** Strong-willed: Susan Archer Weiss, *The Home Life of Poe* (New York, 1907), 58. Account: Ingram 817. Although the account came from Thomas H. Ellis, who disliked Poe, I accept it in outline because of its congruence with established reports of Poe's behavior on other occasions, for instance when courting SHW. Some further support for it appears in the statement by Edward V. Valentine (Ingram 222) that he believed he heard Louisa Allan say that Poe once came to the house, but that she did not identify him. See also BPB, 51–52. Because of my hesitation in fully accepting Ellis's account, however, I have compressed it in the text. Various tellings of the supposed episode exist, and some challenges to them. See, e.g., Ingram 236, 237, 361, and Weiss. It remains uncertain whether Poe saw the second Mrs. Allan once, twice, or never. Plaster: Margaret Ellis to Charles Ellis, als, Richmond, 19 Mar 1834, CR, #62675. Cries: Charles Ellis, Jr., to Charles Ellis, als, Richmond, 27 Mar 1834, CR, #62716. See also Margaret Ellis to James Ellis, als, Richmond, 11 Apr 1834, PL. As "Jack," "Jock"/ Respected, tombstone: Log, 138. Proper: James Ellis to Charles Ellis, als, "Military Academy," 15 Apr 1834, PL. **John Allan had drawn/** The will and codicils are printed in Hervey Allen, *Israfel: The Life and Times of Edgar Allan Poe*, rev. ed. (New York, 1934), 685–98. **What Louisa Allan received/** MS "Accounts of the estate of John Allan & copies of papers in the suit Louisa G. Allan v. James Galt, executor of John Allan," The College of William and Mary Library. **Edgar estimated/** Million: LI, 68. Books: Ingram 494.

The Southern Literary Messenger; *Marriage to Virginia Clemm*

"**This is the golden**/ Frank Luther Mott, *A History of American Magazines 1741–1850* (New York, 1930), q. 341. **The swelling enthusiasm**/ Apprentice: David K. Jackson, *Poe and the Southern Literary Messenger* (Richmond, 1934), 18. Stimulate: *SLM,* I (Aug 1834), 1. Awakening: *SLM,* I (Aug 1834), 32. **But so far as**/ Empress: *SLM,* I (Nov 1834), 126. Vehicle: *SLM,* I (Oct 1834), 33. Waltz: *SLM,* I (Apr 1835), 427. Speculated: Log, 140, 151. **Despite his success**/ "Hard-run": Jackson, 105. Assistance: Jackson, 94. Manager: Log, 156. **A suitable editorial**/ Intention: LI, 57. Virginian: *SLM,* I (Apr 1835), 460. Cant: LI, 57–58. Recommended: LI, 62–63. Praised: Jackson, 59. **Nothing in Poe's**/ Eighty: LI, 61n. Pleasure: LI, 62. Insipid, crude, lethargy: Poe's reviews of *SLM* appeared in the Baltimore *Republican and Commercial Advertiser,* 14 May, 13 Jun, and 10 Jul 1835. I have used photocopies of the texts in the folder "Book Reviews, Essays and News Articles 1831–1849," Iowa. **The dealings between**/ Resources: LI, 54. Thoughtful: Whitty, xxxvii. Coat: Log, 133. Remaining details drawn from Augustus Van Cleef, "Poe's Mary," *Harper's New Monthly Magazine,* LXXVIII (Mar 1889), 635–36, and Thomas Ollive Mabbott, ed., *Merlin: Baltimore, 1827* [by Lambert A. Wilmer] (New York, 1941), 29–30. **Staying presentable**/ Teaching: LI, 56. Purloining: LI, 59. Dinner: LI, 56–57. Verge: Log, 149. Unwell: LI, 60. Sea voyage: LI, 61. **But White's interest**/ Employ: Log, 149. Darling: LI, 69. Son: Harrison, XVII, 380. Her name also sometimes appears as "Muddie," but Poe nearly always wrote it "Muddy." Pension: Arthur Hobson Quinn, *Edgar Allan Poe: A Critical Biography* (New York, 1942), 218; William Clemm to H. Harwood, als, Baltimore, 1 Mar 1822, Maryland Historical Society. Relief: LI, 68. **A real chance**/ Offer: LI, 63. Erudition: James Garnett to T. W. White, als, Fredericksburg, 22 Jun 1835, Virginia Historical Society. **Poe went to Richmond**/ Vacancy: David K. Jackson, "Two Notes: A Joseph H. Clarke Manuscript and Something about a Mr. Persico," *Poe Studies,* IX (Jun 1976), 22. Poe may also have been planning to launch a new monthly magazine of his own, in partnership with Lambert Wilmer. See *Merlin,* 26. Salary: Log, 165. Initially White expected Poe to stay only a month, but their arrangements seem to have changed quickly as Poe settled into the work. See T. W. White to Lucian Minor, als, Richmond, 18 Aug 1835, Pierpont Morgan Library. **Whatever pleasure Poe**/ Shaking: LI, 68. Possibility: BPB, 52. **To Poe the offer**/ Quotations in this and the next paragraph from LI, 69–71. **Adding a fillip**/ Amiable: Jackson, 98. Blonde: MI, 233. Involved: The story of their involvement may be apocryphal, but if authentic Poe apparently treated Eliza as a sort of second best. He published in *SLM* a poem beginning "Eliza! let thy generous heart / From its present pathway part not," I (Sep 1835), 748. Apparently addressed to White's daughter, the poem was but a slightly revised version of one he had earlier written in the album of his cousin Elizabeth Herring. By one account, Eliza White believed that it was to stop Poe from marrying her that Maria Clemm brought about his marriage to Virginia. See Ingram 196 and 233. On the other hand, T. W. White's apprentice stated in old age that Poe and Eliza were never more than friends. See Whitty, xxxix. Given Poe's behavior with women after Virginia's death, when he clearly sought backups for the women he courted, it seems to me that he may have pursued Eliza even while ardently pressing Virginia. Editor: Jackson, 98. Junior: LI, 73. Usurped: LI, 68. **However he exaggerated/** Suffering: LI, 73. Dissipated: Jackson, 98. Poe himself remarked in 1841 that while at the *Messenger* he was sometimes "completely intoxicated" and after each bout of heavy drinking had to spend several days in bed; he would seem to be speaking of the period of Neilson Poe's offer. LI, 156. Console: LI, 73. Cheerful: J. P. Kennedy to Poe, als, 15 Sep 1835, Gris. **But by the time/** Jackson, 100. **Poe had not simply/** Married: Baltimore County Marriage Records, 1832–1839, Maryland Hall of Records, Annapolis. First-cousin: Virginia law at the time did not prohibit marriage between first cousins. See *The Revised Code of the Laws of Virginia,* I (Richmond, 1819), 399. Rare: Daniel Scott Smith, "Parental Control and Marriage Patterns: An Analysis of Historical Trends in Hingham, Massachusetts," *Journal of Marriage and the Family,* XXXV (Aug 1973), 423–24. See also Robert V. Wells, *Revolutions in Americans' Lives: A Demographic Perspective* (Westport, 1982). **Whether married or only/** T. W. White to Poe, als, Richmond, 29 Sep 1835, Gris. **Poe returned to Richmond/** Son: Harrison, XVII, 379. Contributor: Jackson, 104. George: LI, 80. **Poe's return with his/** Bottle: Jackson, 107. Pecuniary: LI, 81. Benefit: Harrison, XVII, 379–81.

Writings in the Southern Literary Messenger

Whether or not called/ Forty: LI, 84. Diplomacy: See, e.g., LI, 86, 90. **Poe's editorial duties/** Neglect: LI, 78. Ludicrous: LI, 57–58. **In creating "Berenice"/** German: See Gerhard Hoffmann, "Edgar Allan Poe and German Literature," in Christoph Wecker, ed., *American-German Literary Interrelations in the Nineteenth Century* (Munich, 1983), 52–104, and Michael Allen, *Poe and the British Magazine Tradition* (New York, 1969), esp. 138–39. Gothic: In the very large literature on Gothicism, I have found the following particularly useful: Donald A. Ringe, *American Gothic: Imagination & Reason in Nineteenth-Century Fiction* (Lexington, 1982); Elizabeth MacAndrew, *The Gothic Tradition in Fiction* (New York, 1979); and Maurice Lévy, "Poe and the Gothic Tradition," *Emerson Society Quarterly,* n.s., XVIII (1972), 19–29. Several times, the paragraph closely paraphrases William Patrick Day's especially fine *In the Circles of Fear and Desire: A Study of Gothic Fantasy* (Chicago, 1985). **Not only does attachment/** Illusion: David Halliburton remarks, accurately I think, that Poe's basic theme is the unity and eternality of being: "Poe's 'saving' myth is the deliverance of being from apparent destruction." *Edgar Allan Poe: A Phenomenological View* (Princeton, 1973), 55. **This insistent questioning/** "Politian": Text from *SLM,* II (Dec 1835), 16. **Other tales concern/** Proboscis: Sentence quoted as it appears in the 1840 version of the tale. Immortality: Bertram D. Lewin speaks of patients to whom success represents "immortality and a defense against a fear of death." *The Psychoanalysis of Elation* (New York, 1961), 156. **While editing the *Messenger*/** Autographs: J. R. Thompson, a later editor of *SLM*, owned autographs of Burns, Lamb, Scott, Napoleon, and Mendelssohn, among many others. See Charles Roberts Autograph Collection, Haverford College Library. Poe's friend Lewis Jacob Cist collected eleven thousand specimens of autographs and old portraits. See Leslie W. Dunlap, ed., *The Letters of Willis Gaylord Clark and Lewis Gaylord Clark* (New York, 1940), 107, n.1. Treatise: Meredith Neill Posey, "Notes on Poe's *Hans Pfaall*," *Modern Language Notes*, XLV (1930), 501–7. Pinakidia: How much originality Poe intended to claim for his selections and commentary remains a question. His oddly self-contradictory preface leaves it uncertain whether he is acknowledging or denying his borrowings. Woodberry believed that a "not" was omitted from a key sentence of the preface, reversing Poe's meaning. But see Pollin's persuasive discussion of the matter in Brev. In "Maelzel's Chess-Player"/ See W. K. Wimsatt, Jr., "Poe and the Chess Automaton," *American Literature*, XI (May 1939), 138–51, and Leroy L. Panek, " 'Maelzel's Chess-Player,' Poe's First Detective Mistake," *American Literature*, XLVIII (Nov 1970), 370–72. **Constricted by White/** Conforming: Edward Pessen, *Jacksonian America: Society, Personality, and Politics,* rev. ed. (Urbana, 1985), q. 17. Emerson: "Self-Reliance," *The Works of Ralph Waldo Emerson*, II (Boston, 1909), 53. **Spurred by British/** Anonymously: *SLM*, I (Apr 1835), 459. Balderdash: *SLM*, II (Dec 1835), 56. Era: Ingram 494. **One elementary critical/** Partisan: *SLM*, II (Jan 1836), 120. Detector: Walker, 333. Constructive: T, 135. **Poe's contempt for ignorant/** Blunders: Sidney P. Moss, *Poe's Literary Battles: The Critic in the Context of His Literary Milieu* (Durham, 1963), q. 46. **Although Poe frequently/** Greek: See Burton R. Pollin, ed., *Edgar Allan Poe: Writings in* The Broadway Journal . . . *Part 2, The Annotations* (New York, 1986), 7. Hebrew: See Harrison, XVII, 42–43, and compare with T, 935–36. French: Jacques Barzun, "A Note on the Inadequacy of Poe as a Proofreader and of his Editors as French Scholars," *Romanic Review*, LXI (Feb 1970), 23–26. Italian: Joseph Chesley Mathews, "Did Poe Read Dante?," *Studies in English 1938* (Austin, 1938), 123–36. German: MI, 237, n. 4; *The Annotations*, 128. C. F. Briggs commented that Poe knew no German at all. **Poe directed his critical/** Well!: *SLM*, II (Dec 1835), 54. Gander: T, 874–75. **Poe made his fullest/** *SLM*, II (Apr 1836), 326–36. **Poe's critical writing generated/** Cincinnati: *SLM*, II (Apr 1836), 343. Flaying: Log, 204. Microscopic: Moss, q. 46. Overkill: *SLM*, II (Jul 1836), 520. **Having yearned for fame/** New Bern: See Moss, 44–62. Puffed: Log, 157. The opportunity to review himself perhaps explains why Poe undertook to write blurbs for White in the first place. Boasting: *SLM*, I (May 1835), 468. Jumped: *SLM*, II (Aug 1836), 599. Gourmont: Jean Alexander, ed., *Affidavits of Genius: Edgar Allan Poe and the French Critics, 1847–1924* (Port Washington, 1971), 232. **While becoming a prominent/** *SLM*, II (Apr 1836), 348.

Second Marriage (?) to Virginia; Break with the Messenger

Poe spent sixteen months/ Climate: Thomas Hale, Jr., to Moses and Josiah Hale, als, Richmond, 16 Dec 1826, HRC; Charles Dickens, *American Notes* *for General Circulation* (Harmondsworth, 1972), 181. Population: *SLM,* I (Feb 1835), 257–60. Atmosphere: Agnes M. Bondurant, *Poe's Richmond* (1942; rpt. Richmond, 1978), 7–8. **During much of his stay/** Arms: LI, 81. Married: Marriage Bond, 16 May 1836, Virginia Historical Society. Fifteen: LI, 82. Child: Susan Archer Weiss, *The Home Life of Poe* (New York, 1907), 85–86. Husband: Frederick W. Coburn, "Poe as seen by the Brother of 'Annie'," *New England Quarterly,* XVI (Sep 1943), 471. **Having brought Sissy/** Regarded: LI, 81. Currency: Arthur H. Quinn, ed., *Edgar Allan Poe: Letters and Documents in the Enoch Pratt Free Library* (New York, 1941), 15. Earned: John Ward Ostrom, "Edgar A. Poe: His Income as Literary Entrepreneur," *Poe Studies,* XV (1982), 2. Wilmer: Thomas Ollive Mabbott, ed., *Merlin: Baltimore, 1827* [by Lambert A. Wilmer] (New York, 1941), 32. Mobile: LI, 80. Furniture: LI, 95. **Poe tried even more/** Bequeathed: LI, 82. Profit: J. P. Kennedy to Poe, als, Baltimore, 26 Apr 1836, University of Virginia Library. Annuity: LI, 92. **Poe's residence in Richmond/** Know: PHR, 160. Bills: Poe Collection Misc., HRC. Pseudoretardation: Erna Furman, "On Trauma: When is the Death of a Parent Traumatic?," *Psychoanalytic Study of the Child,* XL (1986), esp. 199–204. Unhandsome: See folder, "E. V. Valentine's Notes," VM. **However gratified to be/** Circulated: MS memoranda of T. H. Ellis, 1876, VM; Ingram 237. By one account, a party in the city loyal to the second Mrs. Allan tried to discredit Poe. See note on back of envelope, seemingly in the hand of J. H. Whitty, beginning "Poe Mss Correspondence," HRC. Offices: Mary Wingfield Scott, *Old Richmond Neighborhoods* (1950; rpt. Richmond, 1975), 135. Annuity: LI, 54. Will: LI, 68. **Poe's falsifications seem/** "Unparralleled": see MI, illustrated table of contents following p. 474. **Poe's return to Richmond/** Cemetery: Ingram 66. Orphans: LI, 68. String: LI, 78–79. **Whatever else Richmond/** Bragged: LII, 440. Nervous: See his letters in David K. Jackson, *Poe and the Southern Literary Messenger* (Richmond, 1934), *passim.* Quixotic: T. W. White to B. Badger, typed transcript, Richmond, 27 May 1836, PL. White's friend James E. Heath called him a man of integrity but also of *"fickle temperament."* Heath to Lucian Minor, als, Richmond, 26 Feb 1835, Virginia Historical Society. Warily: T. W. White to William Scott, typed transcript, Richmond, 25 Aug 1836, PL. Fretting: Jackson, 102, 105. **By the late fall/** Announced: *SLM,* II (Sep 1836), 668. Press: *SLM,* II (Nov 1836), 788. New Bern: Log, 236. Cancer: Log, 240. **By Christmastime/** Notice: T. W. White to William Scott, typed transcript, Richmond, 15 Dec 1836, PL. Conditions, jackass: Jackson, 109–10. **In the January number/** Tom: LI, 141, 198. Promising: LI, 106. Bombast: Log, 239. Pym: Log, 241. Relief: Jackson, 112. **Poe lingered in Richmond/** Outlive, disgusted: Log, 241–42. Disenchanted: Jackson, 115.

The Blank Period; The Narrative of Arthur Gordon Pym *and* "Ligeia"

After leaving White/ Hawks: Log, 237. Gowans: Isaac S. Lyon, *Recollections of an Old Cartman* (1872; rpt. New York, 1984), 102. Matchless: Ingram 514.

Sedulously: John H. Ingram, *Edgar Allan Poe: His Life, Letters, and Opinions* (1886; rpt. New York, 1965), q. 117. **Poe always felt/** Dinner: Log, 243. Depression: Marvin Meyers, *The Jacksonian Persuasion: Politics and Belief* (1957; rpt. Stanford, 1960), 111. **After about a year/** Left: The earliest known date of Poe's being in Philadelphia is 19 Jul 1838. See LII, 681. Settled: Thomas, 913. Paulding: Log, 248. Wilmer: Thomas Ollive Mabbott, ed., *Merlin: Baltimore, 1827* [by Lambert A. Wilmer] (New York, 1941), 33. **Poe also seems to/** Log, 248. **Ironically, less than/** Place: Ralph M. Aderman, ed., *The Letters of James Kirke Paulding* (Madison, Wis., 1962), 173–74. Declined: Harper and Brothers to Poe, als, New York, 19 Jun 1836, Gris. Announced: Eugene Exman, *The Brothers Harper* (New York, 1965), 97, and Joseph V. Ridgely, "The Growth of the Text," in Burton Pollin, ed., *Edgar Allan Poe: The Imaginary Voyages* . . . (Boston, 1981), 29–36. Quotations of *Pym* in the text are from Pollin's edition. **The novella's lengthy/** Illusion: See the discussion in Patrick F. Quinn, *The French Face of Edgar Poe* (Carbondale, 1957). Constraints of space in the text allow no chance for commenting on Poe's technical achievement. Making Pym's adventures credible posed a problem to which he clearly gave much thought. Probably having in mind the plain realism of *Robinson Crusoe,* one of his favorite works, he contrived a style that was for him singularly unembellished, lacking the erudition and lush atmosphere of his tales of horror. He also narrated his "incredibilities" according to a principle he had laid down in an *SLM* review: not to explain them but rather, as Pym does, to express bafflement over them himself, "as if the author were firmly impressed with the truth, yet astonished at the immensity, of the wonders he relates, and for which, professedly, he neither claims nor anticipates credence," II (10 Sep 1836), 667. Poe also gave Pym's assorted adventures a fairly symmetrical shape, devoting twelve chapters to events on the *Grampus* and twelve to events on the *Jane Guy.* The halves, moreover, contain many parallel actions: among others, the episode aboard the *Grampus* in which Pym is lowered into the submerged hold by ropes, balances the episode on Tsalal where he is let down from the precipice by a handkerchief rope. Smaller-scale contrasts contribute to the balanced effect: white and black, cook's faction and mate's faction, the half-breed Peters and the "hermaphrodite brig" *Jane Guy.* Poe also artfully built the evolving mood of wonder, the powerful copulative closing, and the suspense in such individual episodes as Pym's attempt to illuminate the dark hold by gathering bits of phosphorous from matches, a tour de force of hyperrealism. On the other hand, critics have long noted the many inconsistencies and blunders in the narrative (Augustus dies during the voyage, but Pym mentions speaking with him years after it), and there are many errors in grammar, especially the characteristic dangling participles: "Upon seeing me open my eyes, his exclamations of gratitude and joy excited alternate laughter and tears." Particularly in his account of the *Jane Guy*'s travels southward, too, Poe lifted from encyclopedias and other travel accounts many details of navigation, geography, and exotic flora and fauna. Chapters 14 to 16, occupying some fifteen pages of such description in modern editions, are largely plagiarized. On these matters see also David Ketterer, *The Rationale of Deception in Poe* (Baton Rouge, 1979), and the notes and commentary in Pollin's text. **Not only in this/** Evade: Richard Wilbur acutely calls the novella "an allegory of regeneration." *Responses. Prose Pieces: 1953–1976* (New York, n.d.), 208. **Through Pym's adventures/** Inscriptions: The petroglyphs also reflect a scientific revival of the ancient trope of the book of nature, a sense that nature can be read through its language of fossils, fissures, strata, etc. See Barbara Maria Stafford, *Voyage Into Substance: Art, Science, Nature and the Illustrated Travel Account, 1760–1840* (Cambridge, Mass., 1984). Poe probably modeled his pictographs on those in William Alexander Caruthers's *The Kentuckian in New-York* (1834), I, 146, where similar writing appears as the work of a black slave. Nu-Nu: The Indian heroine of a story by N. P. Willis is named Nunu. See "The Cherokee's Threat" in Rufus Griswold, ed., *The Prose Writers of America* (Philadelphia, 1852), 485–89. **Like some submerged/** Peters: The University of Virginia Library owns a copy of *Pym* inscribed by Poe with respects to "Mrs. Mary Kirk Petrie," suggesting that in creating Dirk Peters he may have had an actual person in mind. "E. Ronald": Richard Wilbur pointed out that *Ronald* anagrammatizes *Arnold,* the name of Poe's mother. His remark is cited in Richard Kopley, "The Hidden Journey of *Arthur Gordon Pym,*" *Studies in the American Renaissance* (Boston, 1982), 29–51. I arrived at my reading of Henry Poe's presence in the novel before seeing Professor Kopley's rich article, which points out several of the parallels between Augustus and Henry, adding that the word *hope,* an anagram for *H. Poe,* permeates the novella, appearing thirty-eight times. The similarity in the dates of death was first pointed out by Marie Bonaparte. **A deeper but also/** Tekeli: David K. Jackson and Burton R. Pollin, "Poe's 'Tekeli-li'," *Poe Studies,* XII (Jun 1979), 19. Eliza also played Ariel, in *The Tempest,* the name of Pym's sloop. Nourisher: Martha Wolfenstein discusses a bereaved child who while his mother was dying became insatiably hungry. "How is Mourning Possible?," *Psychoanalytic Study of the Child,* XXI (1966), 119. On geographical exploration as exploration of the mother see Howard F. Stein and William G. Niederland, eds., *Maps From the Mind: Readings in Psychogeography* (Norman, 1989), *passim.* **Pym attracted perhaps/** Freezing: Burton R. Pollin, "Poe's *Narrative of Arthur Gordon Pym* and the Contemporary Reviewers," *Studies in American Fiction,* II (Spring 1974), 43. Hinted: Log, 249. **Even after Poe published/** Sacrifices: LI, 123. Pushed: LI, 112. Pedder: Log, 248. **However soured on/** Wyatt: Thomas, 952. **During this blank/** Disordered: LI, 161. **In "Ligeia"/** In essence, Poe had of course been writing this story since the time of "Metzengerstein" and "Berenice." He gave "Ligeia," however, a dense economy, directing every detail toward the climactic horror of Ligeia's return. He also braced the narrative with a powerfully rhythmic structure, marked by strong contrasts between Ligeia and Rowena, Germany and England, and by the dramatically plausible repetition at key points of the remark he attributed to the seventeenth-century demonologist Joseph Glanvill. Ligeia's return is subtly heralded and stressed by the repetition of many other elements in the tale, a tale in which everything returns. **The psychological complexity/** See the convincing interpretation in J. Gerald Kennedy, *Poe, Death, and the Life of Writing* (New Haven, 1987). **Poe seems to have/** John Ward Ostrom, "Edgar A. Poe: His Income as Literary Entrepreneur," *Poe Studies,* XV (1982), 2.

Philadelphia; Billy Burton

Neat, clean, quiet/ Perfect, wearisome: J. S. Buckingham, *America, Historical, Statistic, and Descriptive,* II (London, 1841), 26; Frances Trollope, *Domestic Manners of the Americans* (New York, 1984), 221. Clean, Sunday: Frederick Marryat, *A Diary in America With Remarks on Its Institutions* (New York, 1962), 145. **The tranquillity was/** Population: Edward Pessen, *Jacksonian America: Society, Personality, and Politics,* rev. ed. (Urbana, 1985), 54. Newspapers: Buckingham, 75. Gas: Ellis Paxson Oberholtzer, *Philadelphia: A History of the City and its People,* II (Philadelphia, n.d.), 229. Markets, etc.: See Trollope, and Joseph John Gurney, *A Journey in North America* (1841; rpt. New York, 1973). **Poe, Sissy, and Muddy/** Fawn: LI, 129. Small: LI, 111. For further description of the house see Thomas Dunn English, "Reminiscences of Poe," *Independent,* XLVIII (22 Oct 1896), 1415–16, and Thomas, 901–3. Pecuniary: Whitty, xliii. F. W. Thomas is certainly referring here to the Sixteenth Street house. See Log, 379. Acquaintance: English, 1415. **Not yet seventeen/** Refinement: English, 1415. Algebra, music: BPB, 48, and Thomas Ollive Mabbott, ed., *Merlin: Baltimore, 1827* [by Lambert A. Wilmer] (New York, 1941), 32. Starr: Augustus Van Cleef, "Poe's Mary," *Harper's New Monthly Magazine,* LXXVIII (Mar 1889), 639. Singer: Thomas, q. 789. **After two and a half/** Burton: *Frank Leslie's Illustrated Newspaper,* 25 Feb 1860, 202. Vulgar: James Rees to Sol Smith, als, Philadelphia, 23 May 1840, Missouri Historical Society. Avocations: W. E. Burton to G. P. Morris, als, Philadelphia, 26 Jan 1839, Historical Society of Pennsylvania. Vagrant: Leslie W. Dunlap, ed., *The Letters of Willis Gaylord Clark and Lewis Gaylord Clark* (New York, 1940), 58. **Bluff, worldly/** Impudent: Walker, 96. **With whatever misgivings/** Avocation: W. E. Burton to Poe, als, Philadelphia, 10 May 1839, Gris. Over-estimated: T, 492. **But at the same time/** Impudence: Als of 26 Jan 1839. Morbid: W. E. Burton to Poe, als, Philadelphia, 30 May 1839, Gris. **Irked or not/** Log, 262–63.

Writing for Burton's; *"The Fall of the House of Usher" and "William Wilson"; Ciphering;* Tales of the Grotesque and Arabesque

Poe's work for Burton/ Storm: LI, 127. Hodgepodge: In attributing *Burton's* articles to Poe I follow T. O. Mabbott. See the four folders on *Burton's,* Box 2, Material Under Seal, Iowa. Rees: J. O. Bailey, "Poe's 'Stonehenge'," *Studies in Philology,* XXXVIII (Oct 1941), 645. **Burton's cautions about/** Goadings: T, 1061. Dealing: LI, 114. **For many Americans/** Over-rated: LI, 121, 112. Exemption: Harrison, X, 88. **Poe also went after/** Deficient: T, 671–79. Purloined: LI, 161. Stakes: Log, 288–90, 304. **Poe was far from/** Unworthy: T, 504. Brother: W. E. Burton to Poe, als, Philadelphia, 10 May 1839, Gris. Pleaded: LII, 689. Cloying: LI, 159. Inveterate: LI, 117. Evasion:

Ingram 237. **Poe did not exaggerate/** Pressing: LI, 126. "Silence": See MI, 323. The poem first appeared three months earlier in the Philadelphia *Saturday Courier.* Poe based it on a sonnet with the same title by Thomas Hood, reversing Hood's valuation of the two kinds of silence. **Between these extremes/** Hoax: David K. Jackson, "A Poe Hoax Comes Before the U.S. Senate," *Poe Studies,* VII (Dec 1974), 47–48, and Edwin Fussell, *Frontier: American Literature and the American West* (Princeton, 1965), 158–62. **The appearance here/** *Pym:* The Henry Poe-like Augustus is also reborn in Rodman's ailing companion. Thornton, the two being, Poe writes, "as intimate, during our whole expedition, as brothers could possibly be." "Rodman" is quoted from the text in Burton Pollin, ed., *Edgar Allan Poe: The Imaginary Voyages* (Boston, 1981). Pilfering: Pollin correctly calls "Rodman" a "verbal collage" (512) and exhaustively documents Poe's copying. Studies of Poe's borrowings by Bailey and Posey have already been cited, but see also Margaret Alterton, *Origins of Poe's Critical Theory* (Iowa City, 1925); Wayne R. Kime, "Poe's Use of Irving's *Astoria* in 'The Journal of Julius Rodman'," *American Literature,* XL (May 1968), 215–22; Ronald Sterne Wilkinson, "Poe's 'Balloon-Hoax' Once More," *American Literature,* XXXII (Nov 1960), 313–17. **For all this remodeling/** Steam-travel: Nicholas B. Wainright, ed., *A Philadelphia Perspective: The Diary of Sidney George Fisher Covering the Years 1834–1871* (Philadelphia, 1967), q. 49. Windmill: Marvin Meyers, *The Jacksonian Persuasion: Politics and Belief* (1957; rpt. Stanford, 1960), q. 122. On Poe as a social critic see Eric W. Carlson, "Poe's Vision of Man," in Richard P. Veler, ed., *Papers on Poe: Essays in Honor of John Ward Ostrom* (Springfield, Ohio, 1972), 7–20. **Poe also contributed/** Outworn: A Gothic novel popular in America in the late eighteenth century was entitled *Count Roderic's Castle* (1794). Poe had himself used the now-trite last-of-the-line theme in "Metzengerstein." **In "William Wilson"/** Wound: Marie Bonaparte, *The Life and Works of Edgar Allan Poe: A Psycho-Analytic Interpretation* (English ed. 1949; rpt. London, 1971), 544. "Wilson" appeared in *Burton's* for October 1839, but had first appeared a few months earlier in *The Gift for 1840.* Irving: MII, 423. Mann: Benjamin Lease, *Anglo-American Encounters: England and the Rise of American Literature* (Cambridge, England, 1981), q. 77. **It endures in part/** Bewilderingly: For a fine analysis of the mirror scene, see Elizabeth MacAndrew, *The Gothic Tradition in Fiction* (New York, 1979), 220–21. **The past is also/** Performed: See for instance *The Emerald,* 16 Apr 1808, and the earlier discussion of the Ushers. The Ushers had died in 1814, but Poe may have known their children, including the actress Agnes Pye (Pym?) Usher. **For his ninety-five/** Reprinted: John Ward Ostrom, "Edgar A. Poe: His Income as Literary Entrepreneur," *Poe Studies,* XV (1982), 2. Borrow, work: LI, 123, 130, 176. *Alexander's:* Clarence S. Brigham, *Edgar Allan Poe's Contributions to Alexander's Weekly Messenger* (Worcester, 1943). Distance: Brigham, 36. **Poe invited readers/** Brigham, 23, 27. **Although boasting his/** Infallibility: See David Kahn, *The Codebreakers: The Story of Secret Writing* (London, 1967), 783ff. **While working for *Burton's*/** Pecuniary: Lea and Blanchard to Poe, als, Philadelphia, 28 Sep 1839, Gris. Reduced: Thomas, 74. **Poe had been trying/** Grotesque: See Patricia C. Smith, "Poe's Arabesques," *Poe Studies,* VII (Dec 1974), 42–45. G. R. Thompson notes that Schlegel himself confounded the words, and that among romantic writers *arabesque* seems often to be an alternative term for *grotesque*. *Poe's Fiction: Romantic Irony in the Gothic Tales* (Madison, Wis., 1973), 105. Hybrid: Geoffrey Galt Harpham, *On the Grotesque: Strategies of Contradiction in Art and Literature* (Princeton, 1982). **In his peculiar preface/** Improbable: Log, 151–52. Twaddle: LI, 121. Hoffmann's: Gustav Gruener, "Notes on the Influence of E. T. A. Hoffmann upon Edgar Allan Poe," *PMLA*, XIX (1904), 1–25. **While Poe's productive/** Praised: Log, 268, 276, 287. Trash: Walker, 124. Foremost: Walker, 125. **Poe awaited his reviews/** Capital: LI, 125. Praises: Richard Beale Davis, ed., *Chivers' Life of Poe* (New York, 1952), 62. Master-hand, Shelley: Walker, 118, 117. Sonnet, story: Brigham, 66, 29. Conundrum: Brigham, 16.

Break with Burton; "The Penn Magazine"

Despite his success/ Taxed: LII, 687. **More, Poe particularly/** Toto: LI, 125. Connexion: LI, 138. **Once more dressing up/** On the contest see Dwight Thomas, "William E. Burton and his Premium Scheme: New Light on Poe Biography," *University of Mississippi Studies in English*, n.s., III (1982), 68–80. I join Thomas in the now-general discrediting of an older account of the break between Poe and Burton, told to Hyman Rosenbach by the son of Richard Penn Smith. See, e.g., Edwin Wolf 2d, "Horace Wemyss Smith's Recollections of Poe," *University of Pennsylvania Library Chronicle*, XVII (Spring–Summer 1951), 90–103, and Arthur Hobson Quinn, *Edgar Allan Poe: A Critical Biography* (New York, 1942), 296–97. **In replying to Burton's/** LI, 129–32. **Slights to himself/** Reviewer: Walker, 96. Revenge: LI, 129–32. **Much as it had begun/** Cursed: LI, 138. Botched: Log, 307. Barlow: Thomas, 175. Felon: LI, 155–56. **Poe also vigorously/** LI, 156–57. **The truth of the matter/** Reassuring: On the other hand, some evidence that Poe stayed sober at least during his first few months on the *Gentleman's* appears in a letter to him from the new editor of *SLM*, James E. Heath, replying to what was apparently a statement from Poe declaring his sobriety. Heath euphemistically congratulated Poe on the good sense that "enabled you to overcome a seductive and dangerous besetment which too often prostrates the wisest and best by its fatal grasp." Als, Richmond, 12 Sep 1839, Gris. Contributor: Thomas Dunn English, "Reminiscences of Poe," *Independent*, XLVIII (22 Oct 1896), 1416. Interfered: Quinn, 297. **As for Burton's/** LI, 155–57. **Poe no sooner parted/** Dust: LI, 119. Hand: LI, 143. Succeeding: LI, 138. **Poe did not plan/** Quotations in this and the next paragraph from T, 1024–26. **Sometimes using the reverse/** Trips: LI, 140; on a probable business trip to New York see F. W. Thomas to Poe, als, Washington, 24 Aug 1840, Gris. Honor: LI, 143 and n. *Chronicle:* 14 Sep 1840. Predicted: LI, 149. **But no "Penn"/** LI, 145, 150. **So far as Poe's remarks/** Cliques: Frederick Marryat, *A Diary in America With Remarks on Its Institutions* (New York, 1962), 146. Biddle: LII, 693–95 and n. **That was not enough/** Sheet: Joseph J. Moldenhauer, "Beyond the Tamarind Tree: A New Poe Letter," *American Literature*, XLII (Jan 1971), 468–77. Auspices: LI, 157.

Graham's Magazine; *Important Critical Essays;*
"The Murders in the Rue Morgue"

For $3,500/ Log, 309. **Boyish-looking and clean-shaven/** Graham: Frank
Luther Mott, *A History of American Magazines 1741–1850* (New York, 1930),
342, n. 6; John Sartain, *The Reminiscences of a Very Old Man 1808–1897* (1899;
rpt. New York, 1969), 196ff. Liberal: LI, 186. Profession: Mott, 509. **At the
same time/** Things: *GM*, XVIII (Feb 1841), 67. Madrid: *GM*, XVIII (Mar
1841), 105. Valenciennes: *GM*, XVIII (Feb 1841), 96. **The *Graham's* diet/**
Detest: LI, 197. Liberal: LI, 157. Personage: LI, 153, 205. Praised: Log, 299.
Commendation: Log, 320. Hub: J. Albert Robbins, "George R. Graham Philadelphia Publisher," *Pennsylvania Magazine of History and Biography*, LXXV
(Jul 1951), 283, n. 18. **Although listed as/** Solicited: LI, 155. Tales: LI, 182,
200. **Although Poe's circumscribed/** Overwhelmed: LI, 235. Boasted: LI,
172–73. One challenge, written by a man named Frailey, involved Poe in a
particularly revealing controversy, too long and complex to be treated here,
in which he claimed to have discovered a cryptographical plagiarist. See W. K.
Wimsatt, Jr., "What Poe Knew about Cryptography," *PMLA*, LVIII (1943),
754–79, and Log. **As he had been hired/** In attributing *GM* reviews to Poe,
I have again followed Mabbott's attributions. See Box 3, Material Under Seal,
Iowa. Bedizzened: T, 499. Fancied: T, 922. Flogged: T, 824. **For every ten
writers/** Transition: T, 258. Tone: T, 156. Meanings: T, 259. James: Eric W.
Carlson, ed., *The Recognition of Edgar Allan Poe* (Ann Arbor, 1970), 66. **Far
more important/** Excessive: T, 492. Elite: See, e.g., Poe's review of Sprague,
GM, XVII (May 1841), 252. **Within the first six/** "Exordium": All quotations
from T, 1027–32. **These included correctness/** Collection: All quotations
from T, 569–77. **Poe had touched on/** Schlegel: Robert D. Jacobs, *Poe: Journalist & Critic* (Baton Rouge, 1969), 115–16. See also Donald Barlow Stauf-
fer, "Poe's Views on the Nature and Function of Style," *Emerson Society Quarterly*, LX (Summer 1970), 23–30. Design: T, 572–73. **In a review of
Longfellow's/** All quotations from T, 679–96. My remarks in the text are
confined to poetry, but Poe speaks more generally of "Poesy," intending the
quality of supernal beauty as it appears not only in poetry but in other arts as
well. See Mutlu Konuk Blasing, *American Poetry: The Rhetoric of its Forms* (New
Haven, 1987), 24–25. **Belonging "solely to Eternity"/** Fancy: Poe's treatment of Fancy and Imagination presents many more problems than can be
conveniently treated here. It seems clear to me that for Poe the Imagination,
as distinct from the Fancy, was bound up with the denial of death. One of his
fullest discussions of the problem appears in his review of Moore's *Alciphron,*
which deals with the search for Eternal Life. The five long quotations from the
poem which he chooses to illustrate Moore's ideality, all have to do with tran-
scending death. For fuller discussion see Jacobs, 235–40. Excited: LI, 257. **In
these and in/** Shaw: Carlson, 53. **Poe also stepped/** Hyper-patriotic: T, 404.
Miltons: T, 1010, 1013. Defects: T, 405. **Poe moved more systematically/**
Bryant: Harrison, XV, 189. Whipple: Gerald E. Gerber, "E. P. Whipple Attacks Poe: A New Review," *American Literature*, LIII (Mar 1981), 110–13.

"Eleonora"/ Ended: MI, 635. **Poe combined the tale**/ Combined: See David S. Reynolds, *Beneath the American Renaissance: The Subversive Imagination in the Age of Emerson and Melville* (New York, 1988), 35, 46. Reveries: T, 871. Damnable: T, 871. **In the April 1841**/ Ratiocination: LII, 328. Sensational: Reynolds, 160ff., 207. Apes: See Richard Kopley's forthcoming "Edgar Allan Poe and *The Philadelphia Saturday News,*" which Professor Kopley kindly allowed me to read in manuscript. An early account I have not seen mentioned elsewhere is "The Wonderful Ape of Marseilles," in *The American Magazine of Wonders* (New York, 1809), 34–37. It might be added that crime was coming to be regarded aesthetically, as in Thomas de Quincey's essay "Murder Considered as One of the Fine Arts" (1827). See John G. Cawelti, *Adventure, Mystery, and Romance* (Chicago, 1976), 54–56, 95. **Despite its thorough novelty**/ Gothic: See William Patrick Day, *In the Circles of Fear and Desire: A Study of Gothic Fantasy* (Chicago, 1985). Web: LII, 328. Backwards: T, 872. **A 'short story' rather**/ Urban: Dana Brand, "Reconstructing the 'Flaneur': Poe's Invention of the Detective Story," *Genre,* XVIII (Spring 1985), 36–56. The anonymity of people in a crowd was a popular literary motif of the period. See, e.g., Rufus Griswold's poem "Sights from My Window—Alice": "In the crowd how little know they / What griefs its members bear!" *GM,* XX (Jun 1842), 340. Endorsed: I owe this insight to some remarks of a fine graduate student at New York University, Alice Fahs. **For all its Parisian**/ Augustus: On Dupin's name see W. T. Bandy, "Who Was Monsieur Dupin?," *PMLA,* LXXIX (1964), 509–10. Henry is also perhaps acknowledged in the sailor of the story. **Poe understatedly called**/ Key: LII, 328. *Inquirer:* Walker, 132–33. Features: See Cawelti, 81–85. On the psychoanalytic view of detective fiction see Geraldine Pederson-Krag, "Detective Stories and the Primal Scene," in Glenn W. Most and William W. Stowe, eds., *The Poetics of Murder: Detective Fiction and Literary Theory* (New York, 1983), 13–20. On the sociological view see Stephen Knight, *Form and Ideology in Crime Fiction* (London, 1980) and Dennis Porter, *The Pursuit of Crime: Art and Ideology in Detective Fiction* (New Haven, 1981).

Resignation from Graham's; *F. W. Thomas; Virginia's Illness;* "The Mask of the Red Death"

Graham's **prospered from Poe's**/ Planned: Log, 361. Astounding: LI, 185. Earned: John Ward Ostrom, "Edgar A. Poe: His Income as Literary Entrepreneur," *Poe Studies,* XV (1982), 2. Several salary receipts from Graham, signed by Poe, survive at HRC. **Still, Poe's work**/ Disgusted: LI, 170. Climate: LI, 178, and Harrison, XVII, 101–2. Ninnies: LI, 192–93. Coin: LI, 172. **Even while seeing to**/ Partnership: LI, 180. Pecuniary: LI, 164. By his later account, perhaps somewhat distorted, Poe had originally joined Graham as a salaried editor on the understanding that Graham would join him in the new magazine after six months, or certainly after a year. LI, 205. "Penn": LI, 161–70. **Poe intended to launch**/ Lurch: LI, 205. West: LI, 183, 185, and F. W.

Thomas to Poe, als, Washington, 14 Jun 1841, Gris. According to a thirdhand account, Poe at around this time was thinking of relocating in the western reserve. Theodore Pease Stearns, "A Prohibitionist Shakes Dice with Poe," *Outlook,* CXXVI (Sep 1920), 25–26. Triumph: LI, 192. **The hope of a different/** Thomas: See Thomas, 913–17. One of his songs, " 'Tis said that absence," was a favorite of Virginia's. LI, 184. Intimate: F. W. Thomas to Poe, als, Washington, 3 Aug 1841, Gris. Respect: F. W. Thomas to Poe, als, Washington, 21 May 1842, Gris. Leg: Warfield Richardson to W. M. Griswold, als, [n. pl.], 25 Mar 1897, Gris. Smack: F. W. Thomas to Poe, als, Washington, 10 Oct 1844, Gris. Drinking: Warfield Richardson, als of 25 Mar 1897. **The way out of literary/** Novel: F. W. Thomas to Poe, als, Washington, 3 Aug 1841, Gris. Stroll: F. W. Thomas to Poe, als, Washington, 20 May 1841, Gris. **Poe felt, as he said/** LI, 170. **But Thomas doubted his/** Washington: F. W. Thomas to Poe, als, Washington, 1 Jul 1841, Gris. Kennedy: LI, 172. Clerkship: F. W. Thomas to Poe, als, Washington, 7 Jul 1841, Gris. Hurlyburly: F. W. Thomas to Poe, als, Washington, 19 Jul 1841, Gris. **Thomas's efforts for Poe/** Professing: LI, 190. Buzzing: F. W. Thomas to Poe, als, Washington, 30 Aug 1841, Gris. Robert: F. W. Thomas to Poe, als, Washington, 22 Sep 1841 and 26 Feb 1842, Gris. "Penn": LI, 192. **Neither the "Penn" nor/** Weak: LI, 197. Snodgrass: LI, 202–3. **Graham at last made/** Wishes: Log, 372. Respect: LI, 205. Cautionary tale: J. Albert Robbins, "George R. Graham Philadelphia Publisher," *Pennsylvania Magazine of History and Biography,* LXXV (Jul 1951), 286f. **One other event fed/** Perfect: BPB, 48. Ruptured: LI, 191. Death-in-life: Michael McEachern McDowell, "American Attitudes Towards Death, 1825–1865," Ph.D. diss., Brandeis U., 1978, 280. **For nearly two weeks/** Neighbor: Log, 358. Shudder: Walker, 380. Agony: LI, 191. **But Poe could not/** In revised form, "Life in Death" was republished under the more familiar title, "The Oval Portrait."

Virginia's Health; The Custom House; The "Stylus"; Washington

Virginia's condition went/ Michael McEachern McDowell, "American Attitudes Towards Death, 1825–1865," Ph.D. diss., Brandeis U., 1978, 279–84. **Plump but graceful/** Rose-tint: Thomas, 878. Beer: LI, 197–98, 209. Ostrom drew his text of this important letter from the portions of it that were transcribed in the catalogue of an Anderson Galleries auction on 18 Jan 1922. His edition omits significant parts of the transcription, however. T. O. Mabbott saw the original but was not allowed to copy it; he made some brief notes on its content, however, and also copied the entire text of the transcription in the Anderson catalogue. See "Letters" folder, Box 7, Material Under Seal, Iowa. **Poe watched closely/** Risen: LI, 204. Faint: LI, 210. Improved: LI, 212. Grave: Whitty, xliv. Many who saw Virginia commented on her plumpness. Better: LII, 702; on Rosalie's visit see Joseph J. Moldenhauer, "Beyond the Tamarind Tree: A New Poe Letter," *American Literature,* XLII (Jan 1971), 469. Saratoga: Theodore Pease Stearns, "A Prohibitionist Shakes Dice with Poe," *Outlook,* CXXVI (Sep 1920), 25–26. Poe may have made this trip in

September 1843. In an unpublished letter to Edmond Evans, Philadelphia, 21 Sep 1843, he mentions that he has been away from the city for the last few weeks. Estelle Doheny Collection, St. John's Seminary, Camarillo, California. **It may have been hope/** Moved: LI, 198, 211. Quaker: LI, 234. Lean-to: Thomas, 877–78. Neatness: Whitty, xliii. Palings: Thomas, 933–34. Communicant: The Rev. John Coleman, *The Sabbatical Year* (Philadelphia, 1842), 31. Earlier she had been a member of St. Paul's Protestant Episcopal Church in Baltimore. **Poe had disabling bouts/** Succumbed: LI, 237. Drinking: I leave aside here the much-argued question of whether Poe also drank in Philadelphia in the period before Virginia's illness. The matter is not subject to conclusive proof, since knowledge about it is limited to fragmentary evidence of dubious value, such as is preserved in Edwin Wolf 2d, "Horace Wemyss Smith's Recollections of Poe," *University of Pennsylvania Library Chronicle,* XVII (Spring–Summer 1951), 90–103. Poe himself claimed that he stayed away from alcohol between 1838 and 1840. If he did drink some while working for Burton and Graham, it was very little compared with how much he consumed after Virginia became ill. Thomas: LI, 230 n. Binges: Thomas Dunn English, "Reminiscences of Poe," *Independent,* XLVIII (22 Oct 1896), 1415–16. Diarrhea: Ingram 402. Muddy: Maria Clemm to T. H. Chivers, als, Milford, 8 Dec 1852, Huntington Library. **On a trip to New York/** Wallace: LII, 699. Starr: Augustus Van Cleef, "Poe's Mary," *Harper's New Monthly Magazine,* LXXVIII (Mar 1889), 634–40. **Poe tried more than/** Cousin: Poe to Mrs. Elizabeth R. Tutt, transcription, Philadelphia, 7 Jul 1842, "Letters" folder, Box 7, Material Under Seal, Iowa. This letter lends added credence to the account by Mary Starr. Straight: Joseph J. Moldenhauer, *A Descriptive Catalog of Edgar Allan Poe Manuscripts in The Humanities Research Center Library* (Austin, 1973), 55. **Poe's October resolution/** Teetotaler: Log, 412–13. Reprobate: John Tomlin to Poe, als, Jackson, 2 Jul 1843, Gris, and LI, 236. Enemy: William Poe to Poe, als, Baltimore, 15 Jun 1843, Gris. Both Poe's cousin Elizabeth Herring, then living in Philadelphia, and the New York poet William Wallace later claimed that he also took opium. See Thomas, 802–3, and George E. Woodberry, *The Life of Edgar Allan Poe,* I (1909; rpt. New York, 1965), 303. It is true that opium figures in several of Poe's tales, and that in his time opium was easily available as an analgesic and tranquilizer, used for travel sickness, hangovers, and a variety of ailments and nervous conditions. Just the same, it seems unlikely that Poe used the drug for any purpose beyond such general painkilling, if at all. T. D. English saw and spoke with Poe frequently and was moreover a doctor. Although he also detested Poe (as will appear), English denied rumors that Poe took opium and remarked later that had he done so, "I should, both as a physician and a man of observation, have discovered it" during their frequent meetings. Thomas Dunn English, "Reminiscences of Poe," *Independent,* XLVIII (15 Oct 1896), 1381–82. See also Alethea Hayter, *Opium and the Romantic Imagination* (London, 1968), 29–33. **Poe's drinking may also/** Distraction: LI, 198. Little is known in detail about Poe's financial straits at this time, although a few months earlier a promissory note he signed for $104 had become due. MS promissory note, Poe to John W. Albright, Philadelphia, 1 Dec 1841, HRC. Crash: Nicholas B. Wainright, ed., *A Philadelphia Perspective: The Diary of Sidney George Fisher Covering the Years 1834–1871*

(Philadelphia, 1967), 134–35. Bankruptcy: LI, 199; LII, 698. Lot: LII, 703. Wilder: LI, 211, 212; Thomas, 933, 758–59. Employ: John Ward Ostrom, "Edgar A. Poe: His Income as Literary Entrepreneur," *Poe Studies,* XV (1982), 3. Strategies: LI, 200, 201. **Poe saw the clearest/** Hewitt: Thomas, 267. Figures: Carl E. Prince and Mollie Keller, *The U.S. Customs Service: A Bicentennial History* (Washington, 1989). Vacancies: F. W. Thomas to Poe, als, Washington, 21 May 1842, Gris. **Poe's hopes sprang/** Precisely: LI, 197, 199. Prospects: LI, 211–12. **Thomas's visit to Philadelphia/** Penn: LI, 215. Unkempt: Poe impressed the illustrator F. O. C. Darley, for instance, as "exceedingly neat in his person." Mary E. Phillips, *Edgar Allan Poe the Man,* I (Chicago, 1926), q. 793. And T. D. English, among others, remarked that one could always tell when Poe had been drinking by his "slouchy, unkempt dress": Ingram 887. Thomas: Whitty, xliii. **Thomas and Poe agreed/** Consented: LI, 213. **Poe now got a taste/** Claimants: LI, 218. Parties: LI, 215. Appointment: William H. Gravely, Jr., "Poe and Thomas Dunn English: More Light on a Probable Reason for Poe's Failure to Receive a Custom-House Appointment," in Richard P. Veler, ed., *Papers on Poe: Essays in Honor of John Ward Ostrom* (Springfield, Ohio, 1972), 165–93. The author provides a coherent and deeply researched account of Poe's candidacy, but I do not find convincing his argument that T. D. English was instrumental in denying Poe the appointment. **According to Poe/** Quotations in this and the next paragraph from LII, 699–701. **The affair not only/** Station: LII, 681. Ruffians: LI, 218–19. **But this seemingly/** LI, 219. **Poe believed he saw/** Exile, Myrrhine: Richard Beale Davis, ed., *Chivers' Life of Poe* (New York, 1952), 29, 32. Vision: S. Foster Damon, *Thomas Holley Chivers: Friend of Poe* (New York, 1930), 123. No-Man: Emma Lester Chase and Lois Ferry Parks, eds., *The Complete Works of Thomas Holley Chivers,* I (Providence, 1957), 212. **Poe asked Chivers/** LI, 215. **But Chivers was in no/** *The Complete Works,* 19–21. **Early in 1843 Poe/** Partner: LI, 224. Darley: MS "Agreement between Felix O. C. Darley and Thomas C. Clarke with Edgar A. Poe," 31 Jan 1843, Huntington Library. Prospectus: T, 1033–35. **Poe went to Washington/** Missions: Whether Poe considered these complementary or alternative ways of resolving his financial difficulties is uncertain. He may have felt that having a government post would allow him enough time to run his magazine. On the other hand, his agreement with Clarke obliged him to supply all the literary matter during the first year; he decided he would write as much as possible under his own name and pseudonyms, and count on his friends for the rest. Holding down a government job, however much a sinecure, would seem an impossible burden to add to heavy literary labors and editorial duties. It seems likely, then, that Poe thought of his twin plans as mutual safeguards. If one failed, he might count on the other. Dickens: Charles Dickens, *American Notes for General Circulation* (Harmondsworth, 1972), 163–64. Lyell: Charles Lyell, *A Second Visit to the United States of North America,* I (New York, 1849), 200. **Poe's trip to the Capitol/** Money: LI, 225, 227. Cupping: Log, 403. Funds: LI, 227. **Poe was making a sensation/** Thomas, 531. **Just what Poe did/** Peccadilloes: LI, 229. Seedy: John Hill Hewitt, *Recollections of Poe* (Atlanta, 1949), 19. Physician: Whitty, xlvii. **Like Thomas, Dow/** Thomas, 532. **After a week or so/** LI, 228. **As Poe recorded their/** LI, 228–29. **Poe also tried to repair/** Man-talk: F. W.

Thomas to Poe, als, Washington, 27 Mar 1843, Gris. Keen: LI, 230 n. Pride: LI, 236. **Having patched things/** Propping: F. W. Thomas to Poe, als, Washington, 27 Mar 1843, Gris. White: LI, 230, 198; LII, 702. Drawing: James Russell Lowell to Poe, als, Boston, 17 Apr 1843, HRC. Cabbage: Nathaniel Hawthorne to James Russell Lowell, als, Concord, [Jun?, 1843], NYPL. **Whether Rob Tyler sent/** Recommendation: Tyler at least replied, from the White House, that it would gratify him *"very sensibly"* to see Poe appointed. Robert Tyler to Poe, als, "White House," 31 Mar 1843, Gris. Exploded: LI, 234.

Reputation after leaving Graham's; *Charles Dickens and England; Lowell's* Pioneer *and Boston*

At the age of thirty-three/ Restless: In J. E. S[nodgrass]., "American Biography. Edgar Allan Poe," Baltimore *Saturday Visiter,* 29 Jul 1843. Broad: Mary E. Phillips, *Edgar Allan Poe the Man,* I (Chicago, 1926), 793. Process: Clarence S. Brigham, *Edgar Allan Poe's Contributions to Alexander's Weekly Messenger* (Worcester, 1943), 20–21. Daguerreotype: Michael J. Deas, *The Portraits and Daguerreotypes of Edgar Allan Poe* (Charlottesville, 1988), 12f. **The face Poe presented/** LI, 223, 239. **Although the *Museum*/** Log, 402. **Poe transformed his/** Unless otherwise noted, quotations in this and the next paragraph are from the Philadelphia *Saturday Museum,* 4 Mar 1843; Poe's MS autobiographical sketch, Virginia State Library; and the revised version of the sketch in Rufus Griswold, ed., *Poets and Poetry of America* (Philadelphia, 1842), 387. I am very grateful to Dwight R. Thomas for giving me a photocopy of the important *Museum* issue. Debtor: Baltimore City Chancery Court Records B62, fol. 403, Maryland Hall of Records, Annapolis. **In having his readers/** Eventful: Log, 399. The lies and inflations in Poe's accounts seem clearly designed to assuage his sense of his miserable present condition as a near bankrupt, and to restore a feeling of his own importance. But his full motives were more complex than can be treated here. His many misdatings may simply reflect a faulty memory. Like some other orphans he may genuinely have been uncertain of the year of his birth, and the dates and nature of other events in his early life. Eileen Simpson remarks of a group of orphaned boys she knew that they were uncertain about their dates of birth, having no memory of their birthdays ever having been celebrated. *Orphans: Real and Imaginary* (New York, 1987), 6. Many of Poe's remarks also represent belated revenge against John Allan, whom he repeatedly depicts as a debauched scoundrel who when "sixty-five years of age" married a woman "young enough to be his grand-daughter." Allan was fifty-one, his new wife thirty-one. Including more than thirty testimonials to his literary gifts, some quoted from private letters to him, he also designed the *Museum* biography as a puff for the "Stylus." According to F. W. Thomas, he laughingly confessed that the piece was "intended to help the magazine project." See Whitty, xlvii. **Poe sought other means/** Standard: T, 214. **Poe's enthusiasm was/** Boz: David S. Reynolds, ed., *George Lippard:*

Prophet of Protest (New York, 1986), 229–30. Philadelphia: Thomas, 318ff., 345. **Moved by both admiration/** Suggested: Harrison, XVII, 107. Interviews: For the reasoning behind this reconstruction of the meeting, see Thomas, 341–44. Moxon: Harrison, XVII, 124–25. **Poe may not have been/** *Review:* Log, 446. Echoes: LI, 258. Spleen: LI, 246. On the belief that the review was by Dickens see Thomas, 660–61. **Poe made one other/** *Orion:* T, 310. Poe reviewed the fourth edition of the work. Sell: Just when Horne learned of Poe's review of *Orion* is uncertain. Elizabeth Barrett seems to have told him about it even before he received Poe's letter. For the view, unconvincing to me, that Poe's real object in contacting Horne was to bring himself to Barrett's attention, see Francis B. Dedmond, "Poe and the Brownings," *American Transcendental Quarterly,* n.s., I (Jun 1987), 111–21. Tribute: R. H. Horne to Poe, als, London, 16 Apr 1844. For the English version of the tale see Joseph J. Moldenhauer, "Poe's 'The Spectacles': A New Text from Manuscript," *Studies in the American Renaissance 1977* (Boston, 1978), 179–234. Shocked: John H. Ingram, *Edgar Allan Poe: His Life, Letters, and Opinions* (1886; rpt. New York, 1965), q. 204–5. **Poe also sought to extend/** LI, 206. **A chance for Poe to enter/** *Head:* T, 809. Trash: LI, 222 n. **Through Lowell's *Pioneer*/** Piece: LI, 217. Admired: Harrison, XVII, 120, 144. Boasted: LI, 78. Twentieth-century prosodists have faulted Poe for treating English verse as if, like Latin, it were quantitative rather than accentual, and for his quirky (although consistently used) definition of "caesura." See for instance Gay Wilson Allen, *American Prosody* (New York, 1935). **Poe's entry into Boston/** Mortality: Harrison, XVII, 138, 143. Grieved: LI, 238. Blow, concern: LI, 231. Poe waited six months before approaching Lowell directly for money, and then lamented that Lowell could not "imagine how sincerely I grieve that any necessity can urge me to ask this of you." LI, 237. **In addition to its appearance/** Unsaleable: LI, 216. **Poe included reprintings/** Names: In Poe's "Eleonora"—another name close to *Leonard*—Eleonora is succeeded by Ermengarde, whose name contains the name *Edgar.* Ermengarde-Eleonora thus recall the character Edgar-Leonard in Henry Poe's tale "The Pirate." **Although lacking a regular/** Bridal: Alexander G. Rose III and Jeffrey Alan Savoye, eds., *Such Friends as These* (Baltimore, 1986), 39. Pedantic: I take the conundrums as transcribed by T. O. Mabbott in his "Saturday Museum" folder, Box 8, Iowa. In slightly different form, the first and last also appear in Brigham, 14–15. Merry: T, 778. **In "The Mystery of Marie Rogêt"/** Principles: LI, 200. **Poe took particular satisfaction/** Perfect: T, 869. When editing *SLM*—which published several defenses of slavery during his editorship—Poe several times commented incidentally on slavery, in one case praising the antiabolitionist strain in Robert Montgomery Bird's novel *Sheppard Lee.* See also Bernard Rosenthal, "Poe, Slavery, and the *Southern Literary Messenger:* A Reexamination," *Poe Studies,* VII (Dec 1974), 29–38. Galling: *SLM,* II (Jan 1836), 122. Starr: Augustus Van Cleef, "Poe's Mary," *Harper's New Monthly Magazine,* LXXVIII (Mar 1889), 636. **As usual, biting/** Incorporate: A classic statement of the equation between looking at and devouring is Otto Fenichel, "The Scoptophilic Instinct and Identification," in *Collected Papers: First Series* (New York, 1953), 373–97. **A need to unearth/** On unburying the past see William G. Niederland, "An Analytic Inquiry into the Life and Work of Heinrich Schliemann," in Max Schur, ed., *Drives, Affects, Behavior,* II (New York, 1965), 369–96. **If not a financial/** Remarkable: Walker, 136–37. Poe was also accused of collusion with the award committee and of plagiarism, however. See W. T. Bandy, "Poe, Duane and Duffee," *University of Mississippi Studies in English,* n.s., III (1982), 81–95. **In varying degrees/** Sigmund Freud, "The 'Uncanny,' " *Collected Papers,* IV (New York, 1959), 401–2.

Rufus Griswold; Last Days in Philadelphia

However busy during his six/ Reid: Ingram 546, 880. Hirst: Thomas, 809–16; John Sartain, *The Reminiscences of a Very Old Man 1808–1897* (1899; rpt. New York, 1969), 224–25. Du Solle: Roger Butterfield, "Poe's Obscure Contemporaries," *American Notes & Queries,* II (May 1942), 27–29. Lippard: David S. Reynolds, ed., *George Lippard: Prophet of Protest* (New York, 1986), 258. **Poe's work brought him/** Thomas, 325. **The effect of suavity/** Flute-playing: F. W. Thomas to Poe, als, Washington, 29 May 1841, Gris. Enamored: Joy Bayless, *Rufus Wilmot Griswold: Poe's Literary Executor* (Nashville, 1943), q. 10. **For several years after/** Chimney: W. M. Griswold, ed., *Passages from the Correspondence and Other Papers of Rufus W. Griswold* (Cambridge, Mass., 1898), 58. Mother: George Egon Hatvary, *Horace Binney Wallace* (Boston, 1977), q. 79. The author's discussion of Griswold is penetrating. **Griswold's reading and training/** Unrivaled: W. M. Griswold, 66. Boasted: C. W. Briggs to Rufus Griswold, als, New York, 13 Mar 1837, Gris. Peterson: Thomas, 365. **Poe often proudly proclaimed/** Sprague, Earle: *GM,* XVIII (May 1841; Jun 1841), 252, 296. Lauded: B. Bernard Cohen and Lucian A. Cohen, "Poe and Griswold Once More," *American Literature,* XXXIV (Mar 1962), 97–101. **It is uncertain whether/** Vacillates: Harrison, XV, 215. Fouled: Log, 355. **The actual publication of *Poets*/** Humbug: LI, 202. Proposition: LI, 211–12. **Poe may have reported/** Tuberculosis: Rufus Griswold to James T. Fields, als, Philadelphia, 23 Feb 1842, Huntington Library. Cynicism: Log, 37. Tennyson: Thomas, 413. Manuscript: LI, 211. **Having paid Poe to review/** Terms: Log, 377. Humiliating: W. M. Griswold, 120. Dignity: T, 556. **An overlapping event/** Crosscurrents: Charles J. Peterson of *Graham's* later told Ingram that "Griswold hated Poe, but also feared him." Ingram 348. Invited: Thomas, 396, 417. Dissatisfied: LI, 211. Rueful: Thomas, 400. Rumpus: Thomas, 606. Attacks: Thomas, 398. **In the sniping, Poe/** Precious: LI, 216. Stephens: Thomas, 550. Vindictive: Mary E. Phillips, *Edgar Allan Poe the Man,* I (Chicago, 1926), 848. Information: LI, 211. Jackal: Thomas, 612. **What happened to Griswold/** Credited: Rufus Griswold to Bayard Taylor, als, Philadelphia, 16 Apr 1843, Cornell University Library. Midnight: Rufus Griswold to [James T. Fields], als, New York, 10 Nov 1842, Huntington Library. **Forty days after the funeral/** Forehead: Bayless, q. 66. **The two men's troubled/** Blind: Thomas, 638. Absurd: T, 210. Appearances: LI, 241ff. Reviews: Thomas, 667, 645, 663. **The title of Poe's/** Title: Thomas, 689. Scathing: Thomas, 649. Delaware: Clipping from Delaware *State Journal,* 28 Nov 1843, "Lectures" folder, Box 5, Material Under Seal, Iowa. Reported: Log, 443. **Although still ill and still/** Sharply: Thomas, 649. Longfellow: Thomas, 656.

The Brennan Farm; Willis's Mirror; *"The Purloined Letter"*

During the first week/ Future: LI, 253. **Poe left Virginia aboard/** Quotations in this and the next three paragraphs from LI, 251–52. **The elegant hams/** Poorly: Log, 462. Reduced: LII, 707. Dirty: Jacob E. Spannuth and Thomas Ollive Mabbott, eds., *Doings of Gotham by Edgar Allan Poe* (Pottsville, 1929), 31. Leathern: Spannuth and Mabbott, 61. Sissy: LI, 262. **The setting of Poe's/** Mary E. Phillips, *Edgar Allan Poe the Man,* II (Chicago, 1926), 883 ff.; Theodore F. Wolfe, "Poe's Life at the Brennan House," undated clipping from *New York Times Saturday Review of Books,* Poe Scrapbook, University of Rochester Library. Hermit: LI, 262. **But like his Prince/** Exceedingly: LII, 705. Host: LI, 264. Loan: LI, 272n. Cab: MIII, 1092. Pollin doubts that the pieces in the *Ledger* are by Poe. Harrison: "Edgar A. Poe. Reminiscences of Gabriel Harrison, an Actor, Still Living in Brooklyn," *New York Times-Saturday Review,* 4 Mar 1899, 144. In return, Harrison said, Poe would accept nothing but a bag of his best coffee, identifying himself as "Thaddeus K. Perley," a name reminiscent of the young army recruit "Edgar A. Perry." Cf. Thomas, 793–94. **In November and December/** Introduction: Brev, 107–9. **Poe's only steady outlet/** Goethe: Henry A. Beers, *Nathaniel Parker Willis* (Boston, 1885), 262. Tall: N. P. Willis to [W——] Ward, als, Cornwall, 29 Aug 1852, Princeton University Library. Foster: George Foster, *New York in Slices* (New York, 1849), 74. Passive: Willis Gaylord Clark to James Lawson, als, Philadelphia, 2 Sep [no year], South Caroliniana Library. Nancyism: Log, 505. Gondolier: Jedediah Auld to George Duyckinck, als, [New York], [Sep 1847], NYPL. **However maligned as fluffy/** Whip: N. P. Willis to J. Boughton, als, Glenmary, 7 Jun 1842, New York State Library. Brother: C. F. Briggs to James Russell Lowell, typed transcript, 6 Jan 1845, Cornell University Library. **Exactly when and how/** Honored: Log, 462. Invalid: Log, 471. Uncertain: On the problem of ascertaining when Poe joined the paper at its offices, see William H. Gravely, Jr., "The Early Political and Literary Career of Thomas Dunn English," Ph.D. diss., U. of Virginia, 1953, 432–34. If Poe worked in the office in October, he may well have met Walt Whitman, who served on the staff for a few weeks that month. **Poe badly needed/** Trifler: LI, 246. Cologne: *Burton's Gentleman's Magazine,* VI (Mar 1840), 154. Estimable: Spannuth and Mabbott, 34. **Willis in turn genuinely/** Kenneth Walter Cameron, "A Late Defence of Poe by N. P. Willis," *American Transcendental Quarterly,* XXXVI (Fall 1977), 69–74; Ingram 526. **Willis was correct in thinking/** Thousand: Cortland P. Auser, *Nathaniel P. Willis* (New York, 1969), 59. Frivolous: Log, 466. Scott's: *Weekly Mirror,* 17 Nov 1844. Swiss: MIII, 1118. Copyright: *Evening Mirror,* 24, 25, 27, 31 Jan and 3 Feb 1845. **Even while finding something/** Broadside: Log, 457. Besieged: Spannuth and Mabbott, 33–34. Blunderingly: Log, 460. Ignorance: Spannuth and Mabbott, 55. On the general psychological meaning to Poe of flying, see Bernard C.

Meyer, "Notes on Flying and Dying," *Psychoanalytic Quarterly*, LII (1983), 327–52. **The unnamed narrator of "The Premature Burial"/** Life-preserving: MIII, 971. See also J. Gerald Kennedy, "Poe and Magazine Writing on Premature Burial," *Studies in the American Renaissance 1977* (Boston, 1978), 165–78. **The denouement of the tale/** For a similar reading of the tale see David M. Rein, *Edgar A. Poe: The Inner Pattern* (New York, 1960), 5ff. **Sometime in his transition/** Best: LI, 258. Brothers: On the many other instances of doubling in the story see Liahna Klenman Babener, "The Shadow's Shadow: The Motif of the Double in Edgar Allan Poe's 'The Purloined Letter'," in Donald K. Adams, ed., *The Mystery and Detection Annual* (Beverly Hills, 1972), 21–32. "The Purloined Letter" has become the focus of a growing Lacanian literature on Poe. See, e.g., John P. Muller and William J. Richardson, eds., *The Purloined Poe: Lacan, Derrida, and Psychoanalytic Reading* (Baltimore, 1988). **Poe tried in brief space/** LI, 260. **Poe continued to ponder/** Mesmerism: The most thorough treatment of the subject is Maria M. Tatar, *Spellbound: Studies on Mesmerism and Literature* (Princeton, 1978). See also Doris V. Falk, "Poe and the Power of Animal Magnetism," *PMLA*, LXXXIV (1969), 536–46, and Arthur Wrobel, ed., *Pseudo-Science and Society in Nineteenth-Century America* (Lexington, 1987). Republished: MIII, 1029. Misapprehensions: T, 870. Framework: Log, 631.

Poe's "Crisis"; Attack on Longfellow; "The Raven"

Working hard at the Brennan/ Crisis: LI, 271. Dejected: Thomas Dunn English, "Reminiscences of Poe," *Independent*, XLVIII (22 Oct 1896), 1416. Friends: LI, 267. Thomas: F. W. Thomas to Poe, als, Washington, 2 Sep 1844, Gris. See also John Tomlin to Poe, als, Jackson, 23 Feb 1844, Gris. Chivers: Thomas Holley Chivers to Poe, Oaky Grove, 15 May 1844, Gris. **Poe's self-absorbed unhappiness/** Estimated: John Ward Ostrom, "Edgar A. Poe: His Income as Literary Entrepreneur," *Poe Studies*, XV (1982), 4. "DOLLAR": Frances Trollope, *Domestic Manners of the Americans* (New York, 1984), 258–59. Magazinist: LI, 270. Orphanage: LI, 268. **Swimmer of the longest swim/** Parnassus: LI, 259. Poe expressed the opposite sentiment when writing to Lowell the month before: "I am *not* ambitious—unless negatively. I, now and then feel stirred up to excel a fool, merely because I hate to let a fool imagine that he may excel me. Beyond this I feel nothing of ambition." LI, 256. There was of course some truth in the assertion that, where he knew he had ability, Poe was not so much anxious to excel as to prevent others from excelling him. But he remained affected by the old struggle of Conqueror with Cottager, as he sometimes recognized himself: "The truth seems to be that genius of the highest order," he wrote somewhat later, "lives in a state of perpetual vacillation between ambition and *the scorn of it*." Brev, 313. Profit: LI, 266, 269–70. Blocked: LI, 270–71. **In this certainty, or/** Harper: Eugene Exman, *The Brothers Harper* (New York, 1965), 233–34. Remuneration: LI, 271, 267. Anthon: Charles Anthon to Poe, als, New York, 2 Nov 1844, Gris. Trust: Sean Wilentz, *Chants Democratic: New York City & the Rise of the American Working*

Class 1788–1850 (New York, 1984), q. 319. **Ironically, Poe's ten-month/** Lowell: Harrison, XVII, 182. Resembles: LI, 246. **More important, Lowell/** Lowell: Walker, 156–68. Newspaper: Log, 493–94. **Poe himself created/** T, 696–702. **Poe's slaps and clips/** T, 703–5. **Such were the first lunges/** Buffalo: Nelson F. Adkins, " 'Chapter on American Cribbage': Poe and Plagiarism," *Papers of the Bibliographical Society of America*, XLII (1948), 169–210. Abroad: Harrison, XVII, 383–85. **Poe had his say/** Acknowledged: Rufus Griswold to Poe, als, New York, 14 Jan 1845, Gris. Conversation: C. F. Briggs to James Russell Lowell, New York, 6 Jan 1845, in *Charles Frederick Briggs: Correspondence with James Russell Lowell and William Page, 1843–1846,* Archives of American Art microfilm. Novice: LI, 275, 285. **Poe did not do the same/** Cannibalism: *Evening Mirror,* 27 Feb 1845. Davidson: Log, 512. Alacrity: Log, 510. Cant: Log, 508. Boston: Log, 513. **As the opening of Poe's/** Log, 496. **The reception of "The Raven"/** Everybody: Log, 503. Electrified: Elizabeth Oakes Smith, "Ralph Waldo Emerson: Or Recollections of him by Elizabeth Oakes Smith," MS, NYPL. *Inquirer* etc.: Log, 503, 499. **Excitement over the catchy/** Parodies: MI, 352; William H. Gravely, Jr., "The Early Political and Literary Career of Thomas Dunn English," Ph.D. diss., U. of Virginia, 1953, 498; Log, 504–5, 521. **Poe's own fame rose/** Humanized: Log, 554. Francis: Mary E. Phillips, *Edgar Allan Poe the Man,* II (Chicago, 1926), 1107–9. Smith: J. C. Derby, *Fifty Years Among Authors, Books and Publishers* (New York, 1884), 547–48; Elizabeth Oakes Smith, "Autobiographic Notes. Edgar Allan Poe," *Beadle's Monthly,* III (Feb 1867), 154. Saunders: Frederick Saunders, MS "Recollections," photostat, NYPL. **The countless admirers also/** Suit: T, 15. Sapphic: Walker, 141–42. Hardness: T, 24–25. **How commendably Poe realized/** Yeats: Eric W. Carlson, ed., *The Recognition of Edgar Allan Poe* (Ann Arbor, 1970), 77. **In his later comments/** Emblematic: T, 25. Conflict: J. Gerald Kennedy, *Poe, Death, and the Life of Writing* (New Haven, 1987), 68–69. **Obscurely, Poe himself/** Pleasurable: T, 19. **In several details/** Source: Joseph Jones, " 'The Raven' and 'The Raven': Another Source of Poe's Poem," *American Literature,* XXX (May 1958), 185–93.

Return to the City; The Broadway Journal; *The Longfellow War*

Poe, Muddy, and Virginia/ Venice: Frances Trollope, *Domestic Manners of the Americans* (New York, 1984), 297. Metropolis: Edward K. Spann, *The New Metropolis: New York City, 1840–1857* (New York, 1981), 2 *et passim.* Palazzi: Allan Nevins and Milton Halsey Thomas, eds., *The Diary of George Templeton Strong* (New York, 1952), 302. Omnibuses: George Foster, *New York in Slices* (New York, 1849), 63–65. Overturn: Sean Wilentz, *Chants Democratic: New York City & the Rise of the American Working Class 1788–1850* (New York, 1984), q. 110. **Many felt that New York/** Greeley: Frank Luther Mott, *A History of American Magazines 1741–1850* (New York, 1930), q. 376. Houses: See John Tebbel, *A History of Book Publishing in the United States,* I (New York, 1972), 269ff., and William Charvat, *Literary Publishing in America 1790–1850* (Philadelphia, 1959), *passim.* **During the year (again)/** Boardinghouses:

Charles Lyell, *A Second Visit to the United States of North America,* I (New York, 1849), 122. Amity: This structure is now 85 West Third Street, on the north side of the street between Sullivan and Thompson Streets in Greenwich Village. Poe, Muddy, and Virginia had lived before on an Amity Street, in Baltimore. Fashionable: Jacob E. Spannuth and Thomas Ollive Mabbott, eds., *Doings of Gotham by Edgar Allan Poe* (Pottsville, 1929), 31. University: At the time, the school was called the University of the City of New York. **What brought Poe back/** Partnership: MS "Memorandum of a Contract entered into between Charles F. Briggs and John Bisco for publishing a weekly paper," 23 Dec 1844, HRC. Briggs: T, 1133. Metamorphoses: See Bette S. Weidman, "The *Broadway Journal*(2): A Casualty of Abolition Politics," *Bulletin of the New York Public Library,* LXXIII (Feb 1969), 94–113. Imprisoned: C. F. Briggs to James Russell Lowell, typed transcripts, Staten Island, 19 Mar 1845 and 13 Feb 1846, Cornell University Library. **Around the middle of December/** Introduction: On the route of introduction see C. F. Briggs to William Page, New York, 26 Jul 1845, in *Charles Frederick Briggs: Correspondence with James Russell Lowell and William Page, 1843–1846,* Archives of American Art microfilm; C. F. Briggs to James Russell Lowell, typed transcripts, New York, 7 Dec and 19 Dec 1844, Cornell University Library. Dollar: C. F. Briggs to James Russell Lowell, New York, 17 Jan 1845, in *Charles Frederick Briggs.* Indigenous: *Evening Mirror,* 8 Jan 1845. I rely on Mabbott's attribution of this anonymous paragraph. **Poe got what he called/** Stake: MS "Memorandum of an agreement entered into between John Bisco and Edgar A. Poe Feby 21*st* 1845," HRC. Pecuniary: LI, 286. George: LI, 303. **Briggs was pleased with/** Liked: C. F. Briggs to James Russell Lowell, New York, 6 Jan 1845, and Staten Island, 19 Mar 1845, in *Charles Frederick Briggs.* Artistic: C. F. Briggs to James Russell Lowell, "Bishop's Terrace" [Staten Island], 27 Jan 1845, and New York, 11 Feb 1845, in *Charles Frederick Briggs.* Assistant: C. F. Briggs to James Russell Lowell, New York, 8 Mar 1845, in *Charles Frederick Briggs.* **It was not unreasonable/** Consented: C. F. Briggs, letter of 19 Mar 1845. **Whatever Poe's misconception/** Brood: *BJ,* I (4 Jan 1845), 1. **In his first months/** Slave: LI, 286. **Poe also wrote long/** Over-stocked: Stewart E. Desmond, "The Widow's Trials: The Life of Fanny Fern," Ph.D. diss., New York U., 1988, q. 137. **Writing here and there/** Magazine-ward: *BJ,* I (1 Mar 1845), 139. Fulfillment: Mott, 341–42; Spann, 407. Illimitable: *BJ,* I (7 Jun 1845), 354. Poe lifted most of this review of *Peter Snook* from his 1836 review of the same book, although his opening remarks on magazines, including those quoted, were fresh additions in 1845. Condensed: *BJ,* I (1 Mar 1845), 139. Elaboration: *BJ,* I (7 Jun 1845), 354. **"Without an international copyright/** Throats: LI, 210. Bryant: William Cullen Bryant II and Thomas G. Voss, eds., *The Letters of William Cullen Bryant,* II (New York, 1977), 246–47, n.2. Quagmire: *BJ,* II (19 Jul 1845), 27. Anastatic: *BJ,* I (12 Apr 1845), 231. **Because the lack of/** Allegania: *BJ,* I (22 Mar 1845), 186, and I (5 Apr 1845), 223. **Poe had of course/** Capabilities: *BJ,* II (19 Jul 1845), 26. On the basis of a temporary change in Poe's relation with Cornelius Mathews—one of many rapprochements Poe reached with his enemies and near enemies—and other not very convincing evidence, several scholars have claimed that early on in his editorship of the *Journal* Poe expediently took up the Young America banner. See for example Claude Richard, "Poe and 'Young America'," *Studies in Bibliography*, XXI (1968), 25–58. But as mentioned in the text, the endorsements of the movement in the earlier issues of *BJ* cannot confidently be assigned to Poe. On the other hand, the "Editorial Miscellany" on 4 Oct 1845, which certainly is by Poe, reasserts yet once more his opposition to literary nationalism, except as it means regarding British literary opinion with a critical eye and supporting American writers by securing a copyright law. The most that can be claimed, I think, is that for five or six months Poe may have flirted with Young America opinions. **But in being nearby/** Quotations in this and the next paragraph from *BJ*, II (4 Oct 1845), 199–200, and "The Living Writers of America. Some Honest Opinions about their Literary Merits, with Occasional Words of Personality," MS, Pierpont Morgan Library. **Living in New York/** Amusement: *BJ*, I (19 Apr 1845), 242. Eliza: *BJ*, II (19 Jul 1845), 29. **Poe flung his tomahawks/** *Shrew: BJ*, II (2 Aug 1845), 60. Rats: MII, 1244. *Antigone:* Such a review was perhaps inevitable, for Poe crudely dismissed Greek drama in general as meaningless for the present and artistically naive, marked by "insufferable *baldness*, or platitude." *BJ*, I (12 Apr 1845), 236. Observing that Poe attributed Sophocles' *Oedipus at Colonus* to Aeschylus, Elizabeth Barrett remarked that he "sits somewhat loosely, probably, on his classics." Harrison, XVII, 386. Rapped: *BJ*, I (19 Apr 1845), 251. Support: Poe published this article in the *Evening Mirror* on 9 Jan 1845, shortly before he joined the *Journal*. Renewal: *BJ*, I (29 Mar 1845), 220. **Having created a sensation/** T, 714. **Over the next month Poe/** Acquaintance: R. Baird Shuman, "Longfellow, Poe, and 'The Waif'," *PMLA*, LXXVI (1961), 155–56. Complimentary: T, 712. *Alexander's:* Clarence S. Brigham, *Edgar Allan Poe's Contributions to Alexander's Weekly Messenger* (Worcester, 1943), 33. The identification of "Outis" as Poe seems to have begun with Mary Phillips. Yet in a letter to Victor Paltsits (25 Nov 1919, New-York Historical Society), she also identified "Outis" as the Harvard graduate Henry Stevens, who collected Americana for the British Museum. Stevens did use the name Outis, although whether as early as 1845 is uncertain. Poe's perceptive friend G. W. Eveleth, writing to E. C. Stedman about the Outis letter (21 Aug 1896, Columbia University Library), confided his suspicion that "Poe, himself, may have *defied himself* in that article!" The most persuasive proponent of the identification has been Professor Burton Pollin. See, e.g., his notes in *Edgar Allan Poe: Writings in* The Broadway Journal . . . *Part 2, The Annotations* (New York, 1986), 28ff., and his "Poe as Author of the 'Outis' Letter and 'The Bird of the Dream'," *Poe Studies*, XX (Jun 1987), 10–15. See also the exchange of scholarly notes among Professor Pollin, Dwight Thomas, and Kent Ljungquist in *PSA Newsletter*, XVI (Fall 1988); XVII (Fall 1989); and XVIII (Spring 1989). Poe again launched a pseudonymous attack on himself in his extraordinary late essay, "A Reviewer Reviewed" (see ahead). **Some of Poe's essay-length/** All quotations from Poe's reviews of Longfellow during the Longfellow War are from T, 696ff. On the war generally see Sidney P. Moss, *Poe's Literary Battles: The Critic in the Context of His Literary Milieu* (Durham, 1963). **The ongoing "Longfellow War"/** Monomaniac: C. F. Briggs to James Russell Lowell, New York, 8 Mar 1845, in *Charles Frederick Briggs*. Finish: C. F. Briggs to James Russell Lowell, New York, 24 Mar 1845, in *Charles Frederick Briggs*. **Long-**

fellow, although by now/ Brawls: Log, 518. Playful: C. F. Briggs to James Russell Lowell, Staten Island, 19 Mar 1845, in *Charles Frederick Briggs*. Simms: Mary C. Simms Oliphant et al., eds., *The Letters of William Gilmore Simms,* II (Columbia, 1952), 90, 68. **Poe clubbed Longfellow not only/** Negrophilic: The remarks about Longfellow's abolitionism may have been written by T. D. English, editor of the *Aristidean*. In his capacity as a physician, English wrote derogatorily of blacks, remarking that anatomy and microscopy prove "that the Negro is of a distinct and inferior species to the Caucasian." William H. Gravely, Jr., "The Early Political and Literary Career of Thomas Dunn English," Ph.D. diss., U. of Virginia, 1953, q. 766. **Whether in editorial squibs/** Hack: *BJ,* I (14 Jun 1845), 382; II (16 Aug 1845), 88; II (23 Aug 1845), 103. Unaccountably: C. F. Briggs to James Russell Lowell, Staten Island, 19 Mar 1845, in *Charles Frederick Briggs*. Steadfast: *BJ,* II (16 Aug 1845), 93. Principal: T, 1154. **But by this time/** *Town:* Log, 533–34. *Exile:* T, 141, 123. Nonplussed: Francis B. Dedmond, "Poe and the Brownings," *American Transcendental Quarterly,* n.s., 1 (Jun 1987), q. 116. **'Mad with love and hate'/** Graham: Log, 452. Forster: Log, 465. **In itself, the idea of/** Mummy: MII, 1180, 1196, n.6. Lifted: *BJ,* I (7 Jun 1845), 354–57. **Yet in the face of such/** Chapter: Brev, 191. Edmund Bergler speaks of the "plagiaristic hunter" and remarks that "The man who is always compulsively searching for plagiarisms of others is *a priori* to be suspected of wanting to plagiarize himself." *The Writer and Psychoanalysis,* 2d ed. (Madison, Conn., 1986), 207. **And Poe found his financial/** Complained: LI, 286. Chafed: Arthur Hobson Quinn, *Edgar Allan Poe: A Critical Biography* (New York, 1942), 655. Avenge: See Marvin Eisenstadt et al., *Parental Loss and Achievement* (Madison, Conn., 1989), 25–27.

Poe's Condition; The Lyceum War

In the wake/ Saunders: Frederick Saunders, MS "Recollections," photostat, NYPL. Lecture: Log, 526; Ingram 760. **Many others noticed/** Manhandling: James Russell Lowell to C. F. Briggs, als, Boston, 16 Jan 1845, Harvard University Library. Soggy: George E. Woodberry, *The Life of Edgar Allan Poe,* II (1909; rpt. New York, 1965), q. 137. Stilted: Log, 536. The disenchantment was mutual, for on his part Poe confessed himself disappointed in Lowell's appearance. "He was not half the noble-looking person that I expected to see." Richard Beale Davis, ed., *Chivers' Life of Poe* (New York, 1952), 45. Muddy: Log, 536. **By June Poe was badly/** Dreadfully: LI, 290. Devil: LI, 286. Lynch: Anne C. Lynch to Poe, als, [n. pl.], "Friday Morning 27" [probably Jun 1845], Gris. Recruiting: LI, 290. Relapsed: C. F. Briggs to James Russell Lowell, New York, 27 Jun 1845 and 16 Jul 1845, in *Charles Frederick Briggs: Correspondence with James Russell Lowell and William Page, 1843–1846,* Archives of American Art microfilm. **At about this time/** The treatment of Chivers's visit in this and the following paragraphs is based on his own account, printed in Davis, 38–61. Chivers's description of the events often seems bloated, owing to his eccentric language. Nevertheless, his rendering of Maria Clemm's speech is faithful to the language of her letters and suggests that he was generally a reliable recorder of things done and said. **Like Lowell, Chivers/** Praised: *BJ,* II (2 Aug 1845), 55. Recited: Maria Clemm to Thomas Holley Chivers, als, Milford, 8 Dec 1852, Huntington Library. **Chivers found Poe volatile/** Fling: Davis, 112. **Muddy revealed something else/** Commitment: Probably because of his lecturing, Poe was sometimes asked to appear at commencement exercises. He was invited to serve on a jury to judge the literary compositions of the high-school girls at the Rutgers Female Institute. He did appear at this event, on July 11, and recited the prize composition. Log, 538, 549. Difficult: Poe's new writing problems perhaps explain the large proportion of reprinted material he got together for *BJ.* English: Log, 540. English's claim is corroborated by Briggs, who said that "drunkenness prevented" Poe from appearing. See his letter to Lowell, 16 Jul 1845. Informed: Log, 545. **Chivers too much admired/** Discussing: *BJ,* II (16 Aug 1845), 88. Rankled: Charles Eliot Norton, ed., *Letters of James Russell Lowell,* I (New York, 1894), 99–101. **In his misery Poe/** Mislaid: *BJ,* II (26 Jul 1845), 47. *Doubt: BJ,* II (2 Aug 1845), 63. Gracious: Typed fragments, "Unused scraps from Mr. Stoddard's 'Rambling Reminiscences'," NYPL. Confronted: Log, 558. Acknowledged: Burton R. Pollin, ed., *Edgar Allan Poe: Writings in* The Broadway Journal . . . *Part 2, The Annotations* (New York, 1986), 153. **The same month, Poe/** Laughton Osborn to Poe, als, "219 Eighth Avenue," 14 Aug 1845, Free Library of Philadelphia, and typed transcript, "219 Eighth Avenue," 16 Aug 1845, Brown University Library. **Poe felt bad enough/** Lie: LI, 293–94. Missive: Laughton Osborn, letter of 16 Aug 1845. Note: Laughton Osborn to Poe, als, [n. pl.], 2 Nov 1845, Princeton University Library. In the last few issues of *BJ,* Poe did publish several Italian sonnets, but without translation. **In others less emotionally/** Simms: Mary C. Simms Oliphant et al., eds., *The Letters of William Gilmore Simms,* II (Columbia, 1952), 98–99. **The concern took other/** Formal: Woodberry, II, 137. Restraint: Kenneth Walter Cameron, "A Late Defence of Poe by N. P. Willis," *American Transcendental Quarterly,* XXXVI (Fall 1977), 74. Emphatically: T, 121. Froth: Brev, 306. Machinery: *BJ,* II (6 Sep 1845), 136. Genius: Brev, 223, 131. **But Poe's fix would/** Engagement: LI, 247. Squad: C. F. Briggs to James Russell Lowell, typed transcript, [n. pl.], 21 Aug 1845, Cornell University Library. **Poe ranked himself/** Drew: The psychoanalyst Bernard C. Meyer remarked that "it is difficult to avoid the suspicion that ultimately [Boston] represented the underside of the ambivalence he felt toward the mother who abandoned him by her untimely death." "Notes on Flying and Dying," *Psychoanalytic Quarterly,* LII (1983), 350 n. *Clique:* "The Living Writers of America. Some Honest Opinions about their Literary Merits, with Occasional Words of Personality," MS, Pierpont Morgan Library. Quips: T, 1040. Taste: Brev, 492. Emerson: Elizabeth Oakes Smith, "Ralph Waldo Emerson: Or Recollections of him by Elizabeth Oakes Smith," MS, NYPL. **But much of Poe's thinking/** Define: "The Living Writers of America." Mistake: LI, 259. Distinguish: The case is more complicated still, for Transcendentalists like Emerson did not escape the fusion of praise and blame Poe habitually offered in his criticism, the tomahawks hurled through incense, as when he remarked, "When I consider the true talent—the real force of Mr. Emerson, I am lost in amazement at finding in him little more than a respectful imitation of Carlyle." Brev, 314. On Poe and transcendentalism see Ottavio M. Casale, "Edgar Allan Poe," in Joel Myerson, ed., *The Transcendentalists: A Review of Research and Criticism* (New York, 1984), 362–71. **The trouble began even before/** Dilapidated: Harrison, XVII, 438. English left at least four slightly varying accounts of Poe's visits, on all of which I have drawn for details. See Ingram 887; "Reminiscences of Poe," *Independent,* XLVIII (5 Nov 1896), 1480–81; William H. Gravely, Jr., "The Early Political and Literary Career of Thomas Dunn English," Ph.D. diss., U. of Virginia, 1953, 506. Drop: LI, 296. Fee: According to English, Poe's fee was a hundred dollars. Poe may have given him an inflated figure, for other sources also say fifty dollars. **Poe was slated to read/** Testify: Log, 577. Committee: "A Reminiscence of Edgar A. Poe," unidentified newspaper clipping [ca. 1870, beginning "A correspondent of the Boston *Journal* writes . . ."], Material Under Seal, Iowa. **Cushing opened the program/** Apologies: *BJ,* II (1 Nov 1845), 262. Higginson: Ingram 756. **Poe began to read/** Gone: "A Reminiscence of Edgar A. Poe." Fidgeted: Log, 579. **How much Poe saved/** Fatigued: Log, 578. Walter: Sidney P. Moss, *Poe's Literary Battles: The Critic in the Context of His Literary Milieu* (Durham, 1963), 195. **Having devised one 'plan'/** Quizzing: *BJ,* II (25 Oct 1845), 248. Walter: Moss, 197. *Reveille:* Log, 588. **To try to make his 'plan'/** Lowell: Walker, 161. This (to me) convincing argument is made in Ottavio M. Casale, "The Battle of Boston: A Revaluation of Poe's Lyceum Appearance," *American Literature,* XLV (Nov 1973), 423–28. English: Harrison, XVII, 439. **In his bizarre clarification/** All quotations from *BJ,* II (1 Nov 1845), 261–62. **Poe's zany arguings/** Clark: Moss, 206. Frogpondians: This and the quotations in the next paragraph from *BJ,* II (22 Nov 1845), 309–11. **The venom released/** Dried: *BJ,* II (29 Nov 1845), 325. Insanity: Walker, 237.

Ownership and Loss of the Broadway Journal

The *Journal* **came into/** Lowell: C. F. Briggs to James Russell Lowell, typed transcript, New York, 22 Jan 1845, Cornell University Library. **But Briggs's pragmatism/** Bisco: C. F. Briggs to James Russell Lowell, New York, 12 Apr 1845, in *Charles Frederick Briggs: Correspondence with James Russell Lowell and William Page, 1843–1846,* Archives of American Art microfilm. Puff: *BJ,* I (22 Mar 1845), 183. *Liberator:* Log, 521. **Briggs saw nothing wrong/** Reorganize: C. F. Briggs to James Russell Lowell, New York, 27 Jun 1845, in *Charles Frederick Briggs.* Resolved: LI, 290. **But what followed instead/** Whirl: A clarifying account of the complex proceedings is Heyward Ehrlich, "The *Broadway Journal:* (1) Briggs's Dilemma and Poe's Strategy," *Bulletin of the New York Public Library,* LXXIII (Feb 1969), 74–93. Spree: C. F. Briggs to James Russell Lowell, New York, 16 Jul 1845, in *Charles Frederick Briggs.* Editor: "Memorandum of an Agreement between John Bisco and Edgar A. Poe, July 14th, 1845," MS, NYPL. **From "one-third proprietor"/** Right: C. F. Briggs to James Russell Lowell, typed transcript, [n. pl.], 1 Aug 1845, Cornell University Library. Shell, sot: C. F. Briggs to William Page, New York, 26 Jul 1845, and C. F. Briggs to James Russell Lowell, New York, 16 Jul

1845, in *Charles Frederick Briggs*. Theater: C. F. Briggs to James Russell Lowell, typed transcript, "Bishop's Terrace" [Staten Island], 12 Aug 1845, Cornell University Library. **In fact only a month/** Difficulty: LI, 292. Heaven's: LI, 296. Chivers: Thomas Holley Chivers to Poe, als, Oaky Grove, 9 Sep 1845, Gris. Advertisement: *BJ*, II (16 Aug 1845), 95. Ohio: Charles Anthon to the Rev. C. P. McIlvaine, als, New York, 30 Jul 1845, HRC. Baltimore: Log, 571–72. **As the *Journal* limped/** Driveller: *BJ*, II (20 Sep 1845), 168. Secret: C. F. Briggs to James Russell Lowell, typed transcript, "Bishop's Terrace" [Staten Island], 13 Oct 1845, Cornell University Library. Private: C. F. Briggs to James Russell Lowell, typed transcript, "Bishop's Terrace" [Staten Island], 12 Aug 1845, Cornell University Library. Crazy: C. F. Briggs to James Russell Lowell, typed transcript, [n. pl.], 13 Feb 1846, Cornell University Library. **By October, Bisco had/** Borrowed: Log, 573. Note: "Memorandum of an Agreement entered into between John Bisco and Edgar A. Poe this 24th day of October 1845," MS, HRC, and MS promissory note, 14 Oct 1845, HRC. Rid: LI, 299. Masthead: *BJ*, II (25 Oct 1845), 248. **The comma error that Poe/** Multitudinous: LI, 302. Earnings: John Ward Ostrom, "Edgar A. Poe: His Income as Literary Entrepreneur," *Poe Studies*, XV (1982), 5. Earlier in the year, William Gilmore Simms reported hearing that Poe's "poverty . . . has been extreme." Mary C. Simms Oliphant et al., eds., *The Letters of William Gilmore Simms*, II (Columbia, 1952), 43. **Only two days after signing/** Pinch: LI, 298. Griswold: Poe to Rufus Griswold, 1 Nov 1845, in Harrison, XVII, 220–21. Ostrom doubted the authenticity of this letter and omitted it from L. I follow T. O. Mabbott, however, in considering it at least partly genuine. See his notes in "Letters" folder, Box 10, Material Under Seal, Iowa. Kennedy: LI, 299; J. P. Kennedy to Poe, als, Baltimore, 1 Dec 1845, Gris. Greeley: Log, 581. Fortune: LI, 301, 302. Chivers, George: LI, 302, 303. **The unassisted office work/** Utterly: LI, 302. **To fill up pages/** Pronounced: *BJ*, II (13 Dec 1845), 355. Briggs: Kenneth Walter Cameron, "A Late Defence of Poe by N. P. Willis," *American Transcendental Quarterly*, XXXVI (Fall 1977), 74. Hurry: *BJ*, II (1 Nov 1845), 263. **However oppressive the work/** LI, 300. **But how much Poe/** Dogs: *BJ*, II (6 Dec 1845), 339. Skirmishing: *BJ*, II (1 Nov, 27 Dec, 6 Dec 1845), 262, 387, 339. Repaid: *BJ*, II (29 Nov 1845), 321. **By the first of December/** LI, 305. **Poe's new partnership lasted/** English: Thomas Dunn English, "Reminiscences of Poe," *Independent*, XLVIII (15 Oct 1896), 1382. Muddy: Land Records, A. W. B. 36, folio 233, Baltimore Court House. Perished: LII, 315.

The Salons; Fanny Osgood and Elizabeth Ellet

Some rewards of New York's/ Aristocracies: N[athaniel]. Parker Willis, *Hurry-Graphs; or, Sketches of Scenery, Celebrities and Society* (New York, 1851), 265. See also 283–88. Hunters: Anne Marie Dolan, "The Literary Salon in New York, 1830–1860," Ph.D. diss., Columbia U., 1957, 79 *et passim*. **Poe found himself invited/** Lynch: See *Memoirs of Anne C. L. Botta* ["Written by her Friends"] (New York, 1894). Lynchie: *Memoirs*, 322. Sustenance: Anne

Lynch to Poe, als, [n. pl.], "Friday Morning 27" [probably Jun 1845], Gris. **The tone of Lynch's/** Seven: Anne Lynch to SHW, als, "116 Waverly Place" [New York], 20 Jan 1846, Brown University Library. Pleasure: Mary E. Phillips, *Edgar Allan Poe the Man,* II (Chicago, 1926), 953; George Foster, *New York in Slices* (New York, 1849), 58–63. Ninety: Log, 687. Formula: Anne Lynch, letter of 20 Jan 1846. Delightful: *Memoirs,* 89. Distinction: Elizabeth Oakes Smith, untitled MS Autobiography, NYPL, 476. **During 1845 and at least/** Eugene L. Didier, ed., *The Life and Poems of Edgar A. Poe* (New York, 1882), 13. **Anne Lynch found Poe/** Bearing: BPB, 203–4. Others: See for instance Elizabeth Oakes Smith, "Autobiographic Notes. Edgar Allan Poe," *Beadle's Monthly,* III (Feb 1867), 147–56. Duyckinck: Log, 559. Elegant: BPB, 204. McDougall: Several of these features are discussed in Michael J. Deas, *The Portraits and Daguerreotypes of Edgar Allan Poe* (Charlottesville, 1988), 28–32. Like Deas, I believe that the watercolor in fact depicts Poe. **Poe delighted in the company/** Attached: BPB, 204. Poe considered women capable of great poetry (since the sense of beauty, he said, is "in its very essence, feminine"), and needed as literary critics, since male chivalry subjected women writers to "the downright degradation of mere puffery." *BJ,* II (27 Dec 1845), 392; T, 116. He reviewed women writers often himself, treating their works with a circumspection absent from his reviews of male writers; in pointing out what he considered their defects, he usually wielded not the tomahawk but the gallant euphemism. In turn, many women with literary interests found Poe attractive, possessed of an appealing delicacy of expression and a complimentary grace of manner. A few thought him insincere, however, such as Margaret Fuller, to whom he always seemed "shrouded in an assumed character." Robert N. Hudspeth, ed., *The Letters of Margaret Fuller,* V (Ithaca, 1987), 289. To Elizabeth Oakes Smith, "He always seemed to have a design—*to be acting a part.*" "Autobiographic Notes," 153. Griswold: Rufus Wilmot Griswold, "Frances Sargent Osgood," *International Monthly Magazine,* II (Dec 1850), 133. Foster: *New York in Slices,* 62. Glossy: T, 1197. **Fanny Osgood was also/** Griswold: "Frances Sargent Osgood," 134. Lynch: Anne Lynch to SHW, als, New York, 20 Jan 1846, WP. Correspondence: See, e.g., Frances Osgood to John Sartain, als, New York, 5 Dec 1848, Historical Society of Pennsylvania, stating her terms as "$1 for every four lines of poetry & ten dollars a page for prose." **However immature she appeared/** Gossip: See MI, 379, 396, 556. Coquettish: See, e.g., her undated als to "Mr. Peterson" and her MS poem to Bayard Taylor, "Just now, the lark, as home she flew," Harvard University Library. Lament: T, 1190. **Poe's acquaintance with Fanny/** Rosy: Log, 510. Compliment: Log, 518. Raven: Whitty, li–liii. Liaison: In this instance, a letter survives from William Gillespie, a minor writer and friend of Osgood's, which strongly suggests that if she did not exactly initiate their acquaintance, she at least brought herself to Poe's attention. Gillespie wrote to Poe telling him that Osgood was disappointed at having missed his lecture, "which she had so eagerly anticipated." He explained that she had dressed to go but remained with her hat on in the Astor House (where she was living), awaiting a friend who did not show up. He asked Poe to allow him to copy from manuscript the laudatory remarks about Fanny, evidently so that he could pass them on to her. William Gillespie to Poe, als, [New York], [1 Mar 1845], Gris. It seems unlikely that Gillespie would have written such a letter except at Osgood's behest. Moreover, his explanation that she missed the lecture because she had been stood up seems to have been untrue. Osgood herself, in writing to another friend, said she had received four invitations to attend the lecture, but "had company & couldn't." Log, 518. It seems more likely Fanny than Gillespie who might want Poe to think she had been kept from hearing him only through a friend's carelessness, not because of her own commitments. **Whoever made the approach/** Unlucky: LI, 306. Greeted: Whitty, li–liii. Introduced: Log, 518. **For two months following/** *BJ,* I (5 Apr 1845), 215–17. **Poe printed several other/** Seductive: *BJ,* I ("10 May 1845" [actually 17 May 1845]), 317. Availability: *BJ,* I (24 May 1845), 325. **Not much is known/** Noncommittal: PHR, 155. Midnight: John D. Haskell, "Poe, Literary *Soirées,* and Coffee," *Poe Studies,* VIII (Dec 1975), q. 47. Wizard: Ingram 538. Infantile: Thomas Dunn English, "Reminiscences of Poe," *Independent,* XLVIII (29 Oct 1896), 1448. **The dalliance did not stay/** Rival: Sidney P. Moss, *Poe's Major Crisis: His Libel Suit and New York's Literary World* (Durham, 1970), 167, 36. Urged: LI, 291. English brought back a verbal reply that Poe considered "somewhat vague." **Poe considered commencing/** Evidence: Moss, 58. Chivers: Richard Beale Davis, ed., *Chivers' Life of Poe* (New York, 1952), 59–62. **Chivers's account of Poe's/** Imploring: W. M. Griswold, ed., *Passages from the Correspondence and Other Papers of Rufus W. Griswold* (Cambridge, Mass., 1898), 56. Characteristically, Osgood's remarks leave unmentioned her active role in the affair. Chivers, reporting his own conversation with Poe, said that Osgood wrote to Poe, asking him to come on to Providence. Osgood's claim that Poe went to see her in Boston gains some support from the fact that Poe did make an otherwise unexplained trip there during July, probably the first week of the month. See *BJ,* II (23 Aug 1845), 109, and the accompanying note in Burton R. Pollin, ed., *Edgar Allan Poe: Writings in* The Broadway Journal . . . *Part 2, The Annotations* (New York, 1986). I discount, however, the more scandalous stories about Poe's pursuit of Osgood in Providence and elsewhere that were bruited about and published by her brother-in-law, Henry F. Harrington. His remarks, set down forty years after the events, often contradict established facts. See *The Critic,* n.s., IV (3 Oct 1885), 157–58, and Harrington to R. H. Stoddard, als, New Bedford, 4 May and 6 May 1885, NYPL. Grey: MI, 382. **Whatever the motives and results/** Foundation: Moss, 58. In the later libel suit, however, English testified that Poe did not find Thomas's explanations satisfactory. **Once Poe took over/** Compliment: *BJ,* II (13 Dec 1845), 353. Facility: Rufus Wilmot Griswold, "Memoir of the Author," in *The Literati . . . By Edgar A. Poe* (New York, 1850), xxxviii. I follow Mabbott in accepting this letter as genuine. See "Letters" folder, Box 10, Material Under Seal, Iowa. Lulin: Osgood's poem is reprinted in John Evangelist Walsh, *Plumes in the Dust: The Love Affair of Edgar Allan Poe and Fanny Osgood* (Chicago, 1980), Appendix B. **Once in control of the *Journal*/** Poems: *BJ,* II (29 Nov and 6 Sep 1845), 318, 129. See also the notes in Pollin's edition. Barrett: Francis B. Dedmond, "Poe and the Brownings," *American Transcendental Quarterly,* n.s., I (Jun 1987), 118. **Such public praises/** Intrigue: MI, 557n. Poems: *BJ,* II (30 Aug and 22 Nov 1845), 113, 307. **Fanny Osgood even visited/** Restraining: Log, 512. T. D. English, however, reported that Mrs. Clemm came to him one day asking his help in disengaging Poe from Osgood, as their relationship made Virginia uneasy. "Reminiscences of Poe," 1448. Clemm was probably speaking more for herself than for Virginia, who as her death neared asked several other women to look out for Poe. SHW later remarked that she imagined "Mrs. Osgood & Mrs. Clemm had no love for each other." PHR, 96. Worshipped: J. C. Derby, *Fifty Years Among Authors, Books and Publishers* (New York, 1884), 547. Pale: Log, 553. Fear: LI, 291. **Combined with the other/** Encountered: Log, 620. On Ellet generally see Susan Phinney Conrad, *Perish the Thought: Intellectual Women in Romantic America 1830–1860* (New York, 1976). Publishing: For some of Ellet's business correspondence with editors see the collections of her letters at the Pierpont Morgan Library and the Barnard College Library. Club: Elizabeth Ellet to "Prof. Hart," als, New York, 13 Jun [no year], Cornell University Library. Minnetonka: "First Woman to See Tonka," typed transcript of article from the Minneapolis *Journal* of 24 Oct 1909, Minnesota Historical Society. **This formidable and knowledgeable/** Heritage: Elizabeth Ellet, als to "Prof. Hart." Lewis: PHR, 160. Story: W. M. Griswold, 147. Bigamy: Joy Bayless, *Rufus Wilmot Griswold: Poe's Literary Executor* (Nashville, 1943), 152ff. **Yet as 1845 ended/** Feature: Poe had printed poems and essays by Ellet before in *SLM,* and reviewed a volume of her poems. While still working for Willis he had also defended her in the *Mirror* against a charge of plagiarism. Praised: *BJ,* II (4 Oct and 1 Nov 1845), 186, 242, 251. Duyckinck: Log, 603. **The meaning of Poe's/** German: LII, 409n.; Log, 605. Suggested: See Walsh. **While Poe's exact relation/** W. M. Griswold, 256. **To be under the eye/** PHR, 21. See also Ingram 715. **In Poe's account of what/** LII, 407–8. **Poe's account was probably/** Retold: Ingram 881. Possession: "Reminiscences of Poe," 1448. **It was a lopsided/** Menacingly: "Reminiscences of Poe," 1448. Fracas: Moss, 52. Flogging: LII, 322. **The beating, whoever took/** Greeley: Log, 640. Labouring: Moss, 37. **No such letter from/** Innocence: Elizabeth Ellet to Rufus Griswold, als, New York, 4 Jan [after 1849], Gris. Extenuation: Moss, 52. See also LII, 408. **On the circle of literary/** Indiscretion: Log, 651. Lunacy: Ingram 87. Forgetting: Walsh, 93. **By Valentine's Day/** Reunited: Walsh, 48. Puzzle-poem: MI, 388–89. Lynch: Log, 719, 726. Poe's last visit to one of Lynch's evenings may have been on 20 January, during the letters affair. See Log, 620. **But Poe was remembered/** MI, 524.

Other Writing and Editions in 1845; "The Philosophy of Composition"

Poe's disgusting ending/ E. F. Bleiler, "Edgar Allan Poe," in E. F. Bleiler, ed., *Science Fiction Writers* (New York, 1982), 15. Collyer: Harrison, XVII, 225. For similar receptions of Poe's tale see Walker, 150; Arch Ramsey to Poe, als, Stonehaven, 30 Nov 1846, Gris; and Charles Herbert Cottrell to "Dr. Jarvis," als, London, [n.d.], HRC. South: Taylor Stoehr, "Robert H. Collyer's Technology of the Soul," in Arthur Wrobel, ed., *Pseudo-Science and Society in Nineteenth-Century America* (Lexington, 1987), q. 37. **Similar currents of meaning/** Master: Within my reading, the most illuminating discussion of

Poe's essay and of its relation to the French Symbolists appears in Carl Fehrman, *Poetic Creation: Inspiration or Craft,* trans. Karin Petherick (Minneapolis, 1980). Also helpful are Valéry's own essay, "The Place of Baudelaire," in *Leonardo Poe Mallarmé* (Princeton, 1972), 193–211, and the introduction to Jean Alexander, ed., *Affidavits of Genius: Edgar Allan Poe and the French Critics, 1847–1924* (Port Washington, 1971), 5–74. Hyperanalytic: T, 14–15. **Amid the tumult of 1845/** Book-cases: *BJ,* II (19 Jul 1845), 28. **Duyckinck chose brilliantly/** Rogêt: On Poe's revisions see John Walsh, *Poe the Detective: The Curious Circumstances Behind* The Mystery of Marie Rogêt (New Brunswick, 1968). **The 1845 *Tales* was Poe's/** Claimed: *BJ,* II (4 Oct 1845), 200. Succeeded: Burton R. Pollin, "Poe 'Viewed and *Reviewed*': An Annotated Checklist of Contemporaneous Notices," *Poe Studies* XIII (Dec 1980), 17–28. Griswold: Walker, 182. France: Log, 556, 585. Indians: Walker, 203. Track: Walker, 184. Objection: *BJ,* II (1 Nov 1845), 263. **Poe was nettled as well/** *Aristidean: Aristidean,* I (Sep 1845), 234. Poe may have written this piece in collaboration with T. D. English. Dignity: T, 873. **Paltry commendation and worse/** Walker, 264, 227, 241, 238, 236. **English reviewers and readers/** London: Walker, 260. Barrett: Francis B. Dedmond, "Poe and the Brownings," *American Transcendental Quarterly,* n.s., I (Jun 1987), q. 16, 17.

Turtle Bay; Fordham; The "Literati" War

Poe and his family/ Bills: *BJ,* I (22 Feb 1845), 113. Miller: Whitty, lvii, and Mary E. Phillips, *Edgar Allan Poe the Man,* II (Chicago, 1926), 1109–11. **Poe stayed with the Millers/** Sick: LII, 313. DeUnger: Log, 628. Ill: M. E. Hewitt to Poe, als, New York, 14 Apr 1846, Gris. **Poe's continued sickness/** *Reveille:* Log, 634. *Visiter:* Log, 635. Serious: LII, 714. Snodgrass: Log, 640. **For a hundred dollars/** House: Most details of the cottage are taken from Reginald Pelham Bolton, "The Poe Cottage at Fordham," *Transactions of the Bronx Society of Arts Sciences and History,* I (1922), 1–16, and John E. Piper, "Edgar Allan Poe at Fordham," *Bronx County Historical Society Journal,* IX (Jan 1972), 1–18. Greensward: Eugene L. Didier, "Life of Edgar A. Poe," in Didier, ed., *Life and Poems of Edgar Allan Poe* (New York, 1882), 97. Tables: PHR, 162. Books: By one account Poe gave places of honor to the Brownings. See Brev, 109–10, and Mary Gove Nichols, *Reminiscences of Edgar Allan Poe* (New York, 1863), 9. Birds: Sarah Helen Whitman, *Edgar Poe and his Critics* (1860; rpt. New York, 1966), 31. Humble: Augustus Van Cleef, "Poe's Mary," *Harper's New Monthly Magazine,* LXXVIII (Mar 1889), 639. **The Fordham house uniquely suited/** Jesuit: Log, 644. Close-knit: Harrison, XVII, 430. Alike: PHR, 298. Catterina: BPB, 138. **But neither the intimate/** Snug etc.: LII, 325–26. Magnificent: LII, 330. **Poe's deteriorating condition/** LII, 318. **But Virginia could no longer/** Didier, 97. **In the late spring/** Combing: Ingram 958. Proud: LI, 234. Petted: Susan Archer Weiss, *The Home Life of Poe* (New York, 1907), 130. Muddy: PHR, 195. **Poe offered the "Literati"/** All quotations from the "Literati" are from the text in T. **Even before the "Literati"/** *Tribune:* Log, 629. Greeley: Horace Greeley to H. C. Hosmer, als, Boston, 7 May 1846, HRC. Hundreds: Log, 638. **Inevitably, even the first/** Noses: Log, 636. Peculiarities: Log, 636. Godey: Log, 641. **Had Poe contented himself/** Poe's revisions of the "Literati" appear on an undated holograph leaf, NYPL. **Two sketches in particular/** Sidney P. Moss, *Poe's Major Crisis: His Libel Suit and New York's Literary World* (Durham, 1970), 19, 16. **Briggs scored/** Impression: LII, 319. Handsome: Log, 651. *Courier:* Philadelphia *Saturday Courier,* 25 Jul 1846. Simms: Moss, 94. Touchiness: J. Albert Robbins, "Edgar Poe and the Philadelphians: A Reminiscence by a Contemporary," *Poe Studies,* V (Dec 1972), 46. **Full-scale war over the "Literati"/** Genius: William H. Gravely, Jr., "The Early Political and Literary Career of Thomas Dunn English," Ph.D. diss., U. of Virginia, 1953, 268. Grammar: Gravely, 375. Auxiliaries: Gravely, 306–7. **English was actually a virile/** Passenger: Moss, 40. **The violence of English's/** Greeley: Moss, 188. *Press:* Log, 649. Griswold: Rufus Griswold to Evert Duyckinck, als, "Jones's Hotel," 24 [Jul] 1846, NYPL. *Ledger:* Moss, 40. **How much "intellectual force"/** Arising: LII, 344–45. Beating: LII, 322. **"I have never written an article"/** Confidently: LII, 324. Reply: Quotations from "Mr. Poe's Reply," here and in the next two paragraphs, come from the text in Moss, 50–59. Confided: LII, 356. **Poe saved what he considered/** *Mirror:* Moss, 62.

The Libel Suit; "The Cask of Amontillado"; "The Domain of Arnheim"

On July 23, Poe's/ Fancher: Francis P. Desmond, "Willis and Morris add a Partner—and Poe," *Notes and Queries,* CXCVIII (Jun 1953), 253–54. Stated: Sidney P. Moss, *Poe's Major Crisis: His Libel Suit and New York's Literary World* (Durham, 1970), 82, 84. **Poe did not bring/** Insane: Moss, 47. Sheep: Moss, 59. Disgrace: LII, 319. **At a preliminary hearing/** Moss, 60, 70, 98. **Poe was in no condition/** Fowl: LII, 326. Simms: William Gilmore Simms to Poe, als, New York, 30 Jul 1846, Gris. Gates: LII, 326. **Those who would devour/** Cliquism: LII, 333. Parnassus: Only fragments of the projected book got written, but they make it clear that Poe also designed the volume to puff himself and wither his foes. He planned to include Lowell's laudatory essay on his work, as well as the "Reply to Mr. English" and revised portraits of some writers he had already sketched in the "Literati," too casually he now thought. See LII, 333. His amended sketch of English does not suggest he would have drawn them more judiciously, containing as it does the added insult that English had enough talent "to succeed in his father's profession—that of a ferryman on the Schuylkill" (Moss, 32–34). He also intended to describe Louis Godey as "a little round oily man with a fat head." Other surviving notes for the book indicate that he again meant to have a go at Transcendentalism, Frogpondian Boston, and especially Longfellow ("Flowery-trite"). All the same, he seems to have planned a hopeful ending to his survey of American letters, foreseeing the passage of an international copyright law, and prophesying that the works of American writers would excel those of writers in other countries. "The Living Writers of America. Some Honest Opinions about their Literary Merits, with Occasional Words of Personality," MS, Pierpont Morgan Library.

Poe remained under siege/ Bryant: William Cullen Bryant II and Thomas G. Voss, eds., *The Letters of William Cullen Bryant,* II (New York, 1977), 469. Surpassed: William H. Gravely, Jr., "The Early Political and Literary Career of Thomas Dunn English," Ph.D. diss., U. of Virginia, 1953, 627. I agree with Moss in thinking that English's earlier satirical sketch, "Walter Woolfe; or, The Doom of the Drinker," does not concern Poe. Moss, 101. Flighty: Moss, 103. Further quotations from *1844* are from the text in Moss. **If English was a bare-knuckled/** Amontillado: Technically, it deserves being noted, the tale justifies Poe's pride in variety. It differs from most of his serious tales in being told largely through dialogue, anchored to vivid bits of scene painting that unfurl like a cyclorama as murderer and victim wind through the cellar. Its narrative neatness and speed are won by a fine economy of means: the sardonic double-edged dialogue, in which Montresor vengefully dangles his victim's fate before him in innocent-sounding conversation; the highlighting of a few telling sense details, especially the dampness of the catacomb walls and the jingling bells on Fortunato's cap; the spare typographical emphasis, such as the single use of italicized dialogue in Fortunato's desperate cry, *"For the love of God, Montresor!"* **In Montresor, Poe/** Ass: LI, 130. **With a memory no less/** *Godey's:* Log, 671, 673, 703; LII, 349. Praised: T, 574. Condemned: T, 587. **The key to Poe's change/** Philadelphia: Log, 280. Implacable: LI, 214. **Poe exacted still more/** December: I follow Dwight Thomas in dating this piece around December 1846, although Mabbott dated it in 1849. The later date makes nonsense of the opening sentence of the piece, in which Poe refers to the December 1846 issue of *GM* as a "late number" of that magazine. Were he writing in 1849, "late number" would mean an issue two and a half years earlier. **Ironically, as Poe was doing/** Learned: LII, 336. *Quotidienne:* Log, 645. *Commerce:* Log, 666. "Forgues" was the pen name of Paul Émile Daurant. *Presse:* Log, 667. **Other Paris journals/** Gaillard: Log, 667. Lu: Log, 672. **Forgues's libel suit/** Faculty: Moss, 146. Connu: Log, 683. Russia: Joan Delaney, "Poe's 'The Gold-Bug' in Russia: A Note on First Impressions," *American Literature,* XLII (Nov 1970), 375–79. Baudelaire: Walker, q. 403–4. **According to Evert Duyckinck/** Touching: Evert Duyckinck, 1875 memorandum concerning Poe, kindly communicated to me by Professor Donald Yannella. T. D. English also spoke of Poe's "excessive love of approbation." "Reminiscences of Poe," *Independent,* XLVIII (5 Nov 1896), 1480. Grubs: Moss, 42. George: Poe to George W. Poe, als, Philadelphia, 12 Jul 1839, Free Library of Philadelphia. Diaeresis: "The Orang-Outang of Mr. Old Nick," *Spirit of the Times,* 16 Jan 1847. **Taking what satisfaction/** Numbed: Mary Nichols, *Mary Lyndon, or Revelations of a Life* (New York, 1855), 342. I am grateful to Professor Joel Myerson for pointing out this passage to me. **Ultimately the traveler's/** Bonaparte: *The Life and Works of Edgar Allan Poe: A Psycho-Analytic Interpretation* (English ed. 1949; rpt. London, 1971), 288. Poe used as an epigraph for the piece a quotation from Giles Fletcher's poem "Christ's Victorie on Earth," which specifically compares the landscape to an unconscious woman. Expresses: LII, 397.

Virginia's Death; The Libel Suit Won; Loui Shew

By November, Virginia's/ Mary Gove Nichols, *Reminiscences of Edgar Allan Poe* (1931; rpt. Folcroft, 1969), 12; BPB, 108. **Reports reached the city/** Wretchedness: W. M. Griswold, ed., *Passages from the Correspondence and Other Papers of Rufus W. Griswold* (Cambridge, Mass., 1898), 214. Muddy: Nichols, 8; BPB, 20. Distress: Nichols, 12. Hopeless: LII, 338. Harrison: "Edgar A. Poe. Reminiscences of Gabriel Harrison, an Actor, Still Living in Brooklyn," *New York Times-Saturday Review,* 4 Mar 1899, 144. Harrison may have been speaking of some time earlier in the year, however. Shilling: Griswold, 213, 214. **News of the family's/** *Express:* Log, 672. Union: Log, 675–76. Fuller: Log, 673. **The longest and most personal/** Pained: *BJ,* I ("10 May 1845" [actually 17 May 1845]), 316. Gift: See Sotheby's sale catalogue #5530, for New York auction on 15 Dec 1986. Editorial: Sidney P. Moss, *Poe's Major Crisis: His Libel Suit and New York's Literary World* (Durham, 1970), 130–32. **Poe felt buoyed/** Editor: Log, 673. Lawyer: Mary E. Phillips, *Edgar Allan Poe the Man,* II (Chicago, 1926), 1194. Astor: LII, 338, 340. Capacity: LII, 339. **But little of this public/** LII, 347. **Friends came to Fordham/** Herring: Whitty, xxx. Starr: BPB, 102. Shew: See Margaret Blakeley, "Historic Memories Cling to Old Henderson House," Waterville [N.Y.] *Times,* 17, 18, 19 Sep 1929. Doctor's: BPB, 92. Tonic: BPB, 23. **Loui Shew and Mary Starr/** Mary: Augustus Van Cleef, "Poe's Mary," *Harper's New Monthly Magazine,* LXXVIII (Mar 1889), 639. Weeping: BPB, 116. Calm: LII, 340. **On February 1/** *Tribune:* Log, 685. Speak: BPB, 23. Suffering: LII, 340. **Loui helped with the funeral/** Cologne: BPB, 103. Linen: Nichols, 13. Watercolor: BPB, 122, 97. Mrs. Shew believed that the watercolor resembled a picture of Poe's mother, taken while she lay dying in Richmond. **Virginia's funeral took place/** Cold: Van Cleef, 640. Interred: John E. Piper, "Edgar Allan Poe at Fordham," *Bronx County Historical Society Journal,* IX (Jan 1972), 1–18. Cloak: BPB, 108. **To add to Poe's distress/** Deposition: Moss, 166. Jury: Moss, 173. **Poe sent Muddy to the city/** Moss, 177, 189, 199–202, 188, 210–12. **Poe was aware of the uproar/** Unwell: LII, 349, 346, 347. Devastated: BPB, 47. Visited: MS "Statements of Mrs. Maria Clemm. Noted in short-hand by E. L. D.[idier]," Harvard University Library. **Poe now spoke of his/** Serious: LII, 349. Diagnosis: BPB, 92, 94. Phosphates: BPB, 108. Cautioned: BPB, 103. **Loui recalled that Poe/** Grateful: BPB, 23. Unselfish: LII, 350. Sedative: By Mrs. Shew's later account, Poe had been offered twenty dollars for the publication of this poem. But she was about to be married to a man who had "*old fashioned notions* of woman and her sphere," and whose reaction to the poem she dreaded, as it was "so very personal and complimentary." She asked Poe to delay publishing it, and meanwhile gave him a twenty-five dollar check "for his necessities." BPB, 92. **As Loui tried to calm/** BPB, 128–30. **Poe confided to Loui/** BPB, 92, 129. **Especially Virginia's death led/** BPB, 131, 99, 121, 140. **Poe told her this "privately"/** BPB, 121, 141. F. W. Thomas, who had known Henry Poe, commented that he "pretended not to know what had become of his father." Whitty, xxi. **In fashioning a proud/** BPB, 140.

Attempted Recovery; "Ulalume"; Eureka; Parting from Loui Shew

In trying to repair/ Delicacies: J. C. Derby, *Fifty Years Among Authors, Books and Publishers* (New York, 1884), 588–89. Bronson: Carroll D. Laverty, "Poe in 1847," *American Literature,* XX (May 1948), 165. In another reminiscence which may refer to this time, a woman named Phelps recalled in 1897 that as a young girl and a neighbor of Poe's at Fordham, she found his mood "erratic." One day he would "romp with us children . . . with most charming and windsome [*sic*] manners," while the next he would be "in a dreary, pensive mood." Mary E. Phillips, *Edgar Allan Poe the Man,* II (Chicago, 1926), 1122. Leaping: Mary Gove Nichols, *Reminiscences of Edgar Allan Poe* (1931; rpt. Folcroft, 1969), 9–10. **By summertime, Poe/** Fuller: Log, 701. Fuller also printed a report, probably malicious, that Poe "behaved himself in so indecent a manner that we were compelled to send for a posse of the police to take him away." Griswold: Log, 702. Classic: LII, 350. Worship: BPB, 133. Rigmarole: Log, 564. Renewed: LII, 373. **The amber coffee, broad jumping/** Commencement: Log, 703. Ill: LII, 351. Loui Shew may have had this trip in mind when she spoke of Poe experiencing *"a relapse (a few weeks after)* partial recovery." Marie L. Houghton to SHW, als, [n. pl.], 20 May [1876?], Lilly. Bronson: Laverty, 167. Service: Log, 711. **By the New Year/** Best: LII, 355. Rise: LII, 360. Eveleth: Thomas Ollive Mabbott, "The Letters from George W. Eveleth to Edgar Allan Poe," *Bulletin of the New York Public Library,* XXVI (Mar 1922), 177, 192. In their exchange of lengthy letters Eveleth served as Poe's Boswell, eliciting his literary opinions and his glosses on his tales and poems. Their correspondence is thus an important source for Poe's views on his own work. **As Poe told Eveleth/** LII, 356. **Feeling or at least professing/** Re-establish: LII, 357. Arraigned: Log, 629. Textbook: LII, 344, 349. Prison: William H. Gravely, Jr., "The Early Political and Literary Career of Thomas Dunn English," Ph.D. diss., U. of Virginia, 1953, 705. *Messenger:* Walker, 271–72. **Poe saw his best hope/** Fortune: LII, 356. Expedition: LII, 354, 356, 359. World: Log, 714. **Another chance to make/** Reciting: MI, 410. Engraving: Laverty, 167. Complaint: LII, 716 and n. Reader: Derby, 597. Best: Log, 707. Inquiry: LII, 354. Complied: MI, 413. Poe later asked Duyckinck to republish the item in his *Literary World.* **"Ulalume—A Ballad" evinces/** Muddy: MS "Statements of Mrs. Maria Clemm. Noted in short-hand by E. L. D.[idier]," Harvard University Library. For a contrasting account see Log, 714. *"Moment":* LII, 362. **On February 3, Poe/** Date: LII, 358. **His coat tightly buttoned/** Chest: Log, 720. Praised: Log, 722, 724. On the reviews of Poe's lecture see Log, 720–24 and Burton R. Pollin, "Contemporary Reviews of *Eureka:* A Checklist," in Richard P. Benton, ed., *Poe As Literary Cosmologer: Studies in Eureka. A Symposium* (Hartford, 1975), 27–28. Misrepresented: LII, 361. Appreciate: "B." [A. B. Heywood] to Nancy Richmond, typed transcript, Lowell, 8 Nov 1849, University of Virginia Library. **By the end of May Poe/** On the publication see Roland W. Nelson, "Apparatus for a Definitive Edition of Poe's *Eureka,*" *Studies in the American Renaissance 1978* (Boston, 1978), 161–205, which also lists Poe's planned revisions. For a text and useful bibliography see

Richard P. Benton's edition of *Eureka* in *American Transcendental Quarterly*, No. 22 (Spring 1974), 1–77. The most satisfactory available text, based on Nelson's work, is that in Patrick F. Quinn, ed., *Poe: Poetry and Tales* (New York, 1984), which I have followed. From the large critical literature on *Eureka*, I have indicated in the Notes and Appendix only the several essays and books I have found most useful to my purposes. A lucid and enlightening general discussion appears in Frederick Conner, *Cosmic Optimism* (Gainesville, 1949), 68ff. Humboldt: Douglas Botting, *Humboldt and the Cosmos* (New York, 1973), 257. In this period Poe gave special attention to the subject of the nature of genius. See, e.g., Brev, 323, 321, 316. **Inflamed anew by Virginia's/** BPB, 101. **Whatever consolation Poe found/** Hopkins: Walker, 278. Approaches: LII, 361. Received: Log, 735; LII, 364. Jesuit: BPB, 101. **In May, Hopkins saw/** John Henry Hopkins, Jr., to Poe, als, "Gen. Theol. Sem.," 15 May 1848, Gris. **About two weeks after/** Attributed: Loui Shew, however, believed that Hopkins was not the author. BPB, 141. Ecstatic: Walker, 279. Transcendentalists: Walker, 284. **Poe wrote off a long/** LII, 382. **Whether or not young Hopkins/** Hopeless: Log, 735. Griswold: BPB, 95. Puzzlingly: Rufus Griswold, *Statement of the Relations of Rufus W. Griswold with Charlotte Myers (Called Charlotte Griswold)* (Philadelphia, 1856), 27. Osgood: Rufus Griswold to James T. Fields, als, [n. pl., beginning "Every morning since I received your letter"}, {ca. fall 1848}, Huntington Library. **Something apparently stirred/** BPB, 104, 101. **A visit from Poe/** Rejected: LII, 390. Realize: BPB, 99; John Henry Ingram, *Edgar Allan Poe: His Life, Letters, and Opinions* (1886; rpt. New York, 1965), 361–63. **Loui's growing estrangement/** Reason: LII, 364. Conventional: LII, 372–73. **Around June, Loui sent/** LII, 372–74. This letter exists only in Louise Shew's transcription of it, which contains several errors of grammar, punctuation, and spelling that are untypical of Poe's letters, and must be ascribed to her copying. I have silently emended them.

Jane Locke; Nancy Richmond; Sarah Helen Whitman; Elmira Royster

Virginia's approaching death/ Invocation: Log, 674. Charity: John E. Reilly, "Ermina's Gales: The Poems Jane Locke Devoted to Poe," in Richard P. Veler, ed., *Papers on Poe: Essays in Honor of John Ward Ostrom* (Springfield, Ohio, 1972), 208. **A further uncertainty compounded/** LII, 366–67. **What might or might not/** Dickens: Charles Dickens, *American Notes for General Circulation* (Harmondsworth, 1972), 114. Lecture: Log, 741. One listener said that Poe paid marked attention to the rhythm and "almost *sang* the more musical versifications." **If he had not known so/** Learned: According to testimony from Nancy Richmond in 1877, nearly thirty years after the event, Mrs. Locke visited Fordham to meet Poe before he went to Lowell. Presumably, he would at this time have learned about her marriage. The testimony, however, contradicts the contemporary account of Mrs. Richmond's brother, Bardwell, who wrote that Poe did not learn of Mrs. Locke's marriage until he came to Lowell. Bardwell's account, being closer to the time of the event, seems to me more trustworthy. See A. B. Heywood to President Martin Van Buren, typed transcript, Westford, 2 Oct 1848, University of Virginia Library. Resident: A. B. Heywood, letter of 2 Oct. **At the Richmonds' substantial/** Relative: A. B. Heywood to "Dear Friend," typed transcript, Lowell, 25 Apr 1848, University of Virginia Library. Romance: MIII, 741. Impression: Log, 741. **Poe spent a sociable/** A. B. Heywood, letter of 2 Oct. **In describing his detachment/** According to Heywood, Poe also said that for part of the time during the first two years of his marriage, he was "traveling alone in Europe." The story is more likely than Poe's accounts of having visited Europe in his early youth, for one thing because it might explain the year-long lack of information about his life in New York, from about June 1837 to June 1838. My check of ships' passenger lists in the New York *Evening Post* failed to turn up his name, but the absence is inconclusive. **Unlike Jane Locke and Nancy/** Poem: John Grier Varner, "Sarah Helen Whitman: Seeress of Providence," Ph.D. diss., U. of Virginia, 1940, q. 136. Hegelian: SHW to Ida Russell, als, [n. pl.], [1846, ca. 7 Jan], folder 86, WP. See also her brief translation of Goethe's "To the Clouds," undated, Historical Society of Pennsylvania. Disciple: Emerson reportedly called it "not by a Disciple in any ordinary sense." Caroline Ticknor, *Poe's Helen* (New York, 1916), q. 25. **Helen, as she preferred/** Horror: SHW to Mary Hewitt, als, Providence, 10 Oct 1850, HRC. Meeting: Frances Osgood to SHW, als, New York, 16 Mar 1845, folder 186, WP. Effect: Log, 553. Curious: Log, 619, 614. Barrett: SHW to Ida Russell, als, [n. pl.], [1846, ca. 7 Jan], folder 86, WP. Accounts: Anne Lynch to SHW, als, New York, 31 Jan 1847, folder 101, WP. **Through Anne Lynch, Helen/** Solicited: Log, 718. The sending of valentines was so popular in the period that the New York Post Office hired two or three hundred extra carriers to deliver them. *BJ*, I (15 Feb 1845), 108. Complied: SHW to [John Henry Ingram or R. H. Stoddard], [n. pl., beginning "I have a word to say about the valentine"], [n.d.], folder 92, WP. Lynch: Anne Lynch to SHW, als, New York, 21 Feb 1848, folder 101, WP. **Helen evidently wanted Poe/** Discouraged: Anne Lynch to SHW, als, New York, 10 Mar 1848, folder 101, WP. Persisted: Log, 729. Fanny: Frances Osgood to SHW, als, New York, 26 Mar 1848, folder 186, WP. **As it happened, Poe/** Kindly: Log, 536–37. Married: LII, 384–85. **Whatever interest Poe/** MI, 442–43. **Poe answered immediately/** Clipping: Poe's poem-envelope survives at Lilly. Handwriting: Log, 728. **Whether for here, hereafter/** Blackwell: Blackwell said that she visited, not stayed, with the Poes. See Ingram 315. Something: LII, 370. Identified: PHR, 60. **Poe had planned the trip/** Notebook: Alexander G. Rose III and Jeffrey Alan Savoye, eds., *Such Friends as These* (Baltimore, 1986). Pressing: LII, 368. Unfortunately, although the sojourn marked Poe's first return to his childhood home in over ten years, most surviving accounts of his visit are vague or suspect. Rose: Log, 750; Agnes M. Bondurant, *Poe's Richmond* (1942; rpt. Richmond, 1978), 87–88. Coat: John R. Thompson to E. H. N. Patterson, als, Richmond, 9 Nov 1849, Pierpont Morgan Library. Eureka: John R. Thompson to P. P. Cooke, als, Richmond, 17 Oct 1848, HRC. Clerk: Ingram 728. Challenge: PHR, 41. Mania: Log, 750. **Late in July, Poe/** Enthusiastic: Log, 746. Proposing: For two slightly differing accounts of Poe's intentions toward Mrs. Shelton at this time, see Log, 746, and SHW to Mary [Forest], als, Providence, 20 Jun 1859, folder 47, WP. **Poe came close to doing/** Muddy: A. B. Heywood to President Martin Van Buren, typed transcript, Westford, 2 Oct 1848, University of Virginia Library. Love-struck: John E. Reilly, "Ermina's Gales: The Poems Jane Locke Devoted to Poe," in Richard P. Veler, ed., *Papers on Poe: Essays in Honor of John Ward Ostrom* (Springfield, Ohio, 1972), 210. **What stalled Poe's marriage/** Years: Anne Lynch to Rufus Griswold, als, [n. pl.], [9 Aug 1842], Historical Society of Pennsylvania. Jewess: PHR, 213. Health: Rufus Griswold to Bayard Taylor, als, [New York], [Oct 1848], Cornell University Library; Rufus Griswold to James T. Fields, als, [n. pl., beginning "Every morning since I received your letter"], [ca. fall 1848], Huntington Library; Rufus Griswold to the Rev. A. C. Kendrick, New York, 7 Aug [1848], University of Rochester Library. Literati: PHR, 61. McIntosh: Log, 739. In a rare exception, I have here departed from the chronology of events given in the superbly researched Log. Difficulty in the dating arises from two different accounts of the visit of Maria McIntosh given by Sarah Helen Whitman (compare Log, 739, with PHR, 60–62). Griswold seems to have appeared in Providence around mid-July. As both accounts clearly refer to the same evening, I have combined them in describing the event. **Emboldened, Helen wrote/** Stanzas: Log, 747. Acknowledgment: SHW to R. H. Stoddard, als, Providence, 30 Sep 1872, NYPL. **Poe took Helen's meaning/** Grey: LII, 379. McIntosh: Maria Jane McIntosh to SHW, als, New York, 15 Sep 1848, Brown University Library.

Benefit Street

In person, Helen first/ Pale: LII, 387. Poe's impression seems borne out by the remark of a friend, who described SHW's movements as rapid, nervously eager: "she came flitting into the room," the friend said; "she seemed to flutter like a bird." Caroline Ticknor, *Poe's Helen* (New York, 1916), q. 5. **Like himself, in fact/** Ingram 99. In the margin of one of the many articles about Poe which she collected, SHW herself noted that at the time Poe first saw her, she was forty-two years old. See her copy of John Watson Dalby, "Edgar Allan Poe," 484, Lilly. **Whatever her birth date/** Saturn: John Grier Varner, "Sarah Helen Whitman: Seeress of Providence," Ph.D., diss., U. of Virginia, 1940, 21. Doggerel: Varner, 40. Actresses: MS "Items taken down from Mrs. Whitman herself in pencil," folder 28, WP. Odor: Mary E. Phillips, *Edgar Allan Poe the Man,* II (Chicago, 1926), 1282. **Nicholas Power played/** Coronet: SHW to [unaddressed], Providence, 7 Oct 1875, Lilly. Quotations: All texts from Sarah Helen Whitman, *Hours of Life, and Other Poems* (Providence, 1853). **The House of Agonies/** MS "Items taken down from Mrs. Whitman." **The years since Helen's/** Anna: PHR, 129. **No doubt the two women/** Lawyer: Alvin Rosenfeld, "Wilkins Updike to Sarah Helen Whitman. Two New Letters," *Rhode Island History,* XXV (Oct 1966), 97–109. On other suitors at this time see also the letters to SHW in folders 200 and 201, WP. Senior: MS genealogical notes, folder 28, WP. David: *Hours of Life,* 96–98. **Poe remained in Providence/** Restlessly: LII, 387. Reminisced: PHR, 95. It is a sign of how rarely Poe used the Allan name that Helen repeatedly later wrote "Allen" for "Allan." She may never have seen Poe's full signature. Virginia: SHW to R. H. Stoddard, draft letter, [n. pl., beginning "Mr. Bailey has"], [n.d.], Lilly. **Much of their conversation/** Poet-nature: LII, 383. Devoted: Log, 755. Now or maybe later Poe also gave SHW a copy of *Eureka,* inscribed "from the most sincere of her friends." Photostat, Berg Collection, NYPL. Paged: Log, 756. **Some luck helped out/** "Ulalume": PHR, 116. Recited: SHW to "Mr. Montclair," als, Providence, 27 Dec 1867, Lilly. **However much the literary/** Oppressive: LII, 394. Blackwell: Ticknor, 51. **Conflicts and kinship both/** Harrison, XVII, 422; PHR, 104. Maria Clemm later denied Poe's claim that he had seen Jane Stanard only once. See SHW to E. L. Didier, als, Providence, 25 Dec 1876, Lilly. Indeed he may have said so to impress on SHW her likeness to this love of his adolescence, having in view his tale of having glimpsed Helen on his earlier visit to Providence ("I saw thee once, once only"). Following Muddy's disclaimer, SHW changed her own account of what Poe told her at the cemetery to include repeated later visits by Poe to Jane Stanard before her death: "This lady afterward became the confidant of all his boyish sorrows, and her's was the one redeeming influence that saved and guided him in the earlier days of his turbulent and passionate youth." Sarah Helen Whitman, *Edgar Poe and his Critics* (1860; rpt. New York, 1966), 49. **As they sat together/** Loss: Varner, 301. Valueless: See SHW's marginal notes in Ingram 521. Especial: LII, 384. **As they stood by an unmarked/** Ringing: LII, 383. Encircled: LII, 397. **Having known Helen only/** Respond: PHR, 90. Resuscitate: SHW to R. H. Stoddard, als, Providence, 30 Sep 1872, NYPL. **Although the outing to Swan/** Consented: *Hours of Life,* 196. Poer: PHR, 182–83; *Edgar Poe and his Critics,* 77. **Actually the two families/** Unrelated: That Helen's genealogy was unfounded is demonstrated in Sir Edmund Thomas Bewley, *The Origin and Early History of the Family of Poë or Poe* (Dublin, 1906). Likeness: SHW's poems and comments about Poe repeatedly cast him in the idiom of high chivalry which she associated with her father's ancestry. Here or there she remarked on his "haughty valor," his "imperial intellect," his "imagination royally dowered and descended." Doggerel: Varner, 7. Lenore: PHR, 206. Twin: PHR, 183. Cork: SHW said that everyone who had seen Poe remarked the resemblance. It so appalled her mother that she would not remain in the same room. PHR, 191. Whitman's identification with Poe also implies some feeling of maleness. Regarding another set of photographs, showing her face in left and in right profile, she remarked: "Those of the left are both decidedly masculine, the other two as decidedly feminine." Ticknor, 201. **In his similar craving/** Genealogy: A. Wigfall Green, "The Weekly Magazine and Poe," *English Studies in Honor of James Southall Wilson* (Charlottesville, 1951), 56. Portrait: SHW to J. W. Davidson, draft letters, 1858–78, folder 40, WP. **Poe's first meeting with/** PHR, 90.

An Exchange of Letters; Return to Lowell

Poe returned to Fordham/ Quotations from Poe's letter in this and the following six paragraphs come from LII, 382–90. **To overcome Helen's resistance/** Longest: PHR, 39. **Poe waited anxiously for Helen's/** Quotations from Poe's letter in this and the next four paragraphs come from LII, 391–97. **How Helen responded/** Whimsical: William Whitman Bailey, MS "Recollections of Sarah Helen Whitman," 9–10, WP. Cautious: PHR, 504. Repugnant: John Grier Varner, "Sarah Helen Whitman: Seeress of Providence," Ph.D. diss., U. of Virginia, 1940, 605. **In turmoil over Helen's/** Leaf: Arthur H. Quinn, ed., *Edgar Allan Poe: Letters and Documents in the Enoch Pratt Free Library* (New York, 1941), 39. Entrusting: PHR, 346. **In Lowell, Poe put up/** Lockes: LII, 430. **Incurring Jane Locke's wrath/** Ticking: John Henry Ingram, *Edgar Allan Poe: His Life, Letters, and Opinions* (1886; rpt. New York, 1965), 390. Letter: LII, 401. Annie: Mary E. Phillips, *Edgar Allan Poe the Man,* II (Chicago, 1926), 1293. **Poe's romance with Annie/** Charles: Phillips, II, 1295. Brother: A. B. Heywood to [unaddressed], typed transcript, Concord, 24 Dec 1848, University of Virginia Library. **In fact Charles had no/** Sibling: LII, 402–3. Smith: Ingram 233. Referring to her sister, SHW herself later remarked on "the theory which *she first* propounded to me, of Poe's dread of remarriage." PHR, 86. **But Poe's 'dread' of remarriage/** Propriety: *Aristidean,* I (Sep 1845), 234. Commemoration: Sarah Helen Whitman, *Edgar Poe and his Critics* (1860; rpt. New York, 1966), 48. SHW also spoke of "that remorseful sorrow that seems always to have visited him when his thoughts reverted from some dream of present happiness to the memory of a lost love." PHR, 458. **Although Poe had found/** Frederick W. Coburn, "Poe as seen by the Brother of 'Annie'," *New England Quarterly,* XVI (Sep 1943), 473–74; Ingram, *Edgar Allan Poe,* 390; PHR, 347. **Despite her promise to write/** Torn: PHR, 346–47. Unwilling: SHW to R. H. Stoddard, als, Providence, 30 Sep 1872, NYPL. **Before leaving Lowell, Poe/** Quotations in this and the next paragraph from LII, 402.

Suicide Attempt; "Conditional" Engagement

By the time he reached/ LII, 401. **Instead of returning/** LII, 401. **As if to curse the one/** Embrace: "In persons with established pathological mourning," according to Vamik D. Volkan, "the longing for reunion with the dead, accompanied by the dread of such a possibility, is constant. Under certain circumstances, however, the dread loses its power, so to speak, and the mourner attempts suicide, which represents magical reunion." *Linking Objects and Linking Phenomena: A Study of the Forms, Symptoms, Metapsychology, and Therapy of Complicated Mourning* (New York, 1981), 123. Laudanum: Alethea Hayter, *Opium and the Romantic Imagination* (London, 1968), 29–30; Shomer S. Zwelling, *Quest for a Cure: The Public Hospital in Williamsburg, Virginia 1773–*

1885 (Williamsburg, 1985), 37. **What happened then and over/** LII, 401.
Poe arrived at Benefit/ Distressed: SHW's version of the visit, as given in
this and the following paragraphs, is drawn from PHR, 347–49, and SHW to
R. H. Stoddard, als, Providence, 30 Sep 1872, NYPL. Ill: LII, 399. Replied:
LII, 531. **Poe kept up his appeal/** Eternity: PHR, 78. Associates: Log, 766.
Poe spent the evening/ BPB, 221. Lock: This large lock of Poe's hair survives at Lilly, assigned, probably in SHW's hand, to "the evening of Nov 8th
1848." MacFarlane: PHR, 348. A "William McFarlane," possibly the same
person, had attended Poe's wedding in Richmond. Log, 207. **Reportedly in
his shirt sleeves/** Sleeves: Charlotte Field Dailey to [J. A.] Harrison, als, [n.
pl.], 26 Nov 1907, Brown University Library. **Surprisingly perhaps, Poe's/**
Unearthliness: Sarah Helen Whitman, *Edgar Poe and his Critics* (1860; rpt. New
York, 1966), 44. Comely: PHR, 76. Equipoise: PHR, 88. **Whatever other
motives encouraged/** *Conditional:* SHW to Mary Hewitt, [n. pl.], 27 Sep
1850, HRC. Wine: PHR, 193. Mother: PHR, 88. **Understandably, neither
Poe nor Helen/** Conflicts: PHR, 78; SHW, letter to Stoddard of 30 Sep.
Imprudent: PHR, 88. **The joyless engagement became/** Phrenzy: PHR, 78;
SHW to Mary Hewitt, als, Providence, 10 Oct 1850, HRC. Favorite: SHW
to Sarah Robins, als, Providence, [n.d.], New York University Library. Arc-
turus: Undated MS version of "Arcturus," WP. **Poe returned to New York/**
LII, 400, 719 n. **However dismally qualified/** Agitation: LII, 403. Muddy:
Harrison, XVII, 391–92. **Two days after returning/** LII, 401–3. **During
the next month/** Formulaic: LII, 405–10. Agony: LII, 406–7. Aristocracy:
LII, 410. **In trying to gain Helen's/** Fiend: LII, 408. Griswold: Elizabeth
Ellet to [Mrs. R. W. Griswold], als, [n. pl., beginning "As the wife of Mr R.
W. Griswold"], [n.d.], Gris. Ellet accused Griswold of using "the most vitu-
perative, foul, and obscene language." She also later told G. W. Eveleth that
Poe was "frequently in the asylum." BPB, 201. **Whatever the truth in Poe's/**
Slandered: LII, 407. Rankle: LII, 408. Dawn: LII, 410. **Poe was taking no
chances/** LII, 405–6. **So far as Poe had any/** Cheer: Harrison, XVII, 391–
92. December: Ingram 52. In the same letter Mrs. Clemm confided her opinion that SHW was "not calculated to make him happy." **Not much, probably,
could/** Confessed: PHR, 154–55; SHW to Mary Hewitt, als, Providence, 10
Oct 1850, HRC. Charm: Whitty, liv. For all the tears she shed on Helen's
hands, too, Osgood later remarked caustically to Griswold that SHW "besieged him with valentines and letters long before he wrote or took any notice
of her." Whitty, lxvii. **The marriage plans moved another/** Papers: MS document [marked "Copy," beginning "To Charles F. Tillinghast Administrator"],
15 Dec 1848, Lilly. Promise: LII, 412. How much time elapsed between Poe's
two visits is problematic. His name appears as a witness on the document of
December 15. But a note that he sent SHW from New York concerning his
next visit, dated only "Saturday," appears to have been written on December
16. Or at least this is the date assigned to it—plausibly, judging from its content—by Ostrom in the *Letters.* Poe often was hazy about dates, and may have
mistakenly written "Saturday" for "Monday." Or he may have actually signed
the document dated December 15 a week later, when he endorsed an adden-
dum specifying his assent to the transfer. But these are at best unsatisfactory
guesses. See LII, 413. **Poe probably thought all/** Hewitt: MS "Extract from

Mrs Hewitt's Letter," New York, 2 Oct 1850, Gris. This remark, as printed in Griswold's "Memoir," generated much acrimonious discussion after Poe's death in the correspondence of both his supporters and detractors, who denied or insisted on his having made it. The evidence is too extensive and complex to be fully evaluated here. Suffice it to say that SHW later told several correspondents that when Mrs. Hewitt asked Poe whether he was going to Providence to be married, he answered, "No—to deliver a lecture before the Providence Lyceum." See, e.g., BPB, 220. But her remarks in a letter to Mrs. Hewitt a year after Poe's death indicate that she herself accepted the story that Poe had said the marriage would never take place. "I, of course, cannot but regret that Mr Poe should have spoken as he did in relation to our marriage," she wrote, "yet when I consider his strange and wayward nature I ought not to be surprised at it" (als, Providence, 4 Oct 1850, HRC). She believed that Poe's feelings had been changed by a poem recently published by Fanny Osgood, in which the speaker chides a "friend" for ignoring her and dividing his love for her with others, "poorer spirits." Poe believed the lines to be addressed to himself, Helen said, and she surmised that they "must have deeply affected him and have revived remembrances which, for the moment, prevailed over every other feeling." Osgood's poem appeared as "Lines from an Unpublished Drama," *American Metropolitan Magazine*, I (Jan 1849), 45. Even on the basis of SHW's acceptance of the story alone, I am inclined to believe that Poe told Mrs. Hewitt something very like "that marriage will never take place." Planned: LII, 412; Log, 778.

Lyceum Lecture; Marriage Announced and Called Off; Repercussions in Lowell

Poe spoke before the Franklin/ Familiar: Log, 778. Audience: Harrison, XVII, 413. **Poe had written little/** Chivers: Richard Beale Davis, ed., *Chivers' Life of Poe* (New York, 1952), 63. Nancy Richmond's niece had heard Poe read during his visit to Lowell the year before, and remarked that he "insisted strongly upon an even metrical flow" and "almost *sang* the more musical versifications." John Henry Ingram, *Edgar Allan Poe: His Life, Letters, and Opinions* (1886; rpt. New York, 1965), 389. Some listeners found Poe's style too sing-song. Noteworthy among Poe's choice of readings was "Tears, idle tears, I know not what they mean," from Tennyson's volume *The Princess*, published in America earlier in the year. Tennyson had had admirers in America since the 1830s, but none so exuberantly enthusiastic as Poe, who appraised the English poet to his listeners in Providence as "the noblest poet that ever lived." Ethereal, elegiac, and musical, Tennyson's earlier poetry epitomized for Poe the ideal of beauty uncorrupted by flesh and passion: "No poet is so little of the earth, earthy." See John Olin Eidson, *Tennyson in America: His Reputation and Influence from 1827 to 1858* (Athens, Georgia, 1943). Tennyson in turn considered Poe "the most original American genius," and reportedly said that the only thing he ever wanted to see in America was Poe's grave. Gerhard J.

Joseph, "Poe and Tennyson," *PMLA,* LXXXVIII (May 1973), 418. **Poe fashioned his lecture/** Wooing: Mary E. Phillips, *Edgar Allan Poe the Man,* II (Chicago, 1926), 1350. Bostonians: Elsewhere in the essay Poe also attacks the *North American Review,* and implicitly New England in general, and accuses them all of forming a cabal to reduce the reputations of poets from the South. This probably reflects the fact that Poe also delivered the talk later in Richmond, where he very likely added to it remarks condemnatory of New England, just as when speaking in Providence he had inserted comments praising New England. The essay was first printed after Poe's death from his manuscript, which may have contained traces of both his Providence and his Richmond presentations. **Poe thought the lecture/** Audience: LII, 413. Cautioned: SHW to J. W. Davidson, draft letters, 1858–78, folder 40, WP. **Helen's consent to the marriage/** Prevailed: SHW to R. H. Stoddard, als, Providence, 30 Sep 1872, NYPL. Document: MS document, [marked "Copy," beginning "To Charles F. Tillinghast Administrator"], 15 Dec 1848, Lilly. **The same night Poe/** Indolent: PHR, 227. For an example of Pabodie's verse, see his MS "The River of Knowledge" at HRC, which praises Knowledge because it lulls to rest low desires and provides tranquillity in the storm of life. Intoxication: Harrison, XVII, 413. **For the rest of this long/** Promising: LII, 413. Pabodie delayed delivering the note, hoping to the last that the marriage might be prevented. **What happened that afternoon/** The account in this and the next three paragraphs based on SHW to Mary Hewitt, als, [n. pl.], 27 Sep 1850, HRC; SHW to R. H. Stoddard, als, Providence, 30 Sep 1872, NYPL; PHR, 144–46. **In the spirit of its many/** Hymenial: Log, 780. Babies: Log, 786. Greeley: Horace Greeley to Rufus Griswold, als, Washington, 21 Jan 1849, Gris. Embark: MS "Extract from Mrs Hewitt's Letter," New York, 2 Oct 1850, Gris. **Nothing had been said/** Fever: SHW to Mary Hewitt, als, Providence, 10 Oct 1850, HRC. Headache: LII, 419. Lightened: SHW to Mary Hewitt, als, [n. pl.], 27 Sep 1850, HRC. Burden: LII, 414. Mrs. Clemm was relieved also. "I feel so happy in *all* my troubles. Eddy is not going to marry Mrs. W." Log, 781. **It was of course to Annie/** Unworldly: LII, 414. Sister: LII, 418–19. See also 414–35 *passim,* 624–26. **Poe could no longer fall/** Sacrifice: LII, 415. Aftershock: BPB, 165–66. **"I felt *deeply* wounded"/** LII, 419–20. **But a second set of rumors/** Malignant: LII, 430–31. Love: BPB, 166. Knew: SHW had apparently set Mrs. Locke on to reading Emerson. Maria Jane McIntosh to SHW, als, New York, 10 Nov 1844, Brown University Library. God: LII, 430–31. **Poe blamed not only the Lockes/** LII, 431. **The situation in Lowell/** LII, 432. **Like much else that Poe/** Corroborative: LII, 435; Nancy Richmond later said that Poe had sent her a "large package" of "Ermina's" letters, which she destroyed after Mrs. Locke's death. BPB, 166. Denounced: BPB, 168. Richmond's comment would seem to refer to this letter from Poe and not to his letter of 18 February, as implied in the Log, 794. My reason for thinking so is that in his letter of 23 March Poe still remarks on Charles Richmond's suspicions of him. He is unlikely to have made such a remark after knowing that Charles had urged Nancy Richmond to invite him and Muddy to Lowell. **If Poe also succeeded/** Unanswered: Writing in 1877, thirty years after the event, Mrs. Richmond claimed that SHW did reply to Poe's request, and in a way that "exonerated him completely." But this seems highly unlikely, given Mrs. Whitman's many statements that she felt unable and unwilling to write to Poe again, and did not do so. See LII, 421 n. Devil: LII, 425. Immediately: LII, 421. Version: PHR, 193. Thus: LII, 421. **Poe's letter contained much/** Dare: PHR, 145, 35. Submit: SHW to Mary Hewitt, als, Providence, 10 Oct 1850, HRC. Song: Text in Ingram 511. Helen later retitled the poem "Stanzas for Music." Secret: Despite her effort to be discreet, however, SHW found unnamed persons supposing the lines to be addressed to Poe, and blaming her for allowing them to be published. See the above letter to Mary Hewitt, 10 Oct 1850. SHW's account in this document differs considerably from her two later accounts of sending the poem, in PHR, 35–36, and in her letter to R. H. Stoddard, Providence, 30 Sep 1872, NYPL. I have chosen the earlier version as being twenty years closer in time to the event, therefore more likely trustworthy. **Helen maintained her silence/** Sorrow: SHW to Mary Hewitt, als, [n. pl.], 27 Sep 1850, HRC. Allusion: PHR, 36. Osgood: SHW to Rufus Griswold, als, Providence, 12 Dec 1849, Historical Society of Pennsylvania. **As the time of their separation/** Log, 795; SHW to Mary Hewitt, als, [n. pl.], 27 Sep 1850, HRC. **Helen put her wrenched/** Sarah Helen Whitman, *Poems* (Boston, 1879), 88, 90.

New Attempts to Resume a Literary Career; "The Bells," "Hop-Frog," and Other Writings

During eight months or so/ Pottsville: Log, 754. The owner, Eli Bowen, was formerly editor of the *Columbia Spy,* for which Poe had written his 1844 newsletters on the "Doings of Gotham." Earned: John Ward Ostrom, "Edgar A. Poe: His Income as Literary Entrepreneur," *Poe Studies,* XV (1982), 6. **Poe had a hard time/** Frogpondium: LII, 354. Thompson: J. R. Thompson to P. P. Cooke, als, Richmond, 17 Oct 1848, HRC. **With his parting from Helen/** Bestir: LII, 416. Health: LII, 428. *Boston:* LII, 426. Graham: LII, 419. *Rich:* LII, 415, 418. Professions: LII, 427. **But there turned out/** Disappointment: LII, 437–38. Borrowing: MS promissory note to Isaac Cooper, 3 Feb 1849, Pierpont Morgan Library. Annuity: Log, 800. **In his renewed drive/** Proposed: LII, 415–16. "Marginalia": Brev, 376, 379, 382. On Poe's plagiarisms, see Pollin's notes to these items. **But not only the pessimism/** Wallace: George Egon Hatvary, *Horace Binney Wallace* (Boston, 1977), 64–98. Meditations: Brev, 391 and n. **The deterioration of Poe's/** Pretty: MS "Lines on being asked for my Autograph," HRC. Crave: Sarah Anna Lewis to Evert Duyckinck, als, Brooklyn, 28 Nov 1854, NYPL. Temptress: Anne Marie Dolan, "The Literary Salon in New York, 1830–1860," Ph.D. diss., Columbia U., 1957, q. 105. **Poe had known Stella/** Whist: BPB, 201. Fordham: Log, 678–79; Ingram 86. Sylvanus: Sylvanus D. Lewis to Sara Rice, als, Brooklyn, 19 Jan 1876, Enoch Pratt Free Library. Fat: Log, 711. **Poe in part repaid/** Coaching: MI, 493–96; Log, 781. Flattery: Ingram 759; LII, 372. Clippings: Sarah Anna Lewis to Sara Rice, als, London, 15 Nov 1877, Enoch Pratt Free Library. Blurbs: T, 662. Thomas: LII, 428. I have omitted the story of Poe's efforts on Mrs. Lewis's behalf with the publisher George P. Putnam, which puts him in an even worse light. It is based on the letters Poe supposedly wrote to her and to Putnam in May 1849, included in L. Mabbott, with good reason I think, considered these letters possible forgeries. **Poe may have badly/** LII, 436. See also LII, 425, 724. **The identity of the woman/** Cried: Unidentified newspaper clipping [headed "Edgar Allan Poe. Some Personal Reminiscences of the Dead Poet"], Material Under Seal, Iowa. The item purports to be recollections of a Rufus E. Shapley, who met Mrs. Clemm in Alexandria in February 1861, and conversed at length with her about Poe. Intended: On the various claims see MI, 468–76. In her letters and papers, SHW often tries to demonstrate that Poe intended the poem for her. Fanny: Buford Jones and Kent Ljungquist, "Poe, Mrs. Osgood, and 'Annabel Lee'," *Studies in the American Renaissance 1983* (Charlottesville, 1983), 275–80. **The prospecting returns with/** Death: That Poe understood the valley as the scriptural Valley of Death seems to me clear from the fact that the knight is guided there by a shade or spirit, and from considering "The Colloquy of Monos and Una," where Una asks about the deceased Monos's "passage through the dark Valley and Shadow." In Poe's "Dream-Land," too, Eldorado represents the kingdom of the dead. **The most literary-seeming/** Poe worked on "The Bells" off and on for more than a year, beginning with the evening at Loui Shew's home that became a blank to him. By her account, he had remarked that he was obliged to write a poem but lacked inspiration. They drank tea near some open windows, through which came the sound of neighborhood church bells. Imitating Poe's style, Mrs. Shew said, she wrote out the title and first line to a poem: "The Bells, by E.A. Poe," beginning "The Bells, the little silver Bells." Poe finished off the stanza. She suggested for the next stanza "The Heavy iron Bells," which he also expanded. BPB, 98–99. Near the end of 1848 he sold "The Bells" as a poem of eighteen lines to the *Union Magazine,* edited by his Philadelphia acquaintance, the engraver John Sartain. Yet he kept revising it, and resubmitted "The Bells" to Sartain twice, each time lengthened and improved. Sartain paid him for each version, too, so that before its October publication Poe seems to have received forty-five dollars for the poem, more than he earned by any other. Sartain, however, gave discrepant accounts of his payments to Poe. Compare John Sartain to Fred M. Hopkins, als, Philadelphia, 17 Mar 1896, Free Library of Philadelphia, with the contradictory account in John Sartain, *The Reminiscences of a Very Old Man 1808–1897* (1899; rpt. New York, 1969), 202–5. Perhaps the one fact that can be asserted with certainty is that Sartain gave Poe an additional payment of fifteen dollars for the poem on 21 Feb 1849. See his MS Expense Book, Historical Society of Pennsylvania. **Something of this rage/** Wolfish: LII, 428. Silhouette: John E. Reilly, "Poe in Pillory: An Early Version of a Satire by A. J. H. Duganne," *Poe Studies,* VI (Jun 1973), 9–12. **In "About Critics and Criticism"/** Task: T, 1040. Handling: Brev, 410. **The particular 'blue' Poe/** Bumpkins: MI, 394. Jews: The evidence on either side is scanty, but Poe always spoke in friendly terms, for instance, of the Jewish lawyer and playwright Mordecai Noah. See Burton R. Pollin, ed., *Edgar Allan Poe: Writings in* The Broadway Journal . . . *Part 2, The Annotations* (New York, 1986), 113. John Allan had dealt with many Jews in Richmond, such as Manuel Judah, Alexander Levy, and Myer Myers, whose names appear frequently in the company's business records. In one instance Allan wrote to his partner Ellis concerning "our old friend M.[oses] Myers the Jew." See JA to Charles Ellis, als, Richmond, 14 Mar 1810, and als to them from him, Norfolk, 3 Oct 1812, CR, #25126. The story that Poe and the actor Junius Brutus Booth, returning from a drinking bout, hung a "little Jew" by his breeches to a spiked railing, is thirdhand, written long after the supposed event, and almost certainly apocryphal. See Ingram 880. Passion: LII, 427–28. **Poe's chance to award/** *Fable:* Log, 762. Failure: T, 819–21.

New Revival of the "Stylus"; Final Trip to Lowell; Journey to Philadelphia

Alone together at Fordham/ LII, 437–38 and n. **Some possible relief arrived/** M. D. McElroy, "Poe's Last Partner: E. H. N. Patterson of Oquawka, Illinois," *Papers on Language & Literature,* VII (Summer 1971), 252–71. **In April, Poe received/** LII, 443. By the terms of Patterson's proposal, Poe would also furnish the matter for the magazine at his own expense. **Poe found several features/** Argued: LII, 440, 443. Oquawka: Ingram 873. **Having collected Poe's works/** This and the next paragraph based on E. H. N. Patterson to Poe, draft letter, [n. pl.], 7 May 1849, Lilly, and LII, 439–41, 433–44. **Poe went to Lowell/** Cudworth: Ingram 513. **Annie's brother Bardwell spent/** Bardwell: Frederick W. Coburn, "Poe as seen by the Brother of 'Annie'," *New England Quarterly,* XVI (Sep 1943), 474–75. Reassure: LII, 448. **Poe apparently arrived/** Check: LII, 447. Daguerreotypes: Michael J. Deas, *The Portraits and Daguerreotypes of Edgar Allan Poe* (Charlottesville, 1988), 47–54. On the color of Poe's eyes see Ingram 163. **Unknown to Poe, his/** Charm: John E. Reilly, *The Image of Poe in American Poetry* (Baltimore, 1976), 10–11. Professedly: LII, 438. **Poe does not seem/** Harrison, XVII, 420; PHR, 349; SHW to J. W. Davidson, draft letter, [n. pl.], [fall] 1858, folder 41, WP. **Poe's trip to Lowell/** Smith: Elizabeth Oakes Smith, "Autobiographic Notes. Edgar Allan Poe," *Beadle's Monthly,* III (Feb 1867), 156. Point: LII, 446–47. Muddy: BPB, 29. **Poe's delay involved more/** Muddy: Log, 811. The authenticity of Clemm's statement has been doubted, because it appeared in a letter by her prefatory to Griswold's edition of Poe's works, and therefore perhaps emended by Griswold. But it receives some corroboration in a statement by C. F. Briggs: "we were told at the time that his mother-in-law . . . had no expectation of ever again seeing him return. He arranged all his papers so that they could be used without difficulty in case of his death, and told her that if he never came back she would find that he had left everything in order." Walker, 331. It is of course possible that Briggs's account of what Poe said to Muddy also came through Griswold. Muddy later wrote to Thomas Holley Chivers, without further explanation: "You ask me why my dear Eddie, chose Griswold as his Executor? He did not." Als, Milford, 13 Dec 1852, Huntington Library. Osgood: Frances Osgood, MS "Power of attorney to Rufus Wilmot Griswold," 10 Mar 1849, Harvard University Library. Griswold also acted as a literary agent for P. P. Cooke, Alice Carey, and others. See, e.g., W. M. Griswold, ed., *Passages from the Correspondence and Other Papers of Rufus W. Griswold* (Cambridge, Mass., 1898), 193, 250. Cholera: Charles E. Rosenberg, *The Cholera Years: The United States in 1832, 1849, and 1866* (Chicago, 1962), 114. **In the lighthouse keeper/** Eliza: See Philip H. Highfill, Jr., et al., eds., *A Biographical Dictionary of Actors . . . in London, 1660–1800,* I (Carbondale, 1973), 121. As remarked in an earlier note, much evidence exists suggesting that Poe had access to accounts of his parents' acting careers. It may be added here that J. H. Whitty told Mary Phillips that he had a theatrical notebook containing such material, which he thought had belonged to Poe. Mary E. Phillips, *Edgar Allan Poe the Man,* I (Chicago, 1926), 60–61. On the identification of Poe with the lighthouse keeper it is suggestive that the keeper has obtained his appointment to the lighthouse from a man named "De Grät"—'Edgar to a T'? **Poe finally left for Richmond/** Delayed: BPB, 29. Favor: LII, 451. Poe added invitingly, too, that "all cost shall be promptly defrayed." The patron was Lewis's husband, Sylvanus, who promised to give Griswold the $2.60 per page it cost to set the new sketch in type—as Griswold never did. See *Passages from the Correspondence,* 253. Compensation: Harrison, XVII, 395. **Muddy saw Poe aboard/** Dejected: BPB, 29. A different account of Poe's departure was given by the Lewises, who said that Poe took the five o'clock train to Philadelphia, Muddy staying over with them and returning to Fordham the next morning. BPB, 199; Sylvanus Lewis to Sara Rice, als, Brooklyn, 11 Oct 1875, HRC. I have chosen Mrs. Clemm's account as probably more reliable; the Lewises later tried to claim a special intimacy with Poe, and in this case portrayed themselves as the last persons to see him before he left New York. In a later, and to my mind still less trustworthy account, Mrs. Lewis said that Poe stayed the night and departed the next morning. BPB, 201. Adored: BPB, 132. Poe may have acquired the trunk later. **Poe probably intended only/** Spasms: LII, 452. Cases: Nicholas B. Wainright, ed., *A Philadelphia Perspective: The Diary of Sidney George Fisher Covering the Years 1834–1871* (Philadelphia, 1967), 224. Suppurate: Rosenberg, 101–75 *passim*. Congestion: LII, 457. **Poe's diagnosis of his/** Deranged: LII, 452, 455. According to modern medical study, about one-fourth of clinical alcoholics experience hallucinations, either visual, auditory, or mixed, often accompanied by paranoid ideas, such as Poe's fears of a conspiracy to kill him. On the other hand, Poe's remark to Mrs. Clemm that he had been deranged for ten days "although I was not drinking one drop," may also have been accurate. The convulsions and much of the other behavior Sartain ascribed to Poe typify severe alcoholic withdrawal as well. See Marc Galanter, ed., *Recent Developments in Alcoholism,* IV (New York, 1986), 290 *et passim*. **Poe spared Muddy/** Sartain: John Sartain, *The Reminiscences of a Very Old Man 1808–1897* (1899; rpt. New York, 1969), 182 *et passim*. See also the autobiographical sketch in John Sartain to William E. Mitchell, als, Philadelphia, 20 Jun 1891, Haverford College Library. The narrative of Poe's stay with Sartain in this and the next five paragraphs is based on three differing accounts: *Reminiscences,* 206–13; Richard Tuerk, "John Sartain and E. A. Poe," *Poe Studies,* IV (Dec 1971), 21–23; and the undated MS, "Poe's Last Visit to

Philad," Historical Society of Pennsylvania. **Poe borrowed some money/** Die: LII, 452. Poe and Maria Clemm may have discussed the idea of a death pact earlier, as is suggested by her lament to Nancy Richmond two months or so before, "God knows I wish we were both in our graves." It seems clear that having failed to find a surrogate for Eliza Poe through marriage to Helen or someone else, Poe had decided to rejoin her through death. Martha Wolfenstein remarked concerning a patient: "when the improbable union with the surrogate father proved unattainable, she felt impelled to rejoin her father in another way—by dying." "Loss, Rage, and Repetition," *Psychoanalytic Study of the Child*, XXIV (1969), 443. Poe's ardent professions of love for Muddy make a strange contrast, however, with his fantasies about her being chopped to pieces. These recall other women in Poe's tales, from the de-toothed Berenice and the beheaded Pauline Dubourg of "Murders in the Rue Morgue" to the ax-butchered wife of "The Black Cat." Into such figures Poe's imagination evidently invested the rage he felt toward his young mother for departing from him, leaving uncontaminated by it his other, split-off picture of women as earthly angels, the Helens, Annies, and Annabel Lees whom he would beatifically serve on his knees. Speaking of children who have been unable to mourn the death of a parent, Wolfenstein commented: "The rage at being abandoned is diverted from the representation of the lost parent, which is hypercathected as though to guard it against being lost. The surviving parent, others in the environment, and the world at large become the targets of this rage" (459). These feelings of hatred seem to have now been focused on Maria Clemm. Dr. Eugene L. Goldberg remarked to me that such a diversion of anger away from the idealized mother accounts for the myriad jokes about mothers-in-law, which Muddy in fact was to Poe. **On July 12, still/** David S. Reynolds, ed., *George Lippard Prophet of Protest: Writings of an American Radical, 1822–1854* (New York, 1986), 262–66. **Lippard went out soliciting/** LII, 455; Reynolds, 262.

Richmond

Poe reached Richmond/ LII, 453–54. The dating of Ostrom #325, a letter fragment, is problematic. I have treated it and #326 as parts of the same letter. Poe sometimes composed a letter over several days, and it seems to me that "Near Richmond" most likely means that he began the letter before he arrived in the city, and completed it after. His final stay in Richmond presents unusually many problems in chronology, and I recognize that my account is necessarily somewhat hazy about the dates and exact succession of events. **But his mother herself/** Terrible: LII, 455. Alive: LII, 453–54. **Muddy had been more/** Harrison, XVII, 393–94. **When Muddy at last received/** BPB, 29. **Assuring him that his mother/** Magic: LII, 455. Deception: BPB, 30. **Feeling more himself again/** Slaves: Charles Lyell, *A Second Visit to the United States of North America*, I (New York, 1849), 208–9. Residence: LI, 45. Talent: "The Living Writers of America. Some Honest Opinions about their Literary Merits, with Occasional Words of Personality," MS, Pierpont Morgan

Library. Gentleman: SHW said that Poe's habitual manner was one of "gentlemanly reticence & amenity." SHW to Eugene L. Didier, als, Providence, 3 Aug 1876, Harvard University Library. Fanny Osgood spoke of his approach to women he respected as "chivalric." Whitty, liv. World: LII, 684. **Poe roomed at the Swan/** Talley: A poet herself, Talley had published in *SLM* and professed admiration for Poe, who in turn predicted that she would "stand at the head of American poetesses." The praise may not have been disinterested, for he also hoped to secure money from her uncle for the "Stylus." See Susan Talley to Poe, als, Richmond, 29 Nov 1848, Gris. Raven: Susan Archer Weiss, *The Home Life of Poe* (New York, 1907), 180. Like others who have written on Poe's life, I consider Mrs. Weiss's several accounts of him highly unreliable. I have used them very sparingly, mostly when corroborated by other sources. A lady at one of Anne Lynch's New York soirees in 1849 claimed that Poe had recited the poem fifty-two times during the year. See John Howard Payne MS Diary, 7 Feb 1849, NYPL. Black: Susan A. T. Weiss, "Last Days of Edgar A. Poe," *Scribner's Monthly*, XV (March 1878), 709. **At the Mackenzies' handsome/** Willis: Log, 709. Wrinkled: Mary E. Phillips, *Edgar Allan Poe the Man*, II (Chicago, 1926), 1593; Ingram 921. Vexed: Weiss, "Last Days," 713. Submitted: Weiss, *Home Life*, 195. Lamp: "E. V. Valentine's Notes," MS, entry for 6 May 1901, VM. **Poe also began seeing/** LII, 457. **Poe got his way/** Patterson: Harrison, XVII, 365–66. Talley: Weiss, "Last Days," 709. **Poe also began his lectures/** Twenty-five: Log, 825. Newspapers: Unidentified newspaper clipping headed "Edgar A. Poe, Esqu.," "Lectures" folder, Box 5, Material Under Seal, Iowa. Lind: Edward V. Valentine to Mary Phillips, als, Richmond, 3 Jul 1915, Boston Public Library. **Standing in "a graceful attitude"/** Spectator: Log, 825. Manuscript: Poe wrote to Lippard from Richmond asking his help in locating the manuscript, but Lippard and Burr were unable to find it. George Lippard to Rufus Griswold, als, Philadelphia, 22 Nov 1849, Gris. Repeated: Weiss, *Home Life*, 199. Reviews: Log, 826–27. Enthusiasm: LII, 458. **Setting about his second/** Shelton: F. Meredith Dietz, "Poe's First and Final Love," *SLM*, V (Mar 1943), 38–47. Estate: Log, 467; see also Ingram 236. **Widowed some five years/** Sprightly: Edward M. Alfriend, "Unpublished Recollections of Edgar Allan Poe," *Literary Era*, VIII (Aug 1901), 489–91 (a not very reliable memoir). Baptised: "Biographical: WOMEN HE KNEW" folder, Poe Collection, VM. Eternity: Elmira Shelton to Philip A. Fitzhugh, als, Millers [illeg], 11 Dec 1848, HRC. It is unclear whether Mrs. Shelton is speaking in this letter of her widowhood generally, or of some specific recent event. **On a Sunday, probably/** Hesitated: Ingram 261. Rose: Ingram 921 and Weiss, *Home Life*, 194–95. Affectionately: Ingram 263; Log, 840; Alfriend, 490; MI, 474. **By the end of August/** Fascinating: Ingram 261. Jealousy: Log, 840. Remark: Ingram 261. Protest: Dietz, 40. **For Poe too, Elmira/** Cemetery: Poe's boyhood friend Ebenezer Burling was also buried there. See "Poe, Elmira and the Shelton House," TS, VM. Loyalty: Charles Chauncey Burr, the liberal clergyman who aided Poe in Philadelphia, reported that Poe said he accepted the "idea of a second wife," a replacement for Virginia, *only* for Muddy's sake. [Francis Gerry Fairfield], "A Mad Man of Letters," *Scribner's Monthly*, X (Oct 1875), 693. Executrix: Log, 839. Arrangement: SHW to W. F. Gill [in the hand of Charlotte Field Dailey], als, Providence, 5 Mar [no year], folder 56, WP. This information clearly comes from now-lost portions of the fragmentary letters on 4 Aug and 10 Sep 1849, at the New York University Library. **As marriage to Elmira/** Drank: Weiss, "Last Days," 712; Ingram 683. Temperance: Log, 829–30. **Having heard from Poe/** Maria Clemm to Rufus Griswold, als, New York, 27 Aug 1849, HRC; BPB, 29, 31. **When Muddy at last heard/** Clouds: BPB, 33. Spoilt: This and the quotations in the next two paragraphs from LII, 458–59.

Old Point Comfort, Norfolk, Richmond; Death and Burial in Baltimore

Poe spent nearly four/ Madison: Log, 831. Fortress: C. B. Dana to Elias Loomis, als, Baltimore, 6 Jan 1834, Yale University Library; *DeBow's Review,* I (Aug and Oct 1858), 246–47, 484–85. Ingram: [Susan V. C. Ingram], "Was a Friend of Poe," *New York Herald,* 19 Feb 1905. Bidding: LII, 460. **From Point Comfort, Poe/** Poe to Maria Clemm, als, Old Point Comfort, 10 Sep 1849, New York University Library. **Poe's lecture at the Norfolk/** Exquisite: Log, 836. Madison: LII, 461. **The trip out of Richmond/** Severe: BPB, 32. Answered: LII, 461. **Concerned as ever that/** Elmira Shelton to Maria Clemm, als, Richmond, 22 Sep 1849, Enoch Pratt Free Library. **Some literary business called/** Loud: LII, 458, 461. After Poe's death *The International* noted that the volume, entitled *Wayside Flowers,* was in press, and observed that "The late Mr. Poe was accustomed to praise her works very highly, and was to have edited this edition of them" (1 Sep 1850), 265. Thompson: John R. Thompson, *The Genius and Character of Edgar Allan Poe* ([Richmond], 1929), 23–25, 41. Anxious: LII, 458. Thompson had some insight into Poe's mood and situation, for in later remarking on Poe's quarrelsomeness as a critic he compared him to the engraver of the Middle Ages whose motto was, I keep on engraving that I may not hang myself. Poe, Thompson speculated, needed to exchange blows with others "that he might not turn upon his own consciousness" (15). "Annabel": MI, 476. Advanced: John R. Thompson to E. H. N. Patterson, als, Richmond, 9 Nov 1849, Pierpont Morgan Library. **Thompson may also have paid/** Portrait: Thomas H. Ellis to J. H. Whitty, als, Richmond, 4 Apr 1896, HRC. By another account, it was the daguerreotypist himself, William Pratt, who initiated the portrait. Thomas Dimmock, "Notes on Poe," *Century Magazine,* XXVIII (Jun 1895), 315–16. Buttonhole: Mary E. Phillips, *Edgar Allan Poe the Man,* II (Chicago, 1926), 1593. **On September 24/** Conspicuously: Susan Archer Weiss, *Home Life of Poe* (New York, 1907), 200. *Times: Daily Richmond Times,* 26 Sep 1849, typed transcript, J. H. Whitty Papers, PL. **On September 26/** Buoyant: John R. Thompson to Rufus Griswold, als, Richmond, 10 Oct 1849, Historical Society of Pennsylvania. Sad: Phillips, II, 1489. Married: Ingram 237. Understanding: Ingram 263. In this report of his interview with Mrs. Shelton in 1875, Edward V. Valentine also records her saying, in flat contradiction of her earlier remarks to Maria Clemm, that Poe when he left "was in perfect health and appeared to be perfectly well." Again I have preferred the (considerably) earlier account, which has in addition the virtue of coming from Mrs. Shelton herself, not through Edward Valentine. Entreated: "E[dward] V V[alentine]'s Conversation with Mrs. Shelton [19 Nov 1875]," MS notes, VM. Carter: Susan A. T. Weiss, "Last Days of Edgar A. Poe," *Scribner's Monthly,* XV (March 1878), 714, and *Home Life,* 203–4; Log, 843. The copy of Moore is now at HRC, with a note by Carter attesting that Poe left it at his office. **It was Election Day/** Walker: Ingram 64. Weather: "The Weather," Baltimore *Daily Argus,* 3 Oct 1849. **When Snodgrass arrived/** Log, 844–45; see also J. E. Snodgrass, "The Facts of Poe's Death and Burial," *Beadle's Monthly,* III (Mar 1867), 283–87. **Through the chilly wet/** Streets: Ingram 539. Moran: W. T. Bandy, "Dr. Moran and the Poe–Reynolds Myth," in Benjamin Franklin Fisher IV, *Myths and Reality: The Mysterious Mr. Poe* (Baltimore, 1987), 26–36. Only a few days after Poe entered the hospital, its name was officially changed to the Baltimore City and Marine Hospital. Patient: J. J. Moran to Maria Clemm, als, Baltimore City & Marine Hospital, 15 Nov 1849, Enoch Pratt Free Library. As with the sudden deaths of other national celebrities like Abraham Lincoln and John F. Kennedy, wild stories about Poe's last days proliferated for decades after. Unfortunately, the person best situated to know the truth, Dr. J. J. Moran, himself stimulated the process. In later life he became a Poe collector and investigator who joined the crusade to rescue Poe's reputation from Griswold's aspersions. Bidding for attention as someone who could set the record straight, and also clearly hoping to make some money, he produced a succession of increasingly absurd accounts of Poe's last days, climaxed by a lengthy monograph, *A Defense of Edgar Allan Poe* (Washington, 1885). I follow Poe's earlier biographers in ignoring these later accounts as self-interested, often preposterous, and virtually worthless as biographical evidence. For that reason, the recounting of Poe's death in the following paragraphs relies almost entirely on Moran's November 1849 letter to Maria Clemm. **According to Moran/** Wife: For the remarks of Mrs. Moran see Phillips, II, 1510. Neilson: J. J. Moran to Clarence H. Urner, als, Falls Church, 3 Jan 1878, New York University Library; Neilson Poe to Maria Clemm, als, Baltimore, 11 Oct 1849, Enoch Pratt Free Library. Whig: On Neilson Poe's political involvements see, e.g., his two letters to Thurlow Weed, New York, 31 Mar 1840 (Historical Society of Pennsylvania) and Baltimore, 19 Dec 1860 (University of Rochester Library). Dog: LI, 120. **Then Poe seemed to doze/** Uncle-in-law: A visit from Henry Herring would probably have been no more welcome to Poe than one from his cousin Neilson. As a twenty-year-old living in Baltimore, Poe had written two acrostic poems on the name of Herring's daughter Elizabeth, his cousin, but he had also described her father as "a man of unprincipled character." LI, 67. On the visit of one of Herring's daughters—which one is uncertain—see Ingram 821. On the name-calling episode see the convincing article by Bandy, above. **The cause of Poe's/** Disputed: For one of Moran's many denials see J. J. Moran to Charles Marseilles, als, Falls Church, 24 Jun 1885, NYPL. Congestion: Log, 851. Inflammation: Phillips, II, 1508. Euphemistically: See, e.g., W. M. Griswold, ed., *Passages from the Correspondence and Other Papers of Rufus W. Griswold* (Cambridge, Mass., 1898), 230. Encephalitis: Moran, *A Defense,* 71. Explanations: See also Birgit Bramsbäck, "The Final Illness and

Death of Edgar Allan Poe: An Attempt at Reassessment," *Studia Neophilolo-gica*, XLII (1970), 40–59. Baudelaire: Lois and Francis E. Hyslop, Jr., eds., *Baudelaire on Poe* (State College, 1952), 101. In fact to many in Poe's time who had known or read much about him, his death did not come as a surprise. "For some years past he has been more or less ill," one New York newspaper reported, "and the announcement of his death is not unexpected." Walker, 302. **Dr. Moran seems to have/** Letters: Eugene L. Didier to SHW, als, Baltimore, 26 Jun 1876, Lilly. Books: Neilson Poe to Rufus Griswold, als, Baltimore, 1 Nov 1849, NYPL. Hotel: J. J. Moran, letter to Clarence H. Urner. Miniature: BPB, 99. Clemm: Ingram 390. Shroud: Phillips, II, 1510. Hands: Ingram 631. Locks: W. T. D. Clemm to Chevalier Reynolds, als, Govanstown, 15 Jun 1893, NYPL. Corpse: J. J. Moran, letter to Maria Clemm. **With no display and little/** The account of Poe's funeral is based on several sources: Neilson Poe, letter to Maria Clemm; Snodgrass, "Facts of Poe's Death," 285; "The Poe Family of Maryland," TS, James Southall Wilson Poe Collection, University of Virginia Library; George P. Clark, "Two Unnoticed Recollections of Poe's Funeral," *Poe Studies*, III (Jun 1970), 1–2; Log, 848–49.

Muddy

The news of Poe's/ Oregon: Herbert E. Arntson, "A Western Obituary of Poe," *Poe Newsletter,* I (Apr 1968), 24–25. **Having expected that Poe/** Neilson: Maria Clemm to Neilson Poe, als, New York, 9 Oct 1845 [misdated for 1849], Enoch Pratt Free Library. Willis: Walker, 312. Annie: Log, 850. **Muddy's hunger for the details/** Neilson: Neilson Poe to Maria Clemm, als, Baltimore, 11 Oct 1849, Enoch Pratt Free Library. Sources: MS "Statements of Mrs. Maria Clemm. Noted in short-hand by E. L. D.[idier]," Harvard University Library. J. E. Snodgrass later gave it as his firm opinion, however, that Poe had not been beaten. See "The Facts of Poe's Death and Burial," *Beadle's Monthly,* III (Mar 1867), 283–87. **Immediately after receiving certain/** Hirst: Maria Clemm to Henry B. Hirst, als, New York, 23 Oct 1849, Pierpont Morgan Library. Lowell: Arthur H. Quinn, ed., *Edgar Allan Poe: Letters and Documents in the Enoch Pratt Free Library* (New York, 1941), 55–56. Catterina: BPB, 138. **Muddy remained in Lowell/** More: The length of Mrs. Clemm's stay can be documented from letters extending from 1 Nov 1849 to 17 Feb 1851. She may well have stayed longer. Friends: Maria Clemm to Evert Duyckinck, als, Lowell, 25 Jan 1850, NYPL. Maine: Maria Clemm to John Neal, als, Lowell, 8 May 1850, Free Library of Philadelphia. Longfellow: Frederick W. Coburn, "Poe as seen by the Brother of 'Annie'," *New England Quarterly,* XVI (Sep 1943), 475; Maria Clemm to Neilson Poe, als, Lowell, 1 Nov 1849, Enoch Pratt Free Library. **Yet at least some/** Ill: Maria Clemm to Marie Louise Shew, als, Lowell, 27 Jan 1850, Huntington Library. Happy: Maria Clemm to Evert Duyckinck, als, Lowell, 25 Jan 1850, NYPL. Angels: Maria Clemm to Neilson Poe, als, Lowell, 1 Nov 1849, Enoch Pratt Free Library. **Muddy even found herself/** Attorney: Rufus Griswold to John R. Thompson, als, New York, 25 Oct 1849, Lilly. Claiming: John R. Thompson to Rufus Griswold, als, Richmond, 3 Nov 1849, Historical Society of Pennsylvania; Rosalie Poe to Rufus Griswold, als, Richmond, 20 Aug 1850, Free Library of Philadelphia. Indignation: Maria Clemm to Neilson Poe, als, Lowell, 1 Nov 1849, Enoch Pratt Free Library. **But Muddy gained little/** Trunk: Maria Clemm to [J. J. Moran], als, Lowell, 2 Mar 1850, Free Library of Philadelphia; Maria Clemm to Rufus Griswold, als, Lowell, 29 Apr 1850, Gris; BPB, 156. The trunk arrived too late, however, for Poe's manuscripts and revisions to be included in the first two volumes of Griswold's edition of his work. Publishers: See, e.g., Maria Clemm to [unaddressed, beginning "It has been suggested"], als, Lowell, 2 Dec 1850, Free Library of Philadelphia. Rate: Mary E. Phillips, *Edgar Allan Poe the Man,* II (Chicago, 1926), 1558. Eveleth: Ingram 72. **In a different way/** Hastily: Rufus Griswold to John R. Thompson, als, New York, 25 Oct 1849, Lilly; W. M. Griswold, ed., *Passages from the Correspondence and Other Papers of Rufus W. Griswold* (Cambridge, Mass., 1898), 252–53. Scabrous: Rufus Griswold to William J. Pabodie, photostat, New York, 8 Jun 1852, NYPL. **In Lowell, Muddy was prostrated/** Confined: Maria Clemm to Thomas Holley Chivers, als, Milford, 8 Dec 1852, Huntington Library. Feebly: Ingram 75. Despondent: Maria Clemm to Marie Louise Shew, als, Lowell, 23 Sep 1850, Huntington Library. **Rufus Griswold had many/** Spirit: BPB, 214. Unpunished: Joy Bayless, *Rufus Wilmot Griswold: Poe's Literary Executor* (Nashville, 1943), 158, 221–27. Unrecognizable: PHR, 213–14. Friends: W. M. Griswold to Bayard Taylor, als, Paris, 25 Apr [no year], Cornell University Library. Portraits: Bayless, 252. **Muddy had no reason/** Charities: Rosalie Poe to R. H. Stoddard, als, Oakland, 29 [no month] 1873, NYPL. Fits: Flora Mackenzie to J. H. Whitty, als, Danville, 12 May 1914, HRC. Objectionable: BPB, 58–60. Postcard: Susan Archer Weiss, *The Home Life of Poe* (New York, 1907), 214; PHR, 159. Signature: See, e.g., Rosalie Poe to R. H. Stoddard, als, Oakland, 9 May [1873], NYPL. Rewarded: Rosalie Poe to [unaddressed, beginning "My dear Kind friend"], [7?] Jun [1873?], Harvard University Library. **At the age of sixty-four/** Shelter: BPB, 60–63. Unconscious: "Poe's Unhappy Sister," Baltimore *Sun,* 29 Oct 1905. A Washington newspaper gave the cause of Rose Poe's death as "a violent attack of congestive chills." Ingram 583. Receptacle: Margaret Stone to Martha Mackenzie, als, Washington, 22 Jul 1874, HRC. **The Richmonds treated Muddy/** White-haired: Gabriel Harrison, "Edgar A. Poe. Reminiscences of Gabriel Harrison, an Actor, Still Living in Brooklyn," *New York Times-Saturday Review,* 4 Mar 1899, 144. Desolate: Ingram 74. Willis: "Death of Edgar Poe," *Home Journal,* 20 Oct 1849; Ingram 526; "Tribute to Edgar Poe," *Home Journal,* 8 Oct 1864. Begged: See, e.g., John R. Thompson to Rufus Griswold, als, Richmond, 11 Nov 1849, Historical Society of Pennsylvania; Maria Clemm to Thomas Holley Chivers, als, Milford, 8 Dec 1852, Huntington Library; Maria Clemm to Bayard Taylor, als, Lowell, 20 May 1850, Cornell University Library; Maria Clemm to Evert Duyckinck, als, Lowell, 25 Jan 1850, NYPL. **During the first year/** Lowell: Maria Clemm to Marie Louise Shew, 3 Mar 1852, Huntington Library; Maria Clemm to SHW, als, Lowell, 6 May 1852, Lilly. Strongs: Maria Clemm to Marie Louise Shew, als, Lowell, 27 Jan 1850, Huntington Library. Louisiana: Maria Clemm to Thomas Holley Chivers, als, Milford, 13 Dec 1852, Huntington Library. Tennyson: Gerhard J. Joseph, "Poe and Tennyson," *PMLA,*

LXXXVIII (May 1973), q. 427, n. 6. There is no evidence that Tennyson complied, but Mrs. Clemm wrote for a dole to Dickens as well, who is said to have sent her some money. **Muddy's sojourns strained/** Haste: BPB, 105. Letters: BPB, 137; PHR, 161. Destroyed: BPB, 50–51. Stella: Sarah Anna Lewis to Sara Rice, als, London, 15 Nov 1877, Enoch Pratt Free Library; R. H. Stoddard to R. Shelton Mackenzie, als, New York, 5 Sep 1872, Historical Society of Pennsylvania. Confidences: BPB, 160. Superiority: Ingram 79. October: Quinn, 61. Legally: Phillips, II, 1294. **Several times Muddy slyly/** Louisiana: Ingram 76. Pabodie: Maria Clemm to SHW, als, Lowell, 6 May 1852, Lilly. Suicide: PHR, 115. Sickness: SHW to Maria Clemm, als, Providence, 2 Jun [1852], Huntington Library. **Helen was anyway engrossed/** Noises: New York *Tribune,* 26 Mar 1851. I am grateful to Professor Burton Pollin for pointing out this article to me. Channeled: SHW to Mary Hewitt, als, Providence, 4 Dec 1850, HRC. Gould: John Grier Varner, "Sarah Helen Whitman: Seeress of Providence," Ph.D. diss., U. of Virginia, 1940, 391–93. Lines: Varner, q. 740. Embalmed: Eric W. Carlson, ed., *The Recognition of Edgar Allan Poe* (Ann Arbor, 1970), 72. At her death in 1878, SHW left the bulk of her estate to pay for the publication of a volume of poems by herself and/or her mentally fragile sister, and to the Providence Association for the Benefit of Colored Children and the Rhode Island Society for the Prevention of Cruelty to Animals. Will of SHW, 23 Jul 1878, folder 24, WP. **Wandering, spending time/** Taught: Maria Clemm to SHW, als, Alexandria, 17 Mar 1860, Lilly. Cough: Maria Clemm to Neilson Poe, als, Alexandria, 5 Apr 1860, Enoch Pratt Free Library; Ingram 94. **While in Alexandria Muddy/** Warrant: Maria Clemm to Neilson Poe, als, Alexandria, 5 Apr 1860, 19 Feb 1861, Enoch Pratt Free Library. That Mrs. Clemm managed to sell the warrant is suggested by the several references to "my fortune" in her later letters to Neilson. Birthday: Maria Clemm to SHW, als, Alexandria, 17 Mar 1860, Lilly. **Around May 1861, Muddy/** Timing: Maria Clemm to Evert Duyckinck, als, Baltimore, 7 May 1863, NYPL. Europe: Maria Clemm to Neilson Poe, als, Alexandria, 5 Apr 1860, Enoch Pratt Free Library. Insane: Caroline Ticknor, *Poe's Helen* (New York, 1916), q. 168; BPB, 54. **In the spring of 1863/** Home: Maria Clemm to Evert Duyckinck, als, Baltimore, 7 May 1863, NYPL. Favors: Maria Clemm to Neilson Poe, als, Baltimore, 9 Jan 1871 and 19 Oct 1870, Enoch Pratt Free Library. Confined: Maria Clemm to [unidentified], als, Baltimore, 28 Sep 1865, HRC. **The Church Home had/** Picture: MS "Statements of Mrs. Maria Clemm. Noted in short-hand by E. L. D.[idier]," Harvard University Library. Died: Delman-Heyward Files, Maryland Historical Society. Funeral: Ingram 174. **Muddy had of course/** This and the final paragraph based on Maria Clemm to Nancy Richmond, als, Alexandria, 25 Feb 1859, HRC.

APPENDICES

Summary of *The Narrative of Arthur Gordon Pym. Of Nantucket.*

The novella opens with a *trompe l'oeil* preface that ascribes the narrative to A. G. Pym. Pym explains that after his recent return from the South Seas he was urged to write an account of his adventures by "several gentlemen in Richmond," among them "Mr. Poe, lately editor of the Southern Literary Messenger, a monthly magazine, published by Mr. Thomas W. White." He declined, however, in part fearing that his experiences had been too incredible to be believed. Poe suggested that Pym allow him to draw up a narrative of his earlier adventures for the *Messenger,* publishing it as fiction. Pym consented, but stipulated that Poe's name should be affixed to the work so that this "pretended fiction" would be "certainly . . . regarded as fiction." When it turned out that Poe's factual-sounding-fiction was received as factual, he began thinking he had little to fear from "popular incredulity" and felt encouraged to write a narrative of the actual events. This he now presents, he says, however retaining some of Poe's narrative.

The hair-raising adventures at sea begin when, after a night of drinking, Pym and his friend Augustus Barnard, about sixteen and eighteen years old, go out in Pym's sailboat, *Ariel,* which is smashed by a whaling ship during a storm. Far from cooling Pym's eagerness for wild sea adventures, the nearly fatal mishap makes him more than ever anxious to have them. About eighteen months later, he stows away in a crate in the hold of the *Grampus,* an old whaler commanded by Augustus's father. The plan is for Augustus, cabined above, to supply him food and drink until the voyage is under weigh, when Pym can make his presence known. But Augustus fails to appear; Pym nearly dies of hunger and suffocation, and is nearly eaten by his thirst-crazed dog.

When at last released, Pym discovers that a mutiny has occurred, with the butchery of twenty-two crew members and the setting-adrift of Captain Barnard. The mutineers are restrained only by one of their own number, the grotesque half-Indian Dirk Peters, a "hybrid line-manager" no taller than four-foot-eight but enormously strong—as well as bow-legged, possibly insane, and bald, a condition he conceals by wearing toupees of whatever hairlike material comes to hand, "occasionally the skin of a Spanish dog or American grizzly bear." As a division develops among the mutineers, Peters asks Pym and Augustus to join him in opposing the faction that wishes to turn to piracy. During a storm they overpower this group, frightening them to death, bashing in their brains, or turning Pym's dog on their throats, throwing the bodies overboard. But the tremendous seas also inundate the ship, submerging its provisions. Deranged by lack of food and drink, they draw straws to determine who shall be cannibalized to keep the others alive. The choice falls on a sailor named Parker, whose hands, feet, head, and entrails they throw into the sea, drinking his blood and consuming the rest of the body piecemeal over "four ever memorable days."

After surviving another few weeks on hard-won bits of nourishment and witnessing the decay of Augustus into a "mass of putrefaction," Pym and Peters are picked up by the schooner *Jane Guy,* bound with a crew of thirty-five on a sealing and trading voyage. The ship moves through ever stranger territory toward the Antarctic, bypassing at first albatrosses, penguins, and icebergs, then scarlet creatures with ratlike tails and scarlet teeth. On January 19, anchoring off some large islands, the *Jane Guy* is greeted by four canoes of natives, wielding clubs and bellowing *Anamoo-moo!* The complexion of the Tsalalians, as the natives are called, is "jet-black," as are their teeth, and they wear the skins of some black animal, the bottoms of their canoes full of black stones. The kindness they at first show to their visitors is feigned. Eventually they overrun the ship and massacre its crew. Peters and Pym escape to a hill on Tsalal, surviving a few weeks on filberts and a kind of bittern with jet black plumage. From their perch they watch the natives set fire to the *Jane Guy,* which explodes, killing perhaps a thousand natives and provoking the survivors to rush about the beach shouting *Tekeli-li!*

In trying to flee the island, Pym and Peters make their way to a canyon of black granite, on whose walls appear indentations resembling characters of an alphabet. After a harrowing descent from a precipice by means of a rope of pocket handkerchiefs, they reach the coast and, pursued by the natives, push off in a leaky canoe into the Antarctic Ocean. They enter a "region of novelty and wonder," a realm of ever warmer milky water beneath an ever falling mist of white ash, driven with "hideous velocity" by soundless winds toward a horizon that seems a gigantic silent curtain. Above them huge white birds scream *Tekeli-li!* As an ocean chasm opens to receive them there also appears a large, mysteriously shrouded figure, "very far larger in its proportions than any dweller among men. And the hue of the skin of the figure was of the perfect whiteness of the snow."

APPENDIX 2:
Summary of *"The Fall of the House of Usher"*

The unnamed narrator has been summoned by a "wildly importunate" note from his melancholic boyhood friend Roderick Usher. He finds a gloomy decaying mansion overspread with fungi, enveloped in a sort of swamp gas, fractured from roof to foundation by a zigzagging "barely perceptible fissure." Trembling and cadaverous, Usher fears that in his pitiably unnerved state any disturbing incident will overwhelm him. He attributes his condition to both the strange influence of the decaying house and the approaching death of his last and only relative, his beloved twin sister Madeline. The narrator futilely tries to distract Usher by painting, reading, and listening to music with him. But one evening Usher abruptly announces Madeline's death. Wishing to preserve her corpse for a fortnight before burial, he asks the narrator's help in bearing her coffin to a vault beneath the house, formerly a dungeon.

In the following days Roderick seems to drift from agitation into madness. The narrator, his own nerves fraying, starts from sleep one night, seeming to hear beneath the noise of a storm raging outside certain other sounds, low and indefinite. Usher too has awakened, in a state of "evidently restrained hysteria." To quiet him, the narrator reads aloud the story of the "Mad Trist," in which the knight Ethelred slays a dragon. The events in the story seem to spring to life around them; at the moment when the narrator reads of an enchanted shield clanging on the silver floor, at Ethelred's feet, they also hear within the house of Usher itself a "distinct, hollow, metallic, and clangorous, yet apparently muffled reverberation." The doors open their "ebony jaws" to reveal Usher's sister, who has been placed living in her tomb, "the lofty and enshrouded figure of the lady Madeline. . . . blood upon her white robes, and the evidence of some bitter struggle upon every portion of her emaciated frame." The figure reels on the threshold, then with a moan falls heavily upon her brother, killing him in her thrashing death agonies. As the narrator flees the house he sees its zigzag fissure widen and burst under the force of the storm, hearing the collapse and submergence, with a "long tumultuous shouting sound," of the house of Usher.

APPENDIX 3:
Summary of *"William Wilson"*

The protagonist (and storyteller) only assumes the name William Wilson to disguise his identity, years of idleness and "unpardonable crime" having made him an outcast. He traces his infamy to an excitable disposition inherited from his family, and unrestrained by parental guidance. While a schoolboy in England, he finds that one of his classmates is also named William Wilson, although unrelated to him. More than that, his rival shares his height, his features, and even his birthday. The copy angers him, but worse are the second Wilson's attempts to supervise and advise him, always, however, in a whisper, the echo of his own. The second Wilson reappears to cross his will at climactic moments of dissipation and profligacy in his later life: whispering his name as he is about to deliver a profane toast at Eton, exposing him as a card cheat during a game of *écarté* at Oxford, pursuing him to Naples, Vienna, Berlin, Moscow. At a masquerade during carnival in Rome, he is about to seduce the young wife of an aged duke when he feels a hand on his shoulder, "and that ever-remembered, low, damnable whisper within my ear." Enraged, he draws his sword and runs it through the other Wilson repeatedly. In a dazzling transposition of perspectives, the two seem to change but also not change places. No longer whispering, Wilson tells him in a voice he recognizes as his own that the person he has murdered is himself.

APPENDIX 4:
Summary of *"The Murders in the Rue Morgue"*

An unnamed narrator introduces the reader to C. Auguste Dupin. Descended from an "illustrious family," this gloomy, vastly read, and altogether memorable character lives off the little remnant of a patrimony whose loss, through "untoward events," has made him lethargic and withdrawn. But his distinguishing trait is a "peculiar analytic ability"; he boasts that, to him, most men wear "windows in their bosoms." He and the narrator live together behind closed shutters in a "time-eaten and grotesque mansion" in Paris, existing "within ourselves alone." One day they read a newspaper account of a brutal murder: a Madame L'Espanaye has been beheaded by a straight razor, and her daughter's seemingly strangled corpse has been thrust head downward up the chimney. The police have arrested a suspect but are baffled: the bodies have been found in a locked room, and the accounts of witnesses who were standing outside the apartment when the murder took place differ greatly, particularly concerning the languages spoken by the murderer and the victims. Dupin, scornful of police methods, visits the scene of the crime himself. Then he places an ad in a newspaper addressed—to the narrator's and the reader's amazement—to a sailor from a *"Maltese vessel"* who owns *"a very large, tawny Ourang-Outang of the Bornese species."* In a suspenseful confrontation with the sailor, Dupin, gun ready, reveals the orangutan to have been the murderer.

APPENDIX 5:
Summary of *"Mesmeric Revelation"*

Poe himself summarized the main ideas of "Mesmeric Revelation" in a letter to Chivers on July 10, 1844:

There is no such thing as spirituality. God is material. All things are material; yet the matter of God has all the qualities which we attribute to spirit: thus the difference is scarcely more than of words. There is a matter without particles—of no atomic composition: this is God. It permeates and impels all things, and thus *is* all things in itself. Its agitation is the thought of God, and creates. Man and other beings (inhabitants of stars) are portions of this unparticled matter, individualized by being incorporated in the ordinary or particled matter. Thus they exist rudimentally. Death is the painful metamorphosis. The worm becomes the butterfly—but the butterfly is still material—of a matter, however, which cannot be recognized by our rudimental organs. But for the necessity of the rudimental life, there would have been no stars—no worlds—nothing which we term material. These spots are the residences of the rudimental things. At death, these, taking a n[e]w form, of a n[o]vel matter, pass every where, and act all things, by mere volition, and are cognizant of all secrets but *the one*—the nature of the volition of God—of the agitation of the unparticled matter.

As in this concise account, Poe began his dialogue by posing a version of philosophical materialism. The universe consists of "unparticled" matter, infinitely fine and incapable of division. The sum of this unparticled matter, the whole of things, is God. Only in its sum, however, can the unparticled matter be conceived as matter; considered from the point of view of its utterly rarefied ethereality, such matter inevitably glides into what we conceive as spirit. In all, God is matter; in constituent part, spirit: "God, with all the powers attributed to spirit, is but the perfection of matter." God creates by thinking some portion of himself, of unparticled matter, into "particled" matter, combinations of the ethereal substance which appear in familiar forms such as planets or trees. Poe acknowledged difficulties here in understanding the whole of unparticled matter as mind; it is capable of act and volition rather as the merely physical brain is capable of thought. What counts is the notion that the self is not matter endowed with a soul, but rather a piece of the universe rearranging itself, an incarnate portion of the divine mind (unparticled matter).

God does not create casually; what he creates he means to stay created. Once individualized as particled matter, human beings can never divest themselves of their corporeal nature, for they would become God. Rather, every self has two bodies, "the rudimental and the complete," worm and butterfly. Death is the "painful metamorphosis" between these forms. Poe invoked a theory of knowledge to explain both why the first self remains ignorant of the second, and the manner of existence of the "complete" self, the self after death. Human organs of perception are adapted to the human condition. Every creature's sensory organs are suited to perceiving the planetary environment in which it finds itself (Poe believed that other planets were inhabited). In this decidedly eighteenth-century turn of thought, the reverse is true also; the physical environment exists for the purpose of being perceived by creaturely sensory organs: nebulae, planets, suns, and other bodies exist "for the sole purpose of supplying *pabulum* for the idiosyncrasy of the organs of an infinity of rudimental beings."

Because organs vary according to the features of the place inhabited, and vice versa, what we call substance is really only a "sentiment." Organs of creatures in one place are adapted to see substance where organs of creatures from another place would not: "There are many things on the Earth, which would be nihility to the inhabitants of Venus." By contrast, Poe conceives the self after death, the "complete" self, as "unorganized," that is, lacking in sensory organs altogether. This self is, rather, "entire brain." The external world does not reach it through one or several of its organs, but rather reaches "the whole body," making visible to it all things but the nature and will of the Divine.

APPENDIX 6:
Note on *"The Raven"*

Poe probably wrote the poem at the Brennan farm, although he may have had the idea in mind, and even attempted versions of it, a year or more earlier. He probably first tried, unsuccessfully, to sell the poem to Graham, then sold it for around fifteen dollars to a new five-dollar monthly entitled the *American Review: A Whig Journal.*[1] It was slated to appear in the second number of this magazine, for February 1845, under the name "Quarles," a continuation of Poe's practice of sometimes taking over the names of other poets, in this case the English religious poet and emblem writer Francis Quarles. In fact "The Raven" was first printed in the *Review,* but the magazine did not appear for circulation until after the poem was published in the *Mirror,* with the *Review's* consent and under Poe's own name.

Inevitably, despite the poem's considerable originality, many of its main features echo other poems. Coleridge had written a poem entitled "The Raven." *Nevermore* and the words *never more* were common in English and Continental poetry. Examples range from the *Nimmermehr* of Margaret's song in *Faust,* to the refrain of Shelley's "A Lament" ("No more—Oh, never more!"), to such American adaptations of Shelley as "When the Night Wind Bewaileth," verses published in 1843 by Poe's acquaintance Epes Sargent, containing such lines as "the lost one, whose beauty / I used to adore, / To my heart seems to murmur— / No more—never more! / Oh! never more!"[2] The stanzaic pattern, as Poe intimated later, owes much to Elizabeth Barrett's "Lady Geraldine's Courtship" (1844):

> *With a rushing stir, uncertain, in the air, the purple curtain*
> *Swelleth in and swelleth out around her motionless pale brows;*
> *While the gliding of the river sends a rippling noise forever*
> *Through the open casement whitened by the moonlight's slant repose.*

(The first line is especially close to line 13 of "The Raven," "the silken, sad, uncertain rustling of each purple curtain.")[3] Poe drew on himself as well. The student in the poem is far from the only character in his work who solitarily reads rare books in a plushly furnished room. And *raven* was a popular word in the period, often used to describe the hair of heroines; Poe himself used it and its devouring form *ravenous* in "Ligeia," "The Pit and the Pendulum," and other tales.

---

[1] James Russell Lowell to Poe, als, Cambridge, 12 Dec 1844, HRC. For a general discussion of the poem's history and sources see MI.
[2] Gerald E. Gerber, "Epes Sargent and 'The Raven'," *Poe Studies,* XIX (Jun 1986), 24; Robert S. Forsythe, "Poe's 'Nevermore': A Note," *American Literature,* VII (Jan 1936), 439–52.
[3] Francis B. Dedmond, "Poe and the Brownings," *American Transcendental Quarterly,* n.s., I (Jun 1987), 120.

APPENDIX 7:
Note on *Eureka*

T. S. Eliot spoke bluntly for many other readers of *Eureka,* in saying that it "makes no deep impression . . . because we are aware of Poe's lack of qualification in philosophy, theology or natural science."[1] Indeed Poe's cosmology blends his own fantasies about the nature of physical reality with traditional pantheism, popularized versions of nineteenth-century astronomical thought, and related nineteenth-century bunkum like Mesmerism, Spiritualism, and Phrenology. So far as he was doing science at all, he worked in the spirit of his earlier rejection of its methods in "To Science." Insistent on having the sort of universe he wanted, he still preferred the summer dream beneath the tamarind tree, the pleasure principle, to reality. On the other hand, he had a lifelong amateur interest in astronomy, manifested as early as "Al Aaraaf," and he touched on many of its classic problems in *Eureka:* comets, parallax, infinity, tangential velocity, the shape of the Milky Way, why the universe is dark.[2] In treating such questions he did at least as well as might any other intelligent person casually self-taught in astronomy and physics.

Poe was particularly familiar with the so-called nebular hypothesis of the French astronomer-mathematician Pierre-Simon Laplace. Laplace held that the infant solar system resembled a slowly rotating hot nebula. In his *Système du Monde* (1796), he proposed that the sun's atmosphere, in condensing, left equatorial rings which in turn condensed to form the planets. Of great consequence in his theory was the idea that the universe had not been forged forever by a single divine stroke but was still being created.[3] The theory came under attack in Poe's time, as new and more powerful telescopes revealed the so-called nebulae to be in reality large groups of stars. Poe took up these criticisms in *Eureka* and defended Laplace against them. But he emphasized that his own version of the nebular hypothesis differed significantly from the original, for instance in concluding that the sun had condensed at once, not gradually, as Laplace believed.

Poe's understanding of Laplace came to him through the works of Dr. John Nichol, a professor of astronomy at the University of Glasgow. Nichol's *Views of the Architecture of the Heavens* (1837), appearing in seven editions in seven years, was one of the most widely read works of popular science at the time, and the single book most responsible for bringing the nebular hypothesis to the American reading public. Much in *Eureka* derives from it: Nichol, for

---

[1] "From Poe to Valéry," in *To Criticize the Critic and other writings* (New York, 1965), 41.
[2] See Edward Harrison, *Darkness at Night: A Riddle of the Universe* (Cambridge, Mass., 1987). Despite his glorification of intuition in *Eureka,* Poe worked out mathematically in some detail how the density of the planets varies inversely as their rotary periods. See "Edgar A. Poe's Addenda to his 'Eureka,' with Comments," *Methodist Review,* XII (Jan 1896), 9–18.
[3] See Ronald L. Numbers, *Creation by Natural Law: Laplace's Nebular Hypothesis in American Thought* (Seattle, 1977); on the Newtonian background to *Eureka,* see also the notes in Harold Beaver, ed., *The Science Fiction of Edgar Allan Poe* (Harmondsworth, 1976), 395–415.

instance, suggested that the heavenly clusters could be considered single entities that would one day merge into a cluster of clusters and then into a single sun. Only a week or so before Poe spoke on "The Universe," Nichol began a series of lectures on astronomy at the New York Mercantile Library, heavily attended and widely praised as eloquent and masterful. The New York *Tribune* carried only a brief account of Poe's talk but printed Nichol's lectures entire over several issues, on the front page, reporting that the applause was "frequent enough and hearty enough to have satisfied a 'Returned Hero'."[4] Nichol's standing as a matinee idol among scientists perhaps explains why in *Eureka* Poe treated him rather slightingly.

Poe's great enthusiasm for the nebular hypothesis is readily explained. In his view, the theory confirmed with the certainty of scientific demonstration his personal belief in an otherworld of repeated dyings and rebirths. Some seven years before *Eureka,* he remarked in a review: "the *only* irrefutable argument in support of the soul's immortality—or, rather, the only conclusive proof of man's alternate dissolution and re-juvenescence *ad infinitum*—is to be found in analogies deduced from the modern established theory of the nebular cosmogony."[5]

Poe's remark invites the further comment that he attempted to argue much of *Eureka* by analogy, in his time an important mode of philosophic and scientific thought. Many held that by understanding the circulation of blood in humans, for instance, one could reason by analogy to understand, say, the circulation of sap in trees. Laplace himself had analyzed the solar system by analogy with observed rotating nebulae.[6] Such arguments reflect how scientific investigation had begun to focus on light, magnetism, heat, and similar phenomena that resisted direct observation and demanded an un-Baconian willingness to consider hypotheses. They also served Poe in trying to address both a sophisticated and a popular audience. However exalted or arcane his ideas, he hoped to make them accessible and intelligible. In arguing by analogy he tried to build a "chain of *graduated impression*" that would help readers move by easy stages from more limited and simpler to broader and more complex views of the universe, ultimately to afford an "individual impression" of it, a picture of the universe as one entity, one thing. He did create a vivid pictorial sense of the vastness of planets and of interstellar distances, but how well he otherwise succeeded in keeping his meaning clear is arguable. The work abounds in digressions, obscurities, inconsistencies, and some absurdities. Often speaking with urgency, wanting to be heard and believed, he used for emphasis many of the same devices that create the fervid voices of his distraught tale-tellers, but here sow confusion: double and triple negatives, involuted syntax, reiterated dashes that race across sentences like flights of arrows, uncertainly

[4] *New-York Daily Tribune*, 31 Jan 1848. See also Frederick W. Conner, "Poe and John Nichol: Notes on a Source of *Eureka*," in Robert A. Bryan, et al., eds., *All These to Teach* (Gainesville, 1965), 190–208.
[5] Review of Macaulay's *Critical and Miscellaneous Essays, GM*, XVIII (Jun 1841), 295.
[6] For an excellent discussion of this important topic, see Susan Booker Welsh, "Edgar Allan Poe and the Rhetoric of Science," Ph.D. diss., Drew University, 1986, ch. V. On the connections to Baconianism see also George H. Daniels, *American Science in the Age of Jackson* (New York, 1968).

signifying now apposition, now parentheses, now merely breathing space.

Despite the scientific subject matter of *Eureka*, Poe identified it as "an Art-Product alone," in fact a "Prose Poem." (Emerson's comparable *Nature* was in its time also referred to as "A Prose Poem.")[7] Although *Eureka* defies most of Poe's earlier critical pronouncements on the nature of poetry—having truth for its object, for instance, and requiring not a single reading session but several—his description is justified in the sense that he considered the real poem to be the curious and personally distinctive conception the writer tried to embody, and because the universe he depicts is itself an aesthetic object. He found the cosmos controlled by physical laws corresponding to his deeply held views on Unity of Effect and Unity of Action.

The first correspondence depends on Poe's all-important definition of gravity, offered in *Eureka* as his rendering of Newton's law: *"Every atom, of every body, attracts every other atom, both of its own and of every other body."* Harboring within itself the eventual return to Unity, everything in Poe's universe gravitates to everything else. In a perfect (and to Poe unattainable) literary work of art, words have the same omni-attractiveness. Every word is linked, simultaneously, to every other word; the entire work is present at every moment in every word. The second, closely related correspondence reflects Poe's acquaintance with the eighteenth-century tradition of 'physico-theology,' a Christianized version of mechanical ideas about Nature. In exalting the beauty of God's systematic design, "physico-theologians" evidenced a universal "mutuality of adaptation." To cite Poe's own example of this concept, in polar climates the human frame needs, to maintain bodily heat, an abundance of oils; it happens that in such climates the sole food available is the oil of seals and whales. Whether the oil is there because it is needed, or whether it is the only thing needed because the only thing available, cannot be decided. In the "absolute *reciprocity of adaptation*," as Poe calls it, cause and effect are indistinguishable.

Here the cosmos confirmed the concept of a perfect plot that Poe had been developing for years in his criticism. In one review he likened such a plot to a building "so dependently constructed, that to change the position of a single brick is to overthrow the entire fabric."[8] Converting literary criticism into cosmology, or vice versa, in *Eureka* he likened the universal reciprocity of adaptation to a plot so arranged that one cannot tell whether one incident "depends from any one other or upholds this." As he always had, he argued that finite intelligences cannot attain this infinitely complex formal excellence. "The plots of God are perfect. The Universe is a plot of God." The Universe Poe depicted in *Eureka* was for him the supreme and only perfect tale and poem.

It seems hardly necessary to point out that Poe wrote *Eureka* in faltering physical health and mental stability. Just the same, everything about the book suggests not Prince Prospero or the many other protagonists in his work who feel profoundly threatened, but rather the multimillionaire Ellison manipulat-

---

[7] Merton M. Sealts, Jr., and Alfred R. Ferguson, eds., *Emerson's 'Nature': Origin, Growth, Meaning* (New York, 1969), 90.
[8] Review of Bulwer's *Night and Morning*, GM, XVIII (Apr 1841), 197.

ing land empires, or the imperiously independent editor of the "Stylus," someone exultantly in control. In itself, however, Poe's claim to have reached an
ultimate understanding of things seems desperately tonic. As the psychoanalyst Jacob Arlow explains, cosmological theorizing lends itself readily to gratifying consolatory fantasies of divinity and omnipotence. "The power to predict even what one cannot control is something of an antidote to fear and
helplessness. To make oneself the master of time and of change is to conquer
death and annihilation."[9] Poe in fact prefaced and concluded *Eureka* with remarks about his own death.

Poe's uncertainty over whether to grant death dominion not only drives his
view of a ceaselessly reborn universe(s), but also stamps *Eureka* to an unusual
degree with his characteristic oxymorons and halfwayness. For example, matter as he defines it consists entirely of attraction and repulsion; but after the
universe recondenses into the "globe of globes," there is no longer anything
to attract or repel, hence no matter. The ultimate globe is thus "Matter without Matter," Poe says, "Material Nihility"—being and not being, existing but
not existing. Again, some of his most obscure arguments concern the notion
of how the diffused atoms seek unity but do not tend to any center, drawn
toward what is both a core and not a core, a place and not a place: "the tendency to the general centre is not to a centre as such, but because of its being
a point in tending towards which each atom tends most directly to its real and
essential centre, *Unity* [*sic*]." In dismissing the logic of John Stuart Mill, Poe
similarly argues the possibility that something may be both a tree and not a
tree. And like his own Dupin, he acts in *Eureka* at once as poet and mathematician, the result being a work neither of science nor of imagination, but a
yes-and-no "Prose Poem."

[9] Jacob A. Arlow, "Scientific Cosmogony, Mythology, and Immortality," *Psychoanalytic Quarterly,* LI (1982), 191.

APPENDIX 8:
Note on *"The Rationale of Verse"*

Poe proposed deducing the principles of verse not from a study of poems but from "natural law." In his view, all the elements of verse arose from a human delight in equality, symmetry: "To this enjoyment . . . all the moods of verse—rhythm, metre, stanza, rhyme, alliteration, the *refrain,* and other analogous effects—are to be referred." Because thought seeks satisfaction in equality of sound, the "rudiment" of verse may have been the spondee, the word or phrase consisting of two equally accented syllables. (Poe featured a spondaic rhythm in many of his titles, as in "Dream-Land," "The Gold-Bug," "King Pest," and "Hop-Frog.")[1] In his scenario of the evolution of verse, the repetition of this symmetrical rhythm brought with it a "perception of monotone," which sought relief in words formed of differently accented syllables, giving rise to iambuses and trochees, which by the same process gave rise to dactyls and anapests, and ultimately to repetition of sounds at the ends of lines, the grouping of symmetrical units into stanzas, and such devices as the refrain.

Not much can be said in defense of Poe's thinking, according to which the same principles and devices of versification that arose in English should also have arisen in Tagalog, Turkish, and all other human tongues as well. His psychoaesthetic theory of the origin of verse seems no less fanciful than his description of the origins of the cosmos in his "Prose-Poem," *Eureka,* which the essay closely resembles in many features, among them its claim of unrivaled new understanding of the subject, its rather eighteenth-century emphasis on symmetry, and its mathematical reasonings.[2] He went beyond his earlier picture of the poet as a calculating technician (in "The Philosophy of Composition"), conceiving the poet now as a sort of mathematician with words. Nine-tenths of the subject of rhyme, rhythm, meter, and versification, he said, "appertain to the mathematics." He devised an elaborate numerical system of scansion designed to show "the exact relative value of every syllable employed in Verse." The system in effect accounts for verse rhythm with the same fullness by which symbols of the time values of notes and rests are used to map the rhythm in musical notation.[3] Whole numbers and fractions placed above and below the poetic line mark the relative time value of syllables, theoretically making it possible to read lines of verse with metronomic precision, and making poetry to this extent less a matter of inspiration than of counting.

---

[1] See Martin Roth, "Poe's Divine Spondee," *Poe Studies,* XII (Jun 1979), 14–18.
[2] On the similarities see Margaret Alterton, *Origins of Poe's Critical Theory* (Iowa City, 1925).
[3] In his "Notes Upon English Verse" Poe wrote that "rhythm in prosody, is, in its last analysis, identical with time in music." See *The Pioneer: A Literary Magazine* (rpt. New York, 1947), 105.

ACKNOWLEDGMENTS

I am very grateful to the curators and librarians of the following repositories for allowing me to use their manuscript collections and, where indicated in the notes, granting me permission to quote from them: Alderman Library, University of Virginia; Archives of American Art, Smithsonian Institution (William Page Papers, Microfilm Roll D312); Baltimore Court House; Beinecke Rare Book and Manuscript Library, Yale University; Boston Public Library; Butler Library, Columbia University; Cornell University Library; The Edward Laurence Doheny Memorial Library, St. John's Seminary; Fales Library, New York University (with special thanks to Sherlyn Abdoo and Frank Walker); Rare Book Department, Free Library of Philadelphia; Haverford College Library; John Hay Library, Brown University (Sarah Helen Whitman Papers); Historical Society of Pennsylvania, Philadelphia (Gratz Collection and Society Collection); Houghton Library, Harvard University; The Huntington Library, San Marino (HM 7160, 24239, 24240; FI 1471, 1473); University of Iowa Libraries, Iowa City (T. O. Mabbott Collection); The Library of Congress, Washington, D.C.; Lilly Library, Indiana University, Bloomington, Indiana; Maryland Hall of Records, Annapolis; Maryland Historical Society, Baltimore; Massachusetts Historical Society, Boston; Minnesota Historical Society, St. Paul; Missouri Historical Society, St. Louis; Pierpont Morgan Library, New York City (MA 644, 684); National Archives, Washington, D.C.;

537

New-York Historical Society; Rare Book and Manuscripts Division, New York Public Library, Astor, Lenox, and Tilden Foundations (Duyckinck Family Papers; Richard Henry & Elizabeth B. Stoddard Papers; Frederick Saunders Recollections); William R. Perkins Library, Duke University (William Galt, Jr., Papers; Munford-Ellis Papers); The Edgar Allan Poe Museum, Richmond; Enoch Pratt Free Library, Baltimore (Edgar Allan Poe Collection); Princeton University Library (General MSS Miscellaneous ON-OX); Harry Ransom Humanities Research Center, University of Texas at Austin; University of Rochester Library; South Caroliniana Library, The University of South Carolina (James Lawson Papers); Earl Gregg Swemm Library, The College of William and Mary; The Valentine Museum, Richmond; Virginia Historical Society, Richmond; Virginia State Library, Richmond; Wollman Library, Barnard College.

This wide search for information about Poe was made possible by generous grants from four institutions who have my liveliest thanks. The American Philosophical Society supported my research in Boston, Cambridge, and Providence in 1985; the American Council of Learned Societies supported my research the same year in Richmond, Charlottesville, Annapolis, Baltimore, and Washington, D.C. In the summer of 1987, research at the University of Texas, the University of Iowa, and Indiana University was aided by the National Endowment for the Humanities and the Research Challenge Fund of New York University. While writing part of the biography in 1989–90, I also became the happy beneficiary of a fellowship from the John Simon Guggenheim Memorial Foundation. No less helpful and cheering than the foundation's well-known liberality was the personal encouragement of its president, Joel Conarroe, and its vice president, G. Thomas Tanselle. Throughout the research and writing, too, support of all kinds has come from those concerned with the administration of N.Y.U., especially Dean C. Duncan Rice, and from members of the N.Y.U. Biography Seminar.

My gratitude also goes to Drs. Eugene L. Goldberg, Louise J. Kaplan, and Paola Mieli of New York City for several psychoanalytic insights about Poe's inner life. I have learned much, too, from Dr. Dwight R. Thomas and Professor Burton R. Pollin, the preeminent authorities on Poe. Dwight Thomas several times sent me copies of little-known Poe material, and reviewed an earlier version of this biography with the meticulous thoroughness that makes him one of the most brilliant literary research scholars in America.

Whatever errors and misjudgments remain in the text have not escaped his scrutiny but survived it by my stubbornness. The same is true of Burton Pollin, who also carefully read the earlier manuscript, and both in his critique and in many phone calls, postcards, letters, and packages over six years made available to me without limit his prodigious knowledge of Poe's life and career. Finally, I am lucky in having friends who can be counted on for wisdom, help, and fun, sometimes all at once. They include Alfred Owen Aldridge, Roger Asselineau, Paul Baker, Tom Bishop, Sacvan Bercovitch, Luigi Ballerini, Emory Elliott, Frederick R. Karl, Richard Kopley, Leo Lemay, Mason I. Lowance, Joan Peyser, Hugh Rawson, Peter Shaw, John Seelye, and Jack Zipes. Carl E. Prince twice earns his name: royal friend, and star of the court.

New York City and Highland Lake
5 February 1991

INDEX

abolition:
  Briggs and, 271
  Poe and, 207, 405, 484n
"About Critics and Criticism," Poe,
  404
academies, private, 23
acrostic poem by Virginia Poe, 292–93
acting career:
  of David Poe, Jr., 3–4
  of Eliza Poe, 1–8
addiction, as literary motif, 112
adoption of Poe, questions of, 454n
The Adventures of Harry Franco, Briggs,
  243
aesthetic principles, 69, 70, 119, 165–
  69, 321–23, 384
afterlife:
  ideas of, 167–68, 230, 340
  as literary theme, 57, 73, 170–71
Afterworld, vision of, 322–23
age for marriage of women, 107
"Al Aaraaf," Poe, 50–51, 56–59, 69,
  72, 74, 126, 267–70
Al Aaraaf, Tamerlane, and Minor Poems,
  Poe, 54–59
  review of, 93
alcoholism, 514n
  of David Poe, Jr., 7
  of Edgar Poe, 86, 132, 186, 257–62,
    266, 277, 280, 303, 314, 342–
    43, 470n, 481n
    and death of, 433–35
    English and, 309

fictional references, 406
  at *Gentleman's Magazine*, 158–59,
    477n
  Sarah Helen Whitman and, 377,
    386–87
  Philadelphia episode, 415–18
  Richmond episodes, 362, 427–28
  Virginia's illness and, 183–85, 334
  White and, 106, 108, 128
  Willis and, 325
  Washington trip, 192–94
  of Henry Poe, 83–85, 125
  of F. W. Thomas, 176
Alcott, Bronson, 317–18
Alexander's Weekly Messenger, 152–53,
  155, 158–59, 203, 251
Alexandria, Virginia, Muddy in, 444–
  47
aliases of Poe, 37, 41–42, 84, 273,
  429
  See also pseudonyms of Poe
alienation, as poetic theme, 40–41
Allan, Frances ("Fanny"), 11, 14, 16,
  65, 422, 454n
  death of, 46–47, 77
  in London, 17, 19–20
  memories of, 358, 430
  relationship with Edgar, 19, 20, 26,
    34, 461n
Allan, John (Jack, Jock, "Scotch"), 10–
  15, 52, 126, 358, 422
  business of, 15–22, 27–28
  citizenship, 454n